Tourism and Development

ASPECTS OF TOURISM
Series Editors: Professor Chris Cooper, *University of Queensland, Ipswich, Australia*
and Dr Michael Hall, *University of Otago, Dunedin, New Zealand*

Aspects of Tourism is an innovative, multifaceted series which will comprise authoritative reference handbooks on global tourism regions, research volumes, texts and monographs. It is designed to provide readers with the latest thinking on tourism world-wide and in so doing will push back the frontiers of tourism knowledge. The series will also introduce a new generation of international tourism authors, writing on leading edge topics.
The volumes will be readable and user-friendly, providing accessible sources for further research. The list will be underpinned by an annual authoritative tourism research volume. Books in the series will be commissioned that probe the relationship between tourism and cognate subject areas such as strategy, development, retailing, sport and environmental studies. The publisher and series editors welcome proposals from writers with projects on these topics.

Other Books in the Series
Dynamic Tourism: Journeying with Change
    Priscilla Boniface
Journeys into Otherness: The Representation of Differences and Identity in Tourism
    Keith Hollinshead and Chuck Burlo (eds)
Natural Area Tourism: Ecology, Impacts and Management
    D. Newsome, S.A. Moore and R. Dowling
Tourism Collaboration and Partnerships
    Bill Bramwell and Bernard Lane (eds)
Tourism Employment: Analysis and Planning
    Adele Ladkin, Edith Szivas and Michael Riley
Tourism in Peripheral Areas: Case Studies
    Frances Brown and Derek Hall (eds)

Please contact us for the latest book information:
Channel View Publications, Frankfurt Lodge, Clevedon Hall,
Victoria Road, Clevedon, BS21 7HH, England
http://www.multilingual-matters.com

ASPECTS OF TOURISM 5
Series Editors: Chris Cooper (*University of Queensland, Australia*), and Michael Hall (*University of Otago, New Zealand*)

Tourism and Development

Concepts and Issues

Edited by
Richard Sharpley and David J. Telfer

CHANNEL VIEW PUBLICATIONS
Clevedon • Buffalo • Toronto • Sydney

To Olivia and Kyoko

Library of Congress Cataloging in Publication Data
Tourism and Development: Concepts and Issues
Edited by Richard Sharpley and David J. Telfer
Aspects of Tourism: 5
Includes bibliographical references
1. Tourism–Economic aspects. 2. Economic development.
 I. Sharpley, Richard. II. Telfer, David J. III. Series
G155.A1 T589342 2002
338.4'79104–dc21   2001047709

British Library Cataloguing in Publication Data
A catalogue entry for this book is available from the British Library.

ISBN 1-873150-35-0 (hbk)
ISBN 1-873150-34-2 (pbk)

Channel View Publications
An imprint of Multilingual Matters Ltd

UK: Frankfurt Lodge, Clevedon Hall, Victoria Road, Clevedon BS21 7SJ.
USA: 2250 Military Road, Tonawanda, NY 14150, USA.
Canada: 5201 Dufferin Street, North York, Ontario, Canada M3H 5T8.
Australia: Footprint Books, PO Box 418, Church Point, NSW 2103, Australia.

Typeset by Archetype-IT Ltd (http://www.archetype-it.com).
Printed and bound in Great Britain by Cambrian Printers Ltd.

Contents

Contributors

Dr Raoul Bianchi is Research Fellow in Tourism, Culture and Development at the University of North London, UK. He researches into the political economy of tourism development, focusing on entrepreneurship and social change, tourism migration and labour relations and the politics of world heritage, in particular in Spain and the Canary Islands. His lecturing specialisms include tourism and economic development and the political economy of leisure and tourism.

Dr Judith Cukier is an Assistant Professor at the University of Waterloo's Faculty of Environmental Studies and is the Director of the Tourism Policy and Planning Program at the university. Her teaching responsibilities include the geography of tourism, recreation geography and the social construction of tourism, and her current research interests include tourism employment and entrepreneurship, gender and tourism, and tourism impacts in developing countries, with regional interests in Southeast Asia, the South Pacific and the Caribbean. She has published a variety of articles on tourism employment.

Dr Atsuko Hashimoto is an Assistant Professor in the Department of Recreation and Leisure Studies at Brock University, Canada. She lectures on the areas of international tourism and interactive distribution channels in the Tourism Studies Degree. Her research interests lie in cross-cultural studies in tourism, socio-cultural impacts and tourism development, indigenous tourism in Canada and environmental issues in tourism.

Dr Tanja Mihalic is Associate Professor of Tourism Economics and management at the University of Ljubljana, Slovenia. Her current research interests include environmental economics, tourism competitiveness and tourism policy. Her practical work is related to environmental labelling in the tourism and hospitality industry.

Dr Richard Sharpley is Reader in Travel and Tourism at the University of Northumbria at Newcastle, UK. The author of a number of tourism textbooks, his research interests lie in the field of the sociology of tourism, rural tourism and sustainable tourism development, with a particular focus on tourism development in

Cyprus. He currently lectures in tourism and international development and tourism in society.

Dr Chris Southgate is Lecturer in Environmental Management at the University of Central Lancashire, UK. He completed his doctoral thesis at the University of Manchester in 1998 on natural resource management and institutional change in Kenya's Maasailand. He now leads the BSc (Hons) Ecotourism programme at Central Lancashire.

Dr David J. Telfer is an Associate Professor in the Department of Recreation and Leisure Studies at Brock University, Canada, and is the Co-ordinator of the Bachelor of Tourism Studies Degree. He teaches in the areas of tourism planning and heritage tourism. His research interests include linkages between tourism and development theories, economic linkages of tourism with host communities, strategic alliances and rural tourism.

Dr Dallen Timothy is Assistant Professor of Tourism at Arizona State University, USA. His research interests include tourism planning in developing countries, heritage, political boundaries and tourism, and issues of power and sovereignty.

Introduction

There is no doubt that tourism, frequently referred to as 'the world's largest industry', is big business. By the end of the 20th century, international tourism alone was annually generating well over US$450 billion, whilst total global tourism activity (international and domestic) has been estimated to be worth some US$3.5 trillion. Moreover, it is anticipated that these figures will continue to increase for the foreseeable future. Tourism has long been recognised as a growth industry and current expectations of an annual increase of about 4% in international tourist arrivals and spending suggests that, by 2020, international tourism will be generating up to US$2 trillion a year.

It is not surprising, therefore, that many, if not all, nations have jumped on the tourism 'bandwagon'. Few countries do not promote themselves as destinations as a means of gaining a share of the ever-increasing global tourism market – even countries such as oil-rich Abu Dhabi have adopted tourism development policies – and, for many, tourism represents an integral and important element of broader economic and social development policy. Indeed, it is this potential contribution to development that is the fundamental justification for establishing tourism in the first instance. That is, it is highly unlikely that any destination would willingly 'invite' large numbers of people to visit or tolerate the inevitable consequences, such as environmental degradation or the disruption to the daily life of local communities, were it not for the benefits that potentially accrue from the development of tourism. Such benefits, of course, include foreign exchange earnings, employment creation, economic diversification and growth and a variety of other factors, widely discussed in the tourism literature, that collectively justify tourism's alleged role as a vehicle of development.

However, what is surprising is the fact that, despite the widespread adherence, both in practice and within academic circles, to the notion that tourism represents an effective means of achieving development, relatively little attention has been paid to the inherent processes, influences, objectives and outcomes of tourism-related development. Certainly, the economic benefits that flow from the development of tourism are widely researched and understood, as are the negative environmental and sociocultural consequences that, in a sense, represent debits on the tourism balance sheet. At the same time, the almost obsessive focus on sustainable tourism development during the 1990s was primarily driven by the need to optimise the benefits of tourism to host communities and tourists alike (though ironically not, for the most part, by the desire to achieve sustainable development in destination areas).

Nevertheless, until recently a conceptual leap was made between the (economic) benefits of tourism and its contribution to development. In other words, it is generally assumed that tourism, preferably planned and managed in such a way as to minimise social and environmental impacts, provides a variety of economic benefits that contribute to economic growth and, hence, development, economic growth and development being implicitly regarded as synonymous. As a result, many important issues have, by and large, been overlooked, issues which question the alleged contribution of tourism to development.

For example, it is illogical to claim that tourism, as a specific socioeconomic activity, is an effective vehicle of development without defining the desired outcome – that is, 'development'. If development is considered in simple economic growth terms then tourism undoubtedly has a role to play but, to most people, development connotes more than economic well-being. It represents, perhaps, the characteristics of social existence (wealth, education, health, opportunity, freedom, choice, self-reliance) in the 'developed' countries compared with those in 'less-developed' countries. Viewed in these terms, tourism's contribution may be far less than expected.

Similarly, the developmental role of tourism cannot, or should not, be extolled without knowledge and understanding of the processes by which development, however defined, might be achieved. In other words, the achievement of development in any one country may be dependent upon a particular combination of economic, social and political conditions and processes which may or may not be satisfied by tourism.

At the same time, and related, the potential contribution of tourism to development must be put into perspective. That is, much of the literature addresses the socioeconomic process of tourism in isolation from other socioeconomic sectors and processes, the implication being that tourism represents a panacea to the challenges of underdevelopment. However, it is certainly unrealistic to expect any one development 'tool', such as tourism, to be a solution to all the problems faced by less developed countries (or, indeed, to the challenges facing the less developed or 'backward' regions within wealthier, industrialised nations), whilst the scale of tourism-related development also remains an unresolved issue. In other words, tourism and development are frequently related within a national or even global context – in the extreme, it is viewed as a means of achieving a 'new world order' (WTO, 1980) – yet, in practice, tourism may prove to be most effective as a development catalyst at the local, community level.

An essential question to be asked, therefore, is whether tourism is a universally applicable development option? If not, as it is realistic to suggest, are different forms of tourism development more or less suitable to different countries, societies or developmental needs and objectives? Can tourism contribute to development on its own or should it be considered in combination with other economic sectors or activities? On what scale is tourism likely to contribute most to development – at the national, regional or local level? And what are the influences and forces that determine the extent to which tourism can play an effective developmental role?

The purpose of this book is to address these and other questions, thereby challenging the popular assumption, and implicit assertion within much of the literature, that tourism is, in general, an effective vehicle of development. It does so by locating the analysis of tourism as an agent of development within the theoretical framework of development studies. In other words, it attempts to bridge the conceptual divide referred to earlier by exploring the links between the separate yet intimately related disciplines of tourism and development studies, providing a theoretical underpinning to the study of tourism that, for the most part, has been lacking in the tourism literature.

This relationship between tourism and development studies, and the consequential implications for the study and understanding of the potential contribution of tourism to the development of destination areas, is conceptualised in the model in Figure 1. This demonstrates the interdependence not only between tourism and broader sociocultural, political and economic environment within which it operates, but also between the various consequences, of tourism that collectively result in 'development'. In other words, although it is possible to study individual elements of tourism, its specific consequences, and the external factors that influence the nature of tourism development, each element is related to and interacts with the other elements of what is, in effect, a dynamic tourism-development system.

The model also represents the structure and central thesis of this book. That is, it recognises that a multi-directional relationship exists between the nature of tourism development, the consequences of development in destination areas, the nature of local development and the environment external to the tourism system. Thus, although individual chapters address specific issues with respect to tourism and development, collectively they consider the potential developmental role of tourism within a broad conceptual framework founded in development studies.

Part 1 introduces the concept of development and establishes a relationship between development theories and tourism theory, thereby setting the theoretical parameters for the more specific issues addressed in the following part. Chapter 1 reviews the popularly held justification for the promotion of tourism as a means of achieving development, balancing this positive or idealistic picture with an introduction to many of the forces / influences that potentially militate against tourism's contribution to development. The chapter then goes on to ask the fundamental

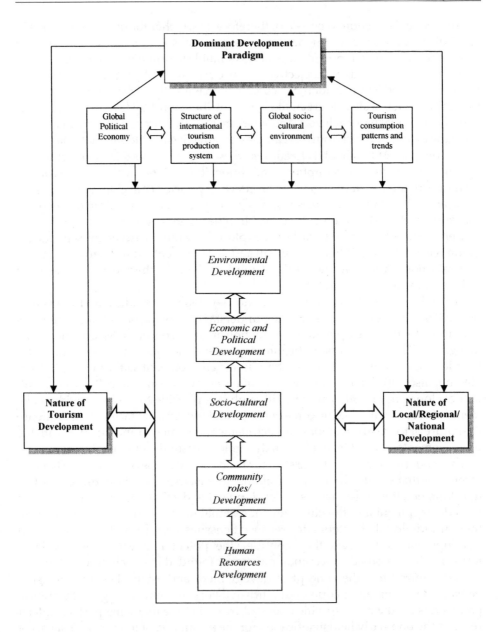

Figure 1 Model showing the relationship between tourism and development studies

question: What is development? Making reference to social, economic and political factors that characterise underdevelopment, it argues that the concept of development has evolved from simply economic growth to a broader achievement of the 'good life' that encompasses social, cultural, political, environmental and economic aims and processes.

Having considered the 'meaning' of development, Chapter 2 goes on to explore the evolution of four development paradigms that have evolved since the Second World War. The chapter starts with an overview of the nature of development before reviewing and critiquing four mainstream development paradigms including modernisation, dependency, economic neoliberalism and alternative development. Parallels are then drawn between the changes in development theory and tourism development assessing the extent to which tourism reflects transformations in development thinking. An analysis of tourism development under the four development paradigms is presented which then forms the basis for the subsequent proposal of a set of considerations that provide a potential framework for the development of appropriate and sustainable tourism.

The purpose of Part 2 of the book is to explore, within the context of specific themes, the relationship between development and tourism. Thus, each chapter in this part of the book, referring to and building upon the theoretical foundation introduced in Part 1, addresses particular issues or challenges related to the use of tourism as a developmental vehicle. Given that this role of tourism is principally referred to in terms of economic benefits, the section commences by addressing, in Chapter 3, economic development issues. Taking economic growth as the fundamental indicator of (economic) development, the chapter introduces economic concepts, such as capital–output ratios and the role of tourism consumption as an expenditure driven economic activity, before discussing a number of issues that challenge the conventional understanding of tourism's economic benefits. This is followed, in turn, by chapters that explore regional development issues, community development issues, human resource issues, sociocultural issues and environmental issues.

Chapter 4 examines the use of tourism as a regional development tool. Governments around the world have selected tourism as a means to promote development or redevelopment in peripheral or economically disadvantaged regions. The chapter begins by examining regional development concepts including innovation, growth poles, agglomeration economies and clusters, which are considered in the context of tourism later in the chapter. The challenge of using tourism as a regional development tool is explored through a number of cases in a variety of different contexts including urban redevelopment, rural regeneration, island tourism, tourism in peripheral regions and tourism across international regions. It is argued for tourism to be an effective tool for regional development so that more than multinational corporations or the local elite benefit, there must be strong economic linkages to a variety of sectors in the local economy. The fundamental thesis of Chapter 5 is that, for the optimisation of benefits accruing to destination societies from tourism (and in accordance with the principles of alternative/sustainable development), there is a need to decentralise tourism development to the community level. The chapter thus proposes the advantages of – and methods of encouraging – community-based tourism development before presenting a number of significant, though not insurmountable, obstacles to its achievement. Chapter 6 then continues the local community theme, focusing on the specific issue the human-resource/employment potential of tourism, particularly in less developed countries. Based upon the argument that much of the analysis of tourism's impacts on employment follows a western-centric, developed country perspective, the chapter addresses a number of central issues, including the dynamics of the formal and informal sectors, the status of tourism employment and gender issues. These are then compared with findings of research undertaken in Bali, which suggests that, contrary to customary opinion, tourism-related employment provides many developmental benefits. The chapter concludes by suggesting that tourism/employment policy, designed to optimise such benefits, could be guided by a model of service-centred employment characteristics.

Chapter 7 explores the relationship between tourism development and sociocultural development. Challenging the traditional, western-centric 'measurement' of development and the resultant inherent bias in assessing the sociocultural impacts of tourism in particular, the chapter reviews a variety of indices against which development is measured. It goes on to examine both the positive and negative sociocultural impacts of tourism before highlighting the contradictions of tourism development and proposing that there is a need to divorce the assessment of tourism's development outcomes from traditional, universalist development paradigms.

Completing Part 2, Chapter 8 considers the relationship between tourism development and the environment. Critiquing mainstream sustainable development theory which is manifested in deterministic and managerialist approaches to the planning and use of tourism's environmental resources, this chapter explores the concept of sustainability as a complex interaction of local social, environmental, political and economic processes. It argues that, despite the recognised negative consequences of tourism development, a focus upon local governance embracing ecological sustainability principles may emphasise the environmental benefits that accrue from tourism.

Finally, Part 3 introduces and addresses what are referred to as 'barriers' to tourism development. It has long been recognised that a variety of externalities serve to limit the growth of tourism and, hence, its economic development potential, such 'limiters' including, for example, government restrictions on inbound/outbound travel, political turbulence, global oil prices, natural disasters, and so on.

However, beyond these specific factors that impact negatively on tourist flows, normally in the shorter term and with respect to specific regions or destinations, tourism's contribution to development is restricted by two important sets of influences. First, as discussed in Chapter 9, the political economy of tourism, in terms of both the internal structure tourism system itself and the global context within which the tourism system operates, has frequently been explained in relation to neocolonialist dependency theory. However, although the power of the nation-state is diminishing within an increasingly globalised political economy, the structure of multinational corporate operations represents a new 'threat' to the achievement of development.

Second, the very nature of tourism as a form of consumption also militates against development (Chapter 10). As an ego-centric social activity, tourism is principally motivated by twin aims of avoidance/escape and ego enhancement/reward. Therefore, despite the alleged spread of environmental awareness and the consequential emergence of the 'new' tourist, not only does tourism remain relatively untouched by the phenomenon of green consumerism but also the ways in which tourism is consumed suggest that, beyond financial considerations, tourists contribute little to the development process.

In addition to these two broad areas of concern, the specific focus on sustainable tourism, the dominant tourism development paradigm of the 1990s, can also be seen as a barrier to development. That is, as Chapter 11 suggests, sustainable tourism development has evolved into a prescriptive and restrictive set of guidelines for tourism development that, whilst offering environmentally appropriate, commercially pragmatic and ethically sound principles for optimising tourism's development role, draws attention away from the potential benefits of other forms of tourism and, indeed, other development agents.

Finally, drawing together the various concepts, themes and issues introduced and discussed throughout the book, the conclusion considers the implications for the role of tourism as a means of achieving development. As such, it raises a number of important points that may encourage further debate amongst students, academic and practitioners of tourism whilst, more generally, it is hoped that this book as a whole will contribute to further understanding and knowledge of the inherent processes, challenges and benefits of tourism as a vehicle of development.

Richard Sharpley and David Telfer
March 2002

Part 1

Development Theories and Tourism Theory

Chapter 1

Tourism: A Vehicle for Development?

RICHARD SHARPLEY

Introduction

Tourism is, without doubt, one of the major social and economic phenomena of modern times. Since the early 1900s when, as a social activity, it was largely limited to a privileged minority, the opportunity to participate in tourism has become increasingly widespread. At the same time, distinctions between both tourism destinations and modes of travel as markers of status have become less defined; tourism, in short, has become increasingly democratised (Urry, 1990b: 16). It now also 'accounts for the single largest peaceful movement of people across cultural boundaries in the history of the world' (Lett, 1989: 277), an international movement of people that, in 1999, amounted to over 662 million arrivals (WTO, 2000). Moreover, if on a global basis domestic tourism trips are also taken into account, this figure is estimated to be between six and ten times higher.

Reflecting this dramatic growth in the level of participation, the so-called 'pleasure periphery' (Turner & Ash, 1975) of tourism has also expanded enormously. Not only are more distant and exotic places attracting ever-increasing numbers of international tourists, but also few countries have not become tourist destinations. For example, in 1997 some 15,000 tourists visited the Antarctic whilst, using the slogan 'From Nebuchadnezzar to Saddam Hussein: 2,240 years of peace and prosperity' (Roberts 1998: 3), even Iraq is now promoting itself as a tourist destination. As evidence of this emergence of tourism as a truly global activity, the World Tourism Organisation (WTO) currently publishes annual tourism statistics for around 200 states.

However, tourism is not only a social phenomenon; it is also big business. Certainly, 'mobility, vacations and travel are social victories' (Krippendorf 1986), yet the ability of ever-increasing numbers of people to enjoy travel-related experiences has depended, by necessity, upon the myriad of organisations and businesses that comprise the 'tourism industry'. In other words, tourism has also developed into a powerful, world-wide economic force. International tourism alone generated over US$453 billion in 1998 (WTO 2000) whilst, according to the World Travel and

Tourism Council (WTTC), global tourism – including domestic tourism – is a US $3.5 trillion industry, accounting for 11% of world GDP and a similar proportion of global employment. Such remarkable figures must, of course, be treated with some caution; as Cooper *et al.* (1998: 87) observe, 'it is not so much the size of these figures that is so impressive, but the fact that anybody should know the value of tourism, the level of tourism demand or to be able to work these figures out'. Nevertheless, there can be no doubting the economic significance that tourism has assumed throughout the world.

Owing to its rapid and continuing growth and associated potential economic contribution, it is not surprising that tourism is widely regarded in practice and also in academic circles as an effective means of achieving development. That is, in both the industrialised and less developed countries of the world, tourism has become 'an important and integral element of their development strategies' (Jenkins, 1991: 61). Similarly, within the tourism literature, the development and promotion of tourism is largely justified on the basis of its catalytic role in broader social and economic development. Importantly, however, relatively little attention has been paid in the literature to the meaning, objectives and processes of that 'development'. In other words, although extensive research has been undertaken into the positive and negative developmental consequences of tourism, such research has, with a few exceptions, been 'divorced from the processes which have created them' (Pearce, 1989b: 15). As a result, tourism's alleged contribution to development is tacitly accepted whilst a number of fundamental questions remain unanswered. For example, what is 'development'? What are the aims and objectives of development? How is development achieved? Does tourism represent an effective or realistic means of achieving development? Who benefits from development? What forces/ influences contribute to or militate against the contribution of tourism to development?

The overall purpose of this book is to address these questions by, in particular, establishing and exploring the links between the discrete yet interconnected disciplines of tourism studies and development studies. In this first chapter, therefore, we consider the concepts of, and inter-relationship between, tourism and development, thereby providing the framework for the application of development theory to the specific context of tourism in Chapter 2 and the more specific issues in subsequent chapters.

Tourism and Development

As previously suggested, tourism is widely regarded as a means of achieving development in destination areas. Indeed, the *raison d'être* of tourism, the justification for its promotion in any area or region within the industrialised or less developed world, is its alleged contribution to development. In a sense, this role of tourism is officially sanctioned, inasmuch as the WTO asserts in the Manila Declaration on World Tourism that

> world tourism can contribute to the establishment of a new international economic order that will help to eliminate the widening economic gap between developed and developing countries and ensure the steady acceleration of economic and social development and progress, in particular in developing countries. (WTO, 1980: 1)

Interestingly, and reflecting the organisation's broader membership and objectives, the focus of the WTO is primarily on the contribution of tourism to development in the less developed countries of the world. In this context, tourism is seen not only as a catalyst of development but also of political and economic change. That is, international tourism is viewed as a means of achieving both 'economic and social development and progress' and the redistribution of wealth and power that is, arguably, necessary to achieve such development. (It is, perhaps, no coincidence that, in 1974, the United Nations had also proposed the establishment of a New International Economic Order in order to address imbalances and inequities within existing international economic and political structures.) This immediately raises questions about the structure, ownership and control of international tourism, issues that we return to throughout this book.

The important point here, however, is that attention is most frequently focused upon the developmental role of tourism in the lesser developed, peripheral nations. Certainly, many such countries consider tourism to be a vital ingredient in their overall development plans and policies (Dieke, 1989) and, as Roche (1992: 566) comments, ' the development of tourism has long been seen as both a vehicle and a symbol at least of westernisation, but also, more importantly, of progress and modernisation. This has particularly been the case in Third World countries.' Not surprisingly, much of the tourism development literature has a similar focus, with many texts and articles explicitly addressing tourism development in less developed countries (for example, Britton & Clarke, 1987; Brohman, 1996b; Harrison, 1992c; Lea, 1988; Mowforth & Munt, 1997; Singh, *et al.* 1989; Weaver, 1998a).

However, the potential of tourism to contribute to development in modern, industrialised countries is also widely recognised, with tourism playing an increasingly important role in most, if not all, OECD countries. In western Europe, for example, there has long been evidence of national government support of the tourism sector, in some cases dating back to the 1920s and 1930s and, more recently, 'tourism – along with some other select activities such as financial services and telecommunications – has become a major component of economic strategies' (Williams & Shaw, 1991: 1). In particular, tourism has become a favoured means of addressing the socioeconomic problems facing peripheral rural areas (Cavaco, 1995; Hoggart *et al.*, 1995) whilst many urban areas have also turned to tourism as a means of mitigating the problems of industrial decline. Indeed, government support for tourism-related development is evident in financial support for tourism-related development or regeneration projects. For example, one method of disbursing EU structural funds for rural regeneration in Europe has been through the LEADER (Liaisons Entre Actions pour la Développement des Économies Rurales) programme. Of 217 projects under the original LEADER scheme, tourism was the dominant business plan in 71 (Calatrava & Avilés, 1993). Thus, just as tourism is a global phenomenon, so too is its developmental contribution applicable on a global basis. What varies is simply the contextual meaning or definition of 'development' or the hoped-for outcomes of tourism development.

Therefore it is important to understand what is meant by the term 'development' and how its meaning may vary according to different contexts. First, however, it is necessary to review the reasons why tourism, as opposed to other industries or economic sectors, is seen as an attractive vehicle for development.

Why Tourism?

Throughout the world, the most compelling reason for pursuing tourism as a development strategy is its alleged positive contribution to the local or national economy. Internationally, tourism represents an important source of foreign exchange earnings; indeed, it has been suggested that the potential contribution to the national balance of payments is the principal reason why governments support tourism development (Oppermann & Chon, 1997: 109). For many developing countries, tourism has become one of the principal sources of foreign exchange earnings whilst even in developed countries the earnings from international tourism may make a significant contribution to the balance of payments in general, and the travel account in particular. For example, in 1998 the UK's international tourism receipts amounted to £12.7 billion. Whilst this represented just 4.6% of total exports, it offset around 65% of the £19.5 billion spent by UK residents on overseas trips that year (British Tourist Authority (BTA), 2000).

Tourism is also considered to be an effective source of income and employment. Reference has already been made to the global contribution of tourism to employment and GDP and, for many countries or destination areas, tourism is the major source income and employment for local communities. In Cyprus, for example, about 25% of the workforce are employed directly and indirectly in tourism. It is also one of the reasons why tourism is frequently turned to as a new or replacement activity in areas where traditional industries have fallen into decline.

The economic benefits (and costs) of tourism are discussed at length in the literature, as are the environmental and sociocultural consequences of tourism. Many of these are considered in the context of development in later chapters. The main point here, however, is that the widely cited benefits and costs of tourism, whether economic, environmental or sociocultural, are just that. They are the measurable or visible consequences of developing tourism in any particular destination and, in a somewhat simplistic sense, tourism is considered to be 'successful' as long as the benefits accruing from its development are not outweighed by the costs or negative consequences. What they do not provide is the justification or reason for choosing tourism, rather than any other industry or economic activity, as a route to development.

From a perhaps cynical point of view, the answer might lie in the fact that, frequently, there is simply no other option (Brown, 1998: 59). For many developing countries, with a limited industrial sector, few natural resources and a dependence on international aid, tourism may represent the only realistic means of earning much needed foreign exchange, creating employment and attracting overseas investment. Certainly this is the case in The Gambia, one of the smallest and poorest countries in Africa. With an estimated average annual per capita income of US$260 amongst its one million population, The Gambia lacks any natural or mineral wealth and its economy is largely based on the production, processing and export of groundnuts. As a result, the country remains highly dependent upon international aid. However, with its fine Atlantic beaches and virtually uninterrupted sunshine during the winter months, The Gambia has, since the mid-1960s, been able to take advantage of the European winter-sun tourism market. Tourism now represents almost 11% of GDP and provides some 7000 jobs directly and indirectly (Dieke, 1993a; Thomson *et al.*, 1995). However, because of the extended family system prevalent in Africa, up to ten Gambians are supported by the income from one job. At the same time, local schools, charitable organisations and environmental projects rely heavily upon income derived directly from tourists whilst, in the absence of scheduled services, regular charter flights to northern Europe provide essential communications and freight services. Thus, despite the fragility of the tourism sector in The Gambia, as evidenced by the collapse of the industry following the military coup in 1994 (see Sharpley *et al.*, 1996), the country had no other realistic choice other than to develop tourism and it now makes a significant contribution to the economy of The Gambia.

More positively, however, a number of reasons may be suggested to explain the attraction of tourism as a development option (see Jenkins, 1980b; 1991).

Tourism is a growth industry

Since 1950, when just over 25 million international tourist arrivals were recorded, international tourism has demonstrated consistent and remarkable growth. In fact, between 1950 and 1998, international tourist arrivals increased by a factor of 25, with the receipts from international tourism growing by a similar amount (see Table 1.1).

Interestingly, the rate of growth in arrivals has been steadily declining. For example, during the 1990s the average annual growth in global tourist arrivals was

Table 1.1 International tourist arrivals and receipts, 1950–98

Year	Arrivals (000s)	Receipts (US$mn)	Year	Arrivals (000s)	Receipts (US$mn)
1950	25,282	2,100	1991	463,951	277,568
1960	69,320	6,867	1992	503,356	315,103
1965	112,863	11,604	1993	519,045	324,090
1970	165,787	17,900	1994	550,471	353,998
1975	222,290	40,702	1995	565,495	405,110
1980	285,997	105,320	1996	596,524	435,594
1985	327,188	118,084	1997	610,763	435,981
1990	458,229	268,928	1998	625,236	444,741

Source: Adapted from WTO (1999a).

4%, the lowest since the 1950s (Table 1.2). Nevertheless, forecasts suggest that international tourism will continue to grow into the new century, with arrivals and receipts predicted to reach 1.6 billion and US$2 trillion respectively by 2020 (WTO, 1998a). Thus, at first sight, tourism as an economic sector has demonstrated healthy growth and, hence, is considered an attractive and safe development option.

However, the overall global figures mask two important factors. First, although international tourism can claim to be a growth sector, certain periods have witnessed low or even negative growth. The OPEC crisis of the mid-1970s, the global recession in the early 1980s and the Gulf conflict in 1991 all resulted in diminished growth figures and, for some countries, an actual drop in arrivals. For example, although world-wide international arrivals in 1991 grew by just 1.25%, Cyprus, as a result of its proximity to the Middle East, experienced a fall of 11.3% in its arrivals figures that year (Cyprus Tourism Organisation, 1992). Thus, tourism is highly susceptible to external influences which, certainly in the short term, may have a

Table 1.2 Tourism arrivals and receipts growth rates, 1950–98

Decade	Arrivals (Average annual increase %)	Receipts (Average annual increase %)
1950–1960	10.6	12.6
1960–1970	9.1	10.1
1970–1980	5.6	19.4
1980–1990	4.8	9.8
1990–1998	4.0	6.5

Source: WTO (1999a).

significant impact at a destinational level on tourism's economic development contribution. Moreover, the highly seasonal character of tourism in many destinations, and the consequential impact on income flows and employment levels, may also weaken tourism's development role.

Second, as Shaw and Williams (1994: 23) point out, the global growth in tourism does not imply that 'global mass tourism has now arrived and that the populations of most countries are caught up in a whirl of international travel'. Despite the growth of international tourism to and within certain regions, in particular the East Asia and Pacific (EAP) area, the flows of international tourism remain highly polarised and regionalised. That is, international tourism is still largely dominated by the industrialised world, with the major tourist flows being primarily between the more developed nations and, to a lesser extent, from developed to less developed countries. Indeed, despite the emergence of new, increasingly popular destinations, such as China, Poland and Thailand, the economic benefits of tourism remain highly polarised, with 'exchanges of money generated by tourism [being] predominantly North–North between a combination of industrialised and newly industrialised countries' (Vellas & Bécherel, 1995: 21). For example, developing countries as a whole received just 30.5% of international tourism receipts in 1997, whilst industrialised countries accounted for 63.8%. At the same time, the largest international movements of tourists occur within well-defined regions, in particular within Europe. Other significant regions include north America, with major flows between Canada and the USA and between the USA and the Caribbean and the EAP region (Table 1.3).

As a result, international tourism contributes most, in an economic sense, to those countries or regions that least require it. Indeed, despite the increasing popularity of long-haul travel, developing countries' share of world tourist arrivals

Table 1.3 Percentage share of international tourist arrivals by region 1960–95

	Africa	*Americas*	*EAP*	*Europe*	*Middle East*	*S. Asia*
1960	1.1	24.1	1.1	72.6	0.9	0.3
1970	1.5	25.5	3.2	68.2	1.1	0.6
1980	2.6	21.6	7.4	65.6	2.1	0.8
1990	3.3	20.6	11.6	62.1	1.7	0.7
1991	3.4	20.9	11.8	61.5	1.5	0.7
1992	3.5	20.6	12.5	60.9	1.7	0.7
1993	3.6	20.3	13.6	60.1	1.7	0.7
1994	3.4	20.0	14.0	60.2	1.6	0.7
1995	3.4	19.6	14.1	59.7	2.4	0.8

Source: WTO (1997: 5).

increased by just 2.2% between 1990 and 1997, growing from 28.4% to 30.6% of total arrivals.

However, the significant tourist flows within the developed world are also evidence of the potential contribution to development in industrialised countries, particularly in deprived urban areas or peripheral rural regions. In Ireland, for example, the government established its 'Programme for National Recovery' in 1987, the aim of which was to create 25,000 jobs and to attract an additional IR£500 million in tourist expenditure through doubling the number of overseas arrivals over a five year period (Hannigan, 1994; Hurley *et al.*, 1994). The success of this policy led to a further tourism-related development policy for the period 1994–99, during which another 35,000 jobs were expected to be created.

Tourism redistributes wealth

Both internationally and domestically, tourism is seen as an effective means of transferring wealth and investment from richer, developed countries or regions to less developed, poorer areas. This redistribution of wealth occurs, in theory, as a result of both tourist expenditures in destination areas and also of investment by the richer, tourist-generating countries in tourism facilities. In the latter case, developed countries are, in principle, supporting the economic growth and development of less developed countries by investing in tourism. However, it has long been recognised that the net retention of tourist expenditures varies considerably from one destination to another, whilst overseas investment in tourism facilities more often than not may lead to exploitation and dependency (see Chapter 2).

No trade barriers to tourism

Unlike many other forms of international trade, tourism does not normally suffer from the imposition of trade barriers, such as quotas or tariffs. In other words, whereas many countries or trading blocks, such as the European Union, place restrictions on imports to protect their internal markets, major tourism-generating countries generally do not normally impose limitations on the rights of their citizens to travel overseas, on where they go and on how much they spend. One notable exception is the 'ban' on American citizens flying directly from the USA to Cuba, whilst currency restrictions may limit international travel from certain less developed countries. For the most part, however, destination countries have free and equal access to the international tourism market, constituting 'an export opportunity free of the usual trade limitations' (Jenkins, 1991: 84). This position is likely to be strengthened by the inclusion of tourism in the General Agreement on Trade in Services (GATS), which became operational in January 1995.

In theory, then, destinations can attract as many tourists as they wish from where they wish, although the lack of trade barriers does not, of course, remove international competition. At the same time, the structure and control of the international travel and tourism industry also limits the ability of destinations to take advantage of this free market. For example, the growth of tourism in Nepal has suffered following the decision by Lufthansa, owing to negative profitability on the route, to suspend flights to Kathmandu from May 1997, thereby limiting demand from one of Nepal's key markets (Cockerell, 1997). Furthermore, although the inclusion of tourism in GATS is widely supported (WTO, 1995), in some quarters it is feared that it will simply lead to greater control of the tourism industry in destination areas by overseas, multinational corporations.

Tourism utilises natural, 'free' infrastructure

The attraction to tourists of many countries or regions lies in the natural resources – the sea, beaches, climate, mountains, and so on. This suggests that the development of tourism (and its subsequent economic contribution) is based upon natural resources that are free or 'of the country', inasmuch as they do not have to be built or created, and that 'economic value can be derived from resources which may have limited or no alternative use' (Jenkins, 1991: 86). Similarly, historic sites and attractions that have been handed down by previous generations may also considered to be free, although costs are, of course, incurred in the protection, upkeep and management of all tourist attractions and resources, whether natural or man-made. The point is that, in the context of tourism as a favoured development option, the basic resources already exist and therefore tourism may be considered to have low 'start-up' costs.

Backward linkages

Owing to the fact that tourists require a variety of goods and services in the destination, including accommodation, food and beverages, entertainment, local transport services, souvenirs, and so on, tourism offers, in principle, more opportunities for backward linkages throughout the local economy than other industries. Such opportunities include both direct links, such as the expansion of the local farming industry to provide food for local hotels and restaurants (Telfer, 1996b), and indirect links with, for example, the construction industry. Again, however, the optimism for this developmental contribution of tourism must be tempered by the fact not all destinations may be able to take advantage of these linkage opportunities. That is, a variety of factors, such as the diversity and maturity of the local economy, the availability of investment funds or the type/scale of tourism development, may restrict the extent of backward linkages. For example, referring back to the case of The Gambia, the economic benefits derived from tourism are very much limited by the fact, as a result of poor quality and a lack of supplies, the majority of tourist hotels import virtually all their food and drink requirements, as well as all fixtures and fittings in the hotels.

A variety of other, secondary reasons may also be suggested for the popularity of tourism as a development option. These include the facts that the development of tourism may lead to infrastructural improvements and the provision of facilities that are of benefit to local communities as well as tourists; that tourism often provides the justification for environmental protection through, for example, the designation of national parks; and, that tourism may encourage the revitalisation of traditional cultural crafts and practices. Together, along with the primary reasons outlined here, they explain why virtually every country in the world has, to a lesser or greater extent, developed a tourism industry.

The Contribution of Tourism Development

The extent to which tourism contributes to the national or local economy or, more generally, to development varies according to a variety of factors. However, as a general rule, it is likely that a greater dependence will be placed on tourism in less developed countries than in industrialised countries. Certainly, in many smaller, less developed nations with highly limited resource bases, in particular island micro-states, tourism has become the dominant economic sector. The Caribbean islands, the Indian Ocean islands of the Seychelles and the Maldives and the islands of the South Pacific fall into this category. However, the importance or scale of the tourism industry is not always related to a country's level of development. For example, in some less developed countries, such as India or Peru, tourism represents an important source of foreign exchange yet is not the main engine of development. In India, international tourism contributes just 0.8% of GDP, whilst in Peru tourism is not considered a primary growth area despite its 6.7% contribution to GDP. Conversely, in some developed states tourism is the dominant economic sector. With a per capita GDP of around $14,000, Cyprus is a high income country and, though non-industrialised, enjoys human development indicators matching those in developed countries. There, tourism is the most significant economic sector, contributing 20% of GDP, 25% of employment and about 40% of exports (Sharpley, 1998). Even in modern, industrialised countries where tourism makes a relatively small contribution to the overall economic activity, it may be the dominant sector in particular regions. In the English Lake District, for example, tourism generated over £500 million in 1996 (BTA, 1997) and supported one-third of all employment in the region.

In all cases, it is evident that the contribution or outcome of tourism development is measured in the quantifiable terms of tourism receipts, contribution to exports, contribution to GDP and employment levels. However, whilst these are certainly indicators of the *economic* contribution of tourism, it is less clear whether they are indicators of the *developmental* contribution of tourism. Therefore, as a basis for exploring the relationship between tourism and development, it is important to define not only the desired outcome of tourism, namely, 'development', but also the means of achieving that outcome.

Defining Tourism

Such has been the growth and spread of tourism over recent decades that it is now 'so widespread and ubiquitous ... that there are scarcely people left in the world who would not recognise a tourist immediately' (Cohen, 1974). However, 'tourism' remains a term that is subject to diverse interpretation, with a wide variety of definitions and descriptions proposed in the literature. This reflects, in part, the multidisciplinary nature of the topic and, in part, the 'abstract nature of the concept of tourism' (Burns & Holden, 1995: 5).

To complicate matters further, there is no single definition of the 'tourist'. In 1800, Samuel Pegge wrote in a book on new English usage that, simply, 'a traveller is now-a-days called a Tour-ist' (cited in Buzard, 1993: 1), although there is some debate as to when the word tourist was first used. Some attribute the origin of the term to Stendhal in the early 1800s (Feifer, 1985), whilst others suggest a number of different sources and dates (Theobald, 1994). Nevertheless, there now exists a diverse array of definitions and taxonomies of tourists, many of which are etic, being structured according to the specific perspective of the researcher.

Despite these difficulties, however, it is important to establish a working definition of tourism as the activity or process that allegedly acts as a catalyst of development. As a starting point, Chambers English dictionary refers to tourism as 'the activities of tourists *and* those who cater for them' (emphasis added), immediately reflecting the dichotomy between tourism as a social activity and tourism as an industry which enables and facilitates participation in that activity. In a similar vein, Burkhart and Medlik (1981: 41–3) identify two main groups or classifications of tourism definitions:

(a) *Technical definitions.* Technical definitions of tourism attempt to identify different types of tourist and different tourism activities, normally for statistical or legislative purposes. The first such definition, proposed by the League of Nations in 1937, defined a tourist as someone who travels for 24 hours or more outside their normal country of residence. It included those travelling for business in addition to pleasure, health or other purposes, and it also introduced the 'excursionist' as someone who stays in a destination for less than 24 hours. A similar definition, though resorting to the more general description of 'visitor', was produced by the United Nations Conference on Travel and Tourism in 1963. It states that a visitor is 'any person visiting a country other than that in which he [sic] has his usual place of residence, for any reason other than following an occupation remunerated from within the country visited', a visitor being either a tourist staying overnight or an excursionist on a day visit. This remains the basis of definitions of tourism adopted, for example, by the WTO, and is used primarily for the quantitative measurement of tourist traffic.

(b) *Conceptual definitions*. In contrast, attempts have also been made to define tourism conceptually from an essentially anthropological perspective. That is, a number of commentators have attempted to inject the meaning or role of tourism (to tourists themselves) into the definitional process. For example, Nash (1981) considers that 'at the heart of any definition of tourism is the person we conceive to be a tourist'. Approaching tourism from the perspective of motivation and touristic practices, he defines tourism as simply the activity undertaken by 'a person at leisure who also travels' (Nash, 1981). Smith develops this theme with a more explicit reference to motivation, a tourist being a 'temporarily leisured person who voluntarily visits a place for the purpose of experiencing a change' (Smith, 1989: 1). Similarly, Graburn (1983) emphasises tourism's functional role inasmuch as it 'involves for the participants a separation from normal 'instrumental' life and the business of making a living, and offers an entry into another kind of moral state in which mental, expressive, and cultural needs come to the fore'.

The technical and conceptual categories of tourism definitions evidently represent two extremes of a 'definition continuum' (Buck, 1978) which are constrained by their disciplinary focus. Ideally, therefore, a balanced, holistic definition that embraces both the factual and theoretical perspectives of tourism is desirable (Gilbert, 1990). Jafari (1977) goes some way to achieving this by epistemologically defining tourism as

> [T]he study of man [sic] away from his usual habitat, of the industry which responds to his needs, and of the impacts that both he and the industry have on the host's sociocultural, economic and physical environments.

However, given the variety of disciplinary treatments of tourism and the variety of forms that tourism takes, it is unrealistic to search for a single, all-embracing, holistic definition. Nevertheless, tourism is primarily a social activity. If people had neither the ability nor the desire to travel from one place to another, tourism would not exist. Thus, tourism is an activity which involves individuals who travel within their own countries or internationally, and who interact with other people and places. It involves people who are influenced and motivated by the norms and transformations in their own society and who carry with them their own 'cultural baggage' of experience, expectations, perceptions and standards. It is, in short, a social phenomenon which involves the movement of people to various destinations and their (temporary) stay there. By implication, therefore, tourists themselves play a fundamental role in the development of tourism and, as considered in Chapter 10, the manner in which tourism is 'consumed' has significant implications for the developmental outcomes of tourism.

At the same time, of course, tourists would not be able to travel without the variety of services provided by the tourism industry, the nature of which also influences the tourism development process. Therefore, tourism can be defined here as a social phenomenon determined by the activities and attitudes of its participants and possessing a number of characteristics which may determine its contribution to development. In particular there are as follows.

- It is normally considered a leisure activity, generally associated with short-term escape from the routine or ordinary and, implicitly, involving freedom from (paid and domestic) work.
- It is socially patterned; that is, the ability to participate in tourism and the nature of tourism consumption is influenced by tourists' sociocultural background.
- It is supported by a diverse, fragmented and multi-sectoral industry, the structure and characteristics of which are significant determinants in the nature of tourism development.
- It is largely dependent upon the physical, social and cultural attributes of the destination and the promise of excitement, authenticity and the extraordinary. It is also, therefore, an 'ecological' phenomenon inasmuch as tourism not only requires an attractive, different environment, but also interacts with and impacts upon that environment.

In effect, these characteristics set an agenda for the study of the developmental contribution of tourism. That is, the nature of tourism, the tourism industry and the destination are all factors which influence the manner or extent to which tourism contributes to development. The next task of this chapter is now to explore what is meant by the term development.

Defining Development

Development, according to Cowen and Shenton (1996: 3), 'seems to defy definition, although not for want of definitions on offer'. It is an ambiguous term that is used descriptively and normatively to refer to a process through which a society moves from one condition to another, and also to the goal of that process; the development process in a society may result in it achieving the state or condition of development. At the same time, it has been suggested that development is a philosophical concept as it alludes to a desirable future state for a particular society (though desirable to whom is not always clear), whilst development plans set out the steps for the achievement of that future state. In short, development can be thought of as a philosophy, a process, the outcome or product of that process, and a plan guiding the process towards desired objectives.

More broadly, development is also considered to be virtually synonymous with progress, implying positive transformation or 'good change' (see Thomas, 2000). In this sense, development is neither a single process or set of events, nor does it suggest a single, static condition. Therefore, although development is most commonly discussed in the context of the developing world, it is a concept that 'relates to all parts of the world at every level, from the individual to global transformations' (Elliot, 1999: 10). A society that is 'developed' does not cease to change or progress; the nature or direction of that change may, however, be different to changes in less developed societies.

Generally, then, development may be seen as a term 'bereft of precise meaning … [and] … little more than the lazy thinkers catch-all term, used to mean anything from broad, undefined change to quite specific events' (Welch, 1984). Its ambiguity is compounded by different uses of the term in different contexts and disciplines and, furthermore, the concept of development has evolved over time. Where at one extreme planners once adhered to 'the myth of development as progress', at the other extreme they denounce it as regression (Goulet, 1992). Nevertheless, for the purposes of this book it is vital to have a working definition of development as the goal of or justification for developing tourism.

The evolution of the development concept

Traditionally, development has been defined in terms of western-style modernisation achieved through economic growth (Redclift, 1987). That is, as the national economy grows, the national productive capacity increases and, as long as output grows at a faster rate than the population growth rate, then development is assumed to be the inevitable consequence.

This perceived 'primary role of economic forces in bringing about the development of a society has often been taken as axiomatic, so that development and economic development have come to be regarded as synonymous' (Mabogunje 1980: 35). Indeed, throughout the 1950s and 1960s, the path from underdevelopment to development was seen to lie along a series of economic steps or stages (Rostow 1960) and, as a result, development came to be defined according to economic measurements, such as GNP or per capita GNP, or according to economic structural criteria. Implicitly, as the economy grows – typically at an annual rate of 5–7% (Todaro, 2000: 14) and as social, economic and political structures modernise (according western parameters – see Figure 1.1) to encourage or accommodate such growth, then development is considered to be occurring.

By the late 1960s it had become clear that, in many countries, economic growth was not only failing to solve social and political problems but was also causing or exacerbating them (Seers, 1969). Some countries had realised their economic growth targets, but 'the levels of living of the masses of people remained for the most part unchanged' (Todaro, 2000: 14).

Moreover, although the aims of development had become more broadly defined with investment in education, housing and health facilities (with corresponding

Traditional	*Modern*

• Traditionalism:
   − orientation to the past/tradition
   − inability to adapt to new circumstances
	• Traditional values less dominant:
	   − ability to change/adapt
	   − challenge to obstacles of tradition

• Kinship system:
   − economic, social, legal structures
     determined by kin relations.
   − ascription as opposed to achievement
	• Open social system:
	   − geographical/social mobility
	   − economic, social, political freedom
	   − achievement as opposed to ascription

• Influence of emotion, superstition, fatalism	• Forward looking society:
	   − innovation, entrepreneurial spirit
	   − objective, rational approach

Figure 1.1 Characteristics of 'traditional' and 'modern' societies
Source: Adapted from Webster (1990).

'social indicator' measurements) becoming part of the development process, economic growth and 'modernisation' remained the fundamental perspective.

Thus, during the 1970s the pendulum began to swing away from development as an economic phenomenon towards the broader concept of development as the reduction of widespread poverty, unemployment and poverty. Increasing numbers of economists called for the 'dethronement of GNP' (Todaro, 2000: 14) although, as has been argued, this was not to suggest that economic growth was unnecessary or destructive. Growth 'may matter a great deal, but, if it does, this is because of some associated benefits that are realised in the process of economic growth' (Sen, 1994: 220). Indeed, even the concept of global sustainable development is, according to the widely cited Brundtland Report, dependent upon growth in the world economy by a factor of five to ten (WCED, 1987: 50).

Nevertheless, the traditional economic growth position was challenged by many, in particular Dudley Seers (1969), who asserted:

> The questions to ask about a country's development are therefore: what has been happening to poverty? What has been happening to unemployment? What has been happening to inequality? If all three of these have declined from high levels, then beyond doubt this has been a period of development for the country concerned. If one or two of these central problems has been growing worse, especially if all three have, it would be strange to call the result 'development', even if per capita income had doubled.

To these three conditions he later added a fourth: self-reliance. The oil crisis of the early 1970s had revealed the cost of dependence of many countries and, for Seers, development now implied '*inter alia*, reducing cultural dependence on one or more of the great powers' (Seers, 1977). Thus, not only had the concept of development expanded beyond simple economic growth to include broader social objectives collectively described by Mabogunje (1980: 39) as 'distributive justice', but also the notion of self-determination also became an essential ingredient of development. In other words, no longer was development considered to be a process lying in the control or 'trusteeship' (Cowen & Shenton, 1996: x) of the advanced, western nations; 'development can be properly assessed only in terms of the total human needs, values and standards of the good life and the good society *perceived by the very societies undergoing change*' (Goulet 1968 – emphasis added).

According to Goulet, three basic values represent this 'good life':

- *The sustenance of life:* all people have basic requirements, such as food, shelter and health, without which 'a state of underdevelopment exists'.
- *Esteem:* all individuals seek self-esteem, a sense of identity, self-respect or dignity. The nature of esteem varies society to the next and may be manifested in increased wealth and material well-being or, conversely, in the strengthening of spiritual or cultural values.
- *Freedom:* in the context of development, freedom represents increased choice for the individual members of society and freedom from servitude to ignorance, nature, other societies, beliefs and institutions.

Similarly, the United Nations Development Programme's *Human Development Report* (UNDP, 1990) defines development as the enlargement of people's choices, the most critical being to lead a long, healthy life, to acquire knowledge and to have access to the resources needed for a decent standard of living.

Thus, the concept of development has evolved, over half a century or so, from a process narrowly defined (by the western, industrialised nations) as economic growth to 'a far-reaching, continuous and positively evaluated change in the totality of human experience' (Harrison, 1988: xiii). The goal of the process is, in effect, the self-actualisation of individuals within a society, embracing at least five dimensions (see Goulet, 1992):

(1) an *economic* component – the creation of wealth and equitable access to resources as a means of overcoming the 'pollution of poverty';
(2) a *social* component – the improvement of health, education, employment and housing opportunities;
(3) a *political* dimension – the recognition of human rights, the creation of political freedom and the enabling of societies to select and operate political systems appropriate to their needs and structures;
(4) a *cultural* dimension – the protection or affirmation of cultural identity and self-esteem; and

(5) the *full-life paradigm* – the preservation and strengthening of the meaning systems, symbols and beliefs of a society.

To these, perhaps, should be added a sixth dimension, namely, an *ecological* component, which reflects the emergence of environmental sustainability as a guiding principle of all development policies. Together, these dimensions are broadly reflected in the global development goals identified at a OECD, UN and World Bank conference (Figure 1.2).

Development, then, is a complex, multidimensional concept which not only embraces economic growth and 'traditional' social indicators, such as healthcare, education and housing, but also seeks to confirm the political and cultural integrity and freedom of all individuals in society. It is, in effect, the continuous and positive change in the economic, social, political and cultural dimensions of the human condition, guided by the principle of freedom of choice and limited by the capacity of the environment to sustain such change.

The Characteristics of Underdevelopment

Having explored the meaning of development, it is also important to consider briefly the opposite side of the coin, namely, underdevelopment. In other words, although many of the problems facing less developed countries, such as pollution, poverty, unemployment, inequality and so on are evident in the goals of development, it is less clear what the specific characteristics of underdevelopment are.

Economic well-being:

- Reducing by half the proportion of people in extreme poverty.

Social development:

- Achieving universal primary education in all countries
- Demonstrating progress towards gender equality and the empowerment of women by eliminating disparities in primary and secondary education.
- Reducing by two-thirds the mortality rates for infants and children under 5 and by three-fourths the mortality rates for mothers
- Providing access to reproductive health services for all individuals of appropriate age.

Environmental sustainability and regeneration:

- Implementing national strategies for sustainable development by 2005 to ensure that the current loss of environmental resources is reversed globally and nationally by 2015.

Figure 1.2 International development goals for 2015

Consequently, also unclear is the extent to which particular development vehicles, such as tourism, are effective means of addressing these problems and challenges.

By definition, it is primarily the less developed countries of the world that experience the problems of underdevelopment. However, in the present context it is important to remember again that tourism also plays a developmental role in the wealthier, industrialised countries. There, specific areas, such as peripheral rural areas, suffer similar problems to less developed countries, albeit to a lesser extent. For example, unemployment, a lack of essential services, a dependence on primary economic sectors and inequality in housing or educational opportunities, as well as the challenge of environmental sustainability, are items high on the rural governance agenda. Nevertheless, it is the problems facing the 160 or so developing countries that are the principal focus of international development policies.

Of course, not all developing countries suffer the same problems, nor to the same extent, reflecting the fact that there exists an enormous diversity of countries that constitute the so-called Third World. As Todaro (2000) explores in detail, developing countries vary greatly according to geographic, historical, sociocultural, political and economic structural characteristics, all of which have some bearing on a country's level and rate of development. Nevertheless, developing countries are typically classified according to either per capita income, non-economic development indicators, such as literacy or life expectancy, or a combination of the two. Such classifications, in turn, draw upon the typical features of developing countries which characterise the condition of underdevelopment. These include the following ones.

Economic dependence upon the agricultural sector and the export of primary products and, conversely, a limited industrial sector

Compared with industrialised nations, most less developed countries are highly dependent upon agricultural production and exports as a source of income and employment. For example, on average almost 60% of the workforce in the less developed world is employed in agriculture compared with just 5% in developed nations. Similarly, agriculture contributes 14% of GDP in less developed countries compared to 3% in industrial countries, although significant variances exist. For example, in some African countries, such as Tanzania, Ethiopia and Uganda, the contribution of agriculture to GDP is 58%, 57% and 50% respectively, whilst in other, particularly South American, countries, the contribution is much lower (UNDP, 1998: 182/3). Frequently, productivity is barely above subsistence levels and a lack of technology and investment finance limit opportunities for increasing output. Therefore, although the export of primary agricultural products represents the principal source of foreign exchange earnings for many developing countries, typically accounting for between 60 and 70% of the foreign currency earnings of the developing world, their share of total world trade continues to decline (Todaro, 2000: 60).

Low levels of living – low incomes and low levels of health and education /literacy

In many less developed countries, a variety of factors contribute to what may be described generally as a low level of living. Principal amongst these is the low level of income, most commonly measured as per capita GDP as a guide to the relative economic well-being of people in different countries. Within the less developed world there are significant variances; the 44 least developed countries (LLDCs) designated by the United Nations, for example, had an average per capita GDP of US$233 in 1995, whilst the Bahamas, classed as a middle-income developing country, had a per capita GDP of over US$10,000 (UNDP, 1998: 5/6). However, the average per capita GDP for all less-developed countries, standing at US$867 in 1995, contrasts starkly with the average per capita GDP of US$12,764 in industrialised countries. Moreover, this income gap between the richer and poorer nations continues to widen. Between 1960 and 1995, per capita GDP grew annually at around 2% in the developed world. However, many less developed countries, particularly in Africa, experienced negative growth over the same period; in Ethiopia, for example, per capita GDP fell by 1.5% annually.

In terms of low levels of health, a variety of measures are utilised to demonstrate the health-related challenges within the developing world. These include life expectancy at birth (51 years in LLDCs; 62 years in all developing countries; 74 years in industrialised countries) and infant mortality (109 per 1000 live births in LLDCs compared with 13 per 1000 in industrialised countries). Table 1.4 lists some key health indicators for developing countries.

As with levels of income, there are significant variations both between different less developed countries and between developing and industrialised countries as a whole, although improvements are in evidence. For example, between 1960 and 1995 life expectancy in developing countries increased on average from 46 to 62

Table 1.4 Selected health indicators for developing countries

	Percentage of population without access to			Child (under 5) mortality rate (per 1000 live births)	Malnourished children under 5 (%)	% of population unlikely to survive to 40 years
	Safe water	Health services	Sanitation			
All developing countries	29	20	58	95	30	14
Least developed countries	43	51	64	171	39	29
Industrial countries	–	–	–	16	–	5

Source: Adapted from UNDP (1998).

years, whilst infant mortality fell from 149 to 65 per 1000 births. Similarly, between 1975 and 1995 adult literacy rates grew from 48% to 70% in developing countries (30% to 49% in LLDCs), though remaining well below the 99% literacy rate in industrialised countries.

High rates of population growth; high unemployment

Over 80% of the world's population live in the Third World, a proportion that will increase as developing countries generally experience higher birth rates than those in developed countries. Indeed, crude birth rates (the annual number of births per 1000 population) in less developed countries vary between 20 and 50, equating to an average annual population growth rate in developing countries of around 2.0%, compared with 0.5% in industrialised countries. This means that, between 1995 and 2025, the populations of many developing countries will double. In addition to inevitable pressures on scarce resources, such rapid population growth will also exacerbate an already serious under- and unemployment problem. It is estimated that unemployment in developing countries varies between 8 and 15% of the labour force, although the figure may be double amongst the 15–24 age group.

Balance of payments problems and high levels of international debt

Amongst the most publicised problems facing less developed countries are their balance of payments deficits and their high level of international debt. With limited natural resources and restricted industrial production, less developed countries, by necessity, import many of their basic needs. However, the opportunity to balance the import bill is severely restricted by their dependence upon the export of primary, agricultural products, the real value of which fell by some 25% during the 1980s alone. Thus, in 1995, exports from LLDCs covered, on average, 64% of their imports. At the same time, many less developed countries suffer high levels of international debt, partly as a result of their inability to pay for imports and partly as a result of excessive borrowing of 'cheap' money during the 1970s. Higher interest rates from the 1980s onwards meant that many countries became ensnared in the debt trap – they were paying out more to service their debt than they had received as borrowing, leading for recent calls from some quarters for western banks to write off Third World debt.

Socio-political structures ill equipped to address the challenges of underdevelopment

As discussed in Chapter 2, and of particular relevance to international tourism, many of the problems associated with underdevelopment are frequently attributed to the evident inequality in the global distribution of economic and political power.

However, social and political structures within many developing countries may also determine the degree to which development strategies are successful.

Recent years have witnessed significant changes in the political structures in many countries, with corresponding impacts on development. The collapse of the Soviet Union, in particular, brought about important changes within Eastern Europe although, as Hewitt (2000) points out, political freedom has been achieved at the cost of reduced aid from the West. Indeed, between 1992 and 1992, aid to the former Soviet Union fell by 14% in real terms. More generally, there has been a dramatic shift in the global patterns of democratisation over the last quarter century. For example, in 1975 there were, globally, 101 authoritarian regimes, 11 partial democracies and 35 liberal democracies, the latter primarily in Europe, North America and Australia. By 1995, there were 43 authoritarian states, whilst the number of partial and liberal democracies had grown to 42 and 79 respectively (Potter, 2000: 369). However, democratisation by itself may not facilitate development, and may even impede it. That is, irrespective of changes in the nature of government, the distribution of power within many less developed countries tends to favour a small, powerful élite (their position often being strengthened and legitimised by the democratic process); experience has shown that successful development is dependent upon fundamental transformations in socioeconomic structures that challenge this traditional dominance of the élite.

This is not, of course, a definitive list of the characteristics of underdevelopment. There are many other indicators of human development, including gender-related issues, access to energy and natural resources, safety and security and so on that must be included as measures of development. At the same time, as the balance sheet of human development (Figure 1.3) shows, there are also many 'developmental' problems facing industrialised countries. Whilst not normally considered to be indicators of underdevelopment, they nevertheless represent, in the context of wealthier, developed nations, challenges to the continuing achievement of development as previously defined.

Many of these issues are discussed in depth in the development studies literature. The main point here, however, is that for tourism to be considered an effective vehicle for development, then it should implicitly represent a means of addressing and providing a solution to many of the developmental challenges outlined earlier. In other words, there is little doubt that, as an economic sector, tourism has much to contribute to countries or specific areas within both the industrialised and less developed worlds; indeed, there are innumerable examples of tourism's positive contribution to income, employment and foreign exchange earnings in destination areas. What is less certain, however, is the extent to which this economic contribution of tourism feeds the developmental process or whether tourism, as a single, identifiable economic sector, represents on its own an effective developmental vehicle. As has been suggested here, the notion that economic growth is synonymous with development has been largely discredited – development is not simply about enrichment in a material sense, but about the enrichment of people's lives in terms of freedom, choice and self-betterment. Tourism undoubtedly creates wealth but, as subsequent chapters question, does it contribute to this broader concept of development?

Interestingly, some would suggest that neither tourism, nor indeed any other economic activity, can be an effective catalyst of development. More specifically, it is argued that 'development' is no longer a viable global process or objective, that we have reached the 'end of development' (Hewitt, 2000). Therefore, this introduction to the role of tourism in development would not be complete without, finally, a consideration of the future of the concept of development as a whole.

The End of Development?

During the 1990s, a number of commentators began to question the very concept of development, concluding that the age of international development as a realistic global process had come to an end. As Sachs (1992: 1) argues, after 40 years of development as the primary objective and aspiration of the less developed world, now 'the idea of development stands like a ruin in the intellectual landscape ... It is time to dismantle this mental structure'. Along with other members of the so-called 'post-development school', Sachs argues that the notion of development is fundamentally flawed, inherently unjust and has never worked and, therefore, should either be simply abandoned or replaced with a less mechanistic, prescriptive approach (Rahnema, 1997).

Two important factors have influenced post-development thinking. Firstly, the 1980s are widely considered to have been a 'lost decade' of development. That is, in many less developed countries the development process either stagnated or went into reverse, with socioeconomic conditions worsening for the majority of people in those countries. A variety of inter-related problems and factors, including high debt repayments, a decline in real non-oil commodity prices, a decline in foreign investment and aid and greater trade protectionism within the industrialised world, contributed to this situation whilst, more generally, the neoliberal economic development policies of the 1980s also came to be widely criticised (Hewitt, 2000). At the same time, the industrialised countries themselves were experiencing severe economic recession, further retarding economic growth in less developed countries.

Second, and more importantly, development has long been criticised as a western-centric philosophy, a process whereby western economic and socio-cultural values have become the objective of development – in short, a process based upon the belief that 'west is best'. Equally, and reinforcing the argument, western-inspired development policies have also been seen as mechanisms for the imposition of economic control over less developed countries to an extent that is equally, if not more, pervasive than the preceding colonial system (Escobar, 1997).

Progress	*Deprivation*
Health	
• By 1992 life expectancy was more than 75 years in 24 of 25 industrial countries.	• Nearly two million people are infected with HIV.
Education	
• Between 1960 and 1990 the tertiary enrolment ratio more than doubled – from 15% to 40%	• More than a third of adults have less than an upper-secondary education.
Income and Employment	
• Between 1960 and 1993 real per capita GNP grew by more than 3% a year. • The average annual rate of inflation during the 1980s was less than 5%.	• The total unemployment rate is more than 8%, and the rate among youths nearly 15%. More than 30 million people are seeking work. • The poorest 40% of households get only 18% of total income.
Women	
• Between 1970 and 1990 the number of female tertiary students per 100 male tertiary students studying science and technology more than doubled – from 25 to 67. • Women now account for more than 40% of the labour force and about a quarter of administrators and managers.	• The wage rate for women is still only two-thirds that for men. • Women hold only 12% of parliamentary seats.
Social Security	
• Social security expenditures account for about 15% of GDP.	• More than 100 million people live below the official poverty line, and more than 5 million are homeless.
Social Fabric	
• There are more than five library books and one radio for every person, one TV set for every two people. One person in three reads a newspaper.	• Nearly 130,000 rapes are reported annually in the age group 15–59.
Environment	
• Aggressive conservation measures and more appropriate pricing policies dramatically reduced energy use per $100 of GDP between 1965 to 1991 – from 166 kg of oil equivalent to 26 kg.	• Each year damage to forests due to air pollution leads top economic losses of about $35 billion – equivalent to the GDP of Hungary. • People in industrial countries consume nearly nine times as much commercial energy per capita as people in developing countries, though they constitute only a fifth of the world's population.

Figure 1.3 Balance sheet of human development – industrial countries
Source: UNDP (1996).

Certainly, the early concepts of development as economic growth and modernisation demonstrated a western bias, but even the most recent concept of sustainable development is criticised for reflecting classic western-centric economic growth principles. For many developing countries, escaping from the pollution of poverty is more vital than the luxury of sustainability.

It is not possible here to explore the idea of post-development in depth (see, for example, Rahnema & Bawtree, 1997), although the criticisms levelled at the development paradigms that comprise the 'age of development' are addressed in Chapter 2. The important point is that doubts have been raised about the validity of development, as an essentially western-inspired concept, as a global process and objective. Indeed, it has been argued (in a rather romantic, idealistic sense) that under-developed, pre-industrial societies may, paradoxically better represent the 'good life' than developed societies: 'the world's most primitive people have few possessions, *but they are not poor*. Poverty is not a certain small amount of goods, nor is it a relation between means and ends; above all it is a relation between people' (Sahlins, 1997: 19; emphasis in the original). Thus, if development itself is a debatable concept, then the potential for any activity, including tourism, to contribute to development must also be in doubt.

Nevertheless, it is an inescapable fact that many countries of the world are 'worse off' than other countries, and that even within the industrialised nations, certain regions are 'poorer' or enjoy fewer opportunities and benefits than others. At the same time, it is also an inescapable fact that tourism represents one (and, in some cases, the only) avenue along which development or the 'good life' may be pursued. The extent to which this is achievable through tourism is the primary focus of this book.

Chapter 2

The Evolution of Tourism and Development Theory

DAVID J. TELFER

Introduction

Development theory and tourism have evolved along similar time lines since the Second World War, yet there has been little work connecting the two fields of study (Telfer, 1996a). This is surprising considering tourism continues to be a growing focus of economic development policy in many regions and nations (Maleki, 1997). Countries around the world are turning to tourism as a strategy for development; however, researchers in this field have given minimal acknowledgement to the overriding development paradigms. Countries are fiercely competing for international tourism receipts, which are forecasted to total over US$2 trillion by 2020 and arrivals are predicted to top 1.6 billion (WTO, 1998a). Locations which can develop and market a tourism product, whether it be a special natural, historic or cultural attraction or an urban or rural destination, can take advantage of this market by attracting revenue from visitors (Maleki, 1997). Tourism is being used to generate foreign exchange, increase employment, attract development capital and promote economic independence (Britton, 1982). Others have also suggested that tourism can be a focus for local economic development tied into the maintenance of the biophysical environment (Wilkinson, 1992).

The purpose in this chapter is to address the theoretical gap between development theory and the use of tourism as a development tool. It focuses on the nature of development and will explore the evolution of development theory since the ending of the Second World War. While it is acknowledged that there is a diversity of approaches and classifications of development theory, for the purposes of this chapter, the main paradigms that have been identified are modernisation, dependency, economic neoliberalism and alternative development (see Telfer, 1996a). While it is not possible to provide a detailed comprehensive study of development theory in this chapter, the key components of each development paradigm are discussed along with relevant criticisms as they form the basis of the analysis to which tourism development is later evaluated. Linking the two fields together, the chapter then moves to indicate the extent to which each development paradigm has influenced tourism. An analysis of the positive and negative attributes of tourism developed under each of the four development paradigms is presented. This information is used as a basis for the establishment of an initial set of considerations for appropriate and sustainable tourism development. The considerations for appropriate and sustainable tourism development are based on elements from the four development paradigms, however, there is a heavy emphasis on the concepts from the alternative development paradigm. It is argued that linkages to local communities are an important component of appropriate and sustainable tourism development, which, in turn, should be planned with other sectors of the economy under the broader concepts of sustainable development.

Nature of Development

While there has been tremendous advancement, the planet still faces a number of new and old problems. Persistent poverty and unfulfilled elementary needs, famines and widespread hunger, violations of political freedoms and basic liberties, neglect of the interests and agency of women, and increasing threats to the environment and the sustainability of economic and social welfare continue to face both rich and poor nations (Sen, 1999). The way in which these problems have been dealt with has varied over time. The definition of development, classified as a normative term, has long been debated (Harrison, 1988; McKay, 1990). As pointed out in Chapter 1, the term has had several meanings including 'economic growth, structural change, autonomous industrialisation, capitalism or socialism, self-actualisation, and individual, national, regional and cultural self-reliance' (Harrison, 1988: 154). Initially the idea of development was conceived narrowly as economic growth after the Second World War and social and cultural factors were only recognised to the extent to which they facilitated growth (Brohman, 1996a; Malecki, 1997). Development was later expanded to incorporate social, moral, ethical and environmental considerations as it came to deal with human betterment and fulfilment through the expansion of choice (Goldsworthy, 1988; Ingham, 1993). Eight years after addressing development in terms of poverty, unemployment and inequality, Seers (1969, 1977) introduced the concept of self-reliance into his definition.

A further expansion of the term can be seen in the work of Todaro (1994) who outlined three core values (sustenance, self-esteem and freedom) and three objectives of development. The first objective is to increase the availability and distribution of basic human needs, the second is to raise the standard of living, which involves higher incomes, better education, the provision of more jobs and greater attention to cultural and humanistic values, thereby promoting greater individual and national self-esteem. The final objective is to expand the range of economic and social choices so that individuals and nations are not dependent on other people or countries. The expansion of freedoms is also at the heart of Sen's (1999) call for expanding freedoms in the areas of economic opportunities, political freedoms, social facilities, transparency guarantees and protective security.

With the growth of the environmental movement, development has expanded to encompass the highly debated term, sustainability (Redclift, 2000). The most cited definition of sustainable development proposed by the World Commission on Environment and Development (WCED, 1987: 43) is defined as 'development that meets the needs of the present without compromising the ability of future generations to meet their own needs'. The 1992 United Nations Conference on the Environment and Development (also known as the Earth Summit or Rio Conference) produced Agenda 21 (see Keating, 1994) which was an action plan for achieving sustainability based on the involvement of local communities using a bottom-up approach. The second Earth Summit (Rio +5) held five years later noted the increasing reliance some developing countries place on tourism and the need to plan appropriately (Holden, 2000). The Rio + 10 Conference is scheduled for 2002 in South Africa.

As a reflection of the changes noted here, not only has the meaning of development altered over time but the way in which development is measured has also changed. The traditional measures of the quality of life, such as per capita income or GNP, have been eclipsed by other more recent measurements such as the Human Development Index (socioeconomic), the Index of Sustainable Economic Welfare (environmental – Daly & Cobb, 1989), and political and civil liberty indices (Dasgupta & Weale, 1992; Brown, 1992). It is not the intention here to develop a new definition of development but rather to recognise the expanding scope of the term. As Hettne (1995) suggests, there can be no final definition of development, only suggestions of what development should imply in particular contexts. Thus development involves structural transformation that implies political, cultural, social and economic changes (Hettne, 1995).

Development Paradigms

> The strength of 'development' discourse comes of its power to seduce, in every sense of the term: to charm, to please, to fascinate, to set dreaming, but to also abuse, to turn away from the truth, to deceive. (Rist, 1997: 1)

The analysis of social change with respect to development encompasses a wide range of perspectives resulting in a variety of social theories and contested notions of change (Preston, 1996). As with the definition of development, development theory has broadened from simplistic economic growth models towards more holistic theories of historical social change (Hettne, 1995). Development theory can be divided into development ideology (the ends) and development strategy (the

Table 2.1 Political ideological underpinnings of development thinking

Conservative	*Liberal*	*Radical*
Market	*Non-structural reformist*	*Social struggle*
– open market competition	– direct assault on poverty	– Marxist
– minimal state role	– basic needs	– class struggle as route to development
Authoritarian	*Structural reformist*	*Commandist*
– strong role of state allied with capital	– broad based reforms for greater social distribution of power and wealth	– Leninist
– top down development	– land reform	– political elite commands economy to organise production in the name of the people

After Goldsworthy (1988).

means). Development strategy is the means of implementing the development process guided by a specific ideology (Hettne, 1995). Goldsworthy (1988) argues that much of development thinking remains politically uninformed and more attention is needed to clarify the ideological underpinnings of development theory as displayed in Table 2.1. Goldsworthy (1988) also suggests that all development theories, policies, plans and strategies consciously or unconsciously express a preferred notion of what development is and these preferences, in turn, reflect values. The recognition of the inherent value systems and political underpinnings in development theories illustrates that development has a powerful normative component.

The development paradigms that evolved after the Second World War were products of three major influences: the US Marshall Plan, which helped to rebuild Europe after the Second World War, resulting in a belief in managed capitalist economic and social development; an optimistic view of the future; and a sense of rising determination of the colonies to follow a path to independence (Dickenson *et. al.*,1986). These influences led to a belief in the superiority of western interventionist economics and that policy development was a linear process leading towards the same political, economic and social structures as those of the West (Dickenson *et. al.*,1986).

Table 2.2 outlines chronologically four main development paradigms and their component parts, which have evolved since the end of the Second World War. It must be stressed that there are a variety of different classification systems for development theories and the information presented in Table 2.2 is only one perspective used to introduce readers to the various concepts which will be used later to examine tourism development. The time frames are only guidelines as it can be difficult to indicate precisely when a development paradigm started. The time frames indicate when the paradigm gained prominence after the Second World War with

Table 2.2 Evolution of development theory

Time guide	Development paradigms	Selected theoretical approaches or models	Key concepts/strategies
1950s and 1960s	Modernisation	Stages	Societies pass through similar development stages as western countries
		Diffusion	Spread of growth impulses from developed areas; growth poles; trickle down effect; state involvement, regional economic development
1950s and 1960s	Dependency	Neocolonialism	Underdevelopment caused by exploitation by developed countries; western cultural influence
		Dualism	Poverty is functional to global economic growth; rich and poor – between countries and within countries, regional inequalities
		Structuralism	Domestic markets, import substitution, social reforms, protectionism, state involvement
mid 1970s and 1980s	Economic neoliberalism	Free market	Supply side macroeconomics; free competitive market; privatisation
		Structural adjustment	Focus on market forces and competitive exports
		One world	New world financial system; deregulation internationalisation of production
1970s early 1980s	Alternative development	Basic needs	Priorities of food, housing, water, health and education
		Grassroots	People-centred development; local control of decision-making, empowerment, NGOs
		Gender	Women in development, gender relations, empowerment
		Sustainable development	Environmental management; meet the needs of the present generation without compromising future needs

After Telfer (1996a). *Sources*: Todaro (1994) and Brohman (1996).

many components still being applicable today. The development paradigms are not all mutually exclusive and some stress directed strategies and policies as to how development should proceed (structural adjustment, basic needs) while others comment more on the underlying reasons for the existence of underdevelopment in a nation (neocolonialism). Each new development paradigm can be viewed, in part, as a reaction against the theories which preceded it. In examining the changes in paradigms, Rist (1997: 2) reminds us that 'every perspective involves a particular point of view, which should be defined so as to dispel the illusion of objectivity or exhaustiveness'.

Modernisation

Modernisation has been defined as socioeconomic development, which follows an evolutionary path from a traditional society to a modern society such as North America or Western Europe (Schmidt, 1989). There is a shift from agriculture to industry and from rural to urban (see Lewis, 1954) and the money market plays a central role. The influence of the family declines and institutions become more differentiated while modern values and institutions opposed by tradition are introduced (Harrison, 1988).

Modernisation has its roots in a variety of different perspectives applied by non-Marxists to developing countries in the 1950s and 1960s (Harrison, 1988). Its early roots can be traced to growth theory grounded in economics based on the transfer of Keynesian models for analysing economic growth developed in the USA and Europe (Brohman, 1996). Thinking in the time period immediately after the Second World War was dominated by functionalist Modernisation (Svenson, 1991) and influenced by Keynesian economics, which advocates a high degree of state involvement (Asimakopulos, 1991). Rostow's (1967) Stages of Economic Growth posited that for development to occur, a country passes through the following stages: traditional society, pre-conditions for take-off, the take-off, the drive to maturity and the age of high mass consumption. It was argued that developed countries had passed the stage of take-off into self-sustaining growth while underdeveloped countries were still in the traditional society or were in the pre-conditions stage. Rostow (1967: 1) argued that the stages were 'in the end, both a theory about economic growth and a more general, if still highly partial, theory about modern history as a whole'. The adherents to the Stages of Economic Growth believed that countries must save and invest a proportion of their GNP in order to have economic growth. Countries able to save 15–20% of GNP would develop at a much faster rate (Todaro, 1994).

The initial economic focus expanded to include the sociological traditions of evolutionism, diffusionism, structural functionalism, systems theory and interactionism along with input from other disciplines such as political science, anthropology, psychology, economics and geography (Harrison, 1988). Economic growth was measured in terms of per capita income and GNP while social development indicators included literacy rates, access to medical services and ownership of consumer durables (Harrison, 1988). Harrison (1992a: 9) identifies modernisation as the process of 'westernization, whereby the internal structures of "developing" societies become more like those of the West allegedly by emulating Western development patterns'.

The theories and strategies of regional economic development which focus, in part, on the transmission or diffusion of growth impulses (Browett, 1980; Schumpeter, 1934, 1961; Perroux, 1995; Myrdal, 1963; Hirschman, 1958; see also Preston, 1984; Higgins & Higgins, 1979) are also considered here briefly as strategies within modernisation. Perroux (1988), for example, discusses development poles, which are locations that contain propulsive enterprises that generate spread effects through investments. A system of urban areas is also seen as a dynamic agent of development (Friedmann, 1978). The regional inequalities, which occur as a result of policies of regional economic development are discussed later in terms of dependency theory. These issues are not often examined in the context of broader development paradigms and, as a result, will be explored in greater detail in Chapter 4 in a separate chapter entitled 'Tourism and Regional Development'.

Critics have challenged the unidirectional path of development of modernisation and also the assumption that traditional values are not compatible with modernity (So, 1990). Criticism has also been directed at the western ethnocentricism embedded in the model and the fact that it does not consider alternative or traditional methods of development (Mehmet, 1995; Said, 1978, 1993; Schmidt, 1989; Galli, 1992; Wiarda, 1983). Modernisation theorists have been criticised for high levels of abstraction (So, 1990). Dependency theorists have suggested that modernisation is an ideology used to justify western involvement and domination of the developing world. Modernisation has also come under attack from those in the post-modernism camp who argue that large-scale top-down meta-theories no longer apply universally across a diversity of environments.

Dependency

The dependency paradigm gained prominence in the 1960s as a critique of modernisation and is one of the best-known neo-Marxist development theories (Schuurman, 1993). Proponents argue that developing countries have external and internal political, institutional and economic structures, which keep them in a dependent position relative to developed countries (Todaro, 1997). International dependence models gained increasing support, especially among intellectuals from developing countries, as a result of growing disenchantment with stages and structural change models (Todaro, 1997). Dependency theorists argued that Europe's development, for example, was based on the 'external destruction: brutal conquest, colonial control and the stripping of non-Western societies of their peoples, resources and surpluses' (Peet, 1999: 107). At the risk of simplifying the theoretical diversity within dependency, Hettne (1995) presented some of the common aspects of the dependency approach to development and underdevelopment. The most important obstacle to development is not the lack of capital or entrepreneurial skills but the international division of labour. This obstacle to development is then seen as an external force as opposed to an internal force. The international division of labour is then analysed in terms of centre and periphery regions with surpluses in the economy moving from the periphery to the centre. With the surpluses moving from the periphery to the centre, development occurred in the centre while simultaneously, underdevelopment was occurring in the periphery. With the periphery doomed to underdevelopment due to its linkages with the centre, it was necessary for a developing nation to 'disassociate itself from the world market, to break the chains of surplus extraction and to strive for national self reliance' (Hettne, 1995: 97).

Similar to modernisation, dependency has roots in a variety of different perspectives and approaches, a few of which are outlined in more detail here. The dependency school emerged from the convergence of two major intellectual trends. The first intellectual trend has its roots in Latin American structuralism which led to the formation of the Economic Commission for Latin America (ECLA) led by Prebisch (Cardoso, 1979; Hettne, 1995) and the second has roots in Marxism including classical Marxism, Marxism–Leninism and neo-Marxism. While some of the approaches related to dependency have been criticised for being vague on policy recommendations (So, 1990), the ECLA developed a series of domestic industrialisation policies based in the context of self-reliance. Theoretically, the ECLA believed that only 'central' nations benefited from trade whereas 'peripheral' nations suffered. The ECLA's development strategy included domestic industrialisation, protectionism and import substitution. Ideologically, the approach of the ECLA constituted a form of economic nationalism (Hettne, 1995). With its focus on domestic industrialisation and self-reliance, this chapter will later return to the structural approach in examining tourism development.

The work of the broadly based school of neo-Marxists has been referred to at various times as dependency theory, world systems theory and underdevelopment theory (Harrison, 1988). Neo-Marxism reflects a transformation of Marxist thinking from the traditional approach, focusing on the concept of development with a Euro-centric view to a more recent approach, which focuses on the concept of underdevelopment and expresses a Third World view (Hettne, 1995). The emergence of the dependency paradigm came not only from some of the perceived weaknesses of the ECLA but also as a more radical response to orthodox development thinking such as that advanced in Rostow's *Stages of Economic Growth*. Oman and Wignaraja (1991) outlined three main currents of dependency in Latin America. The first is found in the writings of Furtado and Sunkel who sought to reformulate the limits of the ECLA and argued that economic policy should be reoriented towards national economic development to overcome the constraints of the centre–periphery relationship. The second current is found in the neo-Marxist views of Frank (1966) who negated the possibility of capitalist development, stating that capitalism itself leads to the 'development of underdevelopment'. Frank argued that 'metropolitan capitalism depends on the exploitation and active under-development of an already capitalist periphery' (Corbridge,1995: 5). Finally the writings of Cardoso and Faletto accepted the possibility of capitalist development and are thus closer to traditional Marxism. They acknowledged that for some parts of the periphery, 'dependent development' was conceivable (Oman & Wignaraja, 1991).

The neo-Marxist, neocolonial dependency model states that the Third World exists in a state of underdevelopment as a result of the 'historic evolution of a highly unequal international capitalistic system of rich–poor country relationships' (Todaro, 1994: 81). Local élites are often presented as serving the interests of, or are dependent on, multinational corporations, national bilateral-aid agencies or multi-lateral assistance organisations such as the World Bank or the International Monetary Fund (IMF), which can result in the perpetuation of underdevelopment (Todaro, 1997). The resulting international system leaves an unequal power rela-tionship between the rich, developed countries (the centre) and the poor, underdeveloped countries (the periphery). Similarly, the dualistic dependency thesis emphasises dual societies (rich and poor) which exist between and within de-veloped and developing countries resulting in areas of wealth surrounded by poverty. The impoverished sectors are indispensable for the wealthy sectors as they supply them with cheap labour. This dualistic system is chronic and the gap between the two sectors is increasing (Todaro, 1994). Finally, the world system ap-proach, often identified with Wallerstein, shares common traits with the dependency school. Within the world system, there are three main economic zones: the core, the semiperiphery and the periphery (Peet, 1999); and underdevelopment occurs as pe-ripheries are incorporated into the world system (Hettne, 1995).

Dependency can also be examined in terms of regional economic development as it applies to regional inequalities. Theorists such as Myrdal (1957) and his discus-sion of backwash effects and Friedman's (1966) centre–periphery model both mention the regional inequalities which result from economic development. While these theorists are not necessarily proponents of dependency, their narratives on the processes and policies of regional economic development illustrate similar con-cepts to those presented in various forms of dependency theory.

The concept of dependency has also been applied to culture. The following comment by Desjeux (1981: 33) illustrates the influence a development project for-mulated in western philosophy and organisational structures can have on a local culture: 'Development projects tend more towards an attempt at normalising social behaviour on the basis of rules and scientific organisation of work or Western or-ganisational models'. According to Desjeux (1981: 33), this trend is based on

sociological or psychological postulates that there is one universal reality and individuals are in agreement with this organisation. This type of thinking places the
weak cultures in developing countries at an extreme disadvantage. The integration
of local culture into development projects also becomes difficult as people who are
removed from and do not participate in the local culture often make decisions on
development in the host's local culture (Desjeux, 1981).

Dependency theory has faced a wide range of criticisms, which mirror its diversity of approaches. Dependency is criticised for being highly abstract, pessimistic,
rhetorical and for emphasising external conditions over internal factors (So, 1990).
Booth's (1985) well-known critique of dependency argued on a number of fronts including the fact that the meta-theoretical influences within Marxism have led to
grand simplifications, which are either wrong or too general to be relevant to the
most important practical issues facing development economists (see also Booth,
1993). Critics argue that the dependency perspective, with the exception of the
structuralist school, is vague on policy recommendations and does not identify concrete plans for newly independent states (So 1990). Friedmann and Douglas (1978)
have published a critique of the development strategy of dualistic dependency
theory. The protectionist policies and isolationism of the structural school have also
been criticised for being overly optimistic about the point that industrialisation
would end all development problems (So, 1990; Cardoso, 1979).

Economic neoliberalism

While some theorists called for the creation of a hybrid approach incorporating
modernisation and dependency-world systems perspectives, others moved in the
direction of neoliberalism (Brohman, 1996a). The development of economic
neoliberalism was a reaction against the policies of strong state intervention, including those promoted by structural dependency theorists. The neoliberal
'counter-revolution' was dedicated to counteracting the impact Keynesianism had
on development theory (Brohman, 1996a). Economic neoliberalism gained popularity with the oil crisis coming at the beginning of the 1970s and the subsequent
restructuring of international capitalism, leading to a redefinition of the role of the
state and, thus, the end of Keynesianism and the welfare state (Schuurman 1993).
The rise of conservative governments in the USA, Canada, Britain and West
Germany in the 1980s continued to influence this revolution in thinking (Todaro,
1994). Neoliberalism draws on neoclassical economic theory which 'treats people as
atomistic individuals who are bound together only through market forces'
(Brohman, 1995: 297). It also has roots in the work of Adam Smith and his principle of
laissez-faire and David Ricardo's theory of comparative advantage, which both call
for a minimalist approach to state involvement in economic transactions (Brohman,
1996a). The movement favours supply-side macroeconomics, free competitive
markets and the privatisation of state enterprises. Developing countries are encour-

aged to welcome private investors from developed countries. As outlined by Lal (1985: 36), the problems of developing countries are not due to market problems but to 'irrational government interventions' including foreign trade controls, price controls and inflationary financing of fiscal deficits. The resulting shift placed new emphasis on 'supply-side factors, private investment, market-led growth and outward development while turning away from older developmentalist policies based in demand stimulation, import substitution, state intervention and centralized development planning' (Brohmam, 1996a: 27).

Early structural adjustment models of development formed part of the modernisation paradigm and focused on mechanisms in the economy which would transform a subsistence agricultural society to a modern urbanised society (see Lewis, 1954; unlimited supplies of labour theory). Chenery and Syrquin's (1975) comparative studies (cross section and longitudinal) on developing countries identified the 'correct' combination of development policies for sustained growth. These policies included a shift from agriculture to industry and a change in consumer demand to manufactured goods and services. More recently, the World Bank, the International Monetary Fund (IMF) and other international development agencies have invested large amounts of resources in Structural Adjustment Lending Programmes (SALPs) (Mosley & Toye, 1988). SALPs are directed at specific policy changes within the receiving countries. The objectives of SALPs focus on financial, macroeconomic and microeconomic adjustments, which include: removing import quotas, reforming budgets, dissolving the powers of state marketing boards, currency devaluation, reducing inflation, downsizing public services, privatisation of public enterprises and export promotion (Mosley & Toye, 1988; Konadu-Agyemang, 2000; Mohan *et al.*, 2000). The SALPs imply that the strategies of the international monetary agencies will lead to the correct path of development (Singer & Ansari, 1992) and it is the endogenous factors that serve as impediments to development and not the exogenous factors that are problems as cited by those in the dependency area (Konadu-Agyemang, 2000). The SALPs of the IMF and neoliberal theory have strong links to monetarist economics. Monetarist economics can be traced to equilibrium theorists of the late 19th and early 20th centuries who advocated using interest rate adjustments for sustained economic equilibrium with lower rates promoting increased growth. In addition, the quantity theory of money is central to monetarism. Macroeconomic problems such as inflationary pressures and indebtedness of developing countries are viewed as monetary problems as a result of excess government spending and other demand stimulation which has driven up the quantity of money in the economy to an unsustainable level (Brohman, 1996a).

McKay (1990) argues that the dominant model, which prevails among policymakers and among those controlling investment funds, is a global model which supports the notion of 'one world'. Like other neoliberal approaches towards development, this model stresses the efficiency of the free market in the allocation of resources, deregulation and export orientation. It attributes, however, even more importance to international money markets in the 'one world' or global market. Neoliberals also support a monoeconomic approach where the problems of developing countries are amenable to general solutions based in standard economic principles rather than proposing different solutions for developing countries (Brohman, 1996a).

Economic neoliberalism has been criticised for its financial strategies (SALPs) and that it is dominated by western countries. SALPs have been criticised for their national or regional outlook. The policies have been criticised for their dire social implications such as declining standards of living and growth of poverty. It is argued that privileged groups who have access to resources and key contacts can take advantage of the new outward economy while the disadvantaged groups face a shrinking domestic economy, falling wages, removal of labour regulations, rising prices for basic consumption and cutbacks in social assistance programmes (Brohman, 1996a). Poor women and children have particularly been noted to suffer the effects of structural adjustment policies (SAPs). Recent criticisms of the IMF including its devaluation policy of the Mexican peso (Drouin, 1995) and its emergency rescue packages for Thailand, Indonesia and South Korea in the context of the Asian economic crisis (Hale, 1998) are a reflection of disillusionment with these policies. Kendie (1995) argues that SAPs need restructuring to include environmental dimensions.

The main focus of SAPs has been to reform the political economy without properly linking the measures to the democratic process. It has been argued that this has resulted in the strengthening of national and transnational élites in the new economic order (Dieke, 1995). Critics, such as Strange (1988, 1996), of the new global economic order argue that governments of all states have been weakened as a result the accelerated integration of national economies into a single global market economy and they criticise the power of international organisations. Recent protests at meetings of the WTO in Seattle, the IMF in Prague and the Summit of the Americas in Quebec City also illustrate the growing disenchantment with the policies of international financial agencies. Neoliberalism has also been criticised for its association with orthodox neoclassical theory. Neoclassical theory, in turn, has been criticised as it neglects sociocultural and political relations, environment and sustainability issues, and the intersubjective realm of meaning and values of development (Brohman, 1995).

> It is usually said that when a development project fails it is because no account has been taken of the qualitative variables, i.e. of culture in the broadest sense of the term: that cultural model, traditions or irrational behaviour restrain the introduction of rational and universal technico-economic innovations. (Desjeux, 1981: 37)

Alternative development

Since the early postwar period, mainstream development strategies have centred on economic growth and the top-down diffusion of growth impulses (Brohman, 1996a). The alternative development paradigm is a pragmatic, broadly based approach, which arose out of the criticisms of these models. Schmidt (1989) argues that there are inherent contradictions in social theories of economic change which were developed by urbanised thinkers, and which were based on development concepts from industrialised countries. Edwards (1989) writes on the irrelevance of development studies arguing for more practical research, which appreciates the indigenous knowledge systems and popular participation. The various alternatives to the Eurocentric, meta-narrative, economic models are centred on people and the environment. The focus of planning often is from the bottom up.

The dissatisfaction with mainstream development models became widespread in the development community in the early 1970s and many international and bilateral aid agencies began searching for alternative, more people-oriented approaches (Brohman, 1996a). The basic needs approach begins with providing opportunities for full physical, mental and social development of the human personality (Streeten, 1977; see Maslow, 1970 for hierarchy of needs). Direct attacks are made on problems such as infant mortality, malnutrition, disease, literacy and sanitation (Streeten, 1977). Meanwhile, indigenous theories of development are promoted as they incorporate local conditions and knowledge systems (Schafer, 1989; Chipeta, 1981). There is a call for increased local involvement in the development process (Bock, 1989; Haq, 1988; Alamgir, 1988; Pretty, 1994; Telfer, in press). Increased participation is then linked to the concepts of empowerment and local control over decision-making (Brohman, 1996a). Within indigenous development theory is the increased recognition of the role of women in local development (Gladwin, 1980; Awa, 1989; Norem et al., 1989; Brohman, 1996a). Moser (1989) identified five historical approaches to gender studies, which include welfare, equity, anti-poverty, efficiency and empowerment. The United Nations declared the decade from 1975–85 as the Decade for Women, which coincided with the Women in Development Approach.

The South Commission (1990) redefined development to be self-directed and focused on self-reliance. The process of involving local populations and empowering them is the focus of Participatory Rural Appraisal (PRA) (Chambers, 1994). Other grassroots approaches include the learning process approach (Korten, 1980), the participatory approach (Edwards, 1989) and the structured flexibility approach (Brinkerhoff & Ingle, 1989). Non-governmental organisations (NGOs) have increasingly played a role in local and community-based development initiatives and, without the burden of government responsibility, NGOs have been able to engage in extensive participatory fieldwork which can generate innovative solutions to local problems rather than standardised state solutions (Brohman, 1996a). Friedmann (1966), who proposed the well-known 'centre–periphery' model, reversed his position (Friedmann & Forest, 1988) and acknowledged the politics of place. He is now an advocate for planning and development based on social learning and indigenous approaches.

Along with a focus on people, alternative development is closely connected to the environment and sustainability. The concept of sustainability has developed with the realisation that environmental resources are limited on our planet (Loening, 1990). Highlighted by the 1987 World Commission on Environment and Development's (WCED) *Our Common Future* (1987) and the 1992 *AGENDA 21* (Keating, 1994), sustainability has come to mean meeting the needs of the present generation without compromising the needs of future generations. As Redclift (1987) suggests, the dominant modernisation, dependency and neoclassical paradigms did not incorporate the environment into development. Now however, ecological processes and resources are being increasingly considered as part of the economic system (Barbier, 1989). The links between the environment and politics have also come to the forefront in the field of political ecology, which attempts to describe the spatial and temporal impacts of capitalism on Third World people and environments (Bryant & Bailey, 1997).

Along with an increased environmental awareness, the concept of sustainability links back to include the recognition of the role of local communities in development. The following comment illustrates the need to understand culture in relation to sustainability.

> Specialists trained in western science often fail to recognise indigenous ecological knowledge because of the culture and religious ways in which indigenous peoples record and transmit that learning. Ways of life that are developed over scores of generations could only thrive by encoding ecological sustainability into the body of practice, myth and taboo that passes from parent to child. (Durning, 1993: 91)

Pretty (1994) developed a typology of seven forms of how people participate in development programmes and projects. Participation ranges from passive participation where people are told what development project is proceeding to self-mobilisation where people take initiatives independent of external institutions. Pretty argues that if development is to be sustainable, then at least the fifth level of participation (functional participation) must be achieved. Functional participation includes the forming of groups by local people to meet predetermined objectives related to the development project. The sixth level is interactive participation, which involves people participating in joint analysis of the development projects, which leads to action plans and institutional strengthening. The seventh stage of participation is self-mobilisation as outlined earlier.

Criticisms of the alternative development are as varied as its approaches. Criticisms of the basic needs approach include: it may impede economic growth in the long term: it underestimates the importance of political change, and it can lead to too much state control (Van Der Hoeven, 1988). Critics of indigenous development theories cite problems of consensus building, barriers to participation, lack of accountability, weak institutions and lack of integration with international funding sources (Brinkerhoff & Ingle, 1989; Wiarda, 1983).

The term sustainable development is criticised for being vague. There are multiple definitions of the term depending on the problem being addressed (Arnold, 1989). Policy-makers are forced to decide what constitutes sustainability criteria and at what level they should be applied (project, regional, national, global). Questions are raised as to what should be sustained, and who decides what should be sustained. One consensus surrounding the definition is that it may be defined differently in terms of each culture, however, Redclift (2000) argues that this is superficially convenient. Difficulties also arise in measuring and quantifying environmental impacts. Graf (1992: 553) argues that the WCED reasserts the 'Northern global ideological hegemony'. There has also been a shift in focus, which has raised criticism. In the 1980s, environmentalists were usually concerned with the local or national space and with ideas such as eco-development or self-reliance that aimed to increase political and economic independence of a place by reconnecting ecological resource flows. However, in more recent years, environmentalists have taken on a global view, in part an outcome of space travel, whereby the planet has become a visible object from space. This shift to global environmental management, however, can also be seen to be in conflict with the aspirations of cultural rights, democracy, self-determination and present a threat to local communities and their lifestyles (Sachs, 1996).

Criticisms aimed at the various paradigms of development covered in this chapter so far have also been raised by those in the post-development camp. The authors of the *Development Dictionary* took aim at the conceptual foundations of the practices of development professionals, criticising not only official declarations on development but also grassroots movements (Peet, 1999). In an often quoted passage, Sachs (1996: 1) stated the following:

> The idea of development stands like a ruin in the intellectual landscape. Delusion and disappointment, failures and crimes have been the steady companions of development and they all tell a common story: it did not work. Moreover, the historical conditions, which catapulted the idea into prominence have vanished: development has become outdated. But above all, the hopes and desires, which made the idea fly, are now exhausted: development has grown obsolete.

In fact, the 1980s have been referred to as the lost decade of development. Those in the post-development camp rejected the way of thinking and the mode of living produced by modern development. They favoured revitalised versions of non-modern or non-western philosophies and cultures. Western development was a destructive force to be resisted (Peet, 1999). While they do criticise development, those in the post-development camp still have positions for social change and political activism. These positions can be generalised into three categories: radical pluralism, simple living and reappraising non-capitalist societies. One of the recurring themes from a variety of these perspectives is the support of local initiatives and the importance of community involvement in the development process (Peet, 1999).

The evolution of developmental thought has become increasingly complex over time. It has moved from being prescriptive to analytical in focus. Impact assessments of development policies are becoming more important as they relate not only to changes in the environment but also in changes to local communities. The linkages to the local community and its role in the development decision-making are becoming more essential as development policies start to operate under the paradigm of sustainability. If tourism is to be developed in a sustainable manner, it is important to utilise local resources. The discussion now turns to conceptualising tourism's role in development before examining tourism under each development paradigm. The discussion will then turn to the creation of an initial tourism and development theory framework.

Conceptualising Tourism's Role in Development Theory

The model presented in the Introduction to this book indicates the complexity of the relationship between tourism and development. Development theory and tourism have evolved along similar time lines since the Second World War and have shared similar focuses. Tourism research has advanced mainly after the Second World War with the rise of mass tourism (Britton, 1982). Papers on tourism can be traced to the 1930s and earlier but the bulk of the literature on tourism evolved from the 1960s (Pearce, 1993). Tourism research initially functioned as an instrument for development with the majority of the research being conducted by planners and economists who worked for organisations including the United Nations, the World Bank and the Organisation for Economic Cooperation and Development (Graburn & Jafari, 1991). During the 1960s, tourism was essentially equated with development, which was part of the modernisation paradigm. There was a belief that tourism created increases in foreign exchange and employment and that tourist expenditures generated a large multiplier effect, which stimulated the local economy (Davis, 1968; Peppelenbosch & Templeman, 1973; Graburn & Jafari, 1991). However, in time, authors began to question the benefits of tourism (Bryden, 1973), indicating that lower multiplier effects and high levels of leakages were closer to reality. This trend was similar to the dependency theorist critique of Modernisation. The title of de Kadt's 1979a book *Tourism – Passport to Development?* indicates the uncertainty involved in using tourism as a development tool. The negative impacts of tourism in developing countries began to be documented more and more (UNESCO, 1976) in disciplines such as anthropology and sociology (Graburn & Jafari, 1991). In the 1980s and 1990s, the neoliberal economic paradigm and tourism studies focused on international markets and competitive exports as tourism is an invisible export industry in the tertiary sector. Mathieson and Wall (1982) likened the tourism industry to banking and insurance where no tangible product is shipped from one place to another. More recently, tourism research has embraced the concept of sustainability, which is part of the alternative development paradigm (Butler, 1993a; Pigram, 1990; Wall, 1993a,b; Holden 2000). Research evaluating alternative types of tourism development, including ecotourism, has become more prevalent (Smith & Eadington, 1992). These changing trends in tourism research were picked up in the analysis of the literature to date by Jafari in 1989 (cited in Smith & Eadington, 1992) who aggregated writings on tourism into four groups: the advocacy platform, the cautionary platform, the adaptancy platform and the knowledge-based platform. Initial support for tourism was called into question when the impacts of tourism were examined leading to calls for more responsible or alternative tourism. The knowledge-based platform is based on a more holistic approach with the aim of creating a scientific body of knowledge on tourism.

Despite a simultaneous evolution, there has been little interaction between the fields of development and tourism. Little has been written in the development literature on tourism despite its increasing economic and social significance and its use as a development strategy by developing countries (Pearce, 1989b). Tourism papers, which refer to development, are more often written in terms of the impacts of tourism (Pearce, 1989b). Authors of tourism literature recognise the importance of tourism as a development strategy but only a small number of studies make any reference to the underlying theoretical constructs of development theory (see Pearce, 1989b; Lea, 1988; Britton, 1991; Oppermann, 1993; Woodcock & France, 1994; Harrison, 1994; Ioannides, 1995; Burns, 1999a; Dieke, 1993, 2000). More integration of the two fields is needed, according to Dann *et al.*, (1988: 1), who found that tourism studies have low levels of theoretical awareness:

> Whether this ideology is located politically to the left (eg. tourism is exploitative in a framework of dependency), or to the right (e.g. tourism provides the basis for universal brotherhood), it still does not explain the phenomena.

More than ten years later, Dann (1999) continues to make the assertion that a better understanding is needed of tourism development. The four main development paradigms profiled earlier (modernisation, dependency, economic neoliberalism and alternative development) are now analysed for the extent to which they have informed or have the potential to inform tourism research.

Modernisation and tourism

Modernisation has been the implicit base for many tourist studies in developing countries. Tourism has been promoted as a development strategy to transfer technology, to increase employment, to generate foreign exchange, to increase the GDP, to attract development capital (Britton, 1982; Cater, 1987), and to promote a modern way of life with western values (Mathieson & Wall, 1982; Harrison, 1992a). It has been argued that tourism generates rural transformations of traditional societies (Pi-Sunyer, 1989).

Initial studies focused on the positive economic aspects of tourism (Davis, 1968; Bond & Ladman, 1972) before later turning to question its value (Diamond, 1977; Bryden, 1973; Young, 1973; de Kadt, 1979a). In accordance with the modernisation paradigm, the United Nations Conference on International Travel and Tourism in 1963 noted that governments should give more attention to tourism with regards to economic development plans and trade agreements (Peters, 1969). The increase in the balance of payments is one of the most publicised economic considerations of tourism (Mathieson & Wall, 1982) (see Chapter 3). Baretje (1982) suggests that the balance of payments should be replaced with a broader concept, namely tourism's external account, which would include tourist expenditures and receipts along with international transactions which are indirectly related to tourism. In time, Baretje (1982) suggests that the adverse social side effects of tourism could be worked into the equation. More recently the tourism satellite account has been promoted as an improved method for keeping track of tourism statistics (S. Smith, 1998).

Van Doorn (1979, cited in Pearce 1989b) argued that tourist development could only be understood in the context of the development stage of the country. This comment can be seen reflected in the proposed evolutionary models of tourism linked to modernisation. Krapf (1961, cited in Pearce 1989b) focused on the economic growth of tourism and drew on Rostow's model. Thurot (1973, cited in Pearce, 1989) linked the development of international tourism to the evolution of airline routes. Plog (1977) differentiated stages of resort development according to interests and activities of tourists. Miossec (1976, cited in Pearce, 1989) developed a model, which depicts the structural evolution of tourist regions and identified hierarchy and specialisation. Van Doorn (1979, cited in Pearce, 1989) proposed a typology, which combined the stage of tourist development with levels of social and economic development. In a widely cited model, Butler (1980) developed an evolutionary model of a tourist area based on the product cycle. Keller (1984) later adapted Butler's model to include increasing levels of international control as the number of tourists increased.

Previously, the theories and strategies of regional economic development were briefly considered under the strategies of the modernisation paradigm. Although it is acknowledged that they are often considered separately, the chapter returns here to examine tourism development within the context of regional development. Chapter 4 will go into the relationship between tourism and regional development in more detail. Tourism, however, has been promoted as a regional development tool as a form of distributive justice (Pearce, 1989). Governments seeking to even out opportunities across the country may use tourism in this context. Oppermann (1992) explored the use of international tourism as a regional development tool in Malaysia. Results of the survey found that active tourists (those who had stayed in at least four different locations in Malaysia) contributed more to regional development while the travel patterns of less active tourists tended to reinforce existing spatial disparities. Similar to the theories of Perroux (1988), Mexican government planners have used a growth pole approach when developing tourist centres along the coast (Kemper, 1979). Infrastructure requirements for tourism have also been used as regional development tools (Peppelenbosch & Tempelman, 1973). The regional economic development work of Myrdal and Hirschman can be seen in tourism studies that have focused on the filtering of economic benefits (direct, indirect and induced – Milne (1992)) through regional, national and local economies. The strategy of utilising growth impulses through the economy falls under the diffusion approach outlined in Table 2.2. Elsewhere, economic concepts such as consumer and production theory, market structure, deductive modelling, cost–benefit analysis, econometric analysis and multiplier analysis have all been applied to tourism (Eadington & Redman, 1991; Archer, 1982, 1977). The inappropriate use and calculations of multipliers have, however, been well-documented (Bryden, 1973; Mathieson & Wall, 1982; Archer, 1983).

The agents of tourism development come from both the private and public sector. In developing countries where there is a weak private sector, the government may have to act as an entrepreneur to attract foreign investment for tourism development (Jenkins, 1980b). This concept is similar to the concepts of modernisation where the state may be required to create the preconditions for economic growth.

Finally, travel and tourism are seen as being part of modern society (WTO, 1983). The production of tourism under modernity takes the form of consumption. Tourism is commoditised and consumed as an end product of experiences and enjoyment. It also appears as symbolic consumption, which is related to the culture of status differentiation and market segmentation (Wang 2000). In the destination however, locals may adopt these western values and migrate to urban and resort areas in search of higher incomes resulting in the demonstration effect (Mathieson & Wall, 1982; Macnaught, 1982).

Dependency and tourism

As mentioned earlier, one of the origins of dependency is the structuralism school, which has domestic industrialism as one of its main strategies of development. During the post-war tourism expansion a number of newly independent states pursued state-led tourism development including the creation of domestic hotel chains to modernise the country and to promote economic self-reliance (Curry, 1990). In Tunisia, for example, 40% of the accommodation was built with state funds between 1960 and 1965 (de Kadt, 1979a). These attempts at focusing on state-led tourism development will be revisited later in the chapter in the creation of tables examining tourism and development. The difficulty with this approach of building a state-led tourism industry will, however, be pointed out in the following section on economic neoliberalism. In the end, many of these countries had to borrow money from international lending agencies for large-scale tourism projects.

In relation to the other perspectives of dependency, it has been argued that tourism is equivalent to a new type of plantation economy. The needs of the metropolitan centre are being met by the developing countries and where the wealth generated is transferred from the 'colony to the motherland' (Mathews, 1978). 'The myths of tourism serve as a smoke screen of this mighty form of domination' ('Impact' 1981: 12). The predominance of foreign ownership in the industry imposes structural dependency on developing countries (Britton, 1989) in a core–periphery relationship which prevents destinations from fully benefiting from tourism (Nash & Smith, 1991). Turner and Ash (1975) refer to tourism destinations as the 'pleasure periphery' which, geographically, is the tourist belt that surrounds the industrialised zones of the world. The pleasure periphery is two to four hours by plane from the large urban centres and is usually toward the equator and the sun. This zone is not static and Turner and Ash (1975: 12) stated that a global pleasure periphery is emerging 'where the rich of the world relax and intermingle'.

Centre–periphery relationships in tourism have been explored by several authors (Christaller, 1963; Murphy, 1985; Smith, 1989; Mathieson & Wall, 1982; Keller, 1984; Hoivik & Heiberg, 1980; Husbands, 1981; Brown & Hall 2000). Lundgren (1973 cited in Mathieson and Wall, 1982) referred directly to Myrdal and Hirschman when commenting on the relationship between the metropolitan centre and the tourist destination (periphery). The migration of workers from the rural areas to the tourist destinations can be equated with backwash effects (Myrdal) or polarisation (Hirschman). In outlining the main tourism issues facing peripheral areas in Europe, Wanhill (1997) noted that there are often limited organisational structures, a lack of planning and direction and little statistical information. As mentioned in the section on dependency, regional economic development theorists, in describing the process of economic growth, have acknowledged the regional inequalities, which can result from economic development.

Dependency has been one of the dominant development theories used in tourism research, especially as it relates to the negative impacts of tourism. The discussion of dependency and tourism has been explored by several authors (Britton,

1989, 1987a,b, 1982; Hills & Lundgren, 1977; Turner, 1976; Mathews & Richter, 1991; Wu, 1982; Wellings & Crush, 1983; Harrison, 1995b; Hoivik & Heiberg, 1980). The basis of the dependency argument lies in the organisation of the tourism industry and in the structure of Third World economies (Lea, 1988). Muller (1979) has argued that multinational corporations have led to the underdevelopment of the Third World. The controlling and integrating force in international tourism has become the large multinational First World companies which control airlines, tour wholesaling and hotel chains. These companies are able to create, coordinate and market the components of the industry to develop a tourism product (Britton, 1982).

Britton (1982) developed a three-tiered structural model of Third World Tourism (headquarters, branch offices, small-scale tourist enterprises) which indicates the lack of control that many Third World countries have over their tourist industry. Developing countries become locked into the marketing system of comprehensive, standardised tourism packages organised in developed countries. Tourist destinations rely on multinational corporations for tourism infrastructure and tourists (Britton, 1982). The control of foreign and local dominant capitalist firms is perpetuated through commercial practices, which include: control over tourism technology (communications), industry expertise, product design and pricing and economies of scale. The dominant firms in the hierarchy are able to control the lower firms and penetrate their markets (Britton, 1982). The inability of the agricultural and manufacturing sectors in many developing countries to guarantee the quality and continuous supply of inputs to the tourist sector often results in the reliance on imported supplies (Britton, 1982). This power structure reinforces the dependency and the vulnerability of the developing countries. In trying to understand the social and institutional processes along with the economic situation of how certain elites come to benefit, Britton (1982) was among the first to examine the political economy of tourism. The structure of developing economies is exploited by the tourist industry as the economy is often linked to the colonial past. Metropolitan companies and governments have maintained the special trading relationships with local elites who gain from the less than equal share of income and profits remaining in the peripheral economy (Lea, 1988). More recently, Dieke (2000) has focused on the political economy of tourism in Africa, arguing that, in the pursuit of tourism as a means of development, one needs to consider that governments responsible for tourism interact with pressure groups, which may lead them to pursue a certain type of development policy. The political economy of tourism is considered in more depth in Chapter 9 in the context of recent transformations in the global capitalist order.

Dependency is also discussed in tourism literature in terms of cultural dependency, which evolves with mass tourism (Nash, 1989, Erisman, 1989). Din (1990) found that in most Muslim countries, the religion does not have a significant influence on tourist operations. 'virtually all ideas and policy precepts which inform tourism planning and management are western-inspired' (Din, 1990: 542). Others have explored the issue of dependency of small islands along with the dangers that are apparent when these islands rely on tourism for their livelihoods (Britton, 1987b; Perez, 1973; Macnaughten, 1982; Oglethorpe, 1984; Boissevain, 1978; Francisco, 1983; Wilkinson, 1987).

Much of the work in tourism has focused on the negative impacts (social, economic and environmental) of tourism (Mathieson & Wall, 1982; Duffield, 1982). Developing countries were seen to be on the receiving end of these impacts but yet dependent upon foreign tourists. Bertram (1986) argues that there are regions such as small islands where 'dependent development' is sustainable and preferable to the drive for self-reliance and that they should pursue migrant labour remittances, licensing fees from foreign fishing vessels and tourism. As will be explored later however, Wall (1995) has suggested that this notion of impacts and dependency needs to be changed as communities are not only impacted by tourism but they respond to it. There have been efforts to apply greater levels of theoretical sophistication to the nature of the impacts of tourism and also how people such as entrepreneurs respond to opportunities (see Bras, 1997).

Economic neoliberalism and tourism

Evidence of economic neoliberalism in tourism research has received less explicit attention than the other three development paradigms. Important aspects of this development paradigm include an emphasis on competitive exports and the use of SALPs. Tourism is an export industry in the tertiary sector and international aid agencies have provided funding to develop tourism plans and tourism infrastructure. These loans started to increase in the 1960s (Diamond, 1977). The European Union, for example, has provided assistance to developing countries in the following areas: infrastructure, human resources, product and market development, preservation of resources and strategy development. More concretely, the EU provided funding to ACP (Africa, Caribbean and Pacific) countries under the Lome Convention. Lome III (1986–90) was the first to mention tourism extensively under new chapters as an integral part of cooperation and trade services (Lee, 1987). The European Union has also provided funding for tourism development through the LEADER programme which is explored in greater detail in Chapter 4. International funding for tourism started within the modernisation framework in the 1960s. The importance of tourism as an economic activity designed to earn foreign exchange increased after the global shift towards economic neoliberalism. 'Serving as a centre piece for the neoliberal strategy of outward-oriented development in many countries is the promotion of new growth sectors such as tourism or nontraditional exports (NTEs)' (Brohman, 1996b: 51). The World Bank has funded a range of tourism policy plans and resorts including the Nusa Dua Resort in Bali (US $14.3

million), Pomun Lake Reso, Republic of Korea (US $25 million), Puerto Plata Resort, Dominican Republic (US $25 million), and the South Antalya Tourism Development Project, Turkey (US $26 million) (Inskeep & Kallenberg, 1992). While the World Bank has not had a department dedicated to tourism since 1979, two of the agencies within the World Bank Group including the International Finance Corporation (IFC) and the Multilateral Investment Guarantee Agency (MIGA), have been actively involved in the sector (see Table 2.3). The IFC's tourism investments involve (1) early investment in transitional economies opening up the private sector, (2) the creation of critical hotel infrastructure for business development and (3) support for the rehabilitation and upgrading of existing and obsolete hotel infrastructure. These investments target countries with few development prospects except tourism where tourism has the potential of becoming an important part of the economy and contribute to the dispersal of economic activity throughout a country (Pryce, 1998). The mandate of MIGA is to promote the flow of foreign investments into and between developing countries. While efforts are underway to raise the profile of tourism within the World Bank Group, most of the projects that are carried out can be classified into one of the following categories: infrastructure; environmental programmes where the focus is frequently on ecotourism; cultural heritage protection; and small (small and medium-sized enterprises) programmes.

Poirier (1995) stated that the future of tourism development in Tunisia, for example, centred on comparative advantage economic thinking and external pressures toward structural adjustment measures. In addition, there is an emphasis on privatisation with the integration of markets. In 1980, the government of Turkey shifted its policies towards the private sector and passed The Foreign Investment Law. This law allowed up to 100% foreign investment in projects or joint ventures with Turkish development banks and companies. The Tourism Encouragement Act

Table 2.3 Regional distribution of the International Finance Corporation Investments in tourism[a]

Region	Investment (US$ mn)	No. of projects
Africa	97.0	41
Asia	99.0	16
Europe	78.0	9
Latin America and Caribbean	90.0	10
Central Asia, Middle East & North Africa	83.0	10
Total	447.0	86

Source: Pryce, 1998.
[a] As of August 1998.

was enacted in 1982 and provided similar encouragement for investment in tourism (Inskeep, 1991). The WTO also made the importance of the international monetary markets for tourism apparent in their study on the impact of the Euro on tourism. The study noted that the Euro will have a direct effect on the business environment for tourism by eliminating exchange-rate fluctuations, guaranteeing price stability and making prices across borders denominated by a single currency, all of which will increase market transparency (WTO, 1998c).

Dieke (1995) is one of the first to examine the relationship between tourism and SAPs explicitly. As a result of the severe economic slump in economic activity from the mid-1970s to the mid-1980s, 29 African countries implemented, to some degree, SAPs. These programmes, inspired by the World Bank and IMF, took the form of: reducing the size of the government work-forces, reducing state monopolies, selling state assets to private companies and liberalising the economy to allow foreign investment. The last of these options relates directly to tourism enterprises (Dieke, 1995).

SAPs have reduced the influence of the state system and highlighted the strategic importance of the private sector in the development of tourism. However, the government has important functions, which are seen as enabling rather than operational for the tourist sector (Dieke, 1995). Governments need to provide assurances for items such as investment incentives and tax holidays, which will stimulate the participation of private companies in the tourism sector. Governments in Africa have permitted an increased role of the private sector in the development of tourism recognising the role of the market in the efficient use of resources (Dieke, 1995). Although economic neoliberalism has received relatively little explicit attention in tourism literature, there are opportunities to explore the effects of government policy changes as a result of SALPs.

Alternative development and tourism

The alternative paradigm has been adopted most recently by tourism researchers and has the greatest potential to inform tourism development as it addresses the concept of sustainability. Within the alternative development paradigm, tourism authors have written on a range of issues in developing countries including indigenous development tourism, local entrepreneurial response, empowerment of local communities in the decision-making process, the role of women in tourism and sustainable tourism development. Similar to the trends in development theory of dissatisfaction with existing development philosophies, many tourism analysts have become disillusioned with mass tourism in favour of 'alternative tourism' (Brohman, 1995). The difficulty in defining alternative tourism development has been raised by Butler (1992) and Brohman (1995). Butler (1992) likens alternative tourism to sustainable development in that it sounds attractive and suggests a new approach and philosophy to an old problem but the phrase can mean almost anything to anyone. Brohman (1995) argues that while the term has been abused, there are a number of recurring themes to alternative tourism, which can be utilised to define the concept. Alternative tourism strategies stress the following: 'small scale, locally-owned developments, community participation, and cultural and environmental sustainability' (Brohman, 1995: 65). Brohman cautions that despite these similarities, it is important to take into consideration the changing conditions and interests of individual countries before any strategies are adopted.

Researchers have begun to explore the fact that indigenous communities are not only impacted by tourism but that they respond to it through entrepreneurial activity (Long & Wall, 1993; Wall, 1995, Shaw & Williams, 1990, 1994, 1998; Wahnschafft, 1982; Lundgren, 1975; Telfer & Wall, 1996). Long and Wall (1993) studied small-scale lodging establishments in Bali. In Tufi, Papua New Guinea, Ranck (1987) found that small-scale guesthouses based on local ownership and management forms a viable industry. They used local labour and construction materials and few imported foods. Archer (1978) found that domestic tourism may be a better generator of local income than international tourism as it relies more on local sources. Telfer and Wall (1996) examined the response of local farmers and fishermen to the introduction of tourism on the island of Lombok, Indonesia. Dahles (1997) has also examined the links between small entrepreneurs and sustainable development. Authors in the field of tourism planning have begun to stress the need for local community involvement and empowerment in the planning process (Murphy, 1983; Jamal & Getz, 1995; Simmons, 1994; Inskeep, 1991; Gunn, 1994). While community involvement is promoted, there are often institutional obstacles in developing countries, which may be difficult to overcome (Sofield, 1993). Some of the obstacles for increased community development are explore in Chapter 5. As part of understanding the empowerment of local people in the tourism industry, authors have also begun to explore the nature of gender, work and tourism (Kinnaird & Hall, 1994a; Sinclair, 1997; Wilkinson & Pratiwi, 1995; Apostolopoulos *et al.*, 2001).

Along with the call for community involvement is the recognition that tourism planning must be guided by principles of sustainable development (Inskeep, 1991; Gunn, 1994; Holden, 2000). The debates and criticisms surrounding the term sustainable development have been incorporated into research on tourism (Hall & Lew, 1998; Mowforth & Munt, 1998; Hall, 2000) and, in the context of this book, are also further explored in Chapters 8 and 11. What is sustainable tourism development and who decides what is sustainable in various contexts have all raised debates. This shift towards sustainability in tourism is evident by the launch of *The Journal of Sustainable Tourism* in 1993. Tourism researchers have also explored the tourism industry's efforts to adopt more sustainable practices including environmental audits, codes of conduct and initiatives such as the Green Globe scheme (international environmental awareness programme for the tourism industry) which arose out of the 1992 Rio Conference and was launched in 1994 (Mowforth & Munt, 1998). Various authors and agencies have outlined principles and guidelines for sustainable tourism development (Eber, 1992; Pigram, 1990; WTO, 1993). An example of the integration of sustainable development and tourism can be found in the Bali Sustainable Development Project (BSDP) which created a sustainable development programme for Bali (Wall, 1993a). The three features of the BSDP definition of sustainable development are (1) the continuity of natural resources and production; (2) the continuity of culture and the balances within culture; and (3) development as the process which enhances the quality of life. A set of criteria was developed for the BSDP concept of sustainable development: ecological integrity, efficiency, equity, cultural integrity, community, integration–balance–harmony and development as a realisation of potential. The BSDP worked within the existing institutions of the local society. Recommendations of the BSDP relating to tourism included:

(a) cultural tourism should be the key to development of tourism;
(b) Balinese culture should have a prominent role in promotion;
(c) 'code of conduct' should be distributed to visitors
(d) collection of more information on tourists should be attempted;
(e) ecotourism and agrotourism should be promoted;and
(f) a moratorium on hotel building should be put into effect. (Wall, 1993a)

With the increased concern for sustainability has also come the promotion of alternative types of tourism. The type that has received the most attention and which is the fastest growing in the industry is ecotourism (Ceballos-Lascurain, 1991; Fennell, 1999). Using the concepts of sustainability and community involvement, ecotourism claims to preserve fragile and protected areas. Rickard and Carmichael (1995: 323) define ecotourism as 'travel to a natural area where the revenue generated by the activity funds conservation efforts to maintain the natural resource base and also achieve sustainable economic development for the local community'. In a special issue of Tourism Recreation Research on tourism NGOs, Horochowski and Moisey (1999) investigated the role of environmental NGOs in sustainable tourism development in Northern Honduras. The study investigated the local populations' support for ecotourism and found that strategies adopted by the NGOs which emphasised local participation were most likely to achieve development and resource sustainability. The implications of these types of alternative developments (small-scale, ecotourism) are explored later. One of the NGOs which has received a great deal of attention in the media is Tourism Concern, based in the UK, with one of its mandates being to draw attention to development issues raised by tourism in developing countries. Given that tourism development is based on physical and cultural resources, a central ethical question arises as to who benefits from tourism development. This extension of environmental ethics into tourism has just begun (Holden, 2000).

Conceptual Framework for Tourism and Development

There have been few attempts to modify development paradigms to make them applicable to tourism studies. Preister (1989) proposed refinements to dependency based on its weaknesses in terms of the analysis of local or specific situations and the failure to address political and social relations. His refined concept of dependency includes the examination of global forces which influence local events as well as the study of the organisation of local residents to respond to these forces and achieve their own goals. It is important to continue to strengthen the theoretical links between tourism and development. Conceptualisation refers to defining the nature of a problem and identifying its parts as well as their relationships (Mitchell, 1989). Figure 2.1 establishes an initial conceptual framework for examining the interface between tourism and development strategies. The main influences of the four development paradigms are highlighted as they relate to tourism development. For example, as illustrated in Figure 2.1, the *focus* of tourism developed under the modernisation paradigm is typically *economic* while tourism developed under the alternative development paradigm is focused on *sustainability*. It should be noted that under the dependency column, the *structuralism* perspective has been taken reflecting the trend that, during the post-war tourism expansion, a number of newly independent states pursued state-led tourism development to modernise the country and to promote economic self-reliance (Curry, 1990). In addition, as suggested by Hettne (1995), one of the elements of a generalised list of common traits of dependency is to strive for national self-reliance. The entire framework presented here is based on a review of the literature and is to be used only to demonstrate the links between tourism and development. The framework can incorporate the many empirical and descriptive case studies on tourism within development paradigms. Each paradigm is described in terms of 26 separate components of development derived from tourism and development literature. It must be stressed that the concepts in Figure 2.1 are not meant as absolutes but are often linked or attributed to the overriding development paradigm and that the dangers of generalisation needs to be acknowledged. The framework is not meant to be comprehensive given the complex nature of development studies. These 26 elements can be classified in two broad categories, which are (A) the scale and control of development; and (B) linkages to the local community and environment. Figures 2.2–2.5 move from the descriptions of Figure 2.1 to analyses where each of the four development paradigms are analysed in terms of their possible positive and negative attributes as they relate to tourism development. For example, in Figure 2.2, while the *focus* of tourism developed under modernisation may generate *high profits* as a positive attribute, it may also be criticised from a negative perspective as also being *less environmentally friendly*. As previously mentioned, the development of a new paradigm was in part a response to the negative attributes of the previous one. Thus, modernisation

(Figure 2.2) has been criticised for neocolonialism and capital flight. Dependency (Figure 2.3) addressed these perceived weaknesses and the structural roots of dependency advocates local control and protectionist policies. Economic neoliberalism (Figure 2.4), on the other hand, represents a return to classical economic policies criticising dependency for too much government interference. Finally, the fourth development paradigm, alternative development (Figure 2.5), criticises the previous paradigms for their lack of recognition of environmental and cultural sustainability and the importance of involving local communities in the development process.

It is readily apparent that the influences of the four development paradigms are not mutually exclusive. The positive and negative attributes of tourism development are shared between categories and paradigms. For example, Bertram (1986) argues that dependent development is preferable and likely to be more sustainable for small islands when compared to a drive for self-reliance. It is not correct to assume automatically that small-scale alternative tourism is sustainable and large-scale tourism is not. It is important to understand the relationships between development paradigms and tourism and to appreciate how that understanding can help lead to the generation of appropriate and sustainable tourism development. It is also important to recognise, as outlined by Wall (1993b), that site-specific considerations must be taken into account.

The next logical step after describing the four development paradigms (Figure 2.1) and analysing their positive and negative attributes (Figures 2.2–2.5) is then to move to making suggestions with regards to considerations for appropriate and sustainable tourism development. The next section explores the literature on the elements of appropriate and sustainable forms of tourism. The literature is divided into the same two components as those in Figures 2.1–2.5: (A) scale and control of tourism development and (B) local community and environmental linkages. Figure 2.6 contains considerations for appropriate and sustainable forms of tourism development at the end of this chapter. It is argued that tourism development must be planned in relation to the broader economy with the overall goal of sustainable development. The alternative development paradigm in Figure 2.1 is relied upon heavily in the development of Figure 2.6 as it emphasises sustainability and linkages with the local community.

Appropriate and Sustainable Forms of Tourism Development

The Third World tourism industry has grown rapidly, but has also encountered many problems common to other outward-oriented development strategies, including: excessive foreign dependency, the creation of separate enclaves, the reinforcement of socioeconomic and spatial inequalities, environmental destruction and rising cultural alienation. (Brohman, 1996b: 48)

Development – Tourism As An Agent of Development				

Components of Development	Modernisation	Dependency Structuralism	Economic Neoliberalism	Alternative Development
(A) Scale and Control of Development				
focus	economic	economic	economic	sustainability
scale of development	large	large/small	large	small
rate of development	fast	fast	fast	incremental
economic distribution	trickle down	local owners	SALP	local owners
planning	top down	top down	top down	bottom up
local involvement	limited	high	limited	high
ownership	foreign	local	foreign	local
industry control	external	internal	external	internal
role of government	high-low	high	low	high-low
management origin	foreign	domestic	foreign	domestic
accommodation type	enclave	mix	enclave	mix
spatial distribution	concentrated	varied	concentrated	disbursed
tourist type	mass tourist	mix	mass tourist	special interest
marketing target	package tours	mix	package tours	independent
employment type	formal	in/formal	formal	in/formal
infrastructure levels	high	high/low	high	low
capital inputs	high	high/low	high	low
technology transfer	high	mix	high	mix
(B) Environmental and Community Linkages				
resource use	high	high/low	high	low
environment protection	low	mix	low	high
hinterland integration	low	high	low	high
intersectoral linkage	low	high	low	high
cultural awareness	exploitative	protective	exploitative	protective
institution development	low	high	low	high
local compatibility	low	high	low	high
adaptive capacity	low	low	low	low

Figure 2.1 Tourism and development theory: A framework for analysis
Source: After Telfer (1996a).

Components of Development	Tourism Developed Under Modernisation		
	Traits	*Positive Attributes*	*Negative Attributes*
(A) Scale and Control of Development			
focus	economic	high profits	less environmental
scale of development	large	high profits	lack of community fit
rate of development	fast	high profits	loss of local control
economic distribution	trickle down	spread effect	élites benefit
planning	top down	expert control	no local input
local involvement	limited	expert control	resident resentment
ownership	foreign	expert control	capital flight
industry control	external	expert control	neocolonialism
role of government	high-low	facilitate investment	low community input
management origin	foreign	expert control	worker resentment
accommodation type	enclave	economies of scale	lack of community fit
spatial distribution	concentrated	economies of scale	limited local access
tourist type	mass tourist	higher profits	near carrying capacity
marketing target	package tour	target mass tourist	capital flight
employment type	formal	trained workers	loss of informal input
infrastructure levels	high	non-touristic uses also	lack of community fit
capital inputs	high	increased multiplier	lack of community fit
technology transfer	high	internationalisation	limited local access
(B) Local Community and Environmental Linkages			
resource use	high	larger multiplier	environmental damage
environment protection	low	minimise costs	environmental damage
hinterland integration	low	supply – stable imports	high leakages
intersectoral linkage	low	familiar suppliers	reduced multiplier
cultural awareness	exploitative	culture as an object	cultural erosion
institution development	low	rely on foreign experts	limited linkages
local compatibility	low	minimise contact	resident resentment
adaptive capacity	low	foreign capital support	open to market change

Figure 2.2 Analysis of modernisation and tourism development
Source: After Telfer (1996a).

Components of Development	Tourism Developed Under Dependency (Structuralism)		
	Traits	Positive Attributes	Negative Attributes
(A) Scale and Control of Development			
focus	economic	higher domestic profits	less environmental
scale of development	large/small	mixed profits	may lack community fit
rate of development	fast	higher domestic profits	may lack community fit
economic distribution	local owners	increased multiplier	elites benefit
planning	top down	public agency control	over regulation
local involvement	high	increased local control	tourism inexperience
ownership	local	increased local control	tourism inexperience
industry control	internal	increased local control	reduced global market
role of government	high	protectionism	over regulation
management origin	domestic	local knowledge	tourism inexperience
accommodation type	mix	use of local resources	reduced profit
spatial distribution	varied	local opportunities	reduced profit
tourist type	mix	travel to new areas	reduced profit
marketing target	mix	increase – local tourists	lack of int'l receipts
employment type	in/formal	employment multiplier	lack of experience
infrastructure levels	high/low	non-touristic uses also	lack of community fit
capital inputs	high/low	may increase multiplier	lack of community fit
technology transfer	mix	self reliance	reduced global market
(B) Local Community and Environmental Linkages			
resource use	high/low	may increase multiplier	environmental damage
environment protection	mix	minimise costs	environmental damage
hinterland integration	high	use of local resources	intermittent supply
intersectoral linkage	high	increased multiplier	intermittent supply
cultural awareness	protective	cultural integrity	tourist restrictions
institution development	high	stronger institutions	tourism inexperience
local compatibility	high	resident acceptance	reduced global market
adaptive capacity	low	self reliance	open to market change

Figure 2.3 Analysis of dependency and tourism development
Source: After Telfer (1996a).

Components of Development	Tourism Developed Under Economic Neoliberalism		
	Traits	*Positive Attributes*	*Negative Attributes*
(A) Scale and Control of Development			
focus	economic	export market	loss of local control
scale of development	large	high profits	lack of community fit
rate of development	fast	high profits	loss of local control
economic distribution	SALP	international funding	elites benefit
planning	top down	expert control	no local input
local involvement	limited	expert control	resident resentment
ownership	foreign	expert control	capital flight
industry control	external	expert control	loss of opportunity
role of government	low	market forces rule	limited protective laws
management origin	foreign	expert control	worker resentment
accommodation type	enclave	economies of scale	lack of community fit
spatial distribution	concentrated	economies of scale	limited local access
tourist type	mass tourist	higher profits	near carrying capacity
marketing target	package tour	target mass tourist	capital flight
employment type	formal	trained workers	loss of informal input
infrastructure levels	high	non-touristic uses also	lack of community fit
capital inputs	high	increased multiplier	lack of community fit
technology transfer	high	internationalisation	limited local access
(B) Local Community and Environmental Linkages			
resource use	high	larger multiplier	environmental damage
environment protection	low	minimise costs	environment damage
hinterland integration	low	supply – stable imports	reduced multiplier
intersectoral linkage	low	familiar suppliers	high leakages
cultural awareness	exploitative	culture as an object	cultural erosion
institution development	low	rely on foreign experts	limited linkages
local compatibility	low	minimise contact	resident resentment
adaptive capacity	low	foreign capital support	open to market change

Figure 2.4 Analysis of economic neoliberalism and tourism development
Source: After Telfer (1996a).

Components of Development	Tourism Developed Under Alternative Development		
	Traits	*Positive Attributes*	*Negative Attributes*
(A) Scale and Control of Development			
focus	sustainability	environment protection	difficult to define
scale of development	small	lower impact	lower profits
rate of development	incremental	community adapts	lower profits
economic distribution	local owners	increase local multiplier	lower profits
planning	bottom up	local involvement	difficult to co-ordinate
local involvement	high	local decision making	tourism inexperience
ownership	local	increased local control	tourism inexperience
industry control	internal	local empowerment	reduced global market
role of government	high-low	sustainable guidelines	over regulation
management origin	domestic	increase local skill	limited experience
accommodation type	mix	local resource usage	loss of profit
spatial distribution	dispersed	less environment stress	diseconomy of scale
tourist type	special interest	environmental concern	lower profits
marketing target	independent	environmental concern	lower profits
employment type	in/formal	increased multiplier	lack of training
infrastructure levels	low	low environment stress	reduced infrastructure
capital inputs	low	low environment stress	smaller investment
technology transfer	mix	increased self reliance	reduced global access
(B) Local Community and Environmental Linkages			
resource use	low	promotes sustainability	reduced multiplier
environment protection	high	promotes sustainability	reduced profit
hinterland integration	high	use of local resources	unreliability of supply
intersectoral linkage	high	increase local multiplier	unreliability of supply
cultural awareness	protective	cultural integrity	restrictions on tourists
institution development	high	stronger institutions	tourism inexperience
local compatibility	high	resident acceptance	demonstration effect
adaptive capacity	low	self reliance	open to market change

Figure 2.5 Analysis of alternative development and tourism development
Source: After Telfer (1996a).

The purpose of this section is to move away from some of the problems related to tourism development identified by Brohman and to move towards creating an initial list of considerations for appropriate and sustainable tourism development. As this chapter continues to move in this direction it is important to ask the following questions: Appropriate for whom? For how long? Under what conditions? And by whose decision is it deemed appropriate? (Butler, 1992). What is deemed as appropriate is situation specific but also needs to be agreed upon in consultation with key stakeholders (Jamal & Getz, 1995; Inskeep, 1991; Gunn, 1994; Murphy, 1985; Nelson, 1993a,b; Smith, 1990). According to Jenkins (1991), a country formulating a tourism policy needs to address the following issues: role of the government (active or passive); ownership and control (public or private); international versus domestic tourism; the scale of tourism development; and integrated versus enclave tourism. If tourism is to fit into a community, appropriate types, scale and industrial organisation of tourist development need to be employed. If the industry is to be a viable force in the economy in the future, it must also be sustainable and use resources wisely. Moreover, local communities must have the opportunity to participate in the planning and operation of the tourist industry. As Brohman (1996b) suggests, the appropriateness of tourism development should be measured according to the changing interests and conditions in the host community and the development should conform to the long-term interests of the majority over an élite minority's short-term goals.

The topics of sustainability, environmental protection and community involvement have moved to the forefront in the tourism literature similar to the trends in the broader development literature (Bock, 1989). Hunter (1995) condensed the principles of sustainable tourism development from a variety of sources. Sustainable tourism development in the long and short term should:

> meet the needs and wants of the local host community in terms of improved living standards and quality of life; satisfy the demands of tourists and the tourism industry, and continue to attract them in order to meet the first aim; and, safeguard the environmental resource base for tourism, encompassing natural, built and cultural components, in order to achieve both of the preceding aims. (Hunter, 1995: 156)

Muller (1994) suggests balanced development using the tourism development magic pentagon. The five points of the pentagon are: economic health, optimum satisfaction of guest requirements, healthy culture, unspoilt nature/protection of resources and subjective well-being. The objective is to develop tourism in a way in which no one point in the pentagon predominates. Principles and guidelines have been developed for sustainable tourism development (Pigram, 1990; Eber, 1992; WTO, 1993). Mowforth and Munt (1998) outlined a list of tools for sustainability under the following eight headings: area protections, industry regulation, visitor

management techniques, environmental impact assessment, carrying capacity calculations, consultation/participation techniques, codes of conduct and sustainability
indicators. The use of indicators as an environmental management tool to help
achieve sustainable development has gained increased acceptance after the adoption of Agenda 21 by many world governments (Holden, 2000). Genot (1995)
analysed voluntary environmental codes of conduct in the tourist sector. After examining codes developed by countries, industry associations and NGOs, Genot
developed the following six principles which are at the core of most industry codes:
overall environmental commitment, recognising overall responsibility toward the
environment, integration of tourism planning and development and other land-use
policies, environmentally sound management practices, cooperation between
various decision-makers, and public awareness. In the development literature, the
adoption of industrial codes of conduct which delineate the terms of trade also have
implications for sustainable tourism development as they represent possible models
for facilitating links between tourism and agriculture (Tester & Drover, 1996).

   While steps have been made by several authors and agencies towards clarifying
the terms related to sustainability, the frustration which exists in trying to define
sustainable development is also found in the field of tourism. Butler (1993a) argues
that there is no universally accepted definition of sustainable development and sustainable tourism, and there are no clear indicators of the acceptability or
sustainability of tourism. What is important is recognising that the planning of
tourism cannot be done in isolation. 'It is important to take into consideration the relationship between tourism, other activities and processes, and the human and
physical environments in which tourism is taking place' (Butler, 1993a, 29). Hunter
(1995) argues that sustainable tourism development needs to be re-conceptualised
in terms of tourism's contribution towards overall sustainable development. More
directly, Wall (1993a) stated that single sector planning is doomed to failure and in
small islands, tourism is such a pervasive force that the concepts of sustainable development and sustainable tourism are inseparable. The following two sections on
(1) scale and control of tourism development and (2) local community and environmental linkages of tourism development set the stage for the introduction of Figure
2.6 – considerations for appropriate and sustainable tourism development.

Scale and Control of Tourism Development

   The concepts of scale and control of tourism development are inter-related and in
the literature it is often stated that large-scale, foreign-owned establishments result
in high leakages, while small-scale, locally owned establishments with internal
control result in smaller leakages. The purpose of this section is to explore the
tourism literature on control and the various forms of tourism development, which
have been debated in the literature as this information is incorporated in Figure 2.6.
Britton (1982) examined the enclave model of tourism where tourists arrive in the

destination areas and are transported to hotels and resort enclaves. Enclave resorts are characterised by the fact that the structure is not intended to benefit the local residents directly, the site is physically separated from the existing community; and it is used almost exclusively by foreign tourists (Jenkins, 1982b). The resort enclaves are dominated by multinationals whose management style creates and controls the physical and cultural environment catering to the tourist's needs (Freitag, 1994). The structure and control of the tourist industry by multinational corporations includes franchising, management contracts, leasing agreements and foreign ownership (Dunning & McQueen, 1982). Freitag (1994) argues that the enclave resort model used in the Dominican Republic exploits local lower classes as cheap labour while national elites and foreign investors earn higher incomes. Wilkinson's (1987) investigations in the Caribbean found that although tourism is a major export earner, a large part of the expenditures leaves the economy 'through payments to international airlines, and major hotel chains, and purchases of foreign food, beverages and supplies' (p. 142). However, in commenting on tourist-based economic development, Lundgren (1975) stated that a centre/periphery relationship existed:

> superior metropolitan economic and political powers have, in the case of tourism, initiated the development of a functional mechanism through which tourist demands are expressed in destination regions, to which local entrepreneurial response tries to react. (Lundgren, 1975: 60)

Integrated tourism development attempts to match the scale of the project to community norms. It is characterised by a smaller scale, more indigenous capital and management and its appeal for tourists with different expectations than those staying in international hotels (Jenkins, 1982b). While recognising that there is little information on this point, Jenkins (1982b) hypothesised that this type of tourism development may be more easily accepted into the host community. Milne (1992) found that guesthouses had a lower propensity to import than hotels and, as a result, higher income and employment were generated from each tourist dollar.

Rodenburg's (1980) evaluation of the social and economic effects of three scales of tourism in Bali (international standard, economy hotels and homestays) found that the best development strategy was not always met through large industrial tourism. Smaller-scale enterprises presented greater opportunities for control and profit by local people. Rodenburg (1980) was criticised by Jenkins (1982b) who states that large-scale tourist developments are more likely due to the market structure of international tourism and external economies of scale. Jenkins (1982b) argued that problems can be mitigated with pre-project planning (see Ascher, 1985). Britton (1987a) argued that decentralised smaller-scale tourism can have a greater impact on 'improving rural living standards, reducing rural-urban migration, rejuvenating rural communities, and countering structural inequalities of income distribution' (p. 183). Pearce (1989) stated that tourism developed gradually over time will allow for a longer period of social and environmental adjustment. This will allow more of the local population to become involved since labour, supplies and capital are more likely to be obtainable from local sources (Pearce, 1989b: 185). This type of incremental development is easier on the local population and may have a better chance of promoting sustainable tourism.

Wall (1993b) developed a tourism typology, which includes attraction types (cultural, natural and recreational), location (water or land based), spatial characteristics (nodal, linear and extensive), and development strategies (highly developed, developed, developing). Within the context of this typology, Wall suggests using quantities and types of accommodation to regulate the levels and types of use in different tourist areas. Wall (1993b) advocates a mix of both tourist types (mass to explorer) and accommodation types (five-star to guesthouses). This typology can be integrated to promote the sustainable development of tourism by protecting both the human and physical environments (Wall, 1993b). A cautionary note is, however, raised by Butler (1999: 72) in that the

> gap between successful integration of tourism and symbolic integration can be wide. A great deal depends on the attitudes of those with responsibility for tourism planning and development and the approaches which they take to co-ordinate and include the full range of viewpoints on proposed developments including those of local residents.

Authors such as Hall (1994a, 2000), Jenkins and Harvey (1982), Nelson (1993a) and Brohman (1996b) have explored the issue of government involvement in tourism development. The level of government involvement in the economy links back to the four development paradigms. Brohman (1996b) argues for state intervention citing that market forces on their own are not capable of resolving issues connected to long-term sustainability or the distribution of costs and benefits generated by tourism. State involvement in tourism planning can ensure that tourism development is integrated with the broader economic and social needs of the host country. Infrastructure development for resorts can be integrated with the rest of the economy. Tourism planning can also be utilised by the state as a regional economic development tool through the encouragement of growth in certain areas and it can also be used as a way to promote traditional arts, culture and the preservation of cultural heritage sites (Brohman, 1996b). Nelson (1993a) developed an action strategy, which outlines the role of government for sustainable tourism development. This 18 point list contains elements such as developing standards and regulations for environmental and cultural impact assessments; monitoring and auditing of existing and proposed tourism developments; design and implementation of public consultation techniques and processes in order to involve stakeholders in making tourism-related decisions; and developing design and construction standards which will ensure that tourism development projects are sympathetic with local culture and natural environments. Nelson (1993a) also calls for an increased understanding of how a region adapts to tourism. The trend of including adaptive capacity for sustainable development is also appearing in the broader development literature. Barlow (1995) suggests that one of the aims of sustainable development is to include adaptive strategies so that it can be resilient and cope with the unforeseen. Lee (1993) argues that through adaptive management and bounded conflict, social learning can occur, which will move us from a condition of unsustainability towards a more durable society.

The extent of local control is an important issue in tourism development. At the early stages of development, the local residents play an important role in the tourist industry and there is a strong local cultural identity. As the industry expands, it becomes increasingly institutionalised and controlled by outside interests (Din, 1990). It has been argued that this process can lead to economic dependency on outside interests. Oliver-Smith *et al.* (1989) argue that an active stance must be taken by local governments to maintain a balance between local and external resource control.

Local Community and Environmental Linkages of Tourism Development

The second major heading, which was used for analysis in Figures 2.1–2.5 was 'Local Community and Environmental Linkages'. This section explores the tourism literature on the links to local community and the environment as this information is also used in the creation of Figure 2.6. Understanding the relationship between both tourists and tourism development with the host communities and host environments is important as it relates to sustainable development. It has been stressed in the literature that one of the essential research opportunities for the future is to 'improve intersectoral linkages' (Eadington & Redman, 1991, also see Bramwell & Lane, 2000). Not only is it important to increase the strength of the linkages to the local community but it is also important to understand the nature of the relationship between tourism and the local community. It has been argued that the view of tourism as an 'exogenous force' impacting upon a static destination area is too simplistic (Wall, 1995). Through examples from Bali, Wall (1995) suggests that tourism is often sought and invited, and local residents take advantage of opportunities provided by tourism. As Mathieson and Wall (1982) point out, the greater the number of internal linkages between sectors of the economy is, the less likelihood that supplies will be required or imported from outside the region, and the multiplier will be larger (see Chapter 3). What is also important to note however is that these linkages need to be made to a number of industries so that it is not just the local élite that benefits. Wall (1995: 16) argues that at a minimum, more comprehensive typologies of tourism are required 'incorporating types of tourists, community characteristics, the nature of visitor-resident interactions and the role of cultural brokers. It may be advisable to include tourism with a number of agents which impact upon communities.'

Various types of tourists have different expectations and demands, which need to be met in the host community. In this sense, tourism has been written about as a promoter of peace and of a promoter of cultural conflict (Robinson, 1999). The type of tourist travelling has implications for the level of interaction with the local community (Cohen, 1972, Smith, 1977) and residents with a commercial stake in the industry are likely to have more definite and positive attitudes towards tourism than those with little or no direct involvement (Murphy, 1985). The tourists' willingness to adapt to local cultures and try local foods can affect the extent to which local people can participate in the industry. Cohen (1972) developed one of the earlier classifications of tourists including the organised mass tourist, the individual mass tourist, the explorer and the drifter. The first two types are identified as having institutionalised tourist roles with most of their arrangements being made by travel agents while the remaining two types of tourists have been classified as having non-institutionalised tourist roles and they try to maximise contact with the locals and search for the less familiar. Those who belong to the institutionalised tourist groups are much more isolated from the residents of the host community staying in star hotels, which often have limited connections to the local economy. The non-institutionalised tourists tend to stay in locally owned accommodation and adapt more to the local society and this interaction increases the economic benefits to the locals (Cohen, 1972).

Another important facet of increasing the linkages to local communities is the inclusion of local community in the planning of tourism developments. This call for more local participation (bottom-up model) in tourism (Jamal & Getz, 1995; Gunn, 1994; Inskeep, 1991; Murphy, 1985; Telfer, 2000c) is also echoed in the development literature (Bock, 1989; Haq, 1988; Alamgir, 1988, Brohman, 1996a). As Meier (2001) noted in tracing the evolution of development thought, under capital accumulation, we have shifted the emphasis from building physical capital to building social capital. McIntosh and Goeldner (1984) advocated establishing a tourism development programme, which is consistent with the social, cultural and economic philosophy of the host community and government. It not only presents the possibility of preserving and sustaining the local culture but also of ensuring that the development project will be better received by the local community. Nelson (1993b) advocated a civics or a more informed, open participatory public process with respect to tourism development decision-making and Jamal and Getz (1995) proposed a collaboration process while Murphy (1983) advocated an ecological model for community-based tourism planning. Although community involvement is seen as an important concept in tourism planning, several authors have found that there is often a lack of knowledge in the community as to how to become involved (Tsartas, 1992; Keller, 1984; Baines, 1987). Richards and Hall (2000: 298) point out that in terms of tourism development, participation is often a problem of power relationships within the community, and empowerment practices, such as bottom-up planning strategies, are not matched by empowering philosophies. Unequal distribution of power and uneven flows of information can disenfranchise members of the community when decisions are taken about tourism development. (See Chapter 5.)

Tourism also stimulates local entrepreneurs in the community to supply tourist establishments (Telfer, 1996a, in press; Telfer & Wall, 1996; 2000). Lundgren's (1975) study in the Caribbean found that tourism stimulated the local food supply network at all levels from small-scale rural producers to larger-scale urban suppliers. The link to local entrepreneurs can help to strengthen backward economic linkages. While considerable literature exists on the economic potential of tourism and the role of multinational firms, little attention until recently has been given to the role of entrepreneurial activity and particularly how tourism enterprises operate in different economies (Shaw & Williams, 1990, 1998). Tourism plans in developing countries often ignore or attempt to eliminate the informal tourist sector from participating in the tourist industry (Wall, 1995). Within the employment sector (formal and informal), it is important to investigate the linkages of women's employment roles in the tourism industry. There is a small but growing body of literature dealing with the relationships between gender, tourism and development (Wilkinson & Pratiwi, 1995; Sinclair, 1997; Apostolopoulos *et al.*, 2001). Cukier and Wall (1994) found in Bali that significantly more men than women were employed in the tourist sector; however, the percentage of women was increasing (see also Chapter 6). Momsen (1994) states that increased incomes as a result of tourism can lead to a redistribution of power in the family and create tensions in gender relations.

Along with calls for strengthening the links to local communities, concerns over the environment with relation to tourism have become more prominent. Holden (2000) categorises the negative environmental consequences of tourism into three main categories. The first is resource use and results when tourism competes with other development forms or human activity for natural resources. The second is human behaviour towards the destination environment and the third is pollution including water, air, noise and aesthetic pollution. All of these potential conflicts can lead to the transformation of ecological habitats and loss of flora and fauna. The need for environmental planning and the monitoring of the scale of tourism development have become noted as important components in promoting environmentally sound tourist developments (Farrell & Runyan, 1991; Inskeep, 1987; Jenkins, 1982b). Governments have a range of policy and legislation to protect the environment. These include establishing protected areas, implementing land-use planning measures, requiring the use of environmental impact analysis and encouraging coordination between government departments over implementing environmental policy as well as opening dialogue with the industry to adopt environmental management schemes (Holden, 2000).

As previously noted in the section on 'Alternative Development and Tourism', alternative tourism developments (ecotourism, small-scale, green tourism) have received a great deal of attention in the literature as they have focused on the need to preserve the environment. Alternative tourism is defined as tourism that is consistent with natural, social and community values, which allows hosts and guests to enjoy worthwhile interaction and shared experiences (Eadington & Smith, 1992). Some have suggested that these types of tourism may even protect the environment. The definition of alternative tourism has been debated and, as Butler (1992) points out, mass tourism is not always uncontrolled and inappropriate and small-scale ecotourism is not always sustainable. Each must be evaluated on its own merits. It is important that comparative research be conducted to determine which types of tourism are appropriate in different situations.

Ecotourism is viewed as a potential path for promoting sustainable development (Tisdell, 1993; Pigram, 1990; Wight, 1993; Gunn, 1994; Boo, 1993). Ecotourism promotes small-scale development with local involvement generating fewer environmental impacts (Cater, 1993). Ecotourism takes advantage of the wide range of natural assets in developing countries; it is free of some of the pitfalls of mass tourism (large scale, high leakages); and, it is nature-based which implies ecological responsibility (Cater, 1993). However, there are strong warnings that not all ecotourism is automatically environmentally sensitive and the term has been used as a marketing tool (Cater, 1993, Butler, 1992; Holden, 2000). Gordon (1992: 42) warns of the dangers of an overly simplistic approach to nature conservation and to preserving indigenous ways of life based on scientific (anthropological) interest and elitist forms of tourism such as ecotourism which attempt to study, preserve and market the wild habitat, its animals and its peoples.

Murphy (1983) and May (1991) emphasised the relationships between tourism, the environment and community development. They argue for a more ecological approach to tourism development. Inskeep (1991) advocates an integrated and sustainable approach to tourism planning arguing that an integrated resort can result in substantial economic and social benefits while minimising environmental, socioeconomic and marketing problems which accompany uncontrolled tourism developments (Inskeep & Kallenberger, 1992) (see Chapter 7 for a discussion of the social and cultural impacts of tourism). Holden (2000: 202) raises the point that in 'a neoliberal global economy, regulation of environmental resources will be critical in determining the success of any alternative tourism policy'. However, he further states that for many less developed countries, the global political economy with international debt repayment and the domination of transnational corporations places the environment under threat in the short term in the pursuit of profits.

Conclusion

This chapter has examined the four main development paradigms – modernisation, dependency, economic neoliberalism and alternative development – which have evolved since the Second World War. Tourism research has evolved along similar patterns as those in the main development paradigms; however, as indicated, there has been very little work connecting the two areas of study. An initial conceptual framework was presented that started with a description of the characteristics of tourism development under the four development paradigms. The positive and negative aspects of each development paradigm with respect to tourism development were analysed. Similar to the trends in development paradigms, the perceived weaknesses in one development paradigm with respect to tourism were subsequently addressed in the following development paradigm.

Modernisation was criticised for its lack of local control of the tourist industry and capital flight, which led to neocolonialism. The structuralist school, which is part of the background to the dependency paradigm, advocated protectionist measures to ensure there was local control of the industry. Economic neoliberalists felt there was too much government control in the previous paradigms and advocated a free market approach to the tourist industry. International tourism is an export industry and, as such, it should be permitted to operate under neoclassical economic principles with limited government involvement. Finally, the alternative development paradigm addressed the weaknesses of the previous three paradigms, which paid little attention to the environment or the concept of sustainability. The importance of linkages to local communities is stressed in alternative development.

Within this framework, considerations for appropriate and sustainable tourism development have been explored. One of the important considerations stressed is the significance of linkages to local communities and the importance of strengthening backward economic linkages, which can increase the multiplier effect and reduces the high levels of leakage that are documented in the literature. Figure 2.6 contains initial considerations for appropriate and sustainable tourism development. The elements of Figure 2.6 were developed from a review of the literature and an analysis of the development paradigms in Figures 2.2–2.5. The weakness raised in the analysis of tourism development under the four development paradigms in Figures 2.2–2.5 were addressed in the creation of Figure 2.6. The suggestions raised here represent a starting point for discussion and not an end point. As Butler (1999a) indicated, there can be a wide gap between tourism development principles and tourism development practices and significant barriers can exist in implementing the suggestions presented in Figure 2.6. The considerations proposed in Figure 2.6 have their closest affinity with the ideas from alternative development as sustainability is stressed; however, they have also been influenced, to some extent, by modernisation, dependency and economic neoliberalism. The following comment by Redclift (1994) clearly illustrates the overlap in development paradigms:

married to the idea of 'development', sustainability represents the high-water mark of the Modernist tradition. At the same time, with the emphasis on cultural diversity, there is a clear expression of Postmodernism.

Elements in Figure 2.6 from modernisation are reflected in the need for profitability and an increase in the multiplier effect. From the various perspectives of dependency comes the realisation that the tourist industry is in danger of being controlled from abroad, which leads to capital flight and exploitation. As a result, suggestions in Figure 2.6 are influenced by the structuralism perspective of dependency that include strong elements of local control and high linkages to local communities to ensure local products are utilised in the tourist industry. The government should facilitate investment and, at the same time, ensure environmental regulations are established and followed. The concern for environmental issues mainly comes from alternative development. The concept of sustainability is promoted in Figure 2.6. However, it is stressed that tourism must be planned within the broader economy in the context of sustainability. Similar to the ideas in the structural school of thought from dependency, alternative development promotes the need to increase linkages to local communities and increase community participation in the planning process, which is reflected in Figure 2.6. It is argued that linkages to local communities and the utilisation of local resources are one of the most important elements of appropriate and sustainable tourism development. The final element of Figure 2.6 is adaptive capacity, which stresses the importance of understanding how a community responds to tourism development.

As has been highlighted in this chapter and throughout this book, the nature of development is a highly contested concept influenced by a wide range of social, political, economic and environmental perspectives each with its own set of values. The development of conceptual frameworks such as presented in Figure 2.6 is not without difficulty and needs to be placed within the context of the environment in which it is being applied. Key questions such as those raised by Lord (1998) in examining the power relations in partnerships also need to be addressed: Who will benefit? Who will be harmed? Is there a common purpose and value? What beliefs about people and change are inherent in the project? How will those differences be addressed? Who will control the process? How will partners work together so that each partner's experience is honoured? How will participation be maximised? How will valued resources be shared? It is important to understand development in terms of development by whom and for whom. The concepts raised in this chapter will be revisited throughout this book. The second section of the book explores specific development issues including economic development, regional development, community development, human resources development, social–cultural development and the environment. The final section of the book examines limits to development by addressing the political economy of tourism, the consumption of tourism and questioning the validity of the term sustainability as it applies to tourism development.

Components of Development	Considerations for Appropriate and Sustainable Tourism Development
(A) Scale and Control of Development	
focus	profitable, part of larger concept of sustainable development
scale of development	mix of small and large scale resorts, restaurants, facilities
rate of development	incremental development according to community size
economic distribution	high level of local participation, use of local resources
planning	participatory with stakeholders, community involvement
local involvement	high level of local involvement at all stages of development
ownership	mix of foreign and local ownership
industry control	local control with foreign input
role of government	facilitate investment, environmental regulations,
management origin	mix of foreign experts with locally trained specialists
accommodation type	mix of types, integrated resorts with small scale establishments
spatial distribution	mix of dispersed and concentrated tourism developments
tourist type	mix of types; mass to explorer, depending on local environment, develop codes of conduct for tourists
marketing target	identify market segmentation best suited to local community
employment type	combination of formal and informal employment
infrastructure levels	accordance with community capacity, integrated with economy
capital inputs	mix of high and low capital inputs
technology transfer	high rates – integration with international tourism industry
(B) Local Community and Environmental Linkages	
resource use	efficient use of resources and management of waste stream
environment protection	sustainable use of environmental resources, use of environmental management tools including E.I.A. sustainability indicators
hinterland integration	high level of linkages to hinterland – use of local products
intersectoral linkage	reduce external leakages and increase local linkages
cultural awareness	maintain cultural integrity; tourists to be aware of local culture
institution development	coordinated efforts to strengthen local institutions, involvement
local compatibility	local considerations influence scale & rate of development

Figure 2.6 Considerations for appropriate and sustainable tourism development
Source: After Telfer (1996a).

Part 2

Relationship Between Development and Tourism

Chapter 3

Tourism and Economic Development Issues

TANJA MIHALIČ

Introduction

Tourism is frequently justified on the basis of its potential contribution to economic development. More specifically, it is widely assumed that tourism can 'help to eliminate the widening economic gap between developed and less developed countries and regions and to ensure the steady acceleration of economic and social development, in particular in developing countries' (WTO, 1980: 1). Certainly, tourism has great potential to fulfil this role through contributing to the (economic) development of destination areas and the economic benefits of tourism, such as income and employment generation, are widely recognised. In practice, however, there are many factors that frequently serve to reduce these potential benefits to the host country. In other words, despite the widespread and justifiable support for tourism as an economic development agent, its potential may not always be fully realised. At the same time, there remain serious doubts whether tourism, without international political intervention and a fundamental transformation in global political structures, can in fact help to establish a more even and equitable economic world order.

Many other questions also surround the role of tourism in economic development. For example, can the widening economic gap between developed and less developed countries be eliminated by the tourism development model? Who actually profits from the development of international tourism? Does tourism development contribute to the establishment of a new form of colonialism? Is it economically healthy to be dependent on the business of tourism? Can the international competitiveness of tourism in developing countries be increased as a result of favourable terms of trade? Are less developed countries, possessing few capital resources but rich in cultural and environmental attractions, able to exploit the latter as a factor of comparative advantage? How high is the general ability to add value to the tourism product? How high is this ability in less developed countries? Who profits from the exploitation of the host country's own natural and human resources? Does the concept of sustainable tourism promote economic development? What, if anything, can be done to achieve a new international economic order through the contribution of tourism development? What will be the future significance of tourism as a generator of economic development in the new emerging countries?

The purpose of this chapter is to address, and to attempt to offer possible answers to, some of these questions. More specifically, it challenges a number of the accepted benefits of tourism referred to in Chapter 1 and proposes alternative ways in which the contribution of tourism to economic development may be assessed and measured. Thus, after locating tourism in a theoretical economic framework, the chapter focuses upon specific economic consequences of tourism, such as contributing to a destination's balance of payments, employment creation and its inflation/ deflation effects, before going on to argue that, in particular, the economic valuation and transfer of property rights over 'free' attractions in destination areas provides a more valid basis for judging the contribution of tourism to economic development.

This is not to suggest from the outset that tourism does not provide positive economic developmental benefits, or that such benefits are less than generally claimed. On the contrary, tourism development brings about many and diverse positive consequences for destination economies which are discussed at length in the literature (for example, Mathieson & Wall, 1982; Bull, 1995; Tribe, 1996). For example, it is a valuable source of foreign currency earnings, it influences the economic development of the host region or country, it creates earnings through the exploitation of the 'free' natural and cultural attractions of the host country and it generates employment opportunities, new investment, new sources of income and governmental revenues. Indeed, there are numerous examples of destinations, regions and countries, both in the developed and less developed worlds, that have benefited significantly from the economic impacts of tourism (see also Chapter 11).

Importantly, however, not only is the magnitude of these impacts determined by various factors but, at the same time, it is also unrealistic to expect that tourism is generally a magic wand that can solve all the problems of underdevelopment and reduce the economic gulf between the developed and less developed worlds. Therefore, this chapter reviews briefly the main economic impacts of tourism but focuses principally on fundamental issues related to, and criticisms of, the potential of tourism to contribute to economic development.

Tourism – The Economic Dimension

Tourism, described as the activities of persons travelling to and staying in places outside their usual environment for not more than one consecutive year for leisure, business and other purposes, can certainly claim to be one of the most remarkable economic and social phenomena of the last century (WTO, 1999c: 1). Moreover, and of vital significance in the context of this chapter, it will undoubtedly maintain this position in the coming decades. Since the completion of economic restructuring following the end of the Second World War, both the number of international and domestic travellers and the value of the consequential tourist receipts/expenditure have been increasing continuously. For example, the number of annual international arrivals worldwide has increased remarkably, growing from a 'mere' 25 million in 1950 to 664 million by 1998. This corresponds to an average annual growth rate of 7%. Receipts from international tourism have also increased dramatically, reaching US$455 billion by 1998, with a further US$93 billion in international fare receipts (WTO, 1999d: 8). If domestic tourism is also taken into consideration, then the figures are even more staggering. Although precise data are not available, it has been estimated that domestic tourism, in terms of volume, is some six to ten times greater than international tourism, meaning that the total gross output of global tourism may be worth around US$4000 billion. Indeed, the World Travel and Tourism Council has suggested that, by 2006, tourism globally will be worth some US$7500 billion, contributing 11.4% of global GDP, supporting 385 million jobs and generating over US$1700 in tax revenues.

Despite this impressive growth and development, however, the economic importance of tourism has, on the one hand, very often been exaggerated, usually for reasons of political expediency. In particular, this is frequently the case in less developed countries that have sought to develop their economies through the development of tourism. On the other hand, the potential economic importance of tourism has frequently been overlooked, particularly in developed countries that are able to build their competitiveness and development on other, very often more productive and more added-value [1] rich industries. For these industrialised areas and cities, tourism is often considered a 'last resort' (Swarbrooke, 2000: 271) where there is little or no chance of attracting other, more traditional industries to help regenerate the local economy. Nevertheless, tourism development can, in addition to the other economic impacts that are widely considered in the literature (for example, Mathieson & Wall, 1982; Sessa, 1983; Bull, 1995; Tribe, 1996), also have a major impact on economic development.

Tourism and Development

As discussed in Chapter 1, development is, both semantically and in terms of its inherent processes and outcomes, an ambiguous concept. Generally, it refers to socioeconomic change and progress, embracing indicators which include increases in per capita income, a reduction in the poverty level among masses, more social justice, modernisation in terms of social changes, higher levels of employment and literacy, improvement in and wider access to medical treatment, a 'better' life with more opportunities for self-improvement, and so on. However, development has various dimensions and, owing to different uses of the term by different disciplines and changes in those uses over time, there is no single, universal definition of it (Pearce, 1989: 6).

Nevertheless, for the specific purposes of this chapter and as a basis for the economic analysis of tourism, the following definition of economic development will be used: economic development is a process of economic transition that involves the structural transformation of an economy and a growth of the real output of an economy over time (Pass *et al.*, 1993). Structural transformation is achieved through industrialisation and is measured in terms of the relative contribution to gross domestic product (GDP)[2] of the agriculture, industry and service sectors. Growth rate is measured by an increase in actual GPD, real GDP or per capita income. Generally speaking, developing countries are characterised by subsistence primary production (i.e. agriculture) and low per capita GDP whilst, conversely, developed countries are characterised by large manufacturing and service sectors, a relatively small agriculture sector and high levels of per capita GDP (see Chapter 1). Frequently, however, and for the sake of simplicity, it is only indicators of economic growth that are taken into account in order to measure economic development or, more precisely, progress in economic development (Ray, 1998: 9).

The different levels of economic growth rates that have been achieved in the past or, indeed, are being achieved today by both the more and less market-oriented economies can be to divide the world into developed and less developed countries. Within less developed countries and regions, of course, tourism is very often considered as a development opportunity – that is, as a contributor to economic growth and as a catalyst of favourable structural changes within the local economy. However, the actual ability of tourism to support economic growth and to make an increasingly significant contribution to GDP remains the subject of intense debate, particularly as there is much evidence to support both sides of the argument. Frequently, this economic argument is derived from capital–output ratio analysis, the capital–output ratio[3] being based upon the amount of capital required to produce a single unit of output in the economy. It represents the ratio between the capital input and the output produced over a particular period of time and, therefore, an increase in the rate at which capital produces a unit of output (i.e. a lower capital–output ratio) will enhance the rate of economic growth.

In the specific context of tourism, capital–output analysis is based upon a comparison between the tourism sector capital–output rate and the equivalent rate calculated for the whole economy. It divides tourism development into three stages, according to its contribution to the growth of the local destination economy. During the first development stage (equivalent, perhaps, to Butler's (1980) exploration stage), tourism development is spontaneous and unsupported by either a tourism development policy or by intensive capital investment. When tourists arrive, their hosts 'get together and rent rooms, offer meals … they purchase a slot machine. One of them gives up fishing and takes the tourists out in his boat, a woman converts her house into a pension … another woman begins to weave for visitors …' (Krippendorf, 1999: 3). In other words, (pioneer) tourists visit attractive places and generate some expenditure in the host region; in response, the local community, without the benefit of any purpose-built tourism infra- and super-structure, improvise in their attempts to satisfy the needs of tourists. At this stage, the average capital–output ratio in the 'tourism sector' is low, and much lower than the average for the economy as a whole. Certainly, tourism businesses contribute to economic growth in the region, although tourism earnings in this first stage are not normally substantial. However, as a result of the non-existent capital investment in tourism businesses, the marginal capital–output ratio[4] suggests that the amount of additional investment required in the tourism sector in order to increase tourism earnings is almost zero.

As the number of visitors and the consequential opportunities for tourism businesses increase, the destination enters the second tourism development stage. Now, tourism development is promoted and politically supported with investment in tourism infra- and super-structure. Significant levels of capital investment are usually required and, since there exists a time lag between invested inputs and generated outputs in the form of tourism earnings, the average capital–output ratio for the tourism sector increases and becomes higher than the average ratio for the economy as a whole. Thus, during the second stage, the capital–output ratio within the tourism sector also increases the overall economy's average capital–output ratio, thereby slowing down the average national economic growth rate. However, during this stage, other benefits of tourism development are promoted, such as improvements in the host population's quality of life in terms of new infrastructure or the opportunity for cultural exchanges with visitors and the multiplier effect of tourism consumption, where the indirect effects of tourism consumption on non-tourism sectors are stressed.

The third stage of tourism development is reached when the average tourism capital–output ratio falls to or below the average ratio for the economy as a whole. This results both from the benefits of the past investment in tourism infra- and super-structure being realised and also from current innovations and improvements in the quality and assortment of tourism products which, together, encourage higher levels of tourist consumption, hence contributing to the economic growth of the local economy. The marginal capital–output ratio is low and little additional tourism capital investment is required for an additional increase in tourism yields. In many destinations, particularly in developed countries, the latter is mainly achieved through the enlargement of daily tourism consumption per visitor whilst the overall number of visitors remains unchanged. However, in many less developed economies, a rise in a tourism destination's yield is predominantly achieved through an increase in the number of visitors by promoting mass tourism and the related advantages of large-scale production. In other words, and as discussed shortly, the potential for increasing per capita tourist spending, based upon the quality and critical mass of facilities and attractions, is, arguably, greater in developed countries than in less developed countries. This suggests that a policy of attracting lower numbers of higher spending tourists may be difficult to achieve in less developed countries, although different destinations must be assessed according to their tourist markets. For example, ecotourists tend to be higher per day spenders yet backpackers, though low spenders on a daily basis, tend to travel for longer and have therefore, somewhat belatedly, been recognised as an economically important tourist market.

There is much evidence to suggest that many destinations have attempted to overcome the lack of financial resources, to by-pass the economically unfavourable second development stage and to speed up the process of tourism infra- and super-structure development with the help of international capital and expertise. That is, they have tried to attract private foreign capital to fund tourism superstructure development, such as accommodation, restaurant or entertainment facilities. At the same time, the development of both general and tourism-specific infrastructure, such as airports, roads, power supply, water supply and sewage, is often seen as the responsibility of the government. Indeed, new growth theorists acknowledge that, in the context of tourism development, such infrastructure represents the secondary tourism resource base (Sinclair & Stabler, 1997: 150). With limited opportunities for local public sector funding, however, international organisations, such as the World Bank and other sources of international development finance, have for many years been the suppliers of capital for such investments (Pearce, 1989b; Bull, 1995).

There is certainly no doubt that foreign capital investment gives rise to extra income and growth, creates new jobs and encourages foreign currency earnings but, at the same time, it unfortunately generates more leakages than domestic capital investment from local private and governmental sources. This is, of course, because profits are remitted to the parent company, more foreign staff are usually employed and more imported goods may be used to support the tourism business, factors which, collectively, serve to reduce the contribution of tourism to GDP (see also Chapter 9).

At the same time, it is evident that the economically favourable third stage of tourism development may not be reached as easily as suggested in theory. The achieved decrease in the average capital–output ratio, based upon the ability of the economy to increase the daily tourism consumption per visitor without much new capital investment, depends upon many factors. For example, international tourism data demonstrate that the more the destination economy is developed, the higher the tourism earnings per visitor and *vice versa*. Thus, Germany earns, per tourist night, approximately twice as much as Hungary, Turkey or Spain (see Table 3.1). In other words, it tends to be the countries with more developed and diverse economies to which the economic benefits of tourism development accrue more ef-

Table 3.1 Selected tourism data by regions and sub-regions, 1997. Division into world's regions according to WTO (1999c)

Region	Receipts (US$ million)	Expenditures (US$ million)	Difference (col 2–col 3) (US$ million)	Arrivals of tourists from abroad (000s)	Receipts per tourist arrival (US$)	GDP per capita (US$)	Receipts as % of GDP	Receipts per foreign tourist night (US$/night)
Africa	**9,018**	**7,001**	**2,017**	**23,157**	**389**	**967**	**1.80**	
Americas	**118,767**	**84,695**	**34,072**	**118,481**	**1002**	**14,887**	**1.13**	
Caribbean	13,776	2,489	11,287	15,286	901	3,964	11.15	
Central America	1,800	873,000	–871,200	2,937	613	2,013	3.31	
Northern America	89,632	66,416	23,216	84,390	1062	24,620	1.01	
Southern America	13,559	14,917	–1,358	15,868	854	5,213	0.90	
East Asia/Pacific	**76,627**	**75,903**	**0,724**	**87,953**	**871**	**3,246**	**1.30**	
• Japan	4,326	33,041	–28,715	4,218	1026	33,265	1.03	
Europe	**218,155**	**202,406**	**15,749**	**361,509**	**603**	**10,199**	**2.54**	
Central/East Europe	25,579	24,058	1,521	79,480	322	2,318	2.93	
• Hungary	2,582	1,153	1,429	17,248	150	4,407	5.65	242
Northern Europe	34,318	47,730	–13,412	40,352	850	24,393	1.69	
Southern Europe	69,191	25,875	43,316	104,793	660	13,476	3.52	
• Spain	26,651	4,467	21,748	43,403	614	13,473	5.02	250
• Portugal	4,277	2,164	2,063	10,172	420	10,271	4.22	189
Western Europe	76,704	99,179	–22,475	123,746	620	24,114	1.82	
• Germany	16,509	46,200	–29,691	15,837	1042	26,868	0.78	452
East Mediterranean	12,468	5,564	6,904	13,138	949	4,793	4.26	
• Turkey	8,088	1,716	6,372	9,040	895	3,397	4.21	224
Middle East	**9,135**	**5,320**	**3,815**	**14,833**	**616**	**3,898**	**1.64**	
South Asia	**4,279**	**2,451**	**1,828**	**4,830**	**886**	**5,889**	**0.63**	

Source: UN, 2000; WTO, 1999a, b.

fectively. Thus, the level of development of the host economy is an important factor in achieving a decrease in the capital–output ratio. Furthermore, industrialised countries may develop other, non-tourism sectors that make a greater contribution to overall economic growth than is possible through tourism. It is important to note, however, that although in these countries the value added in the tourism sector itself may be relatively low, the overall value added, created in response to consumption in both in tourism and other sectors of the economy, may be higher as a result of the involvement of non-tourism sectors. Nevertheless, for some less developed countries or regions, tourism may remain the best development opportunity and the sum of the economic effects of tourism consumption in those countries may be positive.

Tourism Consumption

Tourism is an expenditure-driven economic activity. That is, the consumption of tourism is at the centre of the economic measurement of tourism and the foundation of the economic impacts of tourism and, therefore, understanding tourism consumption is essential for understanding tourism's economic impacts. Within the framework of the previous definition of tourism, the World Tourism Organisation (WTO) defines tourism consumption as 'the total consumption expenditure made by a visitor or on behalf of a visitor for and during his/her trip and stay at the destination' (WTO, 1999c: 20). The sources for tourism consumption are a person's or a household's own cash resources, savings and other personal incomes and social transfers, as well as a company's travel costs for business travellers.

Tourism consumption (in an economic context) always relates to persons travelling or intending to travel. One of its elements refers to the acquisition of goods and services within the normal, home environment (before and after travel) as long as the usage of such goods and services is clearly directed towards a trip or holiday. The other element of tourism consumption relates to all expenditures during the trip, regardless of the nature of the goods and services purchased. The sum of all these expenditures is called *gross* tourism consumption (Planina, 1997: 235). In order to calculate *net* tourism consumption, the reduced, final level of consumption in the place of residence is subtracted from the gross tourism consumption figure. In other words, some consumption (for example, food, drinks and some variable household costs) does not, of course, occur in the home residence context during an individual's trip or holiday and, therefore, represent resources that can be spent on or during the trip. Conversely, other, fixed expenditure (for example, mortgage repayments) occurs irrespective of where the person is. This element of normal, day-to-day variable consumption moves with the traveller to the destination and can be spent on different goods and services, such as on visiting an attraction rather than paying a local energy supplier. Thus, net tourism consumption reveals the increase in personal consumption because a person is travelling.

It may be argued that gross tourism consumption is the most relevant indicator (for international tourism) as it takes into account all tourism consumption effects and the redistribution of national income, both geographically and within sectors of the economy. In the context of domestic tourism, net tourism consumption demonstrates the total increase in consumption within the economy as the tourism consumption of domestic tourists travelling within their own country remains within and contributed to the national economy. In international tourism, however, total consumption represents international tourism receipts or expenditure and is the sum of both inbound and outbound international tourism consumption. Thus, the economic impacts of tourism in the host country are derived from tourism consumption that enters the host economy – that is, through internal tourism consumption from both domestic and foreign tourists. As tourism-generating markets are geographically separate or distant from the host country, a significant part of a foreign traveller's gross tourism expenditure may never enter the host country's economy, but have an impact on other economies. As already mentioned, expenditures may occur at home for goods and services intended for a trip. These may vary from expenditure on personal sport equipment, clothing for the holiday or photo-processing of holiday photographs to the cost of the package tour paid to the national or international outgoing tour operator. In the latter case, only a part of this amount will enter the host economy when the tour operator settles the accounts with local suppliers at the destination. Thus, although the economic contribution of international tourism is usually measured in terms of receipts in the destination country, the value of gross tourism consumption and its influence on economic growth in total may be much higher.

To summarise, then, it is internal tourism consumption, that is, the consumption expenditure of both domestic and international tourists visiting the host economy, that generates national tourism income and influences the rate of growth and development. Nevertheless, the final economic effect of a given amount of internal tourism consumption on economic growth may vary considerably, since it may include different proportions of imported goods and services sold to the tourists in a country visited. In such cases, the tourism consumption for imported goods and services creates leakages, whereby money flows out of the host economy and, as a result, economic growth/development impact is reduced.

The Economic Impacts of Tourism

Sixty years ago, Hunziker and Krapf (1942) showed that tourism has an influence on national economies. They demonstrated that, depending on the inwards or outwards direction of tourist flows, tourism can have both a positive and negative impact upon the quantity of national income. Consequently, tourism first brings about the redistribution of national income, dividing the world into tourist-generating and receiving countries, regions and destinations. Second, it also leads to the redistribution of income between sectors and companies within the economy, the latter resulting from the fact that tourism consumption differs from personal consumption.

Since then, many tourism analysts have studied the different so-called economic impacts of tourism, amongst which the tourism multiplier effect is probably the most widely considered. However, other economic impacts assume more or less importance depending upon the tourism context. For less developed countries, for example, tourism is generally favoured for its potential as a generator of foreign currency whereas, within Europe and in the light of EU policy, it is tourism's role as a source of employment that has been of increasing importance, as well as its contribution to regional development. At the same time, some authors have explored the valuation function of tourism, in particular with respect to the economic valuation of natural and social attractions and attractiveness to the tourism industry. Conversely, the inflation and deflation consequences of tourism remain relatively neglected in tourism economic studies. Importantly, the last two decades have also been dominated by the debate surrounding the environmental impacts of tourism. Although these impacts are usually considered from a non-economic point of view, it can be argued that the environmental issues of tourism development should be also be located within the economic debate. That is, tourism should no longer be viewed only as a reason for environmental protection. The environment is also a financial resource, with the environmental resources that the tourism industry indirectly sells becoming increasingly important economic goods and, hence, an increasingly important element of market economies. Thus, in the context of tourism, environmental protection is becoming an economic activity and, therefore, a part of economic development and a contributor to economic growth.

Tourism development also, of course, has many non-economic developmental impacts, such as sociocultural consequences, educational benefits, peace promotion and so on. However, this chapter is primarily concerned with the economic dimension of tourism, in particular the issues surrounding the potential contribution of tourism to economic development. Therefore, rather than addressing the wide range of topics typically included in the economic analysis of tourism, it focuses principally on specific areas where tourism, from an economic perspective, may contribute to or militate against development. These include:

- the impact of tourism on the balance of payments;
- tourism impacts on general economic development through the multiplier effect;
- the impact of tourism on regional economic development;
- the inflation/deflation consequences of tourism;
- the impact of tourism on employment; and
- environmental goods valuation in tourism.

Tourism and the Balance of Payments

As long ago as the 17th century, the mercantilist Thomas Mun was one of the first to recognise the potential influence of tourism on a country's balance of payments (Planina, 1997: 58). Although the word 'tourism' had yet to enter common usage at that time, nevertheless the 'expenses of travailers' (Mun, 1965: 85) that influence the 'Ballance' (Mun, 1965: 86) were used to describe the impact of international tourism on the balance of payments. Planina (1997: 61) maintains that the tourism impact on the balance of payments was also the first tourism issue to become a matter of scientific debate in the works of Geering (1920), Gebert (1928) and Demeuth (1929). More recently, during the first half of the 20th century and, in particular, during the years of economic recession in Europe, many economists were also concerned with the ability or potential of international tourism to generate foreign currency earnings. At the same time, many countries adopted protectionist measures in order to increase (incoming) tourism receipts and to decrease (outgoing) tourism expenditure, demonstrating the importance of the receipt/expenditure impact of tourism, even for developed countries. Thus, although the United Nations interceded against protectionism in tourism in 1936, governments have continued to promote incoming tourism flows and destimulate outgoing flows through economic controls. For example, in 1966 the British Government, concerned about the deficit in the travel balance, limited the amount of domestic currency taken on trips out of the country to £50 per day. As a result, British foreign tourism expenditure decreased significantly and the tourism balance became positive. Similarly, in 1968 the USA attempted to discourage overseas travel for balance of payments reasons. Although Congress refused to adopt the proposed measures that would limit American's freedom to travel, the then President nevertheless asked American citizens to reduce their foreign travel in the forthcoming years and, in 1968, American overseas tourism expenditures decreased. The tourism balance was thus reduced, aided by increased foreign tourism earnings (Unković, 1981).

In comparison, overseas tourism expenditure by the Japanese increased when they were encouraged by their government to travel more. The reason was again to address an imbalance in the balance of payments although, for Japan, the problem was not a deficit but a surplus in foreign trade with the USA and Europe and tourism was seen as a particularly effective way of reducing the country's international trade surplus (Polunin, 1989: 5). This has proved to be a highly successful policy (see Burns, 1996). Not only has it has evolved into a '10 million programme', but also agreements have been reached with specific countries, such as the 'two million visitors, two-way challenge' with Canada, designed to encourage two million tourists from each country to visit the other. At the same time, in the early 1990s the permitted value of duty free goods brought back into Japan was doubled, from 100,000 to 200,000 yen, thereby increasing the expenditure of Japanese tourists in the destination. However, although the primary intention was to reduce the balance of payments surplus, a goal that has undoubtedly been achieved, it was also seen as a way of addressing social issues in the country. In particular, the Japanese government was keen to develop overseas retirement centres in order to provide more space and lower living costs for its retired population. Not surprisingly, perhaps, these plans were shelved following the negative reaction of the target countries yet, nevertheless, Japan succeeded in increasing its foreign tourism investment in a number of destinations, the capital outflow contributing to a reduction in the total balance of payments surplus.

Thus, although tourism is a powerful tool for balance of payments adjustments, its impact may vary. Certainly, as indicated by WTO and International Monetary Fund (IMF) data, international tourism is the top export category in the world, exceeding both the automobile industry and the chemicals industry, and together with international fare receipts represents about 8% of total export earnings on goods and services worldwide. Tourism is also one of the top five export categories for 83% of all countries, and the main source of foreign currency for at least 38% of them (WTO, 1999d: 13). It is not surprising, therefore, that for many countries, particularly those with a limited industrial sector or with few opportunities for developing alternative export sectors, tourism provides a vital source of foreign exchange earnings. In Cyprus, for example, tourism accounts for about 40% of total exports and, until the mid-1990s, balanced the rapidly increasing imports bill (Sharpley, 2001). Moreover, the true value of tourism to the balance of payments may, in fact, be greater than suggested by focusing on the tourism sector alone. That is, the tourism economy can include all the industries and sectors beyond the direct tourism industry itself. This total contribution can, in theory, be measured by a tourism satellite account (TSA), defined as 'an information system that combines, orders, and interrelates statistics describing all significant and measurable aspects of tourism within a framework that organises tourism data according to the real world relationships from which they originate' (Smith, 1998: 40). Although there are significant problems associated with establishing a TSA, the results they provide (such as those published by the World Travel and Tourism Council) arguably provide a more valid indication of tourism's economic value. As a result, increasing attention is being paid by both the industry and academics to tourism satellite accounting as a cutting edge method of calculating the 'true' value of tourism.

However, tourism's contribution to exports in general, and the balance of international tourism expenditures and receipts in particular, varies considerably from country to country. For instance, within Europe, the countries of western and northern Europe have a negative tourism balance, whereas southern and eastern European countries have a positive balance (see Table 3.1). On a global scale, though, apart from the sun–sea–sand attraction of southern Europe and consequential high level of tourism earnings, the high positive tourism balance tends to belong to less developed countries. Conversely, a deficit in the tourism balance is a characteristic of developed countries. According to the classic view,[5] the less developed, non-industrialised countries may be considered to possess higher tourism attractiveness, due to a less degraded environment. At the same time, they consider tourism to be an export opportunity which has been subject to relatively high growth rates and has the potential for higher earnings than more traditional forms of export.

Indeed, the so-called invisible tourism export is considered to have many advantages over the classic export of goods and services:

- Some goods, which cannot become the subject of exchange within international trade, such as natural and cultural or social attractiveness of the country, can be valorised through tourism. They attract tourism demand and are indirectly 'sold' on the tourism market, in a form of higher prices for tourism products (see the section on environmental goods valuation in tourism).
- Some products that are 'exported' by being sold to foreign tourists visiting the country, such as a bottle of wine or food, may achieve higher prices than if exported 'traditionally' (that is, physically transported for purchase and consumption overseas).
- 'Exporting' by selling to tourists also results in higher profits, because apart from the higher prices mentioned earlier, the costs are lower (for example, lower or no transportation costs or insurance costs).
- Some perishable goods, such as agricultural products, which are sold to the tourists in the country, may simply not be suitable for owing to an insufficiently developed infrastructure and management of export flows.

Tourism is thus seen as a relatively cheap and easy way – and sometimes the only way – of earning the foreign currency required for investing in development. Since many countries face 'balance of payments difficulties because of a deficit in the trade account or capital account, or both' (Witt, 1989: 487), international tourism receipts can help to alleviate such balance of payments problems and contribute to the financial resources needed for economic and social development.

However, the overall contribution of tourism to the current account may be reduced by many factors (Williams & Shaw, 1998: 6). First, it is important to consider the overall balance between international tourism receipts and expenditures. Second, there are leakages of expenditures from the national economy, the level of which is a function of the import propensity of the country, partly a function of the structure of the ownership of the tourism and related industries, and partly a function of the degree of development of domestic industries and their ability to meet the tourist's needs from domestic production. Third, the demonstration effect additionally increases the import expenditures of a country as the local population imitates the consumption patterns of tourists and increases its demand for imported goods.

Tourism's Impact on General Economic Development Through the Multiplier Effect

Although the multiplier effect of tourism is frequently regarded as a separate, identifiable economic impact of tourism and is often treated so in the literature, it is inextricably linked to the direct economic benefits of tourism as a source of income, employment and government revenue. It also contributes to the understanding and calculation of the indirect and induced economic impacts of tourism and is, therefore, a useful tool in exploring the extent of tourism's role in economic development.

The multiplier concept is based upon the recognition that the various industrial sectors of the tourism destination economy are interdependent (Fletcher, 1994: 476). It can be summarised as follows.

Tourism spending represents extra expenditure introduced into an economy which may be the local community, a region within the country, or a country as a whole. This tourism expenditure includes spending on goods and services by tourists, tourism investment by external sources, domestic government spending (in a local community or region only) and foreign government spending such as aid, as well as export of goods stimulated by tourism (WTO, 1981: 1). Tourism expenditure initially accrues to the 'first-round' tourism recipients, such as hotels, accommodation providers and other direct tourism businesses. This is known as the direct effect of tourism consumption and is equal to the amount of tourism consumption (tourism receipts) in the host country. However, because these first-round tourism recipients use the income from tourism to make additional purchases from other sectors within the host economy to support their business, tourism consumption not only benefits the direct producer of tourism services, but also the tourism sector's suppliers, the suppliers' suppliers, and so on. This is referred to as the indirect income effect. As a result of both spending on imports and saving, the amount of money 're-spent' in each subsequent round of expenditure reduces until the remaining income is spent on goods and services in the final round of expenditure in the local economy. At the same time, however, further repercussive effects are generated that add to economic activity in what is known as the induced effect, caused by induced expenditure. This is the increasing consumer spending resulting from increased personal income of the local population, due to tourism expenditure. For example, tourism industry employees use their wages for the purchase of goods and services and generate induced income.

The sum of all these effects – direct, indirect and induced – represents total income which is generated in all rounds in a period of one year as a result of initial tourist expenditure. The ratio between the total income and initial tourist expenditures is known as the normal tourist multiplier (Archer, 1977). It, then, represents the factor by which initial tourist spending is multiplied to equal the sum of direct, indirect and induced income.

Since different calculation methods are used, different kinds of income multipliers [6] are employed. Furthermore, in addition to the variety of income multipliers, a number of other tourism multiplier concepts also exist. Three different types of multiplier in particular are commonly used (Archer, 1977: 2):

- the transactional or sales multiplier, that measures the total business turnover created by an extra unit of tourist expenditure;
- the output multiplier, similar to transaction multiplier but which also takes into account inventory changes; and
- the employment multiplier, which can be calculated as a ratio between primary, indirect, induced employment and initial tourism expenditures or primary employment.

In addition to these widely used tourism multipliers, others can also be calculated, such as the capital or asset (Bull, 1995: 151) and taxation multipliers.

Although there are conflicting concepts of the multiplier (WTO, 1981: 1), the principal weakness is the way, in general, that tourism multipliers have been used and interpreted (Archer, 1977: 2; WTO, 1981: 6; Mathieson & Wall, 1982: 66; Fletcher, 1994: 478). In particular, if the method of calculation is not known, then comparisons are meaningless. Thus for example, the value of a transaction multiplier may be many times higher compared to the normal income multiplier, as suggested by Archer in the case of Gwynedd, North Wales, where the values were 1.16–0.37 (Archer, 1977: 47, 49). Confusion may also arise as many researchers define income differently, and few specify whether or not inventory changes have been taken into account (WTO, 1981: 1–2). In addition, calculation methods have often been incorrectly applied and interpretations have been misleading, such as in the case of the controversial Zinder Report for the Eastern Caribbean (see Mathieson & Wall, 1982: 66–8).

A number of factors can influence the value of the multiplier. For instance, if there a high level of leakages out of the economy exists, either through a dependence upon imported goods or a significant degree of saving, then each subsequent round of expenditure will be proportionally smaller and the value of the tourism income multiplier tends to be lower. Similarly, where the tourism industry in the destination is owned by foreign capital, the subsequent repatriation of income reduces the value of the multiplier, whilst in a tourism sector dominated by expatriate labour or where the great proportion of salaries goes to a more skilled labour force from abroad, the effect would be the same. In such cases, the income multiplier would be small and, since tourism multipliers are a popular means of 'proving' the economic importance of tourism and justifying tourism development policy, its political attractiveness would be lost. Nevertheless, even low-value income multipliers do not necessarily suggest that economic benefits of tourism to the destination are minimal. For example, a normal tourism multiplier below zero, such as 0.7, would mean the generation of 700,000 additional income units from an initial one million units of tourism expenditure. This generated output may be important for the destination economy as a whole or for some sectors, such as the hotel industry or agriculture or transport etc.

As already illustrated in the case of Gwynedd, South Wales, the values of the transaction multipliers are always higher compared to the values of the income multiplier as they refer to total business turnover. Therefore, it can be argued that, in a political context, transaction multipliers are the preferred method of calculation. For example, in the early 1980s when Yugoslavia promoted tourism development, mainly for its foreign exchange contribution, the importance of tourism, was stressed based on a value for the tourism multiplier of 2.77 (Ogorelec *et al.*, 1981: 9). Similarly, in Turkey the political will to support tourism development was justified on the basis of the high value of the tourism multiplier (Dincer, 1999). In reality, however, the economic impact of tourism may not have been as great as these figures suggested. What this suggests is that the real development debate should focus not only on the value of the tourism multiplier but also on the alternative opportunities for development that may be identified in local communities, within the region or nationally. Nevertheless, if tourism remains the only possible development path or is 'the last resort', any additional income or economic activity is likely to be very welcome, irrespective of the multiplier value.

The Impact of Tourism on Regional Economic Development

The relationship between tourism and regional development is explored in some detail in Chapter 4. However, in the context of this chapter, the theory of tourism as a means of achieving economic development embraces two distinct themes. On the one hand, tourism is seen as a vehicle of regional development within a particular developed country, contributing to the alleviation of regional imbalances, in particular between the metropolitan centres and peripheral areas. On the other hand, tourism's developmental role is considered in the context of a world divided into developed and less developed countries, the assumption being that the gap between the two may be reduced through tourism development projects in the latter.

Some authors refer to this theory as 'the dispersion of development to non-industrial regions' (Bryden, 1973: 72). According to this classic view, tourism 'tends to distribute development away from the industrial centres towards those regions in a country which have not been developed' (Peters, 1996, cited in Williams & Shaw, 1998: 12). Conversely, the modern view, based upon the late 20th century development of new forms of tourism, argues that recent changes in tourism markets and investments favour richer regions (Williams & Shaw, 1998: 12).

Although both themes (regional and country) stress the contribution of tourism to development, there are a number of reasons why it is important to distinguish between the two because they have differing implications for the actual contribution of tourism to development. First, at the national level, the attitude towards tourism may vary considerably in less developed and developed countries. In the former, tourism is frequently of much greater economic importance, for example in terms of its share of GDP (see Table 3.1) and as a result, tourism development is often supported, with high expectations, by a national tourism policy (as, for example, in Turkey; see Daoudi and Mihalič (1999: 18).) In developed countries, however, there may not be a specific tourism policy. Rather, tourism development may constitute an element of regional or industrial policy (Keller, 1999: 2), other industries or service sectors may have the potential for much higher added value, and tourism may be seen as a priority economic activity only for less developed regions as opposed to the whole, national economy. Such a situation exists in a number of countries, such as in Switzerland and in many European Union countries, where tourism policy as such is non-existent. Secondly, the negative impacts of tourism development are frequently claimed to be much more evident in less developed countries, primarily as a result of the economic and sociocultural gulf that exists between them and the developed countries that are the principal generators of tourists, and, as a result of both of these factors, much more attention has been given to tourism development theory in the context of the less developed world.

However, it is also important to consider the role of tourism in regional economic development in developed countries. Here, tourism consumption, which is directed mainly towards less developed, peripheral regions that are rich in tourist attractions (natural, cultural and heritage), leads to the redistribution of national income to the benefit of the host region. An increase in the financial resources on the demand side requires increased production in the host region, provoking new directly tourism-related activities, an increase in the production of indirect suppliers to 'first-round' tourism businesses, the creation of new jobs, extra incomes, new additional consumption on the part of new employees, new investment, and so on. As a result, the national per capita income within the incoming region, in theory, increases whilst, other things being equal, the reduced final consumption in the visitor's place of residence slows down economic growth in the more developed region. This gives rise to the concept of convergence. That is, as a result of tourism consumption, the relative differences in per capita income between the incoming and outgoing, less developed and developed regions becomes smaller. In reality, however, the extent to which this may be achieved also depends upon the ability of the tourism businesses to add value in comparison to other activities in the developed region and on the capital–output ratio in the tourism region compared with that in the developed, generating region. If the added value in the tourism in-dustry is lower (and the capital–output ratio higher) compared to added value (capital–output ratio) in other industries in rich regions, then poorer regions can never catch up with the wealthier regions. At the same time, it must be stressed that parity between the metropolitan centres and less developed peripheral regions is rarely, if ever, an objective of tourism development; the goal may simply to gain some economic developmental benefit through tourism.

More generally, the critics of tourism as a development strategy point to leakages from the economy arising from the import of products used in the tourism industry and to the domination of foreign and multinational firms in the hotel, tour operat-ing and transport sectors that redistribute tourism expenditures back to the developed areas where they are located (see Ioannides & Debbage (1998b) for a comprehensive analysis of the influence of supply-side arrangements on tourism development). Some, supporting the theory of dependency, go as far as claiming that tourism is another form of colonialism or imperialism (Harrison, 2000: 147). As previously explained (see Chapter 2), this suggests less developed tourism regions exhibit a reliance upon external factors and, as such, derive their growth from corre-sponding growth in the developed regions. Tourism development may therefore reflect the symptoms of dependency when it results in the enrichment of developed countries or regions at the expense of the poorer (Fletcher, 2000: 142). Although the development of tourism brings an improved infrastructure and external or foreign investments into host regions and countries, at the same time it may make the local economy dependent upon tourism for its survival whilst squeezing out traditional industries, not to mention the other negative, non-economic consequences of tourism development on the natural, social and cultural environment. Further-more, mono-development, based predominantly on one industry, such as tourism, is economically highly risky. Tourism demand tends to be very unstable, frequently changing allegiance from one destination to another. This can happen for a variety of reasons, including unfavourable exchange rates/high prices, inflation, changes in fashion, environmental catastrophes, terrorism, wars and so on. For example, tourism bookings to Rimini, Italy in 1989 dropped by 50% compared with the previ-ous year as a result of algae blooming in the Adriatic Sea (Becheri, 1990: 230). Similarly, American visits to Europe fell dramatically following the Chernobyl ca-tastrophe in 1986, the Balkan wars in the 1990s had a severe negative impact on tourist flows to the region and, following the massacre of 58 tourists at Luxor's Temple of Hatshepsut in Egypt, Egyptian tourism suffered a significant decline (Pizam & Smith, 2000).

The classic view argues that tourism contributes to regional convergence in eco-nomic development. Although this perspective has been widely criticised, the main challenge, as pointed out earlier, is modern, late-20th century tourism develop-ment. Although tourism has traditionally favoured poorer areas, recent transformations in tourism markets and investments have benefited richer regions and countries (Williams & Shaw, 1998: 13). That is, the rapid expansion of new forms of tourism, such as urban tourism, cultural tourism, heritage tourism and theme parks, favours those destinations which are relatively accessible to major metropolitan areas. This has been observed in the UK, in particular in London and the southern counties, as well as in Austria where a significant shift in tourism demand towards richer regions, such as Vienna and Lower Austria, has been noted (Zimmerman, 1998: 30).

This shift in tourism demand towards wealthier, industrialised destinations has, on the one hand, been demand driven by new tourism behavioural patterns towards short breaks and new products. On the other hand, it has been very much supported by the supply side. Many places suffering economic decline as a result of losing major traditional industries, such as coal and steel production, textiles and ship building, as well as others seeking a more general revival, have sought to develop tourism (Kotler *et al.*, 1993). In other words, tourism is expected to bring prosperity to ailing economies (Swarbrooke, 2000), examples being Baltimore and Boston in the 1970s and Essen and Dortmund in Germany in the 1990s. In all cases, however, it was not only a 'take-off' through tourism development that was the hope. That is, there is some evidence that increasing tourism can also increase the attraction of places to foreign investors and, as Sandford and Dong (2000: 217) demonstrate, tourism stimulates direct investments in a wide variety of (non-tourism) industries and, subsequently, gives rise to economic development.

Furthermore, a clear-cut understanding of the relationship between tourism and development based upon the world divided into developed and less developed countries and regions may also be criticised. For example, it neglects the fact that although developed countries may earn substantial absolute amounts of direct tourism expenditure, these are often relatively unimportant as a share of total GDP. At the same time, a developed country's travel balance deficit may be enormous. A good illustration is Germany which, on the one hand, has gained the reputation as 'the world champions of travelling' (Schnell, 1998: 269) but, on the other hand, is also a tourism destination. In 1997, for example, Germany's tourism balance showed a deficit of almost US$29.7 billion, the US$46.2 billion spent by Germans abroad well exceeding the US$16.5 billion the country earned from foreign visitors.

Moreover, an oversimplified theory of tourism development also neglects the fact that tourism expenditure per visitor per day is normally higher if it is a developed country or region being visited (see Table 3.1). From this, it is possible to speculate that developed countries are able to add higher value to their tourism product. Thus, it is logical to suggest convergence in economic development cannot be achieved through the development of tourism. This is not to say that tourism does not represent a development opportunity for less developed countries, helping them to achieve economic growth and restructure their domestic economies. However, from the analysis of added value, it must be concluded that the power of tourism as a means of development is dependent upon the existing level of development in the tourism destination country or region. In other words, it is not only the development level of the tourism sector that is important, but also the degree of development of other sectors of the economy (see also the discussion on the third stage of tourism development and capital–output ratios in the preceding section on tourism and development). Taking into account the dependency of different sectors that, within the host economy, must be involved to satisfy the demand for tourism, it is clear that the better developed economy will be able to earn more, and also retain more of those earnings, within the national economy or region.

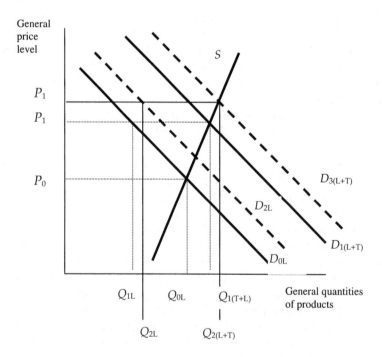

Figure 3.1 Tourism-imported inflation.
Legend: S, supply curve; D_{0L}, local demand (before tourist expenditure enters the economy); $D_{1(L+T)}$, local and tourist demand after tourist expenditure enters the economy (primary or direct effect); D_{2L}, increased local demand due to increased employment and income (secondary effect); $D_{3(L+T)}$, local and tourist demand after the secondary effect took place; P, general price level; Q, general quantities of products

The Inflation/Deflation Consequences of Tourism

Tourism may result in demand–pull inflation/deflation to both the tourism incoming and outgoing economy. International tourists bring additional financial resources into the host country and, if the supply of goods and services cannot adapt to the increased effective demand, the general price level rises, leading to inflation. Conversely, for tourism-generating countries, international tourism represents an outflow of financial resources and has an anti-inflationary influence. Theoretically, it may cause deflation or a reduction in the current rate of inflation.

Figure 3.1 assumes that, in the absence of international tourism, the purchasing funds of local inhabitants equals the funds of goods and services and the economy is in equilibrium P_0Q_{0L}. In this case, tourism expenditures increase the supply of money and bring about inflation. The additional tourism demand shifts total demand from D_{0L} which represents local demand to $D_{1(L+T)}$ which represents the sum of local and tourist demand. A direct or primary effect of tourism expenditure is a new equilibrium at $P_1Q_{1(T+L)}$ where more products are traded, but at a higher price. Since local consumers, whose income remains unchanged, are only able to buy quantities along curve D_{0L} in a new equilibrium at higher prices, they may only buy a lower quantity Q_{2L}. Furthermore, because tourism demand increases production, local employment and salaries will increase (secondary effect). Some of the additional salaries will shift the local demand curve to the right (D_{2L}) as locals are now willing/able to spend more money for available goods and services. At the same time the total demand curve $D_{1(L+T)}$ will move to $D_{3(L+T)}$ and push prices up further. It is the slope of the supply curve that decides how much additional local purchasing power is going to disappear in higher prices.

In the case that a country has higher purchasing funds compared to commodity funds, international tourism will increase the inflation rate; in the opposite case, in an economy with deflation any tendency it will stabilise prices. Conversely, outgoing tourism acts as reductor of purchasing power in an outgoing economy – theoretically it may reduce the inflation rate or cause deflation.

Nevertheless, the influence of tourism development on price levels is related to dependency theory. For example, increased immobility prices which result from an increase in tourism demand may make it impossible for local people to purchase their own homes or to survive in the area whilst remaining engaged in traditional industries. This then leads to the local economy becoming dependent upon tourism for its survival.

Tourism itself is also affected by inflation. Since local inhabitants have to spend more money for basic goods as a result of higher prices, less income remains for discretionary tourism expenditures. Thus, domestic tourism may decline. At the same time, if one tourist country has a faster rate of inflation than that of other, competitive countries, its international competitiveness and, hence, its tourism industry may suffer a decline. For example, a resident of the UK may be contemplating one of two resort holidays in the Mediterranean, one in France and the other in Italy. Should the French franc appreciate in value against sterling while the lira remains unchanged, the British tourist would choose the Italian resort (Sinclair & Stabler, 1997: 24).

In some respects, the impact of tourism on price levels remains under-researched within the tourism literature. In some studies, the influence on immobility prices and prices of consumer goods in tourism destinations are mentioned, but no quantification of the influence of tourism on the inflation/deflation rate is available. On the other hand, the impact of inflation on international tourism demand has been confirmed in many tourism demand models. Besides income and trends, the majority of the models quantify the impact of relative prices, costs of transport and exchange rates (Crouch & Shaw, 1992). Theoretically, since the price elasticity of tourism demand is negative[7] and a cross price elasticity positive,[8] higher prices in country A, all things being equal, will redirect tourist flows to competitive tourism country B, thereby reducing tourism earnings in country A and increasing those of country B. For example, Witt and Witt (1994: 529) have shown that, for the 1965–80 period, British tourists were highly price-sensitive and considered exchange rates in their holiday decision-making process.

Thus, although this consideration of the inflation/deflation consequences of tourism may be oversimplified (and also recognising that many sources of inflation are internal to an economy), it is nevertheless clear that a study into the inflationary effects of international tourism receipts, which are so sought after in terms of their contribution to the balance of payments, may in fact reveal problems that remove much of the political credibility of tourism development in less developed countries. The main tourism flows still follow the direction North to South, that is, from developed countries with relatively stable economies towards less developed counties that, in general, face inflation. Thus, tourism in industrialised generating countries reduces the inflation rate whilst increasing an already high inflation tendency in non-industrialised countries. At the same time, it is logical to deduce that the already rich developed countries stabilise their own prices through 'inflation export' towards less developed tourism countries and increase the gap between developed and less developed economies.

The Impact of Tourism on Employment

Tourism creates valuable employment opportunities. Indeed, commonly regarded as a human-resource intensive activity, tourism represents what may arguably be described as the world's single largest source of employment, the 'tourism economy' – that is, both the direct tourism industry and related sectors, such as construction and finance – providing up to 11% of global employment. Thus, and as considered in Chapter 6, it is inevitable that human resource issues are a central theme in tourism development.

Table 3.2 Contribution of tourism to national employment in selected countries

Country	Travel & Tourism Industry (% of total)	Travel and Tourism Economy (% of total)
Maldives	25.9	54.2
Cayman Islands	18.1	47.3
Malta	15.6	26.3
Cyprus	11.7	22.1
Jordan	10.0	20.9
Mauritius	10.0	21.9
Belize	8.9	22.0
Spain	8.3	20.9
New Zealand	6.2	13.3
United States	5.6	12.6
The Gambia	5.5	12.4
Cuba	5.1	12.1
United Kingdom	4.9	14.8
Australia	4.7	14.5
France	4.3	11.7
Turkey	3.9	8.9
Sri Lanka	3.1	7.4
India	2.7	5.6
Indonesia	2.3	7.4
China	2.0	7.0

Source: World Travel and Tourism Council (2000).

The role and contribution of tourism to employment and, hence, development, varies considerably according to the scale, character, stage of development and relative importance of the tourism industry in any country or destination. Table 3.2 indicates the contribution of tourism to overall employment in a number of selected countries. Generally, however, the tourism-related employment debate in less developed countries tends to focus upon the generation of employment opportunities for lower skilled workers, tourism as a new source of income/wages, and on small-scale entrepreneurship in cottage industries. Similarly, in developed countries, the potential contribution of tourism to employment stresses job creation and entrepreneurship. Frequently, however, it is the impact of tourism on employment in peripheral areas, thereby counteracting rural–urban migration or a population shift towards more developed regions, that is emphasised in particular. Thus, tourism employment is closely connected with regional development issues in the developed world but more usually associated with national economic growth and development in less developed countries. Nevertheless, in some less developed countries, such as Mexico and Indonesia, tourism has been promoted as a regional, as opposed to national, employment generator.

Inevitably, the impact of tourism on employment is widely criticised and it has long been recognised that the promise of high quality, permanent jobs and a reduction in overall unemployment is not always realised in practice. In some societies, for example, negative images are associated with the service sector in general, whilst long and unsociable hours are seen as a particular disadvantage of working in the tourism industry. More specifically, criticism is frequently directed at the part-time, seasonal (i.e. non-permanent) nature of many tourism jobs, and the fact that such jobs often attract individuals, such as students or retired people, who might not be considered part of the working population. At the same time, either a lack of a domestic labour force or the low wages, unsociable hours and the poor image of working in tourism may result in foreign workers, either officially or unofficially, being employed in the sector, resulting in a variety of social tensions. Finally, it is frequently claimed that, particularly in developing economies, the jobs created in tourism for local people are generally menial and lower level, although in many less developed countries, such as Cuba, the potential earnings in the tourism sector may actually be higher than in other professions. For example, the potential for earning tips as a supplement to basic wages in the tourism industry is a major pull, whilst the attraction of other occupations, in particular tourism-related prostitution, is frequently the significant financial gains to be had in comparison with non-tourism employment. Nevertheless, reflecting the inherent dependency of tourism, the higher paid, managerial positions are more often occupied by foreign nationals and, as already observed, this importation of labour usually intensifies leakages that negatively influence economic development.

Nevertheless, the employment contribution of tourism development is currently the (politically) most justified role of tourism in development. In a world where traditional industries in the primary and secondary sectors are employing fewer and fewer people, newer service industries are being increasingly viewed as an effective source of new jobs. Given the enormous variety of businesses which directly and indirectly facilitate travel, tourism is considered a particularly valuable source of employment and, in the light of the positive trends in the growth of travel and tourism, it is likely that there will be significant new job opportunities both directly and indirectly dependent on tourism.

For example, within the EU the tourism sector provides employment for nine million people (Employment 1999) and tourism is acknowledged as being amongst those industries which offer the best prospects for economic growth and job creation. However, this sector's potential has not yet been sufficiently exploited at the

European level and it has been estimated that between 2.2 and 3.3 million new jobs could be created in tourism over the coming decade (Employment, 1999).

From the economic development point of view there is a general consensus that tourism creates employment that is, in general, of benefit to the economy. However, it may also be argued that, rather than creating new, extra jobs, tourism development serves simply to redistribute existing labour. That is, the potential attraction of working within tourism means that traditional industries, in particular in agriculture, lose their labour force and go into decline. As a consequence, more primary products have to be imported, contributing to a negative balance of payments. At the same time, it has also been suggested that working seasonally may be more attractive to the local labour force and thus non-tourist industries that may have a higher value-added potential may not consider it worthwhile locating in the area (Mathieson & Wall, 1982: 81). Despite these problems, however, there is little doubt that tourism, though its employment generation potential, makes an effective contribution to economic development, particularly in those areas where few, if any, alternative employment prospects exist.

Environmental Goods Valuation in Tourism

The theory of the tourism valuation of natural goods – essentially the theory of local public and non-priced goods applied to tourism – states that some, otherwise profitless and, from the standpoint of current market economy order, even value-less aspects of nature and culture may be converted into premium prices[9] if 'sold' on the tourism market. If the supply is fixed, increased demand translates into higher prices, in which the premium to a supplier is known as economic rent. Thus, tourist countries, regions and destinations, and the tourism companies operating in such areas, promote the natural public attractions, such as beautiful countryside, karst caves, pristine beaches, clean waters, and so on because, in the eyes of the tourist, they are part of the tourism supply (Tschurtschenthaler, 1986: 118). The payment from the 'consumption' of natural goods is included in the (higher) price of tourist services which emanates from greater tourist demand resulting from the attractiveness of the natural or cultural goods. For example, British 'green' tourists are willing to pay a premium of £509 for a fortnight's holiday in tropical North Queensland for the unspoiled condition of the natural environment and if the authorities continue to protect it (Huybers & Bennett, 2000: 37).

Since natural goods are usually at everyone's disposal (i.e. public), they have no price and are available free of charge, yet tourism companies realise part of their income through the valuation of such goods. If the property rights to natural goods are not determined, therefore, this part of their income belongs to the domestic or foreign company which has succeeded in usurping the use of some public good for private profit.

In some cases, the premium earnings resulting from the exploitation of the host country's natural and cultural property belong to foreign firms and are transferred out of the host country. Thus, tourism may become a form of neocolonialism whereby control of national property is taken over by foreign capital. On the one hand, this may be seen as being very similar to the colonial exploitation of other natural resources, such as minerals; on the other hand, it is significantly less transparent. That is, international tourism, as an invisible export, may create leakages from the economy before the consumption of tourism even commences in the host country. The great part of financial flows may not accompany travellers but, rather, remain in with foreign or multinational companies based overseas. In particular in the case of package destinations, the payment for goods and services in the host destination pass through the hands of the outgoing tour operator that, normally, enjoys high bargaining power and is able to negotiate low prices with local suppliers.

The consequences are twofold. First, the impact of foreign expenditure in the local host area is, of course, reduced. Second, and of greater relevance here, the premium value for natural and cultural attractions that should, in theory, belong to the host country, is appropriated by the foreign company. As a result, the tourism output in the host economy is lower, the capital–output ratio increases and the economic development effects of tourism are therefore lowered. An extreme case is that of international vessels that 'sell' cruises. Frequently, such ships anchor in the national waters of certain tourism destinations close to beautiful beaches, yet then leave without generating any tourist expenditure if the tourists have not been given the opportunity to visit the mainland.

From the standpoint of traditional foreign trade theory (Heckscher–Ohlin theory), the source of comparative advantage are factor endowments, labour or capital. According to this theory, industrialised countries are able to produce industrial goods (capital intensive production) at lower capital costs than developing countries. Conversely, developing countries have a comparative advantage in service industries, such as tourism. They are able to produce tourism services (labour-intensive production) at a lower factor cost than industrialised countries. The extent to which each will benefit from trade will depend upon the real terms of trade at which they agree to exchange tourism services for industrial goods.

In contrast to this theory based upon the availability of capital and labour, an alternative model is also useful for explaining the international exchange between developing and industrial countries. Countries with rich endowments of natural attractions should, in theory, develop international tourism in order to 'export' products that depend upon them and thus exchange 'island beaches for industrial goods' (Smeral, 1994: 499).

Defenders of this theory claim that the 'selling' of natural and cultural attractions through premium prices does not reduce the wealth of the country as is the case, for instance, with raw material exploitation and export. Indeed, the fact that certain visitors have experienced a particular country's attractions may enhance its appeal and therefore increase its value to others (Ritchie & Crouch, 1993: 35). However, those who criticise the theory point to the issue of environmental damage. The reduction in the value of natural goods resulting from tourist exploitation and pollution may be categorised as a negative external effect; in practice, this is manifested in, for example, the visual pollution of the countryside through inappropriate tourist utilisation of the area, water pollution and other forms of degradation of the environment, such as noise, congestion, destruction of flora and fauna, and negative impacts on the local society and culture. Although the economic success of tourism companies is dependent upon the quality (attractiveness, purity) of natural goods, they are not generally willing to take responsibility for the costs, especially those related to the repair of environmental damage or degradation caused in the past and the consequences of such damage. Thus, the costs of environmental repair and protection are sustained by the host country, irrespective of who has profited from the exploitation of the environment.

The solution, therefore, for countries in transition would be to adopt legislation that will allow the establishment of property rights to natural goods so that they can be efficiently included in economic development processes. If there is no formal owner, then the planning horizon becomes shorter and the use and exploitation of natural goods is less productive. In effect, where no one is responsible for environmental protection and management, environmental quality and, consequently, the attractiveness for tourism, may deteriorate. As a result, premium prices fall and the valuation may even become negative. Tourists would not be willing to 'pay' for poor environmental quality. Indeed, they would require visitor premium (visitor rent) in the form of low prices (Mihalič 2000: 137) or they reject polluted or environmentally spoilt destinations, reducing the economic contribution of tourism to development.

However, an additional problem is that a less developed country may lack the ability to add value to its natural or cultural resources, even when a 'third party' country is not involved in the tourism business. This may be the result of a lack of expertise, poor marketing and promotion, limited access to tourism-generating markets, poor branding, and so on. In the case where the premium value earned is low or zero (or even negative) due to low prices, the tourism output is proportionally lower and thus the value of the capital–output ratio is higher which has, as already argued, negative implications for the economic growth rate and development. Conversely, earned positive tourism rent can bring additional financial resources into the economy which, if used for environmental protection, will generate new economic activities in this sector at the same time as preventing the depreciation of tourism assets. Thus, long-term tourism valuation of (maintained) environmental goods will be assured, as will a sustainable resource for economic growth.

Conclusion

There is no doubt that tourism, as both an incoming and outgoing economic phenomenon, directly influences national, regional and local economies. It is also certainly a fact that tourism development has various potentially beneficial economic impacts that may positively influence the process of economic development in the destination.

However, the justification for promoting tourism on the basis of its alleged positive economic impact is open to criticism, the principal argument being that the magnitude of tourism's economic benefits is variable, being determined by a variety of factors such as the level of economic development in the host country or region, the propensity to import, and so on. Thus, the assertion that tourism development projects in less developed countries can contribute to the establishment of a new world order through reducing the gap between the developed and less developed world all too often overlooks factors that militate against economic development, such as leakages through spending on imports, the external source of investment capital and the international or foreign ownership of tourism organisations and businesses in the host country (see Chapter 9). Even the theory of competitive advantage, whereby destinations in less developed countries benefit from 'natural attractiveness', may be criticised if terms of trade favour the export of industrial goods to the detriment of 'island beaches export'.

According to Butcher (1997: 28), what less developed countries and regions need and require most is 'thoroughgoing development', or fundamental economic development that addresses the poverty of pollution suffered by many in the less developed world. However, reflecting the evolution of development theory from economic growth-based modernisation models to the alternative/sustainable development paradigm, the tourism development debate has similarly moved from support for the positive contribution of tourism to economic development to criticism of tourism development. This criticism, of course, refers mainly to non-economic issues, in particular the negative environmental (natural, social and cultural) consequences of tourism in less developed countries, and is manifested principally in an oversimplified sustainable tourism debate. As argued by Butcher (1997: 28) and elsewhere in this book (see Chapter 11), the focus on sustainable tourism has 'ruled out of order a discussion of ... development'. This is not so much a criticism of the concept of sustainable development as one of its incorrect application, oversimplification and its one-sided emphasis within the context of tourism. Nevertheless, as a result, two fundamental elements of the sustainability concept, namely the economic dimension and the need for equity in development, are often neglected (Inskeep, 1991: 461). (It is conveniently 'forgotten', for example, that the Brundtland Report, the basis for many of the principles of sustainable development, recommended a growth in the world economy by a factor of 5–10 in order to alleviate poverty in less developed countries (WCED, 1987: 50) – something that tourism, as a major economic growth sector, is in a position to contribute to).

As this chapter has demonstrated, despite valid criticism of some of the alleged economic benefits of tourism, there are a variety of economic measures which support the argument that tourism can be an effective vehicle for economic growth. There are also many examples in practice where tourism has been the main engine of economic growth and development in destination countries and regions. At the same time, economic analysis also provides us with two possible solutions to the equity in development issue, thereby increasing the (economic) contribution of tourism to development. First, it would be more equitable or fair to permit host countries to retain the premium value of their own attractions by establishing property rights over natural resources – indeed, some economists believe that inequitable property rights are the basic reason for the division of the world into developed and less developed countries, underpinning the national variations in economic growth rates and GDP (Sotto, 1993: 8). As discussed earlier in this chapter, property rights are a pre-condition for a market to function. The difference between developed and developing countries is not that the former have markets and the latter do not. However, modern market economies generate growth because widespread, formal property rights permit massive, low-cost exchange and facilitate the transfer of resources to their highest-value use (Sotto, 1993: 8).

Second, a possible economic solution to the problem of inequity would be the implementation of national financial compensation for not-travelling (Mihalič, 1999: 128). In other words, travelling represents the 'free' consumption of the environment. Therefore, as it is principally the privilege of people from the developed, industrialised countries to participate in outgoing international tourism, in the global context this free consumption is inequitable. Nevertheless, all the less developed countries and their inhabitants possess the same right (if not ability to exercise that right) to travel and consume (free) resources. The implementation of financial compensation for not travelling (as a payment made by travelling nations to less developed destination countries and regions) would bring money into less developed countries to stimulate future development programmes, promote a new international economic order and, as originally hoped for by the WTO and other organisations, provide a way for tourism to contribute to closing the gap between rich and poorer countries. It is, of course, doubtful that such travel compensation could be implemented in the near future. Nevertheless, it can still be argued that tourism does in fact help to establish a more even and equitable economic world order, and that at the same time may be seen as an instrument for convergence in economic development between poorer and richer countries.

However, one last relevant question remains to be addressed, namely 'What will be the future significance of tourism as a generator of economic development in newly emerging, less developed tourism destinations?'. There is enough evidence to suggest that tourism will remain the 'development hope' for these countries. Examples are numerous. For instance, although keen to keep its borders closed for political reasons, economic necessity forced the North Korean government to open its doors to international exchange in 1998, the government allowing foreign visitors from South Korea to visit the attractive landscape of Kumgang mountain area for US$100 per visitor (Yee, 2001). Similarly, Albania is trying to open its borders and develop tourism based on 'excellent natural resources' (Papa, 1999: 2) whilst, following the collapse of the Soviet bloc, Cuba has also followed a similar path since the early 1990s. Even Kalingrad, a state with newly opened borders in the north of Europe close to the Baltic Sea and which 'doesn't posses too much classically attractive tourism infrastructure' (Steene, 2001) is hoping to attract tourists.

At the same time, it is possible to make a few suggestions as to the future role of tourism in economic development. First, it is likely that tourism will be amongst the most important or valuable international businesses in many of these countries and the foreign currency impact of international tourism will remain an important issue. Second, it is also likely that tourism will be utilised as a means for attracting international development financial aid, particularly for environmental protection. Third, tourism promotional activities will be used as an instrument for improving a country's international recognition and image, the hope being that greater awareness (gained through tourism) will stimulate more direct investment in other industries, thus generating economic development. However, since these countries have few or no resources of their own, a tourism superstructure will be developed by (private) foreign and international capital and so a question mark will still remain over the ability of these countries to eliminate a balance of payments deficit, to overcome the challenge of dependence and, last but by no means least, to reach the desirable or essential third stage of enjoying a low tourism capital–output ratio where tourism's contribution to economic growth and development of the country begins.

Notes

1. Value added is the difference between the total output in terms of revenues and the costs of inputs of raw materials, components or services bought in to produce that output. Value added is the value that the firm, industry or nation adds to its bought-in materials and services through its own production and marketing efforts.

    One has to distinguish between 'value added of the tourism sector' and 'tourism value added'. Value added of the tourism sector sums the total value added of all producers in tourism industry. It includes value added in response to tourism and resident consumption in tourism sector, but it lets out the effect of tourism consumption in other productive sectors which might serve the tourists.

    Tourism value added is defined as the value added generated in the economy by the tourism and other sectors in response to tourism consumption (WTO, 1999c: 57).

2. GDP (Gross Domestic Product) is the total money value of all final goods and services produced in an economy over a one-year period. One way of measuring it is to summa-

rize the value added by each industry. GNP (Gross National Product) is GDP plus net property income from abroad (interest, rent, dividend and profit). National Income or Net National Product is the total money income received by households in return for suplying factor inputs to businesses over a one-year period. It equals the GNP value, reduced by the value of capital consumption.

3. Capital–output ratio R is calculated as follows:
   $R = K(t) / Y(t)$
   where $K(t)$ is the capital over the time t and
   $Y(t)$ is the produced output (GNP) over time t.

4. Marginal capital–output ratio MR is calculated as follows:
   $MR = AK(t) / \ddot{A}Y(t)$
   where $\ddot{A}K(t)$ is the change in capital over the time t
   $\ddot{A}Y(t)$is the change in produced output (GNP) over the time t.

5. See the following section (The Impacts of Tourism on Regional Economic Development) for a consideration of the 'modern' view of tourism flows to the more developed regions and metropolitan areas.

6. Different methods of calculation of income multiplier (Archer, 1977:51) are:

   (1) Ratio multiplier type I ($TM\ I$):
   $TM\ I = (\Delta Y_{direct} + \Delta Y_{indirect})/ \Delta Y_{direct}$
   where ΔY_{direct} is the direct income and
   $\Delta Y_{indirect}$ is the indirect income.

   (2) Ratio multiplier type II ($TM\ II$) or 'orthodox' tourism multiplier
   $TM\ II = \Delta Y / \Delta Y_{direct}$
   where $\Delta Y = \Delta Y_{direct} + \Delta Y_{indirect} + \Delta Y_{induced}$
   with $\Delta Y_{induced}$ the induced income.

   (3) Normal tourism multiplier (TM) or 'unortodox' tourism multiplier
   $TM = \Delta Y / \Delta E$
   with ΔE the tourism expenditure.

7. Price elasticity of tourism demand measures the degree of responsiviness of demand to a given change in price:
$$price\ elasticity\ of\ tourism\ demand = \frac{(\%\ change\ in\ quantity\ of\ tourism\ demand)}{(\%\ change\ in\ price).}$$

8. Cross-elasticity of tourism demand measures the degree of responsiveness of the demand for one destination A to a given change in the price of some other destination B:

$$cross\text{-}elasticity\ of\ tourism\ demand = \frac{(\%\ change\ in\ quantity\ of\ tourism\ demand\ of\ destination\ A)}{(\%\ change\ in\ price\ of\ destination\ B).}$$

9. A premium price for a product over similar products might be charged by a supplier who is able to convince buyers that his/her product is superior, in some respect, to competitors' products. In this case premium price (by fixed supply, also known as tourism rent) refers to valuation value (VV) which is the value placed on tourism products by tourists because of increased demand resulting from the destinations attractiveness (environmental, cultural, etc.) Thus:
   $P = C + PF + VV$
   where P is the price of tourism product; C, the costs of tourism product; PF, the profit ('normal' return on capital involved); and VV, valuation value (tourism rent).

Chapter 4

Tourism and Regional Development Issues

DAVID J. TELFER

Introduction

The sign in front of the construction site for the new multimillion-dollar hotel and casino complex in Niagara Falls, Ontario, Canada reads 'Bringing Jobs and Tourism to Niagara'. This is just one of the many literal and figurative signs that governments and development corporations around the world favour tourism as an economic tool for regional development. Projects ranging in scale from the urban redevelopment schemes of Granville Island in Vancouver, Canada or the Dock-lands in London, England, to the more remote resort complexes of the Lombok Tourism Development Corporation's 1250-hectare development plan for five-star hotels, golf courses and a marina in Indonesia, illustrate the potential use of tourism to generate regional development. As outlined in Chapter 3, the promise of increases in employment, foreign exchange, technology and development capital (Britton, 1982a) is all very attractive to governments as they attempt to reduce economic inequalities among regions. Mabogunje (1980, cited in Pearce, 1989b) suggests that while the goals of regional development may vary, the main concern is to even out or narrow the gap in life chances, employment opportunities and real income of the citizens regardless of which region of the country they come from. Blair (1995) suggests that most communities have three objectives related to economic development, which are job and income creation, fiscal improvement and physical improvements.

In the context of core–periphery, Christaller (1963) argued that tourism can be a means of obtaining economic development in peripheral regions with rich tourists travelling from the metropolitan centre to the periphery, bringing foreign exchange and creating jobs. Coastal, rural or alpine regions represent destinations for metropolitan visitors and, since these regions often fall below national averages on indicators of socioeconomic well-being, tourism can act to redistribute wealth from the richer metropolitan areas to the poorer peripheral regions (Pearce, 1989b). If, however, regional tourism development is based primarily on external inputs of capital, labour, know-how and technical resources, then the resulting high rates of leakage will prevent tourism from being an effective development tool (Pearce, 1989b). For many, tourism represents the potential for regional development (Middleton, 1977); however, as Oppermann and Chon (1997: 35) point out, 'to what extent tourism actually contributes to the regional dispersion of economic development, and to what extent it is a better regional development agent than other industries or services remains largely unexplored'. This double-edged sword of using tourism as a regional development tool was briefly explored in Chapter 2. Within modernisation, it can be argued that the introduction of a new tourism resort development in the form of a growth pole can help to modernise a region. The resulting inequality, which may occur between regions or between the local community and those who control the tourism industry such as the local elite or multinational tourism organisations, can be considered within the dependency paradigm. One of the main factors indicating the success of using tourism for regional development purposes is the extent that the benefits of tourism are spread throughout the surrounding region.

The purpose of this chapter is to explore tourism's potential to contribute to regional development in a variety of different scales and destinations. The chapter will begin by examining the concepts related to regional development. The chapter will then look at the relationship between tourism and regional development by highlighting some of the models developed in the tourism literature, which relate to regional development. The role of the state in regional tourism development is explored, as it is often the state that proposes and plans regional development schemes. The chapter will then move on to consider tourism in a variety of different regions including urban, rural, islands, peripheral regions and tourism regions which cross international borders. As these regions are so diverse, it is important to note at the beginning that the viability and the appropriateness of any tourism development needs to be considered within the parameters of local socioeconomic, geographic and political conditions. The chapter concludes by stressing the need for strong linkages to the surrounding region if tourism is to be used successfully as an agent for regional development.

Before moving on to examine the concepts related to regional development, it is useful to consider the arguments put forward by Higgins and Savoie (1988) as to why it is important to pay particular attention to the regional structure of a national economy.

- Regional disparities create social and political problems that need to be addressed in any political society and especially in countries where 'regions' and gaps among them correspond to states or provinces.
- National economies are aggregations of regional economies, which vary in the degree of integration. Some regions in some countries are more integrated

with the world economy than with other regions of the same country. These regional differences need to be understood in order to develop effective plans.

- Accelerating the growth of a nation as a whole requires an attack on the problems of less developed regions.
- All countries face increasingly complex urban problems. The interactions between cities and regions are a fundamental aspect of these urban problems, and of regional and national social and economic problems.
- Some kinds of resource management – natural and human – are best studied and executed at regional levels as the resources are best defined in terms of space. Examples include river valleys, metropolitan areas, recreation areas and parks.
- Improving the methodology of the social sciences and improving policy and planning requires study of the principal actors where they are at regional and community levels.

While these comments reflect the importance of understanding a region in the context of a national economy, it is also important to keep in mind the changing nature of regions and the fact that they extend beyond national boundaries.

Concepts of a Region

The concept of a region can be quite complex, as regions are often not static but evolve as conditions warrant (Malecki, 1997). Tosun and Jenkins (1996) suggest that, despite the countless attempts to define a region, a satisfactory definition has not been formulated. Blair (1995) considers a region as a part of an area; however, in practice, he refers to the term as a chameleon taking its meaning from the context of use. In other words, a region can be as small as a neighbourhood region or extend across borders to a multinational region, which are receiving increasing amounts of attention as trade between nations increases. While a region is a geographic part of the earth's surface, it is also a space occupied by people who feel affinities of speech, religion, history or way of life (Tosun & Jenkins, 1996).

Different perspectives on regions include (1) the relations of production in a given time and place; (2) regions being defined by a local culture and (3) the region as a setting for social interaction of all types (Malecki, 1997). In identifying the three main types of regions, Smith (1995) lists (1) *a priori* regions, (2) homogeneous regions and 3) functional regions. An *a priori* region is one in which someone has already created a boundary around and assigned it a name such as a political unit. A homogeneous region is defined by an objective set of internal similarities. This is the type of region that planners most often think of when hearing the term region. Important issues with defining such a region is the selection of relevant characteristics and the specification of the degree of similarity that would cause a locale to be included in the region. Smith's (1995) final region is the functional region, which is an area with a high degree of internal interaction. An example of a set of local businesses trading more with each other than they traded with the rest of the world would be a functional region (Blair, 1995).

Malecki (1997) further highlights the concept of a region extending beyond national boundaries. He suggests that there have been major changes, which have occurred in response to technological changes during the 20th century including industrial shifts such as lower transport costs, standardisation of production and increased minimum efficient scale of plants. These changes have resulted in regions being not only subsets of national space but also of international space. Trading blocs such as the European Union (EU) or the Association of Southeast Asian Nations (ASEAN) are also referred to as regions (Malecki, 1997). The more traditional definitions of a region cannot fully address these complex regions such as the EU with its dynamic internal economic and cultural conditions (Malecki, 1997).

With governments selecting tourism as a regional development tool, it is important to consider the definition of regional planning. Tosun and Jenkins (1996) suggest that at a broad level, regional planning is an effort to attain the best possible spatial pattern of development, the central concern being to solve the problems of the sub-national areas and insert the regional plans into the overall national development plan of a country. The WTO (1994) argues that governments should take a lead role in establishing tourism policy and that tourism policy should reflect the overall development policy of the country or region. The role of the state in planning for tourism at the regional level will be considered further in the following section.

The terms tourism region and tourism destination have often been used interchangeably; however, as Tosun and Jenkins (1996) point out, they are not necessarily identical and for the purposes of sub-national tourism planning they need to be clearly defined. Davidson and Maitland (1997) point out the conflict in scales, in that a national tourism organisation may market and promote a whole country as a destination, while within a country, a region may have a defined identity, meaning it constitutes a destination. Further, a destination can also encompass only a single attraction. Smith (1995: 175) defines a tourism region as 'a contiguous area that has been explicitly delineated by a researcher, planner or public agency as having relevance for some aspect of tourism planning, development or analysis'. A destination zone is one type of regionalisation based on an inventory of qualitative characteristics. To define a destination zone is a matter of specifying the characteristics a region should have and then identifying the areas that meet these criteria (Smith, 1995). There is increasing competition between tourism destinations, and Smith (1995: 199) adapted the work of Gunn (1979) to develop a list of criteria to define tourist destination zones:

- The region should have a set of cultural, physical and social characteristics that create a sense of regional identity.

- The region should contain an adequate tourism infrastructure to support tourism development. Infrastructure includes utilities, roads, business services, and other social services necessary to support tourism businesses and to cater to tourists' needs.
- The region should be larger than just one community or one attraction.
- The region should contain existing attractions or have the potential to support the development of sufficient attractions to attract tourists.
- The region should be capable of supporting a tourism planning agency and marketing initiatives to guide and encourage future development.
- The region should be accessible to a large population base. Accessibility may be by road, scheduled air passenger service or cruise ships.

Elsewhere, Davidson and Mailtland (1997) outline the characteristics of a tourist destination in the context of a single district, town, city or clearly defined and contained coastal, rural or mountain area as having a total tourist product based on a variety of resources, other economic activities either in conflict or complementary to tourism, a host community, public authorities responsible for planning the resources and a active private sector.

What is important to note in terms of regional development is the extent to which a tourism region is linked into the domestic and international tourism market, as revealed in the following comment. 'The interactions between capitalist systems, localities, and regions (the local–global linkages) define the regions and its processes of economic development' (Amin & Thrift; Petro cited in Malecki, 1997: 11). In this chapter, the term region will be examined in a wide range of contexts and scales. There is an increasingly competitive stance among tourism regions as they try to attract more tourists. As Kotler *et al.* (1993) point out, with the globalisation of the world's economy and the rate of technological change, places now have to compete with other places and regions in their own country and throughout the world for their economic survival. The importance of competitive advantage will be returned to later in this chapter.

Regional Development Models and Concepts

The processes of the economic development of a region have been studied from a variety of different approaches. Blair (1995) outlines a variety of fundamental theories of regional growth, a few of which are discussed here. (1) Stage models describe key stages that a city or region passes through. As a region develops, it is able to replace imports and develops additional products for exports. (2) The export-based theory of growth is based on the idea that, for a local economy to grow, it must increase its monetary inflow and the only way to do this is through an increase in exports. This model is usually discussed in terms of income or employment. The income which is earned by the export sector is spent and respent locally, thereby

Table 4.1 Early regional economic development theorists

Author	Key concepts
Schumpeter, 1934, 1961	Emphasised innovation and entrepreneurship; rate depends on favourable social climate
Perroux, 1955 (see Perroux, 1988)	Growth pole (theory component); development poles (location containing propulsive enterprises that generate spread effects through investments)
Myrdal, 1963 (1st published 1957)	Circular and cumulative causation; spread effects (positive – economic expansion from growth centre); backwash effects (negative – market forces increase regional inequalities)
Hirschman, 1958	Polarization and trickle-down effects
Friedmann, 1966	Centre – periphery model; economic growth is externally induced; dominant centres feed off less developed regions increasing inequalities; advocates growth centre strategy

Source: Above authors, Preston, 1984, Higgins & Higgins, 1979.

creating additional jobs through the multiplier effect. The size of the multiplier is determined by the degree to which individuals spend money in the local economy. With tourism being an export, there have been numerous studies conducted on tourism multipliers (see Chapter Three for a discussion on multipliers). (3) The supply-side models of economic growth, developed out of the criticisms of the demand-side approaches such as the export-based theory of growth. Supply-side growth theories state that growth occurs in a region due to an increase in the supply of available resources, or because existing resources are used more efficiently. Important determinants of supply include intermediary inputs and primary factors such as land, labour, capital and entrepreneurship. While there are criticisms of both supply and demand based models, what is important to keep in mind is the extent to which development can generate growth throughout a region. On a broader scale, the trickle-down theory suggests that overall growth in gross national product and income per capita would bring benefits (or would trickle down) to the masses in the form of job creation and other economic opportunities (Todaro, 1997). Within the context of tourism, governments have tried to establish the trickle-down effect by creating new resort complexes in hope that economic linkages would spread throughout the region. This section now turns to examine some additional theories and concepts for generating regional development.

Table 4.1 highlights early influential regional economic growth theorists who acknowledge not only growth impulses for regional development but also the resulting regional inequalities, which can occur. The core–periphery dichotomy or dualism is one of the main metaphors of regional development. From an economic perspective, the core is a set of regions where complexity, technology and control are considered the norm and strong linkages to other nodes and the global system are common. The global system marks deep disparities between the core and periphery, not only between nations but also between regions within nations (Malecki, 1997). In the context of developing countries, dualism may be more appropriate, especially as it applies to the linkages between the formal and informal economies (Malecki, 1997). Dualism is the coexistence in one place of two situations (one desirable and the other not) that are mutually exclusive to different groups. Examples include extreme poverty and affluence, modern and traditional sectors and growth and stagnation (Todaro, 1997). Myrdal's (1957) discussion of backwash effects and Friedman's (1966) centre-periphery model both mention the regional inequalities which can result from economic development.

Innovation, growth poles, agglomeration economies and clusters are linked to regional development. Schumpeter (1949) argues that for development to occur, ideas have to produce innovations or new combinations of productive means. This can include the introduction of a new good or a quality of good, the opening of a new market, the introduction of a new means of production or source of supply or the new organisation of a new industry. Perroux (1988) outlined growth pole theory with development poles. Development poles are identified as locations which contain propulsive enterprises that generate spread effects through investments. A growth pole consists of a cluster of expanding industries that are spatially concentrated and set off a chain reaction of minor expansions in the surrounding hinterland (Haggett, 1975). The arguments presented in favour of growth poles are that they will result in agglomeration economies. Agglomeration economies are a result of the cost reductions which occur due to spatial concentration of economic activities. Agglomeration economies can range from savings, which benefit one establishment, to agglomeration economies that spread throughout an entire region. Early work on agglomeration economies and regional development is linked to Weber (1909), Isard (1956), Hirschman (1958) and Myrdal (1963). Myrdal discussed the process of cumulative causation, which refers to the process of change in one direction which can reinforce other tendencies for change in the same direction. For example, a region may start to prosper and self-reinforcing factors can cause cumulative growth. An increased income allows for more amenities, attracts business and thereby increases agglomeration economies (Blair, 1995). In the context of tourism development, an improved infrastructure provided by the government may help to stimulate additional tourism investment.

The process of clustering offers economies of agglomeration, which are linked to external economies of scale. The production unit derives its external economies from its locational association with a larger spatial cluster of economic activities (Lloyd & Dicken, 1977). Agglomeration economies focus on the connections or links between economic activities in a restrictive geographic space. Lloyd and Dicken (1977) outline three main types of links between manufacturing firms, production linkages, service linkages and marketing linkages. Other economies may be derived as association links firms. 'Interindustry agglomeration occurs through both forward and backward linkages. A forward linkage involves suppliers attracting buyers; a backward linkage involves buyers attracting suppliers' (Blair, 1995: 97). Hirschman (1972, cited in Blair, 1995) argued that underdeveloped countries, and hence underdeveloped regions, have weak interdependencies and weak backward and forward linkages. If tourism is to be a successful development tool, it will be essential to strengthen linkages within the local economy.

It is important for economic development officers to understand the existing linkages between firms, how to strengthen these linkages and how to build new linkages between firms (Blair, 1995). With many of the more conventional theories and policies of regional development focusing on the capital–labour production function and responses of the state through various policies, these have now been combined with a new emphasis based on economic competitiveness as a priority for firms, regions and nations (Malecki, 1997). This shift to include competitiveness is best illustrated through the work of Porter and his model of the factors underlying national competitiveness. Malecki (1997) summarised Porter's (1990) diamond-shaped model as follows. The first set of factors called factor conditions embraces the neoclassical or basic factors of production including physical, capital and human resources but it is also extended to include knowledge resources and infrastructure. The second set, called demand conditions, refers to conditions of the home market for product and services. The third set refers to the cluster of related and supporting industries which, if they are internationally competitive, can transmit this quality throughout the network. The fourth element is the legal, cultural and institutional framework that determines a firm's structure, strategy and rivalries. Finally, chance and government are added as variables.

Porter's work on clusters (1998) also suggests a new focus tied to competitive advantage. Porter (1998) states that traditional arguments for agglomeration and the existence of clusters have been undercut by globalisation of supply sources and markets. Traditional concepts of backward and forward linkages emphasised the need to build industries with linkages to many other industries while cluster theory advocates building on 'emerging concentrations of companies and encouraging the development of fields with the strongest linkages to or spillovers within each cluster' (Porter, 1998: 207). There is a greater role for clusters in competition in the current knowledge-based economy. Porter defines clusters as 'geographic concentrations of interconnected companies, specialized suppliers, service providers, firms in related industries, and associated institutions (for example, universities, standards agencies and trade associations) in particular fields that compete but also cooperate' (Porter, 1998: 197).

Effective clusters move beyond hierarchical networks to become 'lattices of numerous overlapping and fluid connections among individual firms and institutions' (Porter, 1998: 226). Clusters highlight the externalities, linkages, spillovers and supporting institutions which are key to competition. Competition is affected by increasing productivity levels, increasing capacity for innovation and stimulating new business formation, which promotes innovation and promotes expansion of the cluster (Porter, 1998). The influence of clusters on competition depends on the extent of personal relationships, and the interaction among networks of individuals and institutions. Porter (1998: 263–66) outlined the common characteristics of successful cluster initiatives as follows:

- a shared understanding of competitiveness and the role of clusters in competitive advantage
- a focus on removing obstacles and easing constraints to cluster upgrading
- a structure that embraces all clusters in a nation or state
- appropriate cluster boundaries
- wide involvement of cluster participants and associated interests
- private sector leadership
- close attention to personal relationships
- a bias towards action
- institutionalisation.

The shift to an increasing focus on competitive advantage will be highlighted throughout this chapter. Not only do destinations have to become more competitive, but government tourism agencies also have to act more in an entrepreneurial manner attracting not only multinational tourism corporations but also major events such as the Olympics. Regional development can also be seen as a process that operates within two complementary characteristics. The first is the linkage with the exterior including the goods, services capital and information and foreign exchange earnings. The second is the level of internal differentiation or internal structural change reflecting a system's capacity to process external linkages, including skill improvement and organisational development (Young in Nuryanti, 1998). How these two forces come into play and who controls these forces will determine how successful tourism will be as a regional development tool.

Finally, two other approaches to regional development need to be addressed as they form part of the alternative development paradigm covered in Chapter 2. Formulated out of criticisms of the functional approach to regional development with growth poles, trickle-down and spread effects as a way to solve regional development problems, they focused on decentralisation and local participation. Integrated regional development planning focuses on the development of integrated small and intermediate urban centres as a way to stimulate growth in rural and peripheral region. The establishment of well-articulated regional hierarchies of spatially dispersed small/medium cities and market towns may developed more balanced equitable growth rather than the propulsive growth of a few large cities (Brohman, 1996a). This concept could be mapped into tourism through for example integrated rural tourism development. The territorial regional planning approach places priority on promoting locally appropriate development by mobilising the human, material and institutional resources of the region to serve the needs of the popular majority. Rather than being subjected to exploitation, peripheral rural regions should pursue a more endogenous form of development, selectively withdrawing from international economic systems (Brohman, 1996a). The two approaches are important in terms of regional development as they both emphasise local participation, a growing trend in the alternative tourism development paradigm.

Tourism and Regional Development

As noted in the Introduction, the role of tourism in regional development is open for debate. Tourism has the potential to generate growth and development but it can also enhance inequalities if only the local elite benefits. A number of the concepts related to regional economic development have been applied to tourism. Christaller (1963) argued that tourism can be a means of obtaining economic development in peripheral regions with rich tourists travelling from the metropolitan centre to the periphery, bringing foreign exchange and creating jobs. Carrying on from the previous section, Porter (1998), for example, suggests that the building of a tourism cluster in developing economies can be a positive force in improving outlying infrastructure and dispersing economic activity. Tourism has been used as a strategy to promote regional development (Oppermann, 1992) in both urban (Beauregard, 1998) and rural areas (Sharpley & Sharpley, 1997). Williams and Shaw (1991) illustrate the potential for tourism to bring development to economically neglected regions of European countries. Peppelenbosch and Tempelman (1973) suggested that infrastructure requirements for tourism could act as regional development tools. Tourism developments have been constructed to act as growth poles to help stimulate regional development. Mexican government planners, for example, have used a growth pole approach when developing tourist centres (Kemper, 1979) including Loreto, Los Cabos, Huatulco and Cancún (Weaver & Oppermann, 2000). In selecting tourism as a growth pole, governments identify a site, which is usually in an economically marginal area that is deemed suitable for sustaining a form of tourism development. With government initiatives and incentives, both public and private investment is injected into the selected area often in the form of subsidised facilities and infrastructure. The incentives attract additional tourism development and their employees. Eventually, economic growth in the area becomes self-sustaining and independent of tourism when a critical mass of residential population is attained. The larger residential population, rather than just tourism, attracts additional development. Government incentives may be withdrawn and the benefits of tourism 'trickle down' from the growth pole to the surrounding area (Weaver & Oppermann, 2000).

Caalders (2000: 187) states that in regional economic planning 'the emphasis has been on attracting foreign industries capable of creating regional growth poles and serving as a pull factor for other economic activities'. This, however, exposed regions to global economic trends and can put them in a dependent situation. This type of vulnerability to multinational tourism companies is often identified in the tourism literature as a negative impact of tourism and calls have been made for more locally controlled development (see Chapter 9 for a discussion on the political economy of tourism). In addition to tourism growth poles, Sinclair and Stabler (1997) examined the importance of economic integration in tourism (vertical, horizontal and conglomerate) between firms as a way to respond to competition. Calls have also been made for increased collaboration and strategic alliances within the tourism industry (Bramwell & Lane, 2000; Telfer, 2000a) for firms and regions to become more competitive.

In his review of the tourism literature, Malecki (1997) evaluates some of the concepts of tourism that make it attractive as a regional development tool. Tourism is a growing focus of economic policy in regions where employment creation through other means of investment is difficult. The industry is labour-intensive and it also provides entrepreneurial activities (see Chapter 6 on tourism employment). Locations which have special natural, cultural or historic attractions can turn these items into exports by attracting tourists. Tourism is also created by the construction of shopping malls, casinos, theme parks, and convention facilities, along with hotels, restaurants and gift shops. Tourism can also be developed around special events and festivals such as the Olympic Games or the Bayreuth Opera Festival in Germany. Along with this list of positives, Malecki (1997) noted a series of negative factors which can prevent tourism from being an effective tool for regional development. Tourism often has low paying jobs that can be very seasonal. The amount of benefit a region receives relates to the level of leakage, which occurs through imports. In some small countries the level of leakage can be quite high, thereby reducing the multiplier effect. Within the international tourism industry, competition can be quite intense and as regions fall out of favour, they will go into decline. In order to develop tourism, a series of barriers have to be overcome, including the building of infrastructure for hotels. Luxury hotels in developing countries also require excessive financial support and can use a disproportionate amount of water, energy, food and construction materials, all of which may be in short supply in the region. If a region pursues concentrated enclave-type tourism development, it is also open to competition from other tourist regions and, over time, the demands of tourists for more amenities tends to increase. Finally, as more countries opt to pursue ecotourism, there is great debate as to whether or not ecotourism can be developed in a sustainable manner. The overall difficulty with the industry is that destinations are trying to respond to demand factors which are beyond their control and often the industry supply is controlled by multinationals (Malecki, 1997).

In discussing the relationship between tourism and regional development, Williams and Shaw (1995) examined three aspects of tourism: (1) tourism is a product which must be consumed at the production point; (2) most forms of tourism are highly temporal; and (3) tourism is an industry subject to restructuring. In the context of mass tourism, the supply points are spatially fixed and subject to a high regard for spatial polarisation. These points are influenced by things like climate and geomorphological distribution of tourist objects, such as beaches/sunshine and mountains/snow. Social construction also has a role in distinguishing what is important for tourists to see. The second feature is that tourism has a degree of seasonality, which can generate a dichotomy betweem core–periphery workers with employees in the periphery holding temporary contracts. The final element of their analysis is the fact that tourism has undergone a process of restructuring that has seen the development of a variety of different forms of tourism such as cultural and industrial heritage exhibits, that have different spatial attributes. Some of these 'newer' types of tourism benefit the core while others benefit the periphery.

There are a number of models which have been developed in the tourism literature that are useful in the context of regional development. Under the diffusionist paradigm, it is assumed that development is inevitable, it occurs in stages and development is diffused from the core to the periphery (Oppermann & Chon, 1997). Butler (1980) developed the Tourism Area Cycle of Evolution, which draws on the product life cycle. Tourism developments go through the following stages: exploration, involvement, development, consolidation, stagnation, decline or rejuvenation. In the context of regional development it is important to note that while initial control of the industry is held locally, eventually larger multinational firms enter the market. If the region stagnates and goes into decline, the usefulness of tourism as a regional development tool will also decline. Miossec (1976 cited in Oppermann & Chon, 1997) also developed a model, which looked at the development process of a resort area. The model examines five different stages for resorts, transport, tourists and hosts. At the final stage, the regions are fully developed with a hierarchy and areas of specialisations. There is maximum connectivity between the resorts and there are also excursion circuits which, in theory, should bring additional income to businesses in these excursion areas. The development of excursion routes on the island of Bali, Indonesia, for example, opened the interior of the island to tourist traffic. Along many of these excursion roads, gold, silver and woodcraft shops have opened to cater to tourists.

There are also models which have been developed and can be placed in the dependency paradigm. These models highlight the difficulties in using tourism as an agent of regional development. In developing his enclave model of tourism development, Britton (1982a) argued that development does not occur through an evolutionary process but was instead dependent upon demands from more developed countries. At the top of Britton's (1982a) model are the head offices of global and national tourism firms, which control the industry. Without control of the industry, such as a domestic hotel chain, funds generated through tourism would be leaked out of the region back to the metropolitan countries. The model also highlights potential inequalities within a country, as attractions in rural areas receive less attention than those in urban areas.

Another model, although developed at a national level, which is also useful for illustrating the potential success for tourism as a regional development tool is the spatio-temporal development model of the tourism space proposed by Oppermann (1993). This model is developed within the context of the sector paradigm, which states that the economy of a developing country is composed of two separate sectors that co-exist side by side but which have few interlinkages. In applying this to tourism, Oppermann notes that there are different types of tourists and different types of tourism suppliers. He differentiates between the formal and informal tourism sector. The formal tourism sector is characterised by such things as international standard hotels, high capital investment costs, high leakages in the form of profit transfers, imported food and construction materials and very little integration into the local economy. Governments of developing countries often only consider this path of tourism development. The informal sector consists mainly of hawkers or street vendors, mini-bus operations and small, locally owned accommodation. This sector is labour intensive with very limited capital. While they are small, they can derive high profits per unit and the money increases the multiplier effect for the local economy (see Chapters 3 and 6). The importance of this model in terms of the discussion in this chapter is that a destination needs to decide which form of tourism it will pursue. While the formal and informal sectors can interact, the formal sector can be closely associated with mass tourism. If the strategy behind regional development is to generate economic benefits for those living in peripheral areas, then governments need to calculate which type of tourism will bring more benefits to the local community. If the informal sector is discouraged then there is a lost opportunity for local entrepreneurial development. The role of government in tourism development is the focus of the next section.

Finally, it is important to mention briefly recent trends in tourism planning as they relate to the concepts of regional development. Sustainable tourism development has received a great deal of attention in the tourism literature (Hall, 2000a). The famous definition of the Bruntland Report reads 'sustainable development is development that meets the needs of the present without compromising the ability of future generations to meet their own needs' (WCED, 1987: 4). Inherent in this definition is the preservation of the environment. As Hall (2000a) suggests, meeting the conditions of sustainability is a major political, economic and environmental issue that requires new ways of thinking about development and growth along with the role of individuals, governments and the private sector. Sustainable development is explored in greater detail in Chapters 8 and 11. The second concept receiving attention and the focus of Chapter 5 is community involvement in the tourism planning process. The work of Murphy (1985) emphasises an ecological, community approach to development and planning which encourages local initiative, local benefits and a tourism product which is in harmony with the local environment and community. The concepts of sustainability and community involvement are part of the alternative development paradigm raised in Chapter 2. If a nation incorporates sustainability and community involvement into regional tourism planning it will mean a decentralisation of power along with an increased focus on the environment.

State Involvement in Regional Tourism Development

The various institutions of the state can have an impact on how tourism is used as a vehicle for regional development. The main institutions of the state include 'the central government, administrative departments, the courts and judiciary, enforcement agencies, other levels of government, government business enterprises, regulatory and assistance authorities and a range of semi-state organisation' (Hall, 1994a: 23). In addition to this list, Hall (1994a) adds components of society such as political parties, trade unions and industry associations (including tourism and hospitality) that receive money from the state. The parliamentary institutions (whether democratic or not) provide the framework for the development of alternative policies and the decision-making process as to which policies are adopted. National or provincial/state ministries of tourism and their related bureaucratic structures influence tourism policy and, as Hall (1994a) points out, one of the significant aspects of the state is the balance of power which exists between the central government and the various regions in the country. All levels of state do not necessarily share the same objectives. The political ideology of a government can determine whether a government favours large resorts or backpacker hostels, ecotourism or casinos (Elliot, 1997).

Ioannides (1995) identifies two broad important roles for governments to play in the tourism sector. The first is establishing a forum enabling the tourism industry suppliers to coordinate their activities. The second major role is that of promoter. Hall (1994) outlines seven roles of government in tourism: coordination, planning, legislation and regulation, entrepreneurship, providing stimulation, social tourism and interest protection. Each of these roles can be adapted to varying degrees of success to help promote regional development and will be reflected in examples in the second half of the chapter. When a government selects certain policies, the government is also choosing between different sets of values and these decisions are made within a complex policy arena (Hall, 1994a). Elliot (1997) argues that the tourism industry could not survive without governments as they have the ability to provide the political stability, security and legal and financial framework which tourism requires. Governments have the power but how it is used depends on factors including 'political culture, political and economic power holders and their perception of the tourism industry' (Elliot, 1997: 4). Governments have the ability to assist tourism by providing services and they have the ability to control the industry to ensure those activities and safety standards are maintained in the public interest. How government performs these activities depends on its public sector management (PSM), which is typically defined as public interest, public service, effectiveness, efficiency and accountability (Elliot, 1997). Oppermann and Chon (1997: 20) indicate that governments of developing countries can influence tourism development through fiscal and investment policies such as:

- investment into the general infrastructure of a destination or region;
- investment into tourism infrastructure;
- investment incentive for companies; and
- influencing exchange rates.

Hall (1994a) cautions, however, that the state is not simply a reflection of the interests of society and at times the state will impose its value preferences, even if they are in contrast with other members of society. This warning is particularly relevant in terms of regional development, as governments in some countries have in the past evicted local residents in the drive to pursue national or regional tourism development plans. It is therefore important to understand the political process which brought the government to power as well as how the government operates and interacts with interest groups inside and outside the country. In examining the nature of the political economy of tourism, Dieke (2000) states that the traditional role of government has been changing towards free-market liberalism, a trend which is supported by several international donor agencies.

Government agencies use geographical scales (national, regional and local) in the application of tourism planning. Theoretically, as in a hierarchy, 'national policies set a broad agenda for development that directly shapes regional-level policies whilst they in turn form a framework for locally implemented plans. As the scale of intervention diminishes, so the level of detail in planning proposals increases' (Williams 1998: 133). In commenting on the role of national plans, Williams (1998: 135) indicates that the national plans designate tourism development regions. Tourism development regions are identified to 'help structure programmes for the redistribution of wealth and to narrow inter-regional disparities; to create employment in areas where unemployment is an issue, or to channel tourism development into zones that possesses appropriate attractions and infrastructure and are therefore considered for tourism.' Regional designation can also be guided by environmental factors such as the need to protect a fragile area from tourism development. Regional tourism plans contain some of the same overriding concepts as national tourism plans as well as containing distinctive elements. Themes, which are carried from national level plans to regional level plans, include:

- concerns for the impact of tourism upon regional economies and employment patterns;
- development of infrastructure, including transport systems to assist in the circulation of visitors within the regions, as well as provision of public utilities such as power and water supplies, both of which are frequently organised at regional levels;
- further spatial structuring in which tourism localities within regions are identified; and
- regional-level marketing and promotion, especially where the region processes a particular identity and/or set of tourism products (Williams, 1998: 133).

Finally, three distinctive aspects which are often included in regional plans are a greater concern over environmental impacts, more detailed consideration of the type and location of visitor attractions along with supporting services, such as accommodation, and greater recognition of visitor management strategies. Management strategies at the regional level encompass strategic placement of key attractions, designation of tourist routes and regional zoning to either concentrate or disperse visitors (Williams, 1998).

Tosun and Jenkins (1996) note, however, that in many developing countries, most of the tourism development is a product of central planning. A shift to a regional planning approach would require decentralisation of power. In the context of Turkey, the authors recommend that the country draw a lesson from the United Kingdom where tourism planning is sub-national.

> Unless there is a mechanism to manage and control tourism development at sub-national level, tourism growth may not be sustainable and contribute to the national development, although it may continue to contribute to the balance of payments. (Tosun & Jenkins, 1996: 530)

Government policy at a variety of levels or regions has been used to direct tourism to less economically developed areas. International tourism development policy for regional development is demonstrated through the EU. The most significant financial interventions for tourism development used by the EU are the Structural Funds and Cohesion Funds (Davidson & Maitland, 1997). These financial instruments are used with the EU's Regional Development Policy to strengthen economic and social cohesion within the EU and to reduce the disparities between the regions of the EU. The main Structural Funds to benefit tourism include the European Regional Development Fund (ERDF) and the European Agricultural Guidance and Guarantee Fund (EAGGF). While the EAGGF has contributed to rural tourism, most of the tourism-related funding has come from the ERDF. This fund has helped disadvantaged regions develop their tourism potential through direct investment in the construction of projects such as marinas, conference centres and airports and indirect investment in the areas of transportation and communication infrastructure. The second type of assistance is targeted at regions which are over dependent on tourism and suffering from its negative impacts. The funds are used to help with environmental problems and to diversify the economy (Davidson & Maitland, 1997).

At a national level, the objectives of the Thailand national growth policies have been to foster growth throughout the country by selectively designating key development areas (Pearce, 1989). The country of Indonesia has a national tourism plan as well as regional tourism plans. In the UK, both national and regional tourism boards have tried to extend the benefits of tourism to all areas of the country. In fact in the UK, applications for EU structural funding are coordinated through Regional Tourist Boards. The UK Government and the British Tourist Authority (BTA) aim to encourage the tourism industry to promote tourism to all areas of the country and more specifically to disperse visitors to areas of high unemployment and urban decay. In 1986, the BTA was asked to prioritise grants to projects assisting the development of tourism in areas of high unemployment (Clewer & Sinclair, 1995). With these policies in place, Clewer and Sinclair (1995) set out to determine whether the policy of dispersing tourism more widely throughout the UK had been successful and hence whether this policy would be an effective means of regional income redistribution. Their study focused on measuring the distribution of demand in the regions across the UK. An examination of inter and intra-regional distribution of tourism demand by nationality found that demand in the regions differs significantly not only from the national pattern but also between regions. While the results show that some dispersal of tourism has occurred, it is debatable as to whether it is due to the policies. One of their main findings was, however, that the peripheral regions did not experience the major share of tourism growth (Clewer & Sinclair, 1995).

In Canada, the Canadian Tourism Commission (CTC) acts in partnership with the tourism industry businesses and associations, provincial and territorial governments and the Government of Canada. The CTC has the authority to plan, direct, manage and implement programmes to generate and promote tourism in Canada. It is made up of industry representatives from across the country (Goeldner *et al.*, 2000). In Canada, the provinces also play a major role in setting tourism policy and initiating programmes. The CTC has established the Product Clubs Programme, which provides funding to small and medium sized businesses in underdeveloped sectors. Many of these Product Clubs, such as the Northern Wilderness Adventure

Product Club, involves companies trying to develop tourism in less developed regions of the country. Similarly, in the Province of Ontario, Canada for example, the Ministry responsible for tourism has established the 'Tourism Marketing Partnership Programme' which helps small diverse independent tour operators join forces and establish tour packages. This programme has significant potential for fostering tourism development in more isolated regions.

In developing a specific region, government officials can attempt to purchase jobs and the related benefits of associated growth by offering businesses a number of different subsidies. These subsidies can include, but are not limited to: tax abatement, infrastructure, and site assistance, low interest loans, labour force training, regulatory relief, sale–lease back and technical assistance (Blair, 1995). Blair suggests that major downtown hotels almost always receive special government incentives, often from more than one level of government. Porter (1998) argues that governments should take an active role in enhancing clusters. 'A location's best chance of attracting foreign investment and promoting exports, for example lies in its existing or emerging clusters' (Porter, 1998: 253). In the Niagara Region of Ontario, Canada, the Niagara Economic and Tourism Corporation (NETCOR) was formed in part to help attract investors to the region. Selected recommendations of a recent report prepared for the agency are:

- engage a tourism-sector investment specialist to work with local industry to develop and implement an investment strategy, including the development of marketing material that promotes Niagara as a premiere tourism investment location internationally;
- promote investment in Niagara's tourism industry to the major, international investment and financial services firms in tourism development, e.g. investment houses in Toronto and New York City;
- initiate and/or strengthen alliances and partnerships between Niagara's tourism sector and government agencies with a mandate for tourism investment and development; and
- promote specific private and public sector tourism development projects within the greater Niagara bi-national region that will result in additional investment in Niagara's tourism sector, e.g. new multimillion dollar attractions. (O'Dell Management Inc., 1999.)

In regard to the promotion of tourism and destination regions, Williams and Shaw (1995) call for additional investigations into the social construction of tourism and tourism images. This is important for economic policy as the attraction of the Olympic Games to Sydney, Australia or the promotion of industrial and ethnic heritage in Bradford, England will determine in part the type of tourist attracted to these regions. As governments pursue tourism as a regional development tool they need to consider what forms of tourism to develop in different areas and what agencies will be responsible for the development project. Ultimately, if regional development is the focus, consideration needs to be directed towards whom will actually benefit from tourism development. The following sections consider the challenges and opportunities of using tourism as a regional development tool in a variety of different scales and regions.

Developing to Developed

Turner and Ash (1975) referred to tourism occurring in the 'pleasure periphery', which has often been taken to be the developing countries. Implied in this concept is that the core is the developed nations while the developing nations are the periphery. In the context of this chapter, it is important to note, however, that there can be a very developed tourism region within a developing country. In the case of the poorest regions, Burns (1999b) proposes a continuum on which tourism planning advice may be placed. The first pole is 'Tourism First', whereby developing the tourism industry is the focus of the planning, and the second pole is 'Development First', whereby planning is framed by national development needs. Whether a government elects to pursue tourism so that national development needs are met and regional disparities are reduced, or whether they let the industry lead by facilitating tourism development, will depend on the agenda of the government. In the context of developing countries, Brohman (1996b) argues for state intervention citing that market forces on their own are not capable of resolving issues connected to long-term sustainability or the distribution of costs and benefits generated by tourism. State involvement in tourism planning can ensure that tourism development is integrated with the broader economic and social needs of the host country. Tourism planning can be utilised by the state as a regional economic development tool through the encouragement of growth in certain areas and it can also be used as a way to promote traditional arts, culture and the preservation of cultural heritage sites (Brohman, 1996b).

Examples from around the world can be used to illustrate tourism being used as a tool to help develop a region. While in many cases government takes an active role in the development process, it is important not to neglect the role of the private sector and small entrepreneurs. The remainder of this chapter will examine cases in a variety of regions (urban, rural, island, peripheral and international). While it is not possible to highlight every possible type of region, it is hoped that these examples highlight the challenges and opportunities associated with tourism and regional development. Some of the cases focus more on government initiatives while others focus more on how smaller entrepreneurs or organisations respond to the introduction of tourism in a region. Before moving on to the regions identified, this section will highlight two types of developments within the developing to developed continuum and the importance of deciding what type of tourism development to pursue to become 'developed'.

The creation of Cancún, Mexico is one example of government involvement in using tourism for regional development in an undeveloped area. The development of Cancún began in the 1970s and 30 years later, it has surpassed Acapulco as the biggest mass resort in Mexico (Hiernaux-Nicolas, 1999). Conceived in the mid-1960s as a large-scale project promoted by the Mexican Government, it was financed by the Mexican Government and the Inter-American Development Bank. The rationale used to justify the project included that it would bring in foreign exchange, generate many new jobs outside of existing overtaxed urban centres such as Mexico City and would counter patterns of regional inequality. Originally planned as a resort complex, recently it has been shifting from a resort enclave to an open urban centre with increasing levels of integration into the neighbouring Mayan region. Although the impact has been substantial, in terms of regional development it is not a clear success. It has not produced substantial improvements in regional conditions (Hiernaux-Nicolas, 1999). The distance continues to grow between local winners and the remaining population, which has been impoverished by national and regional economic crises, and the vast majority of the Mexicans in the region have not benefited from the development in Cancún. The resort is inaccessible to the peasant population as there are no longer positions open to unskilled migrant workers. 'Low wages, unstable labour markets, racism, a high cost of living, and poor housing are some of the conditions the would-be migrants have found in Cancún' (Hiernaux-Nicolas, 1999: 139).

At the other end of the development spectrum are long established coastal resorts such as British seaside resorts. However, within Britain, resort decline has been endemic since the 1970s as demand-side trends associated with changing tastes, which are underpinned by changing demographics and holiday habits, have taken place along supply-side changes. Many of the British seaside resorts are facing severe difficulties including declining visitor numbers, higher than average unemployment and a lack of investment (Agarwal, 1999). The decline has affected regional and local economies that are dependent on mass tourism. Agarwal (1999) investigated the regeneration of seaside tourism in Torbay, Cornwall and Weymouth and Portland. While rejuvenation of seaside tourism has the potential to stimulate local economic development along with wider regional development, there was little evidence that local or regional development was stimulated as a result of the programmes initiated. Additional research is required, however, Agarwal (1999) cautions that once a coastal environment enters a downward spiral, the future of that resort area becomes very uncertain and therefore its role in local and regional development schemes will remain limited.

Decisions also need to be made on which tourism market to pursue. Oppermann (1992) found that in Malaysia, active tourists who stayed in at least four different localities contributed more to the goals of regional development. Wall (1993b) has developed a tourism typology which includes attraction types (cultural, natural and recreational), location (water or land based), spatial characteristics (nodal, linear and extensive) and development strategies (highly developed, developed, developing). Attractions, such as cultural or religious sites, may be more sensitive to high levels of tourist development compared to a recreation facility such as a beach. Accommodation type is seen as an important element in the tourist system with implications for: 'characteristics of tourists, the built environment, economic impacts, degree of local involvement, and critical environmental and sustainability factors including land, capital, water, energy and waste disposal systems' (Wall, 1993b: 52). Within the context of this typology, Wall suggests using quantities and types of accommodation to regulate the levels and types of use in different tourist areas. Wall (1993b) advocates a mix of both tourist types (mass to explorer) and accommodation types (five-star to guest houses). This typology can be integrated to promote the sustainable development of tourism by protecting both the human and physical environments (Wall, 1993b).

Similarly, Britton (1987a) highlights six developing country alternatives to large-scale, capitalist foreign-owned tourism:

- large-scale tourism enterprises owned and controlled by the state;
- large-scale tourism enterprises owned and controlled by national private capital;
- medium-scale tourism enterprises controlled by local companies and individuals;
- small and medium-scale tourism enterprises organised as co-peratives at the village or community level;
- small-scale tourism enterprises organised as individual or family concerns; and
- small-scale tourism enterprises organised by individuals and families as a supplement to simple commodity production.

Britton argues that decentralised, smaller-scale tourism can have a greater impact on 'improving rural living standards, reducing rural-urban migration, rejuvenating rural communities, and countering structural inequalities of income distribution' (Britton, 1987a: 183). Pearce (1989b) states that tourism developed gradually over time will allow for a longer period of social and environmental adjustment. This will allow more of the local population to become involved since labour, supplies and capital are more likely to be obtainable from local sources (Pearce, 1989b: 185). This type of incremental development is easier on the local population and may have a better chance of promoting sustainable tourism. The following sections turn to exploring the use of tourism as a regional development tool in more detail in urban, rural, island, peripheral and international regions.

Tourism and Urban Redevelopment

The use of tourism for regional development can also take place in urban areas as governments attempt to revitalise sections of a city.

> The creation of urban development corporations and enterprise boards is tied in with urban and regional redevelopment programmes seeking to 'rejuvenate' inner-city and industrial lands. Urban revitalisation typically includes the development of inner-city leisure spaces, waterfront redevelopment, festival market-places, casinos, conference centres and sports stadia.' (Hall & Jenkins, 1995: 38.)

In a different context, Jansen-Verbeke and Lievois (1999: 81) comment that 'policies for urban revitalisation are strongly inspired by the possibilities of exploiting the cultural potential of urban historic cities'. In reviewing the pros and cons, Fainstein and Judd (1999) found that the proponents of regeneration through tourism argue that central-city regeneration spurs economic growth through strong multipliers, improves a city's aesthetic and built environment and enhances facilities for residents. In addition, advocates argue that with a lack of alternatives for developing an economic base, if cities do not compete for tourism dollars they will lose out in an increasing global environment (Fainstein & Judd, 1999). Those opposed to this type of renewal argue that its potential as a growth engine falls short of claims made by its proponents. They claim that imitations of publicised festival market places such as those in Boston or Baltimore do not always work in other cities. Detractors cite examples of city-centre retail markets which failed to meet expected visitor flows or incurred losses, such as those in Toledo, OH, Richmond, VA and St Louis, MI. In addition, detractors argue the impact of convention centres have fallen short of expected projections; however, cities are forced to upgrade facilities just to keep up with the competition (Fainstein & Judd, 1999).

In the context of a city, tourism is just one form of industry and how it is integrated into the community can have an impact on its role in regional development. In some cities where there is high urban crime rates, rather than integrating the new tourism development into the surrounding community, it is cordoned off, designed to separate the affluent tourists such as with the Renaissance Centre in Detroit in the United States (Fainstein & Judd, 1999). Instances of success and failure in using tourism to revitalise an urban area can be seen in the city of Vancouver, Canada. Granville Island is a successful mixed-use area, which combines a market, bookstores, tourist shops, a hotel, a theatre, restaurants and cafés along with traditional waterfront businesses such as chandlers, boat repairs and moorings. The project was developed on an incremental scale and benefits not only tourists but also local residents and businesses (Hall 2000a). Not far from Granville Island is the former site of the Expo held in 1986 and, for the most part, it has remained undeveloped for over a decade. Hall (2000a) suggests that appropriate tourism development may mean that relatively small-scale change with public involvement such as in Granville Island is better than large-scale development with limited numbers of owners. While the large-scale projects may be attractive to politicians, gradual change may be more sustainable. An important point is raised by Hall and Jenkins (1995) in that, while local and regional governments may see tourism as a source of employment and income, the role of tourism within the bigger picture of economic and social development processes is often lost.

As governments become more entrepreneurial in trying to attract tourists to their cities either through government agencies or tourism development corporations, such as the case of Baltimore or the Niagara Economic Tourism Corporation (NETCOR) in Niagara Falls, Ontario, Canada, they are turning towards increased place marketing. Some cities have an existing historical image like Paris while others are trying to create an image. Often in a development project, the creation of a landmark, for example the Sydney Opera House or the CN Tower in Toronto, can be valuable attractions as well as giving a city a world class recognisable icon. Other strategies in promoting redevelopment is attracting a world class event to the city: 'The Olympic games represents the biggest prize for cities seeking mega-events' (Holcomb, 1999). The main focus for the Toronto 2008 Olympic bid was a multi-million dollar redevelopment plan of the city's waterfront supported by the city, province and federal government.

Heritage tourism in urban areas has received increased attention (Jansen-Verbeke & Lievois, 1999). In the context of European cities it is suggested that heritage tourism has the mission of marketing nostalgia, authenticity, education and entertainment in a way to safeguard the heritage resources for future generations. This is taking place within the objective of using tourism as a stimulus for urban economy and added value to urban life (Jansen-Verbeke & Lievois, 1999).

Finally, as indicated in the introductory sentence of this chapter, casino complexes have become major tools in development. Las Vegas has had new projects and major expansions, which added nearly 10,000 new hotel rooms to the city between 1996 and 1998. In 1996 alone, three new major casino resorts opened including the Luxor, Treasure Island and MGM Grand Hotel and Casino (Parker, 1999). In the context of Las Vegas, however, this growth strategy and the claims of job creation has to be tempered with increases in compulsive gambling, struggles of citizens to afford housing on service sector jobs, the reduction of public space in favour of private space, bankruptcy of small independent stores, the fiscal difficulties of a local government trying to subsidise profitable gambling establishments while maintaining local infrastructure and environmental degradation.

Tourism and Rural Regeneration

With downturns in rural economies over the last three decades, it is understandable that governments have given a great deal of attention to the economic benefits of tourism, particularly for rural areas attempting to keep pace and adapt to the globalised economy (Hall & Jenkins, 1998). As Grolleau (1994) suggests, growing numbers of city-dwellers are 'getting away from it all' in the countryside. One of the advantages of rural tourism is that it is based on local initiatives, local management, has local spin-offs, is rooted in local scenery and it taps into local culture. In theory, this emphasis on the local can help to generate regional development and according to Sharpley and Sharpley (1997), rural tourism is increasingly being used for socio-economic regeneration and diversification.

While the definition of rural varies in different countries, Sharpley and Sharpley (1997:20) describe rural as all areas, 'both land and water, that lie beyond towns and cities which, in national and regional contexts, may be described as major urban centres'. For tourism to be described as rural tourism then it should mirror the characteristics that signify a rural area including small settlements, low population densities, agrarian-based economies and traditional societies (Sharpley & Sharpley, 1997). Lane (1994) further details the difficulty in attempting to create a definition of rural tourism as not all tourism in rural areas is strictly 'rural' as will be highlighted later. Rural tourism extends beyond farm-based tourism to include

> special-interest nature holidays and ecotourism, walking, climbing and riding holidays, adventure, sport and health tourism, hunting and angling, educational travel, arts and heritage tourism, and in some areas, ethnic tourism. (Lane, 1994: 9).

Opportunities for rural tourism in the public sector often occur in national or provincial parks.

Sharpley and Sharpley (1997) outlined the benefits and costs associated with developing rural tourism. As previously mentioned, many of the business associated with rural tourism are small and independently owned and therefore generate income for the local economy. By developing rural tourism, the local economy becomes more diversified as jobs are created in tourism and tourism-related businesses. Existing services and businesses are supported while new businesses may be attracted to the area further diversifying the economy. One of the more significant components of the rural tourism product in many industrialised countries is vacation farms. There is a long history in Europe of vacation farms and countries such as Australia and New Zealand have experienced recent growth in this sector (Weaver & Fennell, 1997). In terms of social benefits, local transport and health care may be maintained and there may be a revitalisation of local customs, crafts and cultural identities. As rural tourism relies on the natural environment, the industry may be a stimulus for conservation. As with any type of tourism there are associated costs, which are in relation to the importance of the industry, volume of tourists, and the resiliency of the local community. Rural tourism may result in increases in the price of land and goods. In the Muskoka region, north of Toronto, Ontario, the land values for cottages have surpassed the levels at which many locals can afford. Jobs created may also be seasonal and outsiders may control many of the tourism businesses. The dependency on a business, over which they have little control, may also cause difficulties for the local community. Congestion and crowding, which impinges on the daily life of local residents, and the replacement of traditional shops with souvenir shops can have a negative effect on resident attitudes towards tourism development (see Chapter 7 for a discussion of the social and cultural impacts of tourism). Butler and Clark (cited in Page & Getz, 1997) warn that rural tourism may not be the magic solution with its income leakages, volatility, low pay, imported labour and conservative investors. They argue that the least favourite circumstance to promote rural tourism is when the economy is weak since tourism will further create highly unbalanced income and employment distributions. Hall and Jenkins (1998) also warn that tourism can diversify and therefore stabilise a local economy by creating jobs, business opportunities, incomes and a increased tax base. Nevertheless, rural communities are often faced with limited resources, over-extended leaders and volunteers and they are forced to compete with other rural areas that are also developing tourism.

Many countries and regions have developed rural policies which have either directly or indirectly had an impact on rural tourism. In the EU, the Common Agricultural Policy and its subsequent reforms have indirectly had an effect on rural tourism. Within the policy there has been a reduction in the amount of subsidies provided to farmers, some farmers have taken land out of production and others have been given incentives for early retirement, the end result being that a large amount of rural land is available for other uses, the LEADER programme (Liaisons Entre Actions pour la Développement des Économies Rurales) of the EU has particular interest for tourism as it is intended to promote an integrated approach to rural development with emphasis on local support and involvement. Local Action Groups are formed and if their business plan is accepted, the groups receive funding from EU structural funds along with national and private sector funding. Tourism has become one of the dominate concepts of the business plans submitted. In a successful case noted by Sharpley and Sharpley (1997), the South Pembrokeshire Partnership for Action with Rural Communities (SPARC) in the UK covered some 35 rural communities and they were able to help over 100 different projects, many of them related to rural tourism.

Major inflows of capital were put into some rural areas under state socialism including the winter sports centres in Slovenia, Bulgaria and Romania and the holiday complexes along the Black Sea and the Adriatic Coasts. Hall (1998) argues within south-eastern Europe, there is potential for leisure-related activities to influence significantly employment growth. In addition, opportunities exist for rural attractions to act as a resource for tourism organised through locally owned small enterprises and for 'farm-based tourism to act as a vehicle for integrated rural development to raise incomes, stabilise populations, sustain cultures, and redistribute economic roles within the rural household' (D. Hall, 1998: 428). With increases in employment, population retention may be encouraged in rural areas and the availability of abandoned buildings may be an attraction in refurbishing traditional homes for small-scale tourism enterprises as has been attempted in southern Albania. Rural and nature tourism has received substantial promotion in the region by the local governments, NGOs and the private sector. In 1995 the Romanian Ministry of Tourism identified rural tourism as a major growth area. Despite the many opportunities, and the fact the EU PHARE and TEMPUS schemes for education and training in rural tourism have been developed in the Czech Republic, Hungary, Poland and Slovakia, D. Hall (1998) suggests there is limited evidence from south-eastern Europe on the long-term viability of rural tourism, small and medium enterprises, their social impact or multiplier effect.

Cavaco (1995) examined the growth of rural tourism in inland rural areas in Portugal. It was found that rural tourism provided funds to restore manor homes and encouraged families who owned these estates to educate the tourists about nature and rural culture. It also revitalised thermal spas and resorts and also local trade and restoration businesses. However, it was recognised that this sort of tourism occupies a very small niche and is limited to specific areas so the social and economic impacts are very modest. Cavaco (1995) stated that it was unlikely that the National Tourism Plan will fulfil the role it wished to play in raising standards of living in rural areas. The difficulties in using tourism as a regional development tool here included the financial risks required, the remoteness of markets and the local cultural life, the services and other types of activity. The marketing of small-scale tourism products is often handled through an intermediary, which results in a reduction in income for local craft people. The market of mainly middle-aged domestic or foreign tourists in upper to middle income brackets whom usually arrived at the site by their own car or rented vehicle limits the amount of money that can be made in these regions (Cavaco, 1995).

Agritourism has been found to promote community development in the village of Bangunkerto in Indonesia (Telfer, 2000c). The National Tourism Strategy for Indonesia indicated that special interest tourism such as agritourism should be supported. With help from the provincial agricultural department, 4000 salak plants were given to the village which worked on a cooperative basis to establish a salak plantation tourism centre. Traditional dances were performed at the centre and the guides were hired from the surrounding villages. While at the time of investigation the project had not created a lot of additional income for the village, the villagers were hoping in time to expand the facilities.

In the Niagara Region of Ontario, Canada, efforts are now underway to promote the rural areas beyond the well-known attraction of Niagara Falls. The concept of rural or heritage trails have been used to help promote a region and allow visitors to travel on the trail from one location to another. The Niagara Wine Route links over 50 wineries throughout the region. In addition to offering tours and tastings, many of the wineries have moved into the area of wine tourism and offer special events throughout the year (Telfer, 2001a, b, 2000a). The wineries have been successful not in only attracting domestic tourists but also international tourists (Telfer & Hashimoto, 2000; Hashimoto & Telfer, 1999). Part of the development of wine tourism in the area is also due to an organisation called Tastes of Niagara, which promotes the use of local agricultural products in Niagara restaurants. This organisation holds two showcases a year where local producers are paired with a chef from an area restaurant as well as being paired with a winery. This rural festival is one of many in the Niagara Region which encourage people to visit nearby rural areas. 'Rural Routes' have also been successful in the Niagara region as local farmers open their farms for guided tours on select weekends in the summer (Telfer 2000b). One of the key factors for the success of rural tourism in the Niagara Region has been the development of partnerships. As indicated in Telfer (2001a), the success of the wineries, for example, has been the development of competitive advantage of embedded clusters similar to the concepts highlighted by Porter (1998).

Another source of tourism in the rural environment, though it may not meet many of the definitions of small-scale rural tourism (see Lane, 1994), is the introduction of casinos in Native American communities. Nevertheless, it is being used as an agent of economic development. Native American reservations have some of the highest poverty and unemployment rates in the United States and many reservations are turning to the operation of casinos as a strategy for economic development (Baron, 1998). Although it is not possible to generalise, Native American communities, because of their primarily rural nature, have been locked into a pattern of spatial disequilibrium that characterises uneven development (Baron, 1998). Baron warns of the problems in some areas where casinos on reservations are competing for the same market. Ultimately there may be a situation where there is an economic polarisation between tribes with successful casinos and those without.

While rural tourism continues to gain in popularity as a regional development tool, planners need to be aware of the possible conflicts which are caused. The province of Newfoundland is currently experiencing one of the fastest tourism growth rates in Canada. However, once tourists go beyond the main cities, the majority of the province is not equipped to handle the inflow of tourists, which is causing problems for not only the tourists but also the residents. There is also possible migration of labour out of the traditional industries such as agriculture into the tourism sector, leaving fewer people on the farm when needed at harvesting time. Finally, with increased competition between rural areas, Butler and Hall (1998: 117) pose the question: '[h]ow many heritage trails, pioneer museums and villages, historic houses, roadside produce stalls, authentic country cooking, festivals, country shoppes, and Devonshire teas can we stand?' This increased competition has forced rural areas to develop strategic place marketing through imaging or re-imaging.

Island Tourism Development

From the Caribbean to the islands of the Mediterranean or the South Pacific, tourism is the development option of choice for many where there is a lack of resources and a limited range of other economic activities. As Milne (1992) suggests, the microstate category of islands is an amorphous one as it groups relatively large nations with mature tourism industries such as Malta, Fiji or Barbados, alongside extremely small states with limited visitor flows and population of under 30,000, such as the Cook Islands or Niue. In developing tourism, there is a set of common issues which islands face (Butler, 1996). Islands are vulnerable to external influences, have limited local markets, lack a critical mass, and have poor communications and transportation links with potential markets. One of the sources of vulnerability is a high rate of dependence on agencies for providing services such as transportation and finance. In the cases where the government is off island, their priorities may be different from those of the host population. Despite these challenges, many island nations pursue tourism; however, in general, the smaller the island, the less control the local population has had over the nature and scale of the tourism development (Butler, 1996).

Within the theme of this chapter, one could examine the Caribbean, for example, as a region of islands which relies heavily on tourism. Alliances between nations have been building in the Caribbean, including CARICOM (Caribbean Community) developed in 1973, the OECS (Organisation of Eastern Caribbean States) with its common currency (East Caribbean Dollar) and the pan-Caribbean ACS (Association of Caribbean States) formed in 1994 (Wilson, 1996). In the anglophone Caribbean there is a concentration of microstates which are becoming increasingly dependent upon tourism as a source of income. The Windward Islands of Dominica, Grenada, St Lucia, St Vincent and the Grenadines represent tourism at different stages of development. Dominica is in the building phase while St Lucia is more established and tourism is a major foreign exchange earner (Widfelt, 1996). Wilkinson's (1987: 142) investigations in the Caribbean found that although tourism is a major export earner, a large part of the expenditure leaves the economy 'through international airlines, and major hotel chains, and purchases of foreign food'. Widfelt (1996) has raised other potential problems for island nations. The intensive use of coastal zones with the construction of harbours, marinas, hotels and airports has had severe effects on the environment while, at the same time, Caribbean farming and fishing have been marginalised. Rural encroachment also can occur as tourism develops. The economic benefits of tourism in the Caribbean have also been called into question. To build and maintain expanded infrastructure re-quires a great deal of capital and a high proportion of tourism dollars tend to flow out of the region in various forms including profits, payments for imports and other services (Debbage, 1990; Widfelt, 1996).

Regional development can also be examined within the context of a single island. Nuryanti (1998) examined tourism and regional imbalances on the island of Java, Indonesia. She indicated that the success of tourism in generating regional develop-ment depends on the interaction of the following factors: the level of provincial specification or differentiation in terms of sociocultural and economic structures, tourist density, accessibility and the characteristics of the tourism development. A region with a high level of specification or differentiation can absorb tourism impacts in a positive way as the region has the internal capacity:

- to integrate and create the linkages;
- to adapt its organisational structure;
- to increase its level of specification or differentiation; and,
- to handle the long term, more integrated development.

A region with a lower level of differentiation will not be able to respond using its own limited resources. A scenario which often takes place is an immediate in-crease in regional differentiation and regional imbalances. The typical response to this instability has often been to obtain imported assistance such as goods, foreign investment and services to meet the demands set by international tourism (Nuryanti, 1998). If tourism is to be used effectively as a regional development tool, it is necessary for backward and forward linkages to be established through-out the surrounding region. Telfer (1996) and Telfer and Wall (1996, 2000) have explored the linkages between the tourism industry and the agricultural sector on the islands of Lombok and Java in Indonesia. Case studies on both Lombok and Java revealed that large-scale hotels are able to make a wide variety of linkages with the local agricultural sector to purchase local products. The hotels used both small-scale suppliers who visited local markets to purchase products to larger suppliers with broad-based links throughout the region. In the case of Lombok, the resort hired a small-scale fisherman turned supplier to travel to the various fish markets and purchase fresh local seafood. The hotel also provided a local farmer with a variety of seeds for crops, some of which were traditionally not grown on the island. When the crops were ready the hotel would purchase them from the farmer. Lombok is a much smaller island than Java and less fertile so it was difficult for the hotel to get all of the products it required locally. The eco-nomic benefits to the region are improved when linkages with local industry are developed and maintained.

The form of tourism development created can have an impact on the regional benefits of the industry. Weaver (1988) developed a plantation model of tourism, which is based on the Caribbean islands. The evolutionary model has three phases: (1) pre-tourism, (2) transition and (3) tourism domination. The model suggests that the main town area is commonly the dominant focus of tourism development in the initial stages. As Stage 3 is reached, tourism development is not evenly distributed in the peripheral areas and the centre of the island is left as a non-tourism space while the outer edges of the island are more fully developed. McDonnell and Darcy (1998) also examined the form of island tourism development. They compared Bali and Fiji and suggested that one of the possible reasons for the decline in the Australian market share for Fiji compared to Bali was the lack of tourism precincts on Fiji. Tourism precincts are defined as

> an area in which various attractions such as bars, restaurants, places of entertainment or education, accommodation, amenities, and other facilities are clustered in freely accessible public spaces. Tourism precincts by their nature enhance certain aspects of the tourist experience and facilitate social interactions between tourists and locals. (McDonnell & Darcy, 1998: 354).

The term tourism precinct has roots in the following terms: Recreational Business Districts, Peripheral Tourism Areas, Enclaves, Tourist-Historic Cities, Integrated Beach Resort Development, Tourism Shopping Villages, Tourism Business Districts, Tourism Destination Areas and Tourism Districts (McDonnell & Darcy, 1998). While the central and provincial governments of Indonesia and Bali have, in many ways, been the developers of tourism, Fiji's Government has taken on more of a support role. In Bali there are four well-defined tourism areas (Kuta, Sanur, Nusa Dua and Ubud) along with other more minor areas, while in Fiji tourist attractions tend to be scattered over a wide area with no distinctive tourism precincts (McDonnell & Darcy, 1998).

There is debate in the literature as to the merits of enclave resorts *versus* integrated resorts. Enclave resorts are characterised by the following three points: the structure is not intended to benefit the local residents directly; the site is physically separated from the existing community; and they are used almost exclusively by foreign tourists (Jenkins, 1982b). It is argued that resort enclaves are dominated by multinationals with a management style that creates and controls the physical and cultural environment for the tourist (Freitag, 1994). Enclave resort development in the Dominican Republic is blamed for exploiting the local lower classes as cheap labour while national élites and foreign countries are the ones that benefit from higher incomes (Freitag, 1994). This type of development places the destination community in a dependent position. However, integrated tourism development attempts to match the scale of the project to fit within the local community. Integrated tourism development is characterised by a small scale with local capital and management (Jenkins, 1982b). Jenkins hypothesised that this type of tourism development may be more easily assimilated into the host community. Rodenburg's (1980) evaluation of the social and economic effects of international standard hotels, economy hotels, and homestays in Bali found that the best development strategy did not always include large industrial tourism. It was suggested that smaller-scale enterprises may present greater opportunities for control and profit by local people. Jenkins (1982b) criticised Rodenburg (1980) by arguing that large-scale tourist developments were likely to be due to the market structure of international tourism and external economies of scale. He suggested that problems with tourism could be mitigated to some extent if there were pre-project planning. In addition to the form of development, the rate at which tourism develops can also raise concern. In the context of the Baleraic Islands, Morgan (2000) notes that 50 years ago most of the residents were subsistence farmers. Ibiza, for example, is now known for its clubbing scene and mass hedonism. It has been the centre of a construction boom which has spoiled huge areas of coast and countryside and caused a dramatic water shortage. Attempts by the Balearic Government to impose an eco-tax have, however, met with resistance from the industry.

While much of the development in island nations is around mass tourism, others are calling for an increased role in alternative tourism development in island nations (Widfelt, 1996). Alternative tourism has been identified as being more ecologically sound and less detrimental to the environment. Associated with this concept is scale whereby small units are developed and often run by local communities, which keep the economic benefits of tourism in the local community (Widfelt, 1996). In the anglophone Caribbean, local NGOs and NGO networks are becoming increasingly important for national and regional development. Organisations such as the Caribbean Natural Resources Institute (CANARI) are involved in strengthening the capacity of human communities to manage natural resources. This organisation has been promoting nature-based tourism on the south-east coast of St Lucia as part of the project to demonstrate the links between development and conservation.

Within the context of regional development, governments need to decide on the nature of the tourism they want to develop. Large-scale resort enclaves may generate a great deal of income; however, if there are no strong links with the surrounding community then few will benefit. If small-scale alternative tourism development which is locally controlled is pursued, then the benefits may remain in the community but, in an overall regional development context, the amount of money generated may be small. Milne (1992) argues that for tourism to be of maximum benefit for island microstates, the industry needs to be planned and integrated with other parts of the economy taking into account the broader social, political, economic objectives and constraints. Profits derived from tourism should not necessarily be put straight back into further tourism expansion but should be used to secure a regionally, economically and socially balanced pattern of investment and development.

Harrison's (1992a) comment on the work by Smith on the island of Borcay in the Philippines concludes this section. While the once subsistence-based island has been modernised by tourism and is now more closely connected into the world economic system with the expansion of a cash economy along with the introduction of 'western' norms, the question raised is– Was the island developed and who is the judge?

Tourism Development in Peripheral Regions

As the tourism product continues to diversify to satisfy an ever increasingly demanding market, the geographic location to which tourists are travelling to gets further and further away from developed areas and into the periphery. Tourism in the periphery here is considered to be different from the rural tourism discussed earlier and is associated with more remote settings. Botterill *et al.* (2000) outlined the main characteristics of the periphery as follows: low levels of economic vitality and dependence on traditional industries, more rural and remote – often with high scenic values, reliant on imported technologies and ideas, poor information flows, remote from decision-making leading to a sense of alienation and a poor infrastructure. Tourism in these peripheral regions has been identified under a variety of labels such as wildlife tourism, nature tourism, ecotourism and adventure tourism. In order to meet this market, governments are opening up regions that have never had visits from tourists before. Price's (1996a) work on people and tourism in fragile environments focuses on case studies from mountain regions, savannahs and the Arctic.

> Increases in accessibility – whether by land, air or sea may be driven by a government's desire to develop tourism as a means of increasing national incomes or revitalising local economies. (Price, 1996b: 2)

Not only are these fragile ecosystems under threat but they are also home to some of the world's remaining indigenous people whose lifestyle is also under threat. These communities are facing increasing levels of outside involvement in their communities and a potential loss of access to resources. The economic rationale for indigenous tourism development is that it will result in increased economic independence along with a higher rate of self-determination and cultural pride as the shackles of poverty and social welfare are broken (Butler & Hinch, 1996). The second perspective put forward by Butler and Hinch (1996) is that increased participation by indigenous people in tourism will facilitate a better understanding between indigenous and non-indigenous peoples. The increased understanding will generate a more equitable relationship between the two groups.

As indicated in Chapter 2, the alternative development paradigm with its focus on sustainability and appropriate forms of tourism development has recently received a great deal of attention in the tourism literature. Ecotourism has become a favoured label for tourism in untouched ecosystems in many parts of the word (Malecki, 1997) and it is in danger of becoming a marketing label. With many of the beautiful natural environments being located in rural areas of less developed countries where there are often problems of underdevelopment and poverty, the potential economic benefits to be gained from ecotourism also means that there is a potential threat to conservation of these areas (Holden, 2000). Without strict government control over the development, there is little reason to assume the development cycle will be any different from any other form of tourism (Holden, 2000). These strict government controls on the environment may help to protect the environment; however, they may reduce the ability of a region to capitalise on its resources and thereby reduce overall regional development. However, if a region pursues tourism to such a degree that there are major negative impacts on the environment, tourists will no longer want to visit the area.

Other challenges associated with opening up these regions to varieties of tourism, such as ecotourism or adventure, not only include a lack of tourism infrastructure but also the nature of the market. Tourists interested in adventure tourism or ecotourism may not be ready to return to the same site, not only because of the costs involved but they may also want to move on to the next challenge / destination. Therefore, the destination must constantly seek out new customers.

Sinclair and Pack (2000) examined wildlife tourism within the framework of the Communal Areas Management Programme for Indigenous Resources (CAMP-FIRE) in Zimbabwe. The programme attempts to give local communities ownership and control of the wildlife in their domain and to ensure that they receive a return from the resources in terms of cash or community projects. The strategies used to implement the programme are charges, quotas and regulations for wildlife viewing and hunting tourism. 'The community-based wildlife tourism offers a way of improving rural livelihoods in areas where agricultural prospects are at best marginal' (Potts *et al.*, 1996: 217). The difficulties in using this project in regional development are however, indicated in the comment by the authors that while the project has been welcomed in some areas of the country, it has been less successful where economic returns have been relatively low or unequally distributed (Sinclair & Pack, 2000). Tourism development in remote regions can also help to modernise an area. The development of ethnic and adventure tourism in the far north region of Norway has had an important role to play in preserving the indigenous Sami culture. At the same time, tourism has contributed to new ways of living and built new local identities, which fit into modernisation and globalisation processes (Pedersen & Viken, 1996) (see also Chapter 7).

In Belize, the government focused on a tourism policy based on ecotourism as a way to attract foreign investment and protect the environment. However, the majority of the tourists have their travel and accommodations arranged by foreign tour operators, which has led to higher rates of economic leakage. In addition, the

growth in the industry led to inflationary prices along the coastline and it is estimated that 90% of the coastal region is under foreign ownership and the
government has no plans to reduce foreign ownership as it needs the investment
(Holden, 2000). Elsewhere, however, steps have been taken by governments to
reduce tourism development in a peripheral region to protect the environment over
the long term. In 1993, the Queensland Government in Australia decided not to
extend the electricity grid north of the Daintree River in order to limit the possibilities for local governments to attract more tourism development into the isolated Far
North Region. This was a political decision based on ideological grounds, anxiety
about the World Heritage tropical rainforests and Great Barrier Reef, but also in response to the power of the environmental lobby (Elliot, 1997).

Tourism developments in peripheral regions can also be quite large scale. The
Whistler ski resort in British Columbia, Canada, is one such example where
large-scale public and private investment was required to achieve international
resort destination status. A new integrated, comprehensively planned resort community was built with a heavy reliance on public funds used to develop
infrastructure and to ensure a viable economic environment to attract private investment (Gill, 1998). However, in the construction of the Whistler resort, Cubie
(2000) argues that while local contractors were initially involved in the construction
of the Whistler village, many local non-union companies were squeezed out by
union labour as the development proceeded. Larger companies control much of the
remaining development and local companies have moved in a new direction building unique high-end homes showing off their craftsmanship.

While there are both stories of success and failure in using tourism as a regional
development tool in remote peripheral areas, concerns have been raised that the use
of environmental resources for activities such as ecotourism may, in terms of negative impacts of tourism, be more detrimental as ecotourism environments are often
rich in biodiversity and highly susceptible to change (Holden, 2000).

International Regions

As indicated earlier, tourism regions cross international boundaries. The estab-
lishment of international trading blocks such as the Association of Southeast Asian
Nations (ASEAN), the European Union (EU) and the North American Free Trade
Agreement (NAFTA) illustrate the growing trend of cross-border collaboration.
Cross-border collaboration for tourism development has been explored in a
number of different contexts by Timothy (1995, 2000a). The countries of the Carib-
bean, for example, work together to promote the region and the Southern Africa
Development Community (SADCC) developed a tourism sector in 1984 (Teye,
2000). In the Niagara Region, along the border between Canada and the United
States, efforts are underway to promote the Canadian and American side of
Niagara Falls jointly as a regional tourism destination. One of the notable efforts for

encouraging regional development across borders within the ASEAN community is known as the *growth triangle*. The concept originated in 1989 when Singapore invited the Indonesian province of Riau and Malaysia's state of Johor to join forces in an economic union (Timothy, 2000b). One of the goals of the growth triangle was to strengthen the economic and social links between Singapore, Indonesia and Malaysia, including the joint promotion of the area as an investment site for various multinational corporations including those involved in tourism (Timothy, 2000b). A second goal was to decrease barriers within the region and allow greater flows of goods, capital and labour across the borders. With successful industrial development on the Indonesian island of Batam, focus has shifted to the neighbouring island of Bintan. Just a short ferry ride away from Singapore, the island was selected to become a major resort complex over the next two decades. Efforts are under way to develop a 23,000-hectare resort complex on the north coast of Bintan. Singapore and Bintan are marketed together as tourism destinations. Critics of the growth triangle, however, argue that it is Singapore that is the main beneficiary of the developments in the region and the Malaysian state of Johor has been left behind (Timothy, 2000b). While the government of the state of Johor would like to become a more active member of the growth triangle, it needs to wait for approval for action from the federal government. The federal government, in turn, fears that as Johor is already the fastest growing state, further integration would increase growth and the federal government is trying to maintain a national policy of spreading economic growth to other parts of the country (Timothy, 2000b). As with any partnership, there are dangers that there will be an unequal distribution of risks taken and benefits achieved. This can become even more apparent when the partnership crosses political boundaries and various national interests need to be served.

Conclusion

Tourism continues to be a favoured regional development tool for many governments around the world. Regions are complex entities ranging from a small sub-section of a nation to an international region. Where regional imbalances exist, tourism is seen as a way to generate jobs and create new income. Governments have purposely targeted specific undeveloped regions or regions with high unemployment and have created policies to disburse tourists to these regions. Through investment incentives or the provision of infrastructure, governments have taken an active role in the development of tourism. Some of the more classic regional development theories such as growth poles and agglomeration economies can still be seen underlying development projects. However, as is evident in the work of Porter (1998), regions need to move beyond developing traditional agglomeration economies and develop highly competitive clusters with strong linkages in order to become a very competitive destination. The increased competition for investment dollars have forced some governments to act in a more entrepreneurial fashion.

This chapter has examined the use of tourism in a variety of different forms and scales in a variety of different regions. Destinations with special natural, cultural, or historical attractions are adopting tourism for development. Increasingly, tourism is also being created by the construction of convention facilities, shopping districts, hotels, restaurants and theme parks (Malecki, 1997). In urban areas, regional development programmes have been set up to rejuvenate inner city and industrial lands. In rural areas, programmes have been initiated at a variety of government levels to promote rural regeneration in areas where there is agricultural decline or to provide additional sources of income. Tourism is used as a major source of income in island destinations and, depending on the form of development, benefits can spread to the surrounding region if strong linkages are established. In peripheral regions, regions have adopted various types of tourism including nature-based tourism, ecotourism or adventure tourism. This type of development invariably means opening up new regions, which have not previously been exposed to the tourism industry (Wanhill, 1997). Finally, the chapter examined tourism developed on the scale of international regions whereby nations cooperate to promote tourism. Examples were presented to illustrate the challenges associated with using tourism as a regional development tool.

As noted in the Introduction, the role of tourism in regional development is open for debate. Tourism has the potential to generate growth and development but can also exacerbate inequalities if only the local elite benefits. One of the central questions of this book has been to question who benefits from tourism development. As Tosun and Jenkins (1996) suggest, the costs and benefits of tourism are not shared equally. In pursuing tourism, a destination opens itself up to the forces of the market and the forces of globalisation. If countries pursue multinational enterprises to lead tourism development, they face issues of dependency and high rates of leakages when local resources are not used in the industry. Tourism is being moved into more remote regions than ever before and, along with the potential economic benefits which may arise from the new industry, there are social and environmental costs that need to be considered. If a region has high levels of unemployment, the introduction of tourism may cause more disruption when imported labour is used. Workers migrate to areas of opportunity so the development or redevelopment of tourism in a region can introduce migrant workers. Careful examination of the various policies is needed. Questions need to be asked as to who benefits from these regional development policies. Do local people want tourism development? If a region is set up as a growth pole, does it really work and who benefits? How fast does the tourism development occur? Is the development part of the national agenda to generate foreign exchange or is it meant to help out specific regions. What is the image of the destination and how has it been created? Throughout this book, the concept of sustainable tourism development is mentioned along with the importance of local involvement in the decision-making process. If local participation is encouraged, it may require power decentralisation, which national governments may or may not want to undertake. Under the concepts of sustainability, trade-offs need to be made in order to protect the environment. If the policy of regional development is to be successful, there needs to be strong backward economic linkages within the targeted region so that as many people as possible benefit from the industry.

Chapter 5

Tourism and Community Development Issues

DALLEN J. TIMOTHY

Introduction

It is now accepted that tourism's impacts, both positive and negative, are most apparent at the level of the destination community. As a result, researchers in recent years have emphasised the need to decentralise tourism development and integrate it into overall community-defined development goals (Murphy, 1988; Prentice, 1993; Simmons, 1994). The community approach to tourism has been heralded as a way of empowering communities and affording them opportunities to break free from the destructive influences of mass tourism, which grew following the Second World War with economics as its basic rationale. The growth of mass tourism involved largely uncontrolled expansion and blind promotion by forces outside the communities in which tourists' activities were taking place. While not every aspect of mass tourism has been negative, relatively few of its positive impacts have accrued to the host communities. This chapter aims to examine tourism and development from a community perspective, focusing primarily on the empowerment of community members and other stakeholders in decision-making and in the benefits of tourism.

Sustainability and Community-based Tourism

In many insular and less-developed regions, tourism has been developed and controlled by large, multinational tour companies who have little regard for local sociocultural and economic conditions (Timothy & Ioannides, 2002). Most developing destinations and microstates lack significant amounts of wealth and political power, which makes them prone to decision-making that is completely beyond their control. Many decisions governing even domestic matters are made elsewhere by foreign tour companies and service providers (Wilkinson, 1997), which often do not have the destination community's best interest in mind (Timothy & Ioannides, 2002). Thus, as Mitchell and Reid (2001: 114) suggest, 'local people and their communities have become the objects of development but not the subjects'. Shaw and Williams (1994: 115) argue that 'in some respects the geography of tour company operations is the geography of dependency relationships' and, according to Britton (1982a: 331),

> when a Third World country uses tourism as a development strategy, it becomes enmeshed in a global system over which it has little control. The international tourism industry is a product of metropolitan capitalist enterprise. The superior entrepreneurial skills, resources and commercial power of metropolitan companies enable them to dominate many Third World tourist destinations.

Even in cases where individual nations have been in control of tourism development, power has been overwhelmingly concentrated in the hands of a few prominent individuals who have access to wealth and political strength (see Chapter 9 for a discussion on the political economy of tourism). Autocratic power systems have kept grassroots involvement from flourishing in areas of the world where representational democracy has been discouraged (Timothy, 1999). Such conditions are not conducive to sustainable tourism development.

Recent years have seen much debate over the concept of sustainable tourism, which has led scholars and environmental advocacy groups to cry for methods of development, planning and consumption that promote the enduring veracity and quality of cultural and natural resources (Boyd, 2000; Butler, 1999b; Mowforth & Munt, 1998). Advocates have recommended a number of principles that ought to be followed for sustainable tourism development. These include preservation of ecological processes and the protection of biodiversity in the natural realm and, in human terms, preservation of cultural integrity, holistic planning, balance, harmony, efficiency, equity, and integration (Bramwell & Lane, 1993; Hall & Lew, 1998; Timothy, 1998) (see Chapters 2, 8 and 11 on sustainable development).

Community-based tourism is a more sustainable form of development than conventional mass tourism because it allows host communities to break away from the hegemonic grasp of tour operators and the oligopoly of wealthy elites at the national level. Community tourism is about grassroots empowerment as it seeks to develop the industry in harmony with the 'needs and aspirations of host communities in a way that is acceptable to them, sustains their economies, rather than the economies of others, and is not detrimental to their culture, traditions or, indeed, their day-to-day convenience' (Fitton, 1996: 173). Nonetheless, a variety of levels of community involvement exist; some are sustainable and some are not. For example, based on the work of Pretty (1995), France (1998) provides a taxonomy of participation in tourism (Table 5.1). She suggests that resident involvement ranges from an exploitative position on one end of the spectrum to one of self-mobilisation, characterised by independent initiatives where local people are strengthened socially and economically by their involvement.

Table 5.1 Types of participation in tourism

Type	Characteristics	Examples from Tourism
Plantation	Exploitative, rather than developmental. Possibly paternalist. Payment in kind.	No attempt to participate on the part of workers, who are commonly racially and culturally different from 'management' and owners. Purely for material gain of owners.
Manipulative and passive participation	Pretence of participation. Local workers are told what is decided.	Some highly centralized multinational corporations based in developing countries. Neocolonial attitudes prevail through the use of expatriate labour, capital and technology. Those employed in tourism in non-menial jobs are likelyto be expatriates or non-indigenous residents.
Consultation	Residents consulted but external definition of problem and control.	Operations of some MNCs is devolved from metropolitan centers to local elites.
Material incentives	Locals contribute resources but have no stakeholding.	Local employment in tourism services where local expertise is used and locals are hiring in some managerial positions.
Functional participation	Participation seen by outsiders as a way of achieving goals. Major decisions are external.	Increasing use of local technology, capital and expertise. Some small, locally owned hotels. Minority élites often the most likely to participate. In larger hotels, some decisions made locally but according to external forces.
Interactive participation	Residents contribute to planning. Groups take control of local decisions.	Hotels owned by local people or groups of local people. Locally owned taxis, tour agencies, and restaurants. Maintenance of cultural events for the benefit of residents and tourists.
Self-mobilisation	Independent initiatives	Local people who have accumulated capital from tourism strengthen and extend their activities.

Source: After France (1998: 225).

Table 5.2 Types of community empowerment in tourism development

Type	*Signs of empowerment*
Economic	Tourism brings long-term financial benefits to a destination community. Money is spread throughout the community. There are notable improvements in local services and infrastructure.
Psychological	Self-esteem is enhanced because of outside recognition of the uniqueness and value of their culture, natural resources, and traditional knowledge. Increasing confidence in the community leads members to seek out further education and training opportunities. Access to jobs and cash leads to an increase in status for usually low-status residents, such as women and youth.
Social	Tourism maintains or enhances the local community's equilibrium. Community cohesion is improved as individuals and families cooperate to build a successful industry. Some funds raised are used for community development initiatives like education and roads.
Political	The community's political structure provides a representational forum through which people can raise questions and concerns pertaining to tourism initiatives. Agencies initiating or implementing the tourism ventures seek out the opinions of community groups and individual community members, and provide chances for them to be represented on decision-making bodies.

Source: After Scheyvens (1999).

This spectrum is not static, for despite a troubled past in developed and developing countries in tourism terms, levels of empowerment are increasing today among more community members in more places. When outside control turns to local control, several benefits are apparent. Based partly on the work of Friedmann (1992), Scheyvens (1999) provides a useful summary of the signs and benefits of economic, psychological, social, and political forms of empowerment (Table 5.2). Economic empowerment is important because it allows residents and entire communities to benefit financially from tourism (see Chapter 3). Psychological empowerment is critical in developing self-esteem and pride in local cultures, traditional knowledge, and natural resources. Social empowerment helps maintain a community's social equilibrium and has the power to lead to cooperation and enhanced initiatives such as health and education. Finally, signs of political empowerment include representational democracy wherein residents can voice opinions and raise concerns about development initiatives. With political empowerment, agencies and groups initiating tourism ventures seek input from community members and other stakeholders in decision-making (Arnstein, 1969; Friedmann, 1992).

Encompassing these elements of empowerment, community-based tourism can be viewed from at least two perspectives: public participation in decision-making and resident involvement in the benefits of tourism (Timothy, 1999). These two per-spectives form the basis of the following sections.

Public Participation in Decision-making

Participation in decision-making entails community members determining their own goals for development and having a meaningful voice in the organisation and administration of tourism. Better attitudes towards tourism among destination res-idents will result, and the industry will be more successful, for according to Gunn (1994: 111), tourism development 'will bear little fruit unless those most affected are involved from the start'. Likewise, Murphy (1985: 153) argues that tourism 'relies on the goodwill and cooperation of local people because they are part of its product. Where development and planning does not fit in with local aspirations and capac-ity, resistance and hostility can … destroy the industry's potential altogether'. Brohman (1996a: 59) agrees with Murphy and Gunn and maintains that grassroots development 'not only reduce[s] the need for local residents to trade off quality of life and social costs for economic growth, but would also contribute to a more broadly based positive attitude toward tourism'.

Representing a step in this direction, development specialists have begun to see the value of indigenous knowledge and environmental management practices (Berger, 1996; Boonzaier, 1996; Strang, 1996; Tjatera, 1994) and have argued that answers to the most difficult questions about host environments are to be found within the communities themselves. Community control is more likely to be envi-ronmentally sensitive than mass tourism (Fitton, 1996; Timothy & White, 1999) because, in most cases, traditional societies and indigenous groups do not see them-selves as separate from nature. Instead they view themselves as an integral part of the environment and commonly have a detailed knowledge of nature, resources and climate (Berger, 1996; Strang, 1996). Indigenous systems of agriculture, pastoralism and hunting and gathering are often the most sustainable forms of re-source management. For example, the Maasai people of East Africa have long

> used large areas for extensive grazing in ways that have sustained natural eco-systems and allowed relatively harmonious co-existence of wildlife and people. The Maasai did not hunt except in severe famine. In the past, they lim-ited forage offtake levels by restricting access to grazing and water at certain seasons. They practiced rotational grazing and the opportunistic movement of herds to take advantage of spatially and seasonally erratic rainfall. They used fire to encourage new growth of grass, depress bush encroachment, and reduce disease transmission, and kept a variety of stock: cattle, sheep, goats, and don-keys capable of grazing and browsing different types of vegetation. Though pastoralism changes the landscape, it stimulated biological productivity and to some extent promoted biodiversity. The combined impact of fire, grazing,

trampling, and nutrient cycling by livestock and wild herbivores created a mo-
saic of vegetation types inhabited by a rich flora and fauna. (Berger, 1996: 184)

In cultural terms, local control is vital because residents have a greater tendency
to do it in a way that is in harmony with cultural traditions, which might assist in
building ethnic pride. Exogenous power, on the other hand, results in negative
impacts because outsiders do not understand the traditional approaches to different situations. With external control, community cohesion and cooperation are
eroded, and practices, such as unhealthy competition and individualism, develop
in place of the traditional emphasis on group welfare (Berger, 1996). For example,
Baez (1996) attributes the success of tourism in Monteverde, Costa Rica, to the fact
that the people are in control and work in groups toward the common good, as pre-
scribed by traditions of social order. This, in turn, results in more harmonious
efforts on a community-wide basis, consistency and solidarity. Likewise, Tjatera's
(1994) work shows how existing cultural structures can be useful tools in forward-
ing the goals of sustainable development in Bali, and pride in local culture has
potential to grow.

Boonzaier (1996) gives an example of the Nama people of South Africa, who have
long been viewed as primitive and backward, and were assigned the lowest levels
of the social hierarchy. As a result, the Nama themselves 'were induced to participate in this process of denigrating 'indigenousness': they have suppressed the
Nama language and relinquished distinctively Nama customs in an attempt to gain
acceptance as members of the broader category of coloured people' (Boonzaier,
1996: 133). However, since gaining control of their own voice in development decision-making in the mid 1990s, they have begun to take pride in their heritage and
ethnic identity, and they feel that potential tourists might have an interest in experiencing their traditions.

Local control is also instrumental in keeping the most sacred spaces and ceremonies from being defiled by the tourist gaze. Numbers of visitors can be managed,
and cultural/spiritual resources and practices can be protected from the ignorance
of outsiders (Strang, 1996). Examples of this exist on Native American reserves in
the western United States. The Hopi and Taos Indians of Arizona and New Mexico
respectively, control their communities' tourism trade. Some of the most sacred locations and ceremonies on the Hopi reserve are restricted to tribal members only,
and at Taos Pueblo, outsiders have little or no access to some activities, resources
and places of particular spiritual importance. In the case of Taos, many ceremonies
are done in secret, and every February the pueblo is closed to tourists for religious
purposes (Lujan, 1998) (see Chapter 7 for a discussion on the social and cultural
impacts of tourism).

Sustainability now requires the involvement of all community members, in particular those who have traditionally been under-represented. In the past, women
and ethnic minorities have had little voice in policy matters, particularly in the de-

veloping world, and most of their work has been relegated to the economic periphery since it is either domestic in nature or undesirable to those in positions of power. The political rights of women and ethnically diverse residents and their entitlement to participate in tourism planning and decision-making are ill defined in tourism policy and practice. When these people, particularly those in the informal sector, are not given opportunities to participate in decision-making, their positions become even more tangential, for with every new regulation, their work becomes progressively marginalised (Timothy, 2001). Women and racial minorities must be given a louder voice in policy making if the goals of sustainability are to be realised, for these people are an important part of the community who are affected directly and indirectly by tourism (see Chapter 6).

For reasons of equity, harmony, and holistic growth, decision processes should go beyond individual residents to involve additional stakeholders, who have a direct interest in what is taking place. There is now widespread agreement that to achieve the goals of sustainability, planning and development must be done at a grassroots level, involving a wide range of stakeholders in the development process (Murphy, 1985b; 1988; Simmons, 1994; Scheyvens, 1999; Tosun, 2000). Advocacy organizations, business associations, public agencies and NGOs are interest groups, which together with destination residents, are all interdependent stakeholders in a multidimensional arena where no single individual or group can work out tourism issues by acting alone (Brohman, 1996a).

In addition to the groups just mentioned, stakeholder involvement also ought to include lower-level governments – a group generally ignored in the tourism development literature. Most development initiatives in the developing world originate and are driven at the national level, which often results in projects that are inappropriate for local conditions (Rondinelli, 1982; Smith, 1985). Thus, participation of lower-order governments (e.g. municipality, district, province) is critical, for sound tourism development requires critical, local administrative knowledge, something that is often lacking in large, distant capital cities among leaders who are less familiar with regional cultures and local conditions (Timothy, 1998). The inclusion of a wide range of stakeholders in policy processes will assist in bringing about unity of purpose in developing sustainable forms of tourism (Jamal & Getz, 1995; Murphy, 1998; Parker, 1999).

The previous discussion has highlighted the need for community involvement in tourism development, but confusion is common regarding how this can be done. Several techniques have been designed to involve local people in decision-making. For example, Gill (1996) examines the value of an idea known as living room meetings, which involves informal gatherings of small groups of community members in a moderated, yet relaxed, situation in homes throughout the community. Likewise, Fitton (1996: 168) explains the 'planning for real' method, which is a form of town meeting that involves bringing the community together before the planning process begins. Meetings are run and directed by the community rather than the planners, with an exchange of ideas between residents being the primary driving force. Specifically for physical planning, large maps are provided onto which residents place coloured pins to indicate where they think new services are needed, where tourists are the most bothersome and where additional infrastructure is needed. At the end of the session, an in-depth round-table discussion is held where residents can continue to debate and learn about their interests, expectations, desires and concerns for tourism. This approach allows even less outspoken community members to participate and is an excellent tool for informing the planning process. These types of techniques are important in developing tourism, for 'clearly, if communities do not want to be involved in tourism it is difficult and counter-productive to insist' (Fitton, 1996: 169).

Another method that has found considerable success is household questionnaires (Haywood, 1988; Simmons, 1994), which are sometimes combined with the approaches just described. This helps identify issues that are important to an area, focuses on the needs of the community and highlights opportunities for improvement. It gives everyone in the community an opportunity to participate and encourages them to think about tourism, local issues and the environment in depth (Fitton, 1996: 170). By way of example, it was determined through these types of involvement that residents of Llanthony, a small community in southern Wales, were unwilling to choose tourism as an economic development tool. They considered outside visitors to be too ignorant about their community and too disruptive to everyday functions. In contrast, the rural communities in South Pembrokeshire, Wales, opted strongly for tourism, as long as residents would remain in control. Since the 1980s, communities in the area have been directly involved in the development of new tourism opportunities, which has resulted in economic benefits to the local area and a strong community commitment to tourism (Fitton, 1996).

Involvement in the Benefits of Tourism

Resident involvement in the benefits of tourism best resembles Scheyvens' (1999) concepts of economic, social and psychological empowerment, which assume that residents will gain personally from tourism. Opportunities for community members to own businesses, to work in various industry-related jobs, to receive appropriate training, and to be educated about the role and effects of tourism in their community are characteristic of this form of participation (Timothy, 1999). Increased levels of income, employment and education, as well as decreased dependence on external agents and suppliers will be the result (see Chapter 7). An increase in benefits is not the only goal, however. Of equal importance is the distribution of rewards across the population (Scheyvens, 1999). Brohman (1996a: 59) agrees because 'a large proportion of the local population should benefit from tourism, rather than merely bearing the burden of its costs'.

One of the underlying practices in furthering sustainable tourism is the use of small-scale, locally-owned businesses (Brohman, 1996a; Dahles, 1997b; Long & Wall, 1995; Smith, 1998; Timothy & White, 1999). According to Cater (1996), the use of this type of services results in a much higher degree of local participation than traditional mass tourism. Usually, small-scale enterprises are considered more innocuous than large-scale developments because they place less stress on cultural and natural environments (Long & Wall, 1995) and have more direct economic benefits for local communities. Thus, development projects that focus on this genre of tourism enterprise can help decrease economic leakage to the outside and minimise dependency on metropolitan countries and foreign tour operators (Telfer, in press; Timothy & Ioannides, 2002). Similarly, small-scale establishments are more likely to keep control of decision-making in local hands and reduce alienation of indigenous peoples from their land, which has happened in many locations with the development of exogenously controlled mass tourism. Smith (1998: 207) describes these and several additional benefits of allowing local residents to participate in business ownership as follows:

(1) Ownership confers personal community status and promotes expanded networking through memberships in organizations such as Rotary, Soroptimists, Lions Club and Kiwanis with a louder voice in the wider community.
(2) It better enables residents to take control and manage local tourism through existing social networks or to establish *ad hoc* associations to help empower them as decision-makers.
(3) Privatisation can build equity in business terms, to become a family legacy or sellable retirement asset.
(4) The psychological satisfaction of owing one's own business can generate personal opportunities to increase earning power through responsible management and hard work.
(5) Family proprietorships can hire disabled, elderly, juvenile and, in some cases female, family members and friends who might not otherwise be employable.

Costa Rica is often regarded as one of the most community-friendly destinations, where 70% of the hotels are small and locally owned (Griffin, 1998). This has created an environment where residents feel secure in starting small businesses (Baez, 1996). In the Monteverde preserve area, for instance, which is one of the country's most important tourist regions, small-scale development employs dozens of local people and a significant portion of the profits support education programmes, scholarships, infrastructure development and maintenance and garbage collection programmes (Baez, 1996: 115).

While large-scale tourism developments (e.g. mega resorts) have a history of relying on imported supplies and labour, they have the potential to adopt more pro-sustainability policies that require the use of local products and labour where possible (Timothy & Ioannides, 2002). Such action would create a series of back-ward and forward linkages to benefit a broader sector of society. This can be a way of creating employment for fishermen, farmers and other middle people in the supply chain. Based on this notion, Telfer and Wall (1996) examined the linkages between food production and a four-star hotel in Indonesia. They found that insti-tutionalised agreements between local producers and resorts resulted in mutually beneficial relationships, where the hotel was able to acquire high-quality, local veg-etables and fish, and local suppliers profited by having an exclusive contractual agreement with the resort. Such arrangements contribute to changing the depend-ency relationships that have long existed between developing countries and foreign suppliers and moves the relationships between tourism services and local popula-tions from one of conflict to one of symbiosis (Telfer & Wall, 1996: 651).

Another important part of community involvement in the benefits of tourism is education or awareness building. This aspect of community tourism reflects all of Scheyvens' (1999) types of empowerment, as it produces economic, political, social and psychological results. Community awareness of tourism is important, for as Din (1993) suggests, action by destination residents in tourism initiatives requires them to be informed and knowledgeable about the industry and its potential effects. While residents of developed countries may be able to provide valuable insight into tourism development owing to their experiences as host and tourists (Murphy, 1988), in the developing world residents have little first-hand knowledge about being tourists, for relatively few of them have ever been privileged to travel outside their home regions. Thus, effective methods of building public awareness are important if residents are expected to be full participants.

Community awareness-building efforts, in many cases, are necessary in teaching residents how they can support tourism and benefit from it (Inskeep, 1994; Lynn, 1992). By building knowledge in destination communities, local people can be placed in a better position to determine their own needs and direct tourism devel-opment in their own communities (Hall, 1988; Din, 1993; Korten, 1980; Timothy, 2000).

Several actions can be taken by governments to allow residents to become in-volved in the benefits of tourism. As mentioned previously, it is the small-scale, family-run businesses that tend to have the most positive economic benefits in host communities. In this way, residents are employed and local products are utilised, thereby cutting back substantially on economic leakage to the outside. When gov-ernments allow community members to open their own businesses in the formal and informal sectors, benefits of this nature can be spread more broadly through society. Although the government of Indonesia has had problems with this issue in the past to the extent that informal tourism enterprises were threatened by military action (Shoji, 1991), recent years have seen improvements. For example, that street vendors in Yogyakarta, Indonesia, have been legalised and recognised by government officials, which is not the case in many developing countries, is a testimony that efforts are being made to provide opportunities for residents to benefit from tourism. Vendors have been permitted to form cooperatives to assist them in financial matters and in negotiations with government agencies and suppliers (Timothy & Wall, 1997). Similarly, small guesthouses in the heavy tourist areas of Yogyakarta have been afforded legal recognition, are encouraged to function and occasionally even receive small amounts of financial aid from the provincial government (Timothy, 1999).

Officials can also play an important role in building public awareness of tourism through media campaigns, education courses for residents involved in tourism (formally and informally), and public meetings. This is particularly important in regions of the world where economic and social circumstances have kept locals from having experiences as travellers. Some of these efforts are beginning to pay off in the developing world where governments are offering training courses to residents, but are also passing along vital information on being hosts by means of television, newspaper, and brochure campaigns (Lynn, 1992; Timothy, 2000).

Obstacles to Community Tourism Development

While the goals of community-based tourism are commendable and worthwhile to pursue, and their contributions to sustainable development are obvious, many barriers to their operationalisation exist. This is particularly the case in the less developed world.

Power: Socio-political traditions

Perhaps the biggest barrier to community-based tourism is the strong traditional views of power concentration that are still strong in many developing regions. The Big Man system, for example, a long-established village social order of power in the Solomon Islands, now has broad-based implications for business and politics (Lipscomb, 1998). From the community perspective, it is common in traditional societies for people to see the center of power as a leader or group of leaders, who will make decisions that are for the common good of society. From the leaders' perspective, representational democracy is unnecessary, so that dominant national and local groups of elites sometimes deliberately keep residents in a subordinate position (de Kadt, 1979b; Haywood, 1988). According to Tosun (2000: 621),

> in some ... developing nations although there is a formal structure of constitutional, multiparty democracy, these democratic institutions and regulations are not shared with the majority. That is to say, in these countries democracy is limited to business elites and state elites...Elites have a fear that the propertyless and uneducated masses could use their numerical strength to take care of their interests through political power or coercion. Therefore, they do not want to

share fruits of democracy with the hitherto excluded who constitute the major-ity in many developing countries.

This customary view of power nearly always precludes grassroots participation in tourism, and it concentrates decision-making authority in the hands on only a few of the privileged class (see Chapter 9 on the political economy of tourism). On the island of Java, for instance, concepts of power have long centred, and continue to centre, on a single ruler, who personifies the solidarity of society (Geertz, 1967). This person, or group of people, by nature makes decisions for the good of every-one. Common people have little choice but to accept what the head determines, for to disagree would be disrespectful and would bring humiliation upon the source of authority (Anderson, 1972; Moedjanto, 1986). According to Anderson (1972: 52),

> there is no inherent contradiction between the accumulation of central power and the well being of the collectivity, indeed the two are interrelated. The wel-fare of the collectivity does not depend on the activities of its individual components but on the concentrated energy of the center. The center's funda-mental obligation is to itself. If this obligation is fulfilled, popular welfare will necessarily be assured.

Similar traditions of authority are common throughout the developing world (Dwivedi, 1994; Kamrava, 1993; Seligson & Passé-Smith, 1993). Although, this problem is certainly not endemic to less-developed regions alone, for in much of the developed world, democratic traditions have not yet engaged people in control of their communities (Fitton, 1996).

Gender and ethnicity

As mentioned previously, women and ethnic minorities (or majorities who have little power as in South Africa prior to 1994) have customarily been relegated to the margins of decision-making and the benefits of tourism. This treatment also has its roots in the socio-political traditions described earlier, for most power structures are patriarchal, operating at the exclusion of women and minorities. This has led to an under representation of a huge population segment in most countries of the world.

According to some cultural customs, women must be chaperoned when in the company of men and are encouraged (or compelled) not to drive or venture far from home. These stipulations restrict the types of employment that can be undertaken. Similarly, it is often the women's place to keep the closest ties with extended family, home and village life. As a result, they are more likely than men are to return to their villages for important religious and family occasions. In these ways, traditional gender roles sometime determine what types of employment are most suitable or even possible for women (Timothy 2001) and may exclude them from participating in decision-making altogether (see Chapter 6 on tourism employment).

Information accessibility

One of the primary constraints for locally owned businesses is marketing difficulties in less developed countries. The primary target market is an international one, not domestic. Village-based ventures generally lack the capacity to market themselves internationally (Lipscomb, 1998: 192) and can succumb to abandonment when visible success is not apparent immediately at the outset (Edington & Edington, 1997). Limited access to advertising outlets, reservation systems and adequate transportation services also contributes to a lack of ability on some people's part to be business owners (Britton, 1987a). With the growth and spread of the Internet, however, it is likely that more small businesses, even in the developing world, will have more opportunities to participate in the global information system.

Lack of awareness

The relative newness of the industry itself in most places has led to inadequate local expertise in the area of community-based tourism. One manifestation of this is a lack of proper training among tourism officials, which is an important barrier to allowing community input into the process. In the developing world, there appears to be a general dearth of understanding about implementing local involvement in tourism development (Jenkins, 1980a) and a general unawareness of the need for, and benefits of, community tourism development.

Likewise, there is a lack of understanding by residents about tourism. This prevents many people from becoming involved in decision-making and in the benefits of tourism. Lipscomb (1998: 193), for example, relates how villagers in some South Pacific states want to attract tourists, but they have trouble understanding why foreigners would want to visit their villages and what activities they would like to do. Furthermore, a common belief is that if they build a traditional house for accommodating tourists, in spite of location and accessibility, foreigners will come to visit, and they get upset when this does not happen.

A sense of inadequacy also appears to permeate developing societies. Many residents do not feel 'smart enough' or informed enough to participate in critical matters like tourism and feel that locals should not be involved (Timothy & Wall, 1997). Such a feeling is justified, however, for a true lack of knowledge can prevent effective dialogue at the community level (Tosun, 2000).

Economic issues

Unfortunately, opportunities for local ownership are not always equally accessible to the entire population. Distance of residence from key tourist sites, lack of education, social status and family connections may all contribute to this. Unequal access is exacerbated more when significant amounts of start-up capital are necessary.

Insufficient public funding is another limitation to community tourism. Financial constraints at lower levels of administration increase dependence on national governments, thereby strengthening the central government's grip on lower-level administrations (Tjatera, 1994). In addition, the involvement of stakeholders in decision-making is sometimes viewed by budget controllers as a luxury that can hardly be afforded in both money and time (Tosun, 2000).

Residents' low socioeconomic status may also keep them from becoming involved in tourism decision-making, for they are concerned more with making ends meet. For many people, it is difficult to think in the long term when their basic, short-term survival is in question (Timothy, 1999).

Lack of cooperation/partnerships

Tourism by nature is a diverse and multifaceted industry. It is comprised of a wide range of public and private agencies, service providers, residents and tourists. Thus, it is argued that a great deal of collaborative effort is necessary for success in developing tourism (Jamal & Getz, 1995; Parker, 1999). Despite this apparent need, few places have achieved high levels of cooperation in this regard. Timothy (1998) examines four types of cooperation that need to exist in developing sustainable tourism:

(1) cooperation between the private and public sectors (e.g. hotel sector and ministries of tourism);
(2) cooperation between government agencies (e.g. department of transportation and department of cultural affairs);
(3) cooperation between different levels of administration (e.g. national and provincial); and
(4) cross-border cooperation between same-level polities (e.g. state and state).

To this typology should also be added cooperation between private sector services.

Unfortunately, these genres of cooperation, or partnership, are rarely achieved in practice. Many of the constraints discussed so far contribute to a lack of collaborative efforts. A dearth of expertise and perhaps economic issues are good examples of this. From an administrative perspective, in developing countries there has traditionally been a lack of coordinated efforts among producers and regulators of tourism. Sectoral planning traditions, wherein each agency, or service provider, is most interested in achieving its own goals without discussing actions with other agencies and stakeholders who may have related interests, are common. This sometimes results from the existence of too many levels on the governmental hierarchy or the competition between agencies for public funding. It is also a result of ill-defined roles among agencies, overlap of responsibilities of government departments and lack of accountability (Tosun, 2000).

Peripherality

The peripheral nature of many communities throughout the world presents additional limitations. In the global economic sense, developing countries are on the world's periphery, which makes them more vulnerable to outside forces, such as the dependency relationships examined earlier. However, on a national level, peripherality also refers to regions on the physical national margins and areas of physical isolation. Such zones are often viewed by national leaders as unimportant in modernisation and economic development efforts. It is typical throughout the world for the more populated and industrial interiors to be favoured, which leads to a lack of administrative support and funding for economic development, including tourism, in peripheral regions. Peripherality also contributes to the marginalisation of residents' concerns during policy development. Thus, it is not surprising that national-level policies are often at odds with the needs and priorities of distant communities (Timothy & White, 1999).

Conclusion

This chapter has argued that community-based tourism provides a more sustainable alternative in destination areas than traditional mass tourism. Resident involvement in tourism decision-making will give traditionally under-represented groups a voice and will provide a great deal of local knowledge about local conditions. The knowledge base of indigenous groups and other residents has not yet been tapped commensurate with its importance and depth, for it is they who are often the best conservationists, sociologists and economists in matters of local concern and in environments unfamiliar to outside élites. Resident participation will also likely decrease hostility towards tourism developers and tourists themselves, for actions taken and their resultant impacts become the responsibility of the local population.

Likewise, the benefits of tourism must be allowed to accrue to local populations. Tourism development critics have long highlighted the leakage of tourist spending from destination communities or into the hands of local élites. Where possible, governments and community leaders should provide opportunities for residents to benefit financially from tourism by allowing and encouraging entrepreneurial activities. This will stimulate the growth of local economies and increase employment, because small-scale ventures more often have a positive economic effect than large-scale, exogenously motivated endeavors.

Despite the existence of socioeconomic and political barriers to community-based, or alternative, tourism, there is obvious potential for true local involvement. Such an approach may occur at the cost of mass tourism, but we must remember that even community-based tourism has the potential to become massive if not managed properly. In some parts of the world, there is little support for the community approach. However, as the industry's benefits are spread to more segments of society and as more people become aware of the impacts and opportunities of tourism, such notions will likely receive more widespread acceptance. This will, however, require a stronger commitment on the part of governments, developers, interest groups, community members themselves, and yes, foreign operators, than what has heretofore been expressed.

With an increase in political, social, economic, and psychological empowerment along these lines among residents and other stakeholders, tourism will have the potential to help meet local needs for development, bringing to fruition many of the goals of sustainability, including harmony, equity, balance, cultural integrity, and ecological conservation. Resident involvement in decision-making and the benefits of tourism will play a crucial role in making the transition from a destination of dependency to one of empowerment.

Chapter 6

Tourism Employment Issues in Developing Countries: Examples from Indonesia

JUDITH CUKIER

Introduction

Despite widespread and growing interest in tourism research, most studies have focused on aspects of tourism supply and demand, including the analysis of regional data of tourism destination trends (e.g. numbers of visitors, supply of facilities), rather than on more comprehensive views of tourism, including tourism employment and associated impacts. Although some of the literature does address tourism employment, the majority of these studies rely on discourse based on conjecture and not on empirical research (De Kadt, 1979b; Mathieson & Wall, 1982; Murphy, 1985; English, 1986; Pearce, 1987; Lea, 1988; 1993; Baum, 1993). It is argued that studies are needed which focus on tourism employment, specifically empirical studies that examine the consequences of tourism employment for the economies and cultures of developing countries since, to date, very little research exists in this area. The relationships between tourism and employment are complex and, although a number of human resource studies have been undertaken, negligible empirical data exist to shed light on questions such as the relationship between tourism employment and development, impacts on the informal sector, implications for gender roles and the relative status of tourism employment. In addition, research about tourism employment can contribute to the development of new models and concepts, thus contributing to the overall status of knowledge within tourism research. This chapter will present a framework that is well suited to the characteristics of tourism employment in developing countries.

Challenging 'Developed Country' Assumptions

Around the world, destination areas usually elect to become involved in tourism mainly because of the perceived economic benefits, primarily related to the acquisition of hard currency and improvements in balance of payments. However, expected enhancements in individual employee incomes and employment opportunities are also particularly attractive at the local level. Researchers have devoted considerable attention to sales and income generation at national, regional and local levels and, for example, sophisticated economic models incorporating multipliers and leakage have been used to analyse direct, indirect and induced sales and income effects of tourism (Archer, 1982; Fletcher, 1993). When compared with tourism sales and income, however, employment associated with tourism is a relatively neglected area of study. Although it is unclear why this is the case, it may be partially related to the frequent adoption of demand-side definitions of tourism and associated considerations of tourist expenditures when compared with supply-side definitions, as well as the difficulty of defining the tourist industry and those who are employed in it (Smith, 1988).

It is not difficult to find testimony from 'developed countries' concerning the seasonality, servile nature and low remuneration of tourism employment (Young, 1973; Turner, 1973; Duffield, 1982; Vaughan & Long, 1982; Bagguley, 1987; Urry, 1990b; Hudson & Townsend, 1992; Baum, 1993). At the same time, industry representatives frequently bemoan the difficulty of attracting and retaining employees with the required skills and commitment. These two perspectives may well be related. However, while the accuracy of such observations is not in question, at least for much of the 'developed' world, it is difficult to find empirical studies, particularly in developing countries, which provide evidence to support them. Furthermore, such observations may be culture-bound. There is evidence from developing countries that, although the higher managerial positions may often go to people from outside the immediate area, almost all employment opportunities associated with tourism, regardless of the level, may be highly valued and attractive to local residents, particularly when compared with the physically taxing work and low returns gained from many traditional occupations, such as farming and fishing (Cukier & Wall, 1994b, Cukier-Snow & Wall, 1993).

Investigation of employment in developing countries is frequently complicated by the widespread existence of multiple occupations and the prominence of the informal sector. Multiple employment refers to a situation in which an individual is employed in more than one activity, perhaps tending fields or teaching during the day, and performing traditional dances for tourists at night, or farming for part of the year and producing and selling arts and crafts to tourists when the agricultural cycle permits. The tourism informal sector refers to activities such as hawking souvenirs to tourists, acting as an unofficial guide and a variety of other occupations that are excluded from official employment statistics and may be of dubious legality (Cukier & Wall, 1994a). Multiple employment and the magnitude of the informal sector make the interpretation of official tourism employment statistics a speculative art. Thus, there is not a great deal known about the attributes of tourism employment in developing countries and, when other related elements, such as gender, training, working conditions, status and migration impacts are added, it becomes evident that tourism employment, whether direct or indirect, is a subject which awaits empirical examination. Therefore, it is important to examine tourism employment in developing countries in order to establish an empirical basis which may necessitate challenging the limited nature of developed country conceptions and to derive new and more appropriate conceptions which can describe and explain tourism employment in developing countries.

In summary, knowledge about tourism employment has largely been derived from research conducted in a developed country context and what knowledge has been established specifically for developing countries has not been based on empirical research in the tourism sector. This chapter will present results of tourism employment research conducted in Bali, Indonesia from 1991–95 and more recently, in 1999.

Tourism and Employment

Tourism creates a multitude of employment opportunities in both the formal and informal sectors. Additionally, tourism may create three types of employment opportunities: direct, indirect and induced. *Direct employment* refers to employment generated in, for example, hotels, restaurants, tour companies and nightclubs. *Indirect employment* refers to people working in activities that at times are dependent on tourism, and includes the construction trades, professionals such as doctors who occasionally serve hotel employees and tourists, merchants, gasoline station attendants and others who are less dependent but still benefit from tourism. *Induced employment* refers to the additional employment resulting from the effects of the tourism multiplier as local residents re-spend the additional money they have earned (Mathieson & Wall, 1982). Tourism employment can be described as the combination of all direct, indirect and induced employment, in both the formal and informal sectors, resulting from the tourism industry (see Chapter 3 on the economics of tourism).

Tourism employment impacts

Various researchers have attempted to demonstrate the impact of tourism as a formal sector employer. In Bermuda, for example, Dix (1989) estimated that tourism supported 70% of all employment on the island. However, the impact of tourism on employment is underestimated when viewed solely in terms of direct employment. That is, the actual impact is far greater when considering the effect on the economy as a whole through the addition of both indirect and induced employment. Although it is possible to gauge the impact of expected tourist expenditures on direct and indirect employment (Mappisammeng, 1991; Booth, 1988), a lack of accurate figures for the total numbers of people employed in either indirect or induced tourism activities makes it difficult to calculate how many people are affected.[1]

Varley (1978) hypothesised that the volume of indirect employment generated by tourism was dependent on the degree of linkage between the tourism sector and other sectors of the economy. In his studies in Fiji, he noted that the higher the degree of integration and diversification in the economy was, the higher the amount of indirect employment generated. Additionally, cyclical variations in the volume of tourists or their expenditures do not necessarily affect the absolute numbers of people employed, but definitely affect the earnings of those employed in the tourism sector, particularly season to season.

A few researchers have attempted to examine the impacts of tourism employment on the informal sector. In Indonesia, it is estimated that more than 50% of the general labour force is absorbed into the informal sector and that consumer-oriented tertiary activity is the sector that accommodates the greatest number of informal workers (Wirosardjono, 1984). Much of the employment generated by tourism is in the form of self-employed, small-scale entrepreneurs including guides, small store owners, shop workers and vendors (Echtner, 1995). The employment effects of the informal sector are often excluded in the assessment of tourism employment because official employment data do not include this sector. Additionally, the indirect employment effects are dependent on the degree of linkage between the tourism sectors and other producing sectors (Varley, 1978; Sharpley, 1994). The impacts of tourism employment on the informal sector will be discussed in greater detail in a subsequent section.

Although tourism employment is usually analysed in terms of economic benefit, the social and cultural implications of tourism employment also deserve consideration. As stated by Pleumarom (1994), the 'development' of 'underdeveloped areas' requires more than capital input and technology transfer. Cultures too have to be reconciled with economic competition and integration. Tourism provides a means to achieve both. Through the creation of employment, tourism can provide an opportunity for the local population to increase its income and improve its standard of living. Furthermore, from a social viewpoint, tourism employment can positively affect quality of life through increases in social status or the provision of new opportunities for youth and women or negatively by placing additional stress on the society through the influx of new migrants to the area, increased urbanization and increased consumerism as a result of a demonstration effect. The extent to which the population benefits economically and socially is dependent on many factors, including the number of jobs held by expatriates or new migrants to the area, the level of skill required for the job and the type of tourist resort (De Kadt, 1979a: Sharpley, 1994) (see Chapters 5 and 7).

Tourism employment in developing countries

As stated earlier, developing countries become involved in tourism primarily because of expectations of improved economic conditions through an increase in employment and associated income. In contrast to developed countries, where a large proportion of tourism employment is seasonal and low paying, (and thus not considered attractive), employment opportunities in developing countries are more limited and the relative payment higher for employment in the tourism industry than in other economic sectors. Thus, even in the case in which employment is seasonal, tourism jobs may be viewed with great favour. Evidence to support this view has been found in Tahiti where employment in tourism is seen as an 'exciting, clean and modern way to earn one's living' (Cleverdon, 1979: 77). Blanton (1981: 120) provided further support for this view in his statement that 'where there are formal tourism training schools to which students are admitted from the general population, it is not safe to assume that the [tourism] industry worker is a marginal person'. Harrison (1992a; 1994) presented evidence from many Caribbean countries where tourism employment was the predominant employer and was, therefore, looked upon favourably by the local population.

The quality of employment created by tourism is difficult to assess, comprising as it does factors as diverse as money, skill required and options available. English (1986) noted that hotel jobs, for example, appear menial but are usually often better paid than the traditional alternatives. Many authors (Varley, 1978; Pongsapich, 1982; Bridger & Winpenny, 1983) have argued that, in countries in which a large proportion of the population has only primary education, work in tourism can be both appropriate and appealing, especially to the younger generation, who clearly prefer tourism employment over the rigours of traditional sectors such as agriculture and fishing. As one example, salaries for crafts people in Bali were well below the salaries paid by international hotels but, according to Francillon (1979), they were still higher than those paid to local farmers and peasants. Additionally, in Indonesia, it was reported that 'imitation' crafts are produced and sold side-by-side with 'fine art' crafts, the former subsidizing the latter to supplement local income and employment (Dix, 1989). For example, in Tenganen, Bali, authentic, traditional graphic depictions of the Ramayana on Lontar palms sell for US$150 alongside cheap imitations that sell for US$10. Bridger and Winpenny (1983) cautioned that the effect of the labour shift from traditional sectors, especially labour-intensive agriculture, towards tourism should be carefully contemplated.

In their evaluation of the pros and cons of tourism in developing countries, Peppelenbosch and Tempelman (1989) were sceptical of new employment opportunities created. They had misgivings resulting from the perceived seasonal nature of tourism employment, and the anticipated decline in agricultural labour as a result of youth being lured to the 'glamorous' tourism industry, although they did not provide empirical evidence to support this view. Pleumarom (1994) argued that the economic benefits of tourism had been overestimated and that there was a high rate of foreign exchange leakage from developing to developed countries. She further contended that those employed in tourism ventures were poorly paid and their jobs were menial.

A number of researchers (Elkan, 1975; Varley, 1978; Cleverdon, 1979; Smaoui, 1979; Bond & Ladman, 1972; Rodenberg, 1980; Van Houts, 1983; Lever, 1987) have conducted case studies examining the cost of creating tourism employment compared to jobs in other economic sectors, such as manufacturing. Discussion has focused on whether tourism can create employment more 'cheaply' than other sectors of the economy, that is, whether less capital input is required for each job created within the tourism sector than in other economic sectors. Case studies have resulted in different, often contradictory, findings. Varley (1978), in an investigation of tourism in Fiji, found that the cost of a tourism job was high compared to other sectors of the economy. Conversely, Cleverdon (1979) found that, in Tahiti, the cost of creating a tourism job was comparable to that in other sectors of the economy, whilst Elkan (1975) in his work in Kenya and Tanzania, Rodenburg (1980) in his work in Bali, and Bond and Ladman (1972) in their work in Mexico, found that the cost of tourism jobs was lower than for other economic sectors. However, both Elkan and Rodenburg maintained that jobs created in smaller establishments were less expensive than those created in larger establishments. In each of the studies indicated, only direct tourism employment was analysed and conflicting evidence may be due in part to the differing types of tourism development found within each case study country. For example, tourism 'job cost' can vary depending on the stage of tourism development at a particular destination, with some researchers arguing that relatively 'new' tourism developments have associated higher costs of job creation with costs dropping as the age of the development increases.

It is evident from these examples that many of the observations regarding tourism employment are dependent on the relative level of development or wealth of the society, with specific differences between developed and developing countries. From the existing case studies and literature, a number of generalisations can be made about the relationship between tourism and employment in developing countries. First, there is a positive but widely varying correlation between the income-generating effects of tourism and the creation of employment, meaning that high returns from the industry correspond roughly to proportionately more jobs. Second, employment is influenced by the type of tourist product, with some types being more labour intensive or having a higher capital–employment ratio than others. Third, the type of skills available locally will have an effect on the type of employment created, as illustrated by the relatively high demand for unskilled or semi-skilled workers, particularly during earlier stages of tourism development. Fourth, evidence from developing countries indicates that, although managerial positions often go to people from other countries, almost all employment opportunities associated with tourism are highly prized and attractive from the perspective of local residents, particularly when compared to the low-paying and comparatively arduous agricultural labour alternative (Cukier-Snow & Wall, 1993). Fifth, although tourism employment may be seasonal or part-time and, thus, may have little effect in reducing overall unemployment levels, this is partially offset by the prevalence of multiple employment in developing countries.[2] In addition, many seasonal tourism workers may earn enough in the high tourist season to compensate for lower remuneration in the low season. Finally, employment opportunities are created for women and students who previously had little or no opportunity to work within the formal sector (Lea, 1988). Unfortunately, not much can be said about tourism's role in employment generation without reference to the specific case studies, the type of tourism product and the nature of government policies. This renders each case study less broadly applicable to the development of theory than is desirable and thus, case study comparisons are crucial.

Tourism employment: a comparison of developed and developing countries

Numerous differences exist between tourism employment in developed and developing countries. One important difference is the abundance of available labour in developing countries compared to developed countries, resulting in greater pressure among developing country populations to seek employment and higher rates of unemployment, underemployment and multiple employment. In most developing countries, much of the population has more than one occupation and, therefore, single employment data are often misleading. Opportunities for informal labour are created within the tourism industry and, although these occupations are difficult to measure and monitor, they constitute important employment opportunities that should be considered when examining the impact of tourism employment (Mathieson & Wall, 1982).

Although the seasonal nature of tourism employment is roughly similar across developed and developing countries[3], its impact will be different across the two development levels, depending on the prevalence of multiple employment. Although multiple employment is predominantly an issue in developing countries, communities in some developed countries in which unemployment is high, or where

> occupational pluralism (whether through conventional economic activity such as crafting, fishing and knitting, or through domestic commitment) is the accepted norm, part-time or seasonal work in the tourism industry can be an advantage rather than a problem. (Vaughan & Long, 1982: 29).

Related to this is the fact that, in developing countries, a much larger proportion of the economy is devoted to primary sector activities than in developed countries; these primary activities include traditional occupations of fishing and farming which are both physically demanding and relatively poorly paid. Thus, employment in tourism, with its comparatively higher wages and perceived physical ease, becomes an attractive alternative. An associated issue is that developing countries often have less diversified economies than developed countries and thus have a greater dependence upon fewer sectors for overall employment opportunities.

Another difference relates to characteristics of a country's labour force. Generally, populations of developing countries are less educated and have fewer of the necessary skills for higher level jobs within the tourism sector. As mentioned previously, many of the higher level jobs in developing countries are filled by outsiders (English, 1986), whereas in developed countries, these positions are largely filled by the local population (Pearce, 1989a). Migration of workers to the tourism destination is common to both developed and developing countries, although developed countries' tourist destinations may be in a stronger position to absorb new migrants due to their more diversified and stable economic base and presence of integrated social services.

Government policies also have an effect on tourism employment issues. Specifically, the role that developed country and developing country governments adopt regarding employment policy differs. In developing countries, high-level government intervention in, as well as expectations toward returns from, tourism development are common whereas, in developed countries, higher levels of government usually play a smaller role with the private sector, local business lobbyists and municipalities picking up the tourism promotion role. In developed countries, the tourism industry is largely controlled by the private sector and, thus, employment opportunities tend to follow a capitalistic, free-market approach, resulting in high competition and strict regulations against the opportunistic development of the informal sector. In developing countries, where resources are scarce and employment opportunities are more restricted (in part due to high and rapidly expanding populations), explicit government policies are sometimes created which encourage tourism employment in both the formal and informal sectors, although empirical evidence in Wahnschafft (1982) and Kermath and Thomas (1992) negated this view. Jenkins (1980: 27) elaborated on difficulties in the role of government in the tourism industry:

> The governments of developed and developing countries share many areas of responsibility. But in the developing countries the problem of resource scarcity and consequently allocation is acute. Strong government control is necessary to prevent exploitation and obvious waste, and to ensure that the benefits from tourism are optimized. Tourism in developed countries can be regarded as a mainly social activity with economic consequences: in developing countries it is largely an economic activity with social consequences.

It is difficult to point to explicit studies comparing the degree to which the informal sector differs across developed and developing countries. Most studies of tourism employment in both developed and developing countries have dealt almost exclusively with direct employment and, thus, tourism employment studies in both developed and developing countries have predominantly dealt with the formal sector.[4] Additionally, studies that have gone further in attempting measurement of indirect employment experience difficulty since this phenomenon is usually only 'estimated' through the use of employment multipliers. Because of the great difficulty in enumerating and identifying the informal sector, and perhaps due to a research bias introduced through developed country research methods, the informal sector is usually disregarded in studies of tourism employment. The neglect of the informal sector is not surprising when one considers that this sector is virtually non-existent in developed countries where most empirical work to date has occurred.

Employment: The Dynamics of Formal and Informal Sectors

The magnitude of the informal sector in developing countries is extremely significant – it has been estimated that as much as 40–50% of the labour force may be involved in informal sector activities (Winpenny, 1978; Bromley & Gerry, 1979; Hope, 1993) – and thus it is crucial to examine this sector as well as the formal sector in studies of tourism employment. Many researchers have presented theories and concepts regarding the nature of formal and informal employment sectors, ranging from dualistic arguments to broader, continuum-type models. In the 1960s and early 1970s, the prevailing theoretical view of employment's contribution to development was 'economic duality' (Todaro, 2000), in which the labour economy was seen as being divided into both formal and informal sectors. Davies (1979: 88) summed up what he felt was the crucial difference between the two sectors – their 'mode of production':

> The formal sector is based on highly-developed social productive forces; the informal sector is not: both its means of production and its techniques of production are non-capital intensive. In the formal sector the means of production are privately owned by a small class, and are operated on by workers for the benefit of that owning class. In the informal sector the means of production are in general owned by those who operate them. In the formal sector production relations are based on a highly developed division of labour, with hierarchical relations between supervisor and worker, both nationally and internationally, whereas in the informal sector such division of labour as there is, is rudimentary, and horizontal rather than vertical. Thus there are obvious and important differences between the modes of production of the two sectors.

According to the ILO (1972), informal sector activities are characterised by ease of entry, reliance on indigenous resources, family ownership of enterprises, small scale of operation, labour intensive and adaptive technology, skills acquired outside the formal school system and unregulated and competitive markets. This ILO definition of the informal sector has since gained wide acceptance (Cole &

Fayissa, 1991). Hope (1993: 157) defined the informal sector as 'a process of income-generation characterised by the single feature of being unregulated by the institutions of society in an environment in which comparable activities are regulated'. Todaro (2000) interpreted the existence of dualism as characterized by different hierarchical orders which allow for the coexistence and the inter-relation of the strong (formal sector) and the weak (informal sector). He further asserted that this coexistence is chronic in nature rather than a transitional stage, and that the degree of economic disparity between the strong and the weak in developing countries has tended to increase and that the strong actually suppress the development of the weak.

In the early 1970s, the formal and informal sectors were seen as distinct sub-units of the economy, with the formal sector economically dominating the informal sector, largely as a result of government policy that favoured the formal sector (ILO, 1972). However, subsequent research suggested that the informal sector could be further classified into *skilled*, *unskilled* and *semi-skilled* workers (Davies, 1979). This classification was seen as necessary as researchers realized that, as an example, a semi-skilled worker within the informal sector had skills comparable to a semi-skilled worker within the formal sector. Similarly, Winpenny (1978) classified the informal sector into two sub-categories: 'the community of the poor' and the 'intermediate sector', whose latter members were often earning above the minimum wage level. According to Wahnschafft (1982), the formal–informal dichotomy was better represented by a continuum of enterprises, where characteristics varied with mode of production, market structures and government policy. Bromley and Gerry (1979), in attempting to classify types of employment, depicted employment categories along a continuum stretching from the least autonomous, 'stable wage work' to the most autonomous, 'true self-employment'. They described five basic categories of employment formality: (1) stable wage work; (2) short-term wage work; (3) disguised wage work; (4) dependent work; and (5) true self-employment.

Davies (1979) argued that the formal and informal sectors not only complemented each other but that each needed the other in order to exist and, in fact, formed a symbiotic relationship. The informal sector depended on formal wages and demand generated in the formal sector for a great proportion of its markets. It also depended on the formal sector for supplies of certain inputs. Conversely, the formal sector depended on the informal sector for low-cost labour and goods and services (Davies, 1979). Castells and Portes (1989) argued that individual workers may switch between both the formal and informal activities on a daily basis. In reference to Southeast Asia, McGee's (1982) research supported the argument that the two sectors (formal and informal) supported each other and did not necessarily compete. The informal sector, which he found to be growing at a faster rate than the formal sector, filled a niche left empty by the formal sector. Hope (1993) concurred that, in some developing countries, the formal sector must conduct business with the informal sector in order to acquire hard currency, basic goods and services, and to take advantage of the informal sector's efficient production techniques and access to inputs. He argued that this linkage of formal with informal could result in lucrative benefits for workers in the informal sector, a contrast to the widely-held belief that the informal sector is a highly economically marginalized group. Contrasting with this view, Miles-Doan (1992) presented evidence from Jordan in which she found that informal sector workers were often better off financially than those employed within the formal sector. Chu (1992) found further evidence that contradicted the 'marginality thesis',[5] arguing that the income of some informal sector workers was often higher than that of formal sector workers, the division between large and small enterprises was often unclear, women, children and migrants were not always over-represented in the informal sector and the same person may be involved in both sectors simultaneously.

In contrast to traditional employment theory, which stated that the informal sector would 'disappear' as a country achieved 'development', more modern views assert that this dynamic sector should not be simplistically viewed as an economic role that will vanish with the processes of modernization and urbanization (see Chapter 2 for a discussion on development theory). Within tourism, as in other industries in developing countries, the informal sector is a vigorous and notable element and, thus, efforts should be made to better understand informal participation in tourism and its relationship to the formal sector. Within the informal sector there is a growing differential in socioeconomic status among workers. Ebery and Forbes (1985), for example, argued that some hawkers were acquiring a higher status than some formal sector employees because their enterprise required skill, initiative and some capital investment.

The ILO argued that understanding the informal sector provides a key to solving the increasing problems of employment and inequality in developing countries. The informal sector generally operates without legal recognition or protection and has, therefore, been considered by governments to be economically and politically marginalised (Wahnschafft, 1982; Sethuraman, 1992). According to Lewis's neoclassical labour absorption theory (Chu, 1992: 421), 'the marginality thesis argues that overpopulation and rapid migration to the cities have overwhelmed the modern industry's job creation capacity'. Informal sector employment has, thus, emerged as a response by the jobless to cope with their situation and, therefore, informal work is seen to be peripheral to 'modern' industrial production (Chu, 1992). Ebery and Forbes (1985) challenged the traditional belief that the informal sector had an unlimited capacity to absorb labour. In the case of fish distribution in Ujung Pandang, Indonesia (an informal sector activity), the numbers involved in the trade have increased slowly and are unlikely to increase at a rate faster than the population growth rate. The informal sector is no longer seen as merely a receiving station for extra labour but as a complementary alternative to the formal sector (Rachbini, 1991).

Tourism employment 'formality'

The informal sector has generally been described in the employment literature as a marginalized and relatively poor community: a community which barely manages to make ends meet. These descriptions or characteristics of the informal sector as a whole differ from the *tourism* informal sector. One possible reason for this is that the tourism industry involves mainly wealthy consumers (even domestic tourists and 'backpackers' are comparatively wealthy) and, thus, the informal tourism workers fare better than other informal sector workers who predominantly cater to the local poor. The demonstration effect associated with tourism in developing countries may also be a factor that distinguishes the tourism informal sector from the general informal sector. Because the tourism informal sector workers are exposed to foreign lifestyles, languages and materialism, they may be more inclined than the non-tourism informal sector to emulate foreigners, for example, by obtaining higher levels of education or skill or to adopt their mannerisms (Cukier, 1996) (see Chapter 7).

Tourism also creates opportunities for informal sector workers within the formal sector. Many jobs created by the tourism industry do not require a high skill level although, as the industry matures in an area, the number of skilled and professional jobs filled by the local population increases. Thus, particularly in the earlier stages of tourism development, tourism in developing countries has the potential to generate direct benefits for a large proportion of the population. Employees in tourism facilities (hotels, restaurants, shops) are drawn from these lower income groups, since a large number of the jobs require a minimal skill level and, thus, minimal prior training. Many of these jobs are filled by individuals previously making up the informal sector (English, 1986). However, informal sector workers do not always consider employment within the formal sector as a natural, or even desirable, progression. For example, in Nairobi, Winpenny (1978) found that a majority of informal sector workers were content with their occupation and were not seeking employment in the formal sector.

Two notable studies have addressed the issue of the dynamics of the formal and informal sectors within the tourism industry: Wahnschafft (1982) for Thailand, and Kermath and Thomas (1992) in the Dominican Republic. Wahnschafft (1982) found that informal sector tourism workers had developed many skills (foreign languages, marketing techniques, equipment maintenance skills) despite the official discouragement of their activities by the government. The government policy was to restrict informal sector activities to two designated areas – a policy which resulted in heavy economic losses for the workers since tourists did not frequent the designated areas. One of the few studies to address the issue of the dynamics of the formal and informal sectors within the tourism industry was conducted by Kermath and Thomas (1992) in the Dominican Republic. They hypothesised that, as a destination's tourism industry evolved, the informal sector would grow in response to increased employment opportunities, but that as the destination developed, the informal sector, largely as a result of government policies which favoured the formal sector, would either be forced out of the tourism area or would be absorbed into it. Their results, although supportive of their hypothesis, were not conclusive since, although informal sector employees did leave the immediate tourism destination area, their absolute numbers on the periphery of the destination area did not decline. In contrast, I have found that in developing countries, where the presence of the informal sector is well established, accessible and tolerated by government, the sector continues to increase and diversify as the tourism industry develops at a destination and attracts migrants in search of employment opportunities (Cukier, 1996).

The Status of Tourism Employment

The servile nature and low remuneration attributed to tourism occupations in the developed country literature may not be representative of developing countries (Young, 1973; Turner, 1973; Diamond, 1977; Duffield, 1982; Vaughan & Long, 1982; Bagguley, 1987; Urry, 1990b; Pigram, 1990; Johnson & Thomas, 1992; Hudson & Townsend, 1992; Baum, 1993). Almost all employment opportunities associated with tourism in developing countries may be accorded a high status by the local population. The reasons for this include the relatively high salary of tourism occupations (even those within the informal sector); the relative physical ease of many tourism occupations compared to traditional agricultural labour; and the security of some occupations and the flexibility of others. In addition, perspectives on the servile nature often associated with tourism occupations may be strongly culturally based. For example, in many 'non-developed' cultures, service towards others (especially the wealthy) and the service industry in general are allocated a high status and importance in society (Cukier, 1998a).

In developed countries, occupations in the tourism sector are considered to be of low status, partly due to the low remuneration when compared to other sectors and to the comparatively low emphasis many 'developed' cultures place on personal services. Turner (1973), commenting on developed countries, referred to tourism as the most subservient industry and argued, along with Urry (1990b), that tourism work was servile in nature. This view has persisted for decades. For example, Hudson and Townsend (1992) also argued that tourism employment in Britain was characterised by low-quality work and was accorded an associated low status. In contrast, in many developing countries, particularly in Southeast Asia, local cultures have placed a higher value on 'service' towards others, a fact which is reflected in the relatively high status accorded to tourism occupations. The potential for a change in social status and associated shift in attitudes was speculated upon in a 1976 UNESCO report on the sociocultural impacts of tourism. The report identified two traditional employment sectors, fishing and agriculture, whose employees would undergo considerable social change with a shift to tourism employment, primarily due to an increase in social status.

Some developed country researchers have transferred developed country attributes of tourism employment status to those in developing countries, often without any empirical basis (Young, 1973; Turner, 1973; Diamond, 1977; Duffield, 1982; Vaughan & Long, 1982; Richter, 1986; Bagguley, 1987; Rajotte, 1987; Pigram, 1990; Baum, 1993). As noted previously, tourism employment in developed countries is thought by some to be of low status and sometimes degrading. Elkan (1975: 124) adopted this view with reference to tourism employment in Africa. He described the Masai as the 'one time proud [people who] now demean themselves to selling trinkets and begging for sweets'. However, this appeared to be his opinion of the situation rather than a reporting of the Masai opinions on the status of their new-found positions. In contrast, Pongsapich (1982) found that in Thailand, young people who were fluent in English or other foreign languages often became tour guides, a position that was considered a good job in terms of both pay and status. She went on to state that 'guiding', an informal sector job, ranked higher in status than many other formal tourism occupations such as bussing tables, washing dishes or working as a janitor. Pizam *et al.* (1994) compared perceptions toward tourism by tourism employees in both Florida and Fiji. They noted that, overall, Fijian residents accorded a higher status to employment in the tourism industry than Floridians, a finding they attributed to the greater availability of well-paid options in Florida compared to the more limited and less lucrative alternative employment opportunities in Fiji.

Occasionally, the opinion of researchers regarding the status of tourism employment in developing countries is ambiguous. For example, Lovel and Feuerstein (1992) stated that most people working in tourism in New Caledonia, Fiji and Hawaii were given low status positions such as waiters, clerks, maintenance staff and maids. However, in the same article they commented that jobs in tourism were often better paid than the alternatives, resulting in labour being attracted away from other sectors to the tourism sector. They provided the example of nurses in the Pacific region who left their jobs to work in the tourism sector. Such ambiguity regarding the true status of tourism employment suggests that more research is needed.

Gender Role Differentiation within Tourism Employment

Gender and development literature which addresses employment has largely focused on women's work in agricultural and industrial production. However, it should not be assumed that findings of research on agricultural and factory employment are directly applicable to tourism. Only limited gender research has addressed service industries in general, and tourism employment in particular, although in the mid 1990s some publications began to provide overviews of gender and tourism investigations[6]. Because of the relative 'newness' of mass tourism, many new employment opportunities exist for women, both within the formal and informal tourism sectors. In order to appreciate the impact of tourism employment fully, the traditional roles of men and women within a society must be examined. In particular, have the traditional role differentiations in developing countries been transferred to the tourism industry? In order to examine this question, issues such as the traditional and tourism-specific roles of men and women must be considered.

Gender and development: an employment perspective

When considering employment opportunities for women in developing countries, women's 'triple role' must be considered. Moser (1991) describes this role succinctly:

> In most low-income households, women's work includes not only the reproductive work . . . required to guarantee the maintenance and reproduction of the labour force but also productive work, often as secondary income earners. In rural areas this usually takes the form of agricultural work, while in urban areas women frequently work in informal sector enterprises . . . In addition women are involved in community managing work undertaken at a local community settlement level in both urban and rural contexts.

Much of the gender literature dealing with employment has placed blame on the international division of labour, patriarchy and colonial legacy for blocking women's access to formal sector employment which has been seen as conferring higher status and pay and requiring higher formal education (Osirim, 1992). Thus, the informal sector remains a principal employer of women in developing countries, in which a gender-based division of labour is nonetheless apparent (Osirim, 1992).

Gender issues in tourism employment

Kinnaird *et al.* (1994, in Swain, 1995: 249) identified issues crucial for understanding gender in tourism. They pointed out that tourism and its operations are derived from gendered societies structured by gender relations which, over time, 'inform and are informed by the interconnected economic, political, social, cultural and environmental dimensions of all societies involved in tourism development'. Additionally, power, control and equality issues are explained partly through race, class and gender relations, and thus, an examination of gender roles in tourism becomes crucial. Tourism employment both reinforces and transforms gender divisions of labour. Kinnaird *et al.* (1994: 16) asserted that the aspects of tourism employment important for regional development are the quality and type of work available, 'the differential access of men and women to these employment opportunities, the seasonality of employment and the existing and new gender divisions of labour generated . . . '. They further stated that gender relations and roles are an important element of authenticity and tradition, and that these can change according to the demands of the process of tourism development (Kinnaird *et al.* 1994). Hence, gender issues as they pertain to tourism employment merit empirical investigation in a developing country context.

Work within the informal sector has enabled women to more easily fulfil their domestic responsibilities, one of their triple roles (reproductive, productive and community management) (Moser, 1991). Since women in such activities are often self-employed, their work schedules are flexible, allowing them to spend time at home with children when necessary or to bring pre-school-aged children to work with them (Osirim, 1992). According to Hope (1993) and Chu (1992), one important characteristic of the informal economy is the increasing rate of participation of women as an entrepreneurial group. In fact, research in Bali has shown that many women are, in fact, participating in the informal tourism sector (Cukier, *et al.*, 1996; Cukier & Wall, 1995; Bras & Dahles, 1998; Dixon, 2000).

In both developed and developing countries, most tourism researchers agree that tourism employment creates increased job opportunities for women (Turner, 1973; Young, 1973; UNESCO, 1976; De Kadt, 1979b; Mathieson & Wall, 1982; Vaughan & Long, 1983; Van Houts, 1983; Monk & Alexander, 1986; Lever, 1987; Lerch & Levy, 1990). These authors further theorised that the introduction of women into the labour force via tourism employment could cause disharmony at home and threaten traditional family structure and stability. However, Van Doorn (1989: 79,) in his discussion of Cyprus, found that 'the improved financial status of females did not create conflicts between parents and children or husbands and wives, nor did it challenge the authority of the parents or husbands'. Similarly, reports from Bali (UNDP, 1992; Cukier & Wall, 1995) suggest that, while the increase of women in the labour force has changed the traditional family structure, it is not detrimental to family stability. Similar accounts have been reported regarding the influx of youth into the labour force as a result of tourism employment opportunities. However, as with women's tourism employment, the results of this for family stability are debatable (Van Doorn, 1989). Chant (1992) found that in Mexico, in areas in which tourism employment was prevalent, there were greater incidences of female-headed households, which was thought to be a direct result of the greater autonomy achieved by women employed in tourism.

Despite empirical studies which explore gender roles in tourism in developing countries, (Monk & Alexander, 1986; Lever, 1987; Swain, 1989; Miller & Branson, 1989; Lerch & Levy, 1990; Levy & Lerch, 1991; Wilkinson & Pratiwi, 1995, Bras & Dahles, 1998), this is still a relatively new research area. Many of these studies indicate that tourism employment opportunities for women have generally been confined to unskilled, low paid and low status work. Osirim (1992) found that Zimbabwean women working in the informal sector were more likely than men to concentrate their efforts on the tourist market rather than producing or selling goods for export, primarily because the women lacked sufficient capital and knowledge of marketing. Levy and Lerch (1991) found that women who worked in tourism-related jobs in Barbados were generally involved in less stable, lower paid and lower status work than men. However, Pongsapich (1982) claimed that women who found employment within the tourism sector often benefited through acquisition of new skills as well as contributing to the household income. Examples from Greece provided by Castleberg-Koulma (1991) and Leontidou (1994) also depict a more positive influence of gender divisions of labour. Women in Greece have formed tourism cooperatives, enabling them to acquire work and gain independence and financial autonomy. Similar observations were made for Mexico by Chant (1992) and for the Caribbean region by Price (1988) (see Chapters 5 and 7 for further discussions on gender).

Summary

Tourism creates employment opportunities in both developed and developing countries, yet the impacts and implications of this employment are different for developed and developing countries. However, most research in developing countries has relied on concepts first formulated in and based on research in developed countries. Innovative, more appropriate concepts are necessary in order to adequately explain and describe the nature of tourism employment and its impacts on developing countries. It is important to note here that development theories are central and highly relevant to tourism employment research. If tourism employment is positively impacting developing countries, based on social welfare measures, then it is likely that development has occurred. In applying modern development theory to tourism employment research, social welfare (quality of life) aspects should be examined. The general criterion of social welfare, according to Van Doorn (1989), includes the accessibility or provision of health facilities, general measures to ensure one's security, the division of labour and income and job satisfaction. In addition, the rapid growth of the informal sector in developing countries must be considered by governments and policy-makers. Migration, urbanisation and employment formality[7] concepts related to the informal sector need to be broadened in their scope since informal sector activities are becoming increasingly prevalent in almost all areas of economic activity (Hope, 1993) (see Chapter 7 for a discussion on development indicators).

The following sections present and interpret the results of interviews conducted in two coastal resort villages in Bali, Indonesia: Sanur and Kuta. A total of 240 interview questionnaires were completed with tourism workers in four employment categories: (1) front desk staff at starred hotels; (2) drivers/guides who take tourists on tours; (3) workers in kiosk stalls (small shops) who sell souvenirs; and (4) beach and street vendors/hawkers. These target groups were chosen because they represented a range of employment types and included members of both the formal and informal sector. Also, these groups varied in degree of entrepreneurship, job security, job flexibility and capital required. There were 60 respondents for each of the four employment categories, 30 in Sanur and 30 in Kuta. The questionnaire was administered orally by Balinese research assistants and each took approximately 45 minutes to complete. Respondents were approached randomly and, thus, no effort was made to seek out an equal number of male and female respondents. Of the 240 respondents sampled, 159 were male and 81 were female. The data were analyzed through use of frequency counts, cross-tabulations and analysis of variance.

Interpretation of Results and Relation to Literature-based Research Issues

The main empirical research findings of the study are presented and related to the literature discussed earlier.

Formal and informal sector tourism employees

The four employment groups forming the subject of my research, covered a broad range of employment sector formality when evaluated against the criteria which various authors have derived when describing employment sector formality. Figure 6.1, derived from the literature discussed earlier, lists the main criteria used by various authors in identifying the formal and informal economic sectors and applies these criteria to the four employment groups studies in my research.

In general, the criteria indicate a spectrum of tourism employment, with hotel employees judged to be the 'most-formal', followed by guides and kiosk workers with vendors the 'least-formal'. However, within each of the four employment groups, variation exists and degrees of formality vary. For example, if a guide owns his/her own vehicle, he/she would fit within Bromley and Gerry's (1979) 'true self-employment' and Davies' (1979) 'owner operated' categories. He/she would be considered more 'informal' than a guide who drives a vehicle owned by a transportation company or hotel, yet, because he/she does own his own vehicle, his/her potential earnings may be higher than those of the 'formal' guide.

When evaluating employment formality using these criteria, variation occurs in applicability, suitability, and appropriateness. For example, Davies' (1979) 'modes of production' model is least applicable when defining tourism employment formality, mainly because tourism is a service sector and 'mode of production' implies a manufacturing sector. Bromley and Gerry's (1979) continuum is the most applicable when describing the tourism employment through its classification of employees and their labour. The criteria useful in describing employees who are most indicative of the formal sector would be, for example, Bromley and Gerry's (1979) 'stable wage work', Davies' (1979) 'owner operated' and 'hierarchical division of labour'. Tourism employees who are most representative of the informal

Employment formality models	Front desk	Guides	Kiosks	Vendors
Bromley & Gerry (1979)				
Stable wage work	■■	■	□	□
Short-term wage work	□	■	■	■
Disguised wage work	□	■■	■	■■
Dependent work	□	■■	■■	■■
True self-employment	□	■■	■■	■■
Davies (M.O.P.)(1979)				
Capital intensive	■■	□	■	□
Employee operated	□	■	■■	■
Owner operated	■■	■	■	■
Hierarchical division of labour	■■	■	□	□
ILO (1972)				
Ease of entry	□	■■	■	■■
Indigenous resources	□	■	■	■■
Family ownership	□	■	■■	■
Small scale operation	□	■■	■■	■■
Labour intensive	■■	■■	■■	■■
Adaptive technology	N/A	N/A	N/A	N/A
Non-formal skill development	□	■	■■	■■
Unregulated and competitive	■	■	■	■■

Figure 6.1 Tourism employment formality: evaluation by various models
■■, common; ■, somewhat common; and □, uncommon.

sector can be described using, for example, Bromley and Gerry's (1979) 'dependent work' and 'true self-employment' categories, Davies' (1979) 'employee operated' and ILO's (1972) 'ease of entry', 'small scale of operation' and 'non-formal skills development' criteria.

Although there is a growing literature on the emergence of the informal sector in developing countries, very little is known about this sector as it applies to the tourism industry. It has been suggested by a number of authors that, in spite of the considerable number of informal sector tourism workers in developing countries, with the exception of specific activities such as prostitution[9], little is known concerning their character and involvement. The results of my research suggests that, in Bali, the employees most indicative of the informal sector, vendors, were most likely to be single male teenagers or young adults with limited formal education but substantial 'informally acquired' language and other skills (Cukier & Wall, 1994a). Similar characteristics describe the guides surveyed, except that all were male, most were older than the vendors and the majority were married. In contrast, kiosk workers were predominantly female, young married adults in their twenties, had attained higher educational levels than either the vendors or guides and most had children. The formal sector employees (front desk employees) were represented almost equally by men and women, approximately half were married, and education levels were higher than the informal sector employees (Cukier, 1996). Thus, the informal sector should not be viewed as exhibiting similar characteristics to the formal sector; distinctive sub-sets exist within the overall tourism employment population.

The most striking demographic difference between the informal and formal sector employment groups was the level of education. Education levels varied according to the degree of employment formality, with those employees most indicative of the formal sector (front desk employees) having the highest levels of education, followed by kiosk workers, guides and vendors. Almost half of the front desk employees had attained at least some post-secondary education compared with less than 3% of informal sector respondents. Thus, it appears that the level of education varies directly with increased employment formality and that employment is influenced by educational levels. However, despite the relatively low levels of education among vendors, guides and kiosk workers, foreign language skills were highly developed, with the majority speaking at least one foreign language and many speaking at least two foreign languages. Other skills acquired by informal sector employees were marketing skills, for example, promotion of their occupation, and, in the case of guides, equipment maintenance skills. This finding supports Wahnschafft's (1982) view that informal sector tourism workers develop skills which result directly from their employment. The majority of informal sector workers surveyed had not received any formal job training, instead developing the skills necessary for their work on-the-job (Cukier, 1996). Thus, they have compensated for a lack of formal educational training with on-the-job informal education.

The informal sector literature, both general and tourism specific, has predominantly claimed that the informal sector is an economically marginalized group (ILO, 1972; Todaro, 2000), dominated and controlled by the formal sector. More recently, some authors have challenged this view (Chu, 1992; Miles-Doan, 1992; Hope, 1993). The Bali study found that, in fact, most informal sector workers were not marginalised, rather they were earning above minimum wages, often more than the formal sector front desk employees. In fact, all respondents were generally well remunerated, with most earning at least twice the minimum wage for Bali. Additionally, most informal sector employees were relatively independent, entrepreneurial and were not dominated by the formal sector. Thus, the results of this study help to clarify the current contradictory views on the 'degree of marginalization' of the informal sector, indicating that, at least in tourism in Bali, informal sector employees are not as 'marginalized' as much of the academic literature purports.

The employees most indicative of the informal sector, vendors, viewed their current employment as a means of acquiring the skills necessary to gain access to more formalised employment in tourism. However, it is unclear how many are successful in this objective and longitudinal studies would shed light on this matter. One possible indicator of a shift from vending to formal sector employment is the relatively few years the surveyed vendors had worked at their current job when compared to the other employment groups, suggesting that vendors rapidly seek alternative employment after a few years of vending and skills development (Cukier & Wall, 1994a). Unlike vendors, guides, kiosk workers and front desk employees expressed higher levels of satisfaction in their occupations and, thus, were less likely than vendors to seek alternative employment.

While many informal sector workers believed that they had few other employment opportunities, most enjoyed their work and were well remunerated. In fact, expectations of monetary rewards were the main attraction of the position, a finding consistent with the literature (Connell, 1987). Contrasting this finding, formal sector front desk employees were mainly attracted to their occupation because it was viewed as a personally satisfying form of employment. The contention held by some authors that earning a relatively high income results in the belief that the employment is accorded a high status did not hold true for vendors, although it did for both kiosk workers and guides. Although informal sector workers reported longer working hours than the formal sector, their work hours were more flexible. Guides, kiosk workers and vendors were reliant on the presence of tourists to buy their products or use their services, and much of the work day was spent socialising with other group members while waiting for tourists (Cukier, 1998a). In this respect, formal sector employees are at a disadvantage in terms of securing time off to attend family, village or temple ceremonies, which are a factor in maintaining the culture of Bali.

Although Kermath and Thomas (1992) concluded that the informal tourism sector disappears as tourism develops in an area, empirical research findings in Bali do not support this view. As tourism has developed in Bali and informal sector workers have moved to other occupations, perhaps even within the formal sector, new migrants have filled the informal sector employment opportunities left open. Because tourism is so prominent in Bali, the island has a reputation across Indonesia as an ideal place to work, a 'get rich quick' location, and therefore, migrants who initially tend to find work in the informal sector have continued to be attracted to Bali. Consistent with the literature (Connell, 1987; Todaro, 2000), economic considerations have been the primary motivator for migration to Bali. Specifically addressing the issue of female Indonesian internal migrants, Hugo (1992) found that most women migrated to 'follow' husbands or other family members or for education. Work-related reasons and other economic factors were not as significant a motivator as they were for male internal migrants.

Perhaps the most startling empirical finding was that most vendors were not Balinese but, rather, were migrants from other islands in Indonesia, mainly Java. They were typically young migrants who did not speak Balinese and were not Hindu. Thus, many of the individuals with whom tourists come into contact on the beaches and streets of Bali are not Balinese, although they probably do not realise this (Cukier & Wall, 1994a). One might wonder why relatively few Balinese work as beach and street vendors. The reason lies partially in the different economic situations of Bali and Java. Bali is one of the richer islands of Indonesia and it is likely that many Javanese, living on an island on which incomes are lower and employment opportunities are fewer, view Bali as an island of opportunity. Most non-Balinese migrants face restrictions in participating in many of the tourism alternatives to vending, such as owning or working in a kiosk, or hotel or as a guide. Official residence in Bali is a prerequisite to owning a kiosk and therefore, kiosks are predominantly owned by Balinese citizens who are reportedly more likely to hire Balinese family members or friends as employees. Hotel employees generally are required to have a high level of formal education and tourism training, characteristics often lacking in the non-Balinese migrant sample. Working as a guide is an occupation in which local knowledge of traditions and the culture is beneficial as is a detailed knowledge of Bali's tourist sites. New migrants to the island do not usually have this type of knowledge and, thus, initially choose alternative employment such as vending.

Although many authors (Cleverdon, 1977; Monk & Alexander, 1986; Parnwell, 1993; Sharpley, 1994; Krippendorf, 1994) have stated that migrants can place stress on the existing community, and some have specifically argued that migrants cause increased competition (Cleverdon, 1977; Davies, 1979; Todaro 2000), my study revealed that there is little resentment among Balinese toward the non-Balinese employed within the tourism sector. Balinese respondents commented that they are not interested in working at the occupations that non-Balinese employees typically chose, vending, since it was considered a relatively 'low class' job which was culturally inappropriate for Balinese. The fact that many non-Balinese migrants filled a niche left vacant by Balinese employees minimised any possible resentment felt by Balinese towards non-Balinese migrants. Further, non-Balinese vendors often sold products which belonged to Balinese owners of souvenir kiosks. Thus, non-Balinese workers acted as sales agents and received a commission from Balinese kiosk 'contractors'. This finding supports the contention by some researchers that migrants to a tourist area do not cause increased job competition, rather they fill niches left void by the local population (McGee, 1982; Monk & Alexander, 1986; Lever, 1987; Connell, 1987). Although Geertz (1973), in his analysis of Balinese culture, speculated that cultural change would most likely come from outside Bali and most probably from Java, this research has not supported his conclusion for the tourism sector. Despite the large number of non-Balinese tourism employees in Bali (especially vendors), Balinese employees generally felt that little competition was created, and that tolerance was required in order to get along. Finally, although many vendors are 'outsiders' in that they are non-Balinese, they are still Indonesians and thus share many cultural characteristics with the Balinese (including the Indonesian language), which assists in minimising possible negative impacts on the local population.

Tourism employment and gender: An extension of traditional roles?

An expanding tourism industry often creates new employment opportunities for women. In a study on gender and tourism in a Javanese village, Wilkinson and Pratiwi (1995) found that tourism created new opportunities for employment for both men and women in the formal and informal sectors. They found that, despite the double or triple workload, women participating in the informal tourism sector had greater control over their lives and partial economic independence. My empirical research in Bali has also shown that tourism has created employment opportunities for women, although many tourism occupations are gender segregated. Although these employment opportunities benefit both men and women, women's work at home has generally not been alleviated by the shift of work from the primary to the tertiary sector (Ariani & Gregory, 1992), and female tourism employees have had to factor this into their participation in tourism.

The women surveyed in my study predominantly worked in kiosks and as front desk hotel employees. Both these occupations harmonise with women's traditional roles in Bali: front desk staff greet visitors, thus carrying on traditional socialising roles, and kiosk work allows for a cash income while facilitating child-care. Cukier *et al.* (1996) derived similar conclusions in their exploration of women in tourism in Kedewatan, a Balinese village. They found that women were more likely than men to be self-employed, for example, opening kiosks and *warungs* (small restaurants), which facilitated child-care more easily than formal employment. Moser (1991) and Osirim (1992) both reported that informal sector work has enabled women to fulfil their domestic responsibilities due to the flexible nature of this type of work. The literature has argued that the informal sector in Bali is a primary employer of women (see, for example, Ariani & Gregory, 1992). However, these women are not as marginalised as indicated in the literature (Lever, 1987; Lerch & Levy, 1990; Levy & Lerch, 1991). Women work in a variety of tourism occupations (UNDP, 1992), both as employees and as entrepreneurs, and, in Bali, most reported earnings above the minimum wage. Chu (1992) and Hope (1993) argued that the informal sector has increased the participation of women as an entrepreneurial group who, as a result, become relatively well-off financially. The majority of women (57%) surveyed in Bali worked in kiosks, thus lending support to the assertion that the entrepreneurial participation rate of women is increasing through the informal tourism sector. However, the women are 'unofficial' owners of their businesses, since according to traditional Balinese law, *adat*, the business must be registered in the name of the woman's closest living male relative (Ariani & Gregory, 1992).

In my study, gender differences were found in employment type, products sold and tendency to migrate to the tourism areas. Although more men than women worked as vendors in Bali, differences were seen in the products that each sold. For example, clothing was sold by women and sunglasses were sold by men, perhaps reflecting traditional gender perceptions of products and main users in broader society (Cukier & Wall, 1995). The research showed that Balinese women predominantly work in kiosks yet they sell the same products as male mobile vendors. This non-mobile vending option allows women to work in a setting that is favourable to the provision of child-care while working. Women were also less likely than men to migrate to the tourism resort areas, a finding consistent with the literature, which maintains that most migrants are young males (Todaro, 2000). Most women did not travel far from home when they sought employment within the tourism sector, especially when compared to men who were more likely to venture further afield. In addition to traditional customs, which do not encourage women to travel far, there is less societal pressure on women than men to seek employment.

Education and income levels differed between the men and women surveyed in Bali. Within the formal sector (front desk employees), women were paid less than men for similar work despite having attained higher educational levels. Thus, although tourism is providing many new employment opportunities and greater independence for women, access to the highest incomes is still being limited. Within the informal sector (vendors and kiosk workers), incomes varied, with female kiosk workers earning more than male kiosk workers and with female vendors earning less than male vendors. In both these informal sector groups, education levels for women were lower than those for men (Cukier & Wall, 1995). This finding is consistent with the literature on gender and education in Indonesia. Generally, education levels of women employed in the service sector in Indonesia tend to be higher than for other economic sectors, and the tourism sector is well suited to providing challenging occupations to high school and university graduates, one of the goals of the employment strategy for Repelita V (Booth, 1990). Goals for Repelita VI continue along this line with the provision of tourism training opportunities a priority (Booth, 1994). Over half of the women with junior high school education work in the service sector, with this percentage increasing to over two-thirds of those with high school education and almost three-quarters of those with a university education (Gauthama *et al.* 1992). Further supporting this contention, Oey-Gardiner (1991) determined that education was more important than gender in determining access to formal sector employment and that the higher the level of education was, the greater the probability of gaining access to higher status employment became.

Tourism employment in Bali has provided both men and women with greater occupational choices and this has resulted in greater autonomy and independence for women, while increasing their work burden (Ariani & Gregory, 1992). New power relations between men and women are emerging as a result of tourism employment but the long-term implications of these remain to be seen. Women employed in tourism continue to carry out traditional roles within the home, family and religious life. However, instead of making the intricate offerings used for religious ceremonies, more and more working women buy ready-made offerings in the market, creating employment for other women. The significance of the additional work burden that tourism employment creates is difficult to interpret: it is unclear whether this should be interpreted as a contributor to increased economic well-being or as an increase of time pressures, or a combination of both, and whether this signifies cultural degradation or simply cultural change. Similarly, it is uncertain whether the purchase of offerings is a new religious behaviour or a continuation of past behaviours in a modified form congruent with new lifestyles and economic opportunities.

Tourism employment status: A new order

Tourism employment, like any relatively new employment sector, has introduced a new means for determining social status in Indonesia. Wilkinson and Pratiwi (1995) argued that social stratification in Indonesia is increasingly taking on an economic basis as opposed to the traditional class stratification system. They found that people who were considered by their peers to be 'upper-class' were employed in the formal tourism sector or owned tourist accommodations and restaurants, while the 'lower class' individuals were employed in the informal tourism sector.

Many Balinese scholars as well as individuals involved in the tourism sector in Bali believe that tourism employment has, in part, replaced the traditional caste system as an indicator of status (Sukabrata, 1993, pers. comm.; Geriya, 1993, pers. comm.; Sudiyana, 1993, pers. comm.; Mandra, 1993, pers. comm.; Manuaba, 1991, pers. comm.). Everyone in Bali is born into a caste, with the majority of the population belonging to the common *sudra* caste, and a minority belonging to one of the three remaining gentry castes, *brahman* (priests), *satria* (nobles), or *weisa* (merchants) (Geertz & Geertz, 1975). According to Geertz (1973), the caste system dictates religious status and does not affect moral, economic or political status. Wayan Geriya (1993, pers. comm.), a Balinese cultural scholar, has argued that tourism in Bali has caused a shift in status determination. Where previously a person's status was determined by birth caste, it is now more frequently being based upon achievement and type of employment, with the tourism sector providing ample opportunity for both high achievement and prestigious employment. Vickers (1989) supported this view with his argument that poverty in Bali had become associated with a lack of access to tourism income. As stated previously, the results of my research support such contentions: with the exception of vendors, all formal and informal sector tourism workers surveyed ranked their own occupation as having the highest status among tourism jobs. Vendors ranked guides and hotel employees most highly. Overall, hotel employees were accorded the highest rank among tourism occupations, followed by guides and owning a kiosk or another private tourism business.

Tourism occupations in Bali are highly regarded and although vending is not considered the most prestigious, it does provide above-average incomes. Thus, vendors are likely to be perceived by others not employed in tourism as having a higher status simply because of their relative wealth. Front desk employees, kiosk workers and guides were all considered high status occupations by the respondent groups as well as by Balinese scholars. In developing countries, where employment opportunities are limited, vending products to tourists may be an acceptable, remunerative and rewarding activity, contrary to assertations in the literature. According to BPLP (Bali Tourism Training Institute) director, I Nyoman Bagiarta, the tourism training degree programme at BPLP attracts Balinese of a higher caste who are not interested in diploma programmes. For these people, he argued, money is not the important factor: recognition of a degree and status are important. Hotel wages are high compared with wages in other sectors. Bagiarta ranks banking as having the highest wages, followed by hotels, other service sectors and government employees. Working in hotels was accorded a high status, especially if the hotel is large or part of an international chain (Bagiarta, 1991, pers. comm.). At the same time, as a result of remnants of colonial influence, the ability to speak a foreign language is also accorded a high status (Sudiana, 1993, pers. comm.; Sukabrata, 1993, pers. comm.).

Within both the formal and informal sectors, there is a growing differential in socioeconomic status among workers. A number of researchers (for example, Pongsapich, 1982; Ebery & Forbes, 1985; Lovel & Feuerstein, 1992; Pizam *et al.* 1994) have argued that informal sector tourism workers acquired a high status because of the skill, initiative and relatively high remuneration associated with their occupations. The majority of respondents in all four employment groups were well remunerated and had acquired numerous skills, either formally, in the case of front desk employees, or informally, in the case of most members of the remaining three employment groups. As a result, all respondents, with the exception of vendors, considered their own occupation to be high status. In general, perceived status was not strictly linked to income levels, depending also on foreign language ability, the 'honour' of wearing a uniform, the size of the tourism employment venture and the type of tourism employment (Cukier, 1998a).

Sociocultural Implications of Tourism Employment in Bali

The introduction of tourism employment to Bali has had economic, social and cultural implications. Overall, the economic implications have been positive through the raising of individual income levels as well as increased community income. However, it is not clear whether the increase in village income contributes to improved community welfare. According to Geriya (pers. comm. 1993), in order to guarantee improved community welfare, tourism income should contribute to education, maintenance of the environment and religious rituals.

The social benefits of tourism employment are more difficult to assess. Social networks in Bali have been widened as a result of tourism employment. People who work in agriculture are tied to land within their village and, thus, associate predominantly with other village members. In contrast, tourism employees originate from a number of villages and are exposed to many new people, including foreign tourists. An assessment of the impact of these changing patterns on Balinese traditional customs was outside the scope of this research, yet my research undertaken in Bali suggested that some people who have moved from their home village in order to take up tourism employment do not return to their home for all temple ceremonies or to participate in community activities. Instead, these tourism employees pay a fine to compensate for their absence or are represented by family members. Some guides reported they had sold land in order to pay for their vehicle, a finding which has major implications for the maintenance of Balinese culture since so much of the religion and culture of Bali is tied to agricultural land, particularly through the *subak* (traditional water management) system (Lindayati & Nelson, 1995). Geertz saw cultural change in Bali as inevitable, especially in light of the 'new informality of urban life', the growth in importance of youth culture and the consequent 'narrowing . . . of the social distance between generations' (Geertz, 1973: 441). The positive cultural change that might result from tourism employment includes improved harmony between the spiritual and material aspects of life (Geriya, 1993, pers. comm.). To minimise the potential negative impacts, the traditional Balinese institutions (*banjar, subak, desa adat*) need to be maintained.

Balinese culture is still very strong, even among the youth. It is not uncommon to see a guide or a hotel employee leave work and, wearing a traditional outfit adorned with a leather jacket, hop on his / her motorcycle and head off to a temple or village ceremony. Tourism employment has not radically altered traditional customs in Bali. However, because of the relative infancy of tourism in Bali, only one generation has been raised surrounded by and employed within tourism. The young people who are finding work in the tourism sector return home where they are confronted with the traditional customs maintained by their parents and grandparents. A key question is whether these traditions and customs be carried on by future generations. Francillon (1990, 271) optimistically asserted that

> the strength of the people of Bali, their social cohesion and ability to cope with recurrent natural, or other, disruptions have allowed them to resist, and re-

cover from floods, earthquake, and volcanic eruptions many times in the past. Similarly, they could resist, and possibly absorb, tourism

(See Chapter 7 for further analysis of the social and cultural impacts of tourism.)

Research Implications

Historical academic studies that have focused on the overall role of tourism within development have mainly focused on links to regional development (Christaller, 1963; Miossec, 1976). These have emphasised tourism's contribution to economic growth, although not necessarily to development, as defined more widely to include environmental, social and cultural aspects. One primary benefit of the addition of tourism to the economy is diversification of the employment base (assuming tourism is not the only basis of the economy since it is also vulnerable to changes in tourist demand). Stability within the tourism sector of the economy can be achieved through diversification in tourism and the resulting employment that generates additional income for the local population, who then pass on this wealth through the re-spending of earned income. This, in turn, creates more employment opportunities in other non-tourism sectors and perpetuates this economic cycle. Thus, tourism employment is a key link to the stability and strengthening of a developing country's economy.

The research I conducted in Bali contributes to existing knowledge, concepts and research in three main themes: development, particularly related to employment; gender; and tourism employment. Although some level of economic development is required prior to the development of tourism (Harrison, 1994), once tourism has been initiated in a community, further development often results. This has been well documented and modelled by Butler's (1980) evolution of tourist area development concept. This is particularly true when considering broader definitions of development, which incorporate the environmental, social and cultural aspects of development. Tourism employment is beneficial to both the formal and informal economic sectors and contributes economically to both individuals and the community. However, development is not limited to economic factors, with the high status associated with tourism employment resulting in self-fulfillment and self-actualisation of employees (Cukier, 1998a). Furthermore, informal sector employment may be a crucial training ground that leads to cross-overs to the formal sector, thus increasing personal development through increased status, skills and education. The acquisition of skills, whether through formal or informal means, results in a population with skills in demand at the higher levels of tourism employment. Consequently, over the long term, there should be reduced reliance on the use of 'outsiders' to fill higher-level, managerial positions.

The employment literature has predominantly focused on the dualistic nature of employment in the formal and informal sectors. This body of theory has been largely derived from studies of manufacturing and, thus, emphasises issues related to 'modes of production'. However, 'modes of production' concepts do not adequately describe tourism employment and, thus, the main implication of this is that a new, service-centred concept is required. Such a concept is presented in the following section of this chapter. Much of the employment literature has postulated that the informal sector is a marginalised sector, dominated by the formal economy. My research in Bali has demonstrated that the informal tourism sector comprises a range of 'formality' and a subsequent range in employment status, income and skill-levels. Also, the informal tourism sector operates relatively independently from the formal tourism sector, and is associated with substantial skills development, which may eventually lead to formal sector employment.

The employment literature has also discussed the causes and effects of rural–urban migration and the associated urbanisation this causes, yet has largely ignored tourism and related employment as a contributor to migration. Rural–urban migration, although not entirely caused by tourism employment, is certainly exacerbated by it. Tourism employment, thus, must be considered within academic literature as having an impact on the growing urbanisation of areas that surround and are adjacent to tourism resorts (Cukier, 1998b).

Gender and development issues in the academic literature on developing countries have been based largely on analyses of women's work in agricultural and industrial production. This research has demonstrated that conclusions based on agricultural and manufacturing employment are not entirely applicable to tourism employment. Unlike agricultural and manufacturing employment, informal sector tourism employment, because of its flexible nature, has resulted in the facilitation of child-care while 'on-the-job' (Cukier, 1996; Cukier *et al.*, 1996; Long & Kindon, 1997). Additionally, employment opportunities created for women within the tourism sector contribute to overall development by providing full-time, lucrative and high status occupations. Much employment within the tourism sector is gender segregated, possibly reflecting cultural expectations and extensions of traditional roles. According to Osborne (1993), Balinese women are central to the culture and are so indispensable to the tourism sector that, she believed, without women's participation, the industry would collapse.

Much of the academic literature relating to tourism employment in developing countries has adopted a negative stance, focusing on the seasonal and servile nature, low status and high leakages associated with tourism employment. These analyses and criticisms are often based on assumptions which distort the overall picture. Seasonal aspects had a minimal impact on employment creation in Bali, and even where tourist arrivals reflected seasonal variations, employment opportunities were relatively unaffected. Tourism employment, whether part of the formal or informal sector, was generally perceived to have a high status and was not perceived to be 'servile' in nature (Cukier, 1996). Because many of the employment opportunities created within tourism are created within the informal sector and, thus, its employees are independent 'entrepreneurs', the leakages commonly associated with tourism employment are relatively lower when both formal and informal sector employment are considered (Cukier, 2000).

The research has pointed to the considerable positive benefits that accrue to those employed within the tourism sector. However, a cautionary note regarding the negative impacts of tourism for developing countries should also be acknowledged. These negative impacts have been well discussed in the literature, and have generally been grouped under three main categories: economic, social and environmental.[10] Some negative economic impacts mentioned in the literature include high leakages from foreign-owned establishments, high inflation, loss of primary sector labour, rising land values and regional imbalances resulting from the unequal distribution of the economic benefits of tourism development. These issues are discussed further in Chapter 9. Some of the negative social impacts of tourism are an increase in the crime rate, prostitution and community cohesion. As well, tourism can disrupt traditional community bonds through the loss of individuals who have migrated to tourist resorts in search of employment, or can result in resentment of those 'left behind' toward those who have left. Although most of the Balinese sampled in this study indicated that they returned to their home villages for most ceremonies and festivals, other studies in tourism migration 'source' villages (e.g. Lever, 1987) have revealed dissatisfaction with the degree of contact maintained by those employed in tourism, perhaps reflecting a perceptual gap between those who leave the village and those who remain. Some of the most obvious negative impacts of tourism are environmental, resulting largely from physical transformations of the natural landscape. Negative environmental impacts include the transformation of rural agricultural land to a built environment of roads, hotels, restaurants and shops. Damage to natural ecosystems, both marine (e.g. damage to coral reefs, water quality degradation, beach erosion) and terrestrial (pollution, habitat conversion, hydrological change) can be the result of tourism development and is both unpredictable and often irreversible. These issues are explored further in Chapter 8.

A service-centred tourism employment conception

One of the main weaknesses of tourism employment research is that it has had to rely on theories and models 'borrowed' from other research areas. Analysis of the formal and informal sector has largely been based on manufacturing and related 'modes of production' models. A specific service-centred concept is better suited for the analysis of tourism employment in developing countries. Such a concept should incorporate aspects of existing concepts and criteria which describe tourism employment formality through the classification of employees and their labour (such as Bromley and Gerry's (1979) continuum model and the ILO's (1972) characterisation of the informal sector), while de-emphasising production factors (such as Davies (1979) 'modes of production' model).

The following characteristics have been identified through my research as useful in the classification and analysis of tourism employment formality. The use of a continuum model is most valuable in that it allows for variation in employment formality within any one employment group, and thus would serve as the central organising feature of a service-centred tourism employment concept. Additionally, a service-centred concept would analyse:

Ease of entry: The more informal the occupation, the easier it is to gain access to that employment. Migrants, who lack formal tourism skills and training, will be able to seek the most 'informal' employment, such as vending goods or services to tourists.

Flexibility of work hours: The more informal the occupation, the greater the flexibility of work hours. Using Bromley and Gerry's (1979) continuum, 'stable wage work' would be the most restrictive in terms of work hours, with employees' schedules being set by their employer. As working hours become more flexible, the 'informality' of employment increases, with individuals fitting into the 'true self-employment' category having the most flexibility.

Methods and type of skills acquisition: The more formal the system for skills acquisition is, the more formal the type of employment is. In addition, the type of skills acquired may affect tourism employment formality, with entrepreneurial skills (such as marketing, financing and foreign language abilities) denoting more informal sector occupations and management, accounting and administrative skills denoting more formal occupations.

Status: The perceived status of a tourism occupation, both self-perceptions and peer group perceptions, can indicate the degree of tourism employment formality, with those occupations most indicative of the informal sector, such as vending, having the lowest occupational status and those occupations most indicative of formal employment, such as hotel employee, being accorded the highest status.

Degree of market regulation and enforcement: The less regulated the market is, the more informal the occupation becomes. However, the keys to determining the degree of tourism employment formality is the rigour of regulation enforcement and the success of tourism employees in evading such regulation. For example, vendors in Bali are required to obtain a vending license; however, because enforcement of this requirement is weak, many vendors work without a legal permit and are, thus, part of the informal sector. The weaker the enforcement, or more successful the evasion, the more informal the tourism occupation is.

Degree of land dependence: The more formal the tourism occupation, the greater the dependence on access to land. For example, hotel employees and kiosk owners are highly dependent on land on which to base their place of employment. Guides and vendors, on the other hand, are more mobile and do not need to secure access to land in order to operate. Thus, the more mobile the occupation, the more informal it is likely to be.

These descriptors are an initial step toward a service-centred employment conceptual framework. Other relevant factors will undoubtably come to light with additional research.

Policy Implication

A number of policy-related issues arise from the findings of this study. In order to increase the benefits of tourism employment, 'there must be clear consideration and formulation of policy through national plans and an efficient and successful implementation of that policy' (Harrison, 1994: 713). The most obvious issue for policy-making concerns the magnitude and economic structure of the informal tourism sector. According to Todaro (2000), the informal sector should be 'promoted as a major source of employment and income' because of its demonstrated ability to generate employment, income, surplus and training. The research demonstrated that the tourism informal sector is significant in developing countries and its members are relatively well remunerated while exploiting niches left open by sector counterparts. Therefore, it is important for governments to encourage and support this economically viable sector, especially in light of the failure of governments to successfully obliterate or confine informal sector tourism workers (Kermath & Thomas, 1992). The perceived undesirability of the tourism informal sector is very much a policy reality, however. The UNDP-sponsored Comprehensive Tourism Development Plan for Bali (1992: 50) described vendors in Bali as 'undermining the quality of the tourist product and . . . endangering the livelihood of other workers and investors in the industry' and recommended that such vendors be restricted to designated areas through government policies and police support. This proposed 'solution' was similar to that proposed by the government of the Dominican Republic: relocation of vendors to a designated area where tourists could approach them at their leisure. However, by doing so, these informal sector tourism employees are forced to 'formalise', a process which destroys much of the potential for respectable incomes and which has been unsuccessful in other developing countries. In providing support for the informal sector, it is more effective to eliminate barriers which restrict the informal tourism sector from operating efficiently rather than to impose policies which, in attempting to actively support or assist the informal sector, actually hinder it through the need to 'formalise' the government–informal sector relationship.

Another policy implication arising from the research is support for tourism education and training institutes. A deliberate policy to provide a high standard general education as well as specific tourism training will help ensure that the local population will gain access to a variety of higher level management positions within the tourism sector. Blanton (1981: 120) argued that the existence of formal tourism training institutes results in the elimination of the view that the tourism sector employee is a 'marginal person'. Harrison (1994: 715) concurred, arguing that the provision of tourism training institutes enhances the self-image of the tourism employees, 'who might otherwise resent becoming a "nation of bell hops and chambermaids"', especially in developing countries with a history of colonialism. As stated earlier, Bali has a number of tourism training facilities in place, at both the high school and post-secondary levels. The research demonstrated that training institutes such as BPLP enhance employability and facilitate employment that contributes to self-development. Creating a programme to fund or subsidise the annual Rp 700,000 student fee for BPLP, would result in students from lower income families being able to participate in the programmes offered by the school.

As well as providing training for those who will be employed in the tourism sector, education on the impacts of tourism development should be provided to tourism administrators, policy-makers and government tourism planners in developing countries so they can maximise the potential benefits of tourism. These influential groups are often ill informed about tourism and when education is provided, it is not well related to the context and problems specific for that developing country.

Another issue for tourism training is that of implementation. In a study commissioned by the WTO (Rieder, 1992) to define a development programme for village tourism in Bali, one of the recommendations was to invite a team of tourism 'experts' to the villages to train Balinese individuals involved in tourism. Although generally supportive of the idea of the provision of training, it was suggested by an Indonesian tourism planner that it would be more effective to send those requiring training to already established and successful Balinese owned and operated tourism ventures in other parts of Bali. Thus, the trainees could observe first-hand how to operate a successful tourism venture. It is this type of training approach, which may be best suited to Bali and other developing countries.

The research suggests that official government policies promoting cultural tourism should acknowledge the importance of non-Balinese and informal sector tourism employees in the formation of tourists' cultural experiences. Thus, these individuals should be incorporated into the cultural tourism policy framework. Tourism in Bali is being promoted as 'cultural tourism', yet many tourism employees are non-Balinese. For an Indonesian island, which promotes cultural tourism, this finding is significant to government and tourism planners. Guides in Bali act as 'culture brokers' for tourists, yet many guides are 'unofficial', that is, they are not registered and have consequently not received appropriate training. Effective policies, targeting both 'unofficial' guides and non-Balinese tourism employees, would be to recognize these tourism employees as 'cultural emissaries' and to provide them with free or low-cost training courses in Balinese culture, customs and traditions. Similarly, the provision of low-cost or free courses in entrepreneurship, directed at the informal tourism sector, would assist this large and viable tourism sector in acquiring skills, such as marketing, finance, foreign languages and investment knowledge. Such courses have been initiated for informal sector tourism employees in Yogyakarta, Java, and would be particularly beneficial in Bali, where the informal tourism sector is so prominent.

Employment policies in the tourism formal sector need to be altered in Bali in order to grant greater flexibility to both men and women to allow maintenance of the culture through participation in traditional customs. Employers should be flexible in allowing time off for attendance at traditional ceremonies. Additionally, 'indirect' polices, such as encouraging women's self-employment within tourism also fosters this flexibility in allowing women to effectively manage family, social and religious obligations and is particularly attractive to married women with children.

Future Research Directions

There is a need to explore in greater detail how tourism employment has affected the expectations of women in fulfilling their multiple roles and what impact this has on their relationships within the family structure. It is important to examine not only women's experiences with tourism employment, but changes in gender relationships as a result of tourism employment. For example, are gender relations affected by increased family income, by women's increased financial independence or by the new social networks resulting from tourism employment?

Beyond the scope of this study, an important research question is the perceived status of tourism employment by employees in sectors other than tourism. This would shed light on the value of tourism employment and the changing societal structure resulting from shifts in status. Additionally, the perceived status of tourism employment in migrant source villages would assist in identifying whether 'pull' factors are as important as 'push' factors in motivating migration. An initial evaluation of this has been conducted by Wall (1996). In an examination of eight Balinese villages, varying in distance from Bali's main tourism resorts, he found that tourism employment was generally viewed favourably by respondents and was seen by the majority as a desirable employment opportunity for their children. The perceptions towards tourism employment of potential migrants is an area which would benefit from further research. As well, the economic impact upon the source destination is, to date, unknown.

The research was unable to examine the long-term implications of tourism employment on the Balinese culture. In order to assess the 'generational' impact of tourism employment, longitudinal studies of tourism employment's impacts should be carried out. As well, both short- and long-term studies could target a broader spectrum of tourism employment occupations than was presented here or alternatively could focus on one employment sub-sector (e.g. accommodation) in greater detail in order to derive the intricacies and inter-relationships within one employment group, through assessment of accommodation size and type. Although the general findings of this study were that tourism employment is a positive experience for those employed within the sector, it is worth noting that a different perspective may have arisen had the study included individuals not employed in tourism, or those who were previously employed in tourism and had left. There is a relatively high turn-over of hotel employees in Bali (21 month average), although many probably move to other tourism jobs with different establishments. However, individuals surveyed for this study had been employed in tourism between two and seventeen years, suggesting that this group may have been particularly satisfied with their employment. Although there is evidence suggesting that many Balinese who are not employed in the tourism sector have a positive view of tourism in Bali (Wall, 1996), future research targeting those individuals not employed (or previously employed) in tourism could reflect a broader perspective on the attitudes toward tourism employment in Bali.

An additional research question is whether the findings of this study are applicable to other developing country regions with substantial tourism development. The research conducted in Bali could be replicated in other developing regions in order to assess the applicability of the findings. Specifically, research in other regions could help identify whether areas, which have different cultures than Bali are more vulnerable to the negative impacts of tourism employment. Regions with different degrees and type of tourism development than Bali may undergo other experiences than those demonstrated here. Also, variation in government policies toward tourism employment could impact experiences.

Conclusion: Tourism Employment and Development: A Path to the Future?

> [We] asked the kids if they saw anything at the hotel they'd like to do when they grow up, any jobs. People may talk about hotel jobs not being good enough, but those kids were sure excited about them. They talked about being waitresses, lifeguards, desk managers, everything . . . (Knox, 1982: 101)

This research has challenged the knowledge of tourism employment that has largely been derived from a developed country context and has not been based on empirical research within the tourism sector. The study examined the appropriateness of existing conceptions of tourism employment and empirically determined the degree to which these conceptions apply to developing countries. The main conclusion derived from the study was that tourism employment was a generally positive phenomenon from the perspective of tourism employees. Tourism employment was accorded a relatively high status, provided many opportunities for women and migrant workers, and was generally well remunerated, especially when compared to traditional employment options. These findings contrast with many of the prevailing opinions expressed in the literature. Additionally, the study concluded that criteria currently used in the literature to describe formal/informal sectors are inadequate when applied to tourism employment because they have been derived from manufacturing and agricultural sectors. Therefore, a preliminary service-centred concept was devised to define and explain tourism employment 'formality'. For those employed in tourism, tourism employment in Bali has not yet radically altered traditional customs, although it is unknown whether cultural implications will arise in the future.

Tourism in Bali, although still a relatively recent phenomenon, has developed to the point where it is actively promoted by the regional and national governments as an important economic sector and has had an overall positive effect on those employed within that sector. Tourism employment in Bali is increasingly being seen as a desirable alternative to traditional occupations and is considered a provider of high incomes and high status occupations. If people believe their work to be personally satisfying and of high status, 'development' will be positively affected. An official policy of tourism employment promotion should result in greater investment in education, which can benefit the community as a whole and not merely those seeking work in the tourism sector. Murphy (1985) wrote that tourism development can be positive if the needs of the community are placed before the goals of the tourism industry.

Expansion of tourism employment presents both challenges and opportunities. In Bali, tourism employment has stimulated the economy but has exacerbated imbalances in regional economic development. Migration to the resort areas from the interior of the island and from elsewhere in Indonesia has increased as migrants seek employment and have contributed to the urbanization of these areas (Cukier, 1998b). However, tourism employment is more than an economic activity; it has cultural, social and gender implications.

Although I am a western researcher and may thus be influenced by modes of thought formed in a developed country context, it is hoped that the information garnered from the study also reflects the Balinese perspective on tourism employment. The issues raised throughout the study demonstrated that tourism employment is a relatively lucrative, high status, and desirable alternative to traditional occupations. As well as contributing to the existing academic literature, the study made suggestions for policy formulation in Bali and provided direction for future researchers wishing to further extend knowledge based on empirical studies of tourism employment. At the same time, the study findings may be more broadly applicable to tourism employment in *developed* countries which, more and more, are restructuring their economies toward tertiary sector activities (Williams & Montanari, 1995). Although some of the characteristics of tourism employment presented in this study do not generally apply to a *developed* country context (e.g. the informal sector, cultural differences of internal migrants and the relatively high status of tourism jobs), other characteristics have more relevance (e.g. multiple employment, migration for employment, and gender roles in employment) and may contribute to a more complete understanding and analysis in developed countries in which the tourism sector is becoming more dominant. In order to assess tourism employment formality effectively, a service-centred employment concept, such as the one described earlier, must be incorporated into the analysis.

It is most important that regardless of whether tourism employment research is conducted in a developed or developing country context, a sincere effort is made to reflect the culture being studied accurately, and that both the insiders' (emic) and outsiders' (etic) perspectives be, at the very least, acknowledged and, at best, represented equally in the research. This study, through empirical evidence, provides analysis of tourism employment in a developing country and demonstrates the inappropriateness of applying 'developed country' beliefs and assumptions to that of a developing country.

Notes
1. Many researchers (for example, De Kadt, 1979a, Seward & Spinrad, 1982; Mathieson & Wall, 1982; Britton, 1983; Pearce, 1989a) have demonstrated multiplier effects. For a more detailed explanation of the multiplier effect, see Archer (1982).
2. Multiple employment, when it relates to tourism, refers to situations in which a person is employed in more than one occupation, which minimises the negative impact of the seasonal aspect of tourism employment.
3. This is partly due to the seasonality of demand as well as supply.
4. Two notable exceptions are Britton (1983) and Kermath and Thomas (1992).
5. The 'marginality thesis' as described by Chu (1992) refers to those who are economically, politically and socially oppressed.
6. See, for example, Kinnaird and Hall (1994), Norris and Wall (1994) and Swain (1995).
7. Employment formality refers jobs characterised as ranging from informal to formal employment.
8. Each of the four employment groups in Sanur and Kuta consisted of 30 individuals, the minimum sample size required in order to obtain satisfactory results (Daugherty, 1974).
9. For a detailed discussion of prostitution and tourism see Oppermann (1998), Clift and Carter (2000) and Ryan and Hall (2001).
10. For a detailed description of the impacts of tourism, see de Kadt (1979); Mathieson and Wall (1982); Pearce (1989b); and Inskeep (1991).

Chapter 7

Tourism and Sociocultural Development Issues

ATSUKO HASHIMOTO

Introduction

In the pursuit to modernise and promote development within a country, tourism has become the preferred growth mechanism of choice for many developing nations. Within the process of development, it is often the economic indicators that draw the most attention and tourism is seen as attractive as, it is is argued, it generates foreign exchange, increases employment, attracts development capital and promotes economic independence (Britton, 1982). As tourism creates jobs and generates income, 'tourism is therefore said to promote a level of economic development conductive to increase social wellbeing and stability' (Weaver & Oppermann, 2000: 285). Tourism has always been regarded as a means of economic modernisation, but has not been seriously considered as a means of social and cultural modernisation. The concept of socioeconomic modernisation emphasises improvements in various indicators, including improvements in living conditions and the quality of life and well-being of populations. Often, these indicators include decreasing mortality rates, increased literacy rates, access to healthcare and clean water supplies, as well as broader socio-political aims such as improving freedom of choice, increasing political autonomy, promoting the opportunity for endogenous decision-making and the encouragement of self-reliance. To what extent tourism can contribute to the improvement of these indicators is difficult to say. One of the reasons for the lack of a clear understanding of the impact of tourism on a society is partially due to the fact that tourism development is often only a smaller part of larger development schemes, such as national economic development or regional economic improvement plans. In addition, for many of these broader indices, there is no explicit guideline as to what constitutes a necessary level of 'improvement' of these conditions in various cultural and social contexts. Also at issue here is the fact that the concepts of 'improvement' and 'development' of social conditions have evolved from economically developed nations or the western school of thought, and the social and cultural impacts of tourism development are measured against these rather biased indices.

The purpose of this chapter is to examine the nature of the relationship between tourism development and social cultural change. It will also comment on the extent to which tourism development can contribute in a positive as well as in a negative manner towards improving the well-being of the host population. To do this, this chapter will begin by examining the context of broader development theories and the socioeconomic indices used to measure development. By understanding some of the shortcomings of development theories, it will shed light and understanding on how socioeconomic measurement indices used to measure development are influenced by the biases, which underlie western development theories. The chapter will then move on to examine positive and negative examples of the perceived social and cultural modernisation of host communities from the tourism literature.

Relationship of Development Theories to Tourism

As has been discussed earlier in this book, many of the predominant development theories have fundamentally emerged from a western school of thought and they do not consider alternative or traditional methods of development (Said, 1978, 1993) (see Chapter 2). The idea of 'modernisation' started in Europe about 500 years ago and it placed Europe at the centre of a world-system (Dussel, 1998). Later the centre became Euro-America or the West, and it has its own ideas and systems which the rest of the world should embrace (Peet, 1999) in order to go through the 'civilisation process' (Dussel, 1998). This, in turn, implies that there can be only one set of fundamental values and others are, to an extent, derived from these. This set of fundamental values serves as a single universal standard of rationality for the absolute superiority of one standard (Calhoun, 1995). One of the major characteristics of the ideologies from this western school of thought is that there always is the 'them *versus* us' contrast when discussing a concern over differences (Calhoun, 1995). In other word, 'our' (Euro-American) standard is the fundamental index to understand how different 'they' (rest of the world) are from 'us'.

Concepts of development and modernisation of a nation have evolved from the study of Euro-American history (Peet, 1999; Rostow, 1967). According to the previously mentioned fundamental index, the message of development and modernisation theories can be translated as 'our (the developed nations')' value standard is superior to 'their (the developing nations')' value standard, and therefore 'they' should follow the course of development 'we' have taken. In his criticism, Peet (1999) interprets Rostow's stages of economic growth as suggesting that traditional societies should 'copy the already proven examples of the West' and, in order to help out, the 'West will provide armies of modernisers'. Rostow's other suggestion is that the 'backward societies' ought to accept US aid and investment (Peet, 1999: 83).

Rostow's stages of economic growth model is based on the assumption that there is a universal process of modernisation. Likewise, the concept of development widely employed today has a fundamental assumption that every nation in the world should follow the model of the West. According to Peet (1999: 85–86), the four points of 'development' are:

(1) assuming the mental model of the West (rationalisation);
(2) the institutions of the West (the market);
(3) the goals of the West (high mass consumption); and
(4) culture of the West (worship of the commodity).

These assumptions are the backbone of much of the development theory discussed in this book. Although the development theories themselves are sound and conceptually significant, the underlying assumptions of the theories can be a cause for concern. Measurements of the quality of life or level of economic development are always examined against indices which are a reflection of the Euro-American standard of development. The development measurement assumes that the same economic and social systems work perfectly in various nations.

This assumption of homogeneity leads to other shortcomings in current development theories. Within the universalist tradition, development theories apply a single superior standard, which happens to be the western societies' set of values, to the rest of the world. By applying this standard to non-Euro-American nations, the difficulty arises in making sense out of what has been observed (or measured). As interpretation of the unknown has to be derived from the known culture, experience and intellectual traditions (in this case, Euro-American traditions) often fail to understand what is really operative in a non-Euro-American context. Instead, an illusion of what is not working there will be created to 'comprehend' the observed phenomena (Calhoun, 1995; Wuelker, 1993; Bond, 1991; Pick & Pick Jr., 1978). For instance, western philosophies are often described as unidirectional and linear while eastern philosophies are often described as circular. The western idea of development begins with a starting point and progresses over time, but this idea does not openly suggest that the process could be reversed (to regress) or come back to the starting point. Meanwhile, eastern philosophies suggest that the process is circular and will come back to the starting point at the end of the process; therefore, the process is endless. To measure the circular concept of development in the East with the linear concept of development from the West requires a great deal of imagination or a drastic change in world-view.

Another shortcoming of development theories is the unit of comparison. National growth indicators, such as GNP per capita, are often used for comparing one country to another and were initially the main type of indicator used to rank countries on development scales. Quality of life measurement indices have recently been modified to minimise the problem of unit of comparison, however, many indices today are still comparing a unit of 'nation', 'culture' or 'society'. Contrasting units such as 'whole nation' and 'whole society' suggests an assumption that they are internally integrated or there is no diversity within the unit, not even male–female divisions (Calhoun, 1995; Sklair, 1995). It is also suggested that by treating each 'society' or 'culture' as a unit, there is an unspoken understanding that each unit is equal or equivalent without regional or dialectic variations. Within the concept of universalism, there is also the assumption that each society and culture functions in the same way as in the Euro-American model (Calhoun, 1995). As a consequence, these assumptions of integrity within the unit and equality of each unit result in the devaluation of differences. These challenges in comparison also arise when comparing one nation to another in the study of tourism development. In comparisons at the destination level, one destination area may be far more lucrative in terms of economic development than other destination areas in the same country or even in the same region. Different regions within a country may also have different social and cultural values, which will react differently to tourism development and these differences may be lost if only national indices are used. Tourism is often only a small part of larger socioeconomic development plans and, in many cases, it is impossible to isolate the effects of tourism development from other forms of development. In some nations, tourism is the major contributor to social economic development while, in other nations, tourism's overall contribution to development is minimal.

Nevertheless, both the measurement of quality of life and the concepts of development which international and national organisations and agencies employ today are built on the very idea of the western concept of development. The phenomenon of 'globalisation' is a good example of the spread of the universalist idea of development: i.e. encouragement of uniform and homogenised development all over the world regardless of the social, economic and cultural diversity in the characteristics of different nations. If no alternative measurement is suggested, the levels of modernisation and development will be judged against the Euro-American models. This chapter now turns to the examination of the most commonly accepted indices of modernisation and development.

Indices of Social and Economic Development

In this era of globalisation, understanding the state of social economic development of each nation has become highly sought after information. As mentioned earlier, the information from each country typically has been measured against indices created in economically developed nations. The indices used to measure levels of development have become more complex over time from initially focusing on purely economic measurements, such as GNP per capita, to later rating such elements as literacy rates, levels of political freedoms and the status of the environment. The changes in measuring development and underdevelopment were also explored in Chapter 1. The deficiencies of relying on economic growth measures and per capita income as a measure of human well-being can be illustrated in the United Nations Development Programme's 'development diamond'. Two countries may have a similar GDP per capita but when compared to three more indices on the 'development diamond' including life expectancy, adult literacy and infant mortality, it is very apparent that the countries may differ vastly in quality of life (Yeung and Mathieson, 1998). The United States Agency for International Development (USAID) created a broader approach to measuring development using the following variables: economic performance, competitiveness foundations, health, education, environment and democracy and freedom. Sen (1999) concentrates on freedoms in his discussion of development and focuses on economic opportunities, political freedoms, social facilities, transparency guarantees and protective security. For the purposes of discussion here, Sklair's (1995) five types of classifications used by international organisations to measure the level of social economic development are summarised and comments are made on how they relate to tourism development. These classifications are: (1) income-based classifications, (2) trade-based classifications, (3) resource-based classifications, (4) quality of life classifications and (5) bloc-based classifications. However, the fifth classification is disappearing today as socioeconomic blocs (i.e. socialist economic systems as opposed to the capitalist economic system) are rapidly disintegrating and disappearing in today's world. Therefore, the first four major classifications will be briefly outlined here in order to understand their adequacy and significance in measuring the world's social economic development. After this discussion, the chapter turns to examine the social cultural impacts of tourism development.

Income-based classification

This is the most widely used indicator; however, Sklair (1995) warns that this is also one of the most misleading indicators. This classification uses the measurement of poverty and wealth on a per capita basis. Originally, this classification was developed in reaction to the global economic recession during the 1930s and 1940s, with the intention of measuring changes in national and international economic trends (Estes, 1988). Today, the World Bank often uses this classification to rank all nations, except nations of less than one million in population, by GNP per capita. The debatable point of this classification is that this method converts the local currencies into US dollars, regardless of the currency exchange rates. By classifying the countries into low-income nations (GNP per capita up to US$250) and middle-income nations (GNP per capita over US$250), this classification does not report an accurate picture of the social welfare of a nation. This index is useful for the purpose of placing nations into groups based on a common structural characteristic (i.e. GNP); however, this measurement tends to rank the Communist (or ex-Communist) bloc much lower than it should be (Gonzales, 1988). For example, by this classification, countries of centrally planned economies tend to be ranked as low-income nations and countries which accumulate capital surplus through oil exports are ranked as upper-middle-income nations, regardless of the state of welfare of the population. National wealth does not necessarily represent the wealth of a population as so called 'developed' or 'industrialised' nations tend to have smaller populations, thus higher per capita incomes, in comparison to the so called 'developing' or 'underdeveloped' nations, which tend to have larger populations, often termed 'over populated', and thus have a lower per capita income.

Countries turning to tourism as an agent of development often focus on job creation and the extra income that is brought into the economy (see Chapters 3 and 6). Recent advances in the area of Tourism Satellite Accounts are helping to determine more precisely the economic value of the tourism industry to a country (S. Smith, 1998). However, what is of interest in terms of this chapter is to the extent to which the additional income brought in by tourism facilitates the socioeconomic modernisation of a country and affects the quality of life and well-being of the host populations. How the additional income circulates throughout the economy and who benefits both directly and indirectly will have an impact on the overall improvements to the host society. If local people are employed in the tourism industry and governments are able to generate additional revenues to provide more social programmes, the quality of life may improve. However, if multinational corporations and a local élite control the industry, and most of the income leaks out of the country, then there will be little socioeconomic benefit from tourism development (see Chapter 9 for a discussion on the political economy of tourism).

Trade-based classification

In this classification, patterns of trade are important and used as an index for social and economic development. This classification was developed from investigations into the economic growth patterns of currently 'developed' or 'industrialised' nations. The quantity, the value and type of goods and services traditionally imported and exported by these developed nations have a clear pattern (Sklair, 1995). The developed nations historically imported raw materials and exported manufactured goods and capital. This system safeguarded the price of raw materials as being lower relative to manufactured goods, which in turn put the exporter nations of raw materials in an insecure position in the world market. While the importer nations enjoys a diversity of economic activities, the exporter nations tend to rely on one or two main raw materials (also known as a mono-crop economy) and these staples tend to be vulnerable to price instability in the world market (Edwards, 1985; Sklair, 1995). The exporter nation can end up in a dependent position relative to the importer nation. There is criticism that simply adopting the successful pattern followed by the 'developed' nations does not work for the 'developing' nations, as this classification categorises nations by import-led or export-led industries. The nations who adopted export-led industrialisation (ELI) accumulated wealth by successfully manufacturing goods while import substitution industrialisation (ISI) imports components and technologies instead of importing finished goods.

With many nations continuing to shift into service industries, this classification and index may need to be reconsidered. Tourist-generating nations treat tourism as an import and the tourist-receiving nations treat tourism as an export, even though no physical or tangible goods are imported or exported in a strict sense. In this case the tourist-generating countries tend to be developed nations in the North, who already enjoy a diversity of economic activities. Meanwhile the exporter nations who receive tourists are not necessarily in the developing nations of the South (for example, Europe receives more than 50% of world tourist arrivals). However, if the destination country happens to be one of the developing nations in the South, there is a strong possibility that the country is relying on the new mono-crop, namely tourism. By relying on tourism as the dominant industry, a country often suffers from an economically insecure position in the world market. Developing countries, in particular, are often in a dependent position with weak negotiating power as many of the major multinational tourism enterprises have their headquarters in developed countries (see Chapter 9). In addition by relying on tourism as a mono-crop, the destination country is left exposed to changes in tourist demand and seasonality, which can cause a country's tourist industry to go into decline. This not only affects national tourism indicators but also individual tourism workers and entrepreneurs who are left to seek other employment.

Resource-based classification

Resource-based classification is meant to describe the distribution of natural resources in the world, which are currently or potentially of use to human beings. No country in the world is entirely self-sufficient in all of the material it uses and therefore will have to import some products (Sklair, 1995). The extent to which a country needs to import specific products can leave it in a vulnerable and dependent position. When examining resources, usually the following three categories are compared: (1) bioclimatic resources (land surfaces and water bodies), (2) fossil-fuel and non-fuel mineral resources and (3) others (solar energy or geothermal power, etc.) (Cole, 1988). Two such categories of note used to measure levels of self-sufficiency are the level of imports of cereal and oil. In the category of bioclimatic resources, for example, in many developing nations, arable land increases slower than the population growth. However, in the developed nations there has either been little change in the arable land area or loss of arable land due to urbanisation. Some countries rely on the import of cereals because of the lack of agricultural land or due to the fact the countries are growing crops for export and are unable to support the population's needs for staples (Cole, 1988). Meanwhile, Sklair (1995) argues that the needs and consumption of cereal in the 'developing' nations are directly manipulated by transnational practices and, therefore, this index cannot be interpreted as a truthful figure for the needs and consumption of the population.

Indicators such as oil imports are widely interpreted as the ability of a nation to develop or sustain industrialisation. To illustrate what is really the basis of this classification, US energy consumption in 1994 was 7818.53 kg of oil equivalent per capita yearly. The US imported 18.97% of their energy in the same year. The United Arab Emirates consumed 10530.79 kg of oil equivalent per capita yearly and imported 454.42% of its energy in 1994. Meanwhile, Spain consumed 2457.65 kg per capita and imported 69.38% of their energy; Thailand consumed 769.41 kg per capita while importing 60.89% of their energy; and Tanzania consumed 33.87 kg per capita and 83.07% of their energy was imported (Instituto del Tercer Mundo, 1999). Oil and coal represent approximately 70% of global energy consumption. What is important to note, however, is that traditional energy sources such as firewood do not appear in this resource-based classification (Sklair, 1995).

The unequal distribution of natural resources is not the major cause of unequal levels of development and living standards. The industrialised West has homogeneous economic conditions with decreasing natural resources and the Eastern bloc is resource rich with, however, rather limited means of production. Without the successful removal of barriers to flows of people, goods and information (Cole, 1988) and provision of skills, labour technology, capital and trading potential (Bednarz & Giardino, 1988), the abundant resources cannot lead to effective socio-economic development.

While resource-based classifications do not directly measure the quality of life, indirectly they can have an impact on the host population. Many developing countries may have an absolute advantage in natural resources for tourism, such as sandy beaches or pristine wilderness areas. However, they have to import many products such as construction materials, food and even employees. The rate of such imports are often discussed in terms of leakages of the tourism industry and represent potential lost opportunities to develop local supply chains and thus further promote local development. Competition for natural resources within a country between the tourism industry and the local population can cause social and cultural conflicts if locals are denied access. Competition over land and water can also create conflicts within destinations. Modern hotels and golf courses consume a great deal of water leaving less for local farmers. Attempts by the tourism industry to locate near important cultural or historic resources can be another cause of conflict. Such was the case surrounding tourism development on the island of Bali, Indonesia overlooking the temple of Tanah Lot.

Quality of life classification

When the state of a nation's 'quality of life' is measured, it is commonly agreed that economic indicators such as GNP per capita alone cannot describe the welfare of the nation. Indicators such as the distribution of health services, infant mortality rates, life expectancy, literacy rates, and educational services are often employed in an attempt to show the link between the level of economic development and the level of social welfare of the nation. Recently the addition of desirable indicators such as the status of women, distribution of income, housing and consumer durables has been advocated, though it can be difficult to obtain sufficient reliable information on these variables (Sklair, 1995).

Among other innovative indices of quality of life, Estes (1998) developed an Index of Social Progress. This index consists of 44 welfare-relevant social indicators, i.e. the status of women and children, politics, effects of disasters, cultural diversity and defence expenditures. This index has been empirically tested in over 100 countries. Some of the results indicated that some Eastern European countries and Costa Rica ranked higher than the USA and the UK on the quality of life index.

The quality of life index most widely used by international and national organisations today is the United Nations Development Programme (UNDP) Human Development Index (HDI). The HDI calculates the longevity (life expectancy at birth), knowledge (adult literacy and mean years of schooling) and income (real income per capita). The refined version of the HDI is gender sensitive and also sensitive to intra-country differences (for example, sub-cultural groups within a nation) as well as inter-country differences. The HDI is claimed to be one of the most successful indices of quality of life as other indices are based on national averages and do not allow any room to examine disparities within the nation.

The ability of a nation to provide its population with a 'better life' is partly determined by the level of economy and the resources available within the nation. The previously limited acknowledgement of social and cultural impacts when measuring the quality of life could be explained by Parsons' (1966) analysis that the study of economics is a sub-system of a society, and it has been used to understand the general theory of the social system. Cultural changes are seen as a pre-condition for economic development (Hoselitz, 1960) and each society evolves through the processes of adaptation, differentiation and integration (Parsons, 1966). In other words, studying economic impacts naturally encompasses aspects of social and cultural changes, and therefore there is no need to re-emphasise social and cultural aspects. For example, Hoselitz (1960) recognised the distinctive difference between developed and developing countries in many aspects (e.g. practice of distribution of wealth) and came to the conclusion that the level of economic growth in a developing country could be determined by how far the developing country has altered to take on features of the developed countries.

In nations where limited resources can be exploited, such as a small island nation, modernisation by industrialisation or by export is often out of the question. Hall (1998) explains that these disadvantaged nations have to find a way to diversify the economy, meet the needs of increasing pressures of population and generate employment. These nations must enter into the world system of capitalism with limited resources to prove that they are able to provide a 'quality of life' for their population. For 'island states that have very few resources, virtually the only resources where there may be some comparative advantage in favour of [island micro-states] are clean beaches, unpolluted seas and warm weather and water, and at least vestiges of distinctive culture' (Connell, 1988 cited in Hall, 1998: 146). Thus, these nations tend to turn to the service industries like tourism.

Before moving on to the social and cultural impacts of tourism, it is important to reflect further on these indices in terms of tourism development as they apply to improvements in the well-being of the destination's population. As tourism creates jobs and generates income, tourism is, therefore, said to promote economic development, which, in turn, can increase social well-being and stability as Weaver and Oppermann (2000) indicate. With new tourism development and increases in tourist spending, a larger tax base may be generated which governments can use to provide additional social development programmes. In addition, as a destination attempts to improve its international competitiveness, it tends to offer services and health standards that are more acceptable to the tourist-generating countries, which are often more developed. Local residents may then have the opportunity to indirectly derive benefits from these developments, which are primarily aimed at the tourists. Development measures such as the introduction of electricity, the elimination of a malaria hazard, the introduction of anti-crime measures or the paving of roads and the construction of related infrastructure in a resort area can lead to further economic development and thus an increase in social welfare. Moreover, tourism has the potential to moderate the actions of more repressive governments. When Malaysia hosted the 1998 Commonwealth Games, the presence of international athletes and the media had the effect of moderating the government's actions against opposition protestors (Weaver and Oppermann, 2000).

These four main categories of indices (income, trade, resource and quality of life) measure socioeconomic improvements over a wide range of variables. However, as Sklair suggests, all measures are theory laden.

> This is particularly the case for quality of life, for the ways in which the quality of life is measured, and specifically the role and definition of basic needs, virtually define our concepts of development within the global system. (Sklair, 1995: 23)

It is worth reiterating at this point that many of these measures were created in a Euro-American context and may not be applicable in developing countries. In the context of tourism, unfortunately, it is not always possible to pinpoint how many of the improvements in a society are attributable to tourism development. This complex nature of the relationship between tourism development and social cultural change is explored in the remainder of this chapter.

Social and Cultural Impacts of Tourism Development

Tourism development has often wrongly been accused of being the sole agent of rapid social and cultural change in host communities. The whole debate surrounding the negative impacts of rapid modernisation of societies through tourism development has created a series of stereotypical notions. Host communities are often viewed as 'victims', 'having to' accept the social and cultural changes brought about by tourism, while the guests who 'impose' their own values on the host communities are the 'villains'. Generalisations that portray tourism development sponsored by multinational enterprises (MNE) or transnational corporations (TNC) as 'evil invasions' also exist. The positive contributions of tourism to the social and cultural well-being of a host community are overshadowed by the attention given to the negative changes brought about by tourism. Claims that tourism development can preserve and protect traditional cultures are 'attacked' for only commercialising culture. While these arguments may be true to some extent, in some situations, these stereotypical notions are often quite misleading and too simplistic with respect to the social and cultural changes occurring in host communities. Changes may also occur in the visitors to a destination, which is a concept often ignored in the literature.

To begin with, determining the extent to which tourism development is a major agent for sociocultural change in a destination is a grey area. Sociocultural change in destination areas occurs not only through tourism but also due to a range of other reasons such as globalisation forces and the international media. In examining sociocultural change, sociology, for example tends to emphasise different aspects of life such as social structure, action, culture and power functions (Calhoun, 1995). However, the changes in these social conditions have been recorded long before tourism development became a major issue. Ancient Greeks recorded the social and cultural differences among their city-states due to the exchange of social and cultural elements with various other people who came in contact with them (Calhoun, 1995). Exposure to different cultures, peoples and social practices in the form of long-distance trade, military movement, tributary legations, labour migration, pilgrimages, and so forth, has had a gradual influence and resulted in subsequent changes in host societies. Tourism as a new form of exposure to different cultures and social practices in recent years can influence social change, but its extent has never been clearly determined.

Although the basic philosophy of tourism development is deeply rooted in economic development or modernisation theories, one particular aspect of tourism development is the fact that the social and cultural changes in the host communities are not always considered as positive. Tourism development in many developing countries is the major means of economic development. The magnitude of the sociocultural change is, in part, determined by the extent of the differences between the host and guests. Inskeep (1991) suggests that these differences include: basic values and logic systems; religious beliefs; traditions; customs; lifestyles; behavioural patterns; dress codes; sense of time budgeting; and attitudes towards strangers. In addition, the speed at which tourism is developed and the form that the tourism development takes can also have an impact on the rate of sociocultural change.

The tourism industry often sells 'traditions' and 'exotic lifestyles' as tourist attractions. Tourists often demand 'authentic' exhibitions of culture and lifestyles, which are considerably different from their own (Graburn, 1989; Bauman, 1996; Burns & Holden, 1995), even to the extent that *'spectacularisation'* of the host culture takes place (Stanley, 1998). In the name of protecting of traditions and cultures, tourism development ironically prohibits the social and cultural changes that are seen as a precondition for further economic development.

Tourists and the tourism industry do not always welcome modernisation of the host community and the mimicking of Euro-American cultures. While the economic modernisation of the host country has to be judged by the readiness to copy the Euro-American economic model, the level of cultural modernisation does not. Modernisation of culture and lifestyles are often denounced as 'cultural imperialism', 'demonstration effects' and 'assimilation'. With tourists searching for the past and nostalgia through their international travels (Lowenthal, 1985), the modernisation of a host community through the loss of its charm and tradition is disapproved of.

Mathieson and Wall (1982) identified three major types of culture, which are susceptible to change as well as attractive to tourists:

(1) inanimate forms of culture (historical buildings, monuments, traditional arts and crafts);
(2) reflection of normal day-to-day life and activities of the host community;
(3) animated forms of culture (religious events, carnivals and traditional festivals).

It seems the preservation and conservation of *inanimate* forms of culture and *animated* forms of culture are unanimously agreed upon as being important and recommended by international agencies, the tourism industry, tourists and often by the host communities. Preservation and conservation of these forms of cultures can contribute not only to the strengthening of the social and cultural identities of the host communities but also to the stimulation of economic activities. However, it is the change in the 'reflection of normal day-to-day life and activities of the host community' that is often argued as an unwanted, rather than a desirable transformation for further economic improvement.

Having stated this, sociocultural factors that are influenced by tourist activities are the most difficult to measure and quantify. While economic and environmental factors lend themselves to objective measurements, sociocultural impacts are often highly qualitative and subjective in nature (Cooper *et al.*, 1998). Sociocultural changes can range from impacts which are more measurable, such as the outbreak of a particular disease and/or infection, to those which are very hard to measure, such as changes in customs or codes of conduct. Even those factors which appear to be more quantifiable (i.e. increases in crime rates and drug use or prostitution), can be difficult to attribute solely to tourism (Cooper *et al.*, 1998). The two fundamental means of assessing sociocultural impacts in a destination include surveying both residents and tourists, while potential secondary sources of information on sociocultural impacts can include criminal activity statistics, employment data, newspaper reports/articles and other related media and notification of infectious disease statistics. Some of the data sources are quantitative in nature while others are more subjective and careful interpretation is required (Cooper *et al.*, 1998). Researchers at Bournemouth University, UK, have attempted to embed the process of sociocultural change within the more quantifiable economic and environmental models. While it is recognised that the number of sociocultural variables that can be included in a quantifiable level is quite small, they have come up with the following items:

(1) the ratio of tourists to host population;
(2) the number of contacts between hosts and guests for transactions;
(3) the number of contacts between hosts and guests while sharing facilities;
(4) the number of contacts between hosts and guests for sociocultural purposes;
(5) differences between hosts and guests age distributions;
(6) percentage of local population coming into contact with tourists;
(7) percentage of population working in tourism-related industries weighted by indirect and induced employment;
(8) tourist/host clustering; and
(9) nature of tourism (Cooper *et al.*, 1998)

Although the identification of these variables by the Bournemouth researchers may present some interesting results, it also raises further questions surrounding the ability to measure sociocultural change caused by tourism. The socioeconomic indices that were discussed earlier only look at the quantifiable or measurable variables. For example, literacy rate, access to health care and life expectancy are among the variables used as a barometer of social well-being and are seen as a spin-off from economic development. Tourism development as an economic activity for the most part does not contribute directly to these variables but may contribute to them indirectly. As Cooper *et al.* (1998) point out, the areas of social and cultural change that tourism researchers examine are beyond these measurements and are far more qualitative and subjective in nature, which makes numerical measurements almost impossible. This, in turn, questions the validity and reliability of using existing traditional socioeconomic development indices to identify the contribution tourism development makes to the social and cultural modernisation of a host population.

The next two sections will look at the positive and negative social cultural impacts brought about by tourism development. Most of the sociocultural issues discussed in the study of tourism development are not quantifiable in nature. Examples will be used below to examine the most frequently contested topics related to the social cultural impacts of tourism and how these changes have the ability either to improve on or detract from the existing quality of life.

Positive Sociocultural Impacts of Tourism Development

As mentioned at the beginning of the previous section, the relationship between tourism development and sociocultural change is complex and it has led to a variety of stereotypical notions of the impacts of tourism which are often quite misleading. For example, issues of *commoditisation* (or commercialisation) of culture, changing value systems and family structure changes are often discussed as negative impacts of tourism development. However, if managed carefully, tourism development can bring about positive changes in these areas as well. How a host community responds to the introduction of tourism will vary from destination to destination and, if planned correctly, may increase the well-being of the host population.

Tourism development is a means for socioeconomic development and, thus, successful tourism development should bring reasonable economic profit to the involved parties. This, in turn, should improve the quality of life for the local population by providing a modern lifestyle and amenities. As Wall (1995) has suggested, indigenous communities are not only impacted by tourism but they respond to it through entrepreneurial activity. There are numerous success stories of local individuals who have an entrepreneurial mind, and have made a fortune in the tourism business. Tour guides who can speak a few different European languages are living comfortably with modern conveniences (a new car, stereo, satellite dish, etc.) and a fashionable western lifestyle (McCarthy, 1994). A young farmer, who grows vegetables and herbs to cater to tourists at an international hotel on the island of Lombok, Indonesia, had one of the most luxurious houses in his village (Telfer and Wall, 1996). Young men in Kenya (Peake, 1989, cited in Kinnaird *et al.*, 1994) and in The Gambia (Brown, 1992, cited in Kinnaird *et al.*, 1994) found formal and informal lucrative jobs in the tourism industry and gained economic benefits.

If not commoditisation, tourism development can contribute to the *protection and enhancement* of traditions, customs and heritage, which would otherwise disappear through the waves of modernisation. Modernisation and globalisation tend to standardise the world's economic culture by adopting a universal model, and implicitly send a message that indigenous culture and traditions do not bring economic development to a nation. This process encourages the developing nations of the South to embrace things that are Euro-American and devalue their indigenous culture and traditions. Fisher (1988) studied the impacts of modernisation in Sub-Saharan societies and noted that imported goods flooded African markets substituting for traditional items. As a result, indigenous craftsmen were discouraged and dependence on unskilled labour for primary production was encouraged. This is also true in tourism development as a baseline, although, as 'indigenous' culture and traditions are also important commodities in the tourism business, the tourism business urges the local population to maintain their local values, traditions and heritage. Tourism development can create more opportunities for indigenous craftsmen and artists to produce traditional art forms. This also leads to the creation of 'new' traditions such as Canadian Inuit soapstone carvings. Inuit soapstone carving is not a traditional art in a strict sense. It was recently introduced as an alternative means of income for the Inuit population who were losing their traditional means of living such as hunting. It has been established today as an authentic Inuit art and each piece fetches a high price.

With a well-managed small-scale tourism development, *cultural exchange* through tourism can also be possible. It is known that the tourists in general come to the destination with certain stereotypes towards the host culture and their stereotypes are often reinforced by the manipulation of cultural exhibitions (Stanley, 1998). In some cases, tourists' stereotypical images are strengthened during the trip regardless of what they have actually seen in the destination. However, in a small-scale development, where local people are actively involved, direct cultural exchange can be achieved by the use of local guides (Telfer, 2000c) home-stay programmes such as those in South Korea (www.knto.or.kr/english/index.html) and so forth. An open mind is the prerequisite for effective cultural exchange. It does not necessarily mean that everyone agrees with everyone else; however, it does mean that one can accept the existence of different views, opinions and customs without arguing whose opinions and customs are superior. Higher tolerance and the acceptance of eccentricities are required in a close-contact situation often on the host side. Nevertheless, it is important for tourists to acknowledge that they are temporary visitors who have come to see the host community's culture, heritage and natural attractions, and therefore they are the ones to be more tolerant and accepting of different practices and values. It is also important for the host communities to try to remain in control of the guest–host relationship, though external forces may not always allow this to happen.

This kind of cultural exchange cannot, however, be achieved in a mass tourism setting where direct and high-density contact between hosts and guests is minimal. It also may not work for hosts and guests who have such a strongly fixed mindset that they will not understand each other. In this sense, the role of modern and young people, who tend to have more open and inquisitive minds about the outside world, cannot be ignored. Young people in the host communities are drawn to the tourists' culture and value systems. This does not always have to be a one-way process – from the tourists to the host youths. With more education about their cultural values and traditions for the younger generation in the host communities, a positive demonstration of youth culture can be presented both in the host communities and in the tourists' home countries.

With this hope of mutual understanding among young people, between tourists and hosts, the 'Global Summit on Peace through Tourism' was held in Jordan in November 2000. Some academics claim that tourism is a peace time movement (for example, Goeldner *et al.*, 2000) and others take the stance that cultural contacts during the process of travelling can also be a strong drive for world peace. In 1988, the Columbia Charter in Vancouver, Canada was drawn from the 'First Global Conference: Tourism – A Vital Force for Peace'. International tourism can be used as a powerful tool for world peace by educating individual tourists to be more responsible for their words and deeds in the destinations. This is the basic philosophy of Morton-Mar's 'International Institute for Peace through Tourism' in Montreal, Canada (www.iipt.org).

Elsewhere, Tourism Concern in the UK (www.tourismconcern.org.uk) in cooperation with other grassroots organisations use international tourism as a force to change the violation of human rights in Myanmar (Burma). In May 2000, Tourism Concern and The Burma Campaign UK launched a boycott campaign against a tour guidebook on Burma published by Lonely Planet, supporting Aung San Suu Kyi, the Burmese pro-democracy leader who has been under house arrest by the military junta. Burmese pro-democracy leaders are asking potential tourists not to holiday in Burma until it becomes a democratic society. Organisations like Tourism Concern believe that international tourism can be a powerful tool to help resolve political conflicts as well as to pave a path to world peace.

The presence of tourism can also be seen as a force for stability in a society, from which local residents will benefit. With the highly volatile nature of tourist behaviour, any signs of conflict in a destination can lead to mass cancellations of trips. Governments wanting to pursue tourism as an agent of development need to ensure tourist security. A more light-hearted indicator of the link between tourism, peace and stability is the McDonald's theory of conflict prevention developed by Tom Friedman of *The New York Times*. A McDonald's hamburger shop is often one of the main MNE present in more developed tourism destinations. The theory states that two countries with McDonald shop do not go to war with each other (Naím, 2001).

With the recent shift towards sustainability, additional focus has been placed on involving local communities in the planning process (Hall, 2000). As Swarbrooke

(1999: 123) suggests, 'one of the cornerstones of sustainable tourism development is the idea that the host community should be actively involved in tourism planning and should perhaps control the industry and its activities'. The rationale for increasing the level of community involvement in tourism planning is that it is believed to be in keeping with the ideas of democracy, it gives a voice to those who are most affected by impending developments, it makes use of local knowledge in decision-making and it reduces potential conflicts between hosts and guests (Swarbrooke, 1999). This shift in focus has the potential to *empower* local communities and thereby increase local political autonomy and promote the opportunity for endogenous decision-making. The empowerment and enrichment which a community can gain through the involvement of the local population can benefit the overall civics process of a society. In many cases, the consensus is that development should be on a small scale with reasonable government intervention for community development to be successful (Dahles, 2000; Kamsma and Bras, 2000; van der Straaten, 2000; Kappert, 2000).

The *empowerment of communities and women* through tourism are also discussed in detail in other chapters in this book (see Chapters 5 and 6). This section briefly looks at the empowerment issue as a social phenomenon induced by tourism development. Issues of empowerment (especially female empowerment) are considered to be an important indicator of social welfare (Andrews, 1988). Although the United Nations' *Universal Declaration of Human Rights* affirmed the equal rights for men and women in 1948 (Momsen, 1991), it was not until the Danish economist Boserup in 1970 documented the uneven distribution of development benefits to men and women that agencies and governments responded with initiatives to address the situation (Staudt, 1998). In development and modernisation theories, men and women are affected differently. In modernising developing nations primarily based on agriculture, for example, the new and better-paying jobs tend to be given to men with women often losing control or access to resources (Momsen, 1991).

With tourism being a service industry, it is often considered as part of the informal sector and workers are not officially registered. Women in Africa and the Caribbean play a significant role in the retail sector labour force. Ninety-three percent of market traders in Accra, Ghana, 87% of market traders in Lagos, Nigeria and 77% of market traders in Haiti are women (Momsen, 1991). Momsen observed two types of retail workers in the Caribbean: (1) young male beach vendors who sell jewellery or suntan oil for a few years, hoping to meet young female tourists, and (2) older women who braid hair or sell home-made clothing because of the flexibility of work hours, which can accommodate child-care (Momsen, 1991). She also noted many Caribbean women prefer working as a vendor to running a guesthouse due to the caring image of women in retail businesses (Momsen, 1994). Similarly Samoans consider women to be better at hospitality jobs than men, and also the seasonal nature of jobs in tourism also suit women's need to look after domestic chores (Fairbairn-Dunlop, 1994).

As a successful example of empowerment, the West Samoan Women's Advisory Committee began with one woman who started a small-scale hotel business. Her hotel now incorporates historical tours, village tours, business-skill workshops and is even expanding into the area of ecotourism and conservation workshops. The committee helps develop modern handicrafts for tourists and provides necessary workshops for the women who are the producers. The development of this hotel complex features deliberate educational input at each step and the small size of the business enables it to respond to changes (Fairbairn-Dunlop, 1994).

In another example, Indonesia has been operating a national programme primarily funded by UNDP, called P2WIK, since 1981. Under this programme, local women are enabled to become independent *batik* (traditional wax dye textile) producers. Even though on the island of Java, Indonesia, women enjoy equal rights and respect with men in the household, and many families rely on the wife's income, women do not always share the same equality of opportunities (Overholt, 1991). *Batik* production has traditionally been seen as a woman's job and by ensuring the opportunities for women to produce and distribute their finished products, not only do a few households benefit, but also the entire village that participates in this P2WIK project benefit. The finished *batik* products are sold not only to wholesalers but also to tourists (Overholt, 1991). Tourism employment in Bali, Indonesia is also discussed further in Chapter 6 along with the role of women in tourism employment.

While some argue that tourism-related jobs for women often have pitiful working conditions, women who find jobs as cleaners and maids in hotels or as craft producers or inn-keepers can still retain their dignity and economic autonomy. Sex tourism can be viewed by some agencies as another form of job creation for unskilled women and girls, and sometimes for men (see Hall, 1994c). Nevertheless, it is not included as a form of empowerment due to the high-risk nature of this job and the devastating consequences of HIV/AIDS. Prostitution, which often develops in tourism destinations, will be addressed in the next section.

These positive sociocultural changes from tourism have the ability to add to the overall quality of life and well-being in a destination. An infusion of tourists into a destination can generate economic benefits for those involved as well as promoting social and political stability and the protection of cultural and heritage traditions. Additional government revenues from tourism may be used to benefit the wider population further in terms of related social programmes. However, it is difficult to know to what extent these factors can contribute to over riding development indicators. Many of the positive changes outlined above can also be argued from the negative side, as will now be illustrated.

Negative Sociocultural Impacts of Tourism Development

Arguments surrounding the negative sociocultural impacts of tourism development often focus on changes in traditions, customs, festivals, values, language and family structure. Nevertheless, there is little disagreement raised over the modernisation (or westernisation) of accommodation facilities, transportation or even accessibility to cultural attractions in comparison to the criticisms raised over the modernisation of animated culture or reflections on daily life in host communities.

The main areas of discussion are often related to *cultural imperialism* and *assimilation* of the weaker culture. As the majority of tourists come from economically developed nations, they tend to expect familiar amenities and conveniences of life in the destination areas such as they have in their home country, e.g. hot water available 24 hours a day, flushing toilets, air-conditioned rooms, comfortable transportation, familiar food, and so on. The tourists and tourism industry that serve tourists from the developed nations tend to impose their cultural values in the destination. In order to accommodate the lucrative tourism business, the host community often has to accept the tourists' culture. Even though there may be no need for the host community to take the position of a weaker culture, because of the power imbalance, the host community is often placed in a subjugating position.

As part of cultural imperialism and assimilation, changes in *language* will also be observed. Although Mignolo (1998) argues that the relocation of language is nothing but the result of modernisation processes, tourism is a form of modernisation today and transformation in language in the destination areas may partially be because of the introduction of tourism. Most international tourists do not learn or know the language of the host communities and instead, English is used as the common language between tourists and hosts. Those people who serve in the tourism industry or related businesses have to learn a communicable level of English. Languages of young people also change as a form of fashion. Pidgin English is a good example of the fusion of local language and language of communication with the tourists (English in this case). In other areas of the world, as a legacy of colonisation, the common language may be French or Spanish. As the need for a foreign language to communicate with tourists increases, the language curriculum in the school system also changes.

Demonstration effects do contribute to social and cultural changes in the host communities. Although host populations are not always aware of the fact during their brief encounter with individual tourists that the tourists' behaviour is not typical in their home environment (i.e. tourists' being overly self-assertive, extravagant and often promiscuous), often it stirs feelings of envy or disgust in the host population. For example, tension between daring female tourists and local Greek women who are loyal to tradition is mounting (Leontidou, 1994). Balinese communities are becoming aggressive towards tourists as they start seeing the tourists' culture as a threat to Balinese culture (Karyadi, 2000). In Indonesia, an average tourist spends the equivalent of an average Indonesian's annual wage for a few nights in a hotel (Karyadi, 2000) and in Tunisia a tourist spends the equivalent of a Tunisian's annual wage in one week (Tsartas, 1989, cited in Leontidou, 1994). What the tourists possess and how they spend money affect the material culture of the host communities, e.g. cameras and video recorders, electronic gadgets, jewellery and fine clothing or fashionable jeans and T-shirts. McCarthy (1994) warns that particularly youths in the host population, with his example of Indonesian youths, admire everything western without question. The ways tourists behave has an influence on the spiritual or cultural norms of the host populations, i.e. disrespectful attire and behaviours in the context of religious environments, demonstration of affection in public, tourists' diet patterns, and so forth.

The *authenticity* of displayed culture is another debated area. Tourists are seeking 'the past' or 'heritage' (Lowenthal, 1985) in the foreign countries. Although tourists claim to seek the 'authentic' or 'genuine' culture of the host communities, how far they can really accept and appreciate the 'authentic' is always questionable (Hitchcock *et al.*, 1993). It is not uncommon for the 'authentic' culture to be too different, too strange or too complicated for the tourists fully to comprehend. They do not want to spend all day watching the rituals which they may not understand, or they have such a busy travel itinerary that they cannot stay very long at any one site. Safety is the utmost concern for tourists. They want to experience a little bit of a thrill from a safe distance, but they often do not want to risk their safety by participating in cultural activities. But perhaps the factor that causes serious cognitive dissonance is the tourists' stereotypical 'image' or 'idea' of how the authentic culture should be. The modern tourism industry's success relies on successful image creation (Selwyn, 1993; Morgan & Pritchard, 1998) and there are many success stories; for instance, created images of Scotland which are not a true reflection of Scottish history (Butler, 1998b). The information is acquired from travel guidebooks, lure books, travel programmes on TV, travel journals, novels or even from friends and relatives. Bruner (1995) observed that many tourists from North America only wanted to 'see' what was illustrated in the *National Geographic* magazine and did not even bother to wait for the 'authentic' cultural performances in Indonesia, which were running late. Often the tourists' quest for 'authenticity' does not go beyond the confirmation of their stereotypical images. When their images and ideas do not match the 'authentic' cultural exhibitions, tourists tend to reduce dissonance by rejecting the 'authentic' cultural exhibitions.

In addition to the tourists' views, the host communities have different approaches to the display of their own culture. For host populations, it is not a bad idea to maintain and preserve culture, tradition, arts and crafts not only for the tourists but also for future generations. However, the host population will soon learn that the tourists will not understand the true value of their culture. In that case, certain parts of the rituals are too sacred to share with outsiders who probably do not appreciate them. The host populations have also realised that tourists prefer only a certain kind/part of their culture. By accommodating both tourists' and hosts' views, the display of 'authentic' culture becomes merely a 'performance' or 'staged authenticity'. *Staged authenticity* is commonly observed in the following forms: shortened and abbreviated versions of the cultural performances; highlighting the parts/types of cultural performance and crafts which suit tourists' tastes; re-creation of the stage in a more westernised and modern environment; and re-arranging or changing some parts of the host's culture so that it makes sense/is acceptable to tourists. A few examples where these changes have occurred include cultural performances and displays at the Polynesian Culture Centre in Hawaii (Stanley, 1998); performances of the Peking Opera highlights at Taoyuen Theatre in Beijing; the '*touristification*' of Balinese culture in Indonesia (Picard, 1995, 1997); the modification of Pisac pottery to suit tourist's tastes in Peru (Henrici, 1999), the shortening of the Kecak Dance in Bali, and various other changes in culture shows at international hotels and in tourist arts sold at airports.

Family structures and values can also be affected by the introduction of tourism as a form of modernisation. Tourism businesses tend to prefer to use the 'feminine touch' or rely on the friendliness of female workers at different levels. In addition, many tourism-related jobs that are available to the local population are unskilled menial jobs, and hence receive low pay.

These characteristics of tourism jobs give more women an opportunity to work in the tourism industry, both in post-industrial countries and developing countries. Although this phenomenon can be argued to be part of female empowerment through tourism development, it can also be discussed as a changing agent for the family structure and the power game in social structures. In some traditional societies, women are not the main breadwinners of the family. However, by taking up jobs in the tourism industry, suddenly the women starts earning a salary and it is not unusual for their earnings to be steadier and higher than those earned by men in the primary industry (i.e. agriculture or fishery). In his 1995 interview with the manager of a four-star hotel in Senggigi Beach on the island of Lombok, Indonesia, Telfer learned of the case of a young female from a local traditional village who had been hired to work at the hotel. After a period of time the woman's father came from the village to pick the girl up from the hotel and he did not allow her to return to work. He was in an uncomfortable position as his daughter had been making more money than he ever had and he also did not want his daughter working in the presence of foreign male tourists (Telfer, personal communication 2001).

In some countries, highly skilled and trained men such as medical doctors take up jobs in tourism in order to make more money (Szivas & Riley, 1999), which often results in the displacement of professions, particularly in rural areas. Similarly, men who have a limited education are also readily available for tourism jobs. The employment opportunities for these women and men can threaten the authority of chiefs, elders and older men who traditionally hold influential positions in the society (Harrison, 1992a). In some nations like India for example, where retail business employees are traditionally women, many men who are unable to find higher level jobs in the tourism industry or those who have lost their jobs in other sectors, now displace women from their jobs in the retail businesses (Rao, 2000).

It is not economic autonomy that solely results in social changes. Losing women to tourism jobs means the family responsibility for domestic chores, which used to be the responsibility of the women, has to be altered. The practice of a nine-to-five, 40-hour workweek with shifts is alien to many non-western societies. Working in such a system prevents many local employees from participation in social obligations, religious rituals and festivals, which are the basis of the society. This may lead to a disruption in communal life (McCarthy, 1994). Also the sale of their ancestral land, voluntarily or by coercion, for the purpose of tourism development causes problems of ownership, relocation of sacred land and displacement of local populations (McCarthy, 1994; Patterson, 1993).

Migration through tourism can be categorised into two groups: (1) leisure migration (Tomljebivic and Faulkner 2000), especially of retired people; and (2) migration of labour. Leisure migration tends to be less significant in terms of effects on local labour markets and as tourists and retirees migrate semi-permanently to enclave or reserved areas, they contribute to the income in the area. However, *migration of labour* due to tourism has a significant influence on the local labour markets and economic leakage and is widely studied. Anderson (1988) noted the labour migration in the Caribbean Basin, and Szivas and Riley (1998) found highly educated human resources in tourism-related businesses in Hungary. Although most of the tourism jobs are low-paid menial jobs, in the nations/regions where the unemployment rate is high or where farmers and fishermen are barely surviving, tourism jobs are so attractive that many people migrate to the tourist destination areas. Young people, especially young men are drawn to the developed tourist areas where western consumption styles represent the promise of a 'better life' (Dahles, 2000). The story of a taxi-driver who had to ask his passengers for directions is one of the harmless anecdotes. Migration of labour is not only displacing the workforce in the rural and peripheral areas but also destroying family structures as usually one or two family members leave the hometown to seek jobs in the tourist areas. A sudden increase in the population adds pressure to the tourist destination areas and the vicinity, raising issues of employment, low-income housing, welfare insurance, food sufficiency, health issues along with other numerous social issues. Especially where tourism jobs are heavily influenced by seasonality, unemployment during the low seasons becomes a serious problem. These increases in population through labour migrants and tourist influx generate additional pressures and arguably have a negative impact on the quality of life of the host population (see Chapter 6 for a discussion on labour migration). In a yet unproven model, Doxey (1976) suggested that the attitudes of local residents towards increases in tourism (e.g. the number of tourists, infrastructure and facilities, migrant labour, etc.) become progressively more negative.

Migration of labour itself is not the only issue which draws people closer to tourist areas. It can also potentially result in an increase in *crime, drugs, terrorism and prostitution*, as often happens in developed urban zones. *Crimes* targeting tourists, i.e. pick-pocketing, mugging, deception in business, illegal business, sexual and physical assaults and, in some cases, murders and so forth are almost a daily news topic in some fairly developed destination areas. Airports in Florida, USA, offer information leaflets for tourists on how to protect themselves from crime. Many destinations provide a Tourist Police force for the protection of tourists. *Trafficking of illegal drugs* due to tourism is a problem even in nations like The Netherlands and Belgium that have an unusually high tolerance for the possession and sale of soft drugs. As illustrated in the popular films such as *Bangkok Hilton* and *Return to Paradise*, some nations do not hesitate to take extreme measures to prevent drug trafficking by tourists. Illegal drugs not only affect tourism but can also lead to the corruption of the fabric of society.

Terrorists and political activists target international tourists as an effective medium for propaganda, relying on world-wide news coverage. Incidents of tourists being shot at attractions or hotels, the planting of bombs in international hotels and tourist buses, outbreaks of civil riots near tourist areas and tourists being taken as hostage have uncommonly increased in the late 1990s. Although the increase in terrorism acts is not a direct result of tourism development, tourism does lend itself as a perfect venue for terrorist groups to have their agenda noticed. The far-reaching effects of the terrorist attacks in the United States on 11 September 2001 are only beginning to be recognised at the time of writing. The psychological and economic impacts of these attacks are also having direct and indirect impacts on the tourism industry around the world.

Prostitution that specially caters for tourists is also considered to be one of the negative social impacts. Female prostitution is a direct response to local demands rather than tourism demands; however, male prostitution (beach boys) is a direct response to tourist demand (Momsen, 1994). In some Asian nations, government officials turn their heads in toleration of sex tourism (Staudt, 1998), as sex tourism can be an invaluable source of foreign exchange. For instance, sex tourism is the third largest source of foreign exchange for the Philippines. The existence of *Kisaeng* sex tourism is dependent on Japanese clients (tourists and businessmen), and the Thai government took a proactive stance in favour of sex tourism as a form of job creation even when the AIDS/HIV scare became a major issue in the late 1980s, which could no longer be ignored (Hall, 1994c). Nonetheless, women and girls who work in the sex industry for both local men and male tourists 'earn from mere pittance wages to salaries that surpass that of factory jobs' (Staudt, 1998: 106).

The issues associated with prostitution and tourism also include: cross-border human trafficking to satisfy increasing demands, the spread of HIV/AIDS and the resulting deaths, child prostitution to accommodate a paedophile clientele and associated illegal drug use. Certain destinations are already known as 'sex tourism destinations'. It is the stereotypical 'image' creation of the destination with regards to women and children in the destination. Women and children in these destinations are wrongly labelled as 'submissive, obedient, trained to amuse male clients' and 'cheap'. This commercialisation of personal relations (trading a human relationship) in some studies is explained in relation to the loss of male identity in the clients'/tourists' home culture (Kruhse-MountBurton, 1995) and another study suggests that it is a reflection of social values in the clients'/tourists' home culture that approves of the commercialisation of personal relations (Hashimoto, 2000). Sex tourism does not only occur in the tourist destination areas. Trafficking of women often involves the import of women from foreign countries with illegal entry visas (Skrobanek et al., 1997; Seabrook, 1996) to the destination areas to work in the sex industry. Sex tourism also involves exporting local prostitutes to enter illegally the clients' home countries as a mistress or sex slave.

These examples of the negative impacts of tourism illustrate how complicated the relationship between tourism and the host population can be and standard socioeconomic indicators cannot adequately measure these changes. Tourism is a double-edged sword as the industry may bring in more money to the local population and government and thereby raising living standards but at the same time there can be sociocultural costs associated with the development.

Discussions and Conclusions

The issue of tourism as a form of socioeconomic development and modernisation is full of contradictions. First of all, the theories of modernisation and development mainly focus on the economic welfare of the nation as a whole, assuming better economic levels can provide better social welfare, such as a lower unemployment rate, higher GNP, better healthcare and thus longer life expectancy. However, the fundamental assumption of these theories is that the Euro-American model of industrialisation is the preferred model of development and the rest of the world must follow this model to improve economic levels and lifestyles. It has not even been questioned until recently whether or not this model can be applied to different cultures and socioeconomic systems. Second, it has not been questioned whether tourism should be a means of economic development or a means of modernisation to improve living standards. In socioeconomic development theories, both economic development and modernisation of living standards should go hand in hand, and lifestyle and living standards are expected to follow Euro-American models. However, in tourism, indigenous lifestyles and the customs of the host communities are valuable commodities and are not expected to be totally modernised. The question is whether or not it is possible to modernise lifestyles and living standards without changing the traditions and old customs of the host communities.

Tourism development can be reviewed under the concepts of dependency theory and economic neoliberalism, both of which reflect the domination of the economically developed nations in the tourism business, the devaluation of cultural and traditional values of the weaker economy and unfair competition between the North and South (see Chapter 2). According to dependency theory, in the capitalist system, wealth is not equally distributed in the global economic system and within the economic system of a nation. In today's global economy, the top 200 MNE/TNC in nine countries in the North dominated 32% of the world GDP in 1995 (Instituto del Tercer Mundo, 1999). Therefore there is a clear division betweem North and South today, and even within nations there is a visible gap between the rich and poor. Many traditional societies, or developing nations, have cooperatives or community-help networks. As a traditional societies are encouraged to copy the more advanced, complex capitalist society, this old-fashioned system for a more equal distribution of wealth is disappearing.

Most of the destinations in developing nations embrace tourism development, as it is perceived to be a quick foreign exchange earner with little overhead investment, and it is often regarded as a smokeless industry. In destinations that are rich in natural assets such as beaches, mountains, forests, flora and fauna, history and heritage, but lack resources to industrialise, tourism seems to be an ideal form of economic development. However, in reality, the construction of tourist areas which could include hotels, restaurants and infrastructure (airports, roads, water and sewage systems, etc.) requires a large initial capital investment often by MNEs or TNCs. Unless tourism development has investment local entrepreneurs and individual businesses, which often means rather small-scale developments, there are no noticeable economic benefits to the destination's economy due to the high level of leakage of profits back to the MNE/TNC. Alternatively, the money circulates only through the local élite. The demand for the product of tourism is also unreliable in comparison to other more tangible products, i.e. minerals or automobile parts. Trends and tastes in tourism products change quickly and disloyal customers do not repeatedly visit the same destinations. The seasonality of the tourism products does not help provide a steady income to the destinations. In order to maintain the level of demand, many destinations use pricing as a marketing strategy. Such a strategy does not help improve the current economic situation of the destinations. Tourism jobs are often among the lowest-paid jobs. Many tour operators in the developed tourist-generating countries take advantage of exchange rates, Third World payment rates and negotiating power to exploit businesses in the destinations.

Modernisation encourages social and cultural changes, as economic growth needs these changes as a taking-off stage for further economic development. Similar to imperialism and colonisation, tourism development can offer, to a certain extent, improvements in healthcare and the supply of potable water, better infrastructure and sanitation, and better housing and education. While these benefits may be apparent within the tourism complexes in the destination, such as a resort enclave, the extent to which these benefits extend from tourism to the host population's daily life is debatable. There seems to be no systematic reports providing information as to what degree of social benefits result directly from tourism development in an area. For the most part, supranational agencies' statistics do not distinguish tourism development from other forms of economic development in nations. For example, many nations are striving to attain higher literacy rates among the population, as it is an important indicator of social welfare. Information as to whether more educational opportunities were added due to tourism development, however, is not available. Sharing a scarce water supply, especially in island nations, always brings controversy between the tourism industry and the local population. Lea (1988) argues that it is unreasonable to expect skilled medical professionals in a small developing nations even to cater tourists' needs. Even in the tourist destinations in the developed nations, social benefits from tourism development are often perceived to be non-existent (Telfer & Hashimoto, 1999).

Although the principles of tourism development can be debated from the perspectives of dependency and economic neoliberalism, anthropologists, sociologists and psychologists tend to debate the values of indigenous culture and traditions from the stance of alternative development. Tourism development ought to contribute to the protection and maintenance of the culture, traditions and value systems of the host communities. Tourism development should be a catalyst to strengthen the cultural identities and dignity of the host populations. The tourism industry has jumped on the bandwagon for its own purpose. The exotic host culture and traditions are an invaluable commodity as part of the tourism product. However, this argument is a double-edged sword. In an extreme case, a village was designated a historical site, or a museum village, where no alteration or no modernisation was to be allowed in order to maintain historical accuracy. In this case, villagers were not even consulted in the designation process (McCarthy, 1994). Tourists demand to see 'the past' and 'heritage' in an authentic setting but they are unaware of the consequences of their demands. Their demand to see the host communities as they were in yesterday's lifestyles deprives the host populations of their privilege to progress and improve. The tourism industry also creates the images of host communities such as the exotic, the unspoiled, the romantic savage, the backward and the underdeveloped. Such labelling often forces host communities to retain old-fashioned ways of living in order to attract tourists. This clearly goes against the principles of modernisation and economic development. The host community should have a choice of whether or not to comply with such labelling, and it should be able to choose to be modernised. However, as described in dependency theory, power imbalances in tourism development inarguably exists and, when the host community is the vulnerable one in this power game, without strong leadership, the host community has little choice but to choose to survive through this power game.

As is the case for general sociocultural change, empowerment of one gender is also a double-sided issue. Women empowerment is one of the most desirable issues in western concepts of development. It is often argued that post-war industrialis-ation based on capitalism triggered the marginalisation of women today (Staudt, 1998). In many societies, researchers argue that women are subjects of inferior standing through the practice of religion, education, socioeconomic standing and political ideology (Andrews, 1988). Dixon (cited in Andrews, 1988: 126) defined women's inferiority in the society based on 'the degree of women's access to and control over material resources (food, land, income, and other forms of wealth) and social resources (knowledge, power, and prestige) within the family, in the commu-nity and in the society at large'. This may be true in many nations today; however, there still remains the question as to whether or not this condition was aggravated or reinforced by introducing Western ideology of economic development and mod-ernisation. In tourism, in which many so-called developing nations are involved, there are concerns about changes in social structure and social fabric due to tourism development. Women in economically developing nations such as Fiji and Indone-sia, mentioned earlier in this chapter, and women in socialist or communist societies tend to have an equal or more advantageous social status than men. Yet, the introduction of industrialisation and tourism development transformed the value of jobs and created a preference for female workers in the tourism industry, which has inevitably affected women's socioeconomic status. On one hand, women regained the access to material resources (e.g. Aboriginal women's land ownership in Australia) and social resources (e.g. access to higher education) through tourism related jobs. On the other hand, women's income from tourism-related jobs can surpass men's income from agriculture and the fishery. Women who leave home to partake in tourism-related jobs can also cause radical changes in traditional social structures and family values (see Chapter 6).

Social changes such as gender empowerment, family structure and traditional values are clearly inevitable, particularly if developing nations are to copy Euro-American society's lifestyles, value systems and family structures. It is com-monly held that the relationship between economic development and associated social modernisation is inarguably positive. Nevertheless the meaning of the social and cultural changes induced by so-called 'modernisation' is only now being questioned. With alternative development theories gaining in popularity, some people are beginning to question whether it is worth witnessing unexpected drastic changes in sociocultural values and practices in the name of socioeconomic development. Arabic traditionalists are calling for a departure from the urban mod-ernisation paradigm and changes in family values with calls for a revival of Islamic values, including that of dress code (Kamal & Fisher, 1988). In spite of the positive aspects of alternative development theories, including sustainable development, human development, empowerment and the involvement of women and communities, these theories de-emphasise quick economic development, which is the ultimate purpose of 'development' in a capitalist sense. What alternative development theories advocate requires an enormous initial investment in terms of time and capital, and they do not necessary encourage the 'modernisation' that Euro-American societies have achieved.

Even with today's social welfare indices, it is apparent that monetary wealth does not always reflect the social well-being of a population. The income-based index, trade-based index and resource-based index are useful guidelines, though not accurate in many aspects, with which to compare the economic status of nations, which, in turn, might indicate a nation's ability to provide social welfare to its population. However, the definitions of social welfare in these indices are based on western concepts and do not always reflect the state of social welfare or the real interests of people in non-western societies. The UNDP's HDI or quality of life index is one of few indices that place less emphasis on the economic status of a nation and more on its social well-being. Nevertheless, the fundamental concepts of social well-being in this index are also based on western concepts and are not truly cultural-bias free. Moreover, in a study of tourism, the social and cultural aspects being studied cannot be measured by all these indices. These indices are not designed to measure the devaluation of culture and traditions such as levels of cultural assimilation and acculturation. Nor are they designed to judge a nation's level of readiness to copy Euro-American lifestyles and value systems because these indices fundamentally assume that social and cultural transformations in the developing nations are the required steps for an improvement in the quality of life.

Perhaps it is time to review and reconsider the existing development paradigms. Tourism development today raises questions for global economic development theories and modernisation issues, in which many have put their blind trust. Due to the very nature of tourism, sociocultural changes to host communities are often disapproved of as visitors want to see the cultural and historic traditions of the destination. However, without these changes development cannot proceed according to western theories of development. Similarly, many destinations have become aware of the significance of natural and living environments as tourism assets and there is a movement towards natural resource management which does not compromise for short-term economic benefits. For a more efficient and culture-friendly means of community and gender empowerment, smaller scale community-based development is recommended rather than massive multinational investor-oriented development. Changing the foundation of development theory, namely the absolute Euro-American model based on capitalism, may be the most challenging one. This will deny all global 'development' achieved, especially during the post-war period, and deny today's widespread belief in Euro-American values in development and improvements in lifestyle. There is no certain substitute for capitalism after the domino-effect collapse of socialist and communist blocs in the late 1980s and 1990s. Nevertheless, the emergence of alternative development theories with strong support for global cooperation suggests that the concepts of development in the future must be changed one way or another. The social and cultural impacts of tourism development should not just be spin-off concerns as a result of economic development; instead, a more holistic approach is needed. Social and cultural impacts and consequent changes need to be considered on an equal footing with changes not only in the economy of a nation but also with changes in the natural environment. After half a century of blind worship of the Euro-American model of development in the post-war era, its effectiveness is now being questioned; in particular, with respect to the unpredicted side effects on societies, cultures and environments. In response to the Euro-American model, alternative development models have emerged emphasising a more indigenous, more community-centred, more locally controlled type of development, which best suits the locality. Nonetheless, confining alternative development concepts to a limited locality could be as ineffective as following the classic development models. For example, today's social, cultural, economic, environmental and political impacts of tourism development have no boundaries. Environmental pollution can cross political boundaries and sociocultural influences on the host communities cannot be controlled effectively if incoming international tourists are not well informed. Even though alternative development theories continue to gain popularity, development ideologies based on modernisation and economic liberalism are still in operation and tourism development is not exempt from these forces. While small-scale, community-based, incremental tourism development is the main focus of the alternative development model, cooperation is essential for this model at intranational, international and suprantional levels. In particular, cooperation and coordination between government agencies, quasi-government agencies, NGO and interest groups as well as self-regulation and the cooperation of MNE/TNC will become more and more significant in order for successful alternative tourism development to materialise. Without the necessary exogenous cooperation, alternative international tourism development in this era of globalisation is doomed to fail.

Chapter 8

Tourism, Development and the Environment

CHRIS SOUTHGATE AND RICHARD SHARPLEY

Introduction

The inter-relationship between the environment and development has occupied academics and policy-makers alike for several decades. Indeed, the contested ideas as to what could constitute a sustainable future for the planet and its inhabitants have fuelled a now weary intellectual debate. Only latterly has tourism become ensconced at the heart of this debate, not least because 'no other economic activity … transects so many sectors, levels and interests as tourism' (Cater, 1995: 21). However, during a decade in which academic boundaries have become increasingly blurred, a more intricate and complex understanding of tourism, development and the environment has started to emerge. That is, tourism theory has, according to Jafari (1989), passed through four stages, from 'advocacy' to 'knowledge', in particular with respect to tourism's developmental relationship with the environment within which it functions (see Chapters 2 and 11).

The purpose of this chapter is to chart the convergence of once disparate academic niches to establish the extent to which tourism can be developed within the parameters of sustainable resource use. In so doing, it offers a critique of the mainstream sustainable development discourse and the notion of sustainable tourism which it has informed. Since the 1980s, the concept of sustainable development has pervaded almost all avenues of human activity. From its ecocentric origins to it becoming enmeshed in mainstream development discourse, the term has become a focus of debate, discussion and conceptual confusion. Few issues have spurned so many narratives and counter-narratives and Munro (1995: 27), perhaps, typifies a widely shared view in claiming that the term has 'been used to characterize almost any path to the kind of just, comfortable and secure future to which everyone aspires'.

It is argued here that the principles of environmental managerialism which have underpinned tourism development planning in the western world hold little relevance to the social, cultural and ecological characteristics of many developing nations. Indeed, the sustainable tourism discourse offers little beyond a well trodden and, in many ways, superficial reconstitution of mainstream developmentalist ideas, espousing the primacy of economy over ecology, of bureaucratic planning over local participation, and of designation over consultation. A more relevant interpretation of tourism sustainability – both in terms of what it is and how it is to be achieved – is necessary if the competing demands of tourists, governments and host communities are to be reconciled in the future. Sustainability is a more eclectic theoretical concept that broaches diverse natural, social and economic disciplines and which recognises underlying socio-political structures and issues of governance as key factors in environmental management. In the years ahead, the world's poorest nations will be increasingly drawn into the global phenomenon of tourism and if sustainability – in its broadest environmental, economic, social and political context – is to be achieved, important lessons must be learned from the wider environment and development discourse. Indeed, with due consideration to local social and environmental determinants of sustainability, tourism, far from being an agent of degradation, can actively enhance the environment and promote local development.

The concept of sustainable (tourism) development cannot be fully addressed without an understanding of the forces that gave rise to a widespread environmental consciousness and the subsequent adoption of sustainability as a global development objective. Therefore, the chapter begins by briefly reviewing the origins of the alleged 'environmental crisis' facing the global ecosystem and the early responses, manifested in the emergence of the environmental movement in its various guises (see McCormick, 1995). It then considers the origins and differing interpretations of sustainable development as the prevailing development ideology that seeks to establish the middle ground between the competing objectives of, on the one hand, environmental sustainability and, on the other hand, economic development and growth. The manner in which a tourism planning 'blueprint' has embraced sustainable development is then explored before the final part of the chapter argues for the need to go beyond that blueprint, with the issues of environmental governance and ecological sustainability providing the foundation for a new interpretation of the tourism–environment relationship.

The 'environmental crisis'

The United Nations Conference on Environment and Development (UNCED) – the so-called 'Earth Summit' – held in Rio de Janeiro in 1992 drew the world's attention to the vexed question of sustainable development. A myriad of proposals, collectively presented within the wide-ranging Agenda 21, were tabled to reconcile the often conflicting interests of governments, industries and conservationists whilst, more specifically, the intellectual discourse on sustainable development –

initiated some two decades earlier – received a much needed shot in the arm. However, the tangible sense of optimism amongst the leaders of the world's wealthiest nations at the end of the Conference drew media attention away from the vocal environmentalist lobby. Had its voice been heard, the world would have learned that, during the 12 day summit, between 600 and 900 species of plants and animals had become extinct, some 487,200 acres of arable land had turned to desert and well over one million acres of tropical rainforest had been destroyed. Moreover, during the same period, the world's population grew by 3.3 million. Thus, from the environmentalist perspective, there was little ground for optimism.

The message that humanity was facing imminent social and environmental disaster and human tragedy was, by 1992, well rehearsed. Indeed, a similar sense of pessimism was evident at the earlier United Nations Conference on the Human Environment (UNCHE), held in Stockholm in 1972, and was articulated in the ensuing publication *Only One Earth* (Ward & Dubos, 1972). By the early 1970s, increasing rates of deforestation, declining fish stocks, rapidly diminishing supplies of agricultural land and the general reduction of common property resources had all contributed to the environmentalists' concern for the earth's capacity to support prevailing rates of 'development'.

Attracting particular concern was the susceptibility of the Earth to increasing levels of pollution. During the 1970s, radioactive fallout from nuclear tests was seen to be just one of many pollutants which 'ignored' national boundaries, whilst the acidification of Scandinavian lakes and forests and the presence of DDT in Antarctic and Arctic fish brought home the need for development to embrace an understanding of global ecological 'limits'. In short, it became recognised that the 'effluence of affluence' did not respect national borders, that one country's activities could have global consequences. Reid (1995: 3), following Boulding's (1992) description of 'spaceship earth', makes the point that, at that time, the first satellite imagery was reinforcing a perception of the world as a 'precarious and rather vulnerable entity'. Furthermore, by the end of the 1970s, James Lovelock's Gaia hypothesis, which saw the planet as a single homoeostatic organic entity, added to concerns over the potential for human activity to upset the earth's delicate ecological equilibrium (see Lovelock, 1979).

A number of individual catastrophic events served to add substance to the environmentalists' concerns. For example, the disaster in Bhopal in 1984, which cost the lives of some 2500 local inhabitants, and the *Exxon Valdez* catastrophe emphasised the extent to which both human and natural environments were vulnerable to such sudden 'shocks'. In addition to these and other anthropogenic events which fuelled environmental concerns, the 1970s and 1980s also witnessed a number of natural phenomena which suggested the 'limits' of environmental resilience were rapidly approaching. The increasing incidence of floods, drought and famine were well publicised as the media started to reflect widely shared public concerns for the global environment whilst, during the 1970s, the death toll from natural catastrophes increased six-fold over the preceding decade (Reid, 1995).

Inextricably linked to the fears over pollution and resource depletion was the concern over population growth. To many environmentalists, as long as the global population continued to grow, the problems of resource degradation, pollution and human misery would not be solved (Ehrlich, 1968). Quite simply, 'resource problems are not really environmental problems: they are human problems' (Ludwig *et al.*, 1993) and, as long as human exploitation of natural resources increases, so too do the environmental consequences of that activity. Thus, against a background of rapid industrialisation, increasing patterns of inequality and high rates of population growth, the question of sustainability began to dominate the debate over appropriate paths and means of development. Academics and policy-makers from diverse backgrounds and spanning the political continuum reacted to the perceived environmental crises, with tourism being no exception. Even by the late 1970s, with international mass tourism still in relative infancy, commentators criticised the unbridled growth of tourism and its resultant environmental consequences and called for restraint in its development (Young, 1973; Turner & Ash, 1975; Smith, 1977; de Kadt, 1979a). As Mishan (1969: 142) argued,

> travel on this scale... inevitably disrupts the character of the affected regions, their populations and ways of living. As swarms of holiday-makers arrive... local life and industry shrivel, hospitality vanishes, and indigenous populations drift into a quasi-parasitic way of life catering with contemptuous servility to the unsophisticated multitude.

Interestingly, Mishan's élitist 'solution' was to ban international air travel but, more generally, what were the initial responses to this perceived environmental crisis?

Environmental crisis: The neo-Malthusian response

The rise in popular environmental consciousness during the 1970s exhumed many of the founding ideological roots of environmentalism. These resided in mid-19th century Germany and the work of Ernst Haeckel [1834–1919] who coined the term 'ecology'. It was Haeckel who proposed the notion of organic holism, regarding ecosystems as not only comprising many elements – mankind being but one – but also as having intrinsic moral value of their own (Chase, 1995). However, also interwoven with the emergence of the perceived environmental crisis was the resurrection of the Malthusian school of thought founded upon notions of impending social, economic and environmental doom. Such ideas had laid somewhat dormant during the prosperous post-war era of modernisation and the optimism it instilled in the West but the dawn of neo-Malthusianism permeated a wide spectrum of social and environmental literature.

Concerns about the rapidly rising global population started to emerge during the 1950s, the issue receiving attention from, amongst others, Stamp (1953) and Russell (1953), the latter publishing the influential *Man's Role in Changing the Face of the Earth*. The new generation neo-Malthusians of the late 1960s and 1970s firmly placed the 'population problem' at the heart of environmentalism. Paul Ehrlich's (1968) *The Population Bomb* became a standard core text on countless geography-course bibliographies, re-establishing Malthus' ideas of human population limits, maintained by 'natural checks', as the received wisdom in population/environment discourse.

Since then, of course, many of these fears have proved to be unfounded. Nevertheless, by the late 1960s the North's unbridled pursuit of economic growth was certainly leaving its imprint upon the natural environment. The ecological concerns over the break up of the Torrey Canyon oil tanker[1] attracted public interest whilst in the USA, Rachel Carson's (1962) book *Silent Spring* raised awareness over the intensification of agricultural practices. The 1970s also witnessed the publication of several highly pessimistic commentaries on the emerging environment and development debate. For example, Forrester's (1971) *World Dynamics* was one of several attempts to produce global models of a coupled economic and ecological system. The most notable attempt to simulate the consequences of increasing industrialisation was that of the Massachusetts Institute of Technology on behalf of the Club of Rome (an international group of academics backed by European multinational companies). Their work, published as *The Limits to Growth* (Meadows *et al.*, 1972) along with *Blueprint for Survival* (Goldsmith *et al.*, 1972) became the most influential manifestations of 1970s environmentalism. The former, based upon what are today regarded as simplistic and naïve computer simulations, won popular acclaim although, in retrospect, both its methodology and ideology have attracted considerable criticism. Simon (1981), for example, dismissed *The Limits to Growth* as 'a fascinating example of how scientific work can be outrageously bad and yet very influential' (quoted in Adams, 1992: 29).

Not surprisingly, perhaps, the neo-Malthusian uprising of the 1970s initiated a spate of equally emotive counter-arguments about the capacity of the global environment to accommodate rising populations and mankind's continuing quest for prosperity with technocentrists, such as Beckerman (1992), pointing to the contribution of continual technological advance in addressing such challenges. Thus, for example, over the last 30 years average global food supply increased from 2360 to 2740 calories per person per day as a result of agricultural expansion and intensification. At the same time, and contrary to the forecasts of Malthus and his followers, economic growth (as measured in real per capita incomes), has been at its *highest* during periods of rapid population growth. Asian countries experienced economic growth of 25% between 1820 and 1950 whilst their population increased by 84%. From 1950 to 1992, average incomes increased fivefold while their population increased by 128%. India has more than doubled its real per capita income in the past four decades while its population has grown by a factor of four. In the 1960s, the Green Revolution resulted in huge increases in production, particularly for wheat and rice. Thus, the environment and development discourse embraced a new optimism about mankind's resilience, ingenuity and capacity to institute the social and institutional changes to promote effective environmental management (Boserüp, 1965). Moreover, as suggested later and in Chapter 11, this evidence also raises questions about the environmental/developmental contribution of sustainable tourism compared with more intensive (i.e. mass) forms of tourism development.

Yet the ghost of Malthus has not been completely laid to rest and many still forecast an imminent crisis for humanity due to its sheer size. Johnson (1997: 1), commenting on the mistaken pessimism of 1970s environmentalism, states that '[t]he fact that similar claims, made over the past three decades, have all proven to be false always seems to be forgotten'. Today, attention is drawn towards the differentiated allocation of resources and the unjust political economy of globalisation, rather than population growth itself, as an explanation for the many human crises blighting the World's poorest (Bernstein *et al.*, 1995). Nevertheless, despite the methodological deficiencies of *The Limits to Growth* school and the ill-conceived Malthusian interpretation of the 'environmental crisis', the events of the 1970s very much shaped the emergence of a popular environmentalist movement. In the United States, for example, such issues as the preservation of the Spotted Owl at the cost of 'tens of thousands of jobs' (Chase, 1995) propelled environmental issues up the political agenda and fuelled a vitriolic corporate 'green backlash' (Rowell, 1996), testament to the growing political strength of the incongruent but vocal environmental movement.

The emergence of a 'general Green philosophy' (Eckersley, 1992) during the 1970s and 1980s drew partly upon its early philosophical roots, as did, arguably, the 'alternative' tourism perspective that also emerged in the 1980s (Smith & Eadington, 1992). However, the influence of 1960s left-wing ideology and its focus upon participatory politics, alongside the re-emergence of doomsday environmental literature, gave birth to what Eckersley (1992: 8) describes as a new 'ecologically inspired political orientation'. The emergence of 'ecopolitics' – the fusion of politics with environmentalism (see, for example, Doyle and McEachern, 1998) – rapidly gave rise to the formation of protest groups which coalesced into an influential environmental movement, capable of expressing its advocacy for political and social re-orientation in an 'emotive and morally engaged way' (Hughes, 1996).

Thus, the broad environmental movement embraces a variety of frequently competing political philosophies. For example, social ecology, which espouses collective human control over nature, albeit at the local community as opposed to state level, directly opposes deep ecology which pictures an equitable, interconnected ecosystem where no one species is dominant. Conversely, 'eco-feminism' locates gender in the environmental arena, contending that the subordination of women and environmental degradation are linked (see Mellor, 1997). Nevertheless, these political movements have come together within a 'new social movement', manifest in such socio-environmental organizations as Greenpeace and Friends of the Earth. Their influence over single-issue environmental campaigns – most notably in respect to nuclear power, stratospheric ozone depletion and global warming – has transformed the political scene (Mowforth & Munt, 1998).

This politicisation of environmentalism is also, of course, evident in tourism. Generally, calls for more appropriate forms of tourism development have as much, if not more, to do with social equity as they do with environmental concerns, whilst specific campaigns, such as Tourism Concern's Burma Campaign which has, amongst other things, fought against the publication of tourist guide books to that country, are overtly political. However, the important point here is that, collectively, the environmental movement has continued to gain momentum. Not only is it fuelled by over $450 million in grants and a variety of private sources of income (Chase, 1995), but also Green politics has gained prominence in the 1990s, particularly through such channels as the red–green coalition in Germany. By the end of the decade, the environmental ministries in many European countries were lead by 'green politicians' (Bowcott *et al.*, 1999).

Thus, as Eckersley (1992: 7) writes, 'the environmental crisis and popular environmental concern have prompted a considerable transformation in Western politics over the last three decades'. Moreover, 'whatever the outcome of this realignment of Western politics, the intractable nature of environmental problems will ensure that environmental politics … is here to stay (Eckersley, 1992: 7). It is against this background of growing environmental consciousness and the evolution of 'ecopolitics' that the notion of sustainable development has come to permeate development policy and planning, not least within the realm of tourism. The following section briefly reviews its emergence in mainstream development policy.

The origins and contested interpretations of sustainable development

The concept of sustainable development has attracted debate and analysis from virtually all academic standpoints and has transcended the often impenetrable disciplinary boundaries of the social and natural sciences. Many authors have striven to find a single all-purpose definition of sustainable development – according to Steer and Wade-Gery (1993), over 70 different definitions have been proposed! – while others question whether the concept, due to its ambivalence and ambiguity, holds any practical or theoretical relevance to issues of environment and development (Redclift, 1987; Lélé, 1991). Therefore, it is not surprising that sustainable development, both as an overall development paradigm and in its specific guises such as tourism, remains the subject of intense debate.

The origins of the concept can be traced to the 1960s and the coincidence of the perceived environmental crisis and a global institutional response. In 1968, the UNESCO Biosphere Conference held in Paris and the Ecological Aspects of International Development Conference in Washington both addressed concerns about the planet's ecological carrying capacity under growing pressures from human activity. They also heralded the ascendancy of a new environmental awareness in the industrialized West. The 1972 UNCHE in Stockholm, referred to earlier, is noted for being the first concerted international effort to address environmental problems and is described as a milestone in the development of global responses to environmental issues (Reid, 1995). However, whilst the West was concerned primarily with the threat of pollution due to excessive industrial development, developing economies were more concerned that resource conservation was a luxury which only the West could afford to engage in. For them a lack of development was the key to environmental damage, hence the notion of the 'pollution of poverty'. The 26 principles agreed upon by the 119 governments and 400 NGOs reflected both sets of concerns, with 'integrated development' seen as a means of overcoming the perceived paradox between economic growth and environmental protection. However, as Adams (1992) observes, the overall theme of the conference was that development (i.e. growth) need not be impaired by environmental concerns.

However, the Stockholm Conference did succeed in placing issues of environment and development on the international political agenda, whilst its lasting achievement was the creation of the United Nations Environment Programme (UNEP). UNEP has been active in encouraging countries to establish environmental policies and was a key figure in the preparation of the *World Conservation Strategy* (WCS), published in 1980. The WCS was essentially biocentric. Development, defined as 'the modification of the biosphere and the application of human, financial, living and non-living resources to satisfy human needs and improve the quality of human life' (IUCN, 1980: Section 1.3), was regarded primarily as a vehicle for ensuring protection of the global biosphere. For the first time the term 'sustainable development' was adopted and defined as 'the integration of conservation and development to ensure that modifications to the planet do indeed secure the survival and well being of all people' (IUCN, 1980: Section 1.2). The WCS adopted both a utilitarian and moral ethic for conservation, the former articulated in terms of the economic benefits conservation could yield to governments and local communities, the latter summed up by the claim that 'we have not inherited the earth from our parents, we have borrowed it from our children' (IUCN, 1980: Section 1.5). The document also maintained the rhetoric of 1970s global environmentalism by, for example, emphasising that 'human beings, in their quest for economic development and enjoyment of the riches of nature, must come to terms with the reality of resource limitation and the carrying capacities of ecosystems' (IUCN, 1980: *i*).

The WCS has attracted criticism on a number of grounds. It has been described as 'repackaged 1970s environmentalism' with its emphasis on 'limits' (Adams, 1992) and it brought sceptical responses from development pragmatists because of its re-kindled emphasis on environmental ethics and morality. Perhaps the most serious limitation of the WCS, however, was its complete failure to take into account social and political obstacles to development – factors which also militate against sustainable tourism development (Sharpley, 2000) – and consequently it has been described as being both ideological and 'disastrously naïve' (Adams, 1992). As Redclift (1984: 50) argues, 'despite its diagnostic value, the World Conservation Strategy does not even begin to examine the social and political changes that would be necessary to meet conservation goals'.

Shortly after publication of the WCS, the Brandt Commission published its first report, *North–South: A Programme for Survival*, followed three years later by a second: *Common Crisis*. *North–South* declared that 'no concept of development can be accepted which continues to condemn hundreds of millions of people to starvation and despair' (ICIDI, 1980: 50), thereby questioning the main precept of modernism, that faster economic growth provided a panacea for poverty in the South. The message was that too little concern had been given to the *quality* of growth in the past: 'world development is not merely an economic process ... statistical measurements of growth exclude the crucial element of social welfare, of individual rights, of values not measured by money' (ICIDI, 1980: 49). Yet economic growth remained the essential prerequisite for the alleviation of poverty and the protection of the planet's natural resources. The problems experienced in the developing world were considered not to be related to economic growth *per se*, but to external economic forces, such as world recession, high interest rates, and declining terms of trade. Thus, *North–South* proposed a new philosophy of economic growth based on multi-lateralism, international cooperation and increased resources flows from North to South, a theme that was more forcibly pursued in the Commission's second report.

Despite its innovative ideas, few were implemented and the Brandt Commission was disbanded shortly after its second report to the UN General Assembly. In particular, the concept of mutuality of interests (northern economic growth is dependent upon growth in the south) failed to win widespread support, the Commission's proposals again being widely regarded as naïvely failing to take into account the political obstacles to economic and structural reform. The Commission also failed to support explicitly a more participatory form of development.

> The Brandt Commission ... was composed of top people, thinking top down, as such people normally do. The problem with their top-down recommendations was that other top people . . . who would have had to implement them, were and are doing very well out of the status quo. (Ekins, quoted in Reid, 1995: 52)

By the 1980s, the promotion of economic growth in the South, initiated by a re-formed global economic system and based upon a perceived mutuality of economic interest, was seen to hold the key to sustainable development. This was certainly the focus of the widely cited Brundtland (World Commission on Environment and De-velopment (WCED)) report *Our Common Future*, the purpose of which was to 'propose long-term environmental strategies for achieving sustainable develop-ment by the year 2000 and beyond' (WCED, 1987: ix). The Commission set out to address a problem which previous strategies clearly failed to solve: 'many develop-ment trends leave increasing numbers of people poor and vulnerable, while at the same time degrading the environment. How can such development serve next cen-tury's world of twice as many people relying on the same environment?' (WCED, 1987: 4). The report placed much emphasis on sustaining development on a global basis, reiterating the environmentalist message vociferously expressed over a decade earlier that 'the various global crises . . . are not separate crises. They are all one' (WCED, 1987: 4). Poverty was seen as the underlying cause of environmental degradation: 'it is therefore futile to attempt to deal with environmental problems without a broader perspective that encompasses the factors underlying world poverty and international inequality' (WCED, 1987: 3). Therefore, the underlying philosophy of the report is economic growth, although for development to be sus-tainable it must (in the widely cited and adapted phrase) 'meet the needs of the present without compromising the ability of future generations to meet their own needs' (WCED, 1987: 8). However, as Reid (1995) points out, very little attention is given to what these needs are or how they might be met.

The UNCED (the Rio Earth Summit) in 1992 again gave the sustainable develop-ment concept a fresh impetus. The Conference provided a blueprint for securing a sustainable course of development in the 21st century, hence the name of the most important product of the event, Agenda 21. One significant contribution made by Agenda 21 is its rationalisation of environmentalist and developmentalist perspec-tives on sustainability, transcending the ideological and practical discord. Agenda 21 incorporates the philosophy of community empowerment and proactive 'grass roots' development, while articulating the formal structures of planning, legislation and governance in which it should take place. Agenda 21 has been described as the 'sustainable development bible' (Doyle, 1998) and has indeed gone some way to bridge the gulf between green ideology and a politically viable environmental policy. Yet many question whether the fundamental constraints to genuine environ-mental sustainability have been addressed simply by reformulating the means by which development should be pursued. As Hunter (1995: 54) claims, 'sustainability has been seized upon by the political mainstream as a convenient concept for ensur-ing 'sustainable' material growth'.

In short, despite the competing interpretations of sustainable development that, over time, have become amalgamated in successive reports that have accepted, and responded to, the need for global social, economic and political equity, no satisfactory solution has yet been found to the fundamental paradox of sustainable development – that is, how continued global economic growth and development be achieved without the degradation or destruction of the planet's natural resources upon which such development and growth depends? As the next section suggests, this paradox remains a primary challenge to the notion of sustainable tourism development.

Sustainable Development and Tourism

As already noted, the nascent environmentalism of the 1960s and 1970s was reflected in specific concerns about the environmental consequences of tourism development at that time (Dowling, 1992). In particular, and as discussed in the first part of this book, tourism was increasingly considered to be in conflict with the environment, the debate dominated by dependency and limits to growth theorists. However, in parallel with the evolution of sustainable development discourse, concerns about the environmental and social impacts of tourism have escalated in recent years. In this respect, the concepts of ecological limits, sustainable resource use and defined carrying capacities have found wide applicability – as Butler (1991) infers, 'unless specific steps are taken, tourist destination areas and resources will inevitably become over-used, unattractive, and eventually experience declining use'. At the same time, however, it has also been recognised that tourism planning and management must be undertaken in the wider context of global commerce and its social, political, economic and environmental impacts. For example, Garrod and Fyall (1998) claim that

> [t]o the extent that the tourism industry operates by appropriating environmental resources and transforming them for sale in consumer markets, it is really no different in principle to the extraction of petrochemicals, the mining of metals or any other of the 'heavy' industries about which environmental concern is so frequently raised.

Research into the impacts of tourism has embraced the well-established academic pursuit of examining, defining and assessing the applicability of mainstream of sustainable development to the specificities of tourism and recreation. Consequently, a plethora of sustainable tourism definitions has emerged over a decade, reflecting some or all of the social, cultural, economic and environmental connotations of the sustainable development enigma. Typically definitions of sustainable tourism are founded upon the principle of inter-generation equity, but differ according to authors' ideological standpoints (see Figure 8.1 for examples).

The concept of sustainability or, more precisely, sustainable tourism development, has become a guiding principle for both the industry and pressure groups. For example, Tourism Concern advocates that

- To be sustainable (tourism) requires the establishment of an industry which includes consideration of the long-term effects of economic activity in relation to resources and, therefore, concerns for the twin needs for this and future generations. (Curry & Morvaridi, 1992: 131)
- The concept of sustainability is central to the reassessment of tourism's role in society. It demands a long-term view of economic activity ... and ensures that the consumption of tourism does not exceed the ability of the host destination to provide for future tourists. (Archer & Cooper, 1994: 87)
- Sustainable tourism depends on: (a) meeting the needs of the host population in terms of improved standards of living in the short and long term, (b) satisfying the demands of increasing tourist numbers and continuing to attract them to achieve this (c) safeguarding the environment to achieve the two foregoing aims. (Cater & Goodall, 1992: 318)

Figure 8.1 Definitions of sustainable tourism

tourism and associated infrastructures [should], both now and in the future, operate within natural capacities for the regeneration and future productivity of natural resources; recognise the contribution that the people and communities, customs and lifestyles, make to the tourism experience; accept that these people must have an equitable share in the economic benefits of tourism; are guided by the wishes of local people and communities in the host areas' (www.tourismconcern.org.uk.)

Despite the attention paid to the subject, academic ambivalence over what constitutes sustainable tourism continues. In particular, the debate has become polarised between, on the one hand, sustainable tourism development (i.e. sustainable development through tourism as advocated by, for example, the Globe 90 Conference in Canada which recommended that tourism 'must be a recognised sustainable development option, considered equally with other economic activities when jurisdictions are making development decisions' (Cronin, 1990)); and, on the other hand, environmentally sustainable tourism (see Hunter, 1995). As discussed in the literature (Sharpley, 2000), the latter perspective has, inevitably perhaps, come to dominate the planning of tourism in practice – the tourism industry has marched ahead and embraced the 'sustainability imperative' (Garrod & Fyall, 1998) with vigour. A plethora of codes of practice has emerged, and entire (though not necessarily particularly coherent) sub-disciplines such as ecotourism have flourished as the industry has adopted a social and environmental conscience. International, national and industry sectoral organisations have all drawn up codes of practice or lists of guidelines to guide tourism development, whilst tourists themselves have been exhorted to adopt appropriate or sustainable roles and practices (see Mason & Mowforth (1995) for an overview of codes of conduct in tourism).

- The conservation and sustainable use of natural, social and cultural resources is crucial. Therefore, tourism should be planned and managed within environmental limits and with due regard for the long term appropriate use of natural and human resources.
- Tourism planning, development and operation should be integrated into national and local sustainable development strategies. In particular, consideration should be given to different types of tourism development and the ways in which they link with existing land and resource uses and sociocultural factors.
- Tourism should support a wide range of local economic activities, taking environmental costs and benefits into account, but it should not be permitted to become an activity which dominates the economic base of an area.
- Local communities should be encouraged and expected to participate in the planning, development and control of tourism with the support of government and the industry. Particular attention should be paid to involving indigenous people, women and minority groups to ensure the equitable distribution of the benefits of tourism.
- All organisations and individuals should respect the culture, the economy, the way of life, the environment and political structures in the destination area.
- All stakeholders within tourism should be educated about the need to develop more sustainable forms of tourism. This includes staff training and raising awareness, through education and marketing tourism responsibly, of sustainability issues amongst host communities and tourists themselves.
- Research should be undertaken throughout all stages of tourism development and operation to monitor impacts, to solve problems and to allow local people and others to respond to changes and to take advantages of opportunities.
- All agencies, organisations businesses and individuals should cooperate and work together to avoid potential conflict and to optimise the benefits to all involved in the development and management of tourism.

Figure 8.2 Sustainable tourism development: a summary of principles
Source: Eber (1992); WTO (1993); ETB (1991); WTO/WTTC (1996); EC (1993).

The effectiveness of the latter is, as argued in Chapter 10, subject to debate. Those which are directed at tourism development in general, such as those advocated by Tourism Concern, emphasise the breadth of socioeconomic and environmental prerequisites for sustainability so well rehearsed in the sustainable development literature. Such conditions as 'using resources sustainably', 'reducing over-consumption and waste' and 'maintaining diversity' echo the environmental prerequisites for sustainability mooted three decades ago and most famously articulated in Rio in 1992.

It is not possible here to review the varying sets of principles or codes of practice for sustainable tourism. Figure 8.2, however, summarises the key elements of such codes.

What becomes apparent is that, other than serving to draw attention to essential principles, such codes offer little of substance as far as implementation is concerned. For example, a code imploring the sustainable use of natural resources is itself open to a wide range of interpretations. On the one hand, the depletion of natural resources could be justified from a utilitarian standpoint so long as the human-created alternative maintains essential ecological functions. On the other hand, the 'hard sustainability' interpretation of such a code would elevate the need to preserve the natural integrity and biodiversity of the environment above all else. Thus, most codes or lists of principles lack detail and, without definition, explanation and, in some cases quantification, are of limited practical value. Tourism Concern's codes, for example, are reinforced by 98 recommendations as to how they may become operational, but the lack of specificity and quantifiable objectives again limit their practical value. As Garrod and Fyall (1998) argue,

> [s]imple guidelines and codes of practice act as little more than a quack remedy, with sufficient potency to make the patient feel somewhat better but lacking the substance to cure them of their ailments. What is rather worrying is that there are some tourism experts who feel that the treatment is working.

The blueprint for achieving environmentally sustainable tourism

During recent years there has been an increasing tendency towards integrated tourism planning within the wider concerns of social and economic development (Inskeep, 1991) and, in many countries, tourism frequently cuts across several tiers of planning. In the United Kingdom, for example, the received wisdom on how sustainable tourism could and should be achieved falls under the two rather spurious banners of 'planning' and 'designation', the former being concerned with the management or control of development, the latter with identifying particular areas or types of land, such as 'Areas of Outstanding Natural Beauty', within which specific planning measures may be rigorously implemented.

As with its theoretical basis, the practice of planning for sustainable tourism has, in general, been very much guided by the ethos of environmental managerialism implicit in mainstream sustainable development discourse. Central to achieving sustainability is the emphasis on control and the managerial tools employed by planners to ensure environmental 'limits' are respected. At the same time, the rhetoric of sustainability has become institutionalised to the extent that the mere recognition of environmental 'limits' is often regarded as the key facet of sustainable tourism planning. Indeed, tourism planning has become somewhat obsessed with the concept of physical carrying capacity, that is, the degree to which an ecosystem, habitat or landscape can accommodate tourism pressures before unacceptable or irreversible decline occurs. Cooper et al. (1993) suggest that the limits of carrying capacity should really be termed 'saturation limits' rather than carrying capacity, which they define as: 'that level of tourist presence which creates impacts on the host community, environment and economy that are acceptable to both tourists and hosts, and sustainable over future time periods' (Cooper *et al.*, 1993: 95).

Despite the limited appeal of the carrying capacity concept resulting from its inherent fuzziness – what, for example, is 'acceptable' damage, according to whose needs is it determined and how is it measured? – it has nevertheless been embraced widely as an appropriate diagnostic of the environment's capability to accommodate change. The World Tourism Organisation (WTO) considers carrying capacity to be 'fundamental to environmental protection and sustainable development … carrying capacity limits can sometimes be difficult to quantify, but they are essential to planning for tourism and recreation' (WTO, 1992: 23). Similarly, the Brundtland Report enshrines the carrying capacity concept in the more general development context. It states that

> [d]ifferent limits hold for the use of energy, materials, water and land … The accumulation of knowledge and the development of technology can enhance the carrying capacity of the resource base. But ultimate limits there are, and sustainability requires that long before these are reached, the world must ensure equitable access to the constrained resource and reorient technological efforts to relieve the pressure. (WCED, 1987: 45)

Thus, the notion that there is a fixed 'ceiling' to developmental activity in general, and tourism in particular, has long served as the guiding principle informing assessment of tourism's environmental sustainability.

As will be discussed later, not only does the concept of carrying capacity have rather limited applicability in relation to complex socio-environmental systems within which tourism occurs, but without a means of quantifying environmental change the concept is hollow. Not only are measurable environmental indicators pivotal to the application of carrying capacity as a planning and management tool often lacking (not least because concerns over sustainability often surface *after* environmental degradation has occurred), but also the absence of time series data precludes attempts to monitor the processes and rate of environmental change. It is interesting to note, however, that in some cases this can be circumvented through formal Environmental Impact Assessment (EIA) which has evolved into an important proactive and, frequently, legally required planning tool. EIA can be applied to predict and measure the impacts – social as well as environmental – of any development project, and often utilise environmental data as a baseline for monitoring the rate and direction of environmental change, and recording whether the impact falls within the parameters of acceptability.

Planning for environmentally sustainable tourism

As suggested earlier, the conventional approach to environmentally sustainable tourism development is through statutory planning regulations. According to

Green (1995) 'a statutory land use planning system has the capacity to make a significant contribution to the realisation of sustainable tourism development' through resource conservation, by identifying appropriate locations for different activities and by encouraging developers to adopt appropriate approaches to development. In a British context this approach is exemplified by the English Tourist Board (ETB). In response to the Government's national agenda for sustainable development *This Common Inheritance* (Department of the Environment (DoE), 1990), the ETB produced a set of principles to reconcile the growth in tourism with environmental protection (ETB, 1991). Furthermore, these principle are reinforced by the government's planning advice documentation (produced by the then Department of the Environment) which states that regional and local planning should consider:

- the scale and distribution of tourist activity within the area
- the identification of areas within the country where there are problems associated with either the growth or decline of tourism;
- the environmental impact of tourist demand and ways in which any adverse effects can be moderated;
- the need to protect key tourism assets, including such features as characteristic landscapes … unspoilt stretches of undeveloped coastline, areas of special interest for nature conservation, historic buildings and townscape; and
- ways in which tourism can contribute positively to other objectives such as economic development, conservation and urban regeneration. (DoE, 1992: 4.1)

Thus, although tourism planning is a discrete activity it should, nevertheless, be an integral part of the land use planning process, accommodating competing demands for resources and reconciling the interests of all interested parties. For example, in the context of rural Britain, those interested parties are often categorised as, on the one hand, conservationists who seek to protect nature and landscape and, on the other hand, 'commercialists' who seek to exploit the countryside for financial gain. Their mutual interests are often served through the established system of designation which confers specific legislative and institutional control over areas deemed to have significant conservation value. National park status, for example, confers protection to some 10% of the land surface of England and Wales and, as in the United States and elsewhere, the parks were initially established to provide access to 'nature' for the urban population (see Sharpley & Sharpley, 1997: 72–7).

In England and Wales, the control of national parks is established within Town and Country Planning Acts and control over development of tourism and other activities is achieved through strict planning regulations rather than state ownership of the parks' resources.[2] A crucial factor in the achievement of environmental sustainability is the extent to which guidelines articulate with planning procedures and regulations. The parks' planning authorities are required to produce documents outlining policies and proposals relating to activities controlled by the various Planning Acts, and details of management strategies for environmental resources, services and facilities. As a result of complex and often ambiguous planning structures, such activities such as farming, forestry, mineral production and, more recently, large-scale tourism threaten to erode the environmental quality of many UK national parks.

In addition to national parks, a diverse range of designations in the UK confers special protection to coastal areas, areas of outstanding natural beauty, trees and woodland and a range of architectural and historical environments, all of which play host to significant numbers of tourists. A further planning device for promoting sustainable tourism is through coastal zone management (CZM). Owing to the popularity of coastal resorts, the integration of tourism considerations with those for water quality, for example, represents an important step towards achieving the goals of sustainability. However, of the 20 different types of designation denoting protected status (stemming from 30 Acts of Parliament), none guarantees absolute protection from the impacts of development. For example, a study of Sites of Special Scientific Interest (SSSIs) in the UK in 1990 found that 40% had been damaged, most of the permanent damage stemming from activities given planning permission. As one report details (RNU, 2000), the Dorset heaths in south-west England represent a 'microcosm' of the failing conventional protection systems. Two hundred years ago, there were 98,000 acres of heathland in the Poole basin. Now there are only 14,000 acres in scattered fragments. Almost 90% are SSSIs but less than 20% are classified as nature reserves. Ten per cent have been lost in the last 10 years.

To summarise, then, land-use planning and a system of designation collectively provide a framework which, in theory, balances the physical capacities of the resource base against the different interests that are involved in development, providing valuable regulatory mechanisms. However, even within developed countries with established planning systems, sustainable resource use has been sometimes difficult to achieve. Thus, in much of the developing world where tourism is rapidly expanding within a context of diverse and dynamic social, cultural and environmental conditions, the universal relevance of any particular form of development 'blueprint', such as those proposed in many of the sustainable tourism development guides, has been brought into question. The remainder of this chapter will, therefore, move beyond the 'static' blueprint formula for pursuing sustainable tourism, in so doing questioning the western-centric notion of sustainable development.

Beyond the Sustainable Development Blueprint

Before proposing an alternative view of how environmentally sustainable tourism may be achieved, it is useful first of all to return briefly to criticisms of the sustainable development paradigm upon which sustainable tourism is based and, consequently, founders.

Sustainable development: A critique

The irrelevance of mainstream sustainable development theory owes much to the persistence and impenetrableness of now discredited environment and development narrative. Such narratives gain credibility and potency in their acceptance by policy-makers and are enshrined as truisms by the élite interest groups that profit from them. Development agencies disseminate the narratives giving such calamitous hypotheses as *The Tragedy of the Commons* (Hardin, 1968) global recognition and an unquestioned belief in their developmental value. When such narratives become institutionalised as 'received wisdom', their durability and perceived merit become even more entrenched (Leach & Mearns, 1996). As Adams and Hulme (1992: 3) contend, their 'influence and durability is not related to their actual economic, social or environmental achievements... but to the interests of a complex web of politicians, policy makers, bureaucrats, donors, technical specialists and private sector operators whose needs are served by the narrative'.

The perpetuation of sustainable development's underlying assumptions has achieved little more than justifying conventional top-heavy, interventionist approaches to environmental and developmental initiatives in much of the developing world, reinforcing public acceptance of sustainable development rhetoric, and the institutions vested with responsibility for implementing it. As Sneddon (2000: 525) comments, 'sustainable development privileges global environmental problems and institutions, perceives poverty rather than poverty-producing conditions as the root cause of environmental degradation, reproduces economistic and developmentalist biases, and advances a highly reductive interpretation of environment as a 'static' resource'.

In recent years, many of these environment and development truisms have been rejected. Many researchers have been quick to identify the limitations, naïve assumptions and inappropriate recommendations embedded within mainstream sustainable development rhetoric. For example, the very assumption that economic growth must be sustained if national social and environmental objectives are to be met disregards culturally diverse interpretations of what 'development' itself means (Redclift, 1987).

More generally, sustainable development theory is replete with paradoxes. The WCED, in essence, proposed growth and the alleviation of poverty through the much maligned 'trickle-down effect' central to the modernist school of development theory. At the same time, the economic growth envisaged by WCED would necessitate a fivefold increase in energy use in the developing world, yet the Commission went on to say that 'the planetary ecosystem could not stand this, especially if the increases were based on non-renewable fossil fuels' (WCED, 1987: 14). Thus, *Our Common Future* hopes to have its cake and eat it (Adams, 1992).

In search of a more appropriate formula for sustainable development in the developing world, radical commentators have questioned the recurrent emphasis on sustained economic growth. The radical environmentalist perspective on sustainable development is first and foremost biocentric, elevating the intrinsic value of the natural world above the value given to it by mankind. As Rees (1990: 18) contends,

> the emerging ecological crisis reveals fatal flaws in the prevailing world-view. Our mechanical perception of the biosphere is dangerously superficial and our continued belief in the possibility of sustainable development based on the growth-oriented assumptions of neoclassical economics is illusory'.

The *green* perspective gained momentum in the 1970s in reaction to the dominant development paradigm which emphasised modernisation and economic growth. To supporters of the biocentric view, we are no more than stewards of the Earth, holding resources on trust for the future. Emphasis is placed upon the very existence of the Earth's natural resources rather than the income flows which they can generate. The burgeoning green development literature also broaches the otherwise unquestioned mainstream assumptions of what *development* itself should be (Adams, 1992). For example, while the Brundtland Commission emphasised the importance of 'meeting basic human needs' these 'needs' have conventionally been defined according to narrow ideological view of the capitalist western world (Redclift, 1992).

Also central to the mainstream sustainable development thinking is the unquestioned faith in free market institutions as the most effective and efficient means of mitigating against economic 'externalities' associated with development. Environmental policy in much of the industrialised world is today founded upon the principle that 'the power of the market can be harnessed and channelled towards the achievement of environmental goals'(Tietenberg in Rees, 1990: 386). The role of government has become one of ensuring that the operation of the market is programmed to give the 'correct' cost signals to producers and consumers. Command and control solutions or 'state environmentalism', so the neo-liberal argument maintains, lead to political (and hence inefficient) allocation of environmental resources (Doyle, 1998). Again, the applicability of the neoliberal perspective on sustainable development to developing world economies, often in need of a remedy against economic differentiation rather than a catalyst, has attracted criticism from a radical socialist school, one which focuses upon structures of power, the distribution of resources (especially land) and the relations of production which lie at the heart of underdevelopment (Redclift, 1987). Sustainability, according to this view, is constrained by the unequal power relations that exist between the capitalist core and periphery, and the power relations which exist within society at all levels. This argument, of course, holds particular relevance for tourism, the production of which is typified by unequal power relations (see Chapter 9).

Thus, uncoupling the hollow sustainable development meta-narrative from the essential building blocks of a more appropriate notion of environmental sustainability may contribute to a more practical foundation for environmental policy and management, and provide insights into the essential determinants of sustainability for developing world tourism. As Sneddon argues, it is pertinent to examine the concept of sustainability in isolation from its 'problematic partner' of sustainable development, adding that 'the discussion [on sustainable development] rarely transcends abstract notions of 'needs', 'generations' and 'global environment' to confront more intractable, untidy questions at the intersection of ecological degradation and social justice' (Sneddon, 2000: 524). So, let us consider the two essential elements of a potentially more relevant and appropriate connotation of sustainability, one which may offer a clearer basis from which to approach tourism, environment and development.

Environmental governance and sustainability

Central to the concept of sustainability is the issue of appropriate governance or 'the structures and processes of power and authority, cooperation and conflict that govern decision-making and dispute resolution' (Hulme and Woodhouse, 2001: 215). What, then, are the principles of environmental governance as enshrined within the sustainable development discourse?

The evolution of sustainable development has served to institutionalise 'top-down' solutions to socio-environmental problems, regarding local institutional arrangements as necessary components of fundamentally government-driven sustainable development planning (Adams, 1992). As a result, questions of appropriate local governance structures have received little attention. However, by opening our minds to the cultural differences which exist and how they translate into different definitions of 'development' and 'needs', 'we immediately open up the exciting possibility that sustainable development might be defined by people themselves, to represent an ongoing process of self-realisation and empowerment' (Redclift, 1992: 397). Therefore, people must be the 'architects' and 'engineers' of sustainable development, rather than mere recipients of a model of sustainable development created in the industrialised world. Indeed, the notion that governance must be essentially state-managed and based upon the lines of 'an idealised notion of western democracy allied to a Weberian bureaucracy' (Hulme and Woodhouse, 2001: 215) has been largely rejected by development theorists.

Within development studies literature, great advances have been made in understanding the value of institutional diversity and local participation in resource management decision making. In his seminal work *Development Projects Observed*, Hirschmann (1968) drew attention to the tendency for development planners to simplify the world's inherent social and political complexity. When environmental considerations become part of the planning equation, an entirely separate (though comparable) source of uncertainty and complexity further undermines the validity of conventional planning approaches to environment and development. 'Such narratives are operationalised into standard approaches with widespread application, often leading to the standardised "blueprint" approaches to planning that have been so often condemned as ineffective or destructive' (Adams & Hulme, 1992: 2). This is exemplified by conventional approaches to national park planning in much of the developing world. Despite being an essential aid to conservation, their designation has often been to the distinct disadvantage of rural populations. Indeed, governments have often excluding local communities under the misconception that people were disadvantageous to environmental conservation (Murphree & Hulme, 1998).

The crude notion of social sustainability extends into other areas of contemporary environmental management theory, such as the 'new conservation' articulated by Hulme and Murphree (1999). Community conservation implies a more complex and dynamic phenomenon than a mere shift in responsibility from state to community, suggesting similarly a more complex approach to tourism planning than proposed by the traditional 'community' approach (Murphy, 1985, 1988; see also Chapter 5). The concept embraces a web of socio-politcal factors, core concepts including the elevation of indigenous environmental knowledge and need to recognise rural inhabitants as 'citizens not criminals'. Such a eclectic marriage of conservation philosophies sits comfortably with the concept of sustainability. The notion of conservation as preservation is challenged by the emerging sustainability paradigm in which both conservation and development (in the sense of improving security of livelihoods and welfare) are seen as mutually exclusive targets. Natural resources accordingly can be utilised so long as sustainability is not compromised (Hulme & Murphree, 1999).

The value of institutional capital has also become an established part of development thinking. A common critique of neoclassical formulations of sustainable development has been the its oversimplified understanding of social behaviour and, in particular, the social basis of environmental management. For example, neo-classicists consider resources held as common property susceptible to unsustainable rates of consumption because while they are subject to individual use, they are not subject to individual possession. Thus, optimal rates of return from resource consumption can only be achieved through the allocation of exclusive property rights to individuals and the creation of a market in environmental damage (Jacobs, 1994). This perspective on the 'common pool resource' (CPR) problem has long pervaded academic and policy arenas (Berkes, 1989) and has spurred development agencies and governments into measures to dismantle customary CPR management regimes, many of which have consequently succumbed to formal land tenure laws (McKean & Ostrom, 1995), all in the name of 'development'.

Environment and development discourse has, in recent years, begun to reject the conventional wisdom, focusing instead upon the characteristics of indigenous CPR management regimes in both the industrial and developing worlds. A new CPR paradigm has emerged from the (mainly theoretical) research into the problems of collective action, which champions indigenous common property regimes and refutes the conventional state- or market-oriented solutions to the CPR problem. According to this 'new institutionalist' perspective, the solution to the CPR problem rests with endogenously created (rather than imposed) institutional arrangements which generate levels of mutual trust and assurance amongst resource users, and which provide the necessary incentives and constraints to maintain cooperation. An increasing volume of theoretical literature, supported by field observations, suggests cooperation is often achieved, and 'coordination problems' (Ullman-Margalit, 1977) resolved, through rule-systems created by resource users themselves.

These diverse perspectives emphasise the centrality of social and institutional capital. However, evidence is mounting emphasising how decentralised environmental management structures also articulate with market institutions. Recent insights into the dynamics of community conservation have highlighted the essential balance of local governance structures interacting with market institutions. The sustainability of 'nature tourism' in much of the developing world, for example, has revealed the fundamental role market forces play. Be it wildlife, rainforest or cultural heritage, the reality of population growth and economic development has meant that the dictum 'use it or lose it' has found profound relevance (Hulme & Murphree, 1999). Protecting environmental resources from the free market, especially through ineffective or corrupt state regulation, exposes the environment to degradation;

> if species or habitats are to be conserved they must not be protected from market forces as that will place control in the hands of an inefficient state that will allow them to degrade as rent seeking public officials take bribes from poachers and timber companies' (Hulme & Murphree, 1999: 280).

Rather, where the uniqueness and scarcity of natural resources are reflected by their economic value they are more likely to be conserved. Where conservation offers resource managers a higher return as compared to a degrading activity, such as agriculture, the resource managers will have an incentive to conserve rather than consume their natural resource base. The African elephant, for long chastised by communities for destroying crops, damaging property and inflicting injury, has found a new lease of life where its conservation generates local income – be that through hunting (as in Zambia) or wildlife tourism (in Kenya for example).

Ecological sustainability

Appropriate forms of governance therefore lie at the heart of sustainability. However, in the same way as the intrinsically top-down approach of development planners and policy-makers has been discredited, so too must the conventional western conception of ecological management be scrutinised. An emerging school of thought asserts that western ecological principles and the long established environmental management tools which they inform have little relevance to complex socio-environmental systems. It may be argued that rhetorical commitments to environmental conservation as central to sustainable development discourse represents no more than a 'repackaging' of development planning to present a green face to business-as-usual exploitation of people and resources (Sneddon, 2000, Adams, 1992). The often rhetorical commitment to the principles of environmental protection and conservation are subordinated by the primacy of economic growth, forming the ideological basis for mainstream sustainable development theory.

The concept of ecological sustainability has attracted attention, not least because of the catalogue of disastrous development planning initiatives implemented over the years in much of the developing world. As Sneddon writes, 'ecological sustainability as a policy and management guideline … is certainly preferable to a notion of 'sustainable development' wherein ecological concepts and their applications are mere afterthoughts' (Sneddon, 2000: 532). Central to ecological sustainability lies a 'new' ecological understanding which calls into question traditional western Clementian ideas of ecological succession and the western traditions of environmental managerialism that are founded upon them. The new ecology stresses the principles of non-linearity and dynamic equilibria, which contrast with the conventional ecological principles founded upon homeostasis and rigid 'carrying capacities'. As Munro (1995: 31) perceptibly remarks, '[w]e know the carrying capacity of a field for cows is limited; it has objective reality, the factors involved are relatively few and simple… But carrying capacity of the earth for people is subject to a multitude of complex, interacting factors'. A central strand to the new ecology is that environments are inherently dynamic, and not moving towards a climax or equilibrium state, and the recognition that 'natural environments' have long been shaped by human activity.

New ecological theory promotes notions of adaptive management above the rigid positivist models of development planning, emphasising the pre-eminence of locally-specific knowledge over 'blueprint' solutions to environmental management problems. Ironically, it is in the context of African semi-arid environments that the new ecological paradigm has particular reference (Scoones, 1995). Simplistic deterministic 'command and control' strategies of environmental management appear redundant in light of the approach. Adaptive techniques, such as those advocated for a more sustainable approach to pastoral development, are formulated on notions of both institutional and ecological diversity (Adams, 1992). The logic of coupling diverse management strategies with non-linear, unpredictable environmental conditions is well captured by Scoones' (1995) edited text, *Living With Uncertainty*, which seeks to reconstitute the essential element of sustainability so evidently absent from conventional rangeland development planning. The latter positivist approach to environmental managerialism of course runs counter to the philosophy and practice of land-use planning.

The reorientation of ecology has also cast doubt over the conventional understanding of environmental fragility – again particularly in the semi-arid rangelands. Hierarchical relationships within and between interdependent ecological communities promote a much greater degree of resilience than conventionally thought. Biodiversity is now regarded as a critical element of an ecosystem's ability to resist disturbance, whether natural or anthropogenic, and is thus seen as an essential prerequisite for achieving sustainability (Holling *et al.*, 1995). Maintaining ecological diversity is also recognized as a widely employed customary natural resource management strategy. The resilience of ecosystems depends upon many inter-related factors. Resilience is closely related to environmental maturity, so that complex and diverse ecological systems are more stable and capable of absorbing 'shocks', such as those associated with tourism.

Debate over the relevance of the conventional ecology and the concept of carrying capacity concept within tourism literature is nothing new. Butler's (1991) analysis of environment and tourism development utilises the concepts of environmental limits and the notion of definable carrying capacities, and reconciles the life-cycle of tourism from development to stagnation and eventual decline. It espouses the principles of self-regulation and the endogenous environmental feedbacks which limit environmental capacity to sustain resource consumption above a set level (Hunter, 1995). The model engages traditional ecological principles, which state that as a species population increases it will eventually approximate to the environmental determined limits. Due to time lags, the population may temporarily overshoot carrying capacity, but will oscillate around a set limit until a state of dynamic equilibrium is reached. As Hunter (1995: 66) suggests 'such a pattern could be regarded as sustainable over time, and could be taken to represent sustainable tourism development over time, at least in terms of an individual destination area'. Hunter continues to reflect on the popularity of the carrying capacity model as a basis for sustainable tourism; 'an inherently attractive concept for those concerned with the environmental impacts of tourism and for those seeking a rationale for interventionist management' (p. 66). However, a disjuncture evidently exists between the new and emerging paradigm of environmental management and post-positivist ecological theory (based upon notions of non-linearity), and the essentially positivist approach to environmental control implicit in land-use planning. Emerging understandings of ecological dynamics underscore 'the uncertainty of scientific knowledge and its predictive capabilities … (and) … call into question any human attempts to 'manage' ecological systems' (Sneddon, 2000: 531).

To O'Reilly (1986), the value of the carrying capacity concept lies in its ability to foster environmental consideration in tourism planning while promoting a precautionary approach to tourism development and 'respect for local environmental limits' (Hunter, 1995). Several alternative approaches to carrying capacity have been suggested, such as Limits of Acceptable Change (LAC). According to Wight (1998: 82): 'LAC is a planning procedure designed to identify preferred resource and social environmental conditions in a given recreation area and to guide the development of management techniques to achieve and protect these conditions'. LAC bases the whole notion of 'acceptability' on local connotations of positive and negative environmental change, a paradigmatic shift away from the narrow social and environmental basis of carrying capacity.

Allied to the concept of ecological sustainability is the thorny issue of environmental valuation. A major failing of neo-classical economics pertains to the under-valuation of ecological services and its failure to account for the depletion or degradation of natural resources through processes of 'development'. The specific problems of devising and implementing methods of environmental valuation have remained marginal to the far more woolly abstract notions of sustainable development. Today's economic activities bear environmental externalities which must be borne by future generations, and thus the environmental economic contribution to sustainable development theory argues that the present generation must compensate future generations 'to ensure that we pass on to the next generation a stock of ... capital assets no less than the stock we have now' (Pearce, 1992: 4). The fundamental building blocks (Sneddon, 2000) of ecological economics are the notions of intergenerational equity, intragenerational equity and the emphasis placed upon meeting basic human needs, and the integration of ecological processes into economic calculations. Operationalising sustainability depends, therefore, upon the maintenance of a non-depleting stock of natural capital and upon a methodology for valuing environmental goods and services. Costanza (1997) has applied valuation methods to value the planet's global ecosystem in the region of US$33 trillion per year. Other environmental economic prescriptions for achieving sustainability include those that have great theoretical strength but confront political obstruction (such as revamping national accounting systems to accommodate the true costs of natural resource depletion) to others that have become operational within the context of neoliberal approaches to environmental policy (such as 'green taxes' and other market-based instruments).

New Interpretations of Tourism, Environment and Development

The preceding discussion implies a need to rethink the relationship between tourism development, the environment and the communities dependent upon environmental resources. Sustainability in tourism development lies not in the rigid blueprints of development planning but in recognition and utilisation of local social and institutional capital. Evidence is mounting that sustainability is most likely to be achieved where local as well as national interests are respected by tourism developers, where communities engage in decision-making and where market institutions engage with local and national governance structures. Under these circumstances, tourism can actively promote both conservation and development, a far cry from tourism's image as a degrading and exploitative industry.

Throughout the era of mounting public concern for the environmental impact of development, tourism retained its image as a 'smokeless industry', although publications as Turner and Ash's (1974) Golden Hordes drew tourism into the Limits of Growth debate. Since then, the dramatic growth in tourism has redefined it as an industry 'subordinating environmental issues to the primary need to add new products' (Kousis, 2000: 469), whilst since the 1970s, a vast quantity of research has explored the environmental impacts of tourism and recreation, particularly in respect to impacts on soil and vegetation (for example, Goldsmith *et al.*, 1970; Bayfield, 1971).

Significant effort has been dedicated to understanding the factors influencing the environmental impact of tourism (Cohen, 1978; Mathieson & Wall, 1982). Indeed, as Croall (1995: 1) contends, tourism can 'ruin landscapes, destroy communities, pollute the air and water, trivialise cultures, bring about uniformity, and generally contribute to the continuing degradation on our planet'. Is such a critical perspective warranted? Interactions between tourists, developers, policy-makers and planners and the environment are often highly complex (Mieczkowski, 1995). Furthermore, it is often difficult to differentiate between environmental changes caused by tourism from those associated with changing biophysical conditions or those related to other social or economic factors. Mieczkowski (1995) states that tourism is vulnerable to environmental deterioration mediated by socio-political pressures outside the control of the tourism industry. Accordingly, the natural environment both 'constitutes a tourism resource' and is 'part of tourism's product' (Mieczkowski, 1992: 112). Indeed, the damage (environmental, cultural and social) tourism can impart is not an intrinsic product of tourism per se, but a manifestation of the broader socio-environmental hazards of the prevailing mainstream development philosophy which relegates people and resources below the primacy of profit and economic growth. For example, environmental change in and around Kenya's Amboseli National Park, most evidently borne out by vegetation changes within and outside the Park, has occurred over a period of time that has witnessed a marked growth in tourism, a sharp rise in the human population and a related diversification of land use, changing land tenure arrangements, several years of anomalous climatic conditions and increased salinisation of ground water (Lovatt-Smith, 1993). The distant clouds of dust marking the passage of tourist vehicles across the barren Amboseli landscape can easily be correlated with the rapid rise in the number of tourist arrivals yet, in this case, environmental degradation is a culmination of complex inter-related social, political and physical phenomena.

Nevertheless, the tourism industry is often cited as the main culprit as far as negative impacts are concerned and, not infrequently, such criticism is justified. It is true to say, for example, that many commercial operators adopt a short-term perspective on tourism, and are essentially driven by the motive of profit more than any altruistic (or indeed commercial) concern for future generations of the environment upon which they will depend (McKercher, 1993). At the same time, tourists themselves are also agents of environmental change. No longer are vacations to the planet's most remote corners an élitist luxury, but products available to the mass tourism market. Consequently, the numbers of tourists descending upon destinations relatively untouched by the western culture and all it entails have increased alarmingly. Thus, the clear economic benefits of tourism development are often, though not quantifiably, countered by the environmental harm generated by the two-week holiday makers and their own cultural idiosyncrasies. The demands placed upon scarce water resources, for example, particularly in island destinations, may have far-reaching social and environmental consequences for the local populations (although research in Cyprus has demonstrated that tourism accounts for just 3% of total water consumption on the island (Sharpley, 1998)). As Mieczkowski (1995) controversially argues, it is not the quantity of tourists necessarily that inflicts environmental harm, but also the quality of the tourists.

> The involvement of everyone in the market ... has increased the potential for destructive behaviour by individuals with lower educational, and occasionally, even moral levels. Thus, the mass tourism market often includes individuals who lack the eco-conscience that would inhibit them from harming nature. (Mieczkowski, 1995: 164)

Such an overtly élitist position typifies the polarity of the mass *versus* alternative tourism debate (see Chapter 11), yet there is no doubt that, on occasion, the lack of the 'attitudinal prerequisites' gives rise to all manner of environmentally degrading activities, ranging from environmental vandalism, including littering and creating noise pollution, to the unconscious degradation of fragile ecosystems, whether through trampling or the collection of 'souvenirs'.

Not surprisingly, the tourism and development literature is replete with examples of the industry's harmful impacts. Salem (1995) notes that 15,000 cubic metres of water will supply 100 luxury hotel guests for 55 days, while it would serve the needs of 100 rural farmers for three years or 100 urban families for two years. Similarly, Keefe (1995) relates the case of Nahua Indians in Mexico who protested against plans to build a golf course, a five-star hotel and 800 tourist villas, estimated to consume 525,000 gallons of water a day. Pollution is one of the most common negative impacts of tourism. For example, only 30% of the 700 towns on the European Mediterranean coastline treat sewage before discharging it into the sea (Jenner & Smith, 1992) whilst, in the Caribbean, only 10% of the sewage generated by the annual influx of 100 million tourists is treated. Moreover, many emerging tourist destinations in the developing world have no sewage processing infrastructure at all.

However, although there is much evidence of the environmentally degrading consequences of tourism development, the adopted image of tourism as an 'extractive industrial activity' (Garrod & Fyall, 1998) – intrinsically based upon a development and environment dichotomy – often conceals its potential to promote environmental conservation and social and economic development. The Eselenkei Conservation Project in southern Kenya, for example, has evolved through the joint efforts of a commercial operator and the local Maasai Community in Eselenkei Group Ranch. Not only has the community gained significant socioeconomic advantages from the small-scale wildlife safaris conducted on their land, but the mere presence of tourists and the local 'game scouts' has rid the area of poaching. Here, tourism is more than just a malign 'smokeless industry' but a genuine and positive force for change.

Thus, contrary to its reputation as a 'spectre haunting our planet' (Croall, 1995: 1), tourism can justifiably be regarded as a 'smokeless industry' and an 'ecology-oriented sector, a logical partisan of environmental conservation' (Mieczkowski, 1992: 112). In many instances, tourism offers economic incentives for environmental conservation, making protection a more economically profitable option in comparison to other potential resource uses. Wildlife conservation in much of Africa exemplifies the economic and ecological value of conservation, where countless examples of 'community conservation' projects throughout the region are founded on the belief that 'conservation will either contribute to solving the problems of the rural poor who live day to day with wild animals, or those animals will disappear' (Adams & McShane, 1992: xix (in Adams & Hulme, 1992)). Many such projects, most notably the CAMPFIRE programme in Zimbabwe and Kenya's pioneering attempts to promote the linkages between conservation and rural development, have hinged upon the ascendancy of tourism (be it primarily based on hunting in the case of the former and wildlife tourism in the latter) above alternative land uses.

One particular example is Kenya's Maasailand, where scarce 'wetland in dryland' resources have come under increasing pressure due to an increase in small-scale irrigated cultivation. This has started to degrade the water resource base and initiate widescale ecological change. Many Maasai have lost access to customary sources of water and pasture for their herds, and wildlife (in particular elephant herds) have been displaced, creating acute wildlife/human conflict problems elsewhere. However, in recent years and with the support of the Kenya Wildlife Service, commercial investors and local communities, a number of 'community conservation' projects have emerged which have started to generate income for Maasai communities through safari tours. Local institutional arrangements have been created to protect key natural resources for wildlife, to ensure an equitable distribution of income, and to protect wildlife and the community at large from the appropriation of land by outside parties to intensify irrigated cultivation (Southgate & Hulme, 2001).

Similarly, the Galapagos, labelled the 'Enchanted Isles', also provide an insight into the diverse benefits attainable through tourism. Situated some 600 miles off the coast of Ecuador, the cluster of volcanic islands are often regarded as the most precious and fragile of all ecosystems. Remarkably, 95% of the reptiles, 50% of birds, 42% of land plants, between 70 and 80% of insects and 17% of fish found within the Galapagos exist nowhere else in the world. The designation of national park status for 97% of the islands has, without doubt, greatly facilitated conservation although, in doing so, the Ecuadorian government has encountered strong opposition from other groups with vested interests in consuming rather than conserving the archipelago's resources. Only through a blend of strong regulations and due consideration of the needs and wants of the local population, as well as other groups with vested interests in the islands' resources, have positive steps been taken to conserve one of the planet's most valuable enclaves of untouched natural history. The efforts of Ecuador's national park service (Instituto Ecuatoriano Forestal y de Areas Naturales y Vida Silvestre: (INEFAN)) have been aided considerably by the popularity of tourism in the Galapagos. The income generated by tourism has grown considerably over recent years. In 1997, entrance fees were $100 for foreigners, bringing in $5 million directly to the Galapagos National Park (Honey, 1999). Thus, as Honey (1999) notes, conservation has generally benefited from tourism because of the very close relationship between the tourism industry and the state of the environment.

In other cases, tourism has become a 'saviour of ecosystems in crisis' (Mieczkowski, 1995: 121). In Madagascar, for example, much of the natural environment bears the scars of rapid population growth and its dependence upon natural resources. Up to 85% of the country's forests have been felled for charcoal production and to create space for cultivation and livestock production, resulting in a greatly enhanced rate of soil erosion. Mieczkowski quotes an *Economist* report estimating the cost of deforestation to be between $100 million and $300 million a year. However, tourism has provided a lifeline for Madagascar's diminishing forests. In particular, 'nature tourism' has become a major source of income for the Malagasy Government owing to the international interest surrounding Madagascar's unique ecosystem. Species such as the dwarf lemur (*Allocebus trichotis*) have generated considerable interest amongst the growing number of 'nature tourists' and, since 1991, the remaining forests which provide the habitat for this and other lemur species have been protected. At the same time, the Ranomafana National Park has also been established. Importantly, by way of compensating local residents a USAID-funded project has been established in order to train locals as tourist guides and to provide others with the basic skills required for the local tourism and hospitality industry.

Half of the National Park entrance fees contribute towards the running of this project.

As the new century commences, there remains scope for great optimism that tourism may contribute to both sustainable, equitable development and environmental conservation, something that development initiatives have so often failed to achieve. Indeed, what is widely claimed to be the fastest growing sector of the tourism industry – though a claim not generally-substantiated by statistical data (Weaver, 1999) – and often labelled as ecotourism or similar, is that in which the interlinkages between the vacation, conservation and development are most apparent. According to King and Stewart (1996), 'in an idealised model of ecotourism, an integration of conservation and development occurs in which entrepreneurs, government agents, and tourists strive to create sustainable relationships with the environment while improving the welfare of local people'.

Ecotourism is often defined as one of a number of 'sustainable tourism' concepts, alongside 'green tourism' and 'nature tourism' for example. According to Croall (1995: 2) ecotourism 'recognises the fragility of the natural environment, and respects the needs and aspirations of the people that live in the areas affected.' More specifically, Fennell (1999:43) defines it as follows.

> a sustainable form of natural resource-based tourism that focuses primarily on experiencing and learning about nature, and which is ethically managed to be low impact, non-consumptive, and locally oriented… It typically occurs in natural areas, and should contribute to the conservation or preservation of such areas.

Inevitably, perhaps, interpretation of the ecotourism concept varies. Some commentators distinguish between 'deep' and 'shallow' ecotourism (Acott *et al.*, 1998), others relate it to scientific ecological principles (Tyler & Dangerfield, 1999) or local empowerment (Scheyvens, 1999), whilst yet others focus upon tourist experiential aspects (Ryan *et al.*, 2000). Collectively, however, the emphasis is placed on the integration of environmental conservation, socioeconomic development and tourism. With the pressures bearing down on many of the world's most precious islands of natural abundance, often within the poorest of the world's nations, the principle that nature must 'pay its way' has struck a chord with governments and local communities alike. The many variants of nature-based tourism have proven their ability to generate local income, to provide the incentive for conservation over utilisation and to meet the multifaceted demands of tourists, governments, NGOs and commercial operators.

Conclusion

This chapter has explored the concept of sustainability (as distinct from the sustainable development paradigm) both within the broad context of development and with specific reference to tourism. As suggested here and elsewhere in the literature, a disjuncture clearly exists between the rhetoric of sustainable development and its successful implementation both within and beyond the tourism sector. In other words, it has proved difficult, if not impossible, to map the specific socioeconomic process of tourism development onto the more general framework of sustainable development. To an extent, this has resulted from the nature and characteristics of tourism itself but, more particularly in the context of tourism's environmental consequences, it has been argued here that sustainable tourism development has 'failed' as a result of the environmental managerialism inherent in sustainable (tourism) development principles. In other words, the imposition of a universal blueprint for tourism development, a set of 'meta-principles' founded on mainstream planning and designation processes, is inappropriate given the diverse developmental contexts and needs of tourism destinations, particularly in less developed countries.

Importantly, sustainability, which represents the resource element of the sustainable development process (Lélé, 1991), is a broader concept than simply the conservation or protection of natural resources based upon neo-Malthusian principles. Rather, it refers to the capacity for continuance of any one eco-system and is, therefore, a function of complex inter-relationships between society and natural resources, a myriad of socioeconomic and political structures and local-scale management decisions. Thus, although there can be no simple, universal remedy for tourism's troublesome track record, the complex dynamics of human–environment relationships have long been ignored by development planners. It is, therefore, 'not surprising that the target of sustainable tourism remains an illusive one' (Cater, 1995: 26). Nevertheless, the cross-disciplinary approach to sustainable tourism is forging a clearer understanding of those conditions necessary for sustainability to be achieved.

The concept of sustainability not only provides a 'good example of how alternative strategies can challenge the dominant assumptions of development' (Sneddon, 2000: 535), but also adds practical value to understanding the complex socio-environmental conditions influencing, and influenced by, tourism. In particular, it provides the basis for recognising and taking into account the environmental, social, economic and political structures, and their inter-relationship, that are unique to any tourism development context. Of course, the degree to which the concept of sustainability can be operationalised within the tourism destination planning and management process rests partially upon structural context of tourism development, such as national political and economic policies, and aspects of local-level political relationships revolving, for example, around gender and ethnicity. At the same time, the increasingly globalised nature of the tourism production system and its inherent power relationships cannot be ignored.

Nevertheless, there are numerous examples where tourism can sustain communities, conserve environmental resources and genuinely serve the socioeconomic and spiritual rights of future generations. Frequently, this is in the context of local, small-scale ecotourism-type developments, although larger scale (or even mass) tourism developments may be seen as being in accordance with the principles of sustainability, particularly if the twin requirements of local governance and ecological sustainability are taken into account. The important point is that mainstream sustainable development, both generally and in its tourism guise, fails to address a number of questions with respect to, for example, decisions and yardsticks related to 'acceptable damage', the freedom of destinations to develop tourism according to local needs and wishes and their ability to take full and equitable advantage of tourism developmental opportunities. In other words, the managerialist, 'blueprint' character of sustainable tourism serves to reduce the potential environmental and developmental benefits of tourism. Development theorists and practitioners have acknowledged the imperative of community empowerment, participatory development planning, and the value of local indigenous knowledge for two decades. The extent to which tourism engages these same principles will, to a great extent, determine the industry's future.

Notes
1. The Torrey Canyon was the first of the big supertankers to come to grief. On 18 March 1967, she struck Pollard's Rock on a reef between the Scilly Isles and Land's End, England. Some 31 million gallons of crude oil leaked from the ship, killing much marine life along the south coast of Britain and the Normandy shores of France.
2. It must be noted here that the National Parks in Britain differ from the more conservation-oriented international model. Not only is most land within the parks privately, rather than state, owned, but they are also living, working landscapes as opposed to the more widely accepted model of wilderness. Not only do over a quarter of a million people live within the Parks, but the also the land is exploited for farming, forestry, transport, quarrying, water and power supply and, of course, tourism and conservation.

Part 3

Barriers to Tourism Development

Chapter 9

Towards a New Political Economy of Global Tourism

RAOUL V. BIANCHI

> Development must start from the actual conditions and social practices of each people.
>
> (*Michael Barratt Brown*)

Introduction

As pointed out in the Introduction to this book, despite its undoubted significance as an item of international trade, tourism continues to be relatively neglected in the wider development studies literature. While there have been many studies which have sought to evaluate tourism's relative contribution to the economic development of different countries and regions (Bryden, 1973; Cleverdon, 1979), the political economy of tourism has yet to fully establish itself as a discrete field of enquiry. Moreover, there have been few attempts to engage with some of the paradigmatic debates in the theoretical literature on development. Arguably, this has partly been due to the dominance of the neoclassical paradigm in the literature on tourism development, in conjunction with the emphasis on studies of an applied and practical nature. The preponderance of prescriptive and technical studies of tourism's economic impact upon host societies may give some insight into the overall quantitative value of tourism (see Chapter 3), but do little to reveal the complex articulations between technological change and the social relations of power woven into historically specific modes of tourism development.

The principal objective of this chapter, therefore, is to reflect and elucidate upon the systemic sources of power which serve to reproduce and condition different modes of tourism development, as a basis from which to develop a more theoretically informed understanding of the structure and dynamics of the political economy of tourism. This chapter does not claim to provide a comprehensive study of the international political economy of tourism, but rather presents a particular way of looking at tourism development based on the radical theoretical traditions in political economy (cf. Sherman, 1987). The central normative preoccupation of such an approach consists of an analysis of the social relations of power which condition the unequal and uneven processes of tourism development, which are reinforced through particular configurations of ideologies and institutions. In this regard, the following section reviews some of the central 'problems' in the political economy as well as examining some of the earlier applications of the neocolonial dependency model in tourism, before then going on to explore the contemporary tourism political economy in more detail.

Capitalist Development and the Power of Tourism

A radical political economy approach to the analysis of tourism and capitalist development challenges both the neoclassical view of market equilibrium as the central dynamic force of development, as well as reified Marxist models which profess to 'explain' development processes according to a generalised and abstract set of mechanical laws. A radical approach asks how and why asymmetries of power emerge between opposing social class interests and the different geographical regions brought together through inter-locking networks of exchange through tourism. In particular it is concerned with the manner in which market relations between different groups of actors in the tourist system conceal the uneven bargaining powers and underlying material interests of different classes. Before considering existing models of political economy in tourism it is important to dwell briefly upon the principal theoretical assumptions which inform the two main paradigms.

Defining political economy

In its broadest sense the essential distinction between the neoclassical and Marxist traditions in political economy lies in the respective emphasis given to the centrality of *cooperative* and *competitive* instincts in the formation of human societies (Barratt Brown, 1995: xiii). In turn, this has been mirrored by the normative disputes surrounding the appropriate balance between equity and efficiency in the economy (see Levine, 1988: 107–25). The origins of the latter derive from the liberal tradition of economic and political thought in the 18th and 19th centuries, which has consistently emphasised the maximisation of individual liberty (to acquire/dispose of labour and property) as the basis upon which to secure the welfare of society as a whole, in contrast to the former, which is associated with the Marxist tradition, in which it is argued that the formal equality between citizens enshrined within liberal polities, conceals deeper underlying antagonisms brought about by the workings of the market (see Walker, 1989: 22–41). Marxist political economy thus places the emphasis firmly upon the power relations which are constituted by the capitalist *mode of production*,[1] which in turn give rise to the increasingly antagonistic relations between capital and labour. In contrast, scholars in the neoclassical tradition, such as Alfred Marshall, who followed on from the earlier work of Smith and Ricardo (see Larrain, 1989: 7–9), tended to reduce political economy to the study of individual economic behaviour in the market.

Whilst the more deterministic aspects of Marxist political economy have been extensively criticised (see Laclau & Mouffe, 1985; Popper, 1990), the legacy of his work remains central to a radical political economy analysis of the forces of social change and mechanisms of appropriation which condition and structure contemporary patterns of development in the international political economy. Indeed a number of critical scholars, including Cox (1981, 1987), Sherman (1987) and Strange (1994a, b), have demonstrated a more open theoretical approach to political economy whilst retaining the central normative preoccupation of examining the systemic sources of power and inequalities at different levels in the global system. In a seminal paper, Cox (1981) developed the concept of *historical structures*, according to which a particular configurations of forces (material capabilities, ideas and institutions) condition rather than determine the range of actions within the international political economy. Thus, the structures of power which both condition and emerge from a process of social change vary according to the historical–geographical configuration of material capabilities, institutions and ideological forces in particular 'state/society complexes' (Cox, 1981: 134–7). Accordingly, Cox (1987: 5) argues that 'it [production] has no historical precedence; indeed, the principal structures of production have been, if not actually created by the state, at least encouraged and sustained by the state'.

The political economy of tourism should, therefore, seek to elucidate upon the antagonistic forces and social relations which give rise to and are encompassed within specific modes of tourism development. By 'modes of tourism development' I am referring to the specific historical combination of technologies and power relations which underpin the organisation of tourism production in any given historical–geographic context. A radical approach to the political economy of tourism thus challenges the realist perspectives which characterise, for example, technical approaches to tourism policy and planning (e.g. Gunn, 1994). Indeed the weakness of these approaches has already been exposed by Hall (1994a; see Chapter 1) for underplaying the relations of power and bargaining processes between different groups of collective actors, as a result of its emphasis on rational and overt decision-making processes. It is equally critical of the methodological individualism associated with the more pragmatic, management-focused school of tourism development research whereby, for example, the success of tourism is examined in terms of the creativity and innovativeness of individual entrepreneurs (cf. Poon, 1993; Go, 1997). Such analyses do not provide any sustained commentary on the manner in which their ability to do so is constrained by the prevailing distribution of power in a given historical and societal context and, furthermore, ignores the unequal distribution of incomes and power which may result from such 'open' competition in the tourism market.

The attempt to conceive of market behaviour in isolation from the ideologies and values of the different actors and interest groups involved, as reflected in the free market notion of *comparative advantage*, underplays the political nature of markets whereby the state has historically conditioned the activities of economic classes and, furthermore, ignores the uneven consequences of unlimited market competition (see Barratt Brown, 1995: 24–8; Held, 1995: 59–66). Indeed, different economic systems, whether under conditions of capitalist production or centralised planning systems, are inherently political insofar as they serve to mobilise resources and organise people into hierarchical arrangements of power for the purpose of extracting surpluses from a given population (Lummis, 1991). Historically, notions of scarcity have been invoked by those at the apex of any given economic system as a powerful means of legitimising the centralised control of resource allocation. This applies as much to centralised systems of planning as it does to the capitalist free market. As demonstrated by Lummis (1991) and Rowbotham (1998), the free market is nothing of the kind, but rather constitutes a clever means of manipulating consumerist desires whilst simultaneously obfuscating the sources of inequality which arise from the apparent affluence it creates. Thus, the 'free' market traps us in the illusion of choice in so far as we see our assimilated values reflected back at us through a glittering array of consumer items presented to us for our gratification (cf. Williamson, 1978).

Notions of scarcity are articulated through tourism in many different ways, as evidenced in Urry's (1995: 133–40) discussion of the socially constructed and contested nature of tourism carrying capacity. It is also particularly relevant in light of today's conventional wisdom amongst governments and international agencies, that product diversification is a central part of making the tourism development process more sustainable (see Yunis, 2000). The value assumptions which underpin such views involve the implicit acceptance of the political-economic framework within which tourism should operate (i.e. the prevailing logic of the capitalist free market). Furthermore, it ignores the fact that proposed solutions to unsustainable tourism based on, for example, low volume/high spending (quality) tourists, may reproduce the systemic inequalities which characterised previous forms of tourism development whilst doing little to alleviate pressure on the environment. Such views coalesce with a market-based conception of scarcity which serve to conceal underlying arrangements of power, whereby different social groups are struggling for control over the ability to ascribe 'value' to different types of resources.

The approach to the political economy of tourism adopted here can be summarised as follows: the examination of the systemic sources of power which both reflect and constitute the competition for resources and the manipulation of scarcity, in the context of converting people, places and histories into objects of tourism consumption. The questions which need to be posed can be summarised as follows: what are the systemic sources of power which condition and reproduce uneven access to the economic, cultural and political means of production in tourism; how are the relationships between universal mechanisms of change and inequality on the one hand, and historical-geographic specificity on the other, manifest within these processes, and, to what extent is it possible to identify alternative structures of tourism development which challenge the prevailing institutional and economic hegemony of existing actors and institutions? As a precursor to a more in-depth consideration of these issues, the following section reviews the concept of core–periphery relations, one which has played an important part in constructing the neocolonial model of tourism development.

Tourism and core–periphery relations

Earlier research into the political economy of tourism drew heavily on both the liberal economic paradigm, which emphasises the positive economic effects of tourism and analyses tourism policy in terms of practical solutions to its negative environmental and social consequences, as well as the Marxist tradition, specifically, dependency theory (Frank, 1966; Wallerstein, 1979). As considered in detail in Chapter 2, authors in the latter tradition envisaged tourism as an expression of metropolitan hegemony that subordinates peripheral states to a position of dependence on foreign capital and tourists (Leheny, 1995). Although Bryden (1973) and de Kadt (1979a) are rightly credited for some of the earliest critical insights into tourism development, the political economy of tourism is perhaps best associated with Britton's (1980, 1982a) pioneering series of articles in which he elaborated upon the manner in which Third World destinations are exploited by metropolitan capitalist enterprises who organise and control the nature and scope of tourism development in the former. According to the enclave model of Third World tourism he devised, it was emphasised that tourism both exacerbates social and economic inequalities between the core and periphery as well as within destinations themselves. Britton, along with certain others (Hills & Lundgren, 1977; Pérez, 1980), focused predominantly on the unequal relations of exchange between destinations in the so-called 'less developed countries' and the rich generator nations which were rooted in the historical structures of the colonial trading system.

Colonialism had distorted the underlying structure of Third World economies via the imposition of an externally oriented pattern of trade organised around specialised commodity export enclaves producing for the metropolitan market, otherwise known as the 'plantation system' (Beckford, 1972). This resulted in the disintegration of the endogenous economy and the eventual subordination of peripheral states to a position of 'structural dependency' even after formal political independence had been achieved. Thus, the critics argued, international tourism between so-called developed and underdeveloped societies was the expression of the superior affluence and, as a result, superior access to the organised consumption of travel, in the industrialised world (Hiller, 1976; Davis, 1978). Their view offered a stark contrast to the optimistic outlook of developers and governments, who claimed that tourism would help overcome the structural distortions inherited from the colonial economy and promote economic development in many newly independent states (cf. Krapf, 1961; Bond & Ladman, 1972). Thus, rather than stimulate an autonomous dynamic of development, tourism contributed directly towards an extension of metropolitan dominance over weaker destination peripheries and ultimately leads to a loss of self-reliance (Høivik & Heiberg, 1980).

It was therefore claimed that tourism accentuated an enclave pattern of development (Freitag, 1994). In this respect, authors highlighted the structural similarities between the plantation system of agriculture and mass tourism (Butler, 1993b; Hall, 1994b), to the extent that tourism was sometimes referred to as a 'new kind of sugar' (Finney & Watson, 1975). Enclave resorts, controlled by metropolitan capital and generating few linkages to local communities, thus came to symbolise the highly unequal economic and cultural relations which structured tourism development in less developed states. In particular, these patterns of tourism development have been more prevalent in small island states characterised by low levels of economic diversification (Wilkinson, 1989).

The critical perspectives put forward by proponents of the neocolonial model also contained a significant spatial dimension. For example, as evidenced in Fiji (Britton, 1980) and Antigua (Weaver, 1988) the spatial character of tourism development grew out of the pre-existing pattern of the 'colonial space-economy'. Where tourism takes place in small island states which were previously part of the colonial plantation system, as is the case for many resorts in the Caribbean and the Pacific, large-scale resorts operated by expatriate capital have often been built on coastal plantation lands, thus reproducing the plantation economy (Hall, 1994b). Not only did this segregate the relatively affluent tourists from impoverished locals and, in many cases, continues to do so (see Pattullo, 1996: 80–2), it also prevented these lands being transferred to smallholders, thereby exacerbating socio-spatial inequalities between the rural interior and coastal areas (Hills & Lundgren, 1977: 262; Weaver, 1988: 321–8). According to Britton (1982a: 336), this pattern is compounded by the organisational structure of the international tourism industry itself, particularly the monopolistic control exerted by capitalist multinational enterprises within each of the diverse elements which make up the end-product. Their disproportionate control over capital resources, managerial expertise and, most importantly, their ability to dictate consumer demand through marketing and promotion, endows them with an overwhelming competitive advantage compared to local tourism enterprises in the destination countries themselves.

Further to the material relations of unequal exchange perpetuated by tourism in the periphery, others have likened tourism to a form of 'cultural imperialism' (Shivji, 1975: ix) or, rather, the 'hedonistic face of neocolonialism' (Crick, 1989: 322). Here the emphasis lies on the link between tourism and the objectification of native inhabitants by virtue of their incorporation into a system of generalised commodity exchange much like any other form of merchandise. Moreover, it has been argued that tourism and the institutionalisation of hospitality reinforces notions of subservience, particularly where the legacy of colonialism and slavery is strong, as it is in the Caribbean (Husbands, 1983). In this respect it is argued that tourism serves to inculcate a sense of psychological inferiority to metropolitan tourists amongst locals, a situation that is materially reinforced through the proliferation of servile employment and a clearly demarcated ethnic division of labour (Samy, 1980; Pattullo, 1996: 63–5). Erisman (1983), however, warns that these perspectives tend to underplay the ability of Caribbean populations to negotiate and adapt to the penetration of metropolitan cultural forms through tourism. Moreover, international tourism is one amongst numerous mediums through which consumerist values are communicated. It is certainly arguable that the consolidation of a small number of overwhelmingly North American and Western European global media–telecommunications–entertainment corporations, enhances their ability to exercise a far greater degree of influence over local cultural practices and patterns of consumption than tourism does (see Held et al., 1998: 341–60).[2] Nevertheless the historical class and ethnic dimensions of inequality in dependent island economies cannot be ignored, particularly where the symbolism and ideological content of colonial history is refracted through tourism, serving to undermine the emergence of a strong, indigenous, post-colonial identity (cf. Palmer, 1994).

What many of these earlier political economy analyses of international tourism had in common was their overly generalised view of macro-structural processes which, some argue, can be attributed to a disproportionate emphasis on international mass tourism (Oppermannn, 1993). Whilst crucial aspects of local/regional economic development were certainly overlooked and under-theorised, the neocolonial model did nevertheless highlight some of the major structural inequalities between markets and destinations in the international tourism political economy. Before moving onto a more detailed critique of the neocolonial dependency model in tourism, the next section will consider some of the regional patterns of development in the global economic order and their implications for the political economy tourism.

Debt, development and tourism

In the absence of widespread capitalist industrialisation, international mass tourism emerged as one of the principal instruments of the diffusion of capitalist modernity into many non-industrialised or less developed countries, crudely referred to as the 'Third World' (see Chapter 1). Notwithstanding the fact that the geographic and social distribution of benefits which have accrued from international tourism are unevenly distributed (see Harrison, 1995: 4–8), there is no doubt that tourism has provided non-industrialised countries with a valuable source of income and employment in the absence of a diversified economic base. One of the principal advantages of tourism as an export sector resides in the fact that it is less subject to the immense array of tariff barriers which prevent merchandise exports from the developing countries penetrating lucrative western markets, despite proclamations to the contrary by the World Trade Organisation (see Dasgupta, 1998: 151–6). Indeed, international tourism has also been one of the few sectors in which less developed states with weaker, less industrialised economies have consistently achieved trade surpluses (which rose from US$6 billion to US$62.2 billion during the period between 1980 and 1996). Moreover, it has enabled their governments to stabilise their foreign currency receipts and provide some protection against price fluctuations in merchandise export sectors (UNCTAD, 1998: 4). Indeed, were it not for earnings from the tourism sector in 1986, Barbados would have registered a net balance of trade deficit of US$315 million rather than the US$324 million surplus it actually managed to achieve (Allen, 1996: 63).

Yet, according to latest figures from UNDP, much of the Africa and South Asia still suffer from chronic underdevelopment, poverty, famine and reduced life-expectancy (UNDP, 1999). In the Caribbean, where dependence on tourism has historically been high, despite revenues from tourism having reached US$17 billion (£11.6 billion) last year (James, 2000), unemployment is as high as 20% in some islands (e.g. Barbados) and general living standards have fallen since the late 1970s and early 1980s (Wood, 2000: 363). The blame for many of these economic and social ills clearly cannot be solely attributed to tourism, if indeed at all in some cases. Nevertheless, it must be a cause for concern that in those places where tourism has played an instrumental role in economic development, the evidence suggests that it has not brought about the desired / expected benefits for large swathes of the population, as predicted in several well-known studies such as the Zinder and Checchi Reports (see Lea, 1988; Wood, 1979) and promoted by various international agencies (United Nations, 1963). Notwithstanding the expansion of tourism into 'new' destinations, such as Cambodia, Mali, Laos and Myanmar, Uganda and Tanzania (WTO, 1998a: 12), in many cases tourism does not appear to have resulted in a substantial improvement in overall standards of living or stimulated an autonomous dynamic of development beyond the entrance of a minority of members from amongst the national élite into some positions of management such as, for example, in Kenya (Sindiga, 1999: 95).

During the initial phases of post-war tourism expansion, a number of newly independent states deployed a combination of state intervention and limited foreign investment in order to develop tourism, including in Tunisia, where in the space of five years (1960–65) up to 40% of the accommodation capacity was built with state capital (De Kadt, 1979a: 20). The chief aims of such state-led development was to harness tourism in order to modernise their societies and encourage a degree of economic self-reliance (Curry, 1990). However, despite many of the laudable aims of 'Third World' models of socialism which underpinned many of these attempts to develop a state-run tourism industry, the long-term developmental consequences of state-run domestic hotel chains were, on the whole, plagued by bureaucratic inefficiencies and under-investment. As the internal contradictions of their economies became manifest, extensive borrowing linked to large-scale tourism projects soon became encouraged by different lending agencies affiliated to the World Bank between 1969 and 1979, which funded a total of 24 'tourism plants' in 18 countries, amounting to a total investment of US$1.5 billion (Badger, 1996: 21). From the outset, these large-scale tourism development projects contributed to the accumulating debt burdens amongst emerging nations.[3] Nations such as Turkey, Egypt and The Gambia, amongst others, which had borrowed substantial amount of funds in order to develop large-scale tourism infrastructures, found themselves at the mercy of IMF/World Bank structural adjustment programmes (SAPs) by the end of the 1970s (see Badger *et al.*, 1996). As argued in Chapter 2, the significance of these World Bank assisted projects extended beyond the economic sphere into the ideological baggage that accompanied them. Development was seen as axiomatic, and merely depended on the provision of adequate technical expertise and 'a firm belief in economies of scale in relation to infrastructure and communications' (Burns, 1999b: 333).

Technocratic models of tourism master planning constituted one component amongst a cluster of tourism-related policies which aimed to promote a particular kind of tourism rooted in a western economic rationality. A particularly striking example of the paternalistic arrogance of western development agencies towards Africa is provided by the 1973 World Bank/United Nations Development Programme project to develop tourism in The Gambia (Harrell-Bond and Harrell-Bond, 1979). The plans included the facilitation of expatriate investment and the provision of expertise which, it was assumed, 'the Gambians ostensibly lacked', as well the 'total redefinition of indigenous culture' and wholesale social reorganisation of Gambian society which was deemed necessary for the tourism industry to flourish (Harrell-Bond & Harrell-Bond, 1979: 78). Although such explicitly ethnocentric language and inappropriate approaches to tourism planning have, to a certain extent, given way to the language of participatory development and fair trade, albeit in a rather limited way (see Tosun & Jenkins, 1998), the experience of many destinations, including Eritrea (Burns, 1999), Zanzibar (Honey, 1999), Jordan (Hazbun, 2000) and Lombok in Indonesia (Kamsma & Bras, 2000), demonstrates that much contemporary tourism planning advice is still driven by a technocratic rationality, albeit articulated through a neoliberal vision of economic liberalisation and deregulation. In a different context altogether, the legacy of a Soviet bureaucratic political culture combined with the aggressive eastward expansion of neoliberal capitalism, has reinforced the application of top-down (supra-national) models of tourism spatial planning in the Baltic region, despite paying lip-service to local and regional perspectives (Jaakson, 2000).

The historical timing of insertion of many 'developing' countries into the circuits of tourism trade was a key factor conditioning the 'success' of these tourism development projects. As Curry (1982) has demonstrated in the case of Tanzania, the twin effects of the oil shocks and declining commodity prices during the 1970s, combined with a high proportion of investment 'locked into' fixed costs associated with tourism-related infrastructural development, led to worsening terms for the tourism trade precisely at the moment when international tourism was beginning to expand in many other countries, thus intensifying competition. Despite the fact that countries with more diversified economies, such as Kenya, have been able to reduce the leakages from tourism (Dieke, 1995: 79), Sindiga (1999) warns that it is important to disaggregate tourism by sector in order to get a more accurate picture of the manner in which income accrues to the local population. Thus, for example, foreign leakages in the all-inclusive beach tourism sector are generally higher (62–78%) than, for example, safari tourism (34–45%) which relies more on independent, locally run tour companies, tour guides and rangers (Madeley, 1996: 21). These disparities are also reflected in the polarisation of the territorial distribution of benefits. In Kenya, 91% of tourism revenues accrued to Nairobi and Mombasa and the adjacent beach strip in 1981, leaving a mere 9% for the rest of the country (Rajotte, 1987: 84–5).

Notwithstanding varying degrees of participation by an indigenous capitalist bourgeoisie in their domestic tourism industries, notably in Zambia (Teye, 1986), Brown (1998) argues that a combination of oligopolistic corporate *control* by transnational tourism corporations (TTCs) and ineffectual state intervention/regulation continues to sustain an unequal model of tourism development whose benefits flow predominantly to a privileged minority of state officials and TTCs. Indeed by 1975, 47% of all hotels under transnational control were located in less developed countries and, by 1978, only one hotel chain (the Indian-based *Oberoi* chain) out of the top 26 hotel chains was based outside the advanced capitalist countries (Dunning & McQueen, 1982: 72–4). More recently, it is estimated that 13 TTCs, encompassing tour operations, airlines, travel agencies and hotels, exert a substantial degree of control over much of the global tourism industry (Madeley, 1996: 8). Sinclair *et al.* (1995: 60) also point out that, despite significant moves towards the indigenisation of hotel ownership in Kenya, the majority of middle- and upper-category hotels are still predominantly run as joint ventures with foreign companies. Thus, it would appear that the widespread foreign ownership and/or management of tourism facilities, which characterises international tourism in Africa and elsewhere in many 'less developed' states (Sindiga, 1999: 23–31), still presents a considerable structural obstacle to overcoming the developmental inequalities in tourism.

The first signs that the western-inspired model of tourism development in the non-industrialised countries concealed a number of underlying antagonisms, occurred as a result of the combined effects of the 1970s oil crises, extensive over-borrowing from both multilateral and private institutions[4] and declining commodity prices in key export sectors. The principal and most devastating outcome for poorer countries in Africa and Latin America was to precipitate the 'debt crisis' which was to signal a dramatic shift in the balance of power between state and market. The subsequent imposition of SAPs by the IMF/World Bank (see Dasgupta, 1998: 66–136), ostensibly in order to ease their balance of payment deficits and alleviate their debt burdens through export-led economic growth, reflected an ideological shift to the right amongst creditors, who hoped to return these states to a '"proper" economic development path' (Dieke, 1995: 81).

During the 1980s, the architects of the neoliberal capitalist hegemony (the IMF/World Bank, private banks, transnational corporations, globalising politicians, state bureaucrats, various professional actors and journalists) stressed the imperatives of economic growth, deregulation and privatisation. In order to reduce public deficits IMF/World Bank sponsored SAPs encouraged the sell-off of state-owned enterprises, which included government-run tourism enterprises in well-known destinations, such as The Gambia (Sharpley & Sharpley, 1996: 32) and Kenya (Dieke, 1995). Privatisation programmes also stimulated a massive influx of capital into developing nations, precipitating the shift of assets from the public sector into the hands of foreign investors and domestic economic and political elites. In Costa Rica, for example, structural adjustment has led to the displacement of indigenous village entrepreneurs in nature-based tourism, and budget cuts in a number of state-funded conservation services (Place, 1998). Countries in Africa and Latin America have arguably suffered the most from the social, economic and political upheaval as a result of rising debt burdens and the austerity measures imposed by the IMF and World Bank during the 1980s. Where the state had previously played a key interventionist role in the development and planning of tourism resorts in countries such as Mexico (Clancy, 1999) and Peru (Desforges, 2000), the combined influence of the debt crisis and deregulation of global financial markets signalled the decline of state-controlled tourism development. By 1987, it was estimated that 71% of the top two classes of hotel chain in Mexico were operated by TTCs (Clancy, 1999: 13) and, in Peru, the state tourist board had its budget reduced to zero (Desforges, 2000: 186). The extent of neoliberal ideological influence on tourism policy extended to conservation, as manifest by the privatisation of 13 national parks in Thailand (Honey, 1999: 39). Similar proposals were put forward by Peru's national tourism director, who argued that that national parks (including the famous Inca ruins and World Heritage Site of Machu Picchu), should be franchised to private investors (Desforges, 2000: 186).

Indeed, the prevailing neoliberal economic order is clearly reflected in tourism, in which hotels and other strategic assets in the tourism-hospitality sector are seen as, 'part of the essential business infrastructure necessary to attract potential investors and to establish a modern market economy' (Pryce, 1998: 81). Notwithstanding the participation of powerful cliques of Mexican investors in three of the largest Mexican-based hotels chains, each with a considerable presence in other parts of Latin America, by 1994 the USA and Canada were responsible for 70% of total investment in tourism-related activities in Mexico, even before the effects of trade liberalisation under NAFTA had begun to have an effect (Rodríguez & Portales, 1994: 320). Similarly, the move towards a more liberalised international trading regime in tandem with the consolidation of regional trading blocs (NAFTA, EU) further threatens the survival of small-scale Caribbean agricultural and manufacturing producers, as well as domestic tourism businesses, thus intensifying regional dependence on TTC-controlled tourism (Pattullo, 1996: 7). Although it has been argued by some (e.g. Harrison, 2001) that governments have not been particularly effective managers of tourism enterprises, it is rarely mentioned that, where attempts by the state to harness productive capital for tourism have failed, it has usually occurred in countries where productive forces were at a low level of development.

Notwithstanding the disproportionate dominance of national political and economic élites in tourism, as demonstrated in Bali (Hitchcock, 2001), there have traditionally been higher levels of indigenous entrepreneurship and ownership of tourism in many Asian tourism destinations, particularly in peripheral regions beyond the principal circuits of corporate capital exchange and accumulation (e.g. Michaud, 1991, 1997; Dahles, 1997). Even on the island of Bali itself, there has historically been a clear spatial differentiation in the ownership of tourism accommodation facilities. Whilst indigenous entrepreneurial involvement in the former fishing village of Kuta and the inland village of Ubud, particularly in the handicrafts and lodgings sector, has traditionally been high, in nearby Sanur, the coastal strip of hotels has been dominated by external-metropolitan capital (Wood, 1979: 285).

Despite the moves towards an increasingly deregulated global capitalist economy, the structures of ownership and control in tourism cannot simply be read off as linear expansion of capital or, indeed, an expression of neocolonialism. Local and regional conditions of development vary considerably in their relation to globalising capital, which has clear implications for an understanding of the manner in which tourism becomes embedded within and transforms particular social structures. Indeed, Ioannides and Debbage (1998b) argue that tourism is characterised by a polyglot of production forms and strategic alliances in which increased levels of industrial concentration (within TTCs) have arisen in tandem with the proliferation of a loosely federated structure of specialist tour operator subsidiaries, contractors and independent small- to medium-sized enterprises providing a variety of services at different levels. For example, where both informal working practices and production configured predominantly around the family household prevails, as it is in many southern European regions where tourism has a strong presence, capital/labour relations may be quite diverse (e.g. van der Werff, 1980). Moreover, in many of the sub-sectors which make up the tourism industry, including accommodation, retail and local transport services, horizontal distinctions between owners and workers are more often than not intersected by vertical affiliations of ethnicity, gender, religion and kinship (see Michaud, 1991; Galaní-Moutafi, 1993; Zarkia, 1996). In this regard, entrepreneurial agency also needs to be examined in the context of diverse systems of social obligation and relations of trust which are mediated by culturally-defined loyalties to kinship and ethnic groups, rather than impersonal market forces alone (Dahles & Bras, 1997). This pattern can be seen, for example, in the historical presence of an overseas Chinese commercial diaspora in many South-East Asian economies (Arrighi, 1998). Although they comprise distinctive clan groups, the strong presence of ethnic Chinese tourism businesses in Malaysia (particularly in urban areas and along the west coast) and southern Thailand (Phuket) has been indentified by Din (1982) and Cohen (1982).

The manifold non-class ties which characterise much local tourism enterprise must not be seen as mere epi-phenomena but, rather, highlight the need to distinguish between different forms of ownership and control from the point of production to the point of exchange if we are to accurately assess the social relations of power embedded within tourism economic development processes (cf. Narotzky, 1997: 196–7). Where there is a high degree of entrepreneurial independence within the family enterprise, particularly with regard to the control over the labour process, this power may diminish with regard to the production process as a whole. However, at a wider level small-scale entrepreneurs are little able to effect change in the overall relations of production once they enter into market transactions in order to sell their services to tourists (see Bianchi, 1999: 251–7), a situation which is exacerbated where intermediary agencies (tour operators) are involved (see Buhalis 2000).

The 1997 Asian financial crisis served to highlight the fragile foundations of the apparently impregnable East Asian 'Tiger' economies and impacted severely upon small businesses in particular (see Wade & Veneroso, 1998). As the value of Asian currencies collapsed against the US dollar, unemployment soared as 13 million people lost their jobs, real wages fell (by up to 40–60% in Indonesia), and many small businesses went bankrupt due to the escalating value of their debt (UNDP, 1999: 4; 40). Although most East Asian economies and their tourism industries are on their way to recovery (Prideaux, 1999), this has been achieved at the cost of greater foreign involvement (principally Japanese and US firms and banks) in their economies (although it is not clear to what extent tourism assets are implicated) underwritten by IMF-sponsored restructuring initiatives (Wade & Veneroso, 1998: 14–15). Moreover, the rapid growth in tourism and associated infrastructure developments has also been achieved at the expense of considerable ecological and social costs, as demonstrated by the experience of Thailand in recent years (Kontogeorgopoulos, 1999). Clearly then, the geographically uneven nature of capitalist development and its articulation with regional and local socioeconomic formations calls into question the continued validity of a neocolonial dependency model, which envisages an international tourism economy based on the uneven trade between discrete national economies. How, then, can we summarise its conceptual-theoretical shortcomings and what alternative models of analysis can be proposed?

Farewell to the neocolonial model of tourism?

According to the neocolonial model of international tourism outlined earlier, the international organisation of production was conceptualised in predominantly geographic terms in which the organisation and control of the international tourism industry resided in the *northern* metropolitan core countries. Thus, it followed that the 'less developed' countries in the *south* became progressively subordinated to meeting the needs of foreign tourists in return for meagre economic benefits, principally in the form of low wage employment (Turner, 1976). However, in very few cases were attempts made to theorise the 'concrete situations of dependency' in their historical-geographic context (cf. Cardoso & Faletto, 1979). Most critics tended to accept the essential causal link between high levels of foreign ownership and the leakage of economic surpluses back to the metropolitan economy and the underdevelopment of peripheral tourism destinations. For the most part, the neocolonial model of the international tourism system postulated an excessively deterministic relationship between local commercial interests at the destination level, and the metropolitan-controlled agencies higher up the supply chain, whereby the former are rendered functional to the latter by virtue of the disproportionate control exercised by the metropolitan core economies over the overall direction of capital accumulation within the international tourism system (Britton, 1982b: 261). Thus, receiving societies are portrayed as inert objects or 'sub-systems' (Hills & Lundgren, 1977: 255), unable to resist the hegemonic power of metropolitan tourist capital.

These conceptual weaknesses stem, arguably, from two related assumptions which lie at the heart of the dependency model. First of all, there is an *a priori* assumption that underdevelopment is principally the result of the transfer of economic surpluses from the periphery to the core through a process of *unequal exchange* (see Larrain, 1989: 115–45; Kiely, 1995: 48–53). On the one hand, foreign exchange leakages vary widely and are notoriously hard to estimate with any degree of accuracy due to the unreliability of statistical data provided by governments (which tend to play down any negative indicators). On the other hand, a systematic and generalised chain of exploitation is taken for granted where leakages occur, rather than examined in the context of the specific nature of capitalist social relations and class alliances which condition the different forms of foreign capital penetration in the periphery. Although leakages in tourism are typically higher in small island micro-states (50–70% according to the WTO, 1998b: 70) than in larger island states, such as Jamaica (foreign leakages of 37% in 1994), and continental states, such as Kenya (net earnings were equal to 65% of gross foreign exchange earnings in 1992), where higher levels of local ownership and schemes to link local agricultural suppliers with hotels may account for lower import contents (see Sinclair *et al.*, 1995: 59; Dieke, 1995: 79; Pattullo, 1996: 39, 43–6), this does not explain why, for example, many of the poorer states in the Caribbean are those whose tourism trade is weakest.[5]

The second principal shortcoming of the neocolonial model derives from the fact that it tends to overlook the systematic variations in the local conditions of development within which tourism is inserted and to which it contributes. Although Britton (1991: 455) later emphasised that 'the [tourism] production system is not exclusively capitalistic', for the most part, these studies devoted insufficient room to the exploration alternative tourism projects, as well as varied strategies of local adaptation and response to metropolitan-driven tourism development. Related to this, has been the lack of attention paid to significant internal core–periphery relations *within* countries, particularly where uneven patterns of development emerge between dominant islands/continental states and peripheral islands. This has been addressed by Weaver (1998b), who demonstrates how domestic tourism in two peripheral islands within archipelagic states (Tobago and Barbuda) exacerbated historical animosities and disparities in the levels of economic development between the dominant and subordinate islands. Other instances of intra-regional and internal core–periphery relationships include the historically important role played by South Africa in the tourist industries of Lesotho and Swaziland, as a supplier of both capital and tourists (Crush & Wellings, 1983), the targeting of the French-dominated tourism sector by Corsican nationalists seeking independence from the French mainland (Richez, 1994) and the enforced dependence of North Cyprus on Turkey since the partition of the island in 1974 (Scott, 1999).

To summarise, the neocolonial dependency model tended to conflate a generalised system of domination between metropolitan and peripheral states with a specifically unequal capitalist mode of (tourism) production. The inherent tension between theoretical generalisation and historical–geographical specificity has mediated an incomplete understanding of the manner in which the local and regional experiences tourism development articulate with wider circuits of capital and decision-making. Insight into the diverse articulations between tourism capital, national states and local enterprise has also been hindered by the conception of tourism development conditioned predominantly by discrete national economies trading with each other, thus obscuring the increasingly transnational social relations which cut across national boundaries (cf. Hoogvelt, 1997; Sklair, 2001). Increasingly, therefore, we need to examine the differentiated architecture of tourism trade and inequality that has emerged as a result of global capitalist restructuring over the past two decades, in which some regions do well out of tourism and others do not, for reasons that are not entirely to do with geographic location, or indeed, economic dependence on tourism. Thus, we need to ask ourselves to what extent and in what ways have the sources of power and structures of inequality in tourism been transformed in light of the emergence of increasingly powerful transnational tourism corporations, underpinned by the forces of capitalist economic globalisation.

Economic Globalisation and Transnational Relations in Tourism

There are a number of contrasting interpretations regarding the meaning and scope of globalisation, as well as the degree to which powers of the state have receded in the face of global capitalist restructuring (see Hirst & Thompson, 1996; Kiely, 1998; Robertson & Khondker, 1998). It would be hard to deny, however, that a combination of market liberalisation, financial deregulation and technological change have precipitated a dramatic shift towards ever greater economic globalisation and the reconfiguration of power relations within the international political economy. Although manifest in a geographically uneven manner, the process of capitalist economic globalisation principally refers to the emergence of highly integrated cross-border networks of production and finance at many different levels in the global economy. Although ostensibly conditioned by the rigidities of the Fordist mass production model which became increasingly apparent in the late-1960s, particularly in the form of economic stagnation and declining corporate profitability, the shift towards new transnational geographies of production and flows of investment is not reducible to the intrinsic logic of capital accumulation. The processes of economic restructuring and securing a neoliberal capitalist hegemony constitute a political project in which a coalition of neoliberal corporate, financial and political interests have sought to reorganise the ownership of productive assets and thereby shift power away from labour towards capital (Henwood, 1998: 14–15). While international tourism activities have been affected by the process of economic globalisation in much the same way as other economic activities, there are significant qualitative differences in the social and geographical organisation of production within and between different branches of the global tourism industry. Much has already been said in this respect in several recent contributions by Britton (1991), Williams (1995) and Clancy (1998). However, the intention here is to review the implications of these changes in the context of the emerging architecture of power relations which flow from these industrial realignments.

The power of transnational tourism corporations

Recent figures demonstrate that travel and passenger transportation services now account for 7.5% of total world trade in goods and services, exceeding international trade in food, fuels, raw materials and various manufacturing goods (WTO, 1998b: 100–1). Yet, despite the fact that tourism is the world's fastest growing industry in terms of output, income and employment TTCs do not feature in the world's top 100 corporations ranked according to the size of their assets.[6] The fact that the measurement of the international trade in tourism services is plagued by definitional vagueness (it is often incorporated into a residual category encompassing a wide range of different services) is compounded by the manifold and complex network of agents involved in the provision of tourism-related products and services. The difficulty of delineating the precise organisational structure and sequence of tourism 'commodity chains' (cf. Clancy, 1998)[7] is particularly illustrated where, for example, parent companies such as Bass, which owns several transnational hotel chains, including Holiday Inn and InterContinental Hotels, has investments spread across different economic activities ranging from brewing, catering, entertainment and hotels (Griffin, 2000: 27).

According to the new international division of labour theory, the internationalisation of manufacturing production was strongly influenced by the squeeze on profits within industrialised countries which resulted in a shift of investment southwards in search of cheap labour, a process often referred to as 'peripheral Fordism' (Frobel *et al.*, 1980). While the squeeze on corporate profitability and, to a lesser extent, demand for cheap labour did play a part in precipitating the geographical expansion of tourism investment into new destinations from the late 1970s onwards, the territorial distribution of tourism has, to some extent, always been constrained by the intrinsic natural, historical and cultural attributes of the destination locale and the possibilities afforded by the development of transportation infrastructures, both globally and regionally. Even where ostensibly little product differentiation between places exists, tour operators are not as footloose as is often assumed, particularly where tourist loyalties are enhanced by historical familiarity with a destination (e.g. the Balearic Islands). Moreover, destination image and customer identification with a particular place are to some governed by forces beyond the control of corporate marketeers. Certain resorts may develop an iconic status by virtue of their identification with emergent cultural trends (e.g. clubbing in Ibiza and Ayia Napa), thus, in effect, becoming extensions of the very metropolitan centres from where the majority of tourists originate (a trend which, nevertheless, needs to be seen in the context of the growth of powerful club 'empires' and record company merchandising).

Nevertheless, the industrial organisation of the international tourism industry has undergone radical restructuring over the past two decades. Specifically, economic globalisation has been accompanied by increased levels of industrial concentration amongst a few globally integrated TTCs. The precise scope and organisational structure of transnational capital intervention in tourism, which conditions the degree to which TTCs are able to direct the flow of tourists, varies according to the particular segment of the tourism industry involved (i.e. tour operations, hotels, airlines etc.), as well as the historical conditions under which specific destinations became linked to particular markets. Over the past four decades, international tour operators emerged as the principal fulcrum through which different elements of the tourism commodity chain, principally charter airlines and accommodation, could be coordinated and controlled. Technological improvements, particularly the advent of computer reservation systems (CRSs) in the 1970s, together with the internationalisation of tourism demand throughout the 1980s and early 1990s, dramatically increased the scope of their activities and their ability to control a vast network of affiliated companies and contracted suppliers across an ever widening geographical network of resorts. Thus, TTCs derive considerable oligopsonistic powers as a result of their ability to negotiate low prices from an undifferentiated mass of local accommodation suppliers in the destinations themselves (Williams, 1995: 171).

The market power of TTCs is clearly demonstrated, for example, in the case of southern European tourism destinations. The historically peripheral status of southern European states in the European political economy rendered them susceptible to the superior economic power of north European tour operators and investors, upon which they came to depend for tourists, management expertise and, to a certain extent, capital (Gaviria, 1974; Boissevain, 1977; Oglethorpe, 1984; Jurdao, 1990). Whereas approximately 30% of UK tourists travelling to France do so through a tour operator, this figure rises to 80% in the case of UK tourists travelling to Greece (Ioannides, 1998: 142). Thus, the historical dependence of Greece on a relatively undifferentiated market controlled by a small number of tour operators has undermined the bargaining power of local hoteliers who have few alternatives but to accept the contractual conditions demanded by the tour operator for fear of losing their custom (Buhalis, 2000). Many Greek hoteliers suffer significant losses as a result of this power imbalance and, indeed, according to Evans (1999: 9), some may make as little as £10 per bed if revenues are spread across the year. The reduction of fixed costs and risk in this manner is not a characteristic restricted to transnational tour operators alone. Since the 1970s, transnational hotel chains increasingly substituted non-equity forms of ownership, such as management contracts and franchise agreements, for direct ownership of properties (Wood, 1979: 282). In this way, hotel chains sell or rent their firm-specific proprietary expertise and brand name in return for guaranteed levels and quality of accommodation capacity at minimum levels of risk (see Clancy, 1998: 132–3).

Castells (2000: 15) has suggested that the new globalised economy, characterised by *networks* rather than hierarchies, will lead to a greater de-centralisation and coordination of decision-making. In a similar vein, Poon (1993) has argued that information technologies could enhance the creativity and innovativeness of indigenous SMTEs (small–medium sized tourism enterprises). Despite some evidence to this effect, for example, the proliferation of on-line booking which may enable geo-graphically-distant suppliers of tourism facilities to deal directly with customers, even fewer TTCs (14 according to Madeley (1996: 8)) ostensibly control the global tourism industry. Furthermore, notwithstanding the emergence of a small number of TTCs at a regional level, in Latin America (e.g. Grupo Posadas in Mexico) and East Asia (e.g. New World/Renaissance Hotels in Hong Kong), the power of pre-dominantly western-based TTCs is, if anything, more entrenched.

Nowhere is this pattern more in evidence than in the structure of the global airline industry, where the rapid expansion of strategic global alliances (allowing airline corporations to avoid anti-trust legislation) has consolidated the centralisa-tion of control in the hands of a few mega-carriers. Airline deregulation in the USA in 1978 and more recently in Europe in 1997 brought with it a proliferation of CRSs, such as SABRE, which is owned by American Airlines, through which large mega-carriers derive considerable revenue and market share (Clancy, 1998: 138). Thus, despite the existence of almost 400 alliances involving 170 different airlines, the four major alliances now control around 50% of the world market (Blyton et al., 1998). The biggest of these, the Star Alliance (which includes SAS, Lufthansa, United Airlines, Air Canada, Varig, Thai and British Midland), has revenues total-ling US$50 billion and accounts for nearly 20% of employment of the world's top 100 airlines. Out of the world's top 20 airlines, 14 are based in rich industrialised countries and the six that are not are all based in East Asia (Cathay Pacific and Sin-gapore Airlines are also amongst the top 100 TNCs headquartered outside the core of the industrialised countries in the West (UNCTAD, 1999)). Indeed, despite the existence of regional carriers in the Caribbean (BWIA, Air Jamaica), American Air-lines sold 65% of tickets to this region in 1995 (Honey, 1999: 37).

The concentration of ownership has also proceeded apace in the European tour operator sector, where closer EU integration has precipitated an intensification of cross-border mergers and acquisitions in which both EU and non-EU capital is in-volved (Bywater, 1998). In the UK alone, 72% of charter seats are now controlled by just four airlines (Airtours International 18%, Britannia 22%, Air 2000 16%, JMC Air-lines 16%, as well as Monarch, whose 18% is increasingly controlled by Cosmos), each of which is affiliated to one of four major tour operators (*Travel Weekly*, 24 2000: 8). The net effect is to deny this seat capacity to independent tour companies, who only have access to the remaining 28% of seats. Moreover, whereas until recently Club Méditerranée was one of the few European tourism companies to operate outside of its own domestic market, increasingly, leading tour operators are seeking to establish a presence in non-domestic markets and organise their marketing/sales activities at a trans-continental level. Hence, the declining significance of the na-tionality of shareholders, particularly within the EU, is also reflected in an increasingly transnational orientation to the development of tourism products and services. For the most part, this has been achieved via the direct acquisition of retail travel companies outside the country of origin of particular TTCs (e.g. UK-based Airtours plc has recently purchased numerous companies in Holland, Sweden and Germany). There are also signs that travel companies in what were predominantly destination regions, such as Spain, are increasingly beginning to shift their attentions overseas (e.g. Viajes Barceló) in order to expand their operations beyond their domestic markets (Bywater, 1998: 58).

Many of the large tour operators have also sought to consolidate their market share via the acquisition of leading specialist tour operators.[8] In this way, they have been able to capitalise on the specialist knowledge of particular destinations as well as the loyal client base built up over the years by the smaller companies who may not be aware of the change in ownership at the top (O'Connor, 2000). However, it also leaves independent hoteliers in the destination at the mercy of even fewer companies. Although as much as 96% of the European accommodation sector remains in the hands of independent proprietors (Smeral, 1998), leading operators, such as TUI and Airtours, have also made direct investments in the purchase of holdings in luxury hotels in order to guarantee access to high quality accommodation capacity in a highly competitive market (see http://www.tui.com).[9] This reversal of attitude towards investment in accommodation in the Mediterranean may well have been precipitated by an increasingly strict regulatory environment in many regions (e.g. Mallorca), thus heightening competition over scarce capacity (Walters, 2000).

Rather than precipitate a flourishing of independent networked enterprises, the evidence suggests that deregulation and economic globalisation has strengthened the asymmetrical structures of corporate control in tourism. Moreover, the adoption and monopolisation of (costly) distributional technologies by mega-corporations has reinforced the growth of industrial concentration and transnational corporate power while, at the same time, enabling these same globalised firms to provide individually tailored products to their clients (Milne & Gill, 1998). In some respects, such globally oriented mega-corporations preside over mini-fiefdoms with regard to their relationship with certain destinations as, for example, demonstrated in Cyprus, where 20–30% of its tourism industry is controlled by Preussag-Thomson alone (O'Connor, 2000: 4). Unsurprisingly, Mander (1999: 171) has referred to such competitive technologies as the 'central nervous system' through which increasingly centralised corporate power operates. Together with the fluidity of capital movements, they constitute the foundations upon which an increasingly globalised and transnational tourism political economy has emerged.

Changing patterns of work and labour relations in global tourism

As economic globalisation increasingly forces different regions and different types of enterprise to adjust to the pressures of increasingly larger markets, the restructuring of regional/local economies and large firms will have significant implications for the organisation of work and labour relations across the global tourism industry (see Chapter 6). Clearly, however, the effects of capitalist restructuring on the tourism workforce are bound to be uneven given that different regions, sectors and types of enterprise are articulated in different ways to the forces and agencies of globalisation. Nevertheless, notwithstanding the constraints on the mobility of labour that still exist (see Castells, 1996: 232–40; Richards, 2000), there are signs to suggest that the configuration of capital–labour relations within particular networks of firms and across national boundaries has changed in accordance with more flexible systems of production.

Post-Fordist tendencies in the organisational structure of tourism production are clearly demonstrated by the increased out-sourcing of 'non-core' activities. For example, most international airlines now use external contractors to provide routine maintenance and in-flight catering services (Ioannides & Debbage, 1998b: 116). Similarly, many leading airlines have also sought to shift ancillary services to cheaper 'off-shore' locations, as in the case of British Airways, who took the lead in contracting out their ticketing services to India (Blyton, et al., 1998). Deregulation and privatisation have increased the competitive pressures on airlines (e.g. with the emergence of low-cost carriers), leading to a downward pressure on wages and demands for increased productivity from the workforce. Labour is one of the few variable costs in this sector and has, therefore, received the brunt of the cost-cutting exercises (Blyton, et al., 1998). Attempts to reduce costs in this manner led to the sacking of nearly 300 LSG Lufthansa Services/SKYCHEF workers in November 1998, prompting a three-month long strike (International Transport Worker's Federation, 1999).[10]

Despite the fact that tourism has always been characterised by elements of numeric and functional flexibility (Bagguley, 1990; Urry, 1990b), the effects of economic restructuring and trade liberalisation have intensified the flexibilisation of labour and increased job insecurity in the tourism and hospitality sectors in the advanced capitalist countries. The UK hospitality sector, within which only 10% of workers belonged to a trade union in 1996, was at the forefront of the Conservative Government's attempt to re-engineer the balance of power in favour of capital through ever greater flexibilisation of labour (Thomas, 1996). Furthermore, several studies point to an immediate decline in wages across the UK hotel sector since the abolition of wage councils in 1993 (Radiven & Lucas, 1997). Indeed, what this suggests is, to some extent, the decreasing relevance of geographic boundaries with regard to the new class structures of labour exploitation in tourism. Increasingly, the adjustment to global competitiveness has exerted downward pressure on wages in the advanced capitalist countries, thus leading to a situation where job insecurity and increasing levels of income disparity has also become more prevalent in the advanced capitalist countries (UNDP, 1999: 36–9). In the city of Los Angeles, for example, a combination of state budget cuts during the 1980s and industrial restructuring (particularly the closure of aerospace plants and the shift of many labour-intensive manufacturing industries across the border into Mexico), has underpinned the emergence of a low-wage service economy in which a disproportionate number of Mexican immigrants are employed (Davis, 1993: 45–7). Whilst significant numbers of immigrant workers have traditionally been absorbed by the hospitality and catering sectors in major world cities, such as London and New York (Harris, 1996: 35), a recent ILO study suggests that international migrant flows have not only increased in volume, but have also become more diverse in their composition and extensive in scope (Stalker, 2000: 7; see also King, 1995). Moreover, the structural shift towards a more flexible regime of accumulation in the political economy of the industrialised capitalist countries since the 1970s has been accompanied by a dramatic increase in the role of services in which there has been a tendency to reinforce quite visible patterns of inequality within the labour market, in a sector that is characterised by a high degree of segmentation and flexibility (Hudson, 1999: 35–40).

More so, perhaps, than in any other aspect of global tourism activity, the organisational structure of the cruise ship industry both reflects and reproduces increasingly transnational relations of ownership and labour relations. By 1996, three of the world's largest companies, Royal Caribbean, Carnival Corporation and Princess Cruises, controlled nearly 50% of the market (Ioannides and Debbage, 1998b: 112). However, although most of the major cruise companies have their headquarters in the USA, the ability to sail under 'flags of convenience' has enabled them to register in countries where labour laws, taxes and maritime regulations are far more lax (Wood, 2000: 351). Moreover, given the physical mobility of its primary asset, Wood describes cruise ships as mobile chunks of nomadic capital which are able to avoid state regulations (particularly where labour is concerned) wherever possible. Thus, cruise liners draw on a global pool of migrant labour who benefit from far fewer rights than their land-based counterparts. This is of particular concern for the local workforce in the Caribbean which, according to Wood (2000: 354), is mostly unionised and enjoys higher levels of pay, thus deterring cruise companies from recruiting in the region. The ethnic and social stratification of the workforce within cruise ships also points to a substantial reconfiguration of class relations that cuts across national and geographic boundaries. However, Wood (2000: 353–8) demonstrates how the workforce is drawn from cheaper labour markets across the world and segmented according to ethnicity, thus enabling cruise companies to reinforce an internal division of labour which exploits the precarious nature of employment in their respective countries of origin whilst being subject to the labour regulations of none.

With the exception of the cruise ship industry, whilst TTCs are increasingly integrated at a global level, the overwhelming proportion of the global tourism workforce remains ostensibly local, as indeed do workers in most sectors in the global economy (see Castells, 1996: 234–5). Arguably, however, as the intensity of cross-border networks of investment and ownership amongst tourism corporations intensify, a transnational capitalist class as delineated by Sklair (2001) is emerging, in which the nationality of the shareholders and corporate executives who control the commanding heights of the global tourism industry becomes less significant than do the common interests and aspirations which bind them together. Moreover, by virtue of their global orientation, they are increasingly detached from a more marginal rump of local capitalists, small-scale entrepreneurs and workers. Indeed, Sklair (1991: 120–1) has commented:

> The global capitalist system leaves less and less space for exclusively nationalistic capitalist projects. It follows that members of the indigenous bourgeoisie who resist incorporation into the transnational capitalist class are, with few exceptions, going to be trapped in a spiral of declining markets, low technology and uncompetitiveness.

The transnational capitalist classes are not necessarily the direct owners of capital in the traditional Marxist sense but, rather, comprise a flexible coalition of financiers, fund managers, corporate executives (e.g. internationally mobile hotel executives), managers of nationally based tourism firms, powerful entrepreneurial intermediaries (e.g. importers of key foodstuffs for resorts/hotels), neoliberal political cliques and state bureaucrats, oriented primarily towards the global market and with the support of executive bodies within key supra-national institutions (IMF, World Bank and WTO) regardless of national/regional/local developmental interests (see Sklair, 1990: 62–3; 117–6). Nor do they constitute a uniform stratum with a cohesive set of social and cultural characteristics but, rather, a shifting set of alliances committed to the expansion of 'business values' throughout all spheres of social and economic life and accumulation of capital, regardless of state boundaries (Sklair, 2001: 17–21). In the course of pursuing these interests, they serve to reproduce the division of labour between established and non-established interests in the new transnational capitalist division of labour. Although it is clear that transnational corporations are the principal beneficiary of and medium through which capitalist social relations are being restructured on a global scale, it is important not to overstate either the existence of a transnational capitalist class or the power TTC executives are able to wield over the global tourism economy, without further empirical research. As highlighted earlier, not only is tourism constituted by a diversified enterprise structure, particularly at regional and local levels but, equally, strategic state intervention in tourism may serve to challenge the interests of transnational élites and significantly shape the manner in which transnational capital impacts upon the local economic structures, in accordance with distinctive ideological priorities.

Tourism and the State/Capital Nexus

The extension and consolidation of the power of TTCs is not reducible to the forces of economic restructuring brought about by post-Fordist capitalism. The industrial organisation of tourism is conditioned by the actions of governments and, in particular, dominant political classes within the state. However, whilst it is often assumed that the primary role of the state in a deregulated capitalist market is to ensure an appropriate investment climate for business (Pryce, 1998: 86), this confuses the fact that, while states may legislate in the interests of capital, it does not necessarily follow that they are merely executive agents of TTCs (Sklair, 2001: 14–15). State involvement in tourism varies considerably according to the domestic political and ideological conditions which structure the institutional organisation of state bureaucracies. Direct state intervention usually involves the provision of large-scale infrastructure projects, such as airports and transport networks, which precede and prepare the terrain for tourism development, as well as the establishment of legal and regulatory frameworks within which tourism can operate. Governments in developing states have traditionally deployed a range of investment incentives in order to attract investment capital (see Jenkins, 1982), as evidenced by The Gambia's recent decision to reinstate all-inclusives (Bird, 2000: 4). More often than not, however, national governments may incur considerable financial burdens where the state itself contributes a substantial proportion of investment capital. In Senegal, for example, the state contributed 52% of capital to a hotel managed by the French transnational hotel chain, Meridien (Brown, 1998: 240). Government investment incentives can, however, also be directed towards the strengthening of a local capitalist stratum, as occurred in Cyprus after partition in 1974, when refugee hoteliers from the north were given incentives to invest in hotels in the south (Ioannides, 1992: 721).

Both the direct and indirect involvement of the state in tourism perform an important role in the regulation of the conditions of public and private accumulation of capital. Although it is increasingly rare to find places where the state exercises almost complete control over productive capital in the tourism sector, particularly since the transition towards market economies in Eastern Europe (see Hall, 1991), there is clearly still scope for the state to guide and regulate tourism economic development processes in accordance with domestic political priorities. Thus, we need to go further than to merely label particular states as either favourable or antagonistic towards tourism but, rather, seek to identify how and why different fractions within the state respond and adapt to the market and, in particular, the investment decisions of TTCs. For example, during the early 1990s, the municipal government of Calvià on the Balearic island of Mallorca, which plays host to one of the densest concentrations of tourism development in the Mediterranean, developed a strategy of strategic local intervention into the tourism economy in order to alleviate some of the worst excesses of over-construction and speculative tourism/property development (see Selwyn 2000). At the same time, however, the conservative-led regional government was encouraging the construction of roads and associated tourism infrastructure in the island's interior countryside

(Waldren, 1998). Such was the extent of high-level involvement in pushing through large-scale construction projects that it culminated in the resignation, in 1995, of the region's long-standing prime minister on corruption charges (Fidalgo, 1996). More recently, the newly elected left-wing regional government has proposed levying an eco-tax on all tourism arrivals in order to re-direct some of the income from tourism into the financing of environmental conservation (*Mallorca Daily Bulletin*, 5 August 1999). Indeed, the eco-tax can be seen both as a fiscal instrument to mediate the impact of international tourism on the regional economy, as well as a symbol of regional pride and as means of reinforcing autonomous control over sovereign *Balearic* territory in the face of external 'interference' from both the conservative-led central government and international tour operators (Morell, 2001: 56).

In stark contrast, forces of structural adjustment and internal political turmoil have severely undermined the stability of the post-colonial state in Africa. However, whilst this has destabilised the institutions of the state, economic liberalisation has reinforced the participation of African political élites in global financial markets, thus distancing them even further from their citizen populations (Hoogvelt, 1997: 83–4). Controlling factions within the state apparatuses are able to negotiate aid, loans and direct investment within a network of transnational capital flows which may strengthen their own position whilst inhibiting the flourishing of viable indigenous tourism entreprises (see Dieke, 1995: 87–91; Dahles & Bras, 1997: 65). Policy instruments, such as the Land Acquisition Act in the Indian state of Tamil Nadu, rather than promoting balanced development, are often deployed in order to appropriate land from the poor in anticipation of large-scale tourism development programmes (Seifert-Granzin and Jesupatham, 1999: 18). Examples of the restriction of informal working practices in tourism abound (Wahnschafft, 1980; Kermath & Thomas, 1992; Kamsma & Bras, 2000). However, the key distinction here is that local élites are complicit in the underdevelopment of their states, not as instruments of capital but as a result of the prevailing ideological climate of privatisation and deregulation in which the range of developmental options available to them has become even more constrained. In Zanzibar, for example, this pattern has become evident as a result of the move by the Zanzibari Government to encourage greater involvement of private capital in the tourism sector since 1985. The historical absence of a robust democracy in Zanzibar has enabled the state to implement a strategy of economic liberalisation with little opposition and at the expense of the indigenous hotel sector and small-scale entrepreneurs (Honey, 1999: 265–9).

One could argue that these states are constrained in their actions as a result of the conditions created by structural adjustment programmes and competitive pressures at a wider level. However, this should not blind us to the autonomous role of state actors in directing the accumulation process, as indicated earlier. Moreover, one should not assume that 'third world' states are merely parasitic institutions constraining the latent potential within their economies. Given the high proportion of informal economic activity (particularly pertinent with regard to tourism), the imposition of tariffs on international trade is often one of the few sources of revenue for governing élites (Carter, 1995: 608). Given highly competitive external market conditions, inviting TNCs to participate in the national economy may be one of the few ways a cash-strapped host government can obtain valuable technical, managerial and financial resources, notwithstanding the deleterious effects on smaller-scale local enterprise (see Farver, 1984: 261).

Despite the recent proliferation of tourism in places such as Zanzibar, the benefits which accrue from tourism are still monopolised by a select few countries, and capital cities within them (Harrison, 2000b). The structural obstacles to development faced by many weaker economies are compounded by the lack of an integrated domestic or regional tourist market (few amongst the tourism workforce in developing states are themselves tourists),[11] thus reinforcing what development economists often refer to as the 'low equilibrium trap' (Hazbun, 2000: 195–6). This places an enormous burden on the scarce resources of poorer states who, in order to generate a sufficient level of tourism demand that would sustain the cost of developing a tourism-related infrastructure, have little choice other than to impose externally-oriented growth policies. Moreover, those countries that are too poor even to provide basic infrastructure for tourism may become 'structurally irrelevant' to mobile tourist capital, as demonstrated by the consistently low levels of tourist visitation to countries in Sub-Saharan Africa which are considered 'unbankable' and unsafe for tourists, thus further entrenching the dominance of the more powerful regional centres of accumulation. This brings us to the final question to be considered in this chapter. To what extent is a truly global tourism economy emerging, in which capital and decision-making powers are monopolised by a few TTCs? Or rather, as some of the evidence suggests, are regional imbalances in the nature and scope of a globalising tourism dynamic becoming more entrenched in the context of further market liberalisation?

Globalisation or Regionalisation?

Although free market capitalism is undoubtedly the driving force within the global economy, the global reach of capital is still, to some extent, constrained by geography and politics. The structures of globalising capital only draw on the resources of certain regions and countries (Castells, 1996: 102), articulating with a variety of production arrangements throughout many different social formations. Equally, although those actors working through and within transnational corporations may aspire towards the establishment of a borderless global economy, the reality of global economic integration is far more complex and differentiated (Sklair, 2001: 2–3). Indeed, 75% of foreign direct investment (FDI) flows are concentrated in North America, the European Union and Japan while, at the same time, 70% of FDI outside these blocs is absorbed by only 12 countries (Hoogvelt, 1997: 77). Similarly, it has been argued here that economic globalisation and the transnational restructuring of ownership and labour relations in tourism has not been an even process. It is apparent, therefore, that parallel to the processes of market concentration at a global level, the geographical unevenness of development creates the potential for the peripheralisation of regions and populations that cuts across national boundaries.

Thus, there needs to be an element of caution when considering the precise magnitude and scope of globalisation that has been experienced in and through tourism under the conditions of an emergent transnational capitalism. During the early stages of mass tourism expansion in the 1950s and 1960s, the geographic distribution of tourism production to a large extent mirrored former colonial trading networks, as indicated by Britton (1980) and others (e.g. Harrison, 2001).Yet, although the past 20 years has witnessed the opening up of new tourism regions (e.g. the expansion of tourism and capital into Eastern Europe), the dominant tendency has arguably been the growing importance of destinations and intensification of market forces within *existing* tourism regions such as the Mediterranean. This, therefore, represents the 'thickening' of exchanges within particular regions in tandem with the partial widening of flows to others. The uneven geographical distribution of tourism is illustrated by the rapid expansion of tourism in East Asia and the Pacific, which increased its market share of international tourist arrivals from 7.5% to 14.4% during the period 1980–97, while Africa experienced a far less impressive rise from 2.6% to 3.7%, during the same period (WTO, 1999a). Moreover, despite increasing its market share of international tourism arrivals from 2.6 to 3.7% over the period 1980–97, Africa's share of international tourism receipts fell from 2.6 to 2.1% over the same period (WTO, 1999a: 253–4). With the exception of Botswana, there has in fact been little overall change in the composition of the six dominant receiving countries in Africa over the past decade, in which South Africa, Morocco, Tunisia, Kenya, Botswana and Zimbabwe absorb 70% of the region's arrivals (Harrison, 2001).

The growth of business travel and FDI in these countries has meant that transnational corporate involvement tends to be concentrated in urban areas, particularly in capital cities which were formerly colonial administrative centres. The geographical concentration of tourism in urban centres and a few established coastal areas (e.g. Mombasa, Kenya) reinforces the view that new investment tends to gravitate towards already established tourism destinations with an existing infrastructure provision, 'trained' workforce and, more often than not, amenable governments.[12] Elsewhere, 73% of international tourist arrivals in the Americas are concentrated in the USA, Canada and Mexico (WTO, 1997: 49), while India continues to absorb around half of total international arrivals in South Asia (Harrison, 2001). India's position as the dominant regional tourism metropole has been closely tied to policies of economic liberalisation since the mid-1990s, and has attracted the interest of the WTTC which recently opened a regional office in New Delhi (http://www.wttc.org, 13 December 2000). Recent years have also seen the emergence of a number of powerful domestic hotel chains as well as two nationally-based transnational corporations, the Tata Group, whose hotels operate under the name Taj, and the Oberoi, which since 1991 operates 50 hotels outside India through a series of joint ventures set up with the French Accor group (Seifert-Granzin & Jesupatham, 1999: 11).

Whilst the past two decades have witnessed a dramatic increase in the role of transnational capital investments in tourism,[13] this does not represent the linear diffusion of the hegemonic power of any one particular nation-state, notwithstanding the fact that global capitalism is still strongly associated with the globalisation of US business culture (Arrighi, 1998), as indeed is the 'culture of international hospitality' (Baum, 1996: 207). Rather, as emphasised by Hoogvelt (1997: 125), what has become evident is the intensification of a 'global market discipline' to which states, regions, companies and workers must respond in order to remain competitive. Indeed, the neoliberal emphasis on open markets, private enterprise and competitiveness does not discriminate between states but, rather, permeates numerous trade agreements, government policies and lobbying organisations at different levels in the global system (see Balanyá *et al.*, 2000). For a clear exposition of the neoliberal ideological thrust which underpins the interests and activities of TTCs, one need look no further than the World Travel and Tourism Commission, whose role it is to promote the interests of TTCs through public opinion formation, lobbying and policy formulation. Despite their avowedly pro-environmental stance, in a document entitled *Environment and Development*, their corporate affinities and almost paranoid distaste for taxation and regulation are clear to see (see also Honey, 1999: 33):

> In fact, there is no evidence that politicians, lawyers, sociologists, and enforcement agencies have the necessary knowledge of the complexities of international business of Travel and Tourism. They are in no position to use control and command techniques to secure sustainable tourism development. At best they can control supply by establishing barriers, but they cannot positively influence the future of international demand. (WTTC, 1993: 11)

Deregulation and market liberalisation have, thus, increased the capacity for TTCs to hide behind the façade of self-regulation, whilst vigorously promoting the growth of tourism at all costs, as evidenced by the lobbying efforts of the WTTC. In their defence, TTCs would argue that tourism represents the triumph of liberalism, bringing together the values of tolerance, individualism and freedom within a market-led definition of the citizen (see Urry 2000: 184–5). Yet, the foundations of a post-industrial 'consumer citizenship' have been erected upon the unhindered mobility of capital, increasingly detached from the constraints of geography and state power. The contradictory forces of unhindered mobility (of tourists and capital) and the enforced localisation of others (workers, inhabitants of poorer regions) are the social forces which underpin the emergent political economy of tourism as corporate activity becomes increasingly transnational.

Nowhere is this perhaps more evident than in the context of the global cruise ship industry. Liberated from territorial constraints as well as state regulation and unionisation, these 'mobile chunks of capital' as Wood has referred to them, constitute 'destination resorts' in themselves (Wood, 2000: 349).[14] However, not only are many of the land-based disembarkation points controlled by large businesses linked to the cruise companies themselves (Pattullo, 1996: 164–8), there is even a growing tendency for cruise ships to dock at their own private 'themed' islands (Wood, 2000: 361). Thus, rather than disperse capital and tourists amongst different island destinations, cruise ships are able to deprive ports of valuable revenue as well as enable tourists to indulge their fantasies of an island paradise free from the random and unpredictable nature of public spaces of interaction. In this regard, economic globalisation in and through tourism signals the fulfilment of the free marketeers utopian vision of a borderless, albeit striated, global [tourism] economy unencumbered by the intrusion of the state and cleansed of all uncertainties which enrich the experience of travel.

The structural implications of a global market discipline are also poignantly illustrated by the degree to which (western) standards of service quality have increasingly permeated a variety of areas of tourism service provision, from luxury hotels to small-scale ecotourism lodges. Indeed, the power of transnational hotel corporations is derived from their capacity to sell or rent out their firm-specific reputation for quality (Clancy, 1998: 132–3), which enforces a particular mode of operation on local operators. Where local infrastructure or accommodation standards are said to be below international criteria, local hoteliers struggle to compete with better equipped expatriate investors who are familiar with the desired standards of international service, as is the case in Zanzibar, where economic liberalisation since the mid-1980s has lead to the proliferation of luxury 'ecotourism' constructions built by foreign capital (Honey, 1999: Ch. 8).

Although there are no prominent representatives of the tourism industry on the European Roundtable of Industrialists (see Balanyá et al., 2000: Appendix 3), a powerful lobbying organisation comprised of 45 influential European CEOs, its activities and interests coalesce with the dominant corporate players in the tourism industry as well as EU tourism policy. In the White Paper entitled Growth, Competitiveness and Employment (Commission of the European Communities, 1999), the EU clearly emphasised its commitment to market integration based on a neoliberal recipe of competitiveness, low taxation, deregulation and flexible labour markets. In a more recent publication, the EU emphasises the need 'to promote a more business-friendly legislative and regulatory climate' as a means of promoting economic growth and development through tourism (European Economic and Social Committee, 2000: 3). The move towards an integrated economic space across Europe, underpinned by the pursuit of competitiveness, is likely to involve the emergence of new socio-spatial patterns of inequality within and between regions. Over the past 15 years, economic restructuring in response to the rigidities of the mass tourism model (cf. Marchena Gómez, 1995) and the drive towards market integration has reinforced an increasingly liberal model of capitalist development in southern Europe and stimulated the spatial dispersion of capital into areas it had hitherto been denied (particularly the rural hinterlands). At the same time, in densely built-up resort areas, such as Magaluf, Torremolinos, Benidorm in Spain and the Algarve in Portugal, efforts to reconfigure tourism towards higher spending markets via the regeneration of degraded urban infrastructures, implementation of environmental protection measures and diversification of their image, were underwritten by the state. The municipal government of Calvia in Mallorca, alone spent 15,000 million pesetas (approximately US£84 million) over the period 1992–95 on the regeneration of the degraded infrastructure in the resorts in this locality (Pearce, 1997: 168). Notwithstanding the benefits for the local resident communities in terms of improved amenities and employment, the presence of transnational capital and tour operators in local/regional tourism economies has been further consolidated. Regional and national governments have, thus, played an important role in mediating the intervention of transnational capital in local economies in the name of enhancing quality tourism and diversifying the market into new areas of rural/cultural/heritage tourism. Increasingly, this has occurred at the expense of local, small-scale entrepreneurs and long-term ecological sustainability. Nowhere has this been demonstrated more clearly than on the Canary Island of Fuerteventura, once regarded as a tranquil, low-key alternative to the high-rise developments of neighbouring islands. Over the past few years, the intervention of transnational capital (including Club Mediterranée) has precipitated a familiar pattern of large-scale speculative tourism/property development (6000 bed spaces) around the small fishing village of El Cotillo, the future of whose 600 inhabitants remains uncertain (Ben Magec, 2000: 3)

However, the political consensus within institutions such as the EU and, of course, corporate lobbying organisations, such as the WTTC, is that further economic liberalisation and market integration will engender economic growth and spread employment creation to where its needed. Indeed, such is the logic that underpins the emergence of regional cooperation agreements or 'growth triangles', which are intended to facilitate the cross-border mobility of tourists and labour and liberalise investment in tourism (Hall, 2000). Cooperation between poorer countries at similar levels of development may enable African countries to enhance intra-regional tourism and reduce their dependence on long-haul tourism controlled by TTCs (Dieke, 1995: 88–91). However, in the absence of a strong regulatory framework orientated towards the needs of the weakest regions and sectors of society, it is more likely that the deepening of cross-border market integration will foster even fiercer competition between destinations and regions as they compete for foot-loose investment and lucrative tourism markets. Within an enlarged economic space, there is greater scope for the emergence of territorial inequalities between regions. The removal of internal protectionist barriers and the increased ease of inter-state capital mobility enables / enforces regions to respond and realign themselves to the logic of capital flows rather than the specific economic development policies of national governments (although these changes are precipitated / promoted by the actions of governments). Indeed, despite attempts to reduce spatial variations in the level of economic development through the redistribution of structural funds, deepening (and widening) market integration in the EU forces the weaker economies to align themselves to the logic of market forces without undermining the leading position of the more prosperous regions (Perrons, 1999: 189).[15]

The benefits of economic liberalisation are, thus, more likely to accrue to those regions already well endowed with a well-educated and diversified workforce, access to new technologies, and locational advantages in relation to integrated transport networks (see Dunford, 1994). Thus, regional specialisation has, to a certain extent, benefited networks of dynamic regional economies and world cities in which different layers of capital investment, high status jobs and political control functions intersect, at the expense of those regions and cities which are disconnected from 'processes of accumulation and consumption that characterise the informational / global economy' (Castells, 1996: 102–3). The successful advance of regions, such as the 'Third Italy', and regional cities such as Barcelona, underlines the fact that those regions which have had the most success in adapting to a global market economy are those in which flexible yet interventionist government institutions co-exist with cooperative social-business networks (Mackun, 1998). In contrast, although many peripheral and island regions with high levels of dependence on tourism, such as the Balearic Islands, the Canary Islands and the Aegean archipelagos, may have experienced high levels of economic growth in recent years – tourist arrivals to Greece and Spain rose at rates of 7–10% per annum in 1998 and 1999 (Bar-On, 2000) – further liberalisation may reinforce the systemic pressures within capitalism towards high volume production. In the absence of a diversified economic base, this may 'lock' them into even further dependence on high growth, ecologically unsustainable models of tourism development, despite recent moves by interventionist regional governments to impose ceilings on levels of construction.

Thus, despite evidence of some degree of economic 'convergence' within the EU, per capita GDP in Portugal, Spain, Greece and southern Italy (in which important tourism regions are located) still remains at 60–80% of the EU average (Commission of European Communities, 1999: 31). Furthermore, the overall composition of the ten richest and the ten poorest regions has largely remained the same between 1986–96 (Commission of European Communities, 1999: 20). The strong growth of regional GDP per capita in areas of high tourism concentration also disguises the existence of significant internal regional wealth disparities as well as the social distribution of the benefits. This is also starkly demonstrated in the case of the Canary Islands, where high levels of economic growth centred on tourism development (services contribute approximately 70% to regional GDP), which saw its regional GDP per capita increase from 77% to 94% of the national average between 1960–90 (Longhurst, 1993), have persisted alongside pockets of high levels of unemployment (17% in 1998) and poverty. Although it is estimated that structural funds have contributed to a 4% rise in Spain's GDP, and as much as 10% to Greece and Portugal (Commission of European Communities, 1999: 12), these figures do little to highlight the internal socioeconomic distribution of wealth increases.

Conclusion

Notwithstanding the remarkable expansion of tourism in a number of countries and regions in East Asia, and in the Eastern Mediterranean (Turkey, Cyprus, Israel) over the past two decades, the overall hierarchy between winners and losers in tourism development has remained relatively unchanged. However, it has been argued that capitalist restructuring and economic globalisation has precipitated a reconfiguration of power relations that challenges the validity of state-centric approaches to the political economy of tourism, epitomised by the *neocolonial* dependency model. Central to these changes has been the increasing dominance of transnational tourism corporations and the growing structural power of market forces at a global and regional level. Thus, an increasingly complex and differentiated geography of tourism production, distribution and exchange is emerging, underwritten by the forces of economic globalisation and market liberalisation which challenges the straightforward north–south geometries of power articulated in the neocolonial/dependency model of international tourism.

The changing organisational structures of tourism production have, simultaneously, precipitated the increasing transnationalisation of ownership as well as the more visible participation of specific regions and regional growth triangles as relatively autonomous actors competing for a share of mobile tourism capital. Nevertheless, despite moves towards a consolidation of ownership and sales activities at a transnational level, tour companies are still overwhelmingly identified with and, indeed, cater to their respective national markets. Furthermore, the hegemonic power and influence of TTCs must be seen in the context of the diverse arrangements of capital/labour relations that exist within regional and local destination economies. Indeed, many areas are only partially linked into or, indeed, may be entirely marginal to the orbits of transnational tourism capital. However, what gives the emerging transnational networks of ownership and control their potency has been the ability of TTCs to dictate the terms and scope of product diversification and innovation within a wider context of resort restructuring, whilst externalising risk as far as possible via a system of contractual relations with suppliers. Indeed, rather than challenge the structural logic of market forces and the aggressive cycles of competition between barely distinguishable destinations, the shift towards ostensibly sustainable forms of tourism at the beginning of the 1990s through product diversification, has more often than not been a vehicle for renewed speculative tourism / property investment.

Many proponents of globalisation have argued that deregulation and privatisation have reduced the role of the state to that of a mere conduit for geographically mobile investment capital. Although the autonomy of the national state has given way to over-lapping structures of decision-making authority and been challenged by the power of TTCs, different fractions within the state have played a central role in the restructuring of places in accordance with the interests of tourism capital. Although it has been argued that the degree of class cohesion and global economic influence of TTCs should not be exaggerated, particularly where the interests of TTCs and powerful regional investors are constrained by domestic institutional arrangements, a cluster of global institutions, such as the WTO, WTTC, World Trade Organisation, EU and NAFTA, have provided a powerful institutional impetus to the expansion of neoliberal modes of tourism development in different regional contexts.

Notwithstanding the complex and differentiated dynamics of tourism entrepreneurship at local and regional levels, the market power of TTCs serves to intensify the dominance of transnational capital at the expense of economic diversity and social cohesion within tourism destination locales. The central concern for the political economy of tourism is, therefore, not merely whether or not incomes are rising thanks to tourism or, indeed, whether or not TTCs provide a decent wage for their workers but, rather, the extent to which different modalities of global tourism are leading to a reduction or increase in the inequality of access to power and resources. The question remains as to whether the emergent discourses of fair trade and accompanying development programmes represent isolated examples of endogenous development or whether they do indeed begin to challenge asymmetrical structures of tourism production and exchange. Further empirical investigation of the hierarchical relations of power which bind different networks of local, regional, national and transnational tourism actors and institutions together within specific development circumstances is, therefore, needed in order to enable a more concrete assessment of the changing structures of power within an increasingly transnational tourism industry.

Notes

1. The concept of *mode of production* refers to the particular constellation of productive forces and social relations which structure the manner in which human beings confront nature in order to secure their material subsistence, and the dynamic consequences which flow from these relations (see Wolf, 1982: 386–387; Hindness & Hirst, 1975: 9–12).
2. Nearly 80% of the television content in the Caribbean is controlled by Western multi-media and satellite television corporations (Brown, 1995: 48).
3. During the period 1982–90, US$1345 billion in debt repayments alone were transferred from the developing countries to the creditor nations in the north. After taking into consideration other north-south resource flows the total net transfer of wealth from north to south is calculated at US$418 billion (George, 1992: xv).
4. By 1998 private flows of invesment amount to five times the size of official development assistance to developing countries (Pryce, 1998: 78).
5. Despite relatively low leakages, considerable local ownership in the hotel sector as well as strong linkages to local agricultural suppliers, Jamaica still ranks lower than many other Carribean states in terms of per capita income levels (US$3,440) and poverty (in 1997 Jamaica's Human Development Index was 0.734, compared to 0.828 in Antigua and 0.857 in Barbados), a fact which is undoubtedly connected to high levels of debt-servicing which amount to 98% of GNP (Pattullo, 1996: 21, 39, 47; UNDP, 1999).
6. The Canadian based Thomson Corporation (turnover £5bn), which until 2000 had a 19% stake in the Thomson Travel Group, is the highest ranking tourism-related corporation, in 64th place (UNCTAD, 1997: 29–30).
7. The concept of a global commodity chain is deployed by Clancy (1998) as a means of identifying the complex and differentiated organizational structures of the international tourism industry. They are a useful means of understanding the articulations between different stages of production at local, regional and international levels, and the power relations which ensue from these processes.
8. In less than two years the UK-based specialist hiking and rafting tour company, Headwater, was recently purchased by the Simply Travel Group for nearly £5 million, which in turn was subsequently bought by Thomson Holidays (now owned by the German industrial conglomerate, Preussag) for £29 million (Balmer, 1999).
9. Airtours plc recently acquired the Spanish hotel chain, Hoteles Don Pedro, and has also purchased land in the Canary Islands for the purpose of developing luxury hotels. Last year they invested £335m in new acquisitions, which added 17,000 beds to their in-house bed capacity. (http://www.hemscott.com/equities/company/ar/id/016111/htm, 24th July 2000).

    The German-based operator TUI (owned by Preussag) has major investments in a portfolio of luxury hotels (Riu, Iberohotel, Grecohotel, Grupotel, Club Robinson, and Dorfhotel) predominantely located in the Mediterranean and Spain (http://www.tui.com. 24th July 2000)
10. LSG Lufthansa Services/SKYCHEFS are the worlds leading in-flight catering contractor. In 1993 they serviced nearly 200 carriers in 72 different locations (Ioannides and Debbage, 1998b: 117).
11. Domestic and regional tourism flows do exist in certain parts of Africa (Sindiga, 1999: 119–123; 159–161) and Asia (eg. Goa, Wilson (1996)), for example, however indigenous demand for travel is often restricted to VFR and work-related migration.
12. Lower levels of transnational capital intervention in countries such as Tunisia and Tanzania (Harrison, 2000b), stems from explicit policies by their respective governments to

restrict the involvement of expatriate private capital and encourage state-run tourism during the 1960s and 1970s (see Shivji, 1975; Poirier, 1995; Honey, 1999: Chapter 7).

13. Overall, the number of transnational corporations operating in the global economy increased from approximately 10,000 in 1980 to nearly 40,000 in the early 1990s (Madeley, 1996: 8; Arrighi, 1998: 69)

14. The power of transnational cruise companies to resist the regulatory powers of the state was forcefully illustrated in 1993 when Royal Caribbean Cruise Lines threatened to drop St. Lucia from their itinerary in response to proposals to implement a standard passenger head-tax for all ports (Pattullo, 1996: 159–160).

15. In spite of appearances the overall level of structural funds remains meagre. Although structural funds represent nearly a third of total community spending, they comprise less than 0.5% of Community GDP (Hudson & Williams, 1999: 13).

Chapter10

The Consumption of Tourism

RICHARD SHARPLEY

It is a mistake to assume that most tourists are anything more than consumers, whose primary goal is the consumption of a tourism experience. (McKercher, 1993a)

Introduction

A fundamental characteristic of tourism is that the 'product' is consumed on site. That is, whether within their own country or abroad, tourists travel to the destination to enjoy or participate in tourism. At the same time, it is widely recognised that consumers play a direct role in the production and/or delivery of most service products (Cowell, 1984) and tourism, in particular, is no exception. Indeed, it has been suggested that the 'final output' of the tourism production process – the personal tourist experience – is dependent upon the involvement of tourists themselves (Smith, 1994). Certainly, the tourism industry combines primary (land, labour, etc.) and intermediate (hotels, shops, modes of transport, etc.) inputs to produce intermediate outputs, such as accommodation, meals or performances. However, 'in the final stage, the tourist utilises the intermediate outputs (services) to generate the final output: intangible but highly valued experiences such as recreation, business and social contacts' (Smith, 1994).

In short, tourists are an integral element of the tourism production process. As a result, the nature of the tourism product is influenced not only by the industry that provides the basic constituent parts of the product but also by the needs, motivations, expectations and consequent behaviour of tourists. Implicitly, therefore, the manner in which tourists consume tourism experiences is as influential as the activities of the tourism industry in determining the character of tourism development. This, in turn, has a consequential impact on the extent and nature of tourism's contribution to wider social and economic development in destination areas.

The role of tourists in the tourism production process or, more accurately, the potential impact of inappropriate tourist behaviour on tourism-related development, has long been recognised. For example, according to Ousby (1990: 89), in 1848 Thomas Cook wrote in a handbook for visitors:

> It is very seldom indeed that the privileges extended to visitors of the mansions of the nobility are abused; but to the shame of some rude folk from Lincolnshire, there have been just causes of complaint at Belvoir Castle: some large parties have behaved indecorously, and they have to some extent prejudiced the visits of other large companies. Conduct of this sort is abominable, and cannot be too strongly reprobated.

More recently, since the advent of mass, international tourism, increasing concern has been expressed about the nature of the consumption of tourism. Mass, package tourism – and tourists – have, in particular, attracted widespread criticism (Poon, 1993; Croall, 1995) and, in response, there have been calls from a variety of quarters for more appropriate or ethical behaviour on the part of tourists. As previously noted in Chapter 8, numerous codes of conduct have been published with respect to either specific activities or to particular regions (see Mason & Mowforth, 1995) whilst, more generally, people have been exhorted to become 'good' tourists (Wood and House, 1991). More direct approaches have also been adopted. For example, during 1999 one British charter airline introduced 'educational' videos for tourists on flights to holidays in The Gambia.

At the same time, of course, the concept of sustainable tourism development has also 'achieved virtual global endorsement as the new [tourism] industry paradigm since the late 1980s' (Godfrey, 1996: 60). At the international, national, local and industry sectoral levels, a plethora of policy documents, planning guidelines, statements of 'good practice', case studies and other publications have been produced, all broadly concerned with the issue of sustainable tourism development (Diamantis, 1999).

Importantly, however, both sustainable tourism development, whether as a concept or in any of its product manifestations, such as 'ecotourism', and guides to / codes of appropriate tourist behaviour, are based on the fundamental assumption that tourists are responsive to their inherent messages. In other words, it is largely taken for granted that tourists are positively disposed to seeking out appropriate forms of tourism or that they will respond to advice on how to behave as tourists. It is assumed, quite simply, that tourists will willingly adapt their behaviour as consumers in order to optimise the contribution of tourism to local development.

The purpose of this chapter is to argue that this is not the case. That is, the notion that tourists are becoming increasingly aware of and responsive to the consequences of tourism development (and the implications of their own actions as tourists) in destination areas is overly naïve. Few tourists question or have knowledge of the impacts of tourism (Ryan, 1997: 5) and to expect otherwise is to imply that they follow a rational, knowledge-based consumption process that not only best satisfies their identified needs but which also recognises their contribution to the local society and environment. As Ryan (1997: 3) observes generally, 'from a purely pragmatic viewpoint … [tourism] … seems hardly a rational mode of behaviour', whilst many commentators point out that, more often than not, tourists themselves do not understand why they participate in tourism. More specifically, the expectation of appropriate behaviour on the part of tourists also overlooks the social and cultural forces inherent in the consumption of tourism, forces that, as this chapter suggest, may significantly limit the contribution of tourism to development. Therefore, any analysis of the role of tourism in development would not be complete without exploring the framework of consumerism within which the consumption of tourism occurs.

Development – The Role of the Tourist

For tourism to be an effective means of achieving development in destination areas then, according to current thinking, the manner in which tourism is consumed should, ideally, reflect the characteristics of the destination and the desired nature and rate of development (Inskeep, 1991). In some cases, small-scale, integrated tourism may be most appropriate; in others, the development of more traditional, mass forms of tourism may be seen as the most effective strategy. However, in either case, tourist-consumer behaviour should, it is suggested, be appropriate to the setting.

In other words, a balanced, symbiotic relationship should exist between tourists – and the satisfaction of their needs – and the developmental needs and objectives of the destination (Budowski, 1976). Such a relationship is most commonly conceptualised as a triangular interaction between tourists/the tourism industry, the local community and the destination environment (ETB, 1991; Bramwell & Lane, 1993), although it has also been referred to as the 'magic pentagon' of tourism development (Müller, 1994). According to the latter, the optimum satisfaction of tourists needs should be balanced with the health of local culture, the local economy, the local environment and, finally, the 'subjective well-being' of local communities (Müller, 1994). In both models, it is implied that tourists, in addition to benefiting from the tourism experience, should make a positive contribution to the developmental process (see also Chapter 2).

It has long been argued, however, that this does not often occur and, therefore, that tourism development and tourist behaviour should be controlled or influenced to the benefit of the destination. For example, in the late 1960s Mishan (1969: 142) observed that

> as swarms of holiday-makers arrive by air, sea and land … as concrete is poured over the earth, as hotels, caravans, casinos, night-clubs, chalets, and blocks of

sun-flats crowd into the area and retreat into the hinterland, local life and industry shrivel, hospitality vanishes, and indigenous populations drift into a quasi-parasitic way of life catering with contemptuous servility to the unsophisticated multitude.

This somewhat extreme viewpoint was reflected in the proposed solution, namely, to simply ban all international air travel! A more considered approach became evident in the extensive literature on the host–guest relationship that emerged from the 1970s onwards, although even as early as 1980, and in opposition to the perceived consequences of mass tourism consumption, there were calls for tourists to adopt a more responsible, 'good' approach to being tourists (for example, Figure 10.1).

The mass tourist–good tourist dichotomy was further strengthened by the sustainable tourism debate during the 1990s. As concerns grew about the negative consequences of tourism and, implicitly, its failure to contribute effectively to development, it was argued that 'the crisis of the tourism industry is a crisis of mass tourism; for it is mass tourism that has brought social, cultural, economic and environmental havoc in its wake, and it is mass tourism practices that must be radically changed to bring in the new' (Poon, 1993: 3). This view is echoed by others. For

1. Travel in a spirit of humility and with a genuine desire to learn more about the people of your host country.	7. Instead of the western practice of knowing all the answers, cultivate the habit of asking questions.
2. Be sensitively aware of the feelings of other people, thus preventing what might be offensive behaviour on your part. This applies very much to photography.	8. Remember that you are only one of the thousands of tourists visiting this country and do not expect special privileges.
3. Cultivate the habit of listening and observing, rather than merely hearing and seeing.	9. If you really want your experience to be 'a home away from home', it is foolish to waste money on travelling.
4. Realise that often the people in the country you visit have time concepts and thought patterns different from your own; this does not make them inferior, only different.	10. When you are shopping, remember that the 'bargain' you obtained was only possible because of the low wages paid to the maker.
5. Instead of looking for that 'beach paradise', discover the enrichment of seeing a different way of life, through other eyes.	11. Do not make promises to people in your host country unless you are certain to carry them through.
6. Acquaint yourself with local customs – people will be happy to help you.	12. Spend time reflecting on your daily experiences in an attempt to deepen your understanding. It has been said that what enriches you may rob and violate others.

Figure 10.1 A code of ethics for tourists
Source: O'Grady (1980).

example, McLaren (1998: 6) suggests that 'tourism remains a passive luxury for thousands of travellers. This must change, whilst a recent debate hosted by the pressure group Tourism Concern concluded that all-inclusive holidays, arguably the epitome of mass-packaged tourism consumption, should be banned (Farrington, 1999).

Many would agree that the call to transform the 'passive luxury' nature of tourism or to ignore popular tourism markets is naïve and demonstrates a fundamental misunderstanding of the meaning of tourism as a form of consumption. At the same time, it defies commercial reality. For example, following the decision of The Gambia's tourism authorities to ban all-inclusive holidays in 1999, some tour operators reported a significant fall in bookings. Nevertheless, there is also no doubt that, in many instances, there is a need for an aware, responsive approach on the part of tourists if tourism is to make an effective contribution to the development of destination areas. In particular, as suggested in Chapter 2, sustainable tourism development requires the adoption of sustainable tourism consumption practices, reflecting the need for a new social paradigm of sustainable life-styles as a fundamental element of sustainable development (IUCN, 1991; Sharpley, 2000).

The issue, then, is not about the need for appropriate tourist-consumer behaviour, but whether it is a realistic aspiration. In other words, can it be assumed that tourists are willing or able to adapt their consumer behaviour to better match the developmental needs and objectives of destinations? Two important questions immediately follow, forming the basis of this chapter. First, are we witnessing, as some would claim, the emergence of the 'good' tourist? And, second, what influence do the characteristics of the consumption of tourism have on the nature of tourism development?

Green Consumerism and the 'Good' Tourist?

A number of commentators propose that increasing numbers of tourists are adopting what may be described as a more environmentally appropriate approach to the consumption of tourism. In other words, it is alleged that the traditional, mass-package tourist is being replaced by a more experienced, aware, quality-conscious and proactive tourist-consumer; following a shift in general consumer attitudes, tourists 'want more leisure and not necessarily more income, more environmentally sustainable tourism and recreation and less wasteful consumption' (Mieczkowski, 1995: 388). Poon (1993) refers to this apparent phenomenon as the emergence of 'new tourism' and the 'new tourist'. Whereas the 'old', mass tourist was satisfied with a homogeneous, predictable, sun–sea–sand type holiday experience, the new tourist is more experienced, independent and flexible, seeking quality experiences that educate, are different, are environmentally benign and that satisfy special interests. At the same time, according to Poon

(1993: 145) the 'new' tourist also knows how to behave, how to consume tourism 'correctly'.

Importantly, this assumed emergence of the new, implicitly good tourist is frequently used to justify the promotion and development of appropriate, sustainable forms of tourism – that is, tourism that will contribute to the sustainable development of destination areas. Indeed, the rapid growth in demand over the last decade for activities or types of holidays that may collectively be referred to as 'ecotourism' is often cited as evidence that ever increasing numbers of tourists, as a result of their heightened environmental awareness or concern, are seeking out more appropriate and, in a developmental sense, beneficial forms of tourism. For example, Cater (1993) reports that the number of arrivals to three 'selected ecotourism destinations', namely, Belize, Kenya and The Maldives, virtually doubled over a ten year period since 1981. Similarly, others suggest that participation in ecotourism has increased annually by between 20 to 50% since the early 1980s and now accounts for up to 20% of all international tourism arrivals (Hvenegaard, 1994; Fennell, 1999: 163).

The actual size or value of the ecotourism or sustainable tourism market is open to debate, largely because there is little consensus as to the definition of ecotourism itself. Nevertheless, there is little doubt that not only it is an expanding market sector but also that some, but not all, who participate in such forms of tourism do so on the basis of deeply held environmental convictions. According to Diamantis (1999), this position is supported by research which revealed that 64% of UK tourists believe that tourism causes some degree of damage to the environment and that, generally, UK consumers would be willing to pay more for an environmentally appropriate tourism product. Conversely, there is little evidence to suggest that, generally, tourists are becoming more environmentally conscious. For example, Swarbrooke and Horner (1999: 207) conclude that, although different nationalities of tourists may embrace environmental values to varying extents, on the whole 'most tourists do not appear to have a real concern with the environment that determines their behaviour as tourists'. Indeed, studies into the motivation of ecotourists show that the majority seek wilderness scenery, undisturbed nature and the activities that such locations offer as the prime reasons for participating in ecotourism (Eagles, 1992; Eagles & Cascagnette, 1995). In other words, it is the pull of particular destinations or holidays (and the anticipated enjoyment of such holidays) that determines participation rather than the influence of environmental values over the consumption of tourism in general.

To a great extent, this confusion surrounding the extent of 'good' tourist-consumer behaviour has arisen because the concept the 'new, good' tourist relies heavily upon the assumption that increasing environmental awareness, and the alleged emergence of green consumerism in general, has led to more appropriate styles of tourism consumption in particular. As Chapter 8 explores in detail, since the late 1960s environmental concern has become, and continues to be, one of the most widespread social and political issues (Lowe & Rüdig, 1986); moreover, as Macnaghten and Urry (1998) observe, surveys in both the USA and the UK indicate that public concern over environmental issues continued to increase during the 1990s, although becoming relatively less important compared with other issues. Also, this concern appears to have been translated into people's buying habits. Green consumerism first appeared during the latter half of the 1980s (Zimmer *et al.*, 1994) and rapidly gained support with, for example, Elkington and Hailes' book, *The Green Consumer*, published in 1988, selling over 300,000 copies.

Nevertheless, some would argue that green consumerism has been a passing fad, although surveys suggest otherwise. For example, it has been found that, between 1990 and 1994, the numbers of people who considered themselves to be either 'dark green' (i.e. 'always or as far as possible buy environmentally friendly products') or 'pale green' (i.e. 'buy if I see them') consumers both increased, together representing 63% of those questioned (Mintel, 1994).

Importantly, however, there remains 'an elusive understanding' (Smil, 1993) to the cause, effect and public response to global environmental problems. Research has increasingly demonstrated that it is not possible to associate green consumer behaviour with particular social groupings (Young, 1991), and that such behaviour is unlikely to remain constant over time or be applied to all forms of consumption. In short, consumers address environmental issues in complex and ambivalent ways (Macnaghten & Urry, 1998) and, as a result, their consumer behaviour is frequently contradictory. For example, despite about 90% of people in the UK believing that the countryside is an important part of British heritage and should be protected at all costs (Countryside Commission 1996), over 80% of tourist visits to the countryside are made by car. Thus, despite the large number of surveys suggesting widespread green consumerism, it has been observed that up to one half of those who claim to embrace green values never transfer these beliefs into their consumer behaviour;

> despite the earlier evidence of high levels of environmental concern ... the proportion of adults who behave in a consistently environmentally friendly consumerist fashion is very low. *Fewer than one per cent of consumers behave in a consistently environmentally-friendly way.* (Witherspoon, 1994: 125; emphasis added)

In the present context, this suggests that it cannot be assumed that there are increasing numbers of 'good' tourists simply because there has been an identified spread of general environmental awareness (or a growth in demand for 'good', ecotourism holidays). In other words, concern with issues such as global warming, nuclear waste or the ozone hole does not immediately imply that, at the individual level, tourists will be aware of or concerned about the destinational consequences of their consumer behaviour; it does not imply that they will adapt their behaviour to the developmental benefit of the destination's environment and community People choose different products according to factors such as cost, purpose, availability, ease of use, substitutability and expected benefits. Tourism is no exception and it is not surprising, therefore, that 'relatively few tourists seem to make decisions based on environmental concerns' (Swarbrooke & Horner, 1999: 204). Indeed, as the following section argues, the nature of the consumption of tourism is such that the satisfaction of personal needs, utilitarian or otherwise, dominates the tourist-consumer behaviour process, limiting the extent to which tourists will adapt their behaviour to the needs of the destination.

The Consumption of Tourism

Tourist-consumer behaviour is a complex process; it is 'discretionary, episodic, future oriented, dynamic, socially influenced and evolving' (Pearce, 1992a: 114). Typically, it is seen as a process or 'vacation sequence' (van Raaij & Francken, 1984) comprising a number of inter-related stages, from the initial need identification/motivational stage through to the actual consumption and evaluation of tourist experiences (Goodall, 1991; Gilbert, 1991). Each stage may be influenced by personal and external variables, such as time and money constraints, social stimuli, media influences and so on, whilst each consumption experience feeds into subsequent decision-making processes. At the same time, however, the consumption of tourism may also be considered a continual, cyclical and multidimensional process. That is, consuming tourism is, generally, neither a 'one-off' event nor just a simple, uni-directional purchasing sequence. As Pearce (1992a) points out, tourism consumption occurs over a lifetime, during which tourists may progress up or climb a travel career ladder as they become more experienced tourists. As a result, travel needs and expectations may change and evolve, but these may also be framed and influenced by evolving social relationships, life-style factors and constraints, and emerging values and attitudes.

Despite this complexity, however, two specific characteristics of the tourism consumption process deserve consideration here. First, it is generally accepted that the process begins with motivation, the 'trigger that sets off all events in travel' (Parinello, 1993). It is the motivational stage that pushes an individual from a condition of inertia into tourism-consumptive activity, that translates needs into goal-oriented consumer-behaviour. Therefore, the motivation to consume tourism has a direct bearing on the nature of tourist-consumer behaviour. Second, tourism occurs in a world where the practice of consumption in general is playing an increasingly important role in people's social and cultural lives. That is, most tourism-generating societies are becoming characterised by a dominant consumer culture which influences all forms of consumption, including tourism. Therefore, 'consumption choices simply cannot be understood without considering the cultural context in which they are made' (Solomon, 1994: 536).

Tourist motivation

Tourist motivation represents one of the most important yet complex areas of tourism research. It is also a subject that has enjoyed widespread and diverse treatment in the tourism literature, although a generally accepted theory or understanding has yet to emerge (Jafari, 1987). Nevertheless, a brief review of the main contributions to the literature will reveal not only the complexity of the topic but also, more importantly, the fact that the primary motivational factors in tourism are likely to militate against tourists adopting destinationally appropriate consumer behaviour.

The literature on tourist motivation encompasses 'an amalgam of ideas and approaches' (Dann, 1981). Psychology provided one of the earlier disciplinary foundations, the notion of intrinsic need satisfaction being considered the primary arousal factor in motivated behaviour. Indeed, it has been argued that 'motivation is purely a psychological concept, not a sociological one' (Iso-Ahola, 1982). Many papers and texts refer to Maslow's (1943) hierarchy of needs, linking specific needs with identified goal-oriented tourist behaviour, whilst others explicitly adapt it as, for example, in the case of the travel career concept mentioned earlier. Similarly, Crompton (1979) suggested that tourist motivation emanates from the need to restore an individual's psychological equilibrium which may become unbalanced as a result of unsatisfied needs.

These psychological motivational forces were subdivided by Iso-Ahola into two simultaneous influences. On the one hand, motivation results from the need to escape from personal or interpersonal environments whilst, on the other hand, there also exists the tendency to seek intrinsic psychological rewards from tourism. Similarly, Dann (1977) refers to 'anomie and ego enhancement' as primary motivational push factors, anomie being the sense of normlessness or meaninglessness to be escaped from and ego enhancement representing the opportunity to address relative status deprivation. However, like a number of other commentators, Dann (1981) adopts a more sociological perspective on tourist motivation. Needs are viewed 'in terms of the (tourist) group of which the person deliberately or otherwise is a member', rather than from the individual's psychological condition. In this sense, tourist motivation is structured by the nature and characteristics of the society to which the tourist belongs.

For example, Krippendorf (1986) argues that 'the need to travel is above all created by society and marked by the ordinary' and that, functionally, tourism is 'social therapy, a safety valve keeping the everyday world in good working order'. Tourism, therefore, represents non-routine time when the individual is 'emancipated from the ordinary bounds into the unbounded realm of the non-ordinary' (Jafari, 1987). In the new, unbounded world of the destination, the tourist has travelled beyond the margins of the ordinary (Shields, 1991) into a state of anti-structure where ludic or liminoid behaviour is sanctioned or even expected (Lett, 1983;

Passariello, 1983). Moreover, tourists' 'normal' roles may be inverted, playing king/queen for a day (Gottlieb, 1982) or regressing into a child-like existence (Dann, 1996). Thus, fantasy becomes the dominant motivational factor, the rewards of the tourism experience being the immersion into a dreamlike existence that is a temporary escape from the real world.

Conversely, for MacCannell (1989), the tourist is similarly motivated by the condition of modern society but rather than seeking fantasy, it is the experience of reality or authenticity that is the desired outcome. Faced with the inauthenticity of modern society, the tourist becomes, in effect, a secular pilgrim on a quest for reality, tourism representing 'a kind of collective striving for a transcendence of the modern totality, a way of attempting to overcome the discontinuity of modernity' (MacCannell, 1989: 13). Indeed, whether a search for or an escape from reality, tourism may be considered a sacred journey, being 'functionally and symbolically equivalent to other institutions that humans use to embellish and add meanings to their lives' (Graburn, 1989: 22). Tourists are motivated, therefore, by the potentially spiritual experience of the journey (or pilgrimage), of witnessing or gazing upon particular attractions or sights, or the sense of 'communitas' shared with fellow tourists in the non-ordinary tourism culture of the destination.

Other commentators focus on more specific social factors as determinants of tourist motivation. Some explore the relationship between work and leisure/ tourism experiences (Ryan, 1991), whilst Moutinho (1987) refers collectively to cultural and social factors, including social class, reference groups and family roles, as dominant social influences on tourist motivation and behaviour. These latter issues are also addressed individually by others, such as Gitelson and Kersetter (1994), who examine the extent of the influence of friends and relatives in tourism decision-making, and Howard and Madrigal (1990), who consider the decision-making roles of different family members. At the same time, other motivational studies have focused on particular destinational categories (Klenesky *et al.*, 1993), on the measurement of tourist motivation (Fodness, 1994) and on the motivation of specific tourist groups (for example, Cha *et al.*, 1995).

There is, then, enormous diversity in the treatment of tourist motivation. Nevertheless, a number of factors are commonly evident. First, tourist motivation is complex, dynamic and potentially determined by a variety of person-specific psychological factors and extrinsic social forces. That is, a number of different pressures and influences may shape the needs and wants of tourists at any one time. Therefore, identifying specific or dominant determinant factors may be a difficult, if not impossible task, particularly given the fact that tourists may be unwilling or unable to express their real travel motives. Second, however, most commentators suggest either implicitly or explicitly that tourists are motivated primarily by the desire to escape, by 'going *away* from rather than going towards something or somebody' (Krippendorf, 1987: 29). As van Rekom (1994) suggests, 'a central need which has been revealed time and time again in empirical research is the "escape" notion', a view supported by Robie *et al.* (1993) who identify escape as one of the three most common motivating factors in tourism.

Third, and related, tourists are motivated by the potential rewards of participating in tourism. Such rewards may be personal, inter-personal, psychological or physical and, collectively described as 'ego enhancement', they compensate for the deficiencies or pressures and strains of everyday life. Finally, and again consequently, tourists' motivations are markedly self-oriented: 'now I decide what … is good for me' (Krippendorf, 1987: 29). In other words, tourism represents a form of self-reward or self-indulgence.

The implications of this in the context of tourism and development is that it is highly unlikely that tourists will be motivated to 'work' at tourism, or to ensure that their tourist-consumer behaviour will be directed towards optimising the benefits of tourism to the destination. Not only are tourists generally unaware of tourism-related consequences and tensions in destination areas but as tourism is an essentially ego-centric, escapist activity, tourists 'do not want to be burdened with the concerns of the normal world' (McKercher, 1993). More bluntly, tourists pay significant sums of money in search of relaxation, fun and entertainment. They are, therefore, most likely to give priority to satisfying their personal needs rather than demonstrating and responding to a positive concern for the consequences of their actions – their focus will be inwards, on the satisfaction of personal needs and wants, rather than on the external tourism environment. Moreover, as we shall now see, this characteristic of tourist-consumer behaviour is reinforced by the culture of tourism consumption.

Tourism and consumer culture

As previously suggested, the consumption of tourism has long been viewed as a logical, rational process whereby particular needs or wants may be satisfied, in a utilitarian sense, through tourism. As a result, much of the associated research has been concerned with developing models of the tourism demand process, or with particular elements of or influences within that process, in order to explain why people participate in tourism. Conversely, only recently have researchers come to focus upon the broader role of tourism as a specific form of consumption. In other words, tourism has, by and large, been considered in isolation from other forms of consumption in general, and from the wider cultural framework within which it occurs in particular. As a result, although the practice of consumption has become a defining cultural element of many (allegedly postmodern) tourism-generating societies (Bocock, 1993: 4), the influence of a dominant consumer culture on tourism has been generally overlooked. In short, relatively little attention has been paid to not why, but how tourism is consumed in a world where consumption plays an increasingly vital role in social life.

The tourism–culture relationship

Despite this relative paucity of relevant research, the study of tourism consumption has not remained completely divorced from consumer culture theory. Since Urry (1990a) first considered the 'consumption of tourism', a number of commentators have explored the cultural context of tourist-consumer behaviour, in particular the link between tourism and postmodern culture (for example, Urry, 1990b; Munt, 1994; Pretes, 1995). Indeed, it has long been recognised that an identifiable relationship exists between tourism and the cultural 'condition' of those societies within which occurs or is generated. For example, the widespread adoption of sunbathing during the late 1920s, the popularity of the British holiday camp up to the 1960s and the more recent trend towards adventurous, individualistic forms of tourism all reflect broader cultural change in society as a whole.

However, the nature of the tourism–culture relationship has changed over time. During the 19th century, tourism and culture were largely in opposition. That is, contrasting with 'the bourgeois culture with its concerts, museums, galleries, and so on' (Urry, 1994), tourism for the masses was centred upon the rapid development of seaside resorts as places – separated in time and space from the tourist's 'normal' existence – as places of 'ritualised pleasure' (Shields, 1991). Conversely, throughout the twentieth century, up to the 1970s, tourism practices came to reflect cultural change more closely. In particular, the emergence of a modernist culture based upon Fordist mass production/consumption (that is, where consumption was production-led) was manifested in the development of mass forms of tourism and the ubiquitous mass package holiday. Nevertheless, tourism as a social activity remained separate or differentiated from other social activities and institutions, with specific times and places (the holiday, the resort) distinct from 'normal' time and place. More recently, however, this differentiation between tourism and other practices has, arguably, become less apparent. 'Tourism is no longer a differentiated set of social practices with its own and distinct rules, times and spaces' (Urry, 1994); rather, it has merged into other places (for example, urban tourism) and other social activities, such as shopping or watching television, that were previously considered separate from tourist places and behaviour. Indeed, it has been suggested that people are tourists most of the time and that tourism has simply become cultural.

Thus, the tourism–culture relationship has evolved through two distinct stages. First, throughout most of its development, tourism has been separated from other social activities and institutions, reflecting broader distinctions in social class, employment, gender roles and so on. Even tourism itself has been subject to differentiation with, for example, different resorts or activities becoming associated with different social groups. However, more recently, tourism has now entered a second, 'de-differentiated' (Lash, 1990: 11) stage of development, reflecting the emergence of similarly de-differentiated economic, political, social and cultural processes that have been collectively referred to as the condition of postmodernity

(Harvey, 1990). As a result, it is suggested by some that tourism practices in particular have also become postmodern. Not only has tourism fused with other social activities, representing the 'marriage of different, often intellectual, spheres of activity with tourism' (Munt, 1994), but also a variety of 'postmodern tourisms' have also emerged – though no causal relationship between postmodern culture and tourism practices has been established. Nevertheless, such 'postmodern tourisms' include theme parks, heritage tourism and inland-resort/holiday village tourism whilst, in the extreme, it is claimed that tourists themselves have become postmodern – the 'post-tourist' (Urry, 1990b).

Tourism and postmodern consumer culture

The important point here is the fact that, for many, postmodernity is epitomised by the emergence of a consumer society. That is, within postmodern societies the practice of consumption has assumed a dominant and significantly more complex role than simple utilitarian need satisfaction. People now consume goods and services, including tourism, for a variety of reasons and purposes, in particular as a means of compensating for the loss, through the process of de-differentiation, of traditional social markers. In other words, a fundamental feature of postmodern culture is that 'consumption, rather than production, becomes dominant, and the commodity attains the total occupation of social life' (Pretes, 1995).

The emergence of this dominant consumer culture has resulted, in part, from a variety of factors and transformations within the wider social and economic system in post-industrial societies. Such factors include the large, widely available and ever-increasing range of consumer goods and services, the popularity of leisure-shopping, easily accessible credit facilities, the emergence of consumer groups and consumer legislation, pervasive advertising, greater and faster access to goods and services through the Internet, and 'the impossibility of avoiding making choices in relation to consumer goods' (Lury, 1996: 36). In short, the practice of consumption has been simplified and facilitated by socioeconomic transformations – it has become easy to be a consumer.

However, of equal, if not greater has been the increasing significance of consumption. It has long been recognised that commodities, whether goods or services, embrace a meaning beyond their economic exchange or use value (Douglas & Isherwood, 1979).

> The utility of goods is always framed by a cultural context, that even the use of the most mundane objects in daily life has cultural meaning…material goods are not only used to do things, but they also have a meaning, and act as meaningful markers of social relationships. (Lury, 1996: 11).

Indeed, it has been argued that consumption results only from the inherent significance of goods and services, their use value being irrelevant (Baudrillard, 1988), although this is disputed by others (Warde, 1992: 6). Nevertheless, social lives are patterned or even created by the acquisition and use of things, including tourism.

To put it another way, consumption in postmodern capitalist societies 'must not be understood as the consumption of use-values, a material utility, but primarily as the consumption of signs' (Featherstone, 1991: 85). Typically, this significance of consumption is related to status or identity messages or for establishing distinctions between different social groups (Bourdieu, 1986) and, not surprisingly, much contemporary consumer behaviour research is concerned with the symbolism of consumption, with how consumption conveys 'information to us and others about who we are' (Belk, 1995: 64).

At the same time, however, a variety of other topics, such as consumption festivals and rituals, the significance of possession, and gift-giving and exchange are all considered ways in which cultural meaning is transferred from goods/services to the individual. These all provide a valid theoretical framework for the analysis of the consumption of tourism in particular. For example, tourism has long been utilised as a status symbol, whilst the ritualistic elements of tourism consumption represent 'a kind of social action devoted to the manipulation of cultural meaning for purposes of collective and individual communication' (McCracken, 1986). Such actions include the purchase of souvenirs (possession ritual), sending postcards or the taking and showing of holiday photographs.

Importantly, this multitude of ways in which cultural meaning is transferred through consumption suggests that, generally, 'the act of consuming is a varied and effortful accomplishment underdetermined by the characteristics of the object. A given consumption object ... is typically consumed in a variety of ways by different groups of consumers' (Holt, 1995). Thus, although some individual's consumption practices may be identity or status driven – in the case of tourism, a flight on Concorde or, perhaps, a holiday at an exclusive resort – the same consumption objects may be consumed by others in different ways. Holt suggests four different categories of consumption which, as we now consider, may be effectively applied to the specific context of tourist-consumer behaviour.

Categories of (Tourist) Consumer Behavior

According to Holt (1995), consumer research has traditionally conceptualised consumption practices under two broad headings – the purpose of consumption and the structure of consumption. In terms of purpose, consumers' actions may be ends in themselves (autotelic) or means to an end (instrumental). Structurally, consumption may be focused directly upon the object of consumption (object actions) or, conversely, the objects of consumption may serve as a focal point for interpersonal actions. Thus, within a combination of these two dimensions of consumption practices lie four possible 'metaphors' of consumption:

(1) autotelic/object actions: *consuming as experience*
(2) autotelic/interpersonal actions: *consuming as play*
(3) instrumental/object actions: *consuming as integration*
(4) instrumental/interpersonal actions: *consuming as classification.*

Each of these represent different ways in which an object of consumption (including tourism) may be consumed:

Consuming tourism as experience

The consumption-as-experience perspective, focusing upon the subjective or emotional reactions of consumers to particular consumption objects, draws attention to the ways in which consumers make sense of different objects. As Holbrook and Hirschman (1982) explain, 'this experiential perspective is phenomenological in spirit and regards consumption as a primarily subjective state of consciousness'. Moreover, 'how consumers experience consumption objects is structured by the interpretative framework(s) that they apply to engage the object' (Holt, 1995); consumption objects are embedded in a social world which provides the framework for their definition or understanding.

Tourism is no exception to this process. As a form of consumption it is firmly embedded in tourists' social world and the ways in which people experience, or consume, tourism will depend very much on their interpretation of the meaning of tourism within that social world. For example, and following on the earlier discussion of tourist motivation, tourism may be interpreted as a form of sacred consumption – it occurs outside normal (profane) times and places, a 'festive, liminal time when behaviour is different from ordinary work time' (Belk *et al.*, 1989) and is consumed as a sacred or spiritual experience. Tourists' behaviour will, therefore, be framed by this sacralisation of tourism and may be manifested in different ways. Some, for example, may seek the spiritual refreshment of solitary, natural places (Urry, 1990a); for others, the sacred nature of tourism may be reflected in the collective experience of sites and destinations.

The consumption of tourism is also framed by the experiential aspect of modern consumption as a whole, namely, that 'the consumption experience [is] a phenomenon directed towards the pursuit of fantasies, feelings and fun' (Holbrook & Hirschman, 1982). In other words, modern consumption is directed towards the hedonistic pursuit of pleasure which results not from physical (utilitarian) satisfaction but, according to Campbell (1987), from romantic day-dreaming. Thus, tourism represents the consumption of dreams, again an escape to the non-ordinary, the sacred or novel 'other'.

Consuming as play

As a form of consumption that is autotelic and interpersonal, the consuming-as-play perspective suggests that people utilise objects as a resource or focus for interaction with other consumers rather than for the object's experiential characteristics. In other words, from the play perspective, the object of consumption becomes a vehicle for the achievement of broader, interpersonal goals. Thus, in the context of tourism, consuming-as-play does not refer, for example, to the ludic or 'tourist-as-child' (Dann, 1996) character of certain tourist experiences, but to the fact that tourism is used as a means of socialising or sharing particular experiences with fellow consumers.

This highlights the fact that, frequently, tourism is a social experience, an element of which is 'to be able to consume particular commodities in the company of others. Part of what people buy is in effect a particular social composition of other consumers' (Urry, 1990a). In this sense, tourism provides the focus for people to socialise or to fulfil a more 'performative, reciprocal' role in entertaining each other (Holt, 1995). Thus, tourism in resorts such as Agia Napa in Cyprus may be consumed not primarily for the attraction of the clubs and bars in the town, but for the communal enjoyment of those facilities and the contribution to the social atmosphere of the resort.

Equally, tourism may be a means of sharing unusual or extraordinary experiences; the communal interaction with the consumption object allows tourists to commune or experience communitas (Arnould & Price, 1993), the sense of which may be heightened by the collective sharing of challenging or dangerous experiences. In either case, however, the focus is on the communal, social nature of the consumption experience rather than the object of consumption. That is, the actual holiday or destination is of secondary importance to the shared experiences that such holidays or destinations provide.

Consuming as integration

According to Holt (1995), consuming-as-integration is an instrumental action through which consumers are able to 'integrate self and object, thereby allowing themselves access to the objects symbolic properties'. The object becomes a constituent element of their identity through a process of assimilation, either by merging external objects into their self-concept, or by adapting their self-concept to match the socially or institutionally defined identity of the object.

In the tourism context, integration is automatic given the inevitability, as with all services, of tourists' participation in the production of tourism experiences – the inseparability of the production/consumption of tourist services means that the tourist-consumer must integrate into the object of consumption. However, much depends upon the nature or direction of integration desired by the consumer. On the one hand, a tourist who wishes to be identified with a particular destinational culture or type of tourism may adapt his/her self-concept to 'fit' the identity of the destination or tourism-type through a process of assimilation into the local/tourist culture or through personalisation practices (Holt, 1995). This may be achieved by utilising local services or travelling independently or adopting modes of behaviour that are deemed appropriate to particular forms of tourism or travel. On the other hand, certain types of tourism or tourist experience may be integrated into the individual's self-concept in a process of self-extension; for example, Arnould and Price (1993) analyse white-water rafting as one such form of touristic activity that enables personal absorption and integration, providing communitas and personal growth/ renewal.

Consuming as classification

As previously suggested, consumption practices are most commonly considered a status/identity signifier, a means of achieving social distinction. That is, especially within de-differentiated, postmodern societies, consumers utilise consumption objects to create self-identity and to 'classify themselves in relation to relevant others' (Holt, 1995). This process of consuming-as-classification is not, of course, new; in the 1920s, positional consumption (conspicuous consumption) was identified by Veblen (1925) whilst the so-called 'aristocratic model' (Thurot & Thurot, 1983) of tourism development points to the inherent and long-held role of tourism as a social classifier.

The role of consumption in identity creation is widely considered in the literature (Bourdieu, 1986; Featherstone, 1991; Warde, 1992), as is its applicability to tourism (Voase, 1995; Sharpley, 1996). Generally, however, it is interesting to note that, although the consumption of tourism has become increasingly democratised, and 'while travel has remained an expression of taste since the eighteenth century, it has never been so widely used as at present' (Munt, 1994: 109). In response, the travel industry is developing more specialised, niche products which, though relatively affordable and available to the masses, nevertheless have the aura of status or luxury. Examples of such products include eco- (or 'ego') tourism, all-inclusives and package cruise holidays.

Tourism Consumption and Development

At has already been suggested in this chapter, the 'typical' characteristics of tourist motivation indicate that, generally, tourists are unlikely to be positively disposed towards consuming tourism is a manner that is appropriate to the destination. That is, not only are tourists considered to be unaware of the consequences of tourism, in a developmental sense, for the destination, but they are also primarily motivated by ego-centric needs of escape and self-indulgence. This is not to say that all tourists fall into this category. Undoubtedly there are some who purposefully seek out integrated, balanced forms of tourism that make a positive developmental contribution but, for the most part, tourists purchase holidays which are most likely to satisfy personal needs of escape, relaxation and fun.

To a great extent, this position is both reflected and reinforced by the consumer culture of tourism outlined here. Tourists may initially be motivated by escape and 'ego-enhancement' but, at the same time, cultural meaning is transferred to the consumption of tourism in a variety of ways. That is, the consumption of tourism embraces a meaning and significance that goes beyond utilitarian need satisfaction and, importantly, the ways in which this meaning or significance is manifested in consumption practices supports the argument that the consumption of tourism represents a barrier to effective development through tourism. Indeed, of the four categories of consumption described here, only one – consumption as integration – allows for tourists to consume tourism (to both purchase specific types of tourist experience and to act in appropriate ways) in a manner which will contribute to development. Here, those tourists who wish, in particular, to integrate 'self with object' will purchase holidays that permit them to integrate into the destinational environment and culture and, more generally, will follow the code of tourist ethics shown in Figure 10.1.

However, simply purchasing an ecotourism trip, for example, does not imply appropriate behaviour. Ecotourism tends to be expensive, individualistic, adventurous and relatively exotic. Consequently, it may be consumed for the purpose of classification ('ego-tourism'), play (the communal sharing of adventure or the unusual) or experience as defined by the pursuit of fantasy or the sacred experience of nature framed by a normal, urban existence. In each case, the destination provides the foundation for the experience but the primary focus of consumption is on the self – the tourist, and his or her relationship with other tourists and the home environment and society – rather than on the tourist's relationship with the destination.

The same may be said for most, if not all, types of tourism. That is, tourists are simply consumers who, as in other forms of consumption, seek to satisfy personal needs and to enjoy personal experiences. It matters little whether the object of consumption is a holiday, a meal in a restaurant, a house, a car or an item of clothing. The consumer seeks to optimise the utilitarian and cultural benefits through the act of consumption and to single out tourism as somehow different (and to expect tourists to modify their behaviour as consumers) is both illogical and naïve.

However, whilst this suggests that tourists, who play an integral role in the tourism production process, represent a barrier to effective and appropriate development through tourism, it does not imply that such development is unachievable. Rather, it points to the need to refocus the responsibility for tourism planning and development. It is all too easy to 'blame' the tourist, as in the blanket condemnation of mass tourism, for the challenges and problems facing tourism destinations, whereas the ultimate responsibility lies with the destination. Once the nature of tourism consumption is both recognised and understood, then destinations can plan and develop tourism accordingly to optimise their developmental benefits. As the next chapter goes on to argue, this may be through mass tourism or through localised, small-scale tourism, but the emphasis surely must be placed upon planning and providing products to suit the needs of both the consumer-tourist and the destination, rather than expecting tourists to modify their behaviour to suit the destination.

Chapter 11

Sustainability: A Barrier to Tourism Development?

RICHARD SHARPLEY

Introduction

As has been emphasised throughout this book, since international tourism first emerged as a major socioeconomic phenomenon in the 1960s, it has been almost universally adopted as a vehicle of development. Few, if any, countries do not now seek to attract tourists and, for most, tourism represents an integral element of their development policies. In some cases it may be the dominant economic sector, particularly in less developed countries or island economies, and is thus depended upon as the primary engine of economic and social growth and development. In other cases, more commonly in the modern, industrialised world, tourism principally contributes to economic growth and diversification and, hence, its role is less fundamental to the broader development process. Nevertheless, irrespective of its role and importance, it is difficult to identify any nation that has not, to a greater or lesser extent, embraced tourism within its development policies. Even the oil-rich emirate of Abu Dhabi, with more oil reserves per hectare than anywhere else on earth, is favouring the development of tourism, the main objective being economic stability following the upheavals in global oil prices during the 1990s (Camble, 1999).

However, it is not only for the extent to which it has been positively adopted as a development policy that tourism is remarkable. That is, the rapid growth in tourism over the last half century has been mirrored by an almost equally rapid increase in the number of commentators drawing attention to the potentially negative or destructive consequences of tourism development. Initially, concerns were voiced by the 'Limits to Growth' school who, reflecting the contemporary criticism of unbridled economic growth (Schumacher, 1974; Andersen, 1991), called for restraint in the development of tourism (Mishan, 1969; Young, 1973). More specific studies of tourism's consequences followed in the late 1970s and early 1980s (Turner & Ash, 1975; Smith, 1977; de Kadt, 1979A; Mathieson & Wall, 1982) and, arguably, by the

1990s no subject concerned academics, journalists, pressure groups and certain sectors of the tourism industry more than the 'impacts of tourism'.

To a great extent, criticism focused specifically on the phenomenon of mass tourism. In other words, problems associated with the development of tourism were widely considered to reflect, in particular, the alleged 'crisis' of mass tourism (Poon, 1993; Croall, 1995). It is not surprising, therefore, that the concept of 'alternative' (to mass) tourism gained support as a potential means of minimising the negative consequences of tourism whilst optimising the benefits both to the destination and to tourists (see Smith & Eadington, 1992). Proposing new, integrated and environmentally benign forms of tourism development, alternative tourism formed the foundation for the concept of sustainable tourism development which, throughout the last decade, became the dominant approach to the promotion, management and practice of tourism. Reflecting and appropriating the principles and objectives of the broader sustainable development paradigm (see Chapter 2), sustainable tourism development addresses many (and often justifiable) concerns and criticisms of mass tourism and forms the basis of many tourism development policies at destinational and national levels.

Many of the tourism development issues and challenges raised throughout this book are also addressed by the sustainable tourism concept. That is, sustainable tourism as, in principle, a vehicle for (sustainable) development, offers potential solutions to many of the problems and weaknesses of tourism-related development identified in the preceding chapters. For example, increasing and spreading the local retention of income from tourism (Chapter 3), empowering local communities in tourism development (Chapter 5) and minimising negative environmental impacts (Chapter 8) are all, in addition to being desirable characteristics and outcomes of tourism, fundamental objectives of sustainable tourism development. However, despite widespread support for its aims and principles, sustainable tourism development remains – as does its parental paradigm – a contested concept (Redclift, 1987; Sharpley, 2000). Indeed, the validity of sustainable tourism as a practical or realistic model for the development of tourism is questioned in many quarters (again, see Chapter 8).

In particular, sustainable tourism development is considered to be divisive. Evolving from the mass / alternative tourism dichotomy, its principles and policies polarise the debate between, on the one hand, sustainable ('good') forms of tourism and, on the other hand, unsustainable, mass ('bad') forms of tourism. As a result, the notion of sustainable tourism does not allow for the potentially significant contribution that more traditional, or mass, forms of tourism can make to the socioeconomic development of host societies. Moreover, the principal context of sustainable tourism development is the destination. That is, it is primarily concerned with optimising the benefits of tourism to destinational environments and communities (and, of course, with optimising tourists' experiences). Consequently, the other 'half' of the tourism system, namely, the tourist-generating region, is paradoxically – given the fact that sustainable development requires a global, holistic perspective – excluded from the tourism development equation.

The purpose of this chapter, therefore, is explore the extent to which sustainable tourism is an overly prescriptive and restrictive approach to tourism development, in effect acting as a barrier to development. In so doing, it does not seek to write off sustainable tourism (or the broader concept of sustainable development) as unworkable or inappropriate. Indeed, from a variety of viewpoints – environmental, business, ethical, and so on – both the production and consumption of tourism can and does benefit in a general sense from the adoption of the inherent principles of sustainable (tourism) development. At the same time, there is no doubt that, under some circumstances, the achievement of specific developmental objectives, such as optimising local retention of tourism earnings or local empowerment in managing tourism, is best served through sustainable tourism development. However, as this chapter argues, the notion of sustainable tourism suffers from a theoretical fragility that not only calls into question its universal applicability – as one commentator has suggested, 'it will be difficult to come up with useful principles for tourism development which are true for all places and all times (Wall, 1997: 47) – but which has also led to a specific focus on tourism resource conservation and protection. As a result, traditional, large-scale tourism developments which, for some destinations remain the most effective means of achieving desired developmental outcomes, have come to be discredited.

Tourism, Development and Sustainability

As considered in Chapter 2, the concept of sustainable tourism development has 'achieved virtual global endorsement as the new [tourism] industry paradigm since the late 1980s' (Godfrey, 1996: 60). At the international, national, local and industry sectoral levels, a plethora of policy documents, planning guidelines, statements of 'good practice', case studies, codes of conduct for tourists and other publications have been produced, all broadly concerned with the issue of sustainable tourism development.

Such widespread acceptance of the concept is not surprising. Generally, the emergence of environmentalism as a dominant global political and social movement since the late 1960s has meant that a new, environmental dimension has been added to most economic, political and social activities (Yearley, 1992). Certainly, successive international conferences, from the 1972 United Nations Conference on the Human Environment (UNCHE) to the 1992 'Earth Summit' in Rio de Janeiro, and various strategies, such as the World Conservation Strategy (IUCN, 1980), the widely cited Brundtland Report, *Our Common Future* (WCED, 1987) and the Rio 'Agenda 21' have all served to place environmental concern high on the agenda of most public and private sector organisations. In some cases, such strategies have directly informed global tourism development policies, as evidenced by, for example, the publication of 'Agenda 21 for the Travel and Tourism Industry' (WTO/WTTC, 1996).

More specifically, the tourism industry has been obliged to respond to both the mounting criticism directed at certain forms of tourism development, in particular mass tourism development that is considered to pay little or no respect to the local physical and sociocultural environment, and to the alleged demands on the part of tourists for more environmentally appropriate or benign tourism experiences (see Chapter 10). As a result, many destinational organisations have formulated strategies for the development of sustainable tourism. For example, since 1994 the development of tourism in Australia has been guided by the National Ecotourism Strategy which, by identifying eight key programmes addressing specific aspects of tourism development, such as planning, market research and sound environmental practice, has resulted in a 'heightened awareness among Australian tourism destinations of green issues and environmental management' (Diamantis, 1999). Many other destinations, such as Costa Rica, have also adopted ecotourism policies, whilst yet others follow more general sustainable development principles.

At the same time, there is increasing evidence that the tourism industry, at the level of the principals, such as airlines and accommodation providers, are adopting environmentally sound policies (Middleton & Hawkins, 1993, 1994; Diamantis, 1999). Similarly, tour operators are increasingly developing products, in particular 'eco-tours', that at least appear to be based upon environmental principals. Nevertheless, it is also interesting to note that there is little evidence of a common development and business philosophy according to sustainable principles across the travel and tourism industry (Forsyth, 1995) whilst, from a consumption point of view, recent years have witnessed little or no decrease in the demand for the traditional, summer-sun package holiday. For example, in 1998 some 17 million overseas package holidays were sold in the UK, with the most popular destinations being Majorca, followed by Turkey, Ibiza, Cyprus, France, Tenerife and Menorca – for the most part, traditional mass summer-sun tourist destinations.

Despite the apparent widespread support for and adoption of the principles of sustainable tourism development, however, they remain the subject of intense debate. That is, it remains unclear whether the concept of sustainable tourism represents, on the one hand, a viable and realistic set of guidelines for developing and managing tourism, based upon a solid theoretical understanding of the relationship between tourism and the broader development process or, on the other hand, a politically attractive objective that is unachievable in practice.

Certainly, as discussed in Chapter 2, the emergence of sustainable tourism development has mirrored, perhaps accidentally (although it has been argued that it sustainable tourism represents the logical end of a journey from 'idealism to realism' (Dowling, 1992)), the advent of its parental concept, sustainable development, as the dominant paradigm of development. At the same time, as knowledge and understanding of the relationship between tourism, the environment and development has evolved, so too have new perspectives on tourism development theory and practice, suggesting that sustainable tourism is the logical outcome of increased knowledge of tourism theory and practice. This evolution of tourism theory has, according to Jafari (1989), passed through four identifiable stages, namely advocacy, caution, adaptancy and knowledge and, as explored in detail in Chapter 2, it is not coincidental that these stages parallel to a certain extent the evolution of development theory. This process can be reviewed and summarised as follows:

Advocacy

During the 1960s, a period synchronous with its actual rapid growth, tourism was positively viewed as a vehicle for national and international development. Reflecting neoclassical modernisation ideology, the developmental potential of tourism was considered to lie in its contribution to economic growth, its success measured by indicators such as income and employment generation and the multiplier effect. At the same time, tourism was seen as co-existing with its environment (Budowski, 1976; Dowling, 1992). That is, within the prevailing technocentrist environmental ideology, tourism and conservation were considered separate issues and the potential impacts were, for the most part, overlooked.

Cautionary

From the late 1960s onwards, there was growing awareness of increasing conflict between tourism and its physical and sociocultural environment. Such conflict was occurring not only as a result of the rapidly increasing scale and scope of international tourism, but also because tourism was evolving 'in a way that closely matches historical patterns of colonialism and economic dependency' (Lea, 1988: 10). A number of commentators drew parallels between tourism and the centre–periphery dependency model of development (Høivik & Heiberg, 1980; Britton, 1982), arguing that tourism destinations were becoming dependent upon metropolitan centres for capital, technology, expertise and tourists themselves. In other words, tourism theory embraced the dependency paradigm of development, with tourism reflecting the neocolonial dependence model and, in particular, the dualistic development model whereby development reinforces the dualistic, rich/poor dichotomy within and between underdeveloped and developed countries (Todaro, 1994).

Adpatancy

During the 1980s, attempts were made to bridge the ideological gulf between the preceding antithetical positions in tourism theory. Alternatives (to mass tourism) were proposed in the form of 'responsible', 'soft', 'appropriate' or 'green' tourism, all of which attempted to transpose the concept of alternative development – an en-

Conventional Mass Tourism	Alternative Forms of Tourism
General Features	
Rapid Development	Slow development
Maximises	Optimises
Socially/environmentally inconsiderate	Socially/environmentally considerate
Uncontrolled	Controlled
Short Term	Long term
Uncontrolled	Controlled
Sectoral	Holistic
Remote Control	Local Control
Development Strategies	
Development without planning	First plan, then develop
Project-led schemes	Concept-led schemes
Tourism development everywhere	Development in suitable places
Concentration on 'honey-pots'	Pressures and benefits diffused
New building	Re-use of existing buildings
Development by outsiders	Local developers
Employees imported	Local employment utilised
Urban architecture	Vernacular architecture
Tourist Behaviour	
Large groups	Singles, families, friends
Fixed programme	Spontaneous decisions
Little time	Much time
'Sights'	'Experiences'
Imported lifestyle	Local lifestyle
Comfortable/passive	Demanding/active
Loud	Quiet
Shopping	Bring presents

Figure 11.1 Characteristics of mass versus alternative tourism
Source: Adapted from Lane (1990); Butler (1990).

dogenous development process based upon the satisfaction of basic needs, self-reliance and environmental harmony – onto tourism. Thus, the concept of alternative tourism proposes, in direct contrast to mass, Fordist-type tourism production, locally controlled, appropriate small-scale developments with the community as the primary instigators and beneficiaries of tourism (Figure 11.1).

Knowledge

Inevitably, the idealism (Dowling, 1992) of alternative tourism overlooked a number of 'fundamental truths' (McKercher, 1993a) of tourism, in particular both the exogenous factors that influence the scale, style and rate of tourism development and also the behaviour of tourists as consumers of the tourism product.

Moreover, by definition, it represented an alternative, not a solution, to the alleged problems associated with mass tourism development. Therefore, it evolved into the broader perspective of sustainable tourism development which embodies, according to Jafari (1989), a greater knowledge and understanding of tourism's developmental processes underpinned by contributions from a variety of disciplines.

Questions remain, however, about the extent to which sustainable tourism development is achievable in practice. That is, although the last decade has witnessed widespread support for and adherence to the principles of sustainable tourism, it remains the subject of intense debate, reflecting, to a great extent, the ambiguity of both its inherent processes and its objectives. This may, of course, represent one of the strengths of the concept. As one commentator notes, the parental paradigm of sustainable development

> struck a middle ground between more radical approaches which denounced all development, and the idea of development conceived as business as usual. The idea of Sustainable Development, although broad, loose and tinged with lots of ambiguity around its edges, turned out to be palatable to everybody. This may have been its greatest virtue: it is radical yet not offensive. (Skolimowski, 1995)

The same may be said about its tourism offspring, sustainable tourism development. Its vague, ambiguous yet politically attractive principles and aims can be variously interpreted and appropriated to suit the needs of different organisations or interest groups and, as a result, it has become a catch-all phrase; 'to some ... [it is] all about new products or market segments, to others, it is a process of development, while still to others it represents a guiding principle to which all tourism should aspire' (Godfrey, 1996: 61). On the one hand, this universality may be considered beneficial, in that it encourages environmental awareness, in some form or another, throughout the tourism system. On the other hand, however, it also enables the misappropriation of the concept, hence the argument that sustainable tourism development represents little more than a convenient, attractive 'green' mantle behind which the tourism industry has been able to hide.

What is certain is the fact that, as a consequence of its ambiguity, sustainable tourism development defies precise definition. Nevertheless, much of the literature remains concerned with definitional, as opposed to operational issues, to the extent that 'defining sustainable development in the context of tourism has become something of a cottage industry' (Garrod & Fyall, 1998). Such definitions fall primarily into two broad categories, namely 'tourism-centric' definitions (Hunter, 1995), which focus upon the environmental sustainability of tourism as a specific economic activity, and those which view tourism as an integral element of wider sustainable development policies. At the same time, sustainable tourism development has also been referred to as an 'adaptive paradigm', or a set of meta-principles within which 'several different development pathways may be legitimised according to circumstance' (Hunter, 1997). Whilst this particular conceptualisation is undoubtedly attractive, however, it also neatly sidesteps the need for a concise definition, thereby failing to provide a yardstick against which the viability of the concept may be measured.

It is not the purpose here to review the extensive literature on the 'sustainable tourism debate' (see, for example, Nelson *et al.*, 1993; Priestly *et al.*, 1996; France, 1997; Stabler, 1997; Butler, 1999b). Nevertheless, both the justification for, and a recurrent theme throughout, this book is the failure within the literature to explore the relationship between the theoretical foundations of tourism studies and development studies. This is particularly so in the case of sustainable tourism development, where the lack of theoretical grounding has led to an apparently rigid acceptance that the principles and objectives of sustainable development can be easily transposed onto most tourism development contexts (Inskeep, 1991: xviii). As argued elsewhere, this is not necessarily the case (Sharpley, 2000a) and, as a result, not only has sustainable tourism development frequently failed to live up to expectations but also it has arguably been most effective as a politically attractive red herring. In other words, as this chapter now argues, sustainable tourism has acted as a barrier to (sustainable) development owing to its theoretical weakness and its resultant inherent divisiveness based upon its roots as an alternative to mass tourism.

What is Sustainable Tourism Development?

As previously suggested, it has proved difficult, if not impossible, to achieve consensus on a definition of sustainable tourism development. It has been described as a 'positive approach intended to reduce tensions and friction created by the complex interactions between the tourism industry, visitors, the environment and the communities which are host to holidaymakers' (Bramwell & Lane, 1993) whilst, more ambiguously, the Brundland Report's widely cited phrase is unashamedly paraphrased in defining sustainable tourism development as 'development [which] meets the needs of present tourists and host regions while protecting and enhancing opportunity for the future' (WTO/WTTC, 1996: 30). Neither generalisation, however, reveals the objectives, in the developmental sense, of sustainable tourism or the processes by which such objectives might be achieved.

To further complicate matters, a variety of other terms, such as rural tourism, green tourism, low impact tourism (Lillywhite & Lillywhite, 1991), alternative tourism (Holden, 1984; Eadington & Smith, 1992), soft tourism (Kariel, 1989; Krippendorf, 1991), responsible tourism (Harrison & Husbands, 1996) and nature tourism (Whelan, 1991) are employed, with ecotourism – itself subject to various

1. Tourism must be a recognised sustainable economic development option, considered equally with other economic activities when jurisdictions are making development decisions.
2. There must be a relevant tourism information base to permit recognition, analysis and monitoring of the tourism industry in relation to other sectors of the economy.
3. Tourism development must be carried out in a way that is compatible with the principles of sustainable development

Figure 11.2 Principles for sustainable tourism development
Source: Cronin (1990)

definitions – being widely perceived as being synonymous with sustainable tourism development.

However, given the fact that the concept of sustainable tourism development is, in essence, a sector-specific application of sustainable development, it is logical to assert that 'those who insert the word 'tourism' between "sustainable" and "development"… [should]… ensure that, under all circumstances, the resultant principles of sustainable tourism are also principles of sustainable development' (Hunter, 1995). Such an approach was indeed adopted by the Globe 90 Conference in Canada where, in recognition of tourism's role in wider development, three fundamental principles to guide tourism planning and management were proposed (Figure 11.2).

In short, sustainable tourism should be considered a potential means of achieving sustainable development; that is, any form of tourism should itself be (a) environmentally sustainable and (b) be able to contribute indefinitely to broader sustainable development policies and objectives. Evidently, (a) is also a prerequisite to (b).

This logical definition of sustainable tourism development has a number of implications. First, by locating tourism within the wider developmental context, the effectiveness of tourism as a specific means of satisfying the goals of sustainable development is itself questioned. That is, for some communities or states, tourism (in any form) may not represent, either on its own or in tandem with other activities, an appropriate path to sustainable development when compared to other economic development policies. Second, and as a consequence, sustainable tourism is no longer synonymous with competing for the use of scarce resources (Jenner and Smith, 1992; McKercher, 1993a, b) in order to sustain tourism in the longer term; rather, the emphasis is placed upon the most appropriate and efficient shared use of resources, on a global basis, within overall development goals. Third, the inherently divisive character of sustainable tourism as the 'good' alternative to traditional, mass tourism becomes irrelevant as the focus shifts to striving for developing all forms of tourism within the broader principles of sustainable development.

Most typically, however, the principal concern of sustainable tourism development has become the sustainable development of tourism itself (Lanfant & Graburn, 1992). In other words, where attempts have been made to implement sustainable tourism development policies in practice, they most closely reflect the tourism-centric approach referred to earlier. The aim has become to preserve the natural, built and sociocultural resource base upon which tourism depends in a specific space/place in order to permit the long-term survival of tourism, rather than optimising the contribution of tourism to the wider sustainable development of the destination. As one commentator summarises, 'sustainable tourism is essentially an exercise in sustainable resource management' (Pigram, 1990).

To an extent, of course, this makes good business sense. All businesses or industries strive to maintain their resource base for long-term survival and profit and it is widely recognised that sound environmental policies may significantly enhance profitability. However, the important point here is that this inward focus upon sustaining tourism itself, concentrating on issues such as the rate and scale of development, the type of tourist targeted and the degree of local control, not only suggests that 'true' sustainable tourism development (i.e. consistent with the tenets of its parental paradigm) is unachievable in practice, but has also resulted in a highly polarised and value-laden perspective on tourism development. It is necessary, therefore, to consider briefly the theoretical weaknesses of the concept of sustainable tourism development that underpin its role as a potential barrier, as opposed to contributor, to development.

The 'Problem' of Sustainable Tourism Development

Despite the widespread adoption of its principles and objectives, there has been, as suggested earlier, a surprisingly consistent failure to explore the theoretical links between sustainable tourism and sustainable development. As a result, the concept of development as both the justification for and objective of tourism is rarely, if ever, considered; indeed, it is rarely questioned whether tourism, in whatever form, is a suitable or effective vehicle for the achievement of development.

More specifically, only recently have attempts been made to transpose tourism onto the sustainable development template (see Figure 11.3).

These have revealed a number of significant problems or factors which militate against the achievement of 'true' sustainable tourism development (Sharpley, 2000a). In particular the following ones have been identified:

- As evident from Figure 11.3, a fundamental requirement of sustainable development is the adoption of an holistic approach which locates the developmental and environmental consequences of any activity or process within a global socioeconomic, political and ecological context. For tourism, such a perspective is impossible given the fragmented,

Fundamental principles:	• *Holistic approach*: development and environmental issues integrated within a global social, economic and ecological context. • *Futurity*: focus on long-term capacity for continuance of the global ecosystem, including the human sub-system. • *Equity*: development that is fair and equitable and which provides opportunities for access to and use of resources for all members of all societies, both in the present and future.
Development objectives:	• Improvement of the quality of life for all people: education, life expectancy, opportunities to fulfil potential • Satisfaction of basic needs; concentration on the nature of what is provided rather than income. • Self-reliance: political freedom and local decision making for local needs. • Endogenous development
Sustainability objectives:	• Sustainable population levels. • Minimal depletion of non-renewable natural resources. • Sustainable use of renewable resources. • Pollution emissions within the assimilative capacity of the environment
Requirements for sustainable development:	• Adoption of a new social paradigm relevant to sustainable living • International and national political and economic systems dedicated to equitable development and resource use. • Technological systems that can search continuously for new solutions to environmental problems • Global alliance facilitating integrated development policies at local, national and international levels.

Figure 11.3 Sustainable development: principles and objectives
Sources: Streeten (1977); Pearce *et al.* (1989); WCED (1987); IUCN (1991).

multi-sectoral, private-sector-dominated and profit-motivated character of the tourism production system.

- The political economy of tourism can frequently represent a barrier to development (Chapter 9). Thus, although dependency/underdevelopment is by no means inevitable, the structure, ownership and control of the tourism industry and the related regionalised and polarised characteristic of international tourist flows highlight the significant degree of dependency inherent in the global tourism system. Thus, equitable inter- and intra-generational development is unlikely to be achieved through tourism.

- In terms of futurity, the focus of most plans/policies is primarily upon the short-term profitability of tourism businesses and the longer term viability of tourism (i.e. sustaining tourism) rather than long-term sustainable development through tourism.

- As argued in Chapter 10, research has revealed that the adoption of a new social paradigm relevant to sustainable living, a fundamental requirement for sustainable development (IUCN, 1991), is unlikely to occur. More specifically, the emergence of the 'green' tourist, frequently cited as the justification for promoting sustainable forms of tourism, cannot be taken for granted given the characteristics of the consumption of tourism.

This is not to say that specific elements of the sustainable development template are not being addressed to the benefit of resources upon which tourism depends. For example, many organisations and sectors are implementing policies related to environmental sustainability objectives (see Chapter 8). However, the broader principles of sustainable development and most of its development objectives do not, for the most part, fit easily into the tourism context. One exception, perhaps, is where tourism development is localised, small-scale, environmentally benign and based upon optimising the benefits to both host communities and tourists through meaningful, two-way experiences. For example, a number of local rural tourism projects in England were successfully developed according to sustainable principles although, supporting the argument in Chapter 10, all the projects suffered from a low level of interest on the part of visitors (Countryside Commission, 1995). Under such circumstances, greater opportunities may exist for meeting the objectives of satisfying basic needs and encouraging self-reliance through community involvement in tourism. However, not only do such small-scale, site-based developments fail to embrace the wider principles of sustainable development – for example, the relationship between the destinations or project with the rest of the tourism system is frequently overlooked – but also the inevitability, given the inherent weaknesses of the sustainable tourism concept, of the localised site-based perspective serves to amplify the distinction between 'good', small-scale tourism and traditional, large-scale or mass tourism.

As a result, sustainable tourism development has come to be associated primarily with local, small-scale tourism developments; conversely, large-scale, mass tourism, typified by the package-tour experience, is seen as unsustainable (Milne, 1998). More specifically, this inherently divisive characteristic of the sustainable tourism concept implies the following points:

- The development of traditional, large-scale tourism cannot contribute successfully (or sustainably) to broader socioeconomic development in destination areas. As discussed shortly, and as others have suggested, this is quite evidently not the case.
- Localised developments, employing local people and utilising local products (and, by implication, reducing dependency-related consequences such as excessive leakages, expatriate labour, foreign ownership, profit repatriation, and so on), brings greater economic benefit to destinations. One recent example of support for this concept was a debate which concluded that all-inclusive holidays should be banned (Farrington, 1999). However, whilst ignoring commercial realities, the economic benefits of local, small-scale developments tend, of course, to be both localised and small. For example, although a recipient of British Airways' 'Tourism for Tomorrow' awards in 1998, one of the greatest challenges now facing the Central Region Project in Ghana is considered to be the need to increase and spread the benefits of tourism beyond the vicinity of the project (Ampadu-Agyei, 1999).
- Tourism-related development occurs only in destinations. However, tourism-generating regions also benefit significantly from the production of outgoing tourism through, for example, regional airports acting as developmental growth poles. At the same time, tourism has been described as a 'social victory' (Krippendorf, 1986); the ability of large sectors of the population in tourism generating countries to benefit from tourism experiences – whether 'sustainable' or mass package – is as much a part of the developmental process as is the contribution of tourism to destinational development.
- More generally, the path of sustainable development is the 'best' tourism development route to follow. However, sustainable development itself is often criticised for being a western-centric development paradigm which maintains the existing, unbalanced world order (Mehmet, 1995). That is, a number of questions with respect to, for example, equity, freedom of choice, value judgements about acceptable environmental degradation and who benefits from development challenge the global applicability of sustainable development. The same criticism may also be justifiably directed at sustainable tourism, particularly when attempts are made by western-based groups or organisations, such as the pressure group Tourism Concern, to influence or change the nature of tourism development in other countries. For example, The Gambian

Government's decision in 1999 to ban on all-inclusive holidays was undoubtedly influenced by external pressure – although the commercial reality of competition more recently led to the decision being reversed (Bird, 2000).

Sustainability as a Barrier to Destinational Development

Collectively, these points reveal the way in which sustainability may be considered to be a barrier to development. In other words, the lack of 'fit' between tourism in general and the concept of sustainable development as outlined in the preceding section and the consequential primary focus of most sustainable tourism development policies on local, small-scale, 'appropriate' (from a western-centric point of view) projects has resulted in sustainable tourism becoming both a prescriptive and a restrictive perspective on tourism development which limits the potential for development through tourism. Certainly, the emphasis on locally controlled, small-scale, appropriate/traditional style operations, though most suitable and, as experience has demonstrated, successful in particular circumstances and according to specific developmental objectives, has a number of 'anti-development' implications. For example:

- Relatively few people benefit. Indeed, an inherent contradiction of sustainable tourism is that it minimises, rather than optimises the benefits to local people and restricts opportunities for tourists to participate in such forms of tourism. It also highlights the unresolved question as to how to satisfy both the desire of greater numbers of local people to become involved in and benefit from tourism development and to satisfy the alleged increasing demands for 'sustainable' tourism experiences on the part of tourists. Either tourism companies expand their operations or more businesses are permitted to develop, both of which may result in excessive pressure on natural and human resources. Ironically, the response of ecotourism operators in Australia to increasing use of tourism sites has been to relocate to previously untouched areas to maintain the quality of tourist experiences (Burton, 1998)! Beyond the obvious environmental implications, this also points to a second problem.

- Small-scale, traditional, eco/nature tourism developments, as a specific manifestation of sustainable tourism, are frequently justified on the basis of increasing demand for 'authentic', natural traditional tourism experiences. As a result, such tourism operations are designed to verify the expectations of tourists seeking to escape to the 'Other', to environments and cultures that are in opposition to the tourists' modern, developed home environment. Whilst indicative of 'cultural dependency' (Erisman, 1983), it also limits the potential for the development (as in progress from traditional to modern) of destination areas and societies. As Silver (1993) states, 'it seems that … indigenous peoples can only continue to be attractive to tourists as long as they remain undeveloped and, hence, in some way primitive'.

- Business development opportunities are restricted. Many local communities lack the necessary expertise or financial/technological resources to fully exploit tourism-related opportunities and so a necessary ingredient (and fundamental objective) of tourism development is traditionally considered to be the re-distribution of western wealth to poorer, less developed destination areas through investment and ultimately, tourist spending. Whilst this is indicative, as discussed in the conclusion to this chapter, of the inevitable dependency inherent in the global tourism system, it is likely that, without financial, technological or business/marketing support, many small-scale, locally controlled tourism projects could not survive. For example, one of the earliest attempts to develop sustainable village tourism was the Lower Casamance project in Senegal (Saglio, 1979; Gnigue, 1992). Though successful, however, the project primarily attracted, and was dependent upon, tourists leaving the confines of their Club-Med all-inclusive holiday on the coast for a short, 'authentic' experience in the Senegalese hinterland.

More significantly, perhaps, the inherent divisiveness of sustainable tourism principles which implicitly label more traditional, mass forms of tourism development as 'bad' or unsustainable also severely restricts the extent to which tourism can contribute to development. In other words, the increasingly 'entrenched, doom-laden apocalyptic view' (Middleton, 1998: 230) about the 'crisis' of mass tourism during the 1990s, referring to both the product of mass tourism as manifested in extensive and homogenous 'Costa'-type developments and also its modes and patterns of consumption, firmly rejects the possibility that such forms of tourism can not only contribute to development but may also do so more effectively than alternative or sustainable tourism.

There is much evidence, however, to support the defence of mass tourism, from both a destinational and a generating country perspective, as a vehicle of development (Sharpley 2000b). Indeed, there are numerous examples where allegedly unsustainable, mass forms of tourism have, in fact, made a significant developmental contribution, whereas the extent to which other destinations, such as Bhutan with its restrictions on arrivals or Costa Rica and its focus on eco-tourism, have benefited (in a developmental sense) from much-heralded sustainable tourism policies is less clear (Place, 1995, 1998). To put it another way, although most mass tourism destinations undoubtedly suffer a variety of environmental and sociocultural problems associated with the excessive, rapid or unplanned development of tourism, it is unlikely that overall economic and social development would have been achieved otherwise.

One such country is the Dominican Republic, an island tourism destination that over the last 25 years has built a successful tourism industry based almost entirely on the (allegedly unsustainable) all-inclusive market. Despite significant and well-publicised health problems related to poor hygiene in the mid-1990s, by 1999 some 2.6 million visitors were attracted to the island, generating approximately US$2.5 billion. This represents around 15% of GDP and 30% of export earnings, with tourism the single largest source of foreign exchange earnings. As a result of the predominance of all-inclusive package deals, per capita tourism revenue remains the lowest in the Caribbean, whilst it could also be argued that opportunities for linkages throughout the economy and for greater local control over tourism have been minimised. Nevertheless, the Dominican Republic has emerged as a strong player in the growing budget all-inclusive market, with tourism playing an effective economic role. It provides approximately 140,000 direct jobs in a country with a 16% unemployment rate and backward linkages with both the agricultural and construction sectors have been significantly strengthened. Therefore, although the country as a whole remains relatively underdeveloped by Caribbean standards, tourism has become the engine driving economic growth. In particular, it has provided the foundation for economic stability during the last decade and for further growth and diversification in the future.

Similarly, mass tourism development has underpinned successful economic and social development in Cyprus. Since 1974, when the northern third of the island came under Turkish occupation, the Republic of Cyprus has developed into a major Mediterranean tourism destination. During the 1980s in particular, arrivals grew at an average annual rate of 16% and, despite a slowdown in more recent years, over 2.4 million arrivals were recorded in 1999. Earnings from tourism in Cyprus have increased correspondingly; in 1999, tourism receipts totalled CY£1.02 billion (approximately US$1.8 billion).

To a great extent, this dramatic growth of tourism has been fuelled by the no-less rapid growth in resort development on the island. In 1975, for example, there were fewer than 4000 available bedspaces, the majority of which were located in the mountain resorts. Currently there is a total of about 86,000 bedspaces in four major coastal resort areas, the development of which has attracted widespread criticism for being 'unsustainable' (EIU, 1992). However, tourism contributes 22% of GDP in Cyprus, whilst one-quarter of the working population are employed directly or indirectly in tourism. Perhaps more importantly, with a per capita income of over US$14,000, Greek Cypriots enjoy the third highest standard of living of all Mediterranean countries after France and Italy. It would, of course, be naïve to claim that such economic growth is without cost; in common with many other destinations, Cyprus suffers a variety of environmental and social problems, as well as excessive dependence upon tourism itself (Sharpley, 2001). Nevertheless, although the rapid emergence of tourism in Cyprus conforms to what some would describe as unsustainable mass tourism development, the Cypriots have, by and large, benefited greatly both socially and economically.

Tourism and Development in Generating Countries

As suggested in the introduction to this chapter, the principal focus of sustainable tourism is on destinational environments and communities. Conversely little or no attention is paid to tourist-generating regions as potential beneficiaries of the tourism-related development process. Indeed, international (outbound) mass tourism is commonly viewed as a problem, particularly where the spending of nationals overseas is greater than the earnings from inbound tourism. In 1999, for example, the UK earned just over £12.5 billion from incoming tourism, but the British spent almost £22 billion travelling overseas, representing a deficit of over £10 billion (roughly US$15 billion). For Germany, this travel deficit is more significant – a staggering US$31 billion in 1998.

However, the tourism organisations, businesses and other institutions which, through their ownership and/or control of the industry and tourist flows, 'create' the inherent dependency within the international tourism system, also make a significant (economic) developmental contribution within the metropolitan centres. The 'safety valve' effect of large numbers of people participating in regular holidays has evident socioeconomic benefits, yet a frequently overlooked fact is that, in the major tourism-generating countries, the outbound tourism industry employs significant numbers of people. In the UK, for example, the tour operators and travel agents that comprise the membership of the Association of British Travel Agents (ABTA) collectively employ 45,000 people. More specifically, two of the main tour operators, Thomson Travel and Airtours, employ roughly 17,500 and 16,000 people respectively.

However, it is not only direct employment with tour operators, travel agents and other associated organisations that is of relevance here. Again in the UK, the growth of international mass tourism has also necessitated and encouraged the growth in the number of regional airports around the country, such as Newcastle International Airport, Teesside Airport, East Midlands Airport, Liverpool Airport and London-Luton Airport. Some of these airports owe their existence entirely to the growth of the mass-tourism-related charter flight business, whilst others still cater for a predominantly charter flight market. For example, Newcastle Airport in the north-east of England catered for a small number of domestic and international scheduled flights during the 1950s, but the boom in overseas holidays during the 1960s led to a doubling of passenger numbers. In 1999, almost 51% of the three million passengers using Newcastle flew on charter flights. Similarly, charter flights out of East Midlands and Leeds/Bradford airports account for 50% and 53% of business respectively. At Liverpool airport the figure would be over 50% were it not for the rapid growth in the number of passengers carried by the budget airline Easy Jet. Indeed, it is forecast that Easy Jet passengers at Liverpool will total 1.5 million in 2000, representing 75% of the airport's passenger numbers.

Importantly, many of these have become major local employers. London-Luton, for example, which is the base for two of the world's largest charter airlines, employs over 7000 people, significantly more than Luton's traditional motor-man-ufacturing industry. The East Midlands employs around 5000 people, whilst about 1000 work at Liverpool airport and 1500 at Leeds/Bradford Airport. Perhaps more significantly, the development of regional airports undoubtedly acts as a catalyst for wider economic development or regeneration. London-Luton, for example, once infamous as a charter gateway, is consolidating its position as London's 'fourth' airport with 74% of its passengers now flying on scheduled domestic and international services, whilst its economic regenerative role has taken on greater significance following the announcement, in late 2000, that General Motors is to cease car production in Luton by 2002. Other airports have similarly developed in-ternational scheduled links and, although further research is required, this is likely to be a significant factor in new business links and development.

The relationship between tour operators, charter flight companies and associ-ated regional airport development is undoubtedly more pronounced in the UK than in other major tourism-generating countries. Nevertheless, these examples serve to highlight the holistic, global nature of tourism and, in particular, its eco-nomic power as a vehicle of development. In other words, it is not only destinations, whether in wealthy, industrialised countries or in the developing world, that benefit, in a developmental sense, from tourism. Tourism also provides employ-ment and wealth, and acts as an economic growth pole, through the industry that enables people to travel, whether internationally or domestically. In a simplistic sense, therefore, the more people who are, on a global scale, able to participate in tourism, the greater will be the contribution of tourism to development. Con-versely, policies that limit the growth and scale of tourism, such as sustainable tourism, also potentially limit its developmental role.

Conclusions

It has long been recognised that sustainable tourism development requires a global, holistic perspective. That is, sustainable tourism development is, in theory, but one of innumerable socioeconomic processes and institutions that potentially contribute to broader sustainable development policies. Implicitly, therefore, the principles of sustainable development should also be applicable to tourism on a ho-listic, global scale, rather than manifested in discreet, 'alternative' developments. However, as argued here, tourism, as a specific economic sector and social institu-tion, does not fit easily onto the sustainable development template. Issues of ownership and control, scale, political economy and tourism consumption all serve to challenge the fundamental principles of, and requirements for, the achievement of sustainable development and, as a consequence, 'sustainable tourism' has become defined by the local rather than global. Therefore, it is not surprising that, although making reference in particular to a report on Scottish tourism, it has been observed that in general 'no example of the successful application of sustainable development of tourism has been found' (Butler, 1998: 31). The conclusion must be, therefore, that there is a need to divorce tourism, as a development agent, from what has proved to be the restrictive paradigm of sustainable development.

This is not to say, however, that the principles of sustainable development are of no relevance to tourism as a specific socioeconomic activity. As previously stated, in particular circumstances, small-scale, 'ecotourism' developments may, in fact, represent the optimal development option, at least on a local basis. Moreover, there are a number of lessons that are applicable to all forms of tourism development. For example, it is essential to view tourism as an integral element of broader development policy, and one of a variety of potential developmental vehicles, in order to achieve optimal resource allocation. Similarly, environmentally sound production and consumption practices should be encouraged on both ethical and commercial grounds although, at the same time, a degree of pragmatism is required to counterbalance the inherent idealism of 'sustainable tourism', in particular with respect to the consumption of tourism services (Chapter 10).

However, it is also important to recognise that different countries or societies are not only more or less developed, but also have differing developmental needs and objectives. Therefore, different paths to development are, of course, more or less appropriate in different contexts. As this chapter has argued, tourism – though inherently and unavoidably dependent – has frequently proved to be an effective growth pole; indeed, there are many examples where mass tourism has brought about rapid economic and social progress (albeit frequently accompanied by significant social and environmental consequences). It is important to recognise, therefore, that sustainable tourism is not a universally appropriate vehicle for development. It may, in fact, retard progress or, as Wall (1997) suggests, result in unsustainable development and, thus, destinations must be 'allowed' to choose the form of tourism development best suited to their resources, potential markets and developmental needs.

Chapter 12

Conclusion: Tourism and Development

DAVID J. TELFER

This book was compiled in response to the lack of literature in tourism studies which provides a theoretical underpinning of tourism as a vehicle for development. It has attempted to build stronger links between development theory and the processes of tourism development, and to explore the popular assumption that tourism is an effective tool of development. A central question in the book has been 'what is development?' The definition of development has expanded over time from solely looking at economic growth to a more holistic definition that includes economic, social, cultural, political and environmental aspects. Development theory has also evolved since the Second World War moving from modernisation to sustainable development. As Hettne (1995) suggests, development theory can be divided into development ideology (the ends) and development strategy (the means). Development strategy is the means of implementing the development process guided by a specific ideology. Development is a value-laden concept and the authors in this book have evaluated and critiqued some of the dominant development paradigms. Authors such as Sachs (1996: 1) have even gone so far as to argue that 'development stands like a ruin in the intellectual landscape' as problems such as global poverty still exist. If, however, tourism is to be an agent of development, it is important to understand the theoretical concepts behind the term development and what the ideology is behind the strategy driving tourism development. The model presented in the introduction to the book attempted to illustrate the complex nature of the relationship between development paradigms, the nature of tourism development and the nature of local/regional/national development. The question then becomes what role can tourism play in meeting development objectives. As Burns (1999) suggests, it is important to know whether the policy taken on tourism is one of 'Tourism First', which focuses on the industry or 'Development First' whereby planning is framed by national development needs. The organisation in control of the tourism development process, whether it is public or private, can wield a great deal of power. Questions raised in the introduction of the book include whether tourism is a universally applicable development option or whether there are different forms and

338

scales of development more or less suitable to different destinations. Can tourism contribute to development on its own or should it be considered within larger development schemes? These and other related questions are discussed throughout the book, however, what is important, and where this book has tried to add to the body of literature, is to focus on the concept of development itself.

The structure of this concluding chapter will be to highlight the various concepts, themes and issues raised within the chapters. Selected questions will be presented after each chapter summary as a means hopefully to generate further ideas, debates and future research topics surrounding the role of tourism in development for students, researchers and practitioners. At the end of the three parts of the book, consideration will be given to the implications for the role of tourism as a means of achieving development. The chapter will conclude by considering four concepts: the nature of development, the nature of the tourism industry, the nature of tourists and the nature of the destination.

Part 1

In Part 1 the concepts of development and the relationship between tourism and development have been addressed. The chapters in Part 1 tried to answer the questions about the nature of development and how it relates to the processes within tourism. In any form of development, it is prudent to understand development in terms of development by whom and for whom and who it is that ultimately benefits. Many reports extol the benefits of using tourism as an agent of development; however, it is often the economic benefits which receive the most attention. Chapter 1 examined the reasons why tourism is selected for development as well as exploring the changing definition of development. While the contribution of tourism can be more easily identified in a definition of development centring on economic growth, it becomes more complex to identify the role of tourism in a more holistic definition of development that encompasses social, cultural, political, environmental and economic aims and processes. If tourism is used as an agent of development, it is important to consider what represents underdevelopment and to what extent tourism can address the characteristics of underdevelopment. Tourism creates wealth but to what extent does it contribute to the broader concept of development for the individual, the community, the region or the nation? Having examined the definition of development in Chapter 1, Chapter 2 examined the changes in development paradigms which have occurred since the end of the Second World War. While it is acknowledged that the subject matter is vast and there are a variety of ways to categorise development, the four categories presented and critiqued here are modernisation, dependency, economic neoliberalism and alternative development. Highlighted in the chapter is the fact that development is a highly contested notion influenced by a wide range of social, political, economic and environmental perspectives, each with its own set of values. Tourism development was analysed within the four paradigms presented under (a) scale and control of development and (b) environmental and community linkages. What form tourism development can take is guided by an ideology, which will ultimately determine who will benefit from tourism. Questions need to be asked as to what organisation dictates the ideology behind the strategies of tourism development. To what extent is tourism development influenced by dominant development paradigms? A framework for appropriate and sustainable tourism development was presented; however, it is important to understand the degree to which such a framework can be put into practice.

The role of Part 1 was to bridge the gap between development studies and tourism and to provide a theoretical underpinning for the remainder of the book. If tourism is to be used as means of achieving development, it needs to be understood in the context of a broader definition of development. As governments and researchers continue to move towards sustainable development within the alternative development paradigm, the concepts of increased community participation and environmental protection receive more attention. Tourism developed under these concepts may, however, be in conflict with the goals of profit maximisation.

Part 2

Having examined the fundamental links between development theory and tourism development, Part 2 of the book examined specific themes of development in relation to tourism. Chapter 3 began by examining the relationship between tourism and economic development. Economic indicators are the ones often cited to support tourism development. The other issues covered in this section include regional development, community development, human resource development, sociocultural development and the environment and development. While there is little doubt that tourism has various potentially beneficial economic impacts, which may positively influence the process of economic development in a destination, the magnitude of tourism's economic benefits can be highly variable. As indicated in Chapter 3, factors such as the level of economic development in the host country or region, the propensity to import, the external sources of investment capital and international or foreign ownership of tourism organisations in the host country can all mitigate the economic benefits of tourism. The assertion that tourism development projects in developing countries can contribute to the establishment of a new world order through reducing the gap between developed and less developed countries often over looks these mitigating factors. As the focus of development has shifted from being centred on the economic benefits of tourism to exploring the social and environmental impacts of tourism, a question raised in Chapter 3 which deserves further attention is whether the concept of sustainable tourism promotes economic development?

One of the strategies used by governments to help reduce regional imbalances and create employment and income within a country is to use tourism as a regional development tool. Chapter 4 examined the concepts and models of regional development, such as growth poles, agglomeration economies, and competitive clusters, in a variety of tourism regions. Tourism has been used for urban revitalisation, rural regeneration, island development, peripheral development and the development of international regions. As tourism continues to become more competitive, governments are having to adopt a more entrepreneurial role in attracting not only tourists but also investors to their region. The questions raised surrounding tourism as a regional development tool deal with whether or not there can be real regional economic dispersion of the benefits of tourism. As indicated in Chapter 3, there are a series of factors, which can reduce the economic benefits of tourism development. Tourism development projects, which do not build strong linkages to the surrounding community, will have little impact on the citizens who live nearby. Questions need to be asked about the most appropriate forms of tourism development growth poles so that the trickle-down effect can be maximised. While tourism may help to modernise a region, it may also cause the region to become dependent on external organisations.

Chapter 5 continued the connections with the local community under the alternative development paradigm by examining issues related to empowerment and local participation in the tourism planning process. It is argued that community-based, grassroots tourism is a more sustainable form of development than conventional mass tourism as it allows communities to break away from the hegemonic grasp of tour operators and the oligopoly of local élites. It is argued that there needs to be a decentralisation of tourism down to the community level. As well as generating additional funding, which circulates in the local community, self-esteem is enhanced for the community as control over the development process is maintained locally. While the goals of community-based tourism are commendable, questions were raised as to how well the process works in practice. How can existing power structures be changed to facilitate true community involvement? Developing community-based tourism can be especially difficult in developing countries in term of such issues as access to information, lack of awareness and lack of access to finances. The peripheral nature of many communities interested in community-based tourism raises questions as to how they will attract visitors. Can aligning with a local or national tour operator leave a community in a very dependent position? How long can a community maintain control over the tourism project before a local élite develops? What forms of tourism can be controlled successfully at the local level? Is local control always the preferred option for tourism development?

The theme of local community was continued in Chapter 6 where tourism employment is considered in less developed countries. The dynamics of the formal and informal sectors are explored along with the status of tourism employment and gender role differentiation in tourism employment. The chapter demonstrates through empirical evidence from Bali, the inappropriateness of applying developed country beliefs and assumptions surrounding tourism employment to developing countries. Much of the research on tourism employment is based in a western-centric, developed country perspective where tourism positions are often considered as seasonal and low paying. In a developing country context, however, employment opportunities are more limited but have higher relative rates of payment than in other economic sectors. Even if positions are seasonal they are highly sought after. Tourism employment can create opportunities for the local population to increase their income and improve their standard of living. It can also provide new opportunities for youth and women. A model based on service-centred tourism employment was presented as much of the work in tourism employment research has borrowed models from manufacturing and related models of production. The chapter raised several important concepts related to development including questioning the universality of applying western concepts to developing countries. Jobs dismissed in some countries become highly sought after in other countries. Questions need to be asked such as which tourism-related jobs are best suited to generating development in different countries contexts. If tourism employment in developing countries holds significantly more attraction, how can access to these jobs be enhanced? What steps can be taken to ensure that higher managerial jobs are also available to local residents? What is the impact of tourism employment and gender relations in different country contexts? What is the impact of seasonality on tourism employment? Finally, what policies related to tourism employment should governments adopt to ensure that tourism development plans benefit more than just the local élite?

Challenges to western-based development concepts were also raised in Chapter 7. Here, the gap between the concepts of socioeconomic development and sociocultural impacts of tourism development was explored. Many of the predominant theories of development have emerged from western schools of thought without much consideration being given to more traditional methods of development. Classifications of the major indices for social and economic development including income, trade, resource and quality of life are based within a western or modernisation framework. Within this framework, both economic development and the modernisation of living standards are expected to go hand in hand. However, indigenous lifestyles and the customs of some host communities, for example, are valuable commodities and movement to modernise these societies is criticised by the tourism industry. By examining the complex nature of the relationship between the positive and negative impacts of tourism the chapter argued that the applicability of measuring socioeconomic development based in a western framework to understand tourism development needs to be questioned. While the alternative development paradigm holds promise for considering other types of development, cooperation beyond the local level is needed if the alternative development paradigm is to be any more effective than classic development models. This chapter raised a number of interesting questions. How can sociocultural change associated with tourism be accurately measured? Are traditional indices of socioeconomic development of value when examining the sociocultural changes associated with tourism? Are cultures merging through the process of globalisation? How can tourism be singled out among many industries in an age of globalisation to determine its impact on the host's society? If it is necessary to divorce the assessment of tourism's socioeconomic development outcomes from western development theories, what framework should be used?

The final chapter in the second section of the book (Chapter 8) addressed the relationship between tourism and the environment. After tracing the evolution of sustainable development it was then argued that sustainable tourism development has failed as a result of environmental managerialism inherent in sustainable development principles. Attempts at imposing a universal blueprint for tourism development, or the using of a set of 'meta-principles' which are founded on mainstream planning and designation processes, are inappropriate within the complex developmental contexts and the needs of tourism destinations particularly in developing countries. A more relevant interpretation of tourism and sustainability in terms of what it is and how it can be achieved is necessary. It was argued that sustainability is a more eclectic concept that crosses diverse natural, social and economic disciplines and recognises the underlying issues of governance as key factors in environmental management. If due consideration is given to local social and environmental determinants of sustainability, tourism may be able to enhance the environment and promote local development. The concepts related to sustainable development are further examined in Chapter 11; however, the approach taken here raised some intriguing questions. Has the debate on sustainable tourism development reached a saturation point? Can tourism planners afford to ignore sustainable development despite the difficulties in trying to achieve it? Can sustainable development be defined differently in different country contexts or is that just a way of simplifying the term? As development thinking continues to evolve, is there a successor to sustainable development?

The second section of this book was meant to examine a variety of different issues facing tourism development. One of the commonalties of the chapters in this section is the need to rethink traditional notions of development while considering the resulting implications to tourism development. Economic growth plays a central role in most development theory and tourism has become a favoured growth engine with the potential to increase jobs, income, foreign exchange, domestic and international investment and promote regional development. While examples highlighting cases where tourism has been extremely effective were used, other instances in which tourism may not have lived up to expectations were presented. At the centre of many of the issues raised is the question: 'Who really benefits from tourism development?' Debate was also raised as to whether or not tourism is an effective tool for regional development. Different forms of tourism in different country contexts can yield different results. Criticisms over using tourism employment concepts created in a developed country context and applied to developing countries were presented. Western-based development theory and how development has traditionally been measured were also questioned. Even the concept of sustainable development, which has received a great deal of attention within the alternative development paradigm, was criticised for its deterministic and managerial approaches to planning.

Part 3

Finally, Part 3 examined the issues that are considered to be barriers to tourism development. These barriers limit the potential for tourism to contribute to the overall development of a destination and it is the characteristics of tourism itself that present some of these barriers. The first of these barriers, covered in Chapter 9, relates to the structure of the global tourism industry, which was discussed in the context of the political economy of tourism. It is argued that capitalist restructuring and economic globalisation has led to a change in power relations challenging the validity of state-centric approaches to the political economy of tourism, characterised by the neocolonial dependency model. The reason behind these changes relates to the increasing dominance of transnational tourism corporations and the growing structural power of global and regional market forces. In the context of the political economy of tourism it is not merely important to understand whether incomes are rising due to tourism but also to know whether or not the move to global tourism increases or decreases the access to power and resources. Central to the political economy approach is the question as to who wields the power in tourism development. How does study of the political economy of tourism help in understanding the process of development in the tourism industry? Will those who have the power in the tourism industry be willing to share this power with local communities in destinations and will the sharing of power represent a meaningful partnership? Within the context of the alternative development paradigm, linkages are encouraged with local community groups. If these local linkages can be established, it will be important to determine whether it is only the local élite who benefit or whether other members of the community also benefit.

Chapter 10 argues that tourism is a form of consumption, which militates against the development process. The tourists are an integral part of the tourism production process and, as a result, tourism is not only influenced by the industry, but it is also a product of the needs, motivations, expectations and consequent behaviour of tourists. Tourism is an ego-centric social activity motivated by avoidance/escape and ego-enhancement/reward. Within the alternative development paradigm sustainable tourism has come to the forefront and along with it are codes of appropriate behaviour and forms of tourism such as ecotourism. However, one of the key assumptions is that tourists are responsive to the messages within sustainable tourism development and that they will adapt their behaviour as consumers in order to optimise their contribution of tourism to local development. This chapter argues that this is not the case and tourism is largely untouched by green consumerism. The manner in which tourism is consumed contributes little to the development process beyond financial considerations. All is not lost, however, as once the nature of consumption is understood, then destinations can plan and develop accordingly to optimise the benefits of the industry. The question arises as to the way in which destinations and the industry can better adapt to understand the nature of tourism consumption for their benefit. Do tourists pay much attention to issues related to green consumerism or sustainable development if it is going to require a major effort on their part? Do the new forms of tourism such as ecotourism represent more sustainable forms of tourism or do they represent new forms of ego-tourism?

Finally the concept of sustainable tourism was put under the microscope in the last chapter (11) and it was argued that although it has become one of the dominant tourism paradigms in the 1990s, it can also be seen as a barrier to development. The concept of sustainable development has been covered in many of the chapters in this book in terms of empowerment, economic development, backward economic linkages, small-scale and environmental protection. It was argued that while there is widespread support for the aims and principles for sustainable tourism development, it remains a contested notion as does its parent paradigm that, of sustainable development. Sustainable tourism development has evolved into a prescriptive and restrictive set of guidelines for tourism development. While it offers environmentally appropriate and ethically sound principles for optimising the role of tourism, it draws attention away from the potential benefits of other forms of tourism and other development agents. It is argued that large-scale tourism can also contribute to socioeconomic development in a destination and it is not necessarily a bad form of tourism development. Issues of ownership and control, scale, political economy and tourism consumption challenge the implementation of successful sustainable tourism development. In addition, many of the concepts of sustainable development are western based and therefore cannot be easily applied in non-western destinations. It was argued that sustainable tourism is not a universally appropriate vehicle of development. This raised questions regarding the nature of tourism development and what form and function it should take in different country contexts. Should western development concepts be utilised in non-western settings? Again, is there a successor to sustainable tourism development?

The final section in the book sought to identify barriers to using tourism as an agent of development. While tourism has potential to contribute to the economic and social development of a destination, there are characteristics of the industry, which limit its potential as a development tool. The emerging global power structures of the tourism industry can take control out of the hands of the destination leaving only the local élites and multinational corporations to benefit. It was also argued that tourists themselves are more generally interested in themselves and their needs as opposed to altering their form of consumption to maximise the benefits of tourism for the destination. Is there really a growing segment of the tourist population who is becoming more environmentally friendly and concerned that the money they spend circulates throughout the local economy? Finally, the last chapter sought to challenge the current dominate paradigm of sustainable development. The use of a set of restrictive guidelines may actually prevent other forms of development such as large-scale mass tourism from potentially being a very good source of foreign exchange.

The Nature of Tourism and Development

To conclude the book, four concepts will be considered: the nature of development, the nature of the tourism industry, the nature of tourists and the nature of the destination. As stated in the introduction to this chapter, the nature of development and how it is measured has become more complex over time. The question of how a region or a nation moves towards becoming more developed is just as complex. Development has moved from a focus on economic growth to a more holistic approach taking in a wider range of variables. It is important to ask development for whom and development by whom, and what is the goal of development? Many of the development paradigms are based in western thought and consideration needs to be given as to how appropriate they are in a global context. While sustainability under the alternative development paradigm has received a great deal of attention recently in the literature, theoretical debates surrounding the nature of development will continue to evolve on how best to achieve development. It was even argued in one chapter in this book that sustainable development may be a barrier to development. It is also important to keep in mind that real problems of underdevelopment in the world exist and for the individual experiencing problems of day-to-day survival, theoretical debates may not hold much meaning. As Sen (1999) reminds us, at a global level, problems of persistent poverty and unfulfilled elementary needs, famines and widespread hunger, violations of political freedoms and basic liberties, neglect of the interests and agency of women, and increasing threats to the environment and the sustainability of economic and social welfare continue to face both rich and poor nations.

The question posed in this book was: What role can tourism play in trying to bring development to a region? While no single industry can be expected to bring a solution to the development problems identified by Sen (1999), tourism has been selected by many governments to help generate income. In order to understand the role of tourism it is important to understand the nature of the tourism industry. Whether the public or the private sector controls the industry, it is an industry, which seeks to make a profit. Large multinational corporations or a small agritourism operator seek profit to some extent. In an era of sustainable development, can a firm out to maximise profit also adopt sustainable development principles? With the industry comes a series of power structures which can extend across local, regional and national boundaries. In the context of government selecting certain tourism policies, the government is also choosing between different sets of values and these decisions are made within a complex policy arena (Hall, 1994). Those who are in control of the industry can dictate what happens to the benefits of the industry. The scale, type of tourism selected and speed of development will also have an impact on the degree to which tourism can be a successful agent of development. From large-scale resort complexes to remote ecotourism lodges, the diversity of tourism developments has the potential to contribute to the development of the destination. What forms and scales of tourism development are more suitable for different destinations and development objectives is open for debate. How the industry operates, however, can either enhance or exploit the region. If the industry is successfully integrated into the local economy with strong partnerships and backward economic linkages more people will benefit from tourism. Both the formal and informal tourism sectors will respond to tourism developments in order to meet the demands of the tourists. The tourism industry must not be viewed in isolation but needs to be integrated into wider development plans.

Tourists themselves also have a role to play in the development process. As Urry (1995) suggests, central to the idea of modernity is that of movement. It is argued in Chapter 10 that in travelling, tourists are more interested in satisfying their own needs and desires and therefore they contribute very little in terms of development except in the case of financial gains. Again it is important to consider what the aim of development is and how it should be defined. Financial gain may be all a destination or a region seeks. On the other hand, are there alternative types of tourists with different demands? Can we expect tourists to become green consumers and adopt the philosophies of sustainable tourism? Elsewhere in the book in Chapter 7, the positive sociocultural impacts of tourism development are considered and it is suggested that tourism can promote cultural exchange and understanding between hosts and guests. One of the requirements for successful tourism is stability and this suggests that tourists may help contribute to other areas of development besides through economic contributions.

It is in the destination that the interaction between hosts and guests occur and where many of the physical manifestations of the industry are constructed. Policies are formed and plans are initiated. The appropriateness of tourism development must, however, be considered within the parameters of socioeconomic, geographic and political considerations in the destination. It is important to stress that no one sector such as tourism can be viewed in isolation in terms of development but needs to be placed within the wider context of the local economy. There is no universal form of tourism development that will be successful in every destination. How different levels of government in the destination formulate tourism policy may illustrate decentralisation of power or the formulation of a wider regional development plan. Community-based tourism can help to empower the residents of a destination and help enhance self-determination. With tourism creating income and jobs, it has been suggested that tourism can promote a level of economic development conductive to increased social well-being and stability (Weaver and Oppermann, 2000). While tourism also has the ability to contribute to the protection and enhancement of traditions, customs and heritage in a destination, the demonstration effect can have negative implications on society. However, if the protection of these resources is done to such a degree that a society cannot move forward, or the culture is turned into a commodity, then the process of development may be halted. Along with protecting a destination's culture, the environment may also be protected if the concepts of sustainable development are followed. However, the concept of sustainable development is full of contradictions (Redclift, 1987) and environmentally friendly business practices can soon be turned into a marketing ploy. It was also argued in Chapter 7 that sustainable development cannot be achieved by initiatives by isolated host communities – tourism activities are interdependent on actors across borders, and therefore borderless cooperation for sustainable development is required. Finally, consideration also needs to be given to the destination heavily dependent upon tourism which goes into decline, such as the seaside resorts in the United Kingdom. Is there much of chance of rejuvenation or has tourism run its course and should the destination look to get out of the industry? What are the risks of over relying on tourism?

The study of tourism is a relatively recent phenomenon and more research is needed not only on the goals of development but also on how tourism can be used to reach those goals effectively. The aim of this book has been to raise questions surrounding the nature of tourism in development. These questions also represent potential starting points for future research areas. One of the commonalties presented in the chapters of this book is the need to rethink existing notions of development and how they apply to tourism. It is hoped that the book will contribute to a greater understanding and knowledge of the processes, challenges and benefits of using tourism as a development tool. If we have raised debates and developed questions which we have not yet answered, then we will have considered our job complete.

References

Adams, W. (1992) *Green Development: Environment and Sustainability in the Third World*. London: Routledge.

Adams, W. and Hulme, D. (1992) *Conservation and Communities: Changing Narratives, Policies and Practices in African Conservation*. Manchester: IDPM.

Acott, T., La Trobe, H. and Howard, S. (1998) An evaluation of deep ecotourism and shallow ecotourism. *Journal of Sustainable Tourism* 6 (3), 238–53.

Agarwal, S. (1999) Restructuring and local economic development: Implications for seaside resort regeneration in Southwest Britain. *Tourism Management* 20, 511–22.

Alamgir, M. (1988) Poverty alleviation through participatory development. *Development Journal of SID* 2 (3), 97–102.

Allen, T. (1996) Tourism in Barbados: The bittersweet alternative. In A. Badger *et al.* (eds) *Trading Places: Tourism as Trade* (pp. 63–8). London: Tourism Concern.

Ampadu-Agyei, O. (1999) Central Region Project, Ghana: A case study. Paper given at the 'Changing Tastes, Changing Places' Conference. London: Royal Geographical Society.

Anderson, B. (1972) The idea of power in Javanese culture. In C. Holt (ed.) *Culture and Politics in Indonesia* (pp. 1–70). Ithaca, NY: Cornell University Press.

Anderson, T. (1988) The socio-economic 'worlds' of the Caribbean Basin. In J. Norwine and A. Gonzalez (eds) *The Third World: States of Mind and Being* (pp. 172–82). Boston, MA: Unwin Hyman.

Andersen, V. (1991) *Alternative Economic Indicators*. London: Routledge.

Andrews, A. (1988) The state of women in the Third World. In J. Norwine and A. Gonzalez (eds) *The Third World: States of Mind and Being* (pp. 125–37). Boston, MA: Unwin Hyman.

Apostolopoulos, Y., Sönmez, S. and Timothy, D. (2001) *Women as Producers and Consumers in Developing Regions*. Westport, CT: Praeger.

Archer, B.H. (1977) Tourism multipliers: The state of the art. *Bangor Occasional Papers in Economics* 11. Cardiff: University of Wales Press.

Archer, B.H. (1978) Domestic tourism as a development factor. *Annals of Tourism Research* 5 (1), 126–40.

Archer, B.H. (1982) The value of multipliers and the policy implications. *Tourism Management* 3 (4), 236–41.

Archer, B.H. (1983) Economic impact: Misleading multiplier. *Annals of Tourism Research*, 11 (3), 517–22.

Archer, B. and Cooper, C. (1994) The positive and negative impacts of tourism. In W. Theobald (ed.) *Global Tourism: The Next Decade* (pp. 73–91). Oxford: Butterworth-Heinemann.

Ariani, A. and Gregory, A. (1992) Women's participation in the tourist industry in Bali: Characteristics, effects and possible strategies for the future. Fifth International Interdisciplinary Congress on Women, San Jose, Costa Rica.

Arnold, S.H. (1989) Sustainable development: A solution to the development puzzle? *Development Journal of SID* 2/3, 21–5.

Arnould, E. and Price, L. (1993) River magic: Extraordinary experience and extended service encounter. *Journal of Consumer Research* 20 (June), 24–45.

Arnstein, S.R. (1969) A ladder of citizen participation. *Journal of the American Institute of Planners* 35 (4), 216–24.

Arrighi, G. (1998) Globalization and the rise of East Asia. *International Sociology* 13 (1), 59–77.

Ascher, F. (1985) *Tourism: Transnational Corporations and Cultural Identity*. Paris: UNESCO. Vendome: Imprimerie des Presses Universitaires de France.

Asimakopulos, A. (1991) *Keynes's General Theory and Accumulation*. New York: Cambridge University Press.

Awa, N.E. (1989) Underutilization of women's indigenous knowledge in agricultural and rural development programs: The effects of stereotypes. In D.M. Warren, L.J. Slikkerveer and S.O. Titilola (eds) *Indigenous Knowledge Systems: Implications for Agriculture and International Development* (pp. 3–9). Technology and Social Change Program with the Academy for Educational Development, Iowa State University.

Badger, A. (1996) Tourism as trade. In A. Badger *et al.* (eds) *Trading Places: Tourism as Trade* (pp. 9–23). London: Tourism Concern.

Baez, A.L. (1996) Learning from experience in the Monteverde Cloud Forest, Costa Rica. In M.F. Price (ed.) *People and Tourism in Fragile Environments* (pp. 109–22). Chichester: John Wiley and Sons.

Bagguley, P. (1987) Cited in R. Hudson and A. Townsend (1992) Employment and policy for local government. In P. Johnson and B. Thomas (eds) *Perspectives on Tourism Policy*. London: Mansell: 49–68.

Bagguley, P. (1990) Gender and labour flexibility in hotel and catering. *Service Industries Journal* 10 (4), 737–47.

Baines, G.B.K. (1987) Manipulation of islands and men: Sand clay tourism in the South Pacific. In S. Britton and W.C. Clark (eds) *Ambiguous Alternative Tourism in Small Developing Countries* (pp. 1–9). Suva: University of the South Pacific.

Balanyá, B. *et al.* (2000) *Europe Inc. Regional Restructuring and the Rise of Corporate Power*. London: Pluto Press.

Balmer, D. (1999) Thomson's tentacles. *Observer* (Escape supplement) (9 February).

Barbier, E.B. (1989) The contribution of environmental and resource economics to an economics of sustainable development. *Development and Change* 20 (3), 429–59.

Baretje, R. (1982) Tourism's external account and the balance of payments. *Annals of Tourism Research* 9 (1), 57.

Barlow, C. (1995) Sustainable development, concepts, values and practice. *Third World Planning Review* 17 (4), 369–86.

Bar-On, R. (2000) Databank – Europe. *Tourism Economics* 6 (4), 371–91.

Baron, E. (1998) Casino gambling and the polarization of American Indian Reservations. In A. Lew and G. Van Otten (eds) *Tourism and Gaming on American Indian Lands* (pp. 63–171). New York: Cognizant.

Barratt Brown, M. (1995) *Models in Political Economy* (2nd edn). Harmondsworth: Penguin.

Baudrillard, J. (1988) *Selected Writings*. Cambridge: Polity Press.

Baum, T. (1993) Human resources in tourism: An introduction. In T. Baum (ed.) *Human Resource Issues in International Tourism* (pp. 3–21). Oxford: Butterworth-Heinemann.

Baum, T. (1996) Unskilled work and the hospitality industry: Myth or reality? *International Journal of Hospitality Management* 15 (3), 207–9.

Bauman, Z. (1996) From pilgrim to tourist – or a short history of identity. In S. Hall and P. DuGay (eds) *Questions of Cultural Identity* (pp. 18–36). London: Sage.

Bauman, Z. (1998) *Globalization: The Human Consequences*. Cambridge: Polity Press.

Bayfield, N. (1979) Some effects of walking and skiing on vegetation at Cairngorm. In E. Duffey and A. Watt (eds) *The Scientific Management of Animal and Plant Communities for Conservation* (pp. 469–85). Oxford: Blackwell.

Beauregard, R. (1998) Tourism and economic development policy in US urban areas. In D. Ioannides and K.G. Debbage (eds) *The Economic Geography of the Tourist Industry: A Supply Side Analysis* (pp. 220–34). London: Routledge.

Becheri, E. (1990) Rimini and Co – the end of a legend? Dealing with the algae effect. *Tourism Management* 11, 229–35.

Beckerman, W. (1992) Economic growth and the environment: Whose growth? Whose environment? *World Development* 24 (4), 481–96.

Beckford, G. (1972) *Persistent Poverty: Underdevelopment in Plantation Economies of the Third World*. New York: Oxford University Press.

Bednarz, R. and Giardino, J. (1988) Development and resources in the Third World. In J. Norwine and A. Gonzalez (eds) *The Third World: States of Mind and Being* (pp. 67–81). Boston, MA: Unwin Hyman.

Belk, R. (1995) Studies in the new consumer behaviour. In D. Miller (ed.) *Acknowledging Consumption* (pp. 58–95). London: Routledge.

Belk, R., Wallendorf, M. and Sherry, J. (1989) The sacred and the profane in consumer behaviour: Theodicy on the odyssey. *Journal of Consumer Research* 16 (June), 1–38.

Berger, D.J. (1996) The challenge of integrating Maasai tradition with tourism. In M.F. Price (ed.) *People and Tourism in Fragile Environments* (pp. 175–97). Chichester: John Wiley and Sons.

Berkes, F. (1989) Co-operation from the perspective of human ecology. In F. Berkes (ed.) *Common Property Resources: Ecology and Community-Based Sustainable Development* (pp. 70–88). London: Belhaven Press.

Bernstein, H., Crow, B. and Johnson, H. (1995) *Rural Livelihoods: Crises and Responses*. Milton Keynes: Oxford University Press and Open University.

Bertram, G. (1986) Sustainable development in Pacific micro-economies. *World Development* 14 (7), 809–22.

Bianchi, R. (1999) A critical ethnography of tourism entrepreneurship and social change in a fishing community in Gran Canaria. Unpublished PhD thesis, University of North London.

Bird, L. (2000) All-inclusives are back in the Gambia. *Times*, 2 December.

Blair, J. (1995) *Local Economic Development: Analysis and Practice*. London: Sage.

Blanton, D. (1981) Tourism training in developing countries. The social and cultural dimension. *Annals of Tourism Research* 8 (1), 116–33.

Blyton, P., Martínez Lucio, M., McGurk, J. and Turnbull, P. (1998) *Contesting Globalisation: Airline Restructuring and Trade Union Strategies*. University of Cardiff and International Transport Workers Federation. On WWW at http://www.itf.org.uk/PRESS/conglob.html.

Bock, G. (1989) Learning from the poor. *Development and Cooperation* 1, 7–8.

Bocock, R. (1993) *Consumption*. London: Routledge.

Boissevain, J. (1977) Tourism development in Malta. *Development and Change* 8, 523–88.

Boissevain, J. (1979) The impact of tourism on a dependent island: Gozo, Malta. *Annals of Tourism Research* 6 (1), 76–90.

Bond, M. (1991) *Beyond the Chinese Face: Insights from Psychology.* Hong Kong: Oxford University Press.

Bond. M. and Ladman, J. (1972) International tourism an instrument for Third World development. *Nebraska Journal of Economics and Business* 11. Reprinted in I. Voleger and A. De Souza (eds) (1980) *Dialectics of Third World Development* (pp. 231–40). Montclair, NJ: Allanheld, Osmun.

Boo, E. (1993) Ecotourism planning for protected areas. In K. Lindberg and D.E. Hawkins. *Ecotourism: A Guide For Planners and Managers.* North Bennington, VT: Ecotourism Society.

Boonzaier, E. (1996) Negotiating the development of tourism in the Richtersveld, South Africa. In M.F. Price (ed.) *People and Tourism in Fragile Environments* (pp. 123–37). Chichester: John Wiley and Sons.

Booth, A. (1988) *Development of the Indonesian Tourist Sector in the 1980s: Implications for Employment Generation.* Geneva: ILO.

Booth, A. (1990) The tourism boom in Indonesia. *Bulletin of Indonesian Economic Studies* 26 (3), 45–73.

Booth, A. (1994) Repelita VI and the second long-term development plan. *Bulletin of Indonesian Economic Studies* 30 (3), 3–39.

Booth, D. (1985) Marxism and development sociology: Interpreting the impasse. *World Development* 13 (7), 761–87.

Booth, D. (1993) Development research: From impasse to a new agenda. In F. Schuurman (ed.) *Beyond the Impasse New Directions in Development Theory* (pp. 49–76). London: Zed Books.

Boserüp, E. (1965) *The Conditions of Agricultural Growth: The Economics of Agrarian Change under Population Pressure.* London: Allen and Unwin.

Botterill, D., Owen, R., Emanuel, L., Foster, T., Gale, T., Nelson, C. and Selby, M. (2000) Perceptions from the periphery: The experience of Wales. In F. Brown, and D. Hall (eds) *Tourism in Peripheral Areas.* Clevedon: Channel View.

Boulding, K. (1992) The economics of the coming spaceship earth. In A. Markandya and J. Richardson (eds) *The Earthscan Reader in Environmental Economics* (pp. 27–35). London: Earthscan.

Bourdieu, P. (1986) *Distinction: A Social Critique of the Judgement of Taste.* London: Routledge.

Bowcott, O., Traynor, I., Webster, P. and Walker, D. (1999) Analysis: Green politics. *Guardian* (11 March).

Boyd, S.W. (2000) Tourism, national parks and sustainability. In R.W. Butler and S.W. Boyd (eds) *Tourism and National Parks: Issues and Implications* (pp. 161–86). Chichester: John Wiley and Sons.

Bramwell, B. and Lane, B. (1993) Sustainable tourism: An evolving global approach. *Journal of Sustainable Tourism* 1 (1), 1–5.

Bramwell, B. and Lane, B. (2000a) Collaboration and partnerships in tourism planning. In B. Bramwell and B. Lane (eds) *Tourism Collaboration and Partnerships, Politics, Practice and Sustainability* (pp. 1–19). Clevedon: Channel View.

Bramwell, B. and Lane, B. (eds) (2000b) *Tourism Collaboration and Partnerships, Politics, Practice and Sustainability.* Clevedon: Channel View.

Bras, K. (1997) Small-scale entrepreneurship: Strategies of local guides on the island of Lombok. In H. Dahlas (ed.) *Tourism, Small Entrepreneurs, and Sustainable Development: Cases from Developing Countries* (pp. 49–63). Tilburg University: ATLAS.

Bras, K. and Dahles, H. (1998) Women entrepreneurs and beach tourism in Sanur, Bali: Gender, employment opportunities and government policy. *Pacific Tourism Review* 1 (3), 243–56.

Bridger, G.A. and Winpenny, J.T. (1983) *A Practical Guide to the Choice and Appraisal of Public Sector Investments*. London: Her Majesty's Stationery Office.

Brinkerhoff, D.W. and Ingle, M. (1989) Integrating blueprint and process: A structured flexibility approach to development management. *Public Administration and Development* 9 (5), 487–503.

British Tourist Authority (BTA) (1997) *Regional Tourism Facts – Cumbria*. London: BTA.

British Tourist Authority (BTA) (2000) *Tourism Intelligence Quarterly* 21 (3). London: BTA.

Britton, S.G. (1980) The evolution of a colonial space economy. *Journal of Historical Geography* 6 (3), 251–74.

Britton, S.G. (1982a) The political economy of tourism in the Third World. *Annals of Tourism Research* 9 (3), 331–58.

Britton, S.G. (1982b) International tourism and multinational corporations in the Pacific: The case of Fiji. In M. Taylor and N. Thrift (eds) *The Geography of Multinationals* (pp. 252–74). London: Croom Helm.

Britton, S.G. (1983) *Tourism and Underdevelopment in Fiji*. Canberra: Australian National University.

Britton, S. (1987a) Tourism in small developing countries development issues and research needs. In S. Britton and W.C. Clark (eds) *Ambiguous Alternative Tourism in Small Developing Countries* (pp. 167–87). Suva: University of the South Pacific.

Britton, S. (1987b) Tourism in Pacific-islands states: Constraints and opportunities. In S. Britton and W.C. Clark (eds) *Ambiguous Alternative Tourism in Small Developing Countries* (pp. 113–40). Suva: University of the South Pacific.

Britton, S. (1989) Tourism, dependency and development: A mode of analysis. In T.V. Singh, H.L. Theuns and F.M. Go (eds) *Towards Appropriate Tourism: The Case of Developing Countries* (pp. 93–116). Frankfurt: Peter Long.

Britton, S.G. (1991) Tourism, dependency and place: Towards a critical geography of tourism development. *Environment and Planning D: Society and Space* 9, 451–78.

Britton, S. and Clarke, W. (eds) (1987) *Ambiguous Alternative: Tourism in Small Developing Countries*. Suva: University of the South Pacific.

Brohman, J. (1995) Economic and critical silences in development studies: A theoretical critique of neoliberalism. *Third World Quarterly* 16 (2): 297–318.

Brohman, J. (1996a) *Popular Development: Rethinking the Theory and Practice of Development*. Oxford: Blackwell.

Brohman, J. (1996b) New directions in tourism for Third World development. *Annals of Tourism Research* 23 (1), 48–70.

Bromley, R. and Gerry, C. (1979) Who are the casual poor? In R. Bromley and C. Gerry (eds) *Casual Work and Poverty in Third World Cities* (pp. 3–23). Chichester: John Wiley and Sons.

Browett, J. (1980) Development, the diffusionist paradigm and geography. *Progress in Human Geography* 4 (1), 57–79.

Brown, A. (1995) Caribbean cultures and mass communication technology: Re-examining the cultural dependency thesis. In H.S. Dunn (ed.) *Globalization, Communications and Caribbean Identity*. New York: St Martin's Press.

Brown, D.O. (1998) The search for an appropriate form of tourism for Africa: Lessons from the past and suggestions for the future. *Tourism Management* 19 (3), 237–45.

Brown, F. (1998) *Tourism Reassessed: Blight or Blessing?* Oxford: Butterworth-Heinemann.

Brown, L.R. (1992) Economics versus ecology: Two contrasting views of the world. *Ecodecision* (June), 19–22.

Bruner, E. (1995) The ethnographer/tourist in Indonesia. In M.-F. Lanfant, J. Allcock and E. Bruner (eds) *International Tourism: Identity and Change* (pp. 224–41). London: Sage.

Bryant, R. and Bailey, S. (1997) *Third World Political Ecology*. London: Routledge.

Bryden, J.M. (1973) *Tourism and Development: A Case Study of the Commonwealth Caribbean.* London: Cambridge University Press.

Buck, R. (1978) Towards a synthesis in tourism theory. *Annals of Tourism Research* 5 (1), 110–11.

Budowski, G. (1976) Tourism and conservation: Conflict, co-existence or symbiosis? *Environmental Conservation* 3 (1), 27–31.

Buhalis, D. (2000) Relationships in the distribution channel of tourism: Conflicts between hoteliers and tour operators in the Mediterranean region. *International Journal of Hospitality and Tourism Administration* 1 (1), 113–39.

Bull, A. (1995) *The Economics of Travel and Tourism* (2nd edn). Melbourne: Longman.

Burkhart, A. and Medlik, S. (1981) *Tourism: Past, Present and Future* (2nd edn). Oxford: Butterworth-Heinemann.

Burns, P. (1996) Japan's ten million programme: The paradox of statistical success. *Progress in Tourism and Hospitality Management* 2 (2), 181–92.

Burns, P. (1999a) *An Introduction to Tourism and Anthropology*. London: Routledge.

Burns, P. (1999b) Paradoxes in planning: Tourism elitism or brutalism. *Annals of Tourism Research* 26 (2), 329–48.

Burns, P. and Holden, A. (1995) *Tourism: A New Perspective*. Hemel Hempstead: Prentice Hall International.

Burton, R. (1998) Maintaining the quality of ecotourism: Ecotour operators' responses to tourism growth. *Journal of Sustainable Tourism* 6 (2), 117–42.

Butcher, J. (1997) Sustainable development or development? In M. Stabler (ed.) *Tourism and Sustainability: Principles to Practice* (pp. 27–38). Wallingford: CAB International.

Butler, R.W. (1980) The concept of a tourism area cycle of evolution. *Canadian Geographer* 24, 5–12.

Butler, R.W. (1990) Alternative tourism: Pious hope or Trojan horse? *Journal of Travel Research* 28 (3), 40–5.

Butler, R.W. (1991) Tourism, environment and sustainable development. *Environmental Conservation* 18 (3), 201–9.

Butler, R.W. (1992) Alternative tourism: The thin edge of the wedge. In V.L. Smith and W.R. Eadington (eds) *Tourism Alternatives Potentials and Problems in the Development of Tourism* (pp. 31–46). Philadelphia: University of Pennsylvania Press.

Butler, R.W. (1993a) Tourism – An evolutionary perspective. In J.G. Nelson, R.W. Butler and G. Wall (eds) *Tourism and Sustainable Development: Monitoring, Planning, Managing* (Heritage Resources Centre Joint Publication No. 1) (pp. 27–44). University of Waterloo.

Butler, R.W. (1993b) Tourism development in small islands: Past influence and future directions. In D. Lockhart, D. Drakakis-Smith and J. Schembri (eds) *The Development Process in Small Island States* (pp. 71–91). London: Routledge.

Butler, R.W (1996) Problems and possibilities of sustainable tourism: The case of the Shetland Islands. In L. Briguglio, R. Butler, D. Harrison and W. Fiho (eds) *Sustainable Tourism in Islands and Small States, Case Studies* (pp. 11–49). London: Pinter.

Butler, R.W. (1998a) Sustainable tourism – looking backwards in order to progress? In C.M. Hall and A. Lew (eds) *Sustainable Tourism: A Geographical Perspective* (pp. 25–34). Harlow: Longman.

Butler, R.W. (1998b) Tartan mythology: The traditional tourist image of Scotland. In G. Ringer (ed.) *Destinations: Cultural Landscape of Tourism* (Routledge Advances in Tourism Series) (pp. 121–39). London: Routledge.

Butler, R.W. (1999a) Problems and issues of integrating tourism development. In D. Pearce and R. Butler (eds) *Contemporary Issues in Tourism Development* (pp. 65–80). London: Routledge.

Butler, R.W. (1999b) Sustainable tourism: A state-of-the-art review. *Tourism Geographies* 1 (1), 7–25.

Butler, R. and Hall, C.M. (1998) Image and reimaging of rural areas. In R. Butler, C.M. Hall and J. Jenkins (eds) *Tourism and Recreation in Rural Areas* (pp. 115–22). Chichester: John Wiley and Sons.

Butler, R. and Hinch, T. (eds) (1996) *Tourism and Indigenous Peoples.* London: International Thomson Business Press.

Buzard, J. (1993) *The Beaten Track: European Tourism, Literature and the Ways to 'Culture' 1800–1918.* Oxford: Clarendon Press.

Bywater, M. (1998) Who owns whom in the European travel industry. *Travel and Tourism Analyst* 3, 41–59.

Caalders, J. (2000) Tourism in Friesland: A network approach. In G. Richards and D. Hall (eds) *Tourism and Sustainable Community Development* (pp. 185–204). London: Routledge.

Calatrava Requena, J. and Avilés, P. (1993) Tourism: An opportunity for disadvantaged rural areas? *Leader Magazine* 4, 6–9.

Calhoun, C. (1995) *Critical Social Theory: Culture, History and the Challenge of Difference.* Oxford: Blackwell.

Camble, P. (1999) Oil is dead? Long live tourism! *Middle East Insight* 14 (5), 38–42.

Campbell, C. (1987) *The Romantic Ethic and the Spirit of Modern Consumerism.* Oxford: Blackwell.

Cardoso, F.H. (1979) The originality of the copy: The Economic Commission for Latin America and the idea of sevelopment. In K.Q. Hill (ed.) *Toward a New Strategy for Development.* Toronto: Pergamon Press.

Cardoso, F.H. and Faletto, E. (1979) *Dependency and Development in Latin America.* Berkeley, CA: University of California Press

Carson, R. (1962) *Silent Spring.* New York: Houghton Mifflin.

Carter, A. (1995) The nation-state and underdevelopment. *Third World Quarterly* 16 (4), 595–618.

Castells, M. (1996) *The Rise of the Network Society.* Oxford: Blackwell.

Castells, M. (2000) Materials for an exploratory theory of the network society. *British Journal of Sociology* 51 (1), 5–24.

Castells, M. and Portes, A. (1989) World underneath: The origins, dynamics, and effects of the informal economy. In A. Portes, M. Castells and L.A. Benton (eds) *The Informal Economy. Studies in Advanced and Less Developed Countries* (pp. 11–37). Baltimore, MD: Johns Hopkins University Press.

Castleberg-Koulma, M. (1991) Greek women and tourism: Women's cooperatives as an alternative form of organization. In N. Redclift and M.T. Sinclair (eds) *Working Women* (pp. 197–212). London: Routledge.

Cater, E. (1993) Ecotourism in the Third World: Problems for sustainable tourism development. *Tourism Management* 14 (2), 85–93.

Cater, E. (1995) Environmental contradictions in sustainable tourism. *Geographical Journal* 161 (1), 211–28.

Cater, E. (1996) Ecotourism in the Caribbean: A sustainable option for Belize and Dominica? In L. Briguglio, R. Butler, D. Harrison and W.L. Filho (eds) *Sustainable Tourism in Islands and Small States: Case Studies* (pp. 122–46). London: Pinter.

Cater, E. and Goodall, B. (1992) Must tourism destroy its resource base? In A. Mannion and S. Bowlby (eds) *Environmental Issues in the 1990s* (pp. 309–23). Chichester: John Wiley and Sons.

Cavaco, C. (1995a) Rural tourism: The creation of new tourist spaces. In A. Montanari and A. Williams (eds) *European Tourism: Regions, Spaces and Restructuring* (pp. 129–49). Chichester: John Wiley and Sons.

Cavaco, C. (1995b) Tourism in Portugal: Diversity, diffusion and regional and local development. *Tijdschrift voor Economische en Sociale Geografie* 86 (1), 64–71.

Ceballos-Lascurain, H. (1991) Tourism, ecotourism, and protected areas. In K. Lindberg and D.E. Hawkins (eds) *Ecotourism: A Guide For Planners and Managers*. North Bennington, VT: Ecotourism Society.

Cha, S., McCleary, K. and Uysal, M. (1995) Travel motivations of Japanese overseas travellers: A factor-cluster segmentation approach. *Journal of Travel Research* 34 (1), 33–9.

Chambers, R. (1994) The origins and practice of participatory rural appraisal. *World Development* 22 (7), 953–69.

Chant, S. (1992) Tourism in Latin America: Perspectives from Mexico and Costa Rica. In D. Harrison (ed.) *Tourism and the Less Developed Countries* (pp. 85–101). London: Belhaven.

Chase, A. (1995) *In a Dark Wood: The Fight Over Forests and the Rising Tyranny of Environmentalism*. Boston, MA: Houghton Mifflin.

Chenery, H. and Syrquin, M. (1975) *Patterns of Development 1950–1970*. New York: World Bank by Oxford University Press.

Chipeta, C. (1981) *Indigenous Economics: A Cultural Approach*. Smithtown, NY: Exposition Press.

Christaller, W. (1963) Some considerations of tourism location in Europe: The peripheral regions – underdeveloped countries – recreation areas. *Regional Science Association; Papers XII, Lund Congress* 12, 95–105.

Chu, Y.W. (1992) Informal work in Hong Kong. *International Journal of Urban and Regional Research* 16 (3), 420–41.

Clancy, M. (1998) Commodity chains, services and development: Theory and preliminary evidence from the tourism industry. *Review of International Political Economy* 5 (1), 122–48.

Clancy, M. (1999) Tourism and development: Evidence from Mexico. *Annals of Tourism Research* 26 (1), 1–20.

Cleverdon, R. (1979) *The Economic and Social Impact of International Tourism on Developing Countries*. London: Economist Intelligence Unit.

Clewer, A. and Sinclair, M. (1995) Regional concentration and dispersal of tourism demand in the UK. *Regional Studies* 29 (6), 570–6.

Clift, S. and Carter, S. (2000) *Tourism and Sex: Culture, Commerce and Coercion*. New York: Pinter.

Cockerell, N. (1997) Nepal. *International Tourism Reports* 1, 40–57.

Cohen, E. (1972) Towards a sociology of international tourism. *Social Research* 38, 164–82.

Cohen, E. (1974) Who is a tourist? A conceptual clarification. *Sociological Review* 22 (4), 527–55.

Cohen, E. (1978) The impact of tourism on the physical environment. *Annals of Tourism Research* 5, 215–37.

Cohen, E. (1982) Marginal paradises: Bungalow tourism on the islands of southern Thailand. *Annals of Tourism Research* 9 (2), 189–228.

Cole, J. (1988) The global distribution of natural resources. In J. Norwine and A. Gonzalez (eds) *The Third World: States of Mind and Being* (pp. 55–66). Boston, MA: Unwin Hyman.

Cole, W.E. and Fayissa, B. (1991) The urban subsistence labor force: Toward a policy-oriented and empirically accessible taxonomy. *World Development* 19 (7), 779–89.

Commission of European Communities (1993a) *Taking Account of Environment in Tourism Development* (Tourism Unit, DGXXIII). Luxembourg: Commission of European Communities.

Commission of the European Communities (1993b) *Growth, Competitiveness and Employment: The Challenges and Ways Forward into the 21st Century* (White Paper). Luxembourg: Commission of the European Communities.

Commission of the European Communities (1999) *Competitiveness and Cohesion: Trends in the Regions* (Sixth Periodic Report on the Social and Economic Situation and Development of the Regions in the Community). Brussels: EU.

Connell, J. (1987) Migration, rural development and policy formation in the South Pacific. *Journal of Rural Studies* 3 (2), 105–21.

Constanza, R. (1997) The value of the world's ecosystem services and natural capital. *Nature* 387, 253–60.

Cooper, C., Fletcher, J., Gilbert, D. and Wanhill, S. (1993) *Tourism: Principles and Practice.* London: Pitman.

Cooper, C., Fletcher, J., Gilbert, D., Shephard, R. and Wanhill, S. (1998) *Tourism: Principles and Practice* (2nd edn). Harlow: Longman.

Corbridge, S. (1995) *Development Studies: A Reader.* London: Arnold.

Countryside Commission (1995) *Sustainable Rural Tourism: Opportunities for Local Action*, CCP 483. Cheltenham: Countryside Commission.

Countryside Commission (1996) *Public Attitudes to the Countryside,* CCP481. Cheltenham: Countryside Commission.

Cowell, D. (1984) *The Marketing of Services.* Oxford: Butterworth-Heinemann.

Cowen, M. and Shenton, R. (1996) *Doctrines of Development.* London: Routledge.

Cox, R. (1981) Social forces, states and world orders: Beyond international relations theory. *Millenium: Journal of International Studies* 10 (2), 126–55.

Cox, R. (1987) *Production, Power and World Order: Social Forces in the Making of History.* New York: Columbia University Press.

Crick, M. (1989) Representations of international tourism in the social sciences: Sun, sex, sights, savings and servility. *Annual Review of Anthropology* 18, 307–44.

Croall, J. (1995) *Preserve or Destroy: Tourism and the Environment.* London: Calouste Gulbenkian Foundation.

Crompton, J. (1979) Motivations for pleasure vacation. *Annals of Tourism Research* 6 (4), 408–24.

Cronin, L. (1990) A strategy for tourism and sustainable developments. *World Leisure and Recreation* 32 (3), 12–18.

Crouch, G. and Shaw, R. (1992) International tourism demand: A meta-analytical integration of research findings. In P. Johnson and B. Thomas (eds) *Choice and Demand in Tourism* (pp. 175–207). London: Mansell.

Crush, J. and Wellings, P. (1983) The southern African pleasure periphery, 1966–83. *Journal of Modern African Studies* 21 (4), 673–98.

Cubie, R. (2000) The nuts and bolts of building the village. In B. Barnet (ed.) *Whistler, History in the Making.* Whistler: Pique.

Cukier, J. (1996) Tourism employment in Bali: Trends and implications. In R. Butler and T. Hinch (eds) *Tourism and Indigenous Peoples* (pp. 49–75). London: International Thomson Business Press.

Cukier, J. (1998a) Tourism employment and social status in Bali. In G. Ringer (ed.) *Destinations: Cultural Landscapes of Tourism* (pp. 63–79). London: Routledge.

Cukier, J. (1998b). Tourism employment and the urbanization of coastal Bali. In M. Miller, and J. Auyong (eds) *Proceedings of the 1996 Congress on Coastal and Marine Tourism*, 19–22 June 1996, Honolulu, Hawaii, USA (pp. 296–302). Seattle, WA: Washington Sea Grant Program and School of Marine Affairs, University of Washington, and Oregon Sea Grant College Program, Oregon State University.

Cukier, J. (2000) Tourism entrepreneurship in transitional economies: The 'travellers' café' in Vietnam. In J. Cukier and E. Dixon (eds) *Tourism Resources, Impacts and Planning: Geographical Perspectives on New Zealand and International Tourism* (pp. 87–97). New Zealand: University of Waikato.

Cukier, J. and Wall, G. (1994a) Informal tourism employment: Vendors in Bali, Indonesia. *Tourism Management* 15 (6), 464–7.

Cukier, J. and Wall, G. (1994b) Tourism employment in Bali, Indonesia. *Tourism Recreation Research* 19 (1), 32–40.

Cukier, J. and Wall, G. (1995) Tourism employment in Bali: A gender analysis. *Tourism Economics* 1 (4), 389–401.

Cukier Snow, J. and Wall, G. (1993) Tourism employment: Perspectives from Bali. *Tourism Management* 14 (3), 195–201.

Cukier, J., Norris, J. and Wall, G. (1996) The involvement of women in the tourism industry of Bali, Indonesia. *Journal of Development Studies* 33 (2), 248–70.

Curry, S. (1982) The terms of trade and real import capacity of the tourism sector in Tanzania. *Journal of Development Studies* 18 (4), 479–96.

Curry, S. (1990) Tourism development in Tanzania. *Annals of Tourism Research* 17 (1), 133–49.

Curry, S. and Morvaridi, B. (1992) Sustainable tourism: Illustrations from Kenya, Nepal and Jamaica. In C. Cooper and A. Lockwood (eds) *Progress in Tourism, Recreation and Hospitality Management* (vol. 4, pp. 131–9). London: Belhaven Press.

Cyprus Tourism Organisation (1992) *Annual Report 1991*. Nicosia: Cyprus Tourism Organisation.

Dahles, H. (1997) Tourism, petty entrepreneurs and sustainable development. In H. Dahles (ed.) *Tourism, Small Entrepreneurs, and Sustainable Development: Cases from Developing Countries* (pp. 23–33). Tilburg, The Netherlands: ATLAS, Department of Leisure Studies, Tilburg University.

Dahles, H. (1997) *Tourism, Small Entrepreneurs, and Sustainable Development*. Tilburg, The Netherlands: ATLAS, Department of Leisure Studies, Tilburg University.

Dahles, H. (2000) Tourism, small enterprises and community development. In G. Rechards and D. Hall (eds) *Tourism and Sustainable Community Development* (Routledge Advances in Tourism Series) (pp. 154–69). London: Routledge.

Dahles, H. and Bras, K. (1997) The state, the market, and the role of NGOs in the establishment of sustainable tourism development: A discussion. In H. Dahles (ed.) *Tourism, Small Entrepreneurs, and Sustainable Development: Cases from Developing Countries* (pp. 65–73). Tilburg, The Netherlands: ATLAS, Department of Leisure Studies, Tilburg University.

Daly, H. and Cobb, C. (1989) *For The Common Good*. Boston: Beacon Press.

Dann, G. (1977) Anomie, ego-enhancement and tourism. *Annals of Tourism Research* 4 (4), 184–94.

Dann, G. (1981) Tourist motivation: An appraisal. *Annals of Tourism Research* 8 (2), 187–219.

Dann, G. (1996) *The Language of Tourism: A Socio-Linguistic Perspective.* Wallingford: CAB International.

Dann, G. (1999) Theoretical issues for tourism's future development: Identifying the agenda. In D. Pearce and R. Butler (eds) *Contemporary Issues in Tourism Development* (pp. 13–30). London: Routledge.

Dann, G., Nash, D. and Pearce, P. (1988) Methodology in tourism research. *Annals of Tourism Research* 15 (1), 1–28.

Daoudi, A. and Mihalic, T. (1999) Strategic importance of tourism as a part of an integrated development strategy of countries and places. *Revue de Tourisme* 54 (3), 18.

Dasgupta, B. (1998) *Structural Adjustment, Global Trade and the New Political Economy of Development.* London: Zed Books.

Dasgupta, P. and Weale, M. (1992) On measuring the quality of life. *World Development* 20 (1), 119–31.

Davidson, R. and Maitland, R. (1997) *Tourism Destinations.* London: Hodder and Stoughton.

Daugherty, R. (1974) *Science in Geography: Data Collection.* London: Oxford University Press.

Davies, R. (1979) Informal sector or subordinate mode of production? A model. In R. Bromley and C. Gerry (eds) *Casual Work and Poverty in Third World Cities* (pp. 87–104). Chichester: John Wiley and Sons.

Davis, D.E. (1978) Development and the tourist industry in Third World countries. *Society and Leisure* 1, 301–22.

Davis, H. (1968) Potentials for tourism in developing countries. *Finance and Development* 5 (4), 34–9.

Davis, M. (1993) Who killed Los Angeles? Part two: The verdict is given. *New Left Review* 199, 29–54.

De Kadt, E. (ed.) (1979a) *Tourism: Passport to Development? Perspectives on the Social and Cultural Effects of Tourism in Developing Countries.* New York: Oxford University Press.

De Kadt, E. (1979b) Social planning for tourism in the developing countries. *Annals of Tourism Research* 6 (2), 36–48.

Debbage, K. (1990) Oligopoly and the resort cycle in the Bahamas. *Annals of Tourism Research* 17 (4), 513–27.

Demuth, F. (1929) *Fremdenverkehr und Zahlungsbilanz.* Berlin: Stilke.

Department of Environment (1990) *Department of Environment: Planning Policy Guidelines: Tourism,* PPG 21. London: HMSO.

Desforges, L. (2000) State tourism institutions and neo-liberal development: A case study of Peru. *Tourism Geographies* 2 (2), 177–92.

Desjeux, D. (1981) Development as an acculturation process. *Development: Seeds of Change* 3 (4), 33–8.

Diamantis, D. (1999) Green strategies for tourism worldwide. *Travel and Tourism Intelligence* 4, 89–112.

Diamond, J. (1977) Tourism's role in economic development: The case reexamined. *Economic Development and Cultural Change* 25 (3), 539–53.

Dickenson, J.P. *et al.* (1986) *A Geography of the Third World.* New York Methuen.

Dieke, P. (1989) Fundamentals of tourism development: A Third World perspective. *Hospitality Education and Research Journal* 13, 7–22.

Dieke, P. (1993a) Tourism and development policy in the Gambia. *Annals of Tourism Research* 20 (3), 423–49.

Dieke, P. (1993b) Tourism in the Gambia: Some issues in development policy. *World Development* 21 (2), 277–89.

Dieke, P. (1995) Tourism and structural adjustment programmes in the African economy. *Tourism Economics* 1 (1): 71–93.

Dieke, P. (2000) *The Political Economy of Tourism Development in Africa*. New York: Cognizant.

Din, K.H. (1982) Tourism in Malaysia: Competing needs in a plural society. *Annals of Tourism Research* 9, 453–80.

Din, K. (1990) Islam and tourism patterns, issues, and options. *Annals of Tourism Research* 16 (4), 542–63.

Din, K.H. (1993) Dialogue with the hosts: An educational strategy towards sustainable tourism. In M. Hitchcock, V.T. King and M.J.G. Parnwell (eds) *Tourism in South-East Asia* (pp. 327–36). London: Routledge.

Dincer, M. (1999) The Tourism Encouragement Law in Turkey. Unpublished paper presented at the 49th AIEST Conference on Future-Oriented Tourism Policy, Morocco.

Dix, G. (1989) Tourism and the developing economy. *Third World Planning Review* 11 (2), 127–30.

Dixon E. (2000) Women and tourism: An analysis of the impact of tourism on traditional women's roles in Bali, Indonesia. In J.E. Cukier and E. Dixon (eds) *Tourism, Resources, Impacts and Planning: Geographical Perspectives on International Tourism* (pp. 49–60). Hamilton: Department of Geography, University of Waikato.

Douglas, M. and Isherwood, B. (1979) *The World of Goods*. London: Allen Lane.

Dowling, R. (1992) Tourism and environmental integration: The journey from idealism to realism. In C. Cooper and A. Lockwood (eds) *Progress in Tourism, Recreation and Hospitality Management* (vol. 4) (pp. 33–46). London: Belhaven Press.

Doxey,, G.V. (1976) When enough's enough – the natives are restless in old Niagara. *Heritage Canada* 2 (2), 26–9.

Doyle, T. (1998) Sustainable development and Agenda 21: A secular bible of global free markets and pluralist democracy. *Third World Quarterly* 19 (4), 771–86.

Doyle, T. and Mceachern, D. (1998) *Environment and Politics*. London: Routledge.

Drouin, M. (1995) The role of the institution is problematic: Mexican peso crisis raises questions about the IMF. *Financial Post* (15 March).

Duffield, B.S. (1982) Tourism: The measurement of economic and social impact. *Tourism Management* 3 (4), 248–55.

Dunford, M. (1994) Winners and losers: The new map of economic inequality in the European Union. *European Urban and Regional Studies* 1 (2), 95–114.

Dunning, J.H. and McQueen, G. (1982) Multinational corporations in the international hotel industry. *Annals of Tourism Research* 9 (1), 69–90.

Durning, A. (1993) Supporting indigenous peoples. In Lester R. Brown *et al.* (eds) *The State of the World*. New York: W.W. Norton.

Dussel, E. (1988) Beyond Eurocentrism: The world-system and the limits of modernity. In F. Jameson and M. Miyoshi (eds) *The Culture of Globalization* (pp. 3–31). Durham, NC: Duke University Press.

Dwivedi, O.P. (1994) *Development Administration: From Underdevelopment to Sustainable Development*. New York: St Martin's Press.

Eadington, W. and Redman, M. (1991) Economics and tourism. *Annals of Tourism Research* 18 (1), 41–56.

Eadington, W. and Smith, V. (1992) Introduction: The emergence of alternative forms of tourism. In V. Smith and W. Eadington (eds) *Tourism Alternatives Potentials and Problems in the Development of Tourism* (pp. 1–13). Philadelphia: University of Pennsylvania Press.

Eagles, P. (1992) The travel motivations of Canadian ecotourists. *Journal of Travel Research* 32 (2), 3–13.

Eagles, P. and Cascagnette, J. (1995) Canadian ecotourists: Who are they? *Tourism Recreation Research* 20 (1), 22–8.

Eber, S. (ed.) (1992) *Beyond The Green Horizon: Principles for Sustainable Tourism*. Godalming, Surrey: World Wide Fund For Nature.

Ebery, M.G. and Forbes, D.K. (1985) The 'informal sector' in the Indonesian city: A review and case study. In G.H. Krause (ed.) *Urban Society in Southeast Asia: Social and Economic Issues* (pp. 153–70). Hong Kong: Asian Studies Monograph Series.

Echtner, C.M. (1995) Entrepreneurial training in developing countries. *Annals of Tourism Research* 22 (1), 119–34.

Eckersley, R. (1992) *Environmentalism and Political Theory: Towards an Ecocentric Approach*. London: University College London Press.

Edington, J.M. and Edington, M.A. (1997) Tropical forest ecotourism: Two promising projects in Belize. In M.J. Stabler (ed.) *Tourism and Sustainability: Principles to Practice* (pp. 163–8). Wallingford: CAB International.

Edwards, C. (1985) *The Fragmented World: Competing Perspectives on Trade, Money, and Crisis*. London: Methuen.

Edwards, M. (1989) The irrelevance of development studies. *Third World Quarterly* 11 (1), 116–35.

Ehrlich, P. (1972) *The Population Bomb*. London: Ballantine.

EIU (1992) Cyprus. *International Tourism Reports* 2, 43–64.

Elkan, W. (1975) The relation between tourism and employment in Kenya and Tanzania. *Journal of Development Studies* 11 (2), 123–30.

Elkington, J. and Hailes, J. (1988) *The Green Consumer Guide: From Shampoo to Champagne – Shopping for a Better Environment*. London: Victor Gollancz.

Elliott, J. (1997) *Tourism and Public Policy*. London: Routledge.

Elliott, J. (1999) *An Introduction to Sustainable Development*. London: Routledge.

Employment (1999) The tourism sector's potential for job creation. On WWW at http://europa.eu.int/scadplus/leg/en/cha/c10929.htm. Accessed 20.1.01.

English, E.P. (1986) *The Great Escape: An Examination of North-South Tourism*. Ottawa: North-South Institute.

English Tourist Board (ETB) (1991) *Tourism and the Environment: Maintaining the Balance*. London: English Tourist Board.

Erisman, H.M. (1983) Tourism and cultural dependency in the West Indies. *Annals of Tourism Research* 10 (3), 337–61.

Escobar, A. (1997) The making and unmaking of the Third World through development. In M. Rahnema and V. Bawtree (eds) *The Post Development Reader* (pp. 85–93). London: Zed Books.

Estes, R. (1988) Toward a 'quality-of-life' index: Empirical approaches to assessing human welfare internationally. In J. Norwine and A. Gonzalez (eds) *The Third World: States of Mind and Being* (pp. 23–36). Boston, MA: Unwin Hyman.

European Economic and Social Committee Bulletin 1 (2000).

Evans, G. (1999) Fair trade in tourism and local economic strategies. Paper presented to the Conference on Fairly Traded Tourism, University of North London, 9 June.

Fainstein, D. and Judd, D. (1999) Global forces, local strategies, and urban tourism. In D. Judd and S. Fainstein (eds) *The Tourist City* (pp. 1–20). New Haven, CT: Yale University Press.

Fairbairn-Dunlop, P. (1994) Gender, culture and tourism development in Western Samoa. In V. Kinnaird and D. Hall (eds) *Tourism: A Gender Analysis* (pp. 121–41). Chichester: John Wiley and Sons.

Farrell, B. and Runyan, D. (1991) Ecology and tourism. *Annals of Tourism Research* 18 (1), 26–40.

Farrington, P. (1999) All-inclusives – a new apartheid. *Tourism Concern: In Focus* 33, 10–12.

Farver, J.A.M. (1984) Tourism and employment in the Gambia. *Annals of Tourism Research* 11, 249–65.

Featherstone, M. (1991) *Consumer Culture and Postmodernism*. London: Sage.

Feifer, M. (1985) *Going Places*. London: Macmillan.

Fennell, D.A. (1999) *Ecotourism: An Introduction*. London, Routledge.

Fidalgo, L.F. (1996) El túnel que acabó con el cañellismo. *Anuario El Mundo 1996*, 132.

Fiertz, G. (1996) Tourism development in Turkey. In A. Badger *et al.* (eds) *Trading Places: Tourism as Trade* (pp. 43–7). London: Tourism Concern.

Finney, B. and Watson, A. (1975) *A New Kind of Sugar: Tourism in the Pacific*. Honolulu: East-West Culture Learning Institute.

Fisher, H. (1988) Development in Sub-Saharan Africa: Barriers and prospects. In J. Norwine and A. Gonzalez (eds) *The Third World: States of Mind and Being* (pp. 231–42). Boston, MA: Unwin Hyman.

Fitton, M. (1996) Does our community want tourism? Examples from South Wales. In M.F. Price (ed.) *People and Tourism in Fragile Environments* (pp. 159–74). Chichester: John Wiley and Sons.

Fletcher, J. (1993) Input–output analysis and employment multipliers. In T. Baum (ed.) *Human Resource Issues in International Tourism* (pp. 77–85). Oxford: Butterworth-Heinemann.

Fletcher, J. (1994) Economic impact. In S. Witt and L. Moutinho (eds) *Tourism Marketing and Management Handbook* (2nd edn) (pp. 476–9). New York: Prentice Hall.

Fletcher, J. (2000) Dependency theory. In J. Jafari (ed.) *Encyclopaedia of Tourism* (pp. 142–3). Routledge: London.

Fodness, D. (1994) Measuring tourist motivation. *Annals of Tourism Research* 21 (3), 555–81.

Forrester, J. (1971) *World Dynamics*. Cambridge, MA: Wright-Allen.

Forsyth, T. (1995) Business attitudes to sustainable tourism: Self-regulation in the UK outgoing tourism industry. *Journal of Sustainable Tourism* 3 (4), 210–31.

France, L. (ed.) (1997) *The Earthscan Reader in Sustainable Tourism*. London: Earthscan.

France, L. (1998) Local participation in tourism in the West Indian Islands. In E. Laws, B. Faulkner and G. Moscardo (eds) *Embracing and Managing Change in Tourism: International Case Studies* (pp. 222–34). London: Routledge.

Francillon, G. (1979) *Bali: Tourism, Culture, Environment*. Bali: UNESCO.

Francillon, G. (1990) The dilemma of tourism in Bali. In W. Beller, P. d'Ayala, and P. Hein (eds) *Sustainable Development and Environmental Management of Small Islands* (pp. 267–72). Paris: UNESCO.

Francisco, R. (1983) The political impact of tourism dependence in Latin America. *Annals of Tourism Research* 10 (3), 363–76.

Frank, A. (1966) The development of underdevelopment. *Monthly Review* 18 (4). Reprinted in C. Wilber (ed.) (1988) *The Political Economy of Development and Underdevelopment* (4th edn) (pp. 109–20). Toronto: McGraw-Hill.

Freitag, T. (1994) Enclave tourism development: For whom the benefits roll? *Annals of Tourism Research* 21 (3), 538–54.

Friedmann, J. (1966) *Regional Development Policy: A Case Study of Venezuela*. London: M.I.T. Press.

Friedmann, J. (1978) The role of cities in national development. In L.S. Bourne and J.W. Simmons (eds) *Systems of Cities Readings on Structure, Growth, and Policy* (pp. 70–81). New York: Oxford University Press.

Friedmann, J. (1992) *Empowerment: The Politics of Alternative Development*. Cambridge: Blackwell.

Friedmann, J. and Douglas, M. (1978) Agropolitian development: Towards a new strategy for regional planning in Asia. In Fu-Chen Lo and K. Salih (eds) *Growth Pole Strategy and Regional Development Policy Asian Experience and Alternative Approaches* (pp. 163–92). Toronto: Pergamon Press.

Friedmann, J. and Forest, Y. (1988) The politics of place: Toward a political economy of territorial planning. In B. Higgins and D. Savoie (eds) *Regional Economic Development – Essays in Honour of Francois Perroux* (pp. 115–30). Boston, MA: Hyman.

Frobel, F., Heinrichs, J. and Kreye, O. (1980) *The New International Division of Labour*. Cambridge: Cambridge University Press.

Fukuyama, F. (1989) The end of history? *The National Interest* 16 (Summer), 3–18.

Galaní-Moutafí, V. (1993) From agriculture to tourism: Property, labour, gender and kinship in a Greek island village (Part 1). *Journal of Modern Greek Studies* 11, 241–70.

Galli, R. (1992) Winners and losers in development and antidevelopment theory. In R. Galli (ed.) *Rethinking the Third World: Contributions Towards a New Conceptualization* (pp. 1–27). New York: Crane Russak.

Garrod, B. and Fyall, A. (1998) Beyond the rhetoric of sustainable tourism? *Tourism Management* 19 (3), 199–212.

Gauthama, M., Soeseno, E.D. and Tamsil, K. (1992) Female labour in industry. In B. Kettel, F. Carden and J. Soemirat (eds) *The ITB/York University Forum on Gender and Development, December 1990*, Report 35 (pp. 101–8). Toronto: UCE.

Gaviria, M. (1974) *España a Go-Go: Turismo Charter y Neo-Colonialismo del Espacio*. Madrid: Ediciones Turner.

Gebert, E. (1928) *Fremdenverkehr und Zahlungsbilanz*. Salzburg: Tunder und Muller.

Geering, T. (1920) Die Zahlungsbilanz der Schweiz vor und seit dem Kriege. *Schweizerische Zeitschrift fuer Statistik und Volkswirtschaft* 56, 98–117.

Geertz, C. (1973) *The Interpretation of Cultures. Selected Essays*. New York: Basic Books.

Geertz, H. (1967) Indonesian cultures and communities. In R. McVey (ed.) *Indonesia* (pp. 24–96). New Haven, CT: Yale University.

Geertz, H. and Geertz, C. (1975) *Kinship in Bali*. Chicago: University of Chicago Press.

Genot, H. (1995) Voluntary environmental codes of conduct in the tourism sector. *Journal of Sustainable Tourism Development* 3 (3), 166–72.

George. S. (1992) *The Debt Boomerang: How Third World Debt Harms Us All*. London: Pluto Press.

Gilbert, D. (1990) Conceptual issues in the meaning of tourism. In C. Cooper (ed.) *Progress in Tourism, Recreation and Hospitality Management* (vol. 2) (pp. 4–27). London: Belhaven Press.

Gilbert, D. (1991) An examination of the consumer behaviour process related to tourism. In C. Cooper (ed.) *Progress in Tourism, Recreation and Hospitality Management* (vol. 3) (pp. 78–105). London: Belhaven Press.

Gill, A.M. (1996) Rooms with a view: Informal settings for public dialogue. *Society and Natural Resources* 9, 633–43.

Gill, A.M. (1998) Local and resort development. In R. Butler, C.M. Hall and J. Jenkins (eds) *Tourism and Recreation in Rural Areas* (pp. 97–111). Chichester: John Wiley and Sons.

Gitelson, R. and Kerstetter, D. (1994) The influence of friends and relatives in travel decision-making. In J. Crotts and and W. van Raaij (eds) *Economic Psychology of Travel and Tourism* (pp. 59–68). New York: Haworth Press.

Gladwin, H. (1980) Indigenous knowledge of fish processing and marketing utilization by women traders of Cape Coast Ghana. In D.W. Brokensha, D.M. Warren and O. Werner (eds) *Indigenous Knowledge Systems and Development.* Lanham, MD: University Press of America.

Gnigue, A. (1992) Integrated rural tourism, Lower Casamance, Senegal. In S. Eber (ed.) *Beyond the Green Horizon* (pp. 40–2). Godalming: WWF.

Go, F. (1997) Entrepreneurs and the tourism industry in developing countries. In H. Dahles (ed.) *Tourism, Small Entrepreneurs and Sustainable Development: Cases from Developing Countries* (pp. 5–21). Tilburg, The Netherlands: Tilburg University, ATLAS.

Godfrey, K. (1996) Towards sustainability? Tourism in the republic of Cyprus. In L. Harrison and W. Husbands (eds) *Practising Responsible Tourism: International Case Studies in Tourism Planning, Policy and Development* (pp. 58–79). Chichester: John Wiley and Sons.

Goeldner, C., Ritchie, J. and McIntosh, R. (2000) *Tourism: Principles Practices and Philosophies* (8th edn). Toronto: John Wiley and Sons.

Goldsmith, E., Allen, R., Allaby, M., Davoll, J. and Lawrence, S. (1972) Blueprint for survival. *Ecologist* 2, 1–50.

Goldsmith, F., Munton, R. and Warren, A. (1970) The impact of recreation on the ecology and amenity of semi-natural areas: Methods of investigation used in the Isles of Scilly. *Biological Journal, Linnean Society* 2, 287–306.

Goldsworthy, D. (1988) Thinking politically about development. *Development and Change* 19 (3), 505–30.

Gonzalez, A. (1988) Indexes of socio-economic development. In J. Norwine and A. Gonzalez (eds) *The Third World: States of Mind and Being* (pp. 37–49). Boston, MA: Unwin Hyman.

Goodall, B. (1991) Understanding holiday choice. In C. Cooper (ed.) *Progress in Tourism, Recreation and Hospitality Management* (vol. 3) (pp. 58–77). London: Belhaven Press.

Gordon, R. (1992) Antro-tourism: A new market development. *Development Journal of SID* 4, 42–5.

Gottlieb, A. (1982) American's vacations. *Annals of Tourism Research* 9 (2), 165–87.

Goulet, D. (1968) On the goals of development. *Cross Currents* 18, 387–405.

Goulet, D. (1992) Participation in development: New avenues. *World Development* 17 (2), 165–78.

Graburn, N. (1983) The anthropology of tourism. *Annals of Tourism Research* 10 (1), 9–33.

Graburn, N. (1989) Tourism: The sacred journey. In V. Smith (ed.) *Hosts and Guests: The Anthropology of Tourism* (2nd edn) (pp. 21–36). Philadelphia: University of Pennsylvania Press.

Graburn, N. and Jafari, J. (1991) Introduction tourism social science. *Annals of Tourism Research* 18 (1), 1–11.

Graf, W. (1992) Sustainable ideologies and interests: Beyond Bruntland. *Third World Quarterly* 13 (3), 553–9.

Green, H. (1995) Planning for sustainable tourism development. In C. Hunter and H. Green (eds) *Tourism and the Environment: A Sustainable Relationship?* (pp. 93–121). London: Routledge.

Griffin, R. (2000) Bass plays £4bn waiting game. *Guardian* (8 December), 27.

Griffin, R.K. (1998) Small lodging operations in Costa Rica: A case-study analysis. *Cornell Hotel and Restaurant Administration Quarterly* 39 (2), 55–63.

Grolleau, H. (1994) Putting feelings first. In LEADER. *Marketing Quality Rural Tourism.* LEADER Dossiers.

Gunn, C. (1994) *Tourism Planning: Basics, Concepts, Cases* (3rd edn). Washington, DC: Taylor and Francis.

Haggett, P. (1975) *Geography: A Modern Synthesis.* New York: Harper and Row.

Hale, D. (1998) The Asian crisis and the IMF's new role as financial peacekeeper. *World Economic Affairs* 2 (2), 35–9.

Hall, A. (1988) Community participation and development policy: A sociological perspective. In A. Hall and J. Midgely (eds) *Development Policies: Sociological Perspectives* (pp. 91–107). Manchester: Manchester University Press.

Hall, C.M. (1994a) *Tourism and Politics: Policy, Power and Place.* Chichester: John Wiley and Sons.

Hall, C.M. (1994b) Is tourism still the plantation economy of the South Pacific? The case of Fiji. *Tourism Recreation Research* 19 (1), 41–8.

Hall, C.M. (1994c) Gender and economic interests in tourism prostitution: The nature, development and implications of sex tourism in South-East Asia. In V. Kinnard and D. Hall (eds) *Tourism: A Gender Analysis* (pp. 142–63). Chichester: John Wiley and Sons.

Hall, C.M. (1998a) The institutional setting – tourism and the state. In D. Ioannides and K. Debbage (eds) *The Economic Geography of the Tourist Industry* (pp. 199–219). London: Routledge.

Hall, C.M. (1998b) Making the Pacific: Globalization, modernity and myth. In G. Ringer (ed.) *Destinations: Cultural Landscape of Tourism* (Routledge Advances in Tourism Series) (pp. 140–53). London: Routledge.

Hall, C.M. (2000a) *Tourism Planning, Policies, Processes and Relationships.* Harlow: Prentice Hall.

Hall, C.M. (2000b) Territorial economic integration and globalisation. Paper presented to the 7th ATLAS International Conference, North–South: Contrasts and Connections in Global Tourism, Savonlinna, Finland, 18–21 June.

Hall, C.M. and Jenkins, J. (1995) *Tourism and Public Policy.* London: Routledge.

Hall, C.M. and Jenkins, J. (1998) The policy dimensions of rural tourism and recreation. In R. Butler, C.M. Hall and J. Jenkins (eds) *Tourism and Recreation in Rural Areas* (pp. 19–42). Chichester: John Wiley and Sons.

Hall, C.M. and Lew, A. (1998) *Sustainable Tourism A Geographic Perspective.* Harlow: Addison Wesley Longman.

Hall, C.M. and Lew, A.A. (1998) The geography of sustainable tourism development: An introduction. In C.M. Hall and A.A. Lew (eds) *Sustainable Tourism: A Geographical Perspective* (pp. 1–12). Harlow: Longman.

Hall, D.R. (1991) *Tourism and Economic Development in Eastern Europe and the Soviet Union.* London: Belhaven Press.

Hall, D. (1998) Tourism development and sustainability issues in Central and South-Eastern Europe. *Tourism Management* 19 (5), 423–31.

Hannigan, K. (1994) National policy, European structural funds and sustainable tourism: The case of Ireland. *Journal of Sustainable Tourism* 2 (4), 179–92.

Haq, M. (1988) People in development. *Development Journal of SID* 2 (3), 41–5.

Hardin, G. (1968) The tragedy of the commons. *Science* 162, 1243–8.

Harrell-Bond, B.E. and Harrell-Bond, D.L. (1979) Tourism in the Gambia. *Review of African Political Economy* 14, 78–90.

Harris, N. (1996) *The New Untouchables: Immigration and the New World Worker.* Harmondsworth: Penguin.

Harrison, D. (1988) *The Sociology of Modernisation and Development.* London: Routledge.

Harrison, D. (1992) *Tourism and the Less Developed Countries.* London: Belhaven.

Harrison, D. (1992a) International tourism and the less developed countries: The background. In D. Harrison (ed.) *Tourism and the Less Developed Countries* (pp. 1–18). Toronto: Belhaven.

Harrison, D. (1992b) Tradition, modernity and tourism in Swaziland. In D. Harrison (ed.) *Tourism and the Less Developed Countries* (pp. 148–62). Toronto: Belhaven.

Harrison, D. (1994) Learning from the old south by the new south? The case of tourism. *Third World Quarterly* 15 (4), 707–21.

Harrison, D. (1995a) International tourism and the less developed countries: A background. In D. Harrison (ed.) *Tourism and the Less Developed Countries* (pp. 1–18). Chichester: John Wiley and Sons.

Harrison, D. (1995b) Development of tourism in Swaziland. *Annals of Tourism Research* 22 (1), 135–156.

Harrison, D. (2000a) Developing country. In J. Jafari (ed.) *Encyclopaedia of Tourism* (pp. 147–8). Routledge: London.

Harrison, D. (2000b) Tourism in Africa: The social and cultural framework. In P.U.C. Dieke (ed.) *The Political Economy of Tourism in Africa*. New York Cognizant.

Harrison, D. (2001) *Tourism and the Less Developed Countries: Issues and Case Studies*. New York: Cognizant.

Harrison, L. and Husbands, W. (eds) (1996) *Practising Responsible Tourism: International Case Studies in Tourism Planning, Policy and Development*. Chichester: John Wiley and Sons.

Harvey, D. (1990) *The Condition of Postmodernity*. Oxford: Blackwell.

Hashimoto, A. (2000) Young Japanese female tourists: An in-depth understanding of a market segment. *Current Issues in Tourism* 3 (1), 35–50.

Hashimoto, A. and Telfer, D.J. (1999) Marketing icewine to Japanese tourists in Niagara: The case of Inniskillin Winery. *International Journal of Wine Marketing* 11 (2), 29–41.

Haywood, K.M. (1988) Responsible and responsive tourism planning in the community. *Tourism Management* 9 (2), 105–18.

Hazbun, W. (2000) Enclave orientalism: The state, tourism and the politics of post-national development in the Arab world. In M. Robinson *et al.* (eds) *Management, Marketing and the Political Economy of Travel and Tourism* (pp. 191–205). Sunderland: Business Education.

Held, D. (1995) *Democracy and the Global Order*. Cambridge: Polity Press.

Held, D., McGrew, A., Goldblatt, D. and Perraton, J. (1999) *Global Transformations: Politics, Economic and Culture*. Cambridge: Polity Press.

Henrici, J. (1999) Trading culture: Tourism and tourist art in Pisac, Peru. In M. Robinson and P. Boniface (eds) *Tourism and Cultural Conflicts* (pp. 161–80). Wallingford: CAB International.

Henwood, D. (1998) The Americanization of global finance. *NACLA Report on the Americas* 33 (1), 13–20.

Hettne, B. (1995) *Development Theory and the Three Worlds*. New York: Longman.

Hewitt, T. (2000) Half a century of development. In T. Allen and A. Thomas (eds) *Poverty and Development into the 21st Century* (pp. 289–308). Oxford: Oxford University Press.

Hiernaux-Nicolas, D. (1999) Cancún bliss. In D. Judd and S. Fainstein (eds) *The Tourist City* (pp. 124–39). New Haven, CT: Yale University Press.

Higgins, B. and Higgins, J. (1979) *Economic Development of a Small Planet*. New York: W.W. Norton.

Higgins, B. and Savoie, D. (1988) Introduction: The economics and politics of regional development. In B. Higgins and D. Savoie (eds) *Regional Economic Development Essays in Honour of François Perroux* (pp. 1–27). Boston, MA: Unwin Hyman.

Hiller, H.L. (1976) Escapism, penetration and response: Industrial tourism and the Caribbean. *Caribbean Studies* 16 (2), 92–116.

Hills, T.L. and Lundgren, J. (1977) The impact of tourism in the Caribbean. *Annals of Tourism Research* 4 (5), 248–67.

Hindness, B. and Hirst, P. (1975) *Pre-Capitalist Modes of Production*. London: Routledge and Kegan Paul.

Hirschman, A. (1958) *The Strategy of Economic Development*. New Haven, CT: Yale University Press.

Hirschmann, A. (1968) *Development Projects Observed*. Washington, DC: Brookings Institution.

Hirst, P. and Thompson, G. (1996) *Globalization in Question*. Cambridge: Polity Press.

Hitchcock, M. (2001) Tourism and total crisis: The case of Bali. *Asia Pacific Business Review* (forthcoming).

Hitchcock, M., King, V. and Parnwell, M. (1993) Tourism in South-East Asia: Introduction. In M. Hitchcock, V. King and M. Parnwell (eds) *Tourism in South-East Asia* (pp. 1–31). London: Routledge.

Hoggart, K., Buller, H. and Black, R. (1995) *Rural Europe: Identity and Change*. London: Arnold.

Høivik, T. and Heiberg, T. (1980) Centre-periphery tourism and self-reliance. *International Social Science Journal* 32 (1), 69–98.

Holbrook, M. and Hirschman, E. (1982) The experiential aspects of consumption: Consumer fantasies, feelings and fun. *Journal of Consumer Research* 9, 132–40.

Holcomb, B. (1999) Marketing cities for tourism. In D. Judd and S. Fainstein (eds) *The Tourist City* (pp. 54–70). New Haven, CT: Yale University Press.

Holden, A. (2000) *Environment and Tourism*. London: Routledge.

Holden, P. (1984) *Alternative Tourism with a Focus on Asia*. Chiang Mai, Thailand: Ecumenical Coalition on Third World Tourism.

Holling, C., Schindler, D., Walker, B. and Roughgarden, J. (1995) Biodiversity in the functioning of ecosystems: An ecological synthesis. In C. Perrings, K. Maler, C. Folke, C. Holling and B. Jansson (eds) *Biodiversity Loss: Economic and Ecological Issues* (pp. 44–83). Cambridge: Cambridge University Press.

Holt (1995) How consumers consume: A typology of consumption practices. *Journal of Consumer Research* 22 (June), 1–16.

Honey, M. (1999) *Ecotourism and Sustainable Development: Who Owns Paradise?* Washington, DC: Island Press.

Hoogvelt, A. (1997) *Globalisation and the Postcolonial World: The New Political Economy of Development*. London: Macmillan.

Hope, K.R. (1993) The subterranean economy in developing societies: Evidence from Latin America and the Caribbean. *Journal of Development Studies* 9, 156–66.

Horochowski, K. and Moisey, R. (1999) The role of environmental NGOs in sustainable tourism development: A case study in Northern Honduras. *Tourism Recreation Research* 24 (2).

Hoselitz, B. (1960) *Sociological Aspects of Economic Growth*. Glencoe, IL: Free Press.

Howard, D. and Madrigal, R. (1990) Who makes the decision: The parent or the child? The perceived influence of parents and children on the purchase of recreation services. *Journal of Leisure Research* 22 (3), 244–58.

Hudson, R. (1999) The new economy of the new Europe: Eradicating divisions or creating new forms of uneven development? In R. Hudson and A.M. Williams (eds) *Divided Europe: Society and Territory* (pp. 29–62). London: Sage.

Hudson, R. and Townsend, A. (1992) Employment and policy for local government. In P. Johnson and B. Thomas (eds) *Perspectives on Tourism Policy* (pp. 49–68). London: Mansell.

Hudson, R. and Williams, A.M. (1999) Re-shaping Europe: The challenge of new divisions within a homogenized political-economic space. In R. Hudson and A.M. Williams (eds) *Divided Europe: Society and Territory* (pp. 1–28). London: Sage.

Hughes, G. (1996) Tourism and the environment: A sustainable partnership. *Scottish Geographical Magazine* 112 (2), 107–13.

Hugo, G. (1992) Women on the move: Changing patterns of population movement of women in Indonesia. In S. Chant (ed.) *Gender and Migration in Developing Countries* (pp. 174–96). London: Belhaven Press.

Hulme, D. and Murphree, M. (1999) The 'new conservation' in Africa: An introduction to this book. In D. Hulme and M. Murphree (eds) *African Wildlife and Livelihoods: The Promise and Performance of Community Conservation* (pp. 1–15). London: James Currey.

Hulme, D. and Woodhouse, P. (2001) Governance and the environment: Politics and policy. In P. Woodhouse, H. Bernstein and D. Hulme (eds) *African Enclosures? The Social Dynamics of Land and Water* (pp. 215–32). London: James Currey.

Hunter, C. (1995) On the need to re-conceptualise sustainable tourism development. *Journal of Sustainable Tourism* 3 (3), 155–65.

Hunter, C. (1997) Sustainable tourism as an adaptive paradigm. *Annals of Tourism Research* 24 (4), 850–67.

Hunziker, W. and Krapf, K. (1942) *Grundriss der Allgemeinen Fremdenverkehrslehre*. Zürich: Polygraphischer.

Hurley, A., Archer, B. and Fletcher, J. (1994) The economic impact of European Community grants for tourism in the Republic of Ireland. *Tourism Management* 15 (3), 203–11.

Husbands, W. (1981) Centres, peripheries, tourism and socio-spatial development. *Ontario Geography* 17, 37–60.

Husbands, W. (1983) The genesis of tourism in Barbados: Further notes on the welcoming society. *Caribbean Geographer* 2, 107–20.

Huybers, T. and Bennett, J. (2000) Impact of the environment on holiday destination choices of prospective UK tourists: Implications for tropical North Queensland. *Tourism Economics* 6, 21–46.

Hvenegaard, G. (1994) Ecotourism: A status report and conceptual framework. *Journal of Tourism Studies* 5 (2), 24–35.

ICIDI (1980) *North–South: A Programme for Survival*. London: Pan Books.

ILO (1972) *Employment, Incomes and Equity: A Strategy for Increasing Productive Employment in Kenya*. Geneva: ILO.

Ingham, B. (1993) The meaning of development: Interactions between new and old ideas. *World Development* 21 (11), 1803–21.

Inskeep, E. (1991) *Tourism Planning: An Integrated and Sustainable Development Approach*. New York: Van Nostrand Reinhold.

Inskeep, E. (1991) *Tourism Planning: An Integrated and Sustainable Development Approach*. New York: John Wiley and Sons.

Inskeep, E. (1994) Training for tourism in developing countries. In A.V. Seaton, C.L. Jenkins, R.C. Wood, P.U.C. Dieke, M.M. Bennett, L.R. MacLellan and R. Smith (eds) *Tourism: The State of the Art* (pp. 563–70). Chichester: John Wiley and Sons.

Inskeep, E. and Kallenberger, M. (1992) *An Integrated Approach to Resort Development: Six Case Studies* (A Tourism and the Environment Publication). Madrid: World Tourism Organisation.

Instituto del Tercer Mundo (1999) *The World Guide 1999/2000: A View from the South*. Oxford: New Internationalist Publications.

International Transport Worker's Federation (1999) Lufthansa's union busting in Britain. On WWW at http://www.itf.org.uk/SECTIONS/Ca/LSGpress.html. Accessed 4.8.00.

Ioannides, D. (1992) Tourism development agents: The Cypriot resort cycle. *Annals of Tourism Research* 19 (4), 711–31.

Ioannides, D. (1995) Strengthening the ties between tourism and economic geography: A theoretical agenda. *Professional Geographer* 47 (1), 49–60.

Ioannides, D. (1998) Tour operators: The gatekeepers of tourism. In D. Ioannides and K. G. Debbage (eds) *The Economic Geography of the Tourist Industry* (pp. 139–58). London: Routledge.

Ioannides, D. and Debbage, K. (eds) (1998) *The Economic Geography of the Tourist Industry: A Supply-side Analysis*. London: Routledge.

Ioannides, D. and Debbage, K. (1998) Neo-Fordism and flexible specialization in the travel industry: Dissecting the polyglot. In D. Ioannides and K. G. Debbage (eds) *The Economic Geography of the Tourist Industry* (pp. 99–122). London: Routledge.

Isard, W. (1956) *Location and Space Economy*. Cambridge, MA: MIT Press

Iso-Ahola, S. (1982) Towards a social psychological theory of tourism motivation: A rejoinder. *Annals of Tourism Research* 9 (2), 256–62.

IUCN (1991) *Caring for the Earth: A Strategy for Sustainable Living*. Gland, Switzerland: World Conservation Union.

Jaakson, R. (2000) Supra-national spatial planning of the Baltic Sea region and competing narratives for tourism. *European Planning Studies* 8 (5), 565–79.

Jacobs, M. (1994) The limits of neoclassicism: Towards an institutional environmental economics. In M. Redclift and T. Benton (eds) *Social Theory and the Global Environment* (pp. 67–91). London: Routledge.

Jafari, J. (1977) Editors page. *Annals of Tourism Research* 5 (1), 8.

Jafari, J. (1987) Tourism models: The sociocultural aspects. *Tourism Management* 8 (2): 151–9.

Jafari, J. (1989) Sociocultural dimensions of tourism: An English language literature review. In J. Bystrzanowski (ed.) *Tourism as a Factor of Change: A Sociocultural Study* (pp. 17–60). Vienna: Vienna Centre.

Jamal, T. and Getz, D. (1995) Collaboration theory and community tourism planning. *Annals of Tourism Research* 22 (1), 186–204.

James, C. (2000) Caribbean braced for rush of competition in tourism sector. *Financial Times* (19 October).

Jansen-Verbeke, M. and Lievois, E. (1999) Analysing heritage resources for urban tourism in European cities. In D. Pearce and R. Butler (eds) *Contemporary Issues in Tourism Development* (pp. 81–107). London: Routledge.

Jenkins, C.L. (1980a) Education for tourism policy makers in developing countries. *International Journal of Tourism Management* 1, 238–42.

Jenkins, C.L. (1980b) Tourism policies in developing countries: A critique. *International Journal of Tourism Management* 1 (1), 22–9.

Jenkins, C.L. (1982) The use of investment incentives for tourism projects in developing countries. *Tourism Management* (June), 91–7.

Jenkins, C.L. (1982) The effects of scale in tourism projects in developing countries. *Annals of Tourism Research* 9 (2), 229–49.

Jenkins, C.L. (1991) Tourism development strategies. In L. Lickorish (ed.) *Developing Tourism Destinations* (pp. 61–77). Harlow: Longman.

Jenkins, C.L. (1991) Development strategies. In L.J. Lickorish, A. Jefferson, J. Bodlender and C.L. Jenkins (eds) *Developing Tourism Destinations* (pp. 59–118). London: Longman.

Jenkins, C.L. and Henrey, B. (1982) Government involvement in tourism in developing countries. *Annals of Tourism Research* 9 (4), 499–521.

Jenner, P. and Smith, C. (1992) *The Tourism Industry and the Environment* (Special Report no. 2453). London: Economist Intelligence Unit.

Johnson, P. and Thomas, B. (1992) *Perspectives on Tourism Policy*. London: Mansell.

Jurdao, F. A. (1990) *España en Venta* (2nd edn). Madrid: Ediciones Endymion.

Kamal, R. and Fisher H. (1988) Change and development in the Arab world – advance amid diversity: An economic and social analysis. In J. Norwine and A. Gonzalez (eds) *The Third World: States of Mind and Being* (pp. 196–208). Boston, MA: Unwin Hyman.

Kamrava, M. (1993) *Politics and Society in the Third World*. London: Routledge.

Kamsma, T. and Bras, K. (2000) Gili Trawangan – from desert island to marginal paradise: Local participation, small-scale entrepreneurs and outside investors in an Indonesian tourist destination. In G. Rechards and D. Hall (eds) *Tourism and Sustainable Community Development* (pp. 170–84). London: Routledge.

Kappert, J. (2000) Community and rural development in Northern Portugal. In G. Rechards and D. Hall (eds) *Tourism and Sustainable Community Development* (Routledge Advances in Tourism Series) (pp. 258–67). London: Routledge.

Kariel, H. (1989) Tourism and development: Perplexity or panacea? *Journal of Travel Research* 28 (1), 2–6.

Karyadi, N. (2000) Views from around the world. *In Focus* 37 (Autumn), 9.

Keating, M. (1994) *The Earth Summit's Agenda For Change A Plan Language Version of Agenda 21 and the Other Rio Agreements*. Geneva: Centre for our Common Future.

Keller, C.P. (1984) Centre–periphery tourism development and control. In J. Long and R. Heacock (eds) *Leisure, Tourism and Social Change, University of Edinburgh 1983*. Dunfermline, UK: Centre for Leisure Research, Dunfermline College of Physical Education.

Keller, P. (1999) Future-oriented tourism policy – synthesis of the 49th AIEST Congress. *Tourism Review* 54 (3), 2–6.

Kemper, R. (1979) Tourism in Taos and Patzcuaro: A comparison of two approaches to regional development. *Annals of Tourism Research* 6 (1), 91–110.

Kendie, S.B. (1995) The environmental dimensions of structural adjustment programmes: Missing links to sustaining development. *Singapore Journal of Tropical Geography* 16 (1), 42–57.

Kermath, B.M. and Thomas, R.N. (1992) Spatial dynamics of resorts: Sosúa, Dominican Republic. *Annals of Tourism Research* 19 (3), 173–90.

Kiely, R. (1995) *Sociology and Development: The Impasse and Beyond*. London: UCL Press.

King, D. and Stewart, W. (1996) Ecotourism and commodification: Protecting people and places. *Biodiversity and Conservation* 5 (3), 293–305.

King, R. (1995) Tourism, labour and international migration. In A. Montanarai and A. Williams (eds) *European Tourism: Regions, Spaces and Restructuring* (pp. 177–90). Chichester: John Wiley and Sons.

Kinnaird, V. and Hall, D. (eds) (1994) *Tourism: A Gender Analysis*. Chichester: Wiley.

Kinnaird, V., Kothari, U. and Hall, D. (1994) Tourism: Gender perspectives. In V. Kinnaird and D. Hall (eds) *Tourism: A Gender Analysis* (pp. 1–33). Chichester: John Wiley and Sons.

Klenesky, D., Gengler, C. and Mulvey, M. (1993) Understanding the factors influencing ski destination choice: A means-end analytic approach. *Journal of Leisure Research* 25, 362–79.

Knox, J.M. (1982) Resident-visitor interaction: A review of the literature and general policy alternatives. In F. Rajotte (ed.) *The Impact of Tourism Development in the Pacific* (pp. 76–106). Peterborough, ON: Environmental and Resource Studies Program, Trent University.

Konadu-Agyemang, K. (2000) The best of times and the worst of times: Structural adjustment programs and uneven development in Africa: The case of Ghana. *Professional Geographer* 52 (3), 469–83.

Kontogeorgopoulos, N. (1999) Sustainable tourism or sustainable development? Financial crisis, ecotourism, and the 'Amazing Thailand' campaign. *Journal of Sustainable Tourism* 2 (4), 316–32.

Korten, D. (1980) Community organisation and rural development: A learning process approach. *Public Administration Review* 40 (5), 480–51.

Kotler, P, Haider, D. and Rein, I. (1993) *Marketing Places: Attracting Investment, Industry and Tourism to Cities, States and Nations.* New York: Free Press.

Kousis, M. (2000) Tourism and the environment: A social movements perspective. *Annals of Tourism Research* 27 (2), 468–89.

Krapf, K. (1961) Les pays en voie de développement face au tourisme: Introduction méthodologique. *Revue de Tourisme* 16 (3), 82–9.

Krippendorf, J. (1986) Tourism in the system of industrial society. *Annals of Tourism Research* 13 (4), 517–32.

Krippendorf, J. (1987) *The Holiday Makers: Understanding the Impact of Leisure and Travel.* Oxford: Heinemann.

Krippendorf, J. (1991) Towards new tourism policies. In S. Medlik (ed.) *Managing Tourism* (pp. 307–17). Oxford: Butterworth-Heinemann.

Krippendorf, J. (1994) *The Holiday Makers. Understanding the Impact of Leisure and Travel.* Oxford: Butterworth-Heinemann.

Kruhse-MountBurton, S. (1995) Sex tourism and traditional Australian male identity. In M.-F. Laclau, E. and C. Mouffe (1985) *Hegemony and Social Strategy: Towards a Radical Democratic Politics.* London: Verso

Lal, D. (1985) The misconceptions of 'development economics'. *Finance and Development* 22. Reprinted in K. Wilber (ed.) (1988) *The Political Economy of Development and Underdevelopment* (4th edn) (pp. 28–36). Toronto: McGraw-Hill.

Lane, B. (1990) Sustaining host areas, holiday makers and operators alike. *Conference Proceedings, Sustainable Tourism Development Conference.* Queen Margaret College, Edinburgh, November.

Lane, B. (1994) What is rural tourism? *Journal of Sustainable Tourism* 2, 7–12.

Lanfant, J. Allcock and E. Bruner (eds) *International Tourism: Identity and Change* (pp. 192–204). London: Sage.

Lanfant, M. and Graburn, N. (1992) International tourism reconsidered: The principle of the alternative. In V. Smith and W. Eadington (eds) *Tourism Alternatives: Potentials and Problems in the Development of Tourism* (pp. 88–112). Philadelphia: University of Pennsylvania Press.

Larrain, J. (1989) *Theories of Development.* Cambridge: Polity Press.

Lash, S. (1990) *Sociology of Postmodernism.* London: Routledge.

Lea, J. (1988) *Tourism and Development in the Third World* (Routledge Introductions to Development Series). London: Routledge.

Lea, J.P. (1993) Tourism development ethics in the Third World. *Annals of Tourism Research* 20, 701–15.

Leach, M. and Mearns, R. (1996) *The Lie of the Land: Challenging Received Wisdom on the African Environment.* London: James Currey.

Lee, G. (1987) Tourism as a factor in development cooperation. *Tourism Management* 8 (1), 2–19.

Lee, K. (1993) *Compass and Gyroscope Integrating Science and Politics for the Environment.* Washington, DC: Island Press.

Leheny, D. (1995) The political economy of sex tourism. *Annals of Tourism Research* 22 (2), 367–84.

Lélé, S. (1991) Sustainable development: A critical review. *World Development* 19 (6), 607–21.

Leontidou, L. (1994) Gender dimensions of tourism in Greece: Employment, sub-cultures and restructuring. In V. Kinnaird and D. Hall (eds) *Tourism: A Gender Analysis* (pp. 74–105). Chichester: John Wiley and Sons.

Lerch, P.B. and Levy, D.E. (1990) A solid foundation: Predicting success in Barbados' tourist industry. *Human Organization* 49 (4), 355–63.

Lett, J. (1983) Ludic and liminoid aspects of charter yacht tourism in the Caribbean. *Annals of Tourism Research* 10 (1), 35–56.

Lett, J. (1989) Epilogue to touristic studies in anthropological perspective. In V. Smith (ed.) *Hosts and Guests: The Anthropology of Tourism* (2nd edn) (pp. 265–79). Philadelphia: University of Pennsylvania Press.

Lever, A. (1987) Spanish tourism migrants. The case of Lloret de Mar. *Annals of Tourism Research* 14 (4), 449–70.

Levine, D. (1988) *Arguing for Socialism: Theoretical Considerations.* London: Verso.

Levy, D.E. and Lerch, P.B. (1991) Tourism as a factor in development. Implications for gender and work in Barbados. *Gender and Society* 5 (1), 67–85.

Lewis, W.A. (1954) Economic development with unlimited supplies of labour. *The Manchester School* 26 (2). Reprinted in M. Gersovitz (ed.) (1983) *Selected Economic Writings of W. Arthur Lewis* (pp. 311–63). New York: New York University Press.

Lillywhite, M. and Lillywhite, L. (1991) Low impact tourism. In D. Hawkins and J. Brent Ritchie (eds) *World Travel and Tourism Review: Indicators, Trends and Forecasts* (pp. 162–9). Wallingford: CAB International.

Lindayati, R. and Nelson, G. (1995) Land use change in Bali: A study of tourism development in Kelurahan Sanur. In S. Martopo and B. Mitchell (eds) *Bali: Balancing Environment, Economy and Culture* (Department of Geography Publication Series no. 44) (pp. 411–36). Waterloo: University of Waterloo.

Lipscomb, A.J.H. (1998) Village-based tourism in the Solomon Islands: Impediments and impacts. In E. Laws, B. Faulkner and G. Moscardo (eds) *Embracing and Managing Change in Tourism: International Case Studies* (pp. 185–201). London: Routledge.

Lloyd, P. and Dicken, P. (1977) *Location in Space: A Theoretical Approach to Economic Geography* (2nd edn). London: Harper and Row.

Loening, U. (1990) The ecological challenges to growth. *Development Journal of SID* 3 (4), 48–54.

Long V.H. and Kindon, S.L. (1997) Gender and tourism development in Balinese villages. In M. Sinclair (ed.) *Gender, Work and Tourism* (pp. 91–119). London: Routledge.

Long, V. and Wall, G. (1993) Balinese 'homestays': An indigenous response to tourism. Paper presented at 13th International Congress of Anthropological and Ethnological Sciences, Mexico City, 28 July – 2 August.

Long, V.H. and Wall, G. (1995) Small-scale tourism development in Bali. In M.V. Conlin and T. Baum (eds) *Island Tourism: Management Principles and Practice* (pp. 237–57). Chichester: John Wiley and Sons.

Longhurst, C.A. (1993) Regionalism and economic disparities: Three perspectives. *Journal of the Association of Iberian Studies* 6 (1), 32–41.

Lord, J. (1998) Building genuine partnerships: Potential, principles and problems. *Journal of Leisureability* 25, 3–10.

Lovatt-Smith, D. (1993) *Amboseli: Nothing Short of a Miracle*. Nairobi: Kenway.

Lovel, H. and Feuerstein, M.T. (1992) Editorial introduction: After the carnival – tourism and community development. *Community Devleopment Journal* 27 (4), 335–52.

Lovelock, J. (1979) *Gaia: A New Look at Life on Earth*. Oxford: Oxford University Press.

Lowe, P. and Rüdig, W. (1986) Review article: Political ecology and the social sciences – the state of the art. *British Journal of Political Science* 16, 513–50.

Lowenthal, D. (1985) *The Past is a Foreign Country*. Cambridge: Cambridge University Press.

Ludwig, D., Hilborn, R. and Walters, C. (1993) Uncertainty, resource exploitation and conservation: Lessons from history. *Science* 269 (5104), 17 and 36.

Lujan, C.C. (1998) A sociological view of tourism in an American Indian community: Maintaining cultural integrity at Taos Pueblo. In A.A. Lew and G.A. Van Otten (eds) *Tourism and Gaming on American Indian Lands* (pp. 145–59). New York: Cognizant.

Lummis, C.D. (1991) Development against democracy. *Alternatives* 16, 31–66.

Lundgren, J. (1975) Tourist penetration / the tourist product / entrepreneurial response. In F.M. Helleiner (ed.) *Proceedings of The International Geographical Union's Group, Tourism as a Factor in National and Regional Development* (Occasional Paper 4). Peterborough, ON: Department of Geography, Trent University.

Lury, C. (1996) *Consumer Culture*. Cambridge: Polity Press.

Lynn, W. (1992) Tourism in the people's interest. *Community Development Journal* 27 (4), 371–7.

Mabogunje, A. (1980) *The Development Process: A Spatial Perspective*. London: Hutchinson.

MacCannell, D. (1989) *The Tourist: A New Theory of the Leisure Class* (2nd edn). New York: Schocken Books.

Mackun, P. (1998) Tourism in the Third Italy: Labor and social-business networks. In D. Ioannides and K. Debbage (eds) *The Economic Geography of the Tourist Industry* (pp. 256–70). London: Routledge.

Macnaghten, P. and Urry, J. (1998) *Contested Natures*. London: Sage.

Macnaught, T. (1982) Mass tourism and the dilemmas of modernisation in Pacific Islands Communities. *Annals of Tourism Research* 9 (3), 359–81.

Madeley, J. (1996) *Foreign Exploits: Transnationals and Tourism*. CIIR Briefing. London: Catholic Institute for International Relations.

Magec, Ben (2000) *Boletín Informativo Trimestral* 4 (Autumn). Published in association with *Ecologista* 22 (Autumn).

Malecki, E. (1997) *Technology and Economic Development* (2nd edn). Harlow: Longman.

Mander, J. (1999) How cyber culture deletes nature. *Ecologist* 29 (3), 171.

Mappisammeng, A. (1991) Tourism development and human resources in Indonesia. Paper presented at the seminar on Tourism Planning and Development, Jakarta, November.

Marchena Gómez, M. (1995) New spatial trends and the future of Mediterranean Europe. *Tidschrift voor Economische en Sociale Geografie* 86 (1), 21–31.

Maslow, A. (1943) A theory of human motivation. *Psychological Review* 50, 370–96.

Maslow, A. (1970) *Motivation and Personality*. New York: Harper and Row.

Mason, P. and Mowforth, M. (1995) *Codes of Conduct in Tourism* (Occasional Papers in Geography 1). Plymouth: Department of Geographical Sciences, University of Plymouth.

Mathews, H. (1978) *International Tourism A Political and Social Analysis*. Cambridge, MA: Schenkman.

Mathews, H. and Richter, L. (1991) Political science and tourism. *Annals of Tourism Research* 18 (1), 120–35.

Mathieson, A. and Wall, G. (1982) *Tourism: Economic, Physical, and Social Impacts*. London: Longman.

May, V. (1991) Tourism, environment and development: Values, sustainability and steward-ship. *Tourism Management* 12 (2), 112–18.

McCarthy, J. (1994) *Are Sweet Dreams Made of This? Tourism in Bali and Eastern Indonesia*. Northcote, Australia: Indonesia Resources and Information Program.

McCormick, J. (1995) *The Global Environmental Movement* (2nd edn). Chichester: John Wiley and Sons.

McCracken (1986) Culture and consumption: A theoretical account of the structure and movement of the cultural meaning of consumer goods. *Journal of Consumer Research* 13 (June), 71–84.

McDonnel, I. and Darcy, S. (1998). Tourism precincts: A factor in Bali's rise in fortune and Fiji's fall from favour – An Australian perspective. *Journal of Vacation Marketing* 4 (4), 353–67.

McGee, T.G. (1982) *Labor Markets, Urban Systems, and the Urbanization Process in Southeast Asian Countries*. Honolulu: East-West Center.

McIntosh, R. and Goeldner, C.R. (1984) *Tourism: Principles, Practices, Philosophies* (4th edn). Columbus: Grid.

McKay, J. (1990) The development model. *Development Journal of SID* 3, 55–9.

McKean, M. and Ostrom, E. (1995) Common property regimes in the forest: Just a relic from the past? *Unasylva* 180, 3–15.

McKercher, B. (1993a) Some fundamental truths about tourism: Understanding tourism's so-cial and environmental impacts. *Journal of Sustainable Tourism* 1 (1), 6–16.

McKercher, B. (1993b) The unrecognised threat to tourism: Can tourism survive sustainability? *Tourism Management* 14 (2), 131–6.

McLaren, D. (1998) *Rethinking Tourism and Ecotravel*. West Hartford, CT: Kumarian Press.

Meadows, D.H., Meadows, D.L., Randers, J. and Behrens, W. (1972) *Limits to Growth*. London: Pan Books.

Mehmet, O. (1995) *Westernising the Third World: The Eurocentricity of Economic Development Theories*. London: Routledge.

Meier, G. (2001) Introduction: Ideas for development. In G. Meier and J. Stiglitz (eds) *Frontiers of Development Economics* (pp. 1–12). Oxford: Oxford University Press and the World Bank.

Mellor, M. (1997) *Feminism and Ecology*. Cambridge: Polity Press.

Michaud, J. (1991) A social anthropology of tourism in Ladakh (India). *Annals of Tourism Research* 18 (4), 605–21.

Michaud, J. (1997) A portrait of cultural resistance: The confinement of tourism in a Hmong village in Thailand. In M. Picard and R.E. Wood (eds) *Tourism, Ethnicity and the State in Asian and Pacific Societies* (pp. 124–58). Honolulu: University of Hawaii Press.

Middleton, V. (1977) Some implications of overseas tourism for regional development. In B.S. Duffield (ed.) *Tourism: A Tool for Regional Development* (pp. 1–11). Edinburgh: Tourism and Recreation Research Unit, University of Edinburgh.

Middleton, V. (1998) *Sustainable Tourism: A Marketing Approach*. Oxford: Butterworth-Heinemann.

Middleton, V. and Hawkins, R. (1993) Practical environmental policies in travel and tour-ism – Part I: The hotel sector. *Travel and Tourism Analyst* 6, 63–76.

Middleton, V. and Hawkins, R. (1994) Practical environmental policies in travel and tour-ism – Part II: Airlines, tour operators and destinations. *Travel and Tourism Analyst* 1, 83–97.

Middleton, V. and Hawkins, R. (1998) *Sustainable Tourism: A Marketing Perspective*. Oxford: Butterworth-Heinemann.

Mieczkowski, Z. (1995) *Environmental Issues of Tourism and Recreation*. Lanham, MD: University Press of America.

Mignolo, W. (1988) Globalization, civilization processes, and the relocation of languages and culture. In F. Jameson and M. Miyoshi (eds) *The Culture of Globalization* (pp. 32–53). Durham, NC: Duke University Press.

Mihalic, T. (1999) Equity in outgoing tourism through tourist certificates. *International Journal of Contemporary Hospitality Management* 11, 128–31.

Mihalic, T. (2000) Increasing tourism competitiveness through granting concessions to natural goods. In M. Robinson, J. Swarbrooke, N. Evans, P. Long and R.Sharpley (eds) *Reflections on International Tourism: Environmental Management and Pathways to Sustainable Tourism* (pp. 133–51). Sunderland: Business Education.

Miles-Doan, R. (1992) Class differentiation and the informal sector in Amman, Jordan. *International Journal of Middle East Studies* 24, 27–38.

Miller, D.B. and Branson, J. (1989) Pollution in paradise: Hinduism and the subordination of women in Bali. In P. Alexander (ed.) *Creating Indonesian Cultures* (pp. 91–112). Sydney: Oceania.

Milne, S. (1987) Differential multipliers. *Annals of Tourism Research* 14 (4), 499–515.

Milne, S. (1992) Tourism and development in South Pacific microstates. *Annals of Tourism Research* 19 (2), 191–212.

Milne, S. (1998) Tourism and sustainable development: The global-local nexus. In C.M. Hall and A. Lew (eds) *Sustainable Tourism: A Geographical Perspective* (pp. 35–48). Harlow: Longman.

Milne, S. and. Milne, K. (1998) Distribution technologies and destination development: Myths and realities. In D. Ioannides and K.G. Debbage (eds) *The Economic Geography of the Tourist Industry* (pp. 123–38). London: Routledge.

Mintel (1994) *The Green Consumer I: The Green Conscience*. London: Mintel International.

Miossec, J.M. (1976) Elements pour une theorie de l'espace touristique. *Les Cahiers du Tourisme* C-36. CHET, Aix-en-Provence: Mintel.

Mishan, E. (1969) *The Costs of Economic Growth* (2nd edn). Harmondsworth: Penguin.

Mitchell, B. (1989) *Geography and Resource Analysis* (2nd edn). New York: Longman.

Mitchell, R.E. and Reid, D.G. (2001) Community integration: Island tourism in Peru. *Annals of Tourism Research* 28 (1), 113–39.

Moedjanto, G. (1986) *The Concept of Power in Javanese Culture*. Yogyakarta: Gadjah Mada University Press.

Mohan, G. Brown, E., Milward, B. and Zack-Williams, A. (2000) *Structural Adjustment Theory, Practice and Impacts*. London: Routledge.

Momsen, J. (1991) *Women and Development in the Third World* (Routledge Introductions to Development Series). London: Routledge.

Momsen, J. (1994) Tourism, gender and development in the Caribbean. In V. Kinnaird and D. Hall (eds) *Tourism: A Gender Analysis* (pp. 106–20). Chichester: John Wiley and Sons.

Monk, J. and Alexander, C. (1986) Free port fallout: Gender, employment, and migration on Margarita Island. *Annals of Tourism Research* 13, 393–413.

Morell, M. (2001) The Eco-tax in the Balearics: Where politics and the environment meet tourism. Unpublished Masters dissertation, University of North London.

Morgan, H. (2000) A taxing time. *Tourism in Focus* 37, 6–7.

Morgan, N. and Pritchard, A. (1998) *Tourism Promotion and Power: Creating Images, Creating Identities*. Chichester: John Wiley and Sons.

Moser, C. (1989) Gender planning in the Third World: Meeting strategic and practical gender needs. *World Development* 17 (11), 1799–825.

Moser, C.O. (1991) Gender planning in the Third World: Meeting practical and strategic needs. In R. Grant and K. Newland (eds) *Gender and International Relations* (pp. 83–121). Buckingham: Open University Press.

Mosley, P. and Toye, J. (1988) The design of structural adjustment programs. *Development Policy Review* 6 (4), 395–413.

Moutinho, L. (1987) Consumer behaviour in tourism. *European Journal of Marketing* 21 (10), 5–44.

Mowforth, M. and Munt, I. (1998) *Tourism and Sustainability: New Tourism in the Third World*. London: Routledge.

Müller, H. (1994) The thorny path to sustainable tourism development. *Journal of Sustainable Tourism* 2 (3), 131–6.

Muller, R. (1979) The multinational corporation and the underdevelopment of the Third World. In C. Wilber (ed.) *The Political Economy of Development and Underdevelopment* (1st edn) (pp. 124–51). New York: Random House. (Originally published 1973.)

Mun, T. (1965) England's treasure by forraign trade or the balance of our forraign trade is the rule of our treasure. In *Reprints of Economic Classics*. New York: Augustus M. Kelley.

Munro, D. (1995) Sustainability: Rhetoric or reality? In T. Trzyna and J. Osborn (eds) *A Sustainable World: Defining and Measuring Sustainable Development* (pp. 27–35). Sacramento: International Center for the Environment and Public Policy for the World Conservation Union.

Munt, I. (1994) The 'other' postmodern tourism: Culture, travel and the new middle classes. *Theory, Culture and Society* 11 (3), 101–23.

Murphree, M. and Hulme, D. (1998) Communities, wildlife and the 'new conservation' in Africa. *Journal of International Development* 11 (2), 277–85.

Murphy, P.E. (1983) Tourism as a community industry: An ecological model of tourism development. *Tourism Management* 14 (3), 180–93.

Murphy, P.E. (1985) *Tourism: A Community Approach*. London: Routledge.

Murphy, P.E. (1988a) Community driven tourism planning. *Tourism Management* 9 (2), 96–104.

Murphy, P.E. (1998b) Tourism and sustainable development. In W.F. Theobald (ed.) *Global Tourism* (2nd edn) (pp. 173–89). Oxford: Butterworth-Heinemann.

Myrdal, G. (1963) *Economic Theory and Under-Developed Regions*. London: University Paperbacks.

Naím, M. (2001) McAtlas shrugged. *Foreign Policy* 124 (May/June), 26–37.

Narotzky, S. (1997) *New Directions in Economic Anthropology*. London: Pluto Press

Nash, D. (1981) Tourism as an anthropological subject. *Current Anthropology* 22 (5), 461–81.

Nash, D. (1989) Tourism as a form of imperialism. In V. Smith (ed.) *Hosts and Guests: The Anthropology of Tourism* (2nd edn) (pp. 37–52). Philadelphia: University of Pennsylvania Press.

Nelson, J. (1993a) An introduction to tourism and sustainable development with special reference to monitoring. In J.G. Nelson, R.W Butler and G. Wall (eds) *Tourism and Sustainable Development: Monitoring, Planning, Managing* (Heritage Resources Centre Joint Publication 1) (pp. 3–25). University of Waterloo.

Nelson, J.G. (1993b) Are tourism growth and sustainability objectives compatible? Civics, assessment. Informed choice. In J.G. Nelson, R.W Butler and G. Wall (eds) *Tourism and Sustainable Development: Monitoring, Planning, Managing* (Heritage Resources Centre Joint Publication 1) (pp. 259–65). University of Waterloo.

Nelson, J.G., Butler, R.W. and Wall, G. (eds) (1993c) *Tourism and Sustainable Development: Monitoring, Planning, Managing* (Heritage Resources Centre Joint Publication 1). University of Waterloo.

Norem, R., Yoder, H. and Martin, Y. (1989) Indigenous agricultural knowledge and gender issues in Third World agricultural development. In D.M. Warren, L.J. Slikkerveer and S.O. Titilola (eds) *Indigenous Knowledge Systems: Implications for Agriculture and International Development* (pp. 91–100). Iowa State University: Technology and Social Change Program with the Academy for Educational Development.

Norris, J. and Wall, G. (1994) Gender and tourism. *Progress in Tourism, Recreation and Hospitality Management* 6, 57–78.

Nuryanti, W. (1998) Tourism and regional imbalances: The case of Java. *Indonesia and the Malay World* 26 (75), 136–44.

O'Dell Management (1999) *Niagara Investment Opportunities: A Report Prepared for Niagara Economic Tourism Corporation.* Niagara Falls, ON: Niagara Economic Tourism Corporation.

O'Reilly, T. (1986) Tourism carrying capacity: Concepts and issues. *Tourism Management* 8 (2), 254–8.

O'Connor, J. (2000) The big squeeze. *Tourism In Focus* (Summer), 4–5.

Oey-Gardiner, M. (1991) Gender differences in schooling in Indonesia. *Bulletin of Indonesian Economic Studies* 27 (1), 57–79.

Oglethorpe, M.K. (1984) Tourism in Malta: A crisis of dependence. *Leisure Studies* 3, 147–61.

Ogorelec, P., Planina, J. and Sirše, J. (1981) *Turizem v slovenskem gospodarstvu in njegova vloga v dolgorocnem razvoju SR Slovenije.* Ljubljana: Institut za ekonomska raziskovanja.

O'Grady, R. (1980) *Code of Ethics for Tourists.* Geneva: World Council of Churches.

Oliver-Smith, F., Arrones, F.J. and Arcal, J.L. (1989) Tourist development and the struggle for local control. *Human Organization* 48 (4), 345–51.

Oman, C. and Wignaraja, G. (1991) *The Postwar Evolution of Development Thinking.* New York: St Martin's Press.

Oppermann, M. (1992) International tourism and regional development in Malaysia. *Tijdschrift voor Economische en Sociale Geografie* 83 (3), 226–33.

Oppermann, M. (1993) Tourism space in developing countries. *Annals of Tourism Research* 20 (3), 535–56.

Oppermann, M. (1998) *Sex Tourism and Prostitution: Aspects of Leisure, Recreation and Work.* Elmsford, NY: Cognizant.

Oppermann, M. and Chon, K. (1997) *Tourism in Developing Countries.* London: International Thomson Business Press.

Osborne, C. (1993) Making the most out of tourism. *In Focus: Tourism Concern* 10, 10–11.

Osirim, M.J. (1992) The state of women in the Third World: The informal sector and development in Africa and the Caribbean. *Social Development Issues* 14 (2, 3), 74–87.

Ousby, I. (1990) *The Englishman's England: Taste, Travel and the Rise of Tourism.* Cambridge: Cambridge University Press.

Overholt, C. (1991) Case 4: Indonesia: The P2WIK-UNDP Batik Project. In A. Rao, M. Anderson and C. Overholt (eds) *Gender Analysis in Development Planning: A Case Book* (pp. 55–70). West Hartford, CT: Kumarian Press.

Page, S. and Getz, D. (1997) The business of rural tourism. In S. Page and D. Getz (eds) *The Business of Rural Tourism* (pp. 3–37). London: International Thomson Business Press.

Palmer, C. (1994) Tourism and colonialism: The experience of the Bahamas. *Annals of Tourism Research* 21 (4), 792–811.

Papa, M. (1999) Development of tourism in Albania. MA thesis, Faculty of Economics and International Center for Promotion of Enterprises, Ljubljana.

Parker, R. (1999) Las Vegas – casino gambling and local culture. In D. Judd and S. Fainstein (eds) *The Tourist City* (pp. 107–23). New Haven, NJ: Yale University Press.

Parker, S. (1999) Collaboration on tourism policy making: Environment and commercial sustainability on Bonaire, N.A. *Journal of Sustainable Tourism* 7 (3/4), 240–59.

Parnwell, M. (1993) *Population Movements and the Third World*. London: Routledge.

Parrinello, G. (1993) Motivation and anticipation in post-industrial tourism. *Annals of Tourism Research* 20 (2), 233–49.

Parsons, T. (1966) *Societies: Evolutionary and Comparative Perspectives*. Englewood Cliff, NJ: Prentice Hall.

Pass, C., Lowes, B. and Davies, L. (1993) *Collins Dictionary of Economics* (2nd edn). Glasgow: Harper Collins.

Passariello, P. (1983) Never on a Sunday? Mexican tourists at the beach. *Annals of Tourism Research* 10 (1), 109–22.

Patterson, K. (1993) Aloha! ' Welcome to Paradise'. *New Internationalist* 245 (July), 13–15.

Pattullo, P. (1996) *Last Resorts: The Cost of Tourism in the Caribbean*. London: Cassell / Latin American Bureau.

Pearce, D.G. (1987) *Tourism Today: A Geographical Analysis*. New York: Longman.

Pearce, D.G. (1989a) Using the literature on tourism: A personal perspective. *Tourism Review* 3, 5–11.

Pearce, D.G. (1989b) *Tourist Development* (2nd edn). New York: Longman.

Pearce, D.G. (1992) *Towards Sustainable Development through Environmental Assessment* (CSERGE Working Paper PA92-11). Norwich: CSERGE.

Pearce, D.G. (1993) Introduction. In D.G. Pearce and R.W. Butler (eds) *Tourism Research Critiques and Challenges*. New York: Routledge.

Pearce, D.G. (1997) Tourism and the autonomous communities in Spain. *Annals of Tourism Research* 24 (1), 156–77.

Pearce, D.G. and Butler, R.W. (eds) (1993) *Tourism Research Critiques and Challenges*. New York: Routledge.

Pearce, D.G., Markandya, A. and Barbier, E. (1989) *Blueprint for a Green Economy*. London: Earthscan.

Pearce, D.G., Barbier, E. and Markandya, A. (1990) *Sustainable Development: Economics and the Environment in the Third World*. London: Earthscan.

Pearce, P. (1992) Fundamentals of tourist motivation. In D. Pearce and R. Butler (ed.) *Tourism Research: Critiques and Challenges* (pp. 113–34). London: Routledge.

Pedersen, K. and Viken, A. (1996) From Sami nomadism to global tourism. In M. Price (ed.) *People and Tourism in Fragile Environments* (pp. 69–88). Chichester: John Wiley and Sons.

Peet, R. (1999) *Theories of Development*. New York: Guilford Press

Peppelenbosch, P. and Tempelman, G. (1973) Tourism and the developing countries. *Tijdschrift voor Economische en Sociale Geografie* 64 (1), 52–8.

Peppelenbosch, P. and Tempelman, G. (1989) The pros and cons of international tourism to the Third World. In T.V. Singh, L. Theuns and F.M. Go (eds) *Towards Appropriate Tourism: The Case of Developing Countries* (pp. 23–34). Frankfurt: Peter Lang.

Perez Jr, L. (1973) Tourism underdevelops tropical islands. *Science and Society* 37. Reprinted in I. Voleger and A. De Souza (eds) (1980) *Dialectics of Third World Development* (pp. 249–55). Montclair: Allanheld, Osmun.

Pérez, L.A. (1980) How tourism underdevelops tropical islands. In I. Vogeler and A. de Souza (eds) *Dialectics of Third World Development* (pp. 249–55). Montclair, NJ: Allanheld, Osmun.

Perrons, D. (1999) Deconstructing the Maastricht myth? Economic and social cohesion in Europe: Regional and gender dimensions of inequality. In R. Hudson. and A.M. Williams (eds) *Divided Europe: Society and Territory* (pp. 186–209). London: Sage.

Perroux, F. (1988) The pole of development's new place in a general theory of economic activity. In B. Higgins and D. Savoie (eds) *Regional Economic Development: Essays in Honour of Francois Perroux* (pp. 48–76). Boston, MA: Hyman.

Peters, M. (1969) *International Tourism: The Economics and Development of the International Tourist Trade*. London: Hutchinson.

Picard, M. (1995) Cultural tourism in Bali. In M.-F. Lanfant, J. Allcock and E. Bruner (eds) *International Tourism: Identity and Change* (pp. 44–66). London: Sage.

Picard, M. (1997) Cultural tourism in Bali: The construction of a cultural heritage. In W. Nuryanti (ed.) *Tourism and Heritage Management* (pp. 147–64). Yogyakarta: Gadja Mada University Press.

Pick, A. and Pick, H. Jr (1978) Culture and perception. In E. Carterette and M. Friedman (eds) *Handbook of Perception Volume X: Perceptual Ecology* (pp. 19–39). London: Academic.

Pigram, J.J. (1990) Sustainable tourism – policy considerations. *Journal of Tourism Studies* 1 (2), 2–9.

Pi-Sunyer, O. (1989) Changing perceptions of tourism and tourists in a Catalan resort town. In V. Smith (ed.) *Hosts and Guests: The Anthropology of Tourism* (2nd edn) (pp. 187–99). Philadelphia: University of Pennsylvania Press.

Pizam, A. and Smith, G. (2000) Tourism and terrorism: A quantitative analysis of major terrorist acts and their impact on tourist destinations. *Tourism Economics* 6, 123–38.

Pizam, A., Milman, A. and King. B. (1994) The perceptions of tourism employees and their families toward tourism. A cross-cultural comparison. *Tourism Management* 15 (1), 53–61.

Place, S. (1995) Ecotourism for sustainable development: Oxymoron or plausible strategy? *Geojournal* 35 (2), 161–73.

Place, S.E. (1998) How sustainable is ecotourism in Costa Rica? In C.M. Hall and A. Lew (eds) *Sustainable Tourism: A Geographical Perspective* (pp. 107–108). Harlow: Addison Wesley Longman.

Planina, J. (1997) *Ekonomika Turizma*. Ljubljana: Ekonomska Fakulteta.

Pleumarom, A. (1994) The political economy of tourism. *Ecologist* 24 (4), 142–8.

Plog, S. (1977) Why destination areas rise and fall in popularity. In E.M. Kell (ed.) *Domestic and International Tourism* (pp. 26–8). Wellesley, MA: Institute of Certified Travel Agents.

Poirier, R.A. (1995) Tourism and development in Tunisia. *Annals of Tourism Research* 27 (1), 155–71.

Polunin, I. (1989) Japanese travel boom. *Tourism Management* 10, 4–8.

Pongsapich, A. (1982) Interplay of tradition and modernization in the fishing and tourist industries of Thailand. In G.B. Hainsworth (ed.) *Village-Level Modernization in Southeast Asia* (pp. 335–56). Vancouver: University of British Columbia Press.

Poon, A. (1993) *Tourism, Technology and Competitive Strategies*. Wallingford: CAB International.

Popper, K.R. (1990) *The Open Society and its Enemies, Volume 2, Hegel and Marx*. London: Routledge (first published 1945).

Porter. M. (1990) *The Competitive Advantage of Nations*. New York: Free Press.

Porter, M. (1998) *On Competition, A Harvard Business Review Book*. Boston, MA: Harvard Business School.

Potter, D. (2000) Democratisation, 'good governance' and development. In T. Allen and A. Thomas (eds) *Poverty and Development into the 21st Century* (pp. 365–82). Oxford: Oxford University Press.

Potts, F., Goodwin, H. and Walpole, M. (1996) People, wildlife and tourism in and around Hwange National Park, Zimbabwe. In M. Price (ed.) *People and Tourism in Fragile Environments* (pp. 199–219). Chichester: John Wiley and Sons.

Preister, K. (1989) The theory and management of tourism impacts. *Tourism Recreation Research* 14 (1), 15–22.

Prentice, R. (1993) Community-driven tourism planning and residents' preferences. *Tourism Management* 14, 218–27.

Preston, P.W. (1996) *Development Theory: An Introduction*. Oxford: Blackwell.

Preston, R. (1984) Relationships between classical central place theory and growth-centre based regional development strategies. In C. Bryant (ed.) *Waterloo Lectures in Geography Volume 1, Regional Economic Development* (pp. 73–115). Waterloo: Department of Geography, University of Waterloo.

Pretes, M. (1995) Postmodern tourism: The Santa Claus industry. *Annals of Tourism Research* 22 (1), 1–15.

Pretty, J. (1994) Alternative systems of inquiry for a sustainable agriculture. *Institute of Development Studies Bulletin* 25 (2), 37–48.

Pretty, J. (1995) The many interpretations of participation. *Focus* 16, 4–5.

Price, M. (ed.) (1996a) *People and Tourism in Fragile Environments*. Chichester: John Wiley and Sons.

Price, M. (1996b) Fragile environments, fragile communities? An introduction. In M. Price (ed.) *People and Tourism in Fragile Environments* (pp. 1–18). Chichester: John Wiley and Sons.

Price, S. (1988) *Behind the Planter's Back*. London: Macmillan.

Prideaux, B. (1999) Tourism perspectives of the Asian financial crisis: Lessons for the future. *Current Issues in Tourism* 2 (4), 279–93.

Priestly, G., Edwards, J. and Cocossis, H. (eds) (1996) *Sustainable Tourism? European Experiences*. Wallingford: CAB International.

Pryce, A. (1998) The World Bank group and tourism. *Travel and Tourism Analyst* 5, 75–90.

Rachbini, D.J. (1991) Some reflections on dualism in the urban informal economy. *Prisma* 51, 46–59.

Radiven, N. and Lucas, R. (1997) Minimum wages and pay policy in the British hospitality industry: Past impact and future implications. *Progress in Tourism and Hospitality Research* 3, 149–63.

Rahnema, M. (1997) Towards post-development: Searching for signposts, a new language and new paradigms. In M. Rahnema and V. Bawtree (eds) *The Post-Development Reader* (pp. 377–403). London: Zed Books.

Rahnema, M. and Bawtree, V. (1997) *The Post-Development Reader*. London: Zed Books.

Rajotte, F. (1987) Safari and beach resort tourism: The costs to Kenya. In S.G. Britton and W.C. Clarke (eds) *Ambiguous Alternative* (pp. 78–90). Suva: University of the South Pacific.

Ranck, S. (1987) An attempt at autonomous development: The case of the Tufi guest houses, Papua New Guinea. In S. Britton and W. Clark (eds) *Ambiguous Alternative Tourism in Small Developing Countries* (pp. 154–66). Suva: University of the South Pacific.

Rao, N. (2000) Invisible hands. Invisible bodies. *Tourism in Focus* (Summer), 16.

Ray, D. (1998) *Development Economics*. Princeton, NJ: Princeton University Press.

Redclift, M. (1984) *Development and the Environmental Crisis: Red or Green Alternatives?* London: Methuen.

Redclift, M. (1987) *Sustainable Development: Exploring the Contradictions*. New York: Routledge.

Redclift, M. (1992) The meaning of sustainable development. *Geoforum* 23 (3), 395–403.

Redclift, M. (1994) Sustainable development: Economics and the environment. In M. Redclift and C. Sage (eds) *Strategies for Sustainable Development Local Agendas for the Southern Hemisphere* (pp. 17–34). New York: John Wiley and Sons.

Redclift, M. (2000) *Sustainability, Life Chances and Livelihoods*. London: Routledge.

Rees, W. (1990) The ecology of sustainable development. *Ecologist* 20 (1), 370–92.

Reid, D. (1995) *Sustainable Development: An Introductory Guide*. London: Earthscan.

Richards, G. (2000) Tourism and mobility in the European Union: Crossing the North–South divide. Paper presented to the 7th ATLAS International Conference, Savonlinna, Finland, 18–21 June.

Richards, G. and Hall, D. (eds) (2000) *Tourism and Sustainable Community Development*. London: Routledge.

Richez, G. (1994) Le tourisme dans une région périphérique: L'exemple de l'île de Corse (France). *Téoros* 13 (1), 34–7.

Richter, C. (1986) Tourism services. In O. Giarini (ed.) *The Emerging Service Economy* (pp. 213–44). Oxford: Pergamon Press.

Rickard, T. and Carmichael, B. (1995) Linkages between the agricultural and tourism system in sustaining rural development in Jamaica. In C. Bryant and C. Marois (eds) *Proceedings, First Meeting of the IGU Study Group on the Sustainability of Rural Systems* (pp. 316–30). Montreal: Departement de Geographie, Universite de Montreal.

Rieder, L.G. (1992) Bali village tourism mission activities and findings. Unpublished draft report. Indonesia: UNDP.

Rist, G. (1997) *The History of Development from Western Origins to Global Faith*. London: Zed Books.

Ritchie, J. and Crouch, G. (1993) Competitiveness in international tourism – a framework for understanding and analysis. *Competitiveness of Long Haul Destinations* (pp. 23–71). St Gallen: AIEST.

Roberts, M. (1998) Travel and tourism survey. *Economist* (10 January).

Robertson, R. and Khondker, H.H. (1998) Discourses of globalization: Preliminary considerations. *International Sociology* 13 (1), 25–40.

Robie, C., Bateson, A., Ellison, P. and Figler, M. (1993) An analysis of the tourism motivation construct. *Annals of Tourism Research* 20 (4), 773–6.

Robinson, M. (1999) Cultural conflicts in tourism: Inevitability and inequality. In M. Robinson and P. Boniface (eds) *Tourism and Cultural Conflicts* (pp. 1–32). Wallingford: CAB International.

Roche, M. (1992) Mega-events and micro-modernisation: On the sociology of new urban tourism. *British Journal of Sociology* 43 (4), 563–600.

Rodenburg, E. (1980) The effects of scale in economic development: Tourism in Bali. *Annals of Tourism Research* 7 (2), 177–96.

Rodríguez, M. and Portales, J. (1994) Tourism and NAFTA: Towards a regional tourism policy. *Tourism Management* 15 (5), 319–22.

Rondinelli, D.A. (1982) The dilemma of development administration: Complexity and uncertainty in control-oriented bureaucracies. *World Politics* 35 (1), 42–72.

Rostow, W. (1960) *The Stages of Economic Growth: A Non-Communist Manifesto*. Cambridge: Cambridge University Press.

Rostow, W. (1967) *The Stages of Economic Growth A Non-Communist Manifesto* (2nd edn). Cambridge: University Press.

Rowbotham, M. (1998) *The Grip of Death: A Study of Modern Money, Debt Slavery and Destructive Economics*. Charlbury: Jon Carpenter.

Rowell, A. (1996) *Green Backlash: Global Subversion of the Environmental Movement*. London: Routledge.

Russell, E. (1953) *World Population and World Food Supplies*. London: Allen and Unwin.

Ryan, C. (1991) *Recreational Tourism: A Social Science Perspective*. London: Routledge.

Ryan, C. (1997) The chase of a dream, the end of a play. In C. Ryan (ed.) *Tourist Experience: A New Introduction* (pp. 1–24). London: Cassell.

Ryan, C. and Hall, C.M. (2001) *Sex Tourism: Marginal People and Liminalities*. New York: Routledge.

Ryan, C., Hughes, K. and Chirgwin, S. (2000) The gaze, spectacle and ecotourism. *Annals of Tourism Research* 27 (1), 148–63.

Sachs, W. (ed.) (1996) Introduction. *The Development Dictionary: A Guide to Knowledge as Power* (pp. 1–6). London: Zed Books.

Saglio, C. (1979) Tourism for discovery: A project in Lower Casamance, Senegal. In E. de Kadt (ed.) *Tourism: Passport to Development?* (pp. 321–35). New York: Oxford University Press.

Sahlins, M. (1997) The original affluent society. In M. Rahnema and V. Bawtree (ed.) *The Post-Development Reader* (pp. 3–21). London: Zed Books.

Said, E. (1978) *Orientalism*. New York: Pantheon Books.

Said, E. (1993) *Culture and Imperialism*. Toronto: Random House of Canada.

Samy, J. (1980) Crumbs from the table: The workers' share in tourism? In F. Rajotte and R. Crocombe (eds) *Pacific Tourism: As Islanders See It* (pp. 67–82). Fiji: University of the South Pacific.

Sandford, D. and Dong, H. (2000: 217) Investment in familiar territory: Tourism and new foreign direct investments. *Tourism Economics* 6, 205–19.

Schafer, J. (1989) Utilizing indigenous agricultural knowledge in the planning of agricultural research projects designed to aid small-scale farmers. In D.M. Warren, L.J. Slikkerveer and S.O. Titilola (eds) *Indigenous Knowledge Systems: Implications for Agriculture and International Development* (pp. 116–20). Technology and Social Change Program with the Academy for Educational Development, Iowa State University.

Scheyvens, R. (1999) Ecotourism and the empowerment of local communities. *Tourism Management* 20, 245–9.

Schmidt, H. (1989) What makes development. *Development and Cooperation* 6, 19–26.

Schnell, P. (1998) Germany: Still growing an international deficit? In A. Williams and G. Shaw (eds) *Tourism and Economic Development: European Experiences* (3rd edn) (pp. 269–300). Chichester: John Wiley and Sons.

Schumacher, E. (1974) *Small is Beautiful: A Study of Economics as if People Mattered*. London: Abacus.

Schumpeter, J.A. (1934) *The Theory of Economic Development*. Cambridge, MA: Harvard University Press. In B. Higgins, and J. Higgins (eds) (1979) *Economic Development of a Small Planet*. New York: W.W. Norton.

Schumpeter, J.A. (1949) *The Theory of Economic Development*. Cambridge, MA: Harvard University Press.

Schumpeter, J.A. (1961) *The Theory of Economic Development An Inquiry into Profits, Capital, Credit, Interest, and the Business Cycle*. Cambridge, MA: Harvard University Press.

Schuurman, F. (1993) Introduction: Development theory in the 1990s. In F. Schuurman (ed.) *Beyond the Impasse: New Directions in Development Theory* (pp. 1–48). London: Zed Books.

Scoones, I. (ed.) (1995) *Living with Uncertainty: New Directions in Pastoral Development in Africa*. London: Intermediate Technology.

Scott, J. (1997) *Corporate Business and Capitalist Classes*. New York: Oxford University Press.

Scott, J. (1999) Peripheries, artificial peripheries and centres. In F. Brown and D. Hall (eds) *Tourism in the Peripheral Areas of Europe: Case Studies of Tourism in Peripheral Areas* (Report 15) (pp. 73–90). Bornholm, Denmark: Unit of Tourism Research.

Seabrook, J. (1996) *Travels in Skin Trade: Tourism and the Sex Industry*. London: Pluto Press.

Seers, D. (1969) The meaning of development. *International Development Review* 11 (4), 2–6.

Seers, D. (1977) The new meaning of development. *International Development Review* 19 (3), 2–7.

Seifert-Granzin, J. and Jesupatham, D. Samuel (1999) *Tourism at the Crossroads: Challenges to Developing Countries by the New World Trade Order*. Frankfurt am Main: Equations/Tourism Watch.

Seligson, M.A. and Passé-Smith, J.T. (eds) (1993) *Development and Underdevelopment: The Political Economy of Inequality*. Boulder, CO: Reinner.

Selwyn, T. (1993) Peter Pan in South-East Asia: Views from the brochures. In M. Hitchcock, V. King and M. Parnwell (eds) *Tourism in South-East Asia* (pp. 117–37). London: Routledge.

Selwyn, T. (2000) De-Mediterraneanisation of the Mediterranean? *Current Issues in Tourism* 3 (3), 226–45.

Sen, A. (1994) Development: Which way now? In R. Kanth (ed.) *Paradigms of Economic Development* (pp. 211–31). New York: M.E. Sharpe.

Sen, A. (1999) *Development as Freedom*. New York: Anchor Books.

Sessa, A. (1983) *Elements of Tourism Economics*. Roma: Catal.

Seward, S.B. and Spinrad, B.K. (1982) *Tourism in the Caribbean. The Economic Impact*. Ottawa: IDRC.

Sethuraman, S.V. (1992) Urbanisation, employment and the environment. In A.S. Bhalla (ed.) *Environment, Employment and Development* (pp. 121–40). Geneva: ILO.

Sharpley, R. (1994) *Tourism, Tourists and Society*. Cambridgeshire: ELM.

Sharpley, R. (1996) Tourism and consumer culture in postmodern society. In M. Robinson *et al.* (eds) *Tourism and Cultural Change*. Sunderland: Business Education Publishers.

Sharpley, R. (1998) *Island Tourism Development: The Case of Cyprus*. Sunderland: Business Education.

Sharpley, R. (2000) Tourism and sustainable development: Exploring the theoretical divide. *Journal of Sustainable Tourism* 8 (1), 1–19.

Sharpley, R. (2000b) In defence of (mass) tourism. In M. Robinson, J. Swarbrooke, N. Evans, P. Long and R. Sharpley (eds) *Reflections on International Tourism: Environmental Management and Pathways to Sustainable Tourism*. Sunderland: Business Education.

Sharpley, R. (2001) Tourism in Cyprus: Challenges and opportunities. *Tourism Geographies* 3 (1): 64–86.

Sharpley, R. and Sharpley, J. (1996) Tourism in West Africa: The Gambian experience. In A. Badger *et al.* (eds) *Trading Places: Tourism as Trade* (pp. 27–33). London: Tourism Concern.

Sharpley, R. and Sharpley, J. (1997) *Rural Tourism: An Introduction*. London: International Thomson Business Press

Sharpley, R., Sharpley, J. and Adams, J. (1996) Travel advice or trade embargo? The impacts and implications of official travel advice. *Tourism Management* 17 (1), 1–7.

Shaw, G. and Williams, A. (1990) Tourism, economic development and the role of entrepreneurial activity. *Progress in Tourism, Recreation and Hospitality Management* 2, 67–81.

Shaw, G. and Williams, A.M. (1994) *Critical Issues in Tourism: A Geographical Perspective*. Oxford: Blackwell.

Shaw, G. and Williams, A. (1998) Entrepreneurship, small business culture and tourism development. In D. Ioannides and K. Debbage (eds) *The Economic Geography of the Tourist Industry* (pp. 235–55). London: Routledge.

Sherman, H.L. (1987) *Foundations of Radical Political Economy*. Armonk, NY: M.E. Sharpe.

Shields, R. (1991) *Places on the Margin: Alternative Geographies of Modernity*. London: Routledge.

Shivji, I. G. (1975) *Tourism and Socialist Development*. Dar Es Salam: Tanzania Publishing House.

Shoji, N. (1991) The privatisation of Borobudur. *Inside Indonesia* 28, 13–14.

Silver, I. (1993) Marketing authenticity in Third World countries. *Annals of Tourism Research* 20 (2), 302–18.

Simmons, D. (1994) Community participation in tourism planning. *Tourism Management* 15 (2), 98–108.

Sinclair, M.T. (1991) The economics of tourism. *Progress in Tourism, Recreation and Hospitality Management* 3, 1–27.

Sinclair, M.T. (1997) *Gender Work and Tourism*. London: Routledge.

Sinclair, M. and Pack, A. (2000) Tourism and conservation: The application of economic policy instruments to wildlife tourism in Zimbabwe. In P. Dieke (ed.) *The Political Economy of Tourism Development in Africa* (pp. 181–92). New York: Cognizant.

Sinclair, M. and Stabler, M. (1997) *The Economics of Tourism*. London: Routledge.

Sinclair, M.T., Alizadeh, P. and Atieno Adero Onunga, E. (1995) The structure of international tourism and tourism development in Kenya. In D. Harrison (ed.) *Tourism in the Less Developed Countries* (pp. 47–63). Chichester: John Wiley and Sons.

Sindiga, I. (1999) *Tourism and African Development: Change and Challenge of Tourism in Africa*. Aldershot: Ashgate.

Singer, H.W. and Ansari, J.A. (1992) *Rich and Poor Countries. Consequences of International Disorder* (4th edn). New York: Routledge.

Singh, T., Theuns, H. and Go, F. (eds) (1989) *Towards Appropriate Tourism: The Case of Developing Countries*. Frankfurt am Main: Peter Lang.

Sklair, L. (1991) *Sociology of the Global System*. Hemel Hempstead: Harvester Wheatsheaf.

Sklair, L. (1995) *Sociology of the Global System* (2nd edn). Baltimore, MD: Johns Hopkins University Press.

Sklair, L. (2001) *The Transnational Capitalist Class*. Oxford: Blackwell.

Skolimowski, H. (1995) In defence of sustainable development. *Environmental Values* 4, 69–70.

Skrobanek, S., Boonpakdi, B. and Janthakeero, C. (1997) *The Traffic in Women: Human Realities of the International Sex Trade*. London: Zed Books.

Smaoui, A. (1979) Tourism and employment in Tunisia. In E. de Kadt (ed.) *Tourism: Passport to Development* (pp. 101–10). Washington: UNESCO.

Smeral, E. (1994) Economic models. In S. Witt and L. Moutinho (eds) *Tourism Marketing and Management Handbook* (2nd edn) (pp. 497–503). New York: Prentice Hall.

Smeral, E. (1998) The impact of globalization on small and medium enterprises: New challenges for tourism policies in European countries. *Tourism Management* 19 (4), 371–80.

Smil, V. (1993) *Global Ecology: Environmental Change and Social Flexibility*. London: Routledge.

Smith, S. (1989) *Tourism Analysis: A Handbook*. New York: Longman.

Smith, S. (1994) The tourism product. *Annals of Tourism Research* 21 (3), 582–95.

Smith, S. (1995) *Tourism Analysis: A Handbook* (2nd edn). New York: Longman.

Smith, S. (1998) Tourism as an industry, debates and concepts. In D. Ioannides and K. Debbage (eds) *The Economic Geography of the Tourist Industry* (pp. 31–52). London: Routledge.

Smith, S.L.J. (1988) Defining tourism. A supply-side view. *Annals of Tourism Research* 15, 170–90.

Smith, T.B. (1985) Evaluating development policies and programmes in the Third World. *Public Administration and Development* 5 (2), 129–44.

Smith, V. (ed.) (1977) *Hosts and Guests – The Anthropology of Tourism.* Philadelphia: University of Pennsylvania Press.

Smith, V.L. (1990) Responsible tourism some anthropological issues. *Tourism Recreation Research* 18 (1), 45–9.

Smith, V.L. (1998) Privatization in the Third World: Small-scale tourism enterprises. In W.F. Theobald (ed.) *Global Tourism* (2nd edn) (pp. 205–15). Oxford: Butterworth Heinemann.

Smith, V. and Eadington, W. (eds) (1992) *Tourism Alternatives: Potentials and Problems in the Development of Tourism.* Philadelphia: University of Pennsylvania Press.

Sneddon, C. (2000) 'Sustainability' in ecological economics, ecology and livelihoods: A review. *Progress in Human Geography* 24 (4), 521–49.

So, A. (1990) *Social Change and Development Modernisation, Dependency, and World-System Theory.* London: Sage.

Sofield, T. (1993) Indigenous tourism development. *Annals of Tourism Research* 20 (4), 12–24.

Solomon, M. (1994) *Consumer Behaviour: Having, Buying and Being* (2nd edn). Needham Heights, MA: Allyn and Bacon.

Sotto, H. (1993) The missing ingredient. *Economist* (11 November), 8–10.

South Commission (1990) *The Challenge To The South The Report of the South Commission.* Toronto: Oxford University Press.

Southgate, C. and Hulme, D. (2001) Uncommon property: The scramble for wetland in southern Kenya. In P. Woodhouse, H. Bernstein and D. Hulme (eds) *African Enclosures? The Social Dynamics of Wetlands in Drylands.* London: James Currey.

Stabler, M. (ed.) *Tourism and Sustainability: Principles to Practice.* Wallingford: CAB International.

Stalker, P. (2000) *Workers without Frontiers: The Impact of Globalization on International Migration.* Geneva/London: ILO/Lynne Rienner

Stamp, L. (1953) *Our Undeveloped World.* London: Faber and Faber.

Stanley, N. (1998) *Being Ourselves for You: The Global Display of Cultures* (Material Culture Series). London: Middlesex University Press.

Staudt, K. (1998) *Policy, Politics and Gender: Women Gaining Ground.* West Hartford, CT: Kumarian Press.

Steene, A. (2001) Personal correspondence, 14 March.

Steer, A. and Wade-Gery, W. (1993) Sustainable development: Theory and practice for a sustainable future. *Sustainable Development* 1 (3), 23–35.

Strang, V. (1996) Sustaining tourism in far north Queensland. In M.F. Price (ed.) *People and Tourism in Fragile Environments* (pp. 109–22). Chichester: John Wiley and Sons.

Strange, S. (1988) *States and Markets. An Introduction for International Political Economy.* London: Pinter.

Strange, S. (1994a) Wake up Krasner, the world *has* changed! *Review of International Political Economy* 1 (2), 210–19.

Strange, S. (1994b) *States and Markets* (2nd edn). London: Pinter.

Strange, S. (1996) *The Retreat of the State: The Diffusion of Power in the World Economy* (Cambridge Studies in International Relations 49). Cambridge: Cambridge University Press.

Streeten, P. (1977) The basic features of a basic needs approach to development. *International Development Review* 3, 8–16.

Svenson, T. (1991) Theories and mythologies of the Third World. In M. Morner (ed.) *The Transformation of Rural Society in the Third World.* New York: Routledge.

Swain, M.B. (1995) Gender in tourism. *Annals of Tourism Research* 22 (2), 247–66.

Swarbrooke, J. (1999) *Sustainable Tourism Management*. Wallingford: CAB International.

Swarbrooke, J. (2000) Tourism, economic development and urban regeneration: A critical evaluation. In M. Robinson, R. Sharpley, N. Evans, P. Long and J. Swarbrooke (eds) *Reflections on International Tourism: Developments in Urban and Rural Tourism* (pp. 269–85). Sunderland: Business Education.

Swarbrooke, J. and Horner, S. (1999) *Consumer Behaviour in Tourism*. Oxford: Butterworth-Heinemann.

Szivas, E. and Riley, M. (1999) Tourism employment during economic transition. *Annals of Tourism Research* 26 (4), 747–71.

Telfer, D.J. (1996a) Development through economic linkages: Tourism and agriculture in Indonesia. Unpublished PhD dissertation, University of Waterloo, Waterloo.

Telfer, D.J. (1996b) Food purchases in a five-star hotel: A case study of the Aquila Prambanan Hotel, Yogyakarta, Indonesia. *Tourism Economics, The Business and Finance of Tourism and Recreation* 2 (4), 321–38.

Telfer, D.J. (2000a) The Northeast wine route: Wine tourism in Ontario, Canada and New York State. In C.M. Hall *et al.* (eds) *Wine and Tourism From Around the World* (pp. 253–71). London: Butterworth Heinemann.

Telfer, D.J. (2000b) Tastes of Niagara: Building strategic alliances between tourism and agriculture. *International Journal of Hospitality and Tourism Administration* 1 (1), 71–88.

Telfer, D.J. (2000c) Agritourism – a path to community development? The case of Bangunkerto, Indonesia. In G. Richards and D. Hall (eds) *Tourism and Sustainable Community Development* (pp. 242–57). London: Routledge.

Telfer, D.J. (2001a) From a wine tourism village to a regional wine route: An investigation of the competitive advantage of embedded clusters in Niagara, Canada. *Tourism Recreation Research* 26 (2), 23–33.

Telfer, D.J. (2001b) Strategic alliances along the Niagara wine route. *Tourism Management* 22 (1), 21–30.

Telfer, D.J. (in press) Development issues in destination communities. In S. Singh, D.J. Timothy and R.K. Dowling (eds) *Tourism and Destination Communities*. Wallingford: CAB International.

Telfer, D.J. and Hashimoto, A. (1999) Resident attitudes towards tourism development in Niagara-on-the-Lake. Unpublished report, prepared for TEMCO. Department of Recreation and Leisure Studies, Brock University, St Catharines, ON.

Telfer, D.J. and Hashimoto, A. (2000) Niagara icewine tourism: Japanese souvenir purchases at Inniskillin Winery. *Tourism and Hospitality Research: The Surrey Quarterly Review* 2 (4), 343–56.

Telfer, D.J. and Wall, G. (1996) Linkages between tourism and food production. *Annals of Tourism Research* 23 (3), 635–53.

Telfer, D.J. and Wall, G. (2000) Strengthening backward economic linkages: Local food purchasing by three Indonesian hotels. *Tourism Geographies* 2 (4), 421–47.

Tester, F. and Drover, G. (1996) Offsetting corporate trade: Free trade, community development and alternative trade in the South Pacific. *Alternatives Journal* 22 (1), 16–22.

Teye, V. (1986) Liberation wars and tourism development in Africa: The case of Zambia. *Annals of Tourism Research* 13 (4), 589–608.

Teye, V. (2000) Regional cooperation and tourism development in Africa. In P. Dieke (ed.) *The Political Economy of Tourism Development in Africa* (pp. 217–27). New York: Cognizant.

The Myths of Tourism Economic Imperialism in Third World Tourism (1981) *Impact Asian Magazine for Human Development* 16 (1), 12–14.

Theobald, W. (1994) The context, meaning and scope of tourism. In W. Theobald (ed.) *Global Tourism: The Next Decade* (pp. 3–19). Oxford: Butterworth-Heinemann.

Thomas, A. (2000) Meaning and views of development. In T. Allen and A. Thomas (eds) *Poverty and Development into the 21st Century* (pp. 23–48). Oxford: Oxford University Press.

Thomas, R. (1996) Cheap labourers pawns in the takeover game. *Guardian* (19 January).

Thomson, C., O'Hare, G. and Evans, K. (1995) Tourism in the Gambia: Problems and proposals. *Tourism Management* 16 (8), 571–81.

Thurot, J. and Thurot, G. (1983) The ideology of class and tourism: Confronting the discourse of advertising. *Annals of Tourism Research* 10 (1), 173–89.

Timothy, D.J. (1995) Political boundaries and tourism: Borders as tourist attractions. *Tourism Management* 16 (7), 525–32.

Timothy, D.J. (1998) Cooperative tourism planning in a developing destination. *Journal of Sustainable Tourism* 6 (1), 52–68.

Timothy, D.J. (1999) Participatory planning: A view of tourism in Indonesia. *Annals of Tourism Research* 26, 371–91.

Timothy, D.J. (2000a) Cross-border partnership in tourism resource management: International parks along the US–Canada border. In B. Bramwell and B. Lane (eds) *Tourism Collaboration and Partnerships: Politics, Practice and Sustainability* (pp. 20–43). Clevedon: Channel View.

Timothy, D.J. (2000b) Tourism planning in Southeast Asia: Bringing down borders through cooperation. In K. Chon (ed.) *Tourism in Southeast Asia: A New Direction* (pp. 21–38). New York: Haworth Hospitality Press.

Timothy, D.J. (2000c) Building community awareness of tourism in a developing country destination. *Tourism Recreation Research* 25 (2), 111–16.

Timothy, D.J. (2001) Gender relations in tourism: Revisiting patriarchy and underdevelopment. In Y. Apostolopoulos, S. Sönmez and D.J. Timothy (eds) *Women as Producers and Consumers of Tourism in Developing Regions* (pp. 235–48). Westport, CT: Praeger.

Timothy, D.J. and Ioannides, D. (2002) Tour operator hegemony: Dependency and oligopoly in insular destinations. In Y. Apostolopoulos and D.J. Gayle (eds) *Island Tourism and Sustainable Development: Caribbean, Pacific, and Mediterranean Experiences*. Westport, CT: Praeger.

Timothy, D.J. and Wall, G. (1997) Selling to tourists: Indonesian street vendors. *Annals of Tourism Research* 24, 322–40.

Timothy, D.J. and White, K. (1999) Community-based ecotourism – development on the periphery of Belize. *Current Issues in Tourism* 2 (2/3), 226–42.

Tisdell, C. (1993) Project appraisal, the environment and sustainability for small islands. *World Development* 21 (2), 213–19.

Tjatera, W. (1994) A model for integrating sub-provincial traditional and official regional planning institutions to achieve sustainable development in Bali, Indonesia. PhD thesis, University of Waterloo, Canada.

Todaro, M. (1994) *Economic Development* (5th edn). New York: Longman.

Todaro, M. (1997) *Economic Development* (6th edn). New York: Longman.

Todaro, M. (2000) *Economic Development* (7th edn). Harlow: Addison-Wesley.

Tomljenovic, R. and Faulkner, B. (2000) Tourism and older residents in a sunbelt resort. *Annals of Tourism Research* 27 (1), 93–114.

Tosun, C. (2000) Limits to community participation in the tourism development process in developing countries. *Tourism Management* 21, 613–33.

Tosun, C. and Jenkins, C.L. (1996) Regional planning approaches to tourism development: The case of Turkey. *Tourism Management* 17 (7), 519–31.

Tosun, C. and Jenkins, C.L. (1998) The evolution of tourism planning in Third World countries: A critique. *Progress in Tourism and Hospitality Research* 4, 101–14.

Tribe, J. (1996) *The Economics of Leisure and Tourism: Environments, Markets and Impacts.* Oxford: Butterworth-Heinemann.

Tsartas, P. (1992) Socioeconomic impacts of tourism on two Greek isles. *Annals of Tourism Research* 19 (3), 516–33.

Tschurtschenthaler, P. (1986) *Das Landschaftsproblem in Fremdenverkehr dargestellt anhand der Situation des Alperaums.* Bern: Haupt.

Turner, L. (1973) Tourism – the most subversive industry. In *Multinational Companies and the Third World* (pp. 210–29). New York: Hill and Wang.

Turner, L. (1976) The international division of leisure: Tourism and the Third World. *World Development* 4 (3), 253–60.

Turner, L. and Ash, J. (1975) *The Golden Hordes: International Tourism and the Pleasure Periphery.* London: Constable.

Tyler, D. and Dangerfield, J.M. (1999) Ecosystem tourism: A resource-based philosophy for ecotourism. *Journal of Sustainable Tourism* 7 (2), 146–58.

Ullman-Magalit, E. (1977) Co-ordination norms and social choice. *Erkenntnis* 11, 143–55.

United Nations (1963) *Recommendations on International Travel and Tourism.* Geneva

UN (United Nations) (2000) *Statistical Yearbook* 44. New York: United Nations.

UNCTAD (1997) *World Investment Report: Transnational corporations, market structure and competition policy.* Geneva: United Nations Conference on Trade and Development.

UNCTAD (1998) *International Trade in Tourism-Related Series: Issues and Options for Developing Countries.* Geneva: United Nations Conference on Trade and Development.

UNCTAD (1999) Top 50 transnational corporations in developing countries, 1996. On WWW at http://www.unctad.org/en/subsites/dite/1_itncs/1_top50.htm. Accessed 18.1.00.

UNDP (1990) *Human Development Report.* New York: Oxford University Press.

UNDP (1992) *Comprehensive Tourism Development Plan for Bali* (vols I, II and annexes). UNDP.

UNDP (1996) *Human Development Report 1996.* New York: Oxford University Press.

UNDP (1998) *Human Development Report 1998.* New York: Oxford University Press.

UNDP (1999) *Human Development Report.* New York: Oxford University Press

UNESCO (1976) The effects of tourism on socio-cultural values. *Annals of Tourism Research* 4 (2), 74–105.

Unkovic, S. (1981) *Ekonomika turizma.* Beograd: Savremena administracija.

Urry, J. (1990a) The consumption of tourism. *Sociology* 24 (1), 32–5.

Urry, J. (1990b) *The Tourist Gaze.* London: Sage.

Urry, J. (1994) Cultural change and contemporary tourism. *Leisure Studies* 13 (4), 233–8.

Urry, J. (1995) *Consuming Places.* London: Routledge.

Urry, J. (2000) *Sociology Beyond Societies.* London: Routledge.

Van der Hoeven, R. (1988) *Planning for Basic Needs: A Soft Option or a Solid Policy? A Basic Needs Simulation Model Applied to Kenya.* Brookfield, VT: Gower.

Van der Straaten, J. (2000) Can sustainable tourism positively influence rural regions? In G. Rechards and D. Hall (eds) *Tourism and Sustainable Community Development* (Routledge Advances in Tourism Series), (pp. 221–32). London: Routledge.

Van der Werff, P.E. (1980) Polarizing implications of the Pescaia tourists industry. *Annals of Tourism Research* 7 (2), 197–223.

Van Doorn, J.W.M. (1989) A critical assessment of socio-cultural impact studies of tourism in the Third World. In T.V. Singh, L. Theuns and F.M. Go (eds) *Towards Appropriate Tourism: The Case of Developing Countries* (pp. 71–91). Frankfurt: Peter Lang.

Van Houts, D. (1983) Female participation in tourism employment in Tunisia: Some economic and non-economic costs and benefits. *Tourist Review* 38 (1), 25–30.

Van Raaij, W. and Francken, D. (1984) Vacation decisions, activities and satisfactions. *Annals of Tourism Research* 11 (1), 101–12.

Van Rekom, J. (1994) Adding psychological value to tourism products. In J. Crotts and W. van Raaij (eds) *Economic Psychology of Travel and Tourism* (pp. 21–36). New York: Haworth Press.

Varley, C.G. (1978) *Tourism in Fiji: Some Economic and Social Problems.* Wales: University of Wales Press.

Vaughan, R. and Long, J. (1982) Tourism as a generator of employment: A preliminary appraisal of the position in Great Britain. *Journal of Travel Research* 21 (2), 27–31.

Veblen, T. (1925) *The Theory of the Leisure Class: An Economic Study of Institutions.* London: Allen and Unwin.

Vellas, F. and Bécherel, L. (1995) *International Tourism: An Economic Perspective.* Basingstoke: Macmillan.

Vickers, A. (1989) *Bali: A Paradise Created.* Australia: Penguin.

Voase, R. (1995) *Tourism: The Human Perspective.* London: Hodder and Stoughton.

Wade, R. and Veneroso, F. (1998) The Asian crisis: The high debt model versus the Wall Street–Treasury–IMF complex. *New Left Review* 228, 3–22.

Wahnschafft, R. (1982) Formal and informal tourism sectors a case study in Pattaya, Thailand. *Annals of Tourism Research* 9 (3), 429–51.

Waldren, J. (1998) The road to ruin: The politics of development in the Balearic Islands. In S. Abram and J. Waldren (eds) *Anthropological Perspectives on Local Development* (pp. 120–40). Routledge.

Walker, A. (1989) *Marx: His Theory and its Content.* London: Rivers Oram Press.

Wall, G. (1993a) International collaboration in the search for sustainable tourism in Bali, Indonesia. *Journal of Sustainable Tourism* 1 (1), 38–47.

Wall, G. (1993b) Towards a tourism typology. In J.G Nelson, R.W Butler and G. Wall (eds) *Tourism and Sustainable Development: Monitoring, Planning, Managing* (Heritage Resources Centre Joint Publication 1) (pp. 45–58). University of Waterloo.

Wall, G. (1995) Change, impacts and opportunities: Turning victims into victors. Paper presented at Tilbury University, the Netherlands.

Wall, G. (1996) Perspectives on tourism in selected Balinese villages. *Annals of Tourism Research* 23 (1), 123–37.

Wall, G. (1997) Sustainable tourism – unsustainable development. In S. Wahab and J. Pigram (eds) *Tourism, Development and Growth: The Challenge of Sustainability* (pp. 33–49). London: Routledge.

Wallerstein, I. (1979) *The Capitalist World Economy.* Cambridge: Cambridge University Press

Walters, J. (2000) Chaos on the costas. *Observer* (Business supplement) (20 February).

Wang, N. (2000) *Tourism and Modernity: A Sociological Analysis.* New York: Pergamon.

Wanhill, S. (1997) Peripheral area tourism. *Progress in Tourism and Hospitality Research* 3, 47–70.

Ward, B. and Dubos, R. (1972) *Only One Earth: The Care and Maintenance of a Small Planet.* London: Penguin.

Warde, A. (1992) Notes on the relationship between production and consumption. In R. Burrows and C. Marsh (eds) (1992) *Consumption and Class* (pp. 15–31). Basingstoke: Macmillan.

Weaver, D. (1988) The evolution of a 'Plantation' tourism landscape on the Caribbean Island of Antigua. *Tijdschrift voor Economische en Sociale Geographie* 79 (5), 319–31.

Weaver, D. (1998a) *Ecotourism in the Less Developed World*. Wallingford: CAB International.

Weaver, D. (1998b) Peripheries of the periphery: Tourism in Tobago and Barbuda. *Annals of Tourism Research* 25 (2), 292–313.

Weaver, D. (1999) Magnitude of ecotourism in Costa Rica and Kenya. *Annals of Tourism Research* 26 (4), 792–816.

Weaver, D. and Fennell, D. (1997) Rural tourism in Canada: The Saskatchewan vacation farm operator as entrepreneur. In S. Page and D. Getz (eds) *The Business of Rural Tourism* (pp. 77–92). London: International Thomson Business Press.

Weaver, D. and Oppermann, M. (2000) *Tourism Management*. Brisbane: John Wiley and Sons.

Weber, A. (1909) *Theory of the Location of Industries*. Chicago: University of Chicago Press.

Webster (1990) *Introduction to the Sociology of Development* (2nd edn). Basingstoke: Macmillan.

Welch, R. (1984) The meaning of development: Traditional views and more recent ideas. *New Zealand Journal of Geography* 76, 2–4.

Wellings, P.A. and Crush, J. (1983) Tourism and dependency in Southern Africa: The prospects and planning of tourism in Lesotho. *Applied Geography* 3 (3), 205–23.

Whelan, T. (ed.) (1991) *Nature Tourism: Managing for the Environment*. Washington, DC: Island Press.

Wiarda, H. (1983) Toward a nonethnocentric theory of development: Alternative conceptions from the Third World. *Journal of Developing Areas* 17. Reprinted in C. Wilber (ed.) (1988) *The Political Economy of Development and Underdevelopment* (4th edn) (pp. 59–82). Toronto: McGraw-Hill.

Widfelt, A. (1996) Alternative development strategies and tourism in the Caribbean microstates. In L. Briguglio, R. Butler, D. Harrison and W. Fiho (eds) *Sustainable Tourism in Islands and Small States, Case Studies* (pp. 147–61). London: Pinter.

Wight, P. (1988) Tools for sustainability analysis in planning and managing tourism and recreation in the destination. In C.M. Hall and A. Lew (eds) *Sustainable Tourism: A Geographical Perspective* (pp. 75–91). Harlow: Longman.

Wight, P. (1993) Sustainable ecotourism: Balancing economic environmental and social goals within an ethical framework. *Journal of Tourism Studies* 4 (2), 54–66.

Wilkin, P. (1996) New myths for the south: Globalisation and the conflict between private power and freedom. *Third World Quarterly* 17 (2), 227–38.

Wilkinson, P.F. (1987) Tourism in small island nations: A fragile dependence. *Leisure Studies* 6 (2), 128–46.

Wilkinson, P. F. (1989) Strategies for island micro-states. *Annals of Tourism Research* 16 (2), 153–77.

Wilkinson, P.F. (1992) Tourism: Development imperative and environmental problems. In F. Carden (ed.) *Discussion Forum II on the Graduate Programme in Development Studies at the Bandung Institue of Technology* (Research Series Paper 30) (pp. 22–32). Waterloo: University Consortium on the Environment, University of Waterloo.

Wilkinson, P.F. (1997) *Tourism Policy and Planning: Case Studies from the Commonwealth Caribbean*. New York: Cognizant.

Wilkinson, P.F. and Pratiwi, W. (1995) Gender and tourism in an Indonesian village. *Annals of Tourism Research* 22 (2), 238–99.

Williams, A.M. (1995) Capital and the transnationalisation of tourism. In A. Montanari and A.M. Williams (eds) *European Tourism: Regions, Spaces and Restructuring* (pp. 163–76). Chichester: John Wiley and Sons.

Williams, A.M. and Montanari, A. (1995) Introduction: Tourism and economic restructuring in Europe. In A. Montanari and A.M. Williams (eds) *European Tourism. Regions, Spaces and Restructuring* (pp. 1–15). Chichester: John Wiley and Sons.

Williams, A. and Shaw, G. (eds) (1991) *Tourism and Economic Development: Western European Experiences*. London: Belhaven Press.

Williams, A. and Shaw, G. (1995) Tourism and regional development: Polarization and new forms of production in the United Kingdom. *Tijdschrift voor Economische en Sociale Geografie* 86 (1), 50–63.

Williams, A. and Shaw, G. (1998) Tourism and uneven economic development. In A. Williams and G. Shaw (eds) *Tourism and Economic Development: European Experiences* (3rd edn) (pp. 1–16). Chichester: John Wiley and Sons.

Williams, S. (1998) *Tourism Geographies*. London: Routledge.

Williams, S. and Montanari, A. (1995) Tourism regions and spaces in a changing social framework. *Tijdschrift voor Economische en Sociale Geografie* 86 (1), 3–12.

Williamson, J. (1978) *Decoding Advertisements*. London: Marion Boyars.

Wilson, D. (1996) Glimpses of Caribbean tourism and the question of sustainability in Barbados and St Lucia. In L. Briguglio, R. Butler, D. Harrison and W. Fiho (eds) *Sustainable Tourism in Islands and Small States, Case Studies* (pp. 75–102). London: Pinter.

Winpenny, J. (1978) Employment among the urban poor: A case for laissez-faire? *Built Environment* 5 (2), 119–24.

Wirosardjono, S. (1984) The meaning, limitations and problems of the informal sector. *Prisma* 32, 78–83.

Witherspoon, S. (1994) The greening of Britain: Romance and rationality. In R. Jowell *et al.* (eds) *British Social Attitudes: 11th Report* (pp. 107–39). Aldershot: Dartmouth.

Witt, C. and Witt, S. (1994) Demand elasticities. In S. Witt and L. Moutinho (eds) *Tourism Marketing and Management Handbook* (2nd edn) (pp. 522–9). New York: Prentice Hall.

Witt, S. (1989) Receipts/expenditures balance analysis. In S. Witt and L. Moutinho (eds) *Tourism Marketing and Management Handbook* (2nd edn) (pp. 485–7). New York: Prentice Hall.

Wolf, E. (1982) *Europe and the People without History*. Berkeley, CA: University of California Press.

Wood, K. and House, S. (1991) *The Good Tourist: A Worldwide Guide for the Green Traveller*. London: Mandarin.

Wood, R.E. (1979) Tourism and underdevelopment in Southeast Asia. *Journal of Contemporary Asia* 9, 274–87.

Wood, R.E. (2000) Caribbean cruise tourism: Globalization at sea. *Annals of Tourism Research* 27 (2), 345–70.

Woodcock, K. and France, L. (1994) Development theory applied to tourism in Jamaica. In A. Seaton (ed.) *Tourism the State of the Art* (pp. 110–19). Chichester: John Wiley and Sons.

World Commission on Environment and Development (1987) *Our Common Future*. New York: Oxford University Press.

World Tourism Organisation (WTO) (1980) *Manila Declaration on World Tourism*. Madrid: World Tourism Organisation.

WTO (1981) *Tourism Multipliers Explained*. Madrid: World Tourism Organisation and Horwarth and Horwarth International.

WTO (1983) *New Concepts of Tourism's Role In Modern Society: Possible Development Models*. Madrid: World Tourism Organization.

WTO (1985) *The Role of Transnational Tourism Enterprises in the Development of Tourism*. Madrid: WTO.

WTO (1992) *Yearbook of Tourism Statistics*. Madrid: World Tourism Organisation.

WTO (1993) *Sustainable Tourism Development: A Guide for Local Planners*. Madrid: World Tourism Organisation

WTO (1994) *National and Regional Tourism Planning: Methodologies and Case Studies*. London: Routledge.

WTO (1995) *GATS: Implications for Tourism*. Madrid: World Tourism Organisation.

WTO (1997) *Yearbook of Tourism Statistics 1996* (49th edn). Madrid: WTO.

WTO (1998a) *Tourism 2020 Vision – Influences, Directional Flows and Key Trends*. Madrid: World Tourism Organization.

WTO (1998b) *Tourism Economic Report* (1st edn). Madrid: WTO.

WTO (1998c) *The Euro Impact on Tourism 1998*. Madrid: World Tourism Organization.

WTO (1999a) *Yearbook of Tourism Statistics, I* (51st edn). Madrid: World Tourism Organisation.

WTO (1999b) *Yearbook of Tourism Statistics, II* (51st edn). Madrid: World Tourism Organisation.

WTO (1999c) *Tourism Satellite Accounts (TSA): The Conceptual Framework*. Madrid: World Tourism Organisation.

WTO (1999d) *Tourism Highlights 2000* (2nd edn). Madrid: World Tourism Organisation.

WTO (2000) On WWW at http://www.world-tourism.org/pressrel/00_5_11I.htm.

World Travel and Tourism Council (1993) *World Travel and Tourism Review: Environment and Development*. Belgium: WTTC.

World Travel and Tourism Council (1995) *Travel and Tourism's Economic Perspective*. London: World Travel and Tourism Council.

World Travel and Tourism Council (2000) On WWW at http://www.wttc.org/TSA/tsa.htm.

WTO/WTTC (1996) *Agenda 21 for the Travel and Tourism Industry: Towards Environmentally Sustainable Development*. Madrid: World Tourism Organisation/World Travel and Tourism Council.

Wu, C. (1982) Issues of tourism and socioeconomic development. *Annals of Tourism Research* 9 (3), 317–30.

Wuelker, G. (1993) Questionnaires in Asia. In M. Bulmer and D. Warwick (eds) *Social Research in Developing Countries: Surveys and Censuses in the Third World* (pp. 161–6). London: UCL Press. (Originally published 1983 by John Wiley and Sons.)

Yearley, S. (1992) *The Green Case: A Sociology of Environmental Issues, Arguments and Politics*. London: Routledge.

Yee, C.L. (2001) Personal interview, Guildford, 10 March.

Yeung, O. and Mathieson, J. (1998) *Global Benchmarks, Comprehensive Measures of Development*. Washington, DC: Brookings Institution Press.

Young, G. (1973) *Tourism Blessing or Blight?* Baltimore: Penguin Books.

Young, K. (1991) Shades of green. In R. Jowell, L. Brook and B. Taylor (eds) *British Social Attitudes: The 8th Report*. Aldershot: Dartmouth.

Yunis, E. (2000) Tourism sustainability and market competitiveness in the coastal areas and islands of the Mediterranean. In A. Pink (ed.) *Sustainable Travel and Tourism* (pp. 65–8). London: Green Globe 21/IGC. See WWW at http://www.sustravel.com.

Zarkia, C. (1996) Philoxenia: Receiving tourists – but not guests – on a Greek island. In J. Boissevain (ed.) *Coping with Tourists: European Reactions to Mass Tourism* (pp. 143–73). Oxford: Berghahn.

Zimmer, M. Stafford, T. and Stafford, M. (1994) Green issues: Dimensions of environmental concern. *Journal of Business Research* 30 (1), 63–74.

Zimmerman, F. (1998) Austria: Contrasting seasons and contrasting regions. In A. Williams and G. Shaw (eds) *Tourism and Economic Development: European Experiences* (3rd edn) (pp. 175–97). Chichester: John Wiley and Sons.

Index

Abu Dhabi 1, 319
acculturation 229
advocacy 57, 150, 155, 231, 236, 323
agency, public 65,115
Agenda 21 37, 48, 69, 232, 240, 321, 322
agglomeration economies 5, 118, 146, 341
agriculture 28, 40, 45, 69, 84, 96, 105, 139,
    154, 169, 177, 191, 218, 222, 252, 270
agri-tourism (*see also* Agro-tourism) 137, 347
agro-tourism (*see also* Agri-tourism) 60
AIDS 219, 224
airlines 55, 70, 139, 274, 282, 283-285, 322,
    336
airports 86, 128, 140, 222, 224, 227, 288, 331,
    335, 336
alliances 122, 129, 139, 276, 278, 283, 287
alternative development 5, 35, 36, 47-50, 51,
    58-60, 61, 62, 76, 75, 76, 120, 124, 143,
    227, 228, 229, 230, 232, 336, 339, 341, 342,
    344, 346
Amboseli National Park, Kenya 256
assimilation 213, 220, 229, 315
Association of Southeast Asian Nations
    (ASEAN) 115, 145
Australia 31, 129, 135, 141, 145, 228, 322,
    332
authenticity 23, 134, 180, 221, 222, 309, 309

backward linkages 19-20, 119, 334
backwash effects 43, 54, 118
balance of payments 14, 30, 52, 82, 90,
    91-94, 105, 110
Balearic Islands 281, 295
Bali Sustainable Development Project
    (BSDP) 60
Bali, Indonesia 123, 167, 181, 209, 219
barriers 6, 18, 45, 122, 142, 159, 163, 196,
    209, 268, 292, 344, 345
Big Man system, The 159
biodiversity 145, 150, 153, 244, 254
Brandt Commission 239

British Tourist Authority (BTA) 14, 128
Brundtland Report 25, 108, 245, 321
bureaucratic 125, 232, 273
Burma (*see also* Myanmar) 217, 237
Burma campaign 217, 237

CAMPFIRE Programme 144, 258
Canada 91, 112, 128-129, 133, 134, 137, 138,
    145, 217, 242
Canadian Tourism Commission (CTC) 128
Canary Islands 295, 296
capital investment 84, 85, 86, 124, 175, 226,
    292, 295
capitalism 36, 43, 44, 48, 211, 228, 229, 230,
    273, 287, 290, 291, 292, 295
capital-output ratio 84-88
Caribbean 17, 20, 56, 70, 74, 95, 139, 141,
    142, 145, 169, 181, 223, 257, 270-272, 279,
    283, 286
carrying capacity 69, 238, 244-245, 253, 254,
    255, 268
casino 112, 122, 125, 133, 134, 138, 302
centrally planned economy 207
centre-periphery 118
child labour 175
China 17, 103
clusters 118, 119-120, 129, 138, 146, 341
codes of practice 242, 243, 248
collaboration 73, 122, 145
colonialism 39, 40, 62, 76, 81, 98, 106, 197,
    269, 270, 271, 276, 323
colonisation 222, 226
commercialisation
— of culture 215
— of human relationships 225
common pool resource (CPR) 251-252
communist 206, 228, 230
community 3, 6, 47, 50, 59, 60, 62, 70, 72-75,
    85, 94, 113, 124, 125, 132, 133, 136, 137,
    142, 144, 149-164, 176, 191, 200, 212, 213,
    215, 218, 229, 245, 251, 258, 330, 340